CLYMER®
MANUALS

SUZUKI
GSX-R600/GSX-R750 • 2006-2009

WHAT'S IN YOUR TOOLBOX?

More information available at Clymer.com
Phone: 805-498-6703

Haynes Publishing Group
Sparkford Nr Yeovil
Somerset BA22 7JJ England

Haynes North America, Inc
861 Lawrence Drive
Newbury Park
California 91320 USA

ISBN 10: 1-62092-242-8
ISBN-13: 978-1-62092-242-2
Library of Congress: 2016939516

Author: Ed Scott

Technical Photography: Ed Scott, with technical assistance from Jordan Engineering, Oceanside, CA. Motorcycles courtesy of North Country's House of Motorcycles and Motorcycle Gallery, Oceanside, CA.

Technical Illustrations: Errol McCarthy

Cover: Mark Clifford Photography at www.markclifford.com.

© **Haynes North America, Inc. 2016**
With permission from J.H. Haynes & Co. Ltd.

Clymer is a registered trademark of Haynes North America, Inc.

Printed in the U.S.A.

Common spark plug conditions

NORMAL

Symptoms: Brown to grayish-tan color and slight electrode wear. Correct heat range for engine and operating conditions.
Recommendation: When new spark plugs are installed, replace with plugs of the same heat range.

WORN

Symptoms: Rounded electrodes with a small amount of deposits on the firing end. Normal color. Causes hard starting in damp or cold weather and poor fuel economy.
Recommendation: Plugs have been left in the engine too long. Replace with new plugs of the same heat range. Follow the recommended maintenance schedule.

TOO HOT

Symptoms: Blistered, white insulator, eroded electrode and absence of deposits. Results in shortened plug life.
Recommendation: Check for the correct plug heat range, over-advanced ignition timing, lean fuel mixture, intake manifold vacuum leaks, sticking valves and insufficient engine cooling.

CARBON DEPOSITS

Symptoms: Dry sooty deposits indicate a rich mixture or weak ignition. Causes misfiring, hard starting and hesitation.
Recommendation: Make sure the plug has the correct heat range. Check for a clogged air filter or problem in the fuel system or engine management system. Also check for ignition system problems.

PREIGNITION

Symptoms: Melted electrodes. Insulators are white, but may be dirty due to misfiring or flying debris in the combustion chamber. Can lead to engine damage.
Recommendation: Check for the correct plug heat range, over-advanced ignition timing, lean fuel mixture, insufficient engine cooling and lack of lubrication.

ASH DEPOSITS

Symptoms: Light brown deposits encrusted on the side or center electrodes or both. Derived from oil and/or fuel additives. Excessive amounts may mask the spark, causing misfiring and hesitation during acceleration.
Recommendation: If excessive deposits accumulate over a short time or low mileage, install new valve guide seals to prevent seepage of oil into the combustion chambers. Also try changing gasoline brands.

HIGH SPEED GLAZING

Symptoms: Insulator has yellowish, glazed appearance. Indicates that combustion chamber temperatures have risen suddenly during hard acceleration. Normal deposits melt to form a conductive coating. Causes misfiring at high speeds.
Recommendation: Install new plugs. Consider using a colder plug if driving habits warrant.

OIL DEPOSITS

Symptoms: Oily coating caused by poor oil control. Oil is leaking past worn valve guides or piston rings into the combustion chamber. Causes hard starting, misfiring and hesitation.
Recommendation: Correct the mechanical condition with necessary repairs and install new plugs.

DETONATION

Symptoms: Insulators may be cracked or chipped. Improper gap setting techniques can also result in a fractured insulator tip. Can lead to piston damage.
Recommendation: Make sure the fuel anti-knock values meet engine requirements. Use care when setting the gaps on new plugs. Avoid lugging the engine.

GAP BRIDGING

Symptoms: Combustion deposits lodge between the electrodes. Heavy deposits accumulate and bridge the electrode gap. The plug ceases to fire, resulting in a dead cylinder.
Recommendation: Locate the faulty plug and remove the deposits from between the electrodes.

MECHANICAL DAMAGE

Symptoms: May be caused by a foreign object in the combustion chamber or the piston striking an incorrect reach (too long) plug. Causes a dead cylinder and could result in piston damage.
Recommendation: Repair the mechanical damage. Remove the foreign object from the engine and/or install the correct reach plug.

CONTENTS

QUICK REFERENCE DATA

TIRE SPECIFICATIONS

Item	Front	Rear
Tire type	Tubeless	Tubeless
Size	120/70 ZR17 M/C (58W)	180/50 ZR17 M/C (73W)
Minimum tread depth	1.6 mm (0.06 in.)	2.0 mm (0.08 in.)
Inflation pressure (cold)*		
Solo	250 kPa (36 psi])	290 kPa (42 psi])
Rider and passenger	250 kPa (36 psi])	250 kPa (36 psi])

*Tire inflation pressure is for original equipment tires. Aftermarket tires may require different inflation pressure. The use of tires other than those specified by Suzuki may cause instability.

RECOMMENDED LUBRICANTS AND FLUIDS

Fuel	Regular unleaded
USA, California and Canada models	
Pump octane: (R/2 + M/2)	87 or higher
Research octane	90 or higher
All models except USA, California and	
Canada models	95 or higher
Fuel tank capacity (including reserve)	
2006-2007 models	
California models	15.5 liter (4.1 US gal. [3.4 Imp gal.])
All models except California	16.5 liter (4.4 US gal. [3.6 Imp gal.])
2007-2008 models	
California models	16.0 liter (4.2 US gal. [3.6 Imp gal.])
All models except California	17.0 liter (4.5 US gal [3.7 Imp gal.])
Engine oil	
Grade	API SF or SG or API SH/SJ with MA in JASO
Viscosity	SAE 10W/40
Capacity	
Oil change only	2.2 liters (2.3 U.S. qt. [1.9 Imp qt.])
Oil and filter change	2.5 liters (2.6 U.S. qt., [2.2 Imp qt.])
Overhaul (completely dry)	2.9 liters (3.1 U.S. qt., [2.6 Imp qt.])
Brake fluid	DOT 4
Fork oil	
Type	Suzuki SS-05 fork oil or equivalent
Capacity per leg	
2006-2007 models	
GSX-R600 models	413 ml (14.0 U.S. oz.)
GSX-R750 models	408 ml (13.8 U.S. oz.)
2008-2009 models	
GSX-R600 models	410 ml (13.9 U.S. oz.)
GSX-R750 models	418 ml (14.1 U.S. oz.)
Engine coolant	
Type	Anti-freeze/coolant that is compatible with an aluminum radiator.
Mixing Ratio	50-50 with distilled water
Coolant capacity (system total)	
2006-2007 models	2.7 liters (2.9 US. qt. [2.4 Imp qt.])
2008-2009 models	2.65 liters (2.8 US qt. [2.3 Imp qt.])

MAINTENANCE AND TUNE-UP SPECIFICATIONS

Item	Specification
Battery	
Type	YT12A-BS Maintenance free (sealed)
Capacity	
GSX-R600	12 volt 36.0 kC (8 amp hour)/10 HR
GSX-R750	12 volt 36.0 kC (10 amp hour)/10 HR
Brake pedal height	65-75 (2.56-2.95) below the footrest
Compression pressure (at sea level)	
GSX-R600 models	
Standard	1,200-1,600 kPa (12-16 kg/cm² [(171-228 psi])
Service limit	900 kPa (9 kg/cm² [128 psi])
Maximum difference between cylinders	200 kPa (2 kg/cm² [28 psi])
GSX-R750 models	
Standard	1,300-1,700 kPa (13-17 kg/cm² [(185-242 psi])
Service limit	1000 kPa (10 kg/cm² [148 psi])
Maximum difference between cylinders	200 kPa (2 kg/cm² [28 psi])
Clutch cable free play	10-15 mm (0.4-0.6 in.)
Drive chain 21-pin length	319.4 mm (12.6 in.)
Drive chain slack	20-30 mm (0.8-1.2 in.)
Idle speed (2006-2007 models)	
600 cc models	1200-1400 rpm
750 cc models	1100-1300 rpm
Front fork adjustments	
2006-2007 models (standard positions)	
Spring preload	7th turn from softest position
Rebound damping	1 3/4 turns out
Compression damping	1 3/4 turns out
2008-2009 models (standard position)	
Spring preload	7th turn from softest position
Rebound damping	1 ¾ turns out
Compression damping	
GSX-R600	1 ¾ turns out
GSX-R750	
Low speed	2 turn out
High speed	2 ½ turns out
Ignition timing	
GSX-R600 models	6° B.T.D.C. @ 1300 rpm
GSX-R750 models	
2006-2007 models	8° B.T.D.C. @ 1200 rpm
2008-2009 models	5° B.T.D.C. @ 1200 rpm
Oil pressure	100-400 kPa (1.0-4.0 kgf/cm² [14-57 psi])
Radiator cap opening pressure	108-137 kPa (1.1-1.4 kgf/cm² [14-19.5 psi])
Shift pedal height	65-75 mm (2.6-3.0 in.) below the footrest
Shock absorber	
2006-2007 models	
Spring preload	
Standard preload (spring length)	181.4 mm (7.14 ln.)
Max preload (min spring length)	186.4 mm (7.34 in.
Min preload (max spring length)	176.4 mm (6.94 in.)
Rebound damping	
Standard	1 ½ turns out
Low speed	1 ¾ turns out
High speed	3 turns out
Compression damping	
Low speed	2 turns out
High speed	3 turns out
2008-2009 models	
GSX-R600	
Spring preload	
Standard preload (spring length)	181.4 mm (7.14 in.)
Max preload (min spring length)	186.4 mm (7.34 in.
Min preload (max spring length)	176.4 mm (6.94 in.)

(continued)

Item	Specification
Shock absorber (continued)	
2008-2009 models (continued)	
GSX-R600 (continued)	
Rebound damping	2 turns out
Compression damping	
Low speed	2 turns out
High speed	3 turns out
GSX-R750	
Spring preload	
Standard preload (spring length)	182.3 mm (7.18 in.)
Max preload (min spring length)	186.4 mm (7.34 in.
Min preload (max spring length)	176.4 mm (6.94 in.)
Rebound damping	2 turns out
Compression damping	
Low speed	2 turns out
High speed	3 turns out
Spark plug	
Gap	
2006-2007 models	0.7-0.8 mm (0.028-0.031 in.)
2008-2009 models	0.8-0.9 mm (0.031-0.035 in.)
Type	
2006-2007 models	
Standard	NGK: CR9E, Denso: U27ESR-N
Hot type	NGK: CR8E, Denso: U24ESR-N
Cold type	NGK: CR10E, Denso: U31ESR-N
2008-2009 models	
Standard	NGK: CR9EIA-9, Denso: IUD27D
Hot type	NGK: CR8EIA-9, Denso: IU24D
Cold type	NGK: CR10EIA-9, Denso: IU31D
Steering tension range	200-500 grams (7.05-17.66 oz.)
Throttle cable freeplay	2.0 -4.0 mm (0.08-0.16 in)
Throttle position (TP) sensor (2006-2007 models)	
Input voltage	4.5-5.5 volts
Output voltage	
Fully closed	Approx. 1.1 volts
Fully open	Approx. 4.3 volts
	200-500 grams (7.05-17.66 oz.)
Valve clearance*	
Intake	0-08-0.18 mm (0.003-0.007 in.)
Exhaust	0.18-0.28 mm (0.007-0.011 in.)
Wheel rim runout limit	
Axial	2.0 mm (0.08 in.)
Radial	2.0 mm (0.08 in.)

* Below 35° C (95° F)

MAINTENANCE AND TUNE UP TORQUE SPECIFICATIONS

Item	N•m	in.-lb.	ft.-lb.
Brake bleed valve			
Front master cylinder	6.0	53	–
Front caliper	7.5	66	–
Rear caliper	7.5	66	–
Cylinder head cover bolt	14	–	10
Engine sprocket nut	115	–	85
Exhaust header bolt	23	–	17
Exhaust pipe hanger bolt	23	–	17
Fork bridge clamp bolt			
Upper and lower	23	–	17
Front axle	100	–	74

(continued)

MAINTENANCE AND TUNE UP TORQUE SPECIFICATIONS (continued)

Item	N•m	in.–lb.	ft.–lb.
Front axle pinch bolt	23	–	17
Handle bar clamp bolt	23	–	16.5
Muffler connecting bolt	23	–	17
Muffler mounting bolt	23	–	17
Oil drain bolt	23	–	17
Oil pan bolt	10	89	–
Rear axle nut	100	–	74
Rear brake master cylinder locknut	18	–	13
Rear sprocket nut	60	–	44
Spark plug	11	97	–
Timing inspection cap	11	97	–
Water pump air bleed bolt	13	115	–

CHAPTER ONE

GENERAL INFORMATION

This detailed and comprehensive manual covers the Suzuki GSX-R600 and GSX-R750 from 2006-2009.

The text provides complete information on maintenance, tune-up, repair and overhaul. Hundreds of photographs and illustrations created during the complete disassembly of the motorcycle guide the reader through every job. All procedures are in step-by-step format and designed for the reader who may be working on the motorcycle for the first time.

MANUAL ORGANIZATION

A shop manual is a tool and, as in all Clymer manuals, the chapters are thumb tabbed for easy reference. Main headings are listed in the table of contents and the index. Frequently used specifications and capacities from the tables at the end of each individual chapter are listed in the *Quick Reference Data* section at the front of the manual. Specifications and capacities are provided in U.S. standard and metric units of measure.

Some procedures refer to headings in other chapters or sections of the manual. When a specific heading is called out in a step, it will be italicized as it appears in the manual. If a sub-heading is indicated as being "in this section" it is located within the same main heading. For example, the sub-heading (bf ital) Handling Gasoline Safely is located within the main heading (bf ital)SAFETY.

This chapter provides general information on shop safety, tools and their usage, service fundamentals and shop supplies. **Tables 1-7**, at the end of this chapter, list the following:

Chapter Two provides methods for quick and accurate diagnosis of problems. Troubleshooting procedures present typical symptoms and logical methods to pinpoint and repair the problem.

Chapter Three explains all routine maintenance necessary to keep the motorcycle running well. Chapter Three also includes recommended tune-up procedures, eliminating the need to constantly consult the chapters on the various assemblies.

Subsequent chapters describe specific systems such as engine, transmission, clutch, drive system, fuel system, suspension, brakes, fairing and exhaust system. Each disassembly, repair and assembly procedure is discussed in step-by-step form.

WARNINGS, CAUTIONS AND NOTES

The terms WARNING, CAUTION and NOTE have specific meanings in this manual.

A WARNING emphasizes areas where injury or even death could result from negligence. Mechanical damage may also occur. WARNINGS are to be taken seriously.

A CAUTION emphasizes areas where equipment damage could result. Disregarding a CAUTION could cause permanent mechanical damage, though injury is unlikely.

A NOTE provides additional information to make a step or procedure easier or clearer. Disregarding a NOTE could cause inconvenience, but would not cause equipment damage or injury.

SAFETY

Professional mechanics can work for years and never sustain a serious injury or mishap. Follow these guidelines and practice common sense to safely service the motorcycle.

1. Do not operate the motorcycle in an enclosed area. The exhaust gasses contain carbon monoxide, an odorless, colorless and tasteless poisonous gas. Carbon monoxide levels build quickly in small, enclosed areas and can cause unconsciousness and death in a short time. Make sure to properly ventilate the work area or operate the motorcycle outside.

2. *Never* use gasoline or any extremely flammable liquid to clean parts. Refer to *Cleaning Parts and Handling Gasoline Safely* in this section.

3. Never smoke or use a torch in the vicinity of flammable liquids, such as gasoline or cleaning solvent.

4. If welding or brazing on the motorcycle, remove the fuel tank to a safe distance at least 50 ft. (15 m) away.

5. Use the correct type and size of tools to avoid damaging fasteners.

6. Keep tools clean and in good condition. Replace or repair worn or damaged equipment.

7. When loosening a tight fastener, be guided by what would happen if the tool slips.

8. When replacing fasteners, make sure the new fasteners are the same size and strength as the original ones.

9. Keep the work area clean and organized.

10. Wear eye protection *anytime* the safety of the eyes is in question. This includes procedures that involve drilling, grinding, hammering, compressed air and chemicals.

11. Wear the correct clothing for the job. Tie up or cover long hair so it does not get caught in moving equipment.

12. Do not carry sharp tools in clothing pockets.

13. Always have an approved fire extinguisher available. Make sure it is rated for gasoline (Class B) and electrical (Class C) fires.

14. Do not use compressed air to clean clothes, the motorcycle or the work area. Debris may be blown into eyes or skin. Never direct compressed air at anyone. Do not allow children to use or play with any compressed air equipment.

15. When using compressed air to dry rotating parts, hold the part so it does not rotate. Do not allow the force of the air to spin the part. The air jet is capable of rotating parts at extreme speed. The part may

disintegrate or become damaged, causing serious injury.

16. Do not inhale the dust created by brake pad and clutch wear. These particles may contain asbestos. In addition, some types of insulating materials and gaskets may contain asbestos. Inhaling asbestos particles is hazardous to health.

17. Never work on the motorcycle while someone is working under it.

18. When placing the motorcycle on a stand, make sure it is secure before walking away.

Handling Gasoline Safely

Gasoline is a volatile flammable liquid and is one of the most dangerous items in the shop. Because gasoline is used so often, many people forget it is hazardous. Only use gasoline as fuel for gasoline internal combustion engines. Keep in mind when working on the machine, gasoline is always present in the fuel tank, fuel line and throttle body. To avoid a disastrous accident when working around the fuel system, carefully observe the following precautions:

1. *Never* use gasoline to clean parts. Refer to *Cleaning Parts* in this section.

2. When working on the fuel system, work outside or in a well-ventilated area.

3. Do not add fuel to the fuel tank or service the fuel system while the motorcycle is near open flames, sparks or where someone is smoking. Gasoline vapor is heavier than air; it collects in low areas and is more easily ignited than liquid gasoline.

4. Allow the engine to cool completely before working on any fuel system component.

5. Do not store gasoline in glass containers. If the glass breaks, a serious explosion or fire may occur.

6. Immediately wipe up spilled gasoline with rags. Store the rags in a metal container with a lid until they can be properly disposed of, or place them outside in a safe place for the fuel to evaporate.

7. Do not pour water onto a gasoline fire. Water spreads the fire and makes it more difficult to put out. Use a class B, BC or ABC fire extinguisher to extinguish the fire.

8. Always turn off the engine before refueling. Do not spill fuel onto the engine or exhaust system. Do not overfill the fuel tank. Leave an air space at the top of the tank to allow room for the fuel to expand due to temperature fluctuations.

Cleaning Parts

Many types of chemical cleaners and solvents are available for shop use. Most are poisonous and extremely flammable. To prevent chemical exposure, vapor buildup, fire and serious injury, observe each product warning label and note the following:

1. Read and observe the entire product label before using any chemical. Always know what type of chemical is being used and whether it is poisonous and/or flammable.

2. Do not use more than one type of cleaning solvent at a time. If mixing chemicals is required, measure the proper amounts according to the manufacturer.

3. Work in a well-ventilated area.

4. Wear chemical-resistant gloves.

5. Wear safety glasses.

6. Wear a vapor respirator if the instructions call for it.

7. Wash hands and arms thoroughly after cleaning parts.

8. Keep chemical products away from children and pets.

9. Thoroughly clean all oil, grease and cleaner residue from any part that must be heated.

10. Use a nylon brush when cleaning parts. Metal brushes may cause a spark.

11. When using a parts washer, only use the solvent recommended by the manufacturer. Make sure the parts washer is equipped with a metal lid that will lower in case of fire.

Warning Labels

Most manufacturers attach information and warning labels to the motorcycle. These labels contain instructions that are important to personal safety when operating, servicing, transporting and storing the motorcycle. Refer to the owner's manual for the description and location of labels. Order replacement labels from the manufacturer if they are missing or damaged.

SERIAL NUMBERS

Serial numbers are stamped on various locations on the frame, engine, transmission and throttle body. Record these numbers in the *Quick Reference Data* section in the front of the manual. Have these numbers available when ordering parts.

The VIN number label (**Figure 1**) is located on the left side of the frame.

The frame serial number (**Figure 2**) is stamped into the right side of the steering head.

The engine serial number (**Figure 3**) is stamped into a raised pad on the right side of engine adjacent to the oil level window.

FASTENERS

Proper fastener selection and installation is important to ensure the motorcycle operates as designed and can be serviced efficiently. The choice of original equipment fasteners is not arrived at by chance. Make sure replacement fasteners meet all the same requirements as the originals.

Threaded Fasteners

Threaded fasteners secure most of the components on the motorcycle. Most are tightened by turning them clockwise (right-hand threads). If the normal rotation of the component being tightened would loosen the fastener, it may have left-hand threads. If a left-hand threaded fastener is used, it is noted in the text.

Two dimensions are required to match the thread size of the fastener: the number of threads in a given distance and the outside diameter of the threads.

The two systems currently used to specify threaded fastener dimensions are the U.S. standard system and the metric system (**Figure 4**). Pay particular attention when working with unidentified fasteners; mismatching thread types can damage threads.

NOTE
To ensure that the fastener threads are not mismatched or cross-threaded, start all fasteners by hand. If a fastener is hard to start or turn, determine the cause before tightening with a wrench.

The length (L, **Figure 5**), diameter (D) and distance between thread crests (pitch) (T) classify metric screws and bolts. A typical bolt may be identified by the numbers, 8—1.25 X 130. This indicates the bolt has a diameter of 8 mm, the distance between thread crests is 1.25 mm and the length is 130 mm. Always measure bolt length as shown in L, **Figure 5** to avoid purchasing replacements of the wrong length.

The numbers on the top of the fastener (**Figure 5**) indicate the strength of metric screws and bolts. The stronger the fastener will have the higher number. Typically, unnumbered fasteners are the weakest.

Many screws, bolts and studs are combined with nuts to secure particular components. To indicate the size of a nut, manufacturers specify the internal diameter and the thread pitch. The measurement across two flats on a nut or bolt indicates the wrench size.

WARNING
Do not install fasteners with a strength classification lower than what was originally installed by the manufacturer. Doing so may cause equipment failure and/or damage.

Torque Specifications

The materials used in the manufacturing of the motorcycle may be subjected to uneven stresses if the fasteners of the various subassemblies are not installed and tightened correctly. Fasteners that are improperly installed or work loose can cause extensive damage. It is essential to use an accurate torque wrench as described in this chapter.

Torque specifications for various fasteners appear at the end of each chapter. **Table 6** at the end of this

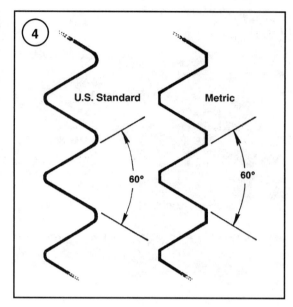

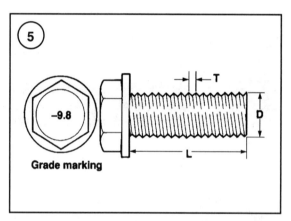

chapter lists general torque recommendations. To use **Table 6**, first measure the size of the fastener as described under Threaded Fasteners *in this section.*

Self-Locking Fasteners

Several types of bolts, screws and nuts incorporate a system that creates interference between the two fasteners. Interference is achieved in various ways. The most common types are the nylon insert nut and a dry adhesive coating on the threads of a bolt.

Self-locking fasteners offer greater holding strength than standard fasteners, which improves their resistance to vibration. Self-locking fasteners cannot be reused. The materials used to form the lock become distorted after the initial installation and removal. Discard and replace self-locking fasteners after removing them. Do not replace self-locking fasteners with standard fasteners.

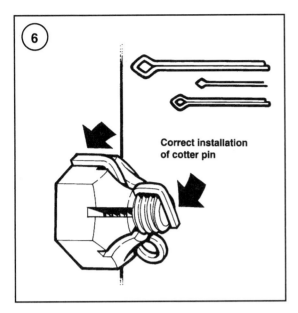

Correct installation
of cotter pin

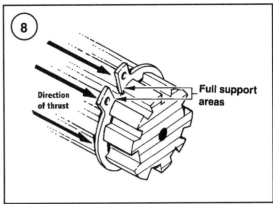

Direction
of thrust

Full support
areas

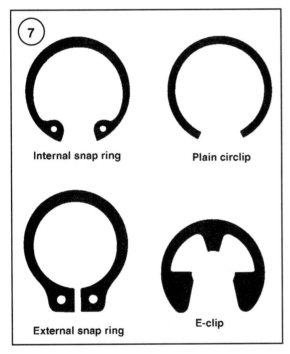

Internal snap ring   Plain circlip

External snap ring   E-clip

Washers

The two basic types of washers are flat washers and lockwashers. Flat washers are simple discs with a hole to fit a screw or bolt. Lockwashers are used to prevent a fastener from working loose. Washers can be used as spacers and seals, or can help distribute fastener load and prevent the fastener from damaging the component.

As with fasteners, when replacing washers make sure the replacement washers are of the same design and quality as the originals.

Cotter Pins

A cotter pin is a split metal pin inserted into a hole or slot to prevent a fastener from loosening. In certain applications, such as the rear axle on a motorcycle or ATV, the fastener must be secured in this way. For these applications, a cotter pin and castellated (slotted) nut is used.

To use a cotter pin, first make sure the diameter is correct for the hole in the fastener. After correctly tightening the fastener and aligning the holes, insert the cotter pin through the hole and bend the ends over the fastener (**Figure 6**). Unless instructed to do so, never loosen a tightened fastener to align the holes. If the holes do not align, tighten the fastener enough to achieve alignment.

Cotter pins are available in various diameters and lengths. Measure the length from the bottom of the head to the tip of the shortest pin.

Snap Rings and E-clips

Snap rings (**Figure 7**) are circular-shaped metal retaining clips. They are required to secure parts and gears in place on parts such as shafts, pins or rods. External type snap rings are used to retain items on shafts. Internal type snap rings secure parts within housing bores. In some applications, in addition to securing the component(s), snap rings of varying thicknesses also determine endplay. These are usually called selective snap rings.

The two basic types of snap rings are machined and stamped snap rings. Machined snap rings (**Figure 8**) can be installed in either direction, because both faces have sharp edges. Stamped snap rings (**Figure 9**) are manufactured with a sharp and a round edge. When installing a stamped snap ring in a thrust application, install the sharp edge facing away from the part producing the thrust.

E-clips are used when it is not practical to use a snap ring. Remove E-clips with a flat blade screwdriver by prying between the shaft and E-clip. To install an E-clip, center it over the shaft groove and push or tap it into place.

Observe the following when installing snap rings:
1. Remove and install snap rings with snap ring pliers. Refer to *Basic Tools* in this chapter.
2. In some applications, it may be necessary to replace snap rings after removing them.
3. Compress or expand snap rings only enough to install them. If overly expanded, they lose their retaining ability.
4. After installing a snap ring, make sure it seats completely.
5. Wear eye protection when removing and installing snap rings.

SHOP SUPPLIES

A variety of shop supplies (lubricants, threadlocking compounds, sealants etc.) are recommenced for the use in this manual. When a particular product is called for in a procedure. always use that product or its equivalent as instructed. The use of a lesser quality product can cause problems that might lead to damage.

Lubricants and Fluids

Periodic lubrication helps ensure a long service life for any type of equipment. Using the correct lubricant is as important as performing the lubrication service, although in an emergency the wrong lubricant is better than none at all. The following section describes the types of lubricants most often required. Make sure to follow the manufacturer's recommendations.

Engine oils

> *CAUTION*
> *Always use oil with a classification recommended by the manufacturer. Using oil with a different classification can cause engine damage. Refer to **Engine Oil and Filter** in Chapter Three for additional information on API, SAE and JASO classifications.*

Engine oil for four-stroke motorcycle engine use is classified by three standards: the American Petroleum Institute (API) service classification, the Society of Automotive Engineers (SAE) viscosity rating and the Japanese Automobile Standards Organization (JASO) T903 Standard rating.

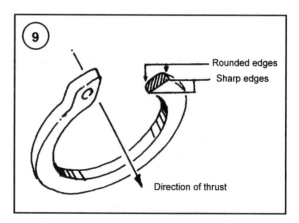

The API and SAE information is on all oil container labels. The JASO information is found on oil containers sold by the oil manufacturer specifically for motorcycle use. Two letters indicate the API service classification. The number or sequence of numbers and letter (10W-40 for example) is the oil's viscosity rating. The API service classification and the SAE viscosity index are not indications of oil quality.

The API service classification indicates that the oil meets specific lubrication standards. The first letter in the classification *S* indicates that the oil is for gasoline engines. The second letter indicates the standard the oil satisfies.

The JASO certification label identifies two separate oil classifications and a registration number to ensure the oil has passed all JASO certification standards for use in four-stroke motorcycle engines. The classifications are: MA (high friction applications) and MB (low friction applications). Only oil that has passed JASO standards can carry the JASO certification label.

Viscosity is an indication of the oil's thickness. Thin oils have a lower number while thick oils have a higher number. Engine oils fall into the 5- to 50-weight range for single-grade oils.

Most manufacturers recommend multi-grade oil. These oils perform efficiently across a wide range of operating conditions. Multi-grade oils are identified by a W after the first number, which indicates the low-temperature viscosity. Refer to *Engine Oil* in Chapter Three. Using other oil can cause engine damage.

Grease

Grease is lubricating oil with and added thickening agent. Grease maintains its lubricating qualities better than oil on long, strenuous rides. Furthermore, water does not wash grease off parts as easily as it does oil.

The National Lubricating Grease Institute (NLGI) grades grease. Grades range from No. 000 to No. 6, with No. 6 being the thickest. Typical multipurpose grease is NLGI No. 2. For specific applications, manufacturers may recommend water-resistant type grease or one with an additive such as molybdenum disulfide (MoS_2).

Various types of greases are needed when servicing a motorcycle. Unless otherwise indicated, use Suzuki Super Grease A (part No. 99000-25030, or equivalent) water-resistant, lithium-based grease—when grease is called for in this manual.

Brake fluid

Brake fluid is the hydraulic fluid used to transmit hydraulic pressure (force) to the wheel brakes. Brake fluid is classified by the Department of Transportation (DOT). Current designations for brake fluid are DOT 3, DOT 4 and DOT 5. This classification appears on the fluid container. Each type of brake fluid has its own definite characteristics.

Use only DOT 4 brake fluid in the motorcycles covered in this manual. Use of the incorrect brake fluid may cause brake failure and component damage. Do not mix different types of brake fluid as this may cause brake system failure. DOT 5 brake fluid is silicone based. DOT 5 is not compatible with other brake fluids or in systems for which it was not designed. Mixing DOT 5 fluid with other fluids may cause brake system failure.

Brake fluid will damage any plastic, painted or plated surface it contacts. Use extreme care when working with brake fluid and wash any spills immediately with soap and water.

Hydraulic brake systems require clean and moisture free brake fluid. Never reuse brake fluid. Keep containers and reservoirs properly sealed.

Coolant

Coolant is a mixture of water and antifreeze used to dissipate engine heat. Ethylene glycol is the most common form of antifreeze. Check the motorcycle manufacturer's recommendations when selecting antifreeze. Most require one specifically designed for use in aluminum engines. These types of antifreeze have additives that inhibit corrosion.

Only mix antifreeze with distilled water. Impurities in tap water may damage internal cooling system passages.

Cleaners, Degreasers and Solvents

Many chemicals are available to remove oil, grease and other residue from the motorcycle. Before using cleaning solvents, consider how they will be used and disposed of, particularly if they are not water-soluble. Local ordinances may require special procedures for the disposal of many types of cleaning chemicals. Refer to *Safety* in this chapter.

Use brake parts cleaner to clean brake system components. Brake parts cleaner leaves no residue. Use electrical contact cleaner to clean electrical connections and components without leaving any residue. Carburetor cleaner is a powerful solvent used to remove fuel deposits and varnish from fuel system components. Use this cleaner carefully, as it may damage finishes.

Generally, degreasers are strong cleaners used to remove heavy accumulations of grease from engine and frame components.

Most solvents are designed to be used with a parts washing cabinet for individual component cleaning. For safety, use only nonflammable or high flash point solvents.

Gasket Sealant

Sealant is used in combination with a gasket or seal. In other applications, such as between crankcase halves, only a sealant is used. Follow the manufacturer's recommendation when using a sealant. Use extreme care when choosing a sealant other than the type originally recommended. Choose sealant based upon its resistance to heat, various fluids and its sealing capabilities.

Before applying any sealant, clean all old gasket residue from the mating surfaces. Remove all gasket material from blind threaded holes to avoid inaccurate bolt torque. Spray the mating surfaces with aerosol parts cleaner and then wipe the surfaces with a lint-free cloth. The area must be clean for the sealant to adhere.

Suzuki recommends the use of the following sealants:

1. Suzuki Bond 1207B (part No. 99000-31140): a silicon-based sealant for vibration-prone, high-heat applications.
2. Suzuki Bond 1215 (part No. 99000-31110): UK, and Europe models.
3. Suzuki Bond 1216 (part No. 99104-31160): a silicon-based sealant for high-crankcase pressure applications.

Removing sealant

Silicone sealant is used on some engine gasket surfaces. When cleaning parts after disassembly, a single-sided razor blade or gasket scraper is required to remove silicone residue that cannot be pulled off by hand from the gasket surface. To avoid damaging gasket surfaces, use Permatex Silicone Stripper (part No.80647) to help soften the residue before scraping.

RTV sealant

Room temperature vulcanization sealant (RTV) is a common sealant that cures at room temperature over a specific time period. This allows the repositioning of components without damaging gaskets.

Moisture in the air causes the RTV sealant to cure. Always install the tube cap as soon as possible after applying RTV sealant. RTV sealant has a limited shelf life and will not cure properly if the shelf life has expired. Manufacturers usually specify a shelf life of one year after the container is opened, though it is recommended to contact sealant manufacturer to confirm shelf life.

Applying RTV sealant

Clean all old gasket residue from the mating surfaces. Remove all gasket material from blind threaded holes to avoid inaccurate bolt torque. Spray the mating surfaces with aerosol parts cleaner and then wipe with a lint-free cloth. The area must be clean for the sealant to adhere, be thorough when cleaning and drying the parts.

Apply RTV sealant in a continuous bead 2-3 mm (0.08-0.12 in.) thick. Circle all the fastener holes unless otherwise specified. Do not allow any sealant to enter these holes.

Drawings in specific chapters show how to apply the sealer to specific gasket surfaces. Assemble and tighten the fasteners to the specified torque within the time frame recommended by the sealant manufacturer.

Gasket Remover

Aerosol gasket remover can help remove stubborn gaskets. This product can speed up the removal process and prevent damage to the mating surface that may be caused by using a scraping tool. Most of these types of products are very caustic. Follow the gasket remover manufacturer's instructions for use.

Threadlocking Compound

> *CAUTION*
> *Threadlocking compounds are anaerobic and will stress, crack and attack most plastics. Use caution when using these products in areas where there are plastic components.*

A threadlocking compound is a fluid applied to the threads of fasteners. When the fluid dries and becomes a solid filler between the threads. This makes it difficult for the fastener to work loose from vibration or heat expansion and contraction. Some threadlocking compounds also provide a seal against fluid leaks.

Before applying a threadlocking compound, remove any old compound from both thread areas and clean them with aerosol parts cleaner. Use the compound sparingly. Excess fluid can run into adjoining parts.

Threadlocking compounds are available in a wide range of compounds for various strengths, temperatures and repair applications. Follow the manufacturer's recommendations regarding compound selection. Always apply the recommended threadlocking compound or its equivalent.

Suzuki recommends the use of the following compounds on the GSX-R600 and GSX-R750.
1. Suzuki Thread Lock Super 1303 (part No. 99000-32030): a high-strength, retaining type compound.
2. Suzuki Thread Lock Super 1322 (part No. 99000-32110) UK, and Europe models.
3. Suzuki Thread Lock 1215 (part No. 99000-31110) UK, and Europe models.
4. Suzuki Thread Lock 1207B (part No. 99000-31140) UK, and Europe models.
5. Suzuki Thread Lock 1342 (part No. 99000-32050): low-strength compound recommended for frequent repairs.
6. Suzuki Thread Lock Super 1360 (part No. 99000-32130): medium-strength, high temperature compound.

TOOLS

Most of the procedures in this manual can be carried out with simple hand tools and test equipment familiar to the home mechanic. Always use the correct tools for the job at hand. Keep tools organized and clean. Store them in a tool chest with related tools organized together.

Quality tools are essential. The best are constructed of high-strength alloy steel. These tools are light, easy to use and resistant to wear. Their working surface is devoid of sharp edges and carefully polished.

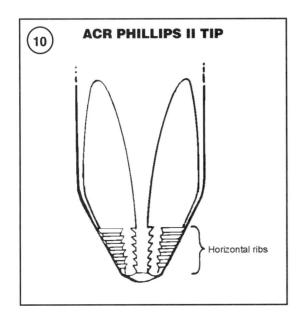

ACR PHILLIPS II TIP

Horizontal ribs

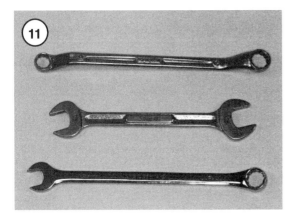

They have an easy-to-clean finish and are comfortable to use. Quality tools are a good investment.

Some of the procedures in this manual specify special tools. In many cases the tool is illustrated in use. Those with a large tool kit may be able to use a suitable substitute or fabricate a suitable replacement. However, in some cases, the specialized equipment or expertise may make it impractical for the home mechanic to attempt the procedure. When necessary, such operations come with the recommendation to have a dealership or specialist perform the task. It may be less expensive to have a professional perform these jobs, especially when considering the cost of equipment.

Consider the tool's potential frequency of use when purchasing tools to perform the procedures covered in this manual. If a tool kit is just now being started, consider purchasing a basic tool set from a quality tool supplier. These sets are available in many tool combinations and offer substantial savings when compared to individually purchased tools. As work

experience grows and tasks become more complicated, specialized tools can be added.

Screwdrivers

Two basic types are the slotted tip (flat blade) and the Phillips tip. These are available in sets that often include an assortment of tip sizes and shaft lengths.

As with all tools, use a screwdriver designed for the job. Make sure the size of the tip conforms to the size and shape of the fastener. Use them only for driving screws. Never use a screwdriver for prying or chiseling metal. Repair or replace worn or damaged screwdrivers. A worn tip may damage the fastener, making it difficult to remove.

Phillips-head screws are often damaged by incorrectly fitting screwdrivers. Quality Phillips screwdrivers are manufactured with their crosshead tip machined to Phillips Screw Company specifications. Poor quality or damaged Phillips screwdrivers can back out (camout) and round over the screw head. In addition, weak or soft screw materials can make removal difficult.

The best type of screwdriver to use on Phillips screws is the ACR Phillips II screwdriver, patented by the Phillips Screw Company. ACR stands for the horizontal anti-camout ribs found on the driving faces or flutes of the screwdriver's tip (**Figure 10**). ACR Phillips II screwdrivers were designed as part of a manufacturing drive system to be used with ACR Phillips II screws, but they work well on all common Phillips screws. A number of tool companies offer ACR Phillips II screwdrivers in different tip sizes and interchangeable bits to fit screwdriver bit holders.

Another way to prevent camout and to increase the grip of a Phillips screwdriver is to apply valve grinding compound or Permatex Screw & Socket Gripper onto the screwdriver tip. After loosening/tightening the screw, clean the screw recess to prevent engine oil contamination.

Wrenches

Open-end, box-end and combination wrenches (**Figure 11**) are available in a variety of types and sizes.

The number stamped on the wrench refers to the distance between the work areas. This size must match the size of the fastener head.

The box-end wrench is an excellent tool because it grips the fastener on all sides. This reduces the chance of the tool slipping. The box-end wrench is designed with either a 6- or 12-point opening. For stubborn or damaged fasteners, the 6-point provides

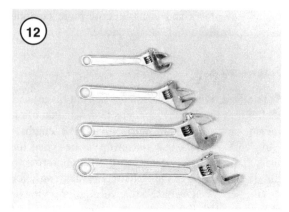

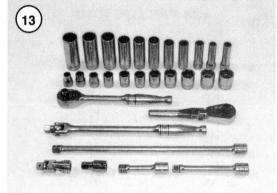

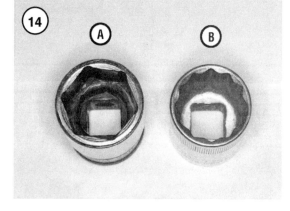

superior holding because it contacts the fastener across a wider area at all six edges. For general use, the 12-point works well. It allows the wrench to be removed and reinstalled without moving the handle over such a wide arc.

An open-end wrench is fast and works best in areas with limited overhead access. It contacts the fastener at only two points and is subject to slipping if under heavy force, or if the tool or fastener is worn. A box-end wrench is preferred in most instances, especially when breaking loose and applying the final tightness to a fastener.

The combination wrench has a box-end on one end and an open-end on the other. This combination makes it a convenient tool.

Adjustable Wrenches

An adjustable wrench or Crescent wrench (**Figure 12**) can fit nearly any nut or bolt head that has clear access around its entire perimeter. An adjustable wrench is best used as a backup wrench to keep a large nut or bolt from turning while the other end is being loosened or tightened with a box-end or socket wrench.

Adjustable wrenches contact the fastener at only two points, which makes them more subject to slipping off the fastener. Because one jaw is adjustable and may become loose, this shortcoming is aggravated. Make certain the solid jaw is the one transmitting the force.

Socket Wrenches, Ratchets and Handles

> *WARNING*
> *Do not use hand sockets with air or impact tools because they may shatter and cause injury. Always wear eye protection when using impact or air tools.*

Sockets that attach to a ratchet handle (**Figure 13**) are available with 6-point (A, **Figure 14**) or 12-point (B, **Figure 14**) openings and different drive sizes. The drive size indicates the size of the square hole that accepts the ratchet handle. The number stamped on the socket is the size of the work area and must match the fastener head.

As with wrenches, a 6-point socket provides superior-holding ability, while a 12-point socket needs to be moved only half as far to reposition it on the fastener.

Sockets are designated for either hand or impact use. Impact sockets are made of thicker material for more durability. Compare the size and wall thickness of a 19-mm hand socket (A, **Figure 15**) and the 19-mm (B) impact socket. Use impact sockets when using an impact driver or air tools. Use hand sockets with hand-driven attachments.

Various handles are available for sockets. Use the speed handle for fast operation. Flexible ratchet heads in varying lengths allow the socket to be turned with varying force and at odd angles. Extension bars allow the socket setup to reach difficult areas. The ratchet is the most versatile. It allows the user to install or remove the nut without removing the socket.

Sockets combined with any number of drivers make them undoubtedly the fastest, safest and most

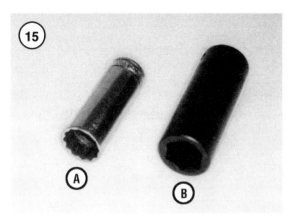

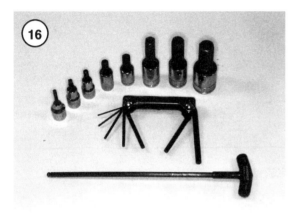

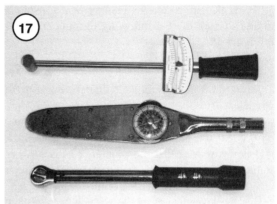

convenient tool for fastener removal and installation.

Impact Drivers

> *WARNING*
> *Do not use hand sockets with air or impact tools because they may shatter and cause injury. Always wear eye protection when using impact or air tools.*

An impact driver provides extra force for removing fasteners by converting the impact of a hammer into a turning motion. This makes it possible to remove stubborn fasteners without damaging them. Impact drivers and interchangeable bits are available from most tool suppliers. When using a socket with an impact driver, make sure the socket is designed for impact use. Refer to *Socket Wrenches, Ratchets and Handles* in this section.

Allen Wrenches

Use Allen or setscrew wrenches (**Figure 16**) on fasteners with hexagonal recesses in the fastener head. These wrenches are available in L-shaped bar,

socket and T-handle types. A metric set is required when working on most motorcycles. Allen bolts are sometimes called socket bolts.

Torque Wrenches

Use a torque wrench with a socket, torque adapter or similar extension to tighten a fastener to a measured torque. Torque wrenches come in several drive sizes (1/4, 3/8, 1/2 and 3/4) and have various methods of reading the torque value. The drive size indicates the size of the square drive that accepts the socket, adapter or extension. Common methods of reading the torque value are the deflecting beam, the dial indicator and the audible click (**Figure 17**).

When choosing a torque wrench, consider the torque range, drive size and accuracy. The torque specifications in this manual provide an indication of the range required.

A torque wrench is a precision tool that must be properly cared for to remain accurate. Store torque wrenches in cases or separate padded drawers within a toolbox. Follow the manufacturer's instructions for their care and calibration.

Torque Adapters

Torque adapters or extensions extend or reduce the reach of a torque wrench. The torque adapter shown in **Figure 18** is used to tighten a fastener that cannot be reached because of the size of the torque wrench head, drive, and socket. If a torque adapter changes the effective lever length (**Figure 19**), the torque reading on the wrench will not equal the actual torque applied to the fastener. It is necessary to recalibrate the torque setting on the wrench to compensate for the change of lever length. When using a torque adapter at a right angle to the drive head, calibration is not required, because the effective length has not changed.

To recalculate a torque reading when using a torque adapter, use the following formula and refer to **Figure 19**:

$$TW = \frac{TA \times L}{L + A}$$

TW is the torque setting or dial reading on the wrench.

TA is the torque specification and the actual amount of torque that is applied to the fastener.

A is the amount that the adapter increases (or in some cases reduces) the effective lever length as measured along the centerline of the torque wrench.

L is the lever length of the wrench as measured from the center of the drive to the center of the grip.

The effective length is the sum of *L* and A.

Example:

TA = 20 ft.-lb.

A = 3 in.

L = 14 in.

$$TW = \frac{20 \times 14}{14 + 3} = \frac{280}{17} = 16.5 \text{ ft. lb.}$$

In this example, the torque wrench should be set to the calculated torque value of 16.5 ft.-lb. Although the torque wrench is set to 16.5 ft.-lb., the applied torque is 20 ft.-lb. When using a beam-type wrench, tighten the fastener until the pointer aligns with 16.5 ft.-lb, the actual torque is 20 ft-lb.

Pliers

Pliers come in a wide range of types and sizes. Pliers are useful for holding, cutting, bending, and crimping. Do not use them to turn fasteners. **Figure 20** and **Figure 21** show several types of useful pliers. Each design has a specialized function. Slip-joint pliers are general-purpose pliers used for gripping and bending. Diagonal cutting pliers are needed to cut wire and can be used to remove cotter pins. Use needlenose pliers to hold or bend small objects. Locking pliers (**Figure 21**), sometimes called Vise-Grips, are used to hold objects very tightly. They have many uses ranging from holding two parts together, to gripping the end of a broken stud. Use caution when using locking pliers, as the sharp jaws will damage the objects they hold.

Snap Ring Pliers

WARNING
Snap rings can slip and fly off when removing and installing them. Also, the snap ring pliers' tips may break. Always wear eye protection when using snap ring pliers.

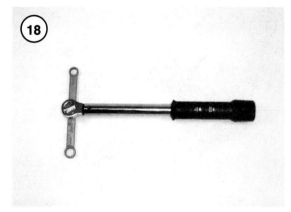

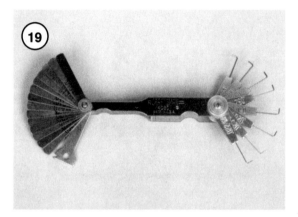

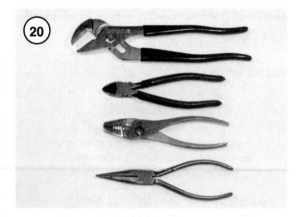

Snap ring pliers are specialized pliers with tips that fit into the ends of snap rings to remove and install them.

Snap ring pliers (**Figure 22**) are available with a fixed action (either internal or external) or convertible (one tool works on both internal and external snap rings). They may have fixed tips or interchangeable ones of various sizes and angles. For general use, select a convertible type of pliers with interchangeable tips (**Figure 22**).

Hammers

Various types of hammers are available to fit a number of applications. Use a ball-peen hammer to

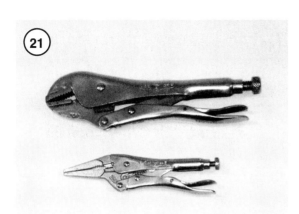

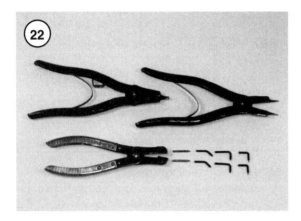

PRECISION MEASURING TOOLS

The ability to accurately measure components is essential to perform many of the procedures described in this manual. Equipment is manufactured to close tolerances, and obtaining consistently accurate measurements is essential to determine which components require replacement or further service.

Each type of measuring instrument is designed to measure a dimension w with a certain degree of accuracy and within a certain range. When selecting the measuring tool, make sure it is applicable to the task.

As with all tools, measuring tools provide the best results if cared for properly. Improper use can damage the tool and cause inaccurate results. If any measurement is questionable, verify the measurement using another tool. A standard gauge is usually provided with micrometers to check accuracy and calibrate the tool if necessary.

Precision measurements can vary according to the experience of the person taking the measurement. Accurate results are only possible if the mechanic possesses a feel for using the tool. Heavy-handed use of measuring tools produces inaccurate results. Hold the tool gently by the fingertips to easily feel the point at which the tool contacts the object. This feel for the equipment produces more accurate measurements and reduces the risk of damaging the tool or component. Refer to the following subsections for specific measuring tools.

Feeler Gauge

Use feeler or thickness gauges (**Figure 23**) for measuring the distance between two surfaces.

A feeler gauge set consists of an assortment of steel strips of graduated thickness. Each blade is marked with its thickness. Blades can be of various lengths and angles for different procedures.

A common use for a feeler gauge is to measure valve clearance. Use wire (round) type gauges to measure spark plug gap.

Calipers

Calipers (**Figure 24**) are excellent tools for obtaining inside, outside and depth measurements. Although not as precise as a micrometer, they allow reasonable precision, typically to within 0.05 mm (0.001 in.). Most calipers have a range up to 150 mm (6 in.).

Calipers are available in dial, vernier or digital versions. Dial calipers have a dial readout that provides convenient reading. Vernier calipers have marked

strike another tool, such as a punch or chisel. Use soft-faced hammers when a metal object must be struck without damaging it. *Never* use a metal-faced hammer on engine and suspension components because damage occurs in most cases.

Always wear eye protection when using hammers. Make sure the hammer face is in good condition and the handle is not cracked. Select the correct hammer for the job and make sure to strike the object squarely. Do not use the handle or the side of the hammer to strike an object.

scales that must be compared to determine the measurement. The digital caliper uses a liquid-crystal display (LCD) to show the measurement.

Properly maintain the measuring surfaces of the caliper. There must not be any dirt or burrs between the tool and the object being measured. Never force the caliper to close around an object. Close the caliper around the highest point so it can be removed with a slight drag. Some calipers require calibration. Always refer to the manufacturer's instructions when using a new or unfamiliar caliper.

Figure 25 shows a measurement taken with a metric vernier caliper. The fixed scale is marked in 1-mm increments. Ten individual lines on the fixed scale equal 1 cm. The movable scale is marked in 0.05 mm (hundredth) increments.

The value of a measurement equals the reading on the fixed scale plus the reading on the movable scale.

To determine the reading on the fixed scale, look for the line on the fixed scale immediately to the left of the 0-line on the movable scale. In **Figure 25**, the fixed scale reading is 1 centimeter (or 10 millimeters).

To determine the reading on the movable scale, note the one line on the movable scale that precisely aligns with a line on the fixed scale. Look closely. A number of lines will seem close, but only one lines up precisely with a line on the fixed scale. In **Figure 25**, the movable scale reading is 0.50 mm.

To calculate the measurement, add the fixed scale reading (10 mm) to the movable scale reading (0.50 mm) for a value of 10.50 mm.

Micrometers

A micrometer (**Figure 26**) is an instrument designed for linear measurement using the decimal divisions of the inch or meter. While there are many types and styles of micrometers, most of the procedures in this manual call for an outside micrometer. Use an outside micrometer to measure the outside diameter of cylindrical forms and the thickness of materials.

A micrometer's size indicates the minimum and maximum size of a part that it can measure. The usual sizes are 0-25 mm (0-1 in.), 25-50 mm (1-2 in.), 50-75 mm (2-3 in.) and 75-100 mm (3-4 in.).

Micrometers that cover a wider range of measurements are available. These use a large frame with interchangeable anvils of various lengths. This type of micrometer offers a cost savings, but its overall size may make it less convenient.

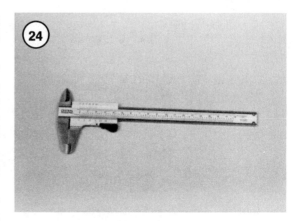

Adjustment

Before using a micrometer, check its adjustment as follows:
1. Clean the anvil and spindle faces.
2A. To check a 0-1 in. or 0-25 mm micrometer:
  a. Turn the thimble until the spindle contacts the anvil. If the micrometer has a ratchet stop, use it to ensure that the proper amount of pressure is applied.
  b. If the adjustment is correct, the 0 mark on the thimble will align exactly with the 0 mark on the sleeve line. If the marks do not align, the micrometer is out of adjustment.
  c. Follow the manufacturer's instructions to adjust the micrometer.
2B. To check a micrometer larger than 1 in. or 25 mm, use the standard gauge supplied by the manufacturer. A standard gauge is a steel block, disc or rod that is machined to an exact size.
  a. Place the standard gauge between the spindle and anvil, and measure its outside diameter or length. If the micrometer has a ratchet stop, use it to ensure that the proper amount of pressure is applied.
  b. If the adjustment is correct, the 0 mark on the thimble will align exactly with the 0 mark on the sleeve line. If the marks do not align, the micrometer is out of adjustment.
  c. Follow the manufacturer's instructions to adjust the micrometer.

Care

Micrometers are precision instruments. They must be used and maintained with great care. Note the following:
1. Store micrometers in protective cases or separate padded drawers in a toolbox.
2. When in storage, make sure the spindle and anvil faces do not contact each other or another object.

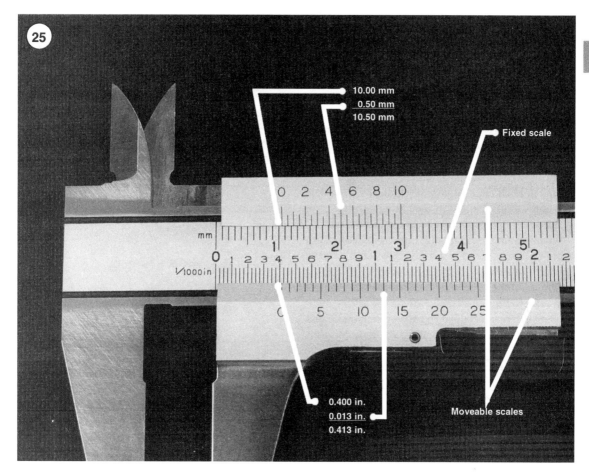

10.00 mm
0.50 mm
10.50 mm

Fixed scale

mm

1/1000 in

0.400 in.
0.013 in.
0.413 in.

Moveable scales

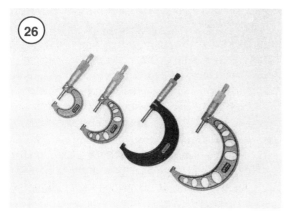

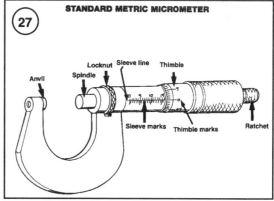

STANDARD METRIC MICROMETER

Locknut Sleeve line Thimble
Anvil Spindle
Sleeve marks Thimble marks Ratchet

If they do, temperature changes and corrosion may damage the contact faces.

3. Do not clean a micrometer with compressed air. Dirt forced into the tool will cause wear.

4. Lubricate micrometers with WD-40 to prevent corrosion.

Reading

When reading a micrometer, numbers are taken from different scales and added together. The follow-ing subsections describe how to read the measure-ments of various types of outside micrometers.

For accurate results, properly maintain the mea-suring surfaces of the micrometer. There cannot be any dirt or burrs between the tool and the measured object. Never force the micrometer to close around an object. Close the micrometer around the highest point so it can be removed with a slight drag.

The standard metric micrometer (**Figure 27**) is accurate to one one-hundredth of a millimeter (0.01 mm). The sleeve line is graduated in millimeter and half millimeter increments. The marks on the upper half of the sleeve line equal 1.00 mm. Each fifth mark above the sleeve line is identified with a number. The number sequence depends on the size of the micrometer. A 0-25 mm micrometer, for example, will have sleeve marks numbered 0 through 25 in 5 mm increments. This numbering sequence continues with larger micrometers. On all metric micrometers, each mark on the lower half of the sleeve equals 0.50 mm.

The tapered end of the thimble has 50 lines marked around it. Each mark equals 0.01 mm. One complete turn of the thimble aligns its 0 mark with the first line on the lower half of the sleeve line or 0.50 mm.

When reading a metric micrometer, add the number of millimeters and half-millimeters on the sleeve line to the number of one one-hundredth millimeters on the thimble. To read a standard metric micrometer, refer to **Figure 28** and perform the following:

1. Read the upper half of the sleeve line and count the number of lines visible. Each upper line equals 1 mm.

2. See if a half-millimeter line is visible on the lower sleeve line. If so, add 0.50 mm to the reading in Step 1.

3. Read the thimble mark that aligns with the sleeve line. Each thimble mark equals 0.01 mm.

NOTE
If a thimble mark does not align exactly with the sleeve line, estimate the amount between the lines. For accurate readings in two-thousandths of a millimeter (0.002 mm), use a metric vernier micrometer.

4. Add the readings from Steps 1-3.

Telescoping and Small Hole Gauges

Use telescoping gauges (**Figure 29**) and small hole gauges (**Figure 30**) to measure bores. Neither gauge has a scale for direct readings. Use an outside micrometer to determine the reading.

To use a telescoping gauge, select the correct size gauge for the bore. Compress the movable post and carefully insert the gauge into the bore. Carefully move the gauge in the bore to make sure it is centered. Tighten the knurled end of the gauge to hold the movable post in position. Remove the gauge and measure the length of the posts. Telescoping gauges are typically used to measure cylinder bores.

To use a small hole gauge, select the correct size gauge for the bore. Carefully insert the gauge into the bore. Tighten the knurled end of the gauge to carefully expand the gauge fingers to the limit within the

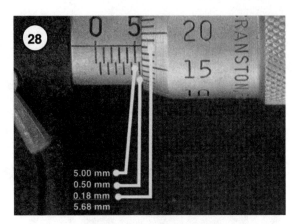

5.00 mm
0.50 mm
0.18 mm
5.68 mm

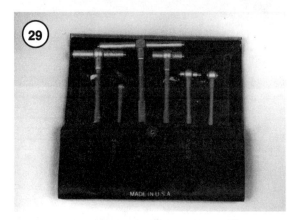

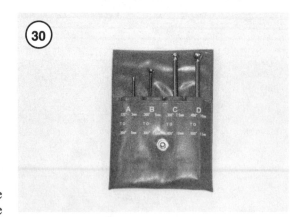

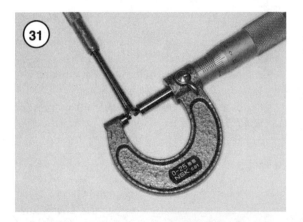

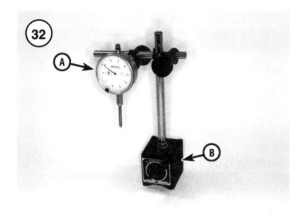

bore. Do not overtighten the gauge because there is no built-in release. Excessive tightening can damage the bore surface and damage the tool. Remove the gauge and measure the outside dimension (**Figure 31**). Small hole gauges are typically used to measure valve guides.

Dial Indicator

A dial indicator (A, **Figure 32**) is a gauge with a dial face and needle used to measure variations in dimensions and movements. Measuring brake rotor runout is a typical use for a dial indicator.

Dial indicators are available in various ranges and graduations and with three basic types of mounting bases: magnetic (B, **Figure 32**), clamp, or screw-in stud. When purchasing a dial indicator, select one with a continuous dial (A, **Figure 32**).

Cylinder Bore Gauge

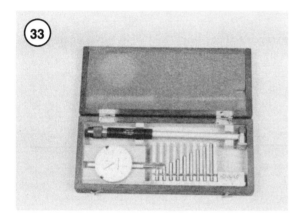

A cylinder bore gauge is similar to a dial indicator. The gauge set shown in **Figure 33** consists of a dial indicator, handle, and different length adapters (anvils) to fit the gauge to various bore sizes. The bore gauge is used to measure bore size, taper and out-of-round. When using a bore gauge, follow the manufacturer's instructions.

Compression Gauge

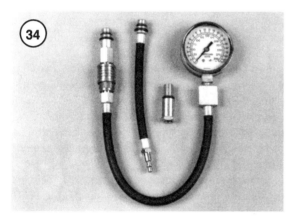

A compression gauge (**Figure 34**) measures combustion chamber (cylinder) pressure, usually in psi or kg/cm². The gauge adapter is either inserted or screwed into the spark plug hole to obtain the reading. Disable the engine so it does not start and hold the throttle in the wide-open position when performing a compression test. An engine that does not have adequate compression cannot be properly tuned. Refer to Chapter Three.

Multimeter

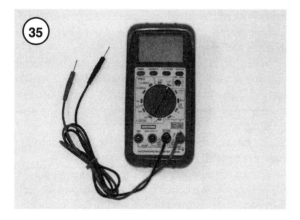

A multimeter (**Figure 35**) is an essential tool for electrical system diagnosis. The voltage function indicates the voltage applied or available to various electrical components. The ohmmeter function tests circuits for continuity and measures the resistance of a circuit.

Some manufacturers' specifications for electrical components are based on results using a specific test meter. Results may vary if a meter not recommended by the manufacturer is used. Such requirements are noted when applicable.

Ohmmeter (Analog) Calibration

Each time an analog ohmmeter is used or if the scale is changed, the ohmmeter must be calibrated. Refer to the manufacturer's instructions.

ELECTRICAL SYSTEM FUNDAMENTALS

A thorough study of the many types of electrical systems used in today's motorcycles is beyond the scope of this manual. However, a basic understanding of electrical basics is necessary to perform simple diagnostic tests.

Refer to *Electrical Testing* in Chapter Two for typical test procedures and equipment. Refer to Chapter Nine for specific system test procedures.

Voltage

Voltage is the electrical potential or pressure in an electrical circuit and is expressed in volts. The more pressure (voltage) in a circuit, the more work can be performed.

Direct current (DC) voltage means the electricity flows in one direction. All circuits powered by a battery are DC circuits.

Alternating current (AC) means the electricity flows in one direction momentarily and then switches to the opposite direction. Alternator output is an example of AC voltage. This voltage must be changed or rectified to direct current to operate in a battery powered system.

Resistance

Resistance is the opposition to the flow of electricity within a circuit or component. It is measured in ohms. Resistance causes a reduction in available current and voltage.

Resistance is measured in an inactive circuit with an ohmmeter. The ohmmeter sends a small amount of current into the circuit and measures how difficult it is to push the current through the circuit.

An ohmmeter, although useful, is not always a good indicator of a circuit's actual ability under operating conditions. This is because of the low voltage (6-9 volts) the meter uses to test the circuit. The voltage in an ignition coil secondary winding can be several thousand volts. Such high voltage can cause the coil to malfunction, even though it tests acceptable during a resistance test.

Resistance generally increases with temperature. Perform all testing with the component or circuit at room temperature. Resistance tests performed at high temperatures may indicate high resistance readings and cause unnecessary replacement of a component.

Amperage

Amperage is the unit of measurement for the amount of current within a circuit. Current is the actual flow of electricity. The higher the current, the more work can be performed up to a given point. If the current flow exceeds the circuit or component capacity, it will damage the system.

SERVICE METHODS

Most of the procedures in this manual are straightforward and can be performed by anyone reasonably competent with tools. However, consider personal capabilities carefully before attempting any operation involving major disassembly.

1. In this manual, the term Front refers to the front of the motorcycle. The front of any component is the end closest to the front of the motorcycle. *Left* and right refer to the position of the parts as viewed by the rider sitting on the seat facing forward.
2. Whenever servicing an engine or suspension component, secure the motorcycle in a safe manner.
3. Label all similar parts for location and mark all mating parts for position. If possible, photograph or draw the number and thickness of any shim as it is removed. Identify parts by placing them in sealed and labeled plastic sandwich bags. It is possible for carefully laid out parts to become disturbed, making it difficult to reassemble the components correctly without a diagram.
4. Label disconnected wires and connectors with masking tape and a marking pen. Connectors must be reconnected to the mates. Do not rely on memory alone.
5. Protect finished surfaces from physical damage or corrosion. Keep gasoline and other chemicals off painted surfaces.
6. Use penetrating oil on frozen or tight bolts. Avoid using heat where possible. Heat can warp, melt or affect the temper of parts. Heat also damages the finish of paint and plastics.
7. When a part is a press fit or requires a special tool for removal, the information or type of tool is identified in the text. Otherwise, if a part is difficult to remove or install, determine the cause before proceeding.
8. To prevent objects or debris from falling into the engine, cover all openings.
9. Read each procedure thoroughly and compare the illustrations to the actual components before starting the procedure. Perform the procedure in sequence.

10. Recommendations are occasionally made to refer service to a dealership or specialist. In these cases, the work can be performed more economically by the specialist than by the home mechanic.

11. The term *replace* means to discard a defective part and replace it with a new part. Overhaul means to remove, disassemble, inspect, measure, repair and/or replace parts as required to recondition an assembly.

12. Some operations require using a hydraulic press. If a press is not available, have these operations performed by a shop equipped with the necessary equipment. Do not use makeshift equipment that may damage the motorcycle.

13. Repairs are much faster and easier if the motorcycle is clean before starting work. Degrease the motorcycle with a commercial degreaser; follow the directions on the container for the best results. Clean all parts with cleaning solvent when removing them.

CAUTION
Do not direct high-pressure water at steering bearings, fuel hoses, wheel bearings, suspension and electrical components. Water may force grease out of the bearings and possibly damage the seals.

14. If special tools are required, have them available before starting the procedure. When special tools are required, they are described at the beginning of the procedure.

15. Make diagrams of similar-appearing parts. For instance, crankcase bolts are often not the same lengths. Do not rely on memory alone. Carefully laid out parts can become disturbed, making it difficult to reassemble the components correctly.

16. Make sure all shims and washers are reinstalled in the same location and position.

17. Whenever rotating parts contact a stationary part, look for a shim or washer.

18. Use new gaskets if there is any doubt about the condition of old ones.

19. Replace self-locking fasteners, with new ones. Do not install standard fasteners in place of self-locking ones.

20. Use grease to hold small parts in place if they tend to fall out during assembly. Do not apply grease to electrical or brake components.

Heating Components

WARNING
Wear protective gloves to prevent burns and injury when heating parts.

CAUTION
Do not use a welding torch when heating parts. A welding torch applies excessive heat to a small area very quickly, which can damage parts.

A heat gun or propane torch is required to disassemble, assemble, remove and install some parts and components in this manual. Read the safety and operating information supplied by the manufacturer of the heat gun or propane torch while also noting the following:

1. The work area must be clean and dry. Remove all combustible components and materials from the work area. Wipe up all grease, oil and other fluids from parts. Check for leaking or damaged fuel system components. Repair or remove these parts before beginning work.

2. Never use a flame near the battery, fuel tank, fuel lines or other flammable materials.

3. When using a heat gun, remember that the temperature can be in excess of 540° C (1000° F).

4. Have a fire extinguisher near the job.

5. Always wear protective goggles and gloves when heating parts.

6. Before heating a part installed on the motorcycle, check areas around the part and those parts *hidden from view* that could be damaged or possibly ignite. Do not heat surfaces than can be damaged by heat. Shield materials near the part or area to be heated. For example, cables and wiring harnesses.

7. Before heating a part, read the entire procedure to make sure the required tools are available. This allows quick work while the part is at its optimum temperature.

8. The amount of heat recommended to remove or install a part is typically listed in the procedure. However, before heating parts without a specific recommendation, consider the possible effects. To avoid damaging a part, monitor the temperature with heat sticks or an infrared thermometer, if possible. Another way, though not as accurate, is to place tiny drops of water on the part. When the water starts to sizzle, the part is hot enough. Keep the heat in motion to prevent overheating.

Removing Frozen Fasteners

If a fastener cannot be removed, several methods may be used to loosen it. First, apply penetrating oil such as Liquid Wrench or WD-40. Apply it liberally and let it penetrate for 10-15 minutes. Rap the fastener several times with a small hammer. Do not hit it hard enough to cause damage. Reapply the penetrating oil if necessary.

For frozen screws, apply penetrating oil as described, and then insert a screwdriver into the slot and rap the top of the screwdriver with a hammer. This loosens the rust so the screw can be removed in the normal way. If the screw head is too damaged to use this method, grip the head with locking pliers and twist the screw out.

Avoid applying heat unless specifically instructed. Heat may melt, warp or remove the temper from parts.

Removing Broken Fasteners

If the head breaks off a screw or bolt, several methods are available for removing the remaining portion. If a large portion of the remainder projects out, try gripping it with locking pliers. If the projecting portion is too small, file it to fit a wrench or cut a slot in it to fit a screwdriver (**Figure 36**).

If the head breaks off flush, use a screw extractor. To do this, center punch the exact center of the remaining portion of the screw or bolt. Drill a small hole into the screw and tap the extractor into the hole. Back the screw out with a wrench on the extractor (**Figure 37**).

Repairing Damaged Threads

Occasionally, threads are stripped through carelessness or impact damage. Often the threads can be repaired by running a tap (for internal threads on nuts) or die (for external threads on bolts) through the threads (**Figure 38**). To clean or repair spark plug threads, use a spark plug tap.

If an internal thread is damaged, it may be necessary to install a Helicoil or some other type of thread insert. Follow the manufacturer's instructions when installing their insert.

If it is necessary to drill and tap a hole, refer to **Table 6** for metric tap and drill sizes.

Stud Removal/Installation

A stud removal tool (**Figure 39**) is available from most tool suppliers. This tool makes the removal and installation of studs easier. If one is not available, thread two nuts onto the stud and tighten them against each other. Remove the stud by turning the lower nut (**Figure 40**).

1. Measure the height of the stud above the surface.
2. Thread the stud removal tool onto the stud and tighten it, or thread two nuts onto the stud.
3. Remove the stud by turning the stud remover or the lower nut.

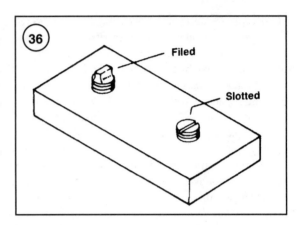

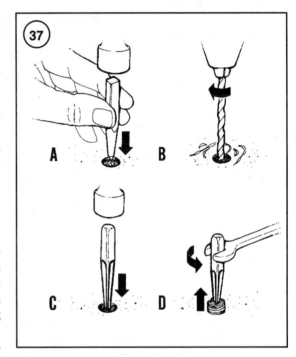

4. Remove any threadlocking compound from the threaded hole. Clean the threads with an aerosol parts cleaner.
5. Install the stud removal tool onto the new stud or thread two nuts onto the stud.
6. Apply threadlocking compound to the threads of the stud.
7. Install the stud and tighten with the stud removal tool or the top nut.
8. Install the stud to the height noted in Step 1 or its torque specification.
9. Remove the stud removal tool or the two nuts.

Removing Hoses

Do not exert excessive force on the hose or fitting when removing stubborn hoses. Remove the hose clamp and carefully insert a small screwdriver or

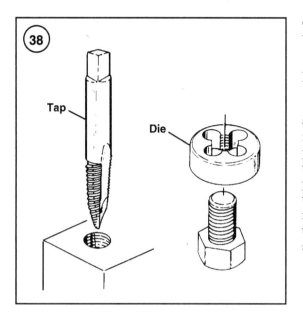

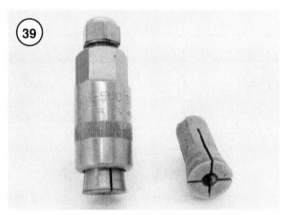

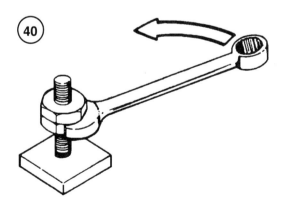

cant may allow the hose to come off the fitting, even with the clamp secure.

Bearings

Bearings are used in the engine and transmission assembly to reduce power loss, heat and noise resulting from friction. Because bearings are precision parts, they must be maintained with proper lubrication and maintenance. If a bearing is damaged, replace it immediately. When installing a new bearing, take care to prevent damaging it. Bearing replacement procedures are included in the individual chapters where applicable; however, use the following subsections as a guideline.

NOTE
Unless otherwise specified, install bearings with the manufacturer's mark or number facing outward.

Removal

While bearings are normally removed only when damaged, there may be times when it is necessary to remove a bearing that is in good condition. However, improper bearing removal will damage the bearing and possibly the shaft or case. Note the following when removing bearings:
1. Before removing the bearings, note the following:
   a. Refer to the bearing replacement procedure in the appropriate chapter for any special instructions.
   b. Remove any seals that interfere with bearing removal. Refer to *Seal Replacement* in this section.
   c. When removing more than one bearing, identify the bearings before removing them. Refer to the bearing manufacturer's numbers on the bearing.
   d. Note and record the direction in which the bearing numbers face for proper installation.
   e. Remove any set plates or bearing retainers before removing the bearings.
2. When using a puller to remove a bearing from a shaft, take care that the shaft is not damaged. Always place a piece of metal between the end of the shaft and the puller screw. In addition, place the puller arms next to the inner bearing race. Refer to **Figure 41**.
3. When using a hammer to remove a bearing from a shaft, do not strike the hammer directly against the shaft. Instead, use a brass or aluminum rod between the hammer and shaft (**Figure 42**) and make sure to

pick tool between the fitting and hose. Apply a spray lubricant under the hose and carefully twist the hose off the fitting. Clean any corrosion or rubber hose material from the fitting with a wire brush. Clean the inside of the hose thoroughly. **Do not** use any lubricant when installing the new or old hose. The lubri-

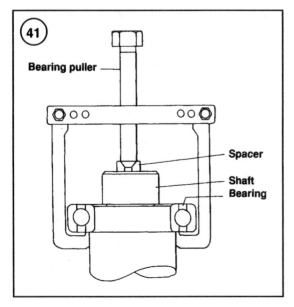

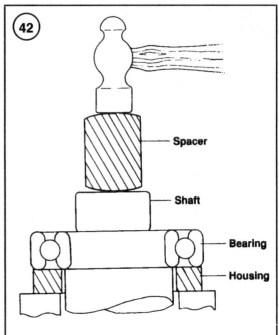

support both bearing races with wooden blocks as shown.

4. The ideal method of bearing removal is with a hydraulic press. Note the following when using a press:

    a. Always support the inner and outer bearing races with a suitable size wooden or aluminum spacer (**Figure 43**). If only the outer race is supported, pressure applied against the balls and/or the inner race will damage them.

    b. Always make sure the press arm (**Figure 43**) aligns with the center of the shaft. If the arm is not centered, it may damage the bearing and/or shaft.

    c. The moment the shaft is free of the bearing, it drops to the floor. Secure or hold the shaft to prevent it from falling.

    d. When removing bearings from a housing, support the housing with 4 × 4 in. wooden blocks to prevent damage to gasket surfaces.

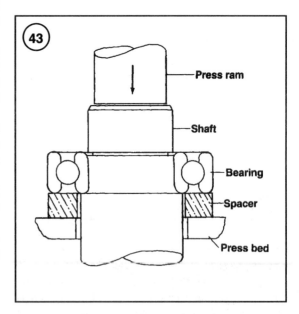

Installation

1. When installing a bearing into a housing, apply pressure to the outer bearing race (**Figure 44**). When installing a bearing on a shaft, apply pressure to the inner bearing race (**Figure 45**).

2. When installing a bearing as described in Step 1, some type of driver is required. Never strike the bearing directly with a hammer or it will damage the bearing. When installing a bearing, use a piece of pipe or a driver with a diameter that matches the bearing inner race. **Figure 46** shows the correct way to use a driver and hammer to install a bearing.

3. Step 1 describes how to install a bearing in a case half or over a shaft. However, when installing a bear-

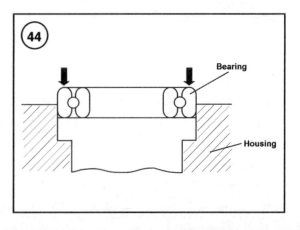

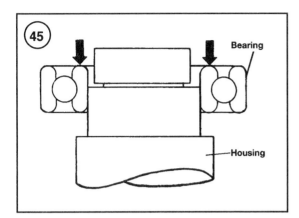

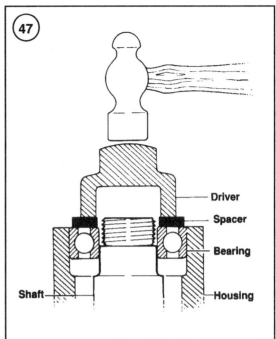

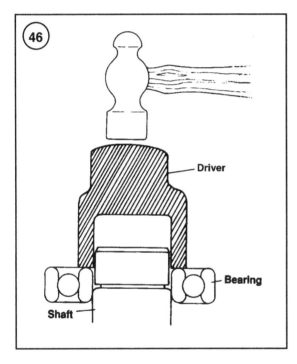

ing over a shaft and into the housing at the same time, a tight fit is required for both outer and inner bearing races. In this situation, install a spacer underneath the driver tool so that pressure is applied evenly across both races. Refer to **Figure 47**. If the outer race is not supported as shown, the balls will push against the outer bearing race and damage it.

Interference fit

1. Follow this procedure when installing a bearing over a shaft. When a tight fit is required, the bearing inside diameter is smaller than the shaft. In this case, driving the bearing on the shaft using normal methods may cause bearing damage. Instead, heat the bearing before installation. Note the following:

   a. If possible, place the shaft in a freezer for ¾ hour to reduce the outer diameter of the shaft.

   b. Secure the shaft so it is ready for bearing installation.

   c. Clean all residues from the bearing surface of the shaft. Remove burrs with a file or sandpaper.

   d. Fill a suitable pot or beaker with clean mineral oil. Place a thermometer rated above 120° C (248° F) in the oil. Support the thermometer so it does not rest on the bottom or side of the pot.

   e. Remove the bearing from its wrapper and secure it with a piece of heavy wire bent to hold it in the pot. Hang the bearing in the pot so it does not touch the bottom or sides of the pot.

   f. Turn the heat on and monitor the thermometer. When the oil temperature rises to approximately 120° C (248° F), remove the bearing from the pot and quickly install it. If necessary, place a socket on the inner bearing race and tap the bearing into place. As the bearing chills, it will tighten on the shaft, so installation must be done quickly. Make sure the bearing is installed completely.

2. Follow this step when installing a bearing in a housing. Bearings are generally installed in a housing with a slight interference fit. Driving the bearing into the housing using normal methods may damage the housing or cause bearing damage. Instead, heat the housing before the bearing is installed. Note the following:

CAUTION
Before heating the housing in this procedure, wash the housing thoroughly with detergent and water. Rinse and rewash the cases as required to remove all traces of oil and other chemical deposits.

a. Heat the housing to approximately 100° C (212° F) in an oven or on a hot plate. An easy way to check that it is the proper temperature is to place tiny drops of water on the housing; if they sizzle and evaporate immediately, the temperature is correct. Heat only one housing at a time.

CAUTION
Do not heat the housing with a propane or acetylene torch. Never bring a flame into contact with the bearing or housing. The direct heat will destroy the case hardening of the bearing and will likely warp the housing.

b. Remove the housing from the oven or hot plate and hold onto the housing with welding gloves. It is hot!

NOTE
Remove and install the bearings with a suitable size socket and extension.

c. Hold the housing with the bearing side down and tap the bearing out. Repeat for all bearings in the housing.
d. Before heating the bearing housing, place the new bearing in a freezer if possible. Chilling a bearing slightly reduces its outside diameter while the heated bearing housing assembly is slightly larger due to heat expansion. This makes bearing installation easier.

NOTE
Always install bearings with the manufacturer's mark or number facing outward.

e. While the housing is still hot, install the new bearing(s) into the housing. Install the bearings by hand, if possible. If necessary, lightly tap the bearing(s) into the housing with a driver placed on the outer bearing race (**Figure 44**). Do not install new bearings by driving on the inner-bearing race. Install the bearing(s) until it seats completely.

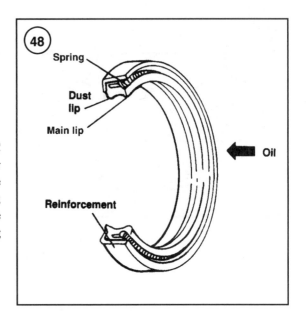

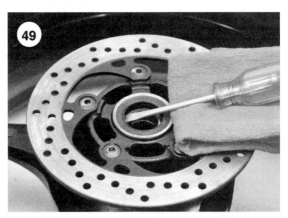

Seal Removal/Installation

Seals (**Figure 48**) contain oil, water, grease or combustion gasses in a housing or shaft. Improperly removing a seal can damage the housing or shaft. Improperly installing the seal can damage the seal. Note the following:

1. Prying is generally the easiest and most effective method of removing a seal from the housing. However, always place a rag underneath the pry tool (**Figure 49**) to prevent damage to the housing. Note the seal's installed depth or if it is installed flush.
2. Pack waterproof grease into the seal lips before the seal is installed.
3. In most cases, install seals with the manufacturer's numbers or marks facing out.
4. Install seals with a socket or driver placed on the outside of the seal as shown in **Figure 50**. Drive the seal squarely into the housing until it is to the correct depth or flush (**Figure 51**) as noted during removal. Never install a seal by hitting against the top of it with a hammer.

STORAGE

Several months of non-use can cause a general deterioration of the motorcycle. This is especially true in areas of extreme temperature variations. This deterioration can be minimized with careful preparation for storage. A properly stored motorcycle is much easier to return to service.

Storage Area Selection

When selecting a storage area, consider the following:

1. The storage area must be dry. A heated area is best but not necessary. It should be insulated to minimize extreme temperature variations.

2. If the building has large window areas, mask them to keep sunlight off the motorcycle.

3. Avoid buildings in industrial areas where corrosive emissions may be present. Avoid areas close to saltwater.

4. Consider the area's risk of fire, theft or vandalism. Check with an insurer regarding motorcycle coverage while in storage.

Preparing the Motorcycle for Storage

The amount of preparation a motorcycle should undergo before storage depends upon the expected length of non-use, storage area conditions and personal preference. Consider the following list the minimum requirement.

1. Wash the motorcycle thoroughly. Make sure all dirt, mud and road debris is removed.

2. Start the engine and allow it to reach operating temperature. Drain the engine oil regardless of the riding time since the last service. Fill the engine with the recommended type of oil.

3. Fill the fuel tank with fuel mixed with a fuel stabilizer. Mix the fuel and stabilizer in the ratio recommended by the stabilizer manufacturer. Run the engine for a few minutes so the stabilized fuel can enter the fuel injection system.

4. Remove the spark plugs and pour a tablespoon (45-60 ml) of engine oil into the cylinders. Place a rag over the openings and slowly turn the engine over to distribute the oil. Reinstall the spark plugs.

5. Remove the battery. Store the battery in a cool and dry location. Charge the battery once a month.

6. Use oily rags to cover the muffler output opening and intake openings in the air filter housing.

7. Apply a protective substance to the plastic and rubber components. Make sure to follow the manufacturer's instructions for each type of product being used.

8. Place the motorcycle on its stand. Rotate the front tire periodically to prevent a flat spot from developing and damaging the tire.

9. Cover the motorcycle with old bed sheets or something similar. Do not cover it with any plastic material that will trap moisture.

Returning the Motorcycle to Service

The amount of service required when returning a motorcycle to service after storage depends on the length of non-use and storage conditions. In addition to performing the reverse of the above procedure, make sure the brakes, clutch, throttle and engine stop switch work properly before operating the motorcycle. Refer to Chapter Three and evaluate the service intervals to determine which areas require service.

Table 1 FRAME SERIAL NUMBERS

Model	Year	Frame number.
GSX-R600K6 and K7		
U.S., California and Canada	2006-2007	JS1GN6DA 62100001-on
U.K. and European U1	2006-2007	JS1CE111100100001-on
European U2	2006-2007	JS1CE211100100001-on
European U3	2006-2007	JS1CE311100100001-on
Australia	2006-2007	JS1CE312100100001-on
GSX-R600K8 and K9		
U.S., California and Canada	2008-2009	JS1GN7EA 82100001-on
U.K. and European U1	2008-2009	JS1CV111100100001-on
European U2	2008-2009	JS1CV211100100001-on
European U3	2008-2009	JS1CV311100100001-on
Australia	2008-2009	JS1CV11200100001-on
GSX-R750K6 and K7		
U.S., California and Canada	2006-2007	JS1GR7KA 62100001-on
U.K. and European U1	2006-2007	JS1CF111100100001-on
European U2	2006-2007	JS1CF211100100001-on
Australia	2006-2007	JS1CF121300100001-on
GSX-R750K8 and K9		
U.S., California and Canada	2008-2009	JS1GR7LA 82100001-on
U.K. and European U1	2008-2009	JS1CW111100100001-on
European U2	2008-2009	JS1CW211100100001-on
Australia	2008-2009	JS1CW111200100001-on

Table 2 VEHICLE DIMENSIONS AND WEIGHT

Overall length	2040 mm (80.3 in.)
Overall width	715 mm (28.1 in.)
Overall height	1150 mm (45.3 in.)
Seat height	810 mm (31.9 in.)
Wheelbase	1400 mm (55.1 in.)
Ground clearance	130 mm (5.1 in.)
Dry mass	
2006-2007 GSX-R600	
All models except California	161 kg (354 lb.)
California models	162 kg (357 lb.)
2008-2009 GSX-R600	
All models except California	165 kg (363 lb.)
California models	166 kg (365 lb.)
2006-2007 GSX-R750	
All models except California	163 kg (359 lb.)
California models	164 kg (361 lb.)
2008-2009 GSX-R750	
All models except California	167 kg (368 lb.)
California models	168 kg (370 lb.)

Table 3 CONVERSION TABLES

Multiply:	By:	To get the equivalent of:
Length		
Inches	25.4	Millimeter
Inches	2.54	Centimeter
Miles	1.609	Kilometer
Feet	0.3048	Meter
Millimeter	0.03937	Inches
Centimeter	0.3937	Inches
Kilometer	0.6214	Mile
Meter	3.281	Feet

(continued)

Table 3 CONVERSION TABLES (continued)

Multiply:	By:	To get the equivalent of:
Fluid volume		
U.S. quarts	0.9463	Liters
U.S. gallons	3.785	Liters
U.S. ounces	29.573529	Milliliters
Imperial gallons	4.54609	Liters
Imperial quarts	1.1365	Liters
Liters	0.2641721	U.S. gallons
Liters	1.0566882	U.S. quarts
Liters	33.814023	U.S. ounces
Liters	0.22	Imperial gallons
Liters	0.8799	Imperial quarts
Milliliters	0.033814	U.S. ounces
Milliliters	1.0	Cubic centimeters
Milliliters	0.001	Liters
Torque		
Foot-pounds	1.3558	Newton-meters
Foot-pounds	0.138255	Meters-kilograms
Inch-pounds	0.11299	Newton-meters
Newton-meters	0.7375622	Foot-pounds
Newton-meters	8.8507	Inch-pounds
Meters-kilograms	7.2330139	Foot-pounds
Volume		
Cubic inches	16.387064	Cubic centimeters
Cubic centimeters	0.0610237	Cubic inches
Temperature		
Fahrenheit	$(°F - 32) \times 0.556$	Centigrade
Centigrade	$(°C \times 1.8) + 32$	Fahrenheit
Weight		
Ounces	28.3495	Grams
Pounds	0.4535924	Kilograms
Grams	0.035274	Ounces
Kilograms	2.2046224	Pounds
Pressure		
Pounds per square inch square centimeter	0.070307	Kilograms per
Kilograms per square centimeter	14.223343	Pounds per square inch
Kilopascals	0.1450	Pounds per square inch
Pounds per square inch	6.895	Kilopascals
Speed		
Miles per hour	1.609344	Kilometers per hour
Kilometers per hour	0.6213712	Miles per hour

Table 4 DECIMAL AND METRIC EQUIVALENTS

Fractions	Decimal in.	Metric mm	Fractions	Decimal in.	Metric mm
1/64	0.015625	0.39688	33/64	0.515625	13.09687
1/32	0.03125	0.79375	17/32	0.53125	13.49375
3/64	0.046875	1.19062	35/64	0.546875	13.89062
1/16	0.0625	1.58750	9/16	0.5625	14.28750
5/64	0.078125	1.98437	37/64	0.578125	14.68437
3/32	0.09375	2.38125	19/32	0.59375	15.08125
7/64	0.109375	2.77812	39/64	0.609375	15.47812
1/8	0.125	3.1750	5/8	0.625	15.87500
9/64	0.140625	3.57187	41/64	0.640625	16.27187
5/32	0.15625	3.96875	21/32	0.65625	16.66875
11/64	0.171875	4.36562	43/64	0.671875	17.06562
3/16	0.1875	4.76250	11/16	0.6875	17.46250
13/64	0.203125	5.15937	45/64	0.703125	17.85937
7/32	0.21875	5.55625	23/32	0.71875	18.25625

(continued)

Table 4 DECIMAL AND METRIC EQUIVALENTS (continued)

Fractions	Decimal in.	Metric mm	Fractions	Decimal in.	Metric mm
15/64	0.234375	5.95312	47/64	0.734375	18.65312
1/4	0.250	6.35000	3/4	0.750	19.05000
17/64	0.265625	6.74687	49/64	0.765625	19.44687
9/32	0.28125	7.14375	25/32	0.78125	19.84375
19/64	0.296875	7.54062	51/64	0.796875	20.24062
5/16	0.3125	7.93750	13/16	0.8125	20.63750
21/64	0.328125	8.33437	53/64	0.828125	21.03437
11/32	0.34375	8.73125	27/32	0.84375	21.43125
23/64	0.359375	9.12812	55/64	0.859375	22.82812
3/8	0.375	9.52500	7/8	0.875	22.22500
25/64	0.390625	9.92187	57/64	0.890625	22.62187
13/32	0.40625	10.31875	29/32	0.90625	23.01875
27/64	0.421875	10.71562	59/64	0.921875	23.41562
7/16	0.4375	11.11250	15/16	0.9375	23.81250
29/64	0.453125	11.50937	61/64	0.953125	24.20937
15/32	0.46875	11.90625	31/32	0.96875	24.60625
31/64	0.484375	12.30312	63/64	0.984375	25.00312
1/2	0.500	12.70000	1	1.00	25.40000

Table 5 TECHNICAL ABBREVIATIONS

ABDC	After bottom dead center
AP sensor	Atmospheric pressure sensor
ATDC	After top dead center
BBDC	Before bottom dead center
BDC	Bottom dead center
BTDC	Before top dead center
C	Celsius (centigrade)
cc	Cubic centimeters
CDI	Capacitor discharge ignition
cid	Cubic inch displacement
CKP sensor	Crankshaft position sensor
CLP switch	Clutch lever position switch (clutch switch)
CMP sensor	Camshaft position sensor
cu. in.	Cubic inches
ECM	Electronic control module
ECT sensor	Engine coolant temperature sensor
EVAP	Evaporative emission control system
EXC valve	Exhaust control valve
EXCVA	Exhaust control valve actuator
F	Fahrenheit
ft.	Feet
ft.-lb.	Foot-pounds
gal.	Gallons
GP sensor	Gear position sensor
H/A	High altitude
hp	Horsepower
IAP sensor	Intake air pressure sensor
IAT sensor	Intake air temperature sensor
in.	Inches
in.-lb.	Inch-pounds
I.D.	Inside diameter kg Kilograms
kgm	Kilogram meters
km	Kilometer
kPa	Kilopascals
L	Liter
m	Meter
MAG	Magneto
ml	Milliliter
mm	Millimeter

(continued)

Table 5 TECHNICAL ABBREVIATIONS (continued)

N•m	Newton-meters
O.D.	Outside diameter
oz.	Ounces
PAIR	Pulsed Secondary AIR Injection
psi	Pounds per square inch
PTO	Power take off
pt.	Pint
qt.	Quart
rpm	Revolutions per minute
STP sensor	Secondary throttle position sensor
STV	Secondary throttle valve
STVA	Secondary throttle valve actuator
TP sensor	Throttle position sensor
TPC	Tank pressure control valve
TO sensor	Tip over sensor

Table 6 GENERAL TORQUE RECOMMENDATIONS

Thread diameter	N•m	in.-lb.	ft.-lb.
5 mm			
Bolt and nut	5	44	–
Screw	4	35	–
6 mm			
Bolt and nut	10	88	–
Screw	9	80	–
6 mm flange bolt and nut	12	106	–
6 mm bolt with 8 mm head	9	80	–
8 mm			
Bolt and nut	22	–	16
Flange bolt and nut	27	–	20
10 mm			
Bolt and nut	35	–	26
Flange bolt and nut	40	–	30
12 mm			
Bolt and nut	55	–	41

*Torque recommendations for fasteners without a specification. Refer to the torque specification table(s) at the end of the respective chapter(s) for specific applications.

Table 7 METRIC TAP DRILL SIZE

Metric	Drill	Decimal size equivalent fraction	Nearest fraction
3 × 0.50	No. 39	0.0995	3/32
3 × 0.60	3/32	0.0937	3/32
4 × 0.70	No. 30	0.1285	1/8
4 × 0.75	1/8	0.125	1/8
5 × 0.80	No. 19	0.166	11/64
5 × 0.90	No. 20	0.161	5/32
6 × 1.00	No. 9	0.196	13/64
7 × 1.00	16/64	0.234	15/64
8 × 1.00	J	0.277	9/32
8 × 1.25	17/64	0.265	17/64
9 × 1.00	5/16	0.3125	5/16
9 × 1.25	5/16	0.3125	5/16
10 × 1.25	11/32	0.3437	11/32
10 × 1.50	R	0.339	11/32
11 × 1.50	3/8	0.375	3/8
12 × 1.50	13/32	0.406	13/32
12 × 1.75	13/32	0.406	13/32

Notes

CHAPTER TWO

TROUBLESHOOTING

The troubleshooting procedures described in this chapter provide typical symptoms of a problem and logical methods for isolating its causes. There may be several ways to solve a problem, but only a systematic approach will successfully avoid wasted time and unnecessary parts replacement.

Begin troubleshooting by gathering as much information as possible and precisely describing the symptoms of the problem. Never assume anything, and do not overlook the obvious. For example, make sure there is fresh fuel in the tank, that the engine stop switch is in the RUN position, or that the spark plug wires are securely connected to the plugs.

If a quick check does not resolve the problem, find the troubleshooting procedure in this chapter that best describes the symptoms being experienced. Perform the listed tests to isolate the problem to a particular system (fuel, electrical, mechanical, etc.) and then isolate it to a particular component. Repair or replace that component, and test ride the motorcycle to confirm the problem has been corrected.

In most cases, expensive and complicated test equipment is not needed to determine whether repairs can be performed at home. A few simple checks could prevent an unnecessary repair charge and lost time while the motorcycle is at a dealership's service department. On the other hand, be realistic and do not attempt repairs beyond one's personal capabilities. Many service departments will not take work that involves the reassembly of damaged or abused equipment. If they do, expect the cost to be high.

If the motorcycle does require the attention of a professional, describe the symptoms, conditions and previous repair attempts accurately and fully. The more information a technician has, the easier it is be to diagnose the problem.

By following maintenance schedule described in Chapter Three, the need for troubleshooting can be reduced by eliminating potential problems before they occur. However, even with the best of care a motorcycle may require troubleshooting.

ENGINE STARTING

1. A sidestand ignition cutoff system is equipped on all models. Consequently, the position of the sidestand affects engine starting. Note the following:
   a. The engine cannot start when the sidestand is down and the transmission is in gear.
   b. The engine can start when the sidestand is down and the transmission is in neutral. The engine will stop, however, if the transmission is put in gear while the sidestand is down.
   c. The engine can start when the sidestand is up and the transmission is in neutral.
   d. If the sidestand is up, the engine will also start if the transmission is in gear and the clutch lever is pulled in.

2. Before starting the engine, shift the transmission into neutral and confirm that the engine stop switch (A, **Figure 1**) is set to run.

3. Turn the ignition switch on. The neutral indicator light should turn on if transmission is in neutral.

4. The engine is now ready to start. Refer to the starting procedure in this section that best describes the air temperature and engine conditions.

5. If the engine idles at a fast speed for more than five minutes or if the throttle is repeatedly snapped on and off at normal air temperatures, the exhaust pipes may discolor.

NOTE
Do not operate the starter motor for more than five seconds at a time. Wait approximately ten seconds between starting attempts.

Cold Engine

1. Shift the transmission into neutral.
2. Make sure the engine stop switch (A, **Figure 1**) is in the run position.
3. Turn the ignition switch on.

WARNING
The warning lights should turn off after a few seconds or after the engine starts. If a light stays on, turn the engine off and check the oil level and coolant level as described in Chapter Three.

4. The following indicator lights should turn on when the ignition switch is turned on.
   a. The neutral indicator light (when the transmission is in neutral)
   b. Low oil pressure indicator LED
   c. Coolant temperature LCD.
   d. Fuel level indicator LCD.
   e. The tachometer needle swings to its maximum setting and then returns to zero.

NOTE
When a cold engine is started with the throttle open and the fast idle lever on, a lean mixture will result and cause hard starting.

5. Completely close the throttle, press the starter button (B, **Figure 1**) and start the engine.
6. The engine is warm when it cleanly responds to the throttle.

Warm or Hot Engine

1. Shift the transmission into neutral.
2. Turn the ignition switch to on.
3. Make sure the engine stop switch (A, **Figure 1**) is in the run position.

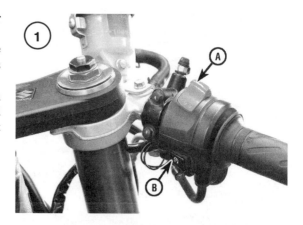

4. Open the throttle slightly and press the starter button (B, **Figure 1**).

Engine Flooded

If the engine will not start and if a strong gasoline smell is present, the engine is probably flooded. To start a flooded engine:
1. Turn the engine stop switch to the off position.
2. Open the throttle fully.
3. Turn the ignition switch to the on position and operate the starter button for five seconds.
4. Wait ten seconds, and turn the engine stop switch to the on position.
5. If the engine starts but idles roughly, vary the throttle position slightly until the engine idles and responds smoothly.

ENGINE WILL NOT START

Identifying the Problem

If the engine will not start, perform the following steps in this order. Because there are so

many things that cause a starting problem, it is important to narrow the possibilities by following a specific troubleshooting procedure. If the engine

7. Check the engine compression as described in Chapter Three. If the compression is low, check for one or more of the following:

    a. Leaking head gasket.

    b. Cracked or warped cylinder head.

    c. Worn piston rings, pistons and cylinder.

    d. Valve(s) stuck open.

    e. Worn or damaged valve seat(s).

    f. Incorrect valve timing.

Spark Test

A spark test determines if the ignition system is producing adequate spark. The following procedure describes the use of a spark tester (MotionPro part No. 08-0122) (**Figure 3**). If the tester is not available, use a new spark plug.

1. Remove the fuel tank and air filter housing as described in Chapter Eight.

> *WARNING*
> *Step 2 must be performed to disable the fuel system. Otherwise, fuel will enter the cylinders when the engine is turned over during the spark test, flooding the cylinders and creating explosive fuel vapors.*

2. Disconnect the fuel pump electrical connector (**Figure 4**) from its harness mate.

3. With the transmission in neutral, turn the engine run/stop switch to the run position (A, **Figure 1**). Start the engine and let it run using the remaining fuel in the fuel rail. Turn the ignition switch off when the engine sputters and shuts off.

4. Remove the spark plugs as described in Chapter Three. Check for the presence of water in the plug caps.

5. Reconnect each spark plug to its original ignition coil/plug cap. Then attach a jumper wire between each spark plug and a known good ground. If the following spark tester is being used, ground it in the same way.

> *CAUTION*
> *Do not ground the spark plug onto the cylinder head cover as the electrical spark will damage the magnesium cover.*

6. If using the spark tester, set the gap to 0.7-0.8 mm (0.028-0.031 in.).

7. Insert the spark plug, or spark tester, into its plug cap and ground the spark plug base to a good engine ground. Position the spark plug so the electrode is visible.

fails to start after performing these checks, refer to the troubleshooting procedures indicated in the steps. If the engine starts but idles or runs roughly, refer to *Engine Performance* in this chapter.

1. Refer to *Engine Starting* in this chapter to make sure all switches and starting procedures are correct.

2. If the starter does not operate, refer to *Electrical Troubleshooting* in this chapter.

3. If the starter operates, and the engine seems flooded, refer to *Engine Starting, Engine Flooded* in this chapter.

4. Make sure there is sufficient fuel. Turn the ignition switch on and check the fuel level warning light on the meter. The fuel level is low if the warning light remains on.

5. Support the fuel tank, and remove the air filter housing (Chapter Eight). Make sure the 2-pin electrical connector (A, **Figure 2**) is securely connected to each ignition coil/plug cap (B). If necessary, carefully push and slightly rotate each ignition coil.

6. Test the ignition system by performing *Spark Test* in this section. If the test produces good spark, proceed to Step 7. If the spark is weak or if there is no spark, refer to Chapter Nine, and perform the troubleshooting procedures in the diagnostic flow chart.

WARNING
Even though the engine was run out of fuel in Step 3, mount the spark plug, or tester, away from the spark plug hole on the cylinder head so that the spark or tester cannot ignite the remaining gasoline vapors in the cylinder. The firing of the spark plug can ignite fuel that is ejected through the spark plug hole.

WARNING
*Do **not** hold the spark plug, wire or connector, or a serious electrical shock may result.*

8. Operate the starter button (B, **Figure 1**) and turn the engine over with the starter. A crisp blue spark should be evident across the spark plug electrode or spark tester terminals. Repeat for each cylinder.

9. If the spark is good, check for one or more of the following possible malfunctions:
   a. Obstructed fuel line or fuel filter.
   b. Refer to *Fuel System* in this chapter.
   c. Low engine compression or engine damage.
   d. Incorrect ignition timing.

10. If the spark is weak or if there is no spark, troubleshoot the ignition system as described in Chapter Nine.

11. Install the spark plugs (Chapter Three).

12. Install the air filter housing and the fuel tank (Chapter Eight).

Engine is Difficult to Start

1. After attempting to start the engine, remove one of the spark plugs as described in Chapter Three and check for the presence of fuel on the plug tip. Note the following:
   a. If fuel is not visible on the plug, remove the other spark plugs. If there is no fuel on this plug, perform Step 2.
   b. If there is fuel present on the plug tip, go to Step 5.
   c. If there is an excessive amount of fuel on the plug, check for a clogged or plugged air filter, incorrect throttle valve operation (stuck open).

2. Perform the fuel pump operation test as described in Chapter Eight. Note the following:
   a. If the fuel pump operation is correct, go to Step 3.
   b. If the fuel pump operation is faulty, test the fuel pump relay and the tip-over sensor as described in Chapter Eight. If both of these components are within specification, replace the fuel pump.

3. Perform the fuel pump discharge test described in Chapter Eight. Note the following:
   a. If the fuel flow is low, replace the fuel pump.
   b. If the fuel flow is within specification, proceed to Step 4.

4. Perform the fuel pressure test described in Chapter Eight. Note the following:
   a. If the fuel pressure is within specification, proceed to Step 5.
   b. If the fuel pressure is low, check for a leak in the fuel system, a clogged air filter, or faulty pressure regulator or fuel pump.

5. Perform the spark test as described in this chapter. Note the following:
   a. If the spark is weak or if there is no spark, go to Step 6.
   b. If the spark is good, go to Step 7.

6. If the spark is weak or if there is no spark, check the following:
   a. Fouled spark plug(s).
   b. Damaged spark plug(s).
   c. Loose or damaged ignition coil wire(s).
   d. Dirty or loose-fitting terminals.
   e. Loose or damaged ignition coil/plug cap(s).
   f. Damaged engine run/stop switch.
   g. Faulty direct ignition coil(s).
   h. Damaged ignition switch.
   i. Damaged crankshaft position sensor.
   j. Damaged ECM.

7. If the engine turns over but does not start, the engine compression is probably low. Check for the following possible malfunctions:
   a. Leaking cylinder head gasket.
   b. Incorrect valve clearance.
   c. Bent or stuck valve(s).
   d. Worn valve guides(s).
   e. Incorrect valve timing.
   f. Worn cylinders and/or pistons rings.
   g. Improper valve-to-seat contact.

8. If the spark is good, try starting the engine by following normal starting procedures. If the engine starts but then stops, check the following conditions:
   a. Leaking or damage rubber intake boots.
   b. Contaminated fuel.
   c. Incorrect ignition timing due to failed ignition system components.

Engine Does Not Crank

If the engine will not run over, check for one or more of the following:
1. Blown fuse.
2. Discharged or defective battery.
3. Defective starter motor, starter relay or starter switch.
4. Faulty starter clutch.

5. Seized piston(s).
6. Seized crankshaft bearings.
7. Broken connecting rod.
8. Locked-up transmission or clutch assembly.

ENGINE

If the engine runs but, performance is unsatisfactory, refer to the following procedure(s) that best describes the symptom(s).

Will Not Idle

1. Clogged air filter element.
2. Poor fuel flow.
3. Incorrect idle speed adjustment.
4. Incorrect throttle cable free play.
5. Fouled or improperly gapped spark plug(s).
6. Leaking head gasket or vacuum leak.
7. Leaking or damaged intake manifold(s).
8. Incorrect ignition timing: faulty ignition system component.
9. Low engine compression.
10. Incorrect throttle valve synchronization.
11. Obstructed or defective fuel injector(s).

Poor Overall Performance

1. Support the motorcycle with the rear wheel off the ground, and spin the rear wheel by hand. If the wheel spins freely, perform Step 2. If the wheel does not spin freely, check for the following conditions:
    a. Dragging rear brake.
    b. Excessive rear axle torque.
    c. Damaged rear axle/bearing.
    d. Damaged drive chain.
2. Check the clutch adjustment and operation. If the clutch slips, refer to *Clutch* in this chapter.
3. If Step 1 and Step 2 did not locate the problem, test ride the motorcycle and accelerate lightly. If the engine speed increases according to throttle position, perform Step 4. If the engine speed does not increase, check for one or more of the following problems:
    a. Clogged air filter or air ducts.
    b. Restricted fuel flow.
    c. Pinched fuel tank breather hose.
    d. Clogged or damaged muffler.
4. Check for one or more of the following problems:
    a. Incorrect oil level.
    b. Contaminated oil.
    c. Worn or fouled spark plugs.
    d. Incorrect spark plug heat range.
    e. Low engine compression.
    f. Clogged or defective fuel injector(s).

g. Worn or damaged valve train assembly.
h. Incorrect ignition timing due to a faulty ignition component, damaged ECM or CKP sensor.
i. Engine overheating. Refer to *Engine Overheating* in this section.
5. If the engine knocks when it accelerates or when running at high speed, check for one or more of the following possible malfunctions:
    a. Incorrect type of fuel.
    b. Lean fuel mixture.
    c. Advanced ignition timing due to a damaged ignition system component.
    d. Excessive carbon buildup in the combustion chamber(s).
    e. Worn pistons and/or cylinder bores.

Poor Idle or Low Speed Performance

1. Check the valve clearance. Adjust the valves as necessary (Chapter Three).
2. Check for damaged intake manifolds and loose throttle body or air filter clamps.
3. Check throttle valve synchronization.
4. Check the fuel pump circuit and the fuel injectors (Chapter Eight).
5. Perform the spark test described in this chapter. If the spark is weak, test the ignition system as described in Chapter Nine.

Poor High Speed Performance

1. Faulty engine or electrical component
    a. Weak valve springs.
    b. Worn camshaft.
    c. Improper valve timing.
    d. Spark plug gap too narrow.
    e. Insufficiently advanced ignition timing.
    f. Defective ignition coil/plug cap(s).
    g. Faulty CKP sensor.
    h. Clogged air filter element.
    i. Clogged fuel line.
    j. Faulty fuel pump.
    k. Defective TP sensor.
    l. Faulty STP sensor or STV actuator sensor.
    m. Faulty ECM.
2. Air flow fault.
    a. Clogged air filter element.
    b. Faulty throttle valve
    c. Faulty secondary throttle valve.
    d. Leaking intake manifold(s).
    e. Improperly synchronized throttle valves.
    f. Defective ECM.
3. Control circuit fault.
    a. Low fuel pressure.

b. Faulty TP sensor.
c. Faulty IAT sensor.
d. Faulty CMP sensor.
e. Faulty CKP sensor.
f. Faulty GP sensor.
g. Faulty IAT sensor.
h. Faulty AP sensor.
i. Incorrectly adjusted TP sensor.
j. Faulty STP sensor or STP sensor actuator.
k. Faulty ECM.

Overheating

Cooling system malfunction

1. Low coolant level.
2. Air in cooling system.
3. Improper coolant in system.
4. Damaged fan motor.
5. Faulty radiator fan relay of circuit
6. Faulty ECM.
7. Defective ECT sensor.
8. Clogged radiator, hose or engine coolant passages.
9. Worn or damaged radiator cap.
10. Thermostat stuck closed.
11. Clogged or damaged oil cooler.
12. Damaged water pump.
13. Damaged cylinder head gasket.
14. Warped or cracked cylinder head/cylinder block.

Lean air/fuel mixture

1. Short in the IAP sensor or its wire.
2. Short in the IAT sensor or its wire.
3. Air leak through intake manifold(s).
4. Defective fuel injector(s).
5. Defective ECT sensor.

Other causes

1. Low oil level.
2. Improper oil viscosity.
3. Oil not circulating properly.
4. Improper spark plug heat range.
5. Faulty throttle valve adjustment.
6. Valves leaking.
7. Heavy engine carbon deposits in combustion chamber(s).
8. Dragging brake(s).
9. Clutch slip.

Not Reaching Operating Temperature

1. Faulty ETC sensor.
2. Excessively cold weather.
3. Faulty thermostat.
4. Defective cooling fan relay or circuit.
5. Defective ECM.

Preignition

Preignition is the premature burning of fuel caused by hot spots in the combustion chamber, inadequate cooling or an overheated spark plug can cause preignition. This is first noticed as a power loss but may eventually damage internal engine parts because of higher combustion chamber temperatures.

Detonation

Sometimes referred to as spark knock or fuel knock, detonation is the violent explosion of fuel in the combustion chamber before the proper time for ignition. Engine damage can result. Use of low octane gasoline is common cause of detonation.

Even when using high-octane gasoline, detonation can occur due to over-advanced ignition timing, lean air/fuel mixture, inadequate cooling or excessive accumulation of carbon deposits in the combustion chamber(s).

Noises

Unusual noises are often the first indication of a developing problem. Investigate any new noises as soon as possible. Some times that may be a minor problem, if corrected, could prevent the possibility of more extensive damage.

Use a mechanic's stethoscope or a small section of hose held near your ear (not directly on your ear) with the other ear closed to the source of the noise to isolate the location. Determining the exact cause of a noise can be difficult. If this is the case, consult with professional mechanic to determine the cause. Do not disassemble major components until all other possibilities have been eliminated.

Consider the following when troubleshooting engine noises:

1. Knocking or pinging during acceleration is caused by the use of a lower octane fuel than recommended. It may also be caused by poor fuel, spark plugs of the wrong heat range or carbon buildup in the combustion chamber.
2. Slapping or rattling noises at low speed or during acceleration may be caused by excessive piston-to-cylinder clearance (piston slap). Piston slap is easier

to detect when the engine is cold and before the pistons have expanded. Once the engine has warmed up, piston expansion reduces piston-to-cylinder clearance.

3. Knocking or rapping while decelerating is usually caused by excessive connecting rod bearing clearance.

4. Persistent knocking and vibration during every crankshaft rotation is usually caused by worn connecting rod or main bearing(s). This can also be caused by broken piston rings or damaged piston pins.

5. Rapid on-off squeal indicates a compression leak around cylinder head gasket or spark plug(s).

6. To troubleshoot a valve train noise, check for the following:

    a. Excessive valve clearance.
    b. Excessively worn or damaged camshaft.
    c. Damaged cam chain tensioner.
    d. Worn or damaged valve lifters and/or shims.
    e. Damaged valve bore(s) in cylinder head.
    f. Valve sticking in guide.
    g. Broken valve spring.
    h. Low oil pressure.
    i. Clogged cylinder oil hole or oil passage.
    j. Excessively worn or damaged cam chain.
    k. Damaged cam chain sprockets.

7. For rattles, start checking where the sound is coming from. This may require the removal of fairing components (Chapter Fifteen). If a rattle is coming from the lower left side of the engine, check for a broken exhaust pipe flange assembly.

ENGINE LUBRICATION

Insufficient engine lubrication system quickly leads to engine seizure. Check the engine oil level before each ride and top off the oil as described in Chapter Three.

High Oil Consumption or Excessive Engine Smoke

1. Too much engine oil in engine.
2. Worn valve guides or valve stem(s).
3. Worn valve stem seal(s).
4. Worn or damaged piston ring(s).
5. Scuffed or scored cylinder wall(s).
6. Worn or damage piston oil ring(s).

Low Oil Pressure

1. Low oil level.
2. Worn or damaged oil pump.
3. Clogged oil strainer screen.

4. Clogged oil filter.
5. Clogged oil cooler.
6. Internal oil leakage.
7. Incorrect type of engine oil.
8. Oil pressure relief valve stuck open.

High Oil Pressure

1. Clogged oil filter.
2. Clogged oil cooler.
3. Clogged oil gallery or metering orifices.
4. Incorrect type of engine oil.

No Oil Pressure

1. Damaged oil pump.
2. Low oil level.
3. Damaged oil pump drive shaft.
4. Damaged oil pump drive sprocket.
5. Incorrect oil pump installation.

Low Oil Level

1. Insufficient amount of oil.
2. Worn piston ring(s).
3. Worn cylinder(s).
4. Worn valve guide(s).
5. Worn valve stem seals.
6. Piston rings incorrectly installed during engine overhaul.
7. External oil leakage.
8. Oil leaking into the cooling system.

Oil Contamination

1. Blown head gasket allowing coolant to leak into the engine.
2. Water contamination.
3. Oil and filter not changed at specified intervals or when operating conditions demand more frequent changes.

CYLINDER LEAKDOWN TEST

A cylinder leakdown test can locate engine problems caused by leaking valves, blown head gasket or broken, worn or stuck piston rings. This test is performed by applying compressed air through the cylinder head and then measuring the leak percentage or pressure loss.

1. Run the engine until it is warm, and then turn the engine off.
2. Remove the air filter housing (Chapter Eight). Secure the throttle in its wide-open position.

3. Set the No. 1 cylinder to top dead center on the compression stroke as described in Valve Clearance *in Chapter Three*.

> *WARNING*
> *The crankshaft may spin when compressed air is applied to the cylinder; remove any tools attached to the end of the crankshaft.*

4. Remove the spark plug from the No. 1 cylinder.
5. Thread the appropriate tester adapter into the No. 1 cylinder spark plug hole following the manufacturer's instructions. Connect the leakdown tester onto the adapter. Connect an air compressor hose onto the tester's fitting.
6. If the engine is not too hot, remove the radiator cap.

> *NOTE*
> *To prevent the engine from turning over as compressed air is applied to the cylinder; shift the transmission into sixth gear and have an assistant apply the rear brake.*

7. Apply compressed air to the leakage tester and perform a cylinder leakdown test following the manufacturer's instructions. Read the gauge. Note the following:
   a. For a new or rebuilt engine, a leakage rate of 0 to 5 percent per cylinder is desirable. A pressure loss of 6 to 14 percent is acceptable and means the engine is in good condition.
   b. Note the difference between cylinders. On a used engine, a pressure loss of 10 percent or less between cylinders is satisfactory. A pressure loss exceeding 10 percent between cylinders points to an engine in poor condition.
8. With air pressure still applied to the combustion chamber, listen for air escaping from the following areas. Use a mechanic's stethoscope to help listen for air leaks in the following areas:
   a. Air leaking through the exhaust pipe indicates a leaking exhaust valve.
   b. Air leaking through the throttle bodies indicates a leaking intake valve.
   c. Air leaking through the crankcase breather suggests worn piston rings or a worn cylinder bore.
   d. Air leaking through the radiator (coolant bubbles) indicating a blown head gasket or a cracked cylinder head or cylinder block.
9. Remove the leakdown tester, and repeat these steps for each cylinder. Note difference between cylinders.

CLUTCH

Clutch Lever Hard to Pull In

1. Clutch cable requires lubrication (non-nylon lined cables).
2. Clutch cable improperly routed or bent.
3. Damaged clutch lifter bearing.

Rough Clutch Operation

Rough operation can be caused by excessively worn, grooved or damaged clutch hub and clutch housing slots.

Clutch Slip

If the engine speed increases without an increase in motorcycle speed, the clutch is probably slipping. Some main causes of clutch slipping are:
1. Insufficient clutch lever free play.
2. Weak clutch springs.
3. Worn clutch plates or friction discs.
4. Damaged pressure plate.
5. Clutch release mechanism.
6. Clutch contaminated by engine oil additive.

Clutch Drag

If the clutch will not disengage or if the motorcycle creeps with the transmission in gear and the clutch disengaged, the clutch is dragging. Inspect for the following:
1. Excessive clutch lever free play.
2. Warped clutch plates.
3. Damaged clutch lifter assembly.
4. Loose clutch housing locknut.
5. Engine oil level too high.
6. Incorrect oil viscosity.
7. Engine oil additive being used.
8. Damaged pressure plate, clutch hub splines or clutch housing slots.

GEARSHIFT LINKAGE

The gearshift linkage assembly connects the shift pedal to the internal shift mechanism, which includes the shift drum, shift forks and shift stopper lever. The external shift mechanism can be examined after the clutch has been removed. The internal shift mechanism can only be accessed by splitting the crankcase.

Transmission Jumps out of Gear

1. Loose stopper lever mounting bolt.
2. Damaged stopper lever.
3. Weak or damaged stopper lever spring.
4. Incorrect shift pedal position.
5. Bent or worn shift fork(s).
6. Bent shift fork shaft(s).
7. Gear groove worn.
8. Damaged stopper bolt.
9. Worn gear dogs or slots.
10. Damaged shift drum grooves.
11. Weak or damaged gearshift linkage springs.
12. Worn shift cam.

Difficult Shifting

1. Improperly assembled clutch.
2. Incorrect engine oil viscosity.
3. Loose or damaged stopper lever assembly.
4. Bent shift fork shaft(s).
5. Bent or damaged shift fork(s).
6. Worn gear dogs or slots.
7. Damaged shift drum grooves.
8. Weak or damaged gearshift linkage springs.
9. Worn or broken shift cam.
10. Worn shift pawl.

Shift Pedal Does Not Return

1. Bent shift shaft.
2. Weak or damaged shift shaft return spring.
3. Shift shaft incorrectly installed.
4. Improper shift pedal linkage adjustment.
5. Bend shift fork shaft.
6. Damaged shift fork.
7. Seized transmission gear.
8. Improperly assembled transmission.

TRANSMISSION

Transmission symptoms are sometimes hard to distinguish from clutch symptoms Before working on the transmission, make sure the clutch and gearshift linkage assemblies are working properly. Refer to Chapter Seven for transmission service procedures

Jumps Out of Gear

1. Improperly adjusted shift pedal position.
2. Loose or damaged shift drum stopper lever.
3. Bent or damaged shift fork(s).
4. Bent shift fork shaft(s).
5. Damaged shift drum grooves.
6. Worn gear dogs or slots.

Incorrect Shift Lever Operation

1. Bent shift pedal or linkage.
2. Stripped shift lever splines.
3. Damaged shift lever linkage.
4. Improperly adjusted shift pedal.

Excessive Gear Noise

1. Worn bearings.
2. Worn or damaged gears.
3. Excessive gear backlash.

ELECTRICAL TESTING

This section describes the basics of electrical testing and the use of test equipment. Refer to *Electrical Troubleshooting* in this chapter for system-specific testing.

Electrical Component Replacement

Most motorcycle dealerships and parts suppliers will not accept the return of any electrical part. If the exact cause of an electrical system malfunction cannot be determined, have a dealership retest the specific system to verify the test results. If a new electrical component is installed and the system still does not work, the unit cannot be returned for a refund.

Consider any test results carefully before replacing a component that tests only slightly out of specification, especially resistance. A number of variables can affect test results dramatically. These include: the test meter's internal circuitry, ambient temperature, and the conditions under which the machine has been operated. All instructions and specifications have been checked for accuracy. However, successful test results depend to a great degree upon individual accuracy.

Preliminary Checks and Precautions

Perform the following before starting any electrical troubleshooting:

1. Check the main fuse (Chapter Nine). If the fuse is blown, replace it.
2. The various circuit fuses are mounted in the fuse box (Chapter Nine). Inspect the fuse protecting the suspect circuit. Replace the fuse as necessary.
3. Inspect the battery (Chapter Nine). Make sure it is fully charged. Check that the battery leads are clean and securely attached to the battery terminals.
4. Refer to the wiring diagrams at the end of this manual for component and connector identifica-

tion. Use the wiring diagrams to determine how the circuit works by tracing the current path from the power source through the circuit components to the ground.

5. Check any circuits that share the same fuse, ground or switch. If the other circuits work properly and the shared wiring is good, the cause must be in the wiring used only by the suspected circuit. If al related circuits are faulty at the same time, the probable cause is a poor ground connection or a blown fuse(s).

6. Electrical connectors are often the cause of electrical system problems. Inspect the connectors as follows:

    a. Disconnect each electrical connector in the suspect circuit, and examine the terminals in each connector. A bent or damaged pin will not connect to its mate in the other half of the connector causing an open circuit.

    b. Make sure the terminal on the end of each wire is pushed all the way into the connector. If not, carefully push it in with a narrow blade screwdriver.

    c. Check all electrical wires where they attach to the terminals for damage.

    d. Make sure all electrical terminals within the housing are clean and free of corrosion. Clean them, if necessary, and pack the connectors with dielectric grease.

    e. Push the connector halves together. Make sure the connectors are fully engaged and locked together.

    f. Never pull the electrical wires when disconnecting an electrical connector. Only pull the connector housings.

7. Never use a self-powered test light on circuits that contain solid-state devices. The solid-state device may be damaged.

Back Probing a Connector

Some tests, such as voltage or peak voltage tests, require back probing a connector. In these instances, insert a small wire, or back probe pin, into the connector at the indicated terminal. Then connect the multimeter test probe to the back probe pin. The pin must not exceed 0.5 mm (0.02 in.) in diameter.

Make sure the pin contacts the metal part of the terminal. Use caution so the pin does not deform either the terminals in the connector or damage the wire. If necessary, seal the probed area with silicone sealant

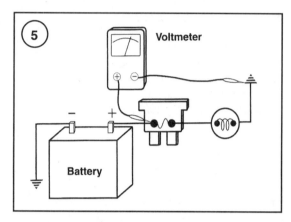

Test Light or Voltmeter

Use a test light to check voltage in a circuit. Attach one lead to the ground and the other lead to various points in the circuit. The bulb lights when battery voltage is present.

Use a voltmeter in the same manner as the test light to find out if battery voltage is present in any given circuit. The voltmeter, unlike the test light, also indicates how much voltage is present at each test point.

Ammeter

Use an ammeter measures the flow of current (amps) in a circuit. When connected in series in a circuit (**Figure 5**), the ammeter determines if current is flowing through the circuit and if that current flow is excessive because of a short in the circuit. Current flow is often referred to as current draw. Comparing actual current draw in the circuit or component to the manufacturer's specified current draw provides useful diagnostic information.

Self-powered Test Light

A self-powered test light can be constructed from a 12-volt light bulb, a pair of test leads and a 12-volt battery. When the test leads are touched together the light bulb should go on.

Use a self-powered test light as follows:

1. Touch the test leads together to make sure the light bulb turns on. If not, correct the problem before using the test light in a test procedure.

2. Disconnect the motorcycle's battery or remove the fuse(s) (Chapter Nine) that protects the circuit to be tested.

3. Select two points within the circuit where there should be continuity.

4. Attach one lead of the self-powered test light to each point.

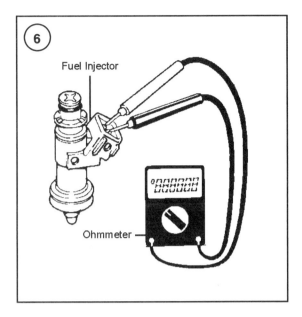

6

Fuel Injector

Ohmmeter

5. If there is continuity, the self-powered test light bulb will turn on.

6. If there is no continuity, the self-powered test light bulb will not come on indicating an open circuit.

Ohmmeter

CAUTION
To prevent damage to the ohmmeter, never connect it to a circuit which has power applied to tit. Always disconnect the battery negative lead before using an ohmmeter.

Use an ohmmeter measures the resistance (in ohms) a circuit or component.

Ohmmeters may be analog (needle scale) or digital (LCD or LED readout). Both types of ohmmeters have a switch that allows you to select different ranges of resistance for accurate readings. The analog ohmmeter also has a set-adjust control, which is used to zero or calibrate the meter. Refer to the manufacturer's instructions to determine the correct scale setting. Digital ohmmeters do not require calibration.

An ohmmeter is used by connecting its test leads to the terminals or leads of the circuit or component to be tested (**Figure 6**). If an analog meter is used, it must be calibrated by touching the test leads together and turning the set-adjust knob until the meter needle reads zero. When the leads are uncrossed, the needle should move to the other end of the scale indicating infinite resistance.

During a continuity test, a reading of infinity indicates that there is an open in the circuit or compo-

nent. A reading of zero indicates continuity, that is, the circuit is good. There is no measurable resistance in the circuit or component being tested.

Jumper Wire

Use a jumper wire to bypass a potential problem and isolate it to a particular point in a circuit. If a faulty circuit works properly with a jumper wire installed, an open exists between the two jumper points in the circuit.

To troubleshoot with a jumper wire, first use the wire to determine if the problem is on the ground side or the load side of a device. Test the ground by connecting a jumper between the lamp and a good ground. If the lamp comes on, the problem is the connection between the lamp and ground. If the lamp does not come on with the jumper installed, the lamp's connection to ground is good so the problem is between the lamp and the power source.

To isolate the problem, connect the jumper between the battery and the lamp. If it comes on, the problem is between these two points. Next, connect the jumper between the battery and the fuse side of the switch. If the lamp comes on, the switch is good. By successively moving the jumper from one point to another, the problem can be isolated to a particular place in the circuit.

Note the following when using a jumper wire:

1. Make sure the jumper wire gauge (thickness) is the same as that used in the circuit being tested. A smaller gauge wire will rapidly overhead and could melt.

2. Install insulated boots over alligator clips. This prevents accidental grounding, sparks or possible shock when working in cramped quarters.

3. Jumper wires are temporary test measures only. Do not leave a jumper wire installed as a permanent solution. This creates a hazard that could damage the wiring harness.

4. When using a jumper wire always install an inline fuse/fuse holder (available at most auto supply stores or electronic supply stores) to the jumper wire.

5. Never use a jumper wire across any load (a component that is connected and turned on). This would result in a direct short and will blow the fuse(s).

Voltage Test

Unless otherwise specified, all voltage tests are made with the electrical connectors still connected. Insert the test leads into the backside of the connector and make sure the test lead touches the electrical wire or metal terminal within the connector housing.

Touching the wire insulation will yield a false reading.

Always check both sides of a connector as one side may be loose or corroded thus preventing electrical flow through the connector. This type of test can be performed with a test light or a voltmeter. A voltmeter provides a reading, whereas a test light only indicates voltage is present.

NOTE
If using a test light, it does not make any difference which test lead is attached to ground.

1. Attach the voltmeter negative test lead to a good ground (bare metal). Make sure the part used for ground is not insulated with a rubber gasket or rubber grommet.
2. Attach the voltmeter positive test lead to the point (electrical connector, etc.) being tested (**Figure 7**).
3. If necessary, turn the ignition switch on. If using a test light, the test light will come on if voltage is present. If using a voltmeter, note the voltage reading. The reading should be within one volt of battery voltage. If the voltage is less, a problem exists in the circuit.

Voltage Drop Test

Because resistance causes a drop in voltage, a voltmeter can be used to determine the resistance in an active circuit by performing a voltage drop test. A voltage drop test measures he difference between the voltage at the beginning of a circuit and the available voltage at the end of the circuit when the circuit is operating. If the circuit has no resistance, voltage in the circuit does not drop so the voltmeter should indicate zero voltage drop. A voltage drop of one or more volts indicates that circuit has excessive resistance.

It is important to remember that zero reading on a voltage drop test is good. Battery voltage, on the other hand, indicates an open in the circuit. A voltage drop test ia an excellent way to check the condition of the solenoids, relays, battery cables and other high-current electrical components.
1. Connect the voltmeter positive test lead to the end of the sire or device to the battery.
2. Connect the voltmeter negative test lead to the ground side of the wire or device (**Figure 8**).
3. Turn the component(s) on the circuit.
4. The voltmeter should indicate zero volts. If it reads one volt or more, there is a problem within the circuit. A voltage drop reading of 12 volts indicates an open in the circuit.

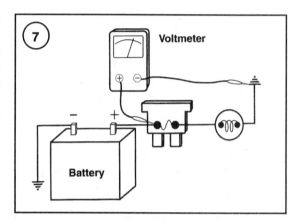

Peak Voltage Test

A peak voltage test checks the voltage output of a component. This test accurately measures a component's output voltage under operating conditions.

A given peak voltage specification is a minimum value. If the measured voltage meets or exceeds this specification, the test results are satisfactory. The tested component is operating within specification. In some instances, the measured voltage may greatly exceed the minimum specification.

The multicircuit tester (Suzuki part No. 09900-25008, or equivalent) and a peak voltage adapter, are needed to perform a peak voltage test. Refer to the manufacturer's instructions when using these tools.

Continuity Test

A continuity test is used to determine the integrity of a circuit, wire or component. A circuit has continuity if it forms a complete circuit; that is if there are no opens in either the electrical wires or components within the circuit. A circuit with an open has no continuity.

A continuity test can be performed with a self-powered test light or an ohmmeter. The ohmmeter gives the best results.
1. Disconnect the cable battery negative terminal (Chapter Nine).
2. Attach one test lead (test light or ohmmeter) to one end of the part of the circuit to be tested.
3. Attach the other test lead to the other end of the part or the circuit to be tested.
4. The self-powered test light comes on if there is continuity. An ohmmeter reads zero or very low resistance if there is continuity. A reading of infinite resistance indicates no continuity; the circuit has an open.

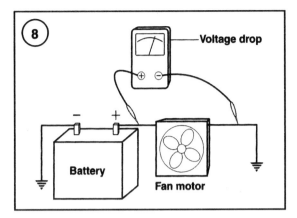

Short Test

An analog ohmmeter or one with an audible continuity indicator works best for short testing. A self-powered test light may also be used.

1. Disconnect the cable from the negative battery terminal.
2. If necessary, remove the blown fuse from the fuse panel.
3. Connect one test lad of the ohmmeter to the load side (battery side) of the fuse terminal in the fuse panel.
4. Connect the other ohmmeter test lead to a good ground location. Make sure the ground is not insulated. If possible, use the battery ground connection.
5. Wiggle the wiring harness related to the suspected circuit at approximately 15.2 cm (6 in.) intervals. Watch the ohmmeter while progressing along the harness.
6. If the ohmmeter needle moves or the ohmmeter beeps, there is a short-t-ground at that point in the harness.

ELECTRICAL TROUBLESHOOTING

Refer to the system-specific procedures and star with the first inspection in the list, and perform the indicated checks in order. If the test indicates that a component is working properly, reconnect the electrical connections and proceed to the next step.

Systematically work through the troubleshooting checklist until the source of the problem is identified. Repair or replace faulty parts as described in the appropriate section of the manual.

Refer to *Electrical Testing* in this chapter for general test procedures. Refer to Chapter Nine for specific component testing procedures. Refer to *Diagonstic System* in Chapter Eight for code malfunction information.

Charging System

A malfunction in the charging system generally causes the battery to remain undercharged.

1. Check the connections at the battery. If polarity is reversed, check for a damaged regulator/rectifier (Chapter Nine).
2. Check for loose or corroded battery cable connectors.
3. Check battery condition. Clean and recharge as required.
4. Perform the *Current Draw Test* (Chapter Nine).
   a. If current draw is excessive, check for a short in the wiring harness.
   b. If the current draw is within specification, proceed to Step 5.
5. Perform the *Regulated Voltage Test* (Chapter Nine).
   a. If voltage is within specification, the battery is faulty.
   b. if voltage is out of specification, proceed to Step 6.
6. Perform *Stator Coil Resistance Test* (Chapter Nine).
   a. If the resistance is out of specification, replace the stator.
   b. If the resistance is within specification, proceed to Step 7
7. Perform the *No-load Voltage Test* (Chapter Nine).
   a. If the voltage is within specification, proceed to Step 8.
   b. If the voltage is out of specification, the alternator is faulty. Replace the stator and retest. If the problem persists, the rotor is faulty.
8. Perform *Regulator/Rectifier* (Chapter Nine).
   a. If any test is out of specification, replace the regulator/rectifier.
   b. If the test readings are within specification, proceed to Step 9.
9. Inspect the charging system wiring for a short or for corroded connectors.
   a. Repair the wiring or connector.
   b. If the wiring is good, replace the battery.

Ignition System

Ignition system problems generate malfunction codes. Refer to *Diagnostic System* in Chapter Eight.

Starting System

1. Check the main fuse.
2. Check the battery as described in Chapter Nine.

3. With the transmission in neutral and engine stop switch in the run position, disengage the clutch and turn the ignition switch on. Listen for the operation of the starter relay. The relay should click.

    a. If the relay clicks, perform Step 4.

    b. If a click is not heard, perform Step 5.

4. Perform the starter motor operation test (Chapter Nine).

    a. If the motor does not run, replace it.

    b. If the motor runs, check the starter motor lead for a loose or corroded connection. If the starter motor lead is in good condition, perform Step 5.

5. Perform the starter relay input voltage test (Chapter Nine).

    a. If the relay has battery voltage, perform Step 6.

    b. If it does not have battery voltage, perform Step 7.

6. Perform the starter relay bench test (Chapter Nine).

    a. If the relay tests within specification, check for poor contacts at the starter relay.

    b. If the relay is out of specification, replace the relay.

7. Check the continuity of the ignition switch (Chapter Nine).

8. Check the continuity of the engine stop switch (Chapter Nine).

9. Check the continuity of the clutch switch (Chapter Nine).

10. Check the continuity of the starter button (Chapter Nine).

11. Perform the sidestand switch test (Chapter Nine).

12. Check the gear position sensor by performing the gear position sensor voltage test and the gear position sensor continuity test (Chapter Nine).

13. Perform the sidestand relay test and the diode test (Chapter Nine).

14. Check the wiring and each connector in the starting circuit.

STEERING AND SUSPENSION

Steering is Sluggish

1. Tire pressure too low.
2. Worn or damaged tire.
3. Incorrect steering stem adjustment (too tight).
4. Improperly installed upper or lower fork bridge.
5. Damaged steering stem.
6. Damaged steering head bearings.

Handlebar Wobble

1. Tire pressure too low.
2. Worn or damaged tire.
3. Loose steering head bearings.
4. Front fork legs not balanced.
5. Damaged fork leg.
6. Incorrect front fork oil level.
7. Damaged front axle.
8. Worn steering stem bearing or race.

Steers to One Side

1. Front and rear wheels are not aligned.
2. Incorrect drive chain adjustment.
3. Incorrectly installed wheels.
4. Uneven front fork adjustment.
5. Front fork legs positioned unevenly in the fork bridges.
6. Bent front or rear axle.
7. Worn or damaged wheel bearings.
8. Worn or damaged swing arm pivot bearings.
9. Damaged steering head bearings.
10. Bent swing arm.
11. Bent frame or fork.

Suspension Noise

1. Low fork oil level.
2. Loose fasteners.
3. Damaged front fork or rear shock absorber.
4. Loose or damaged fairing mounts.
5. Worn swing arm or suspension linkage bearings.

Wheel Wobble/Vibration

1. Unbalanced tire and wheel assembly.
2. Damaged tire(s).
3. Damaged wheel rim(s).
4. Loose wheel axle.
5. Loose fasteners.
6. Loose or damaged wheel bearing(s).
7. Loose swing arm pivot bolt.
8. Loose or damaged swing arm or suspension linkage bearings.

Hard Suspension (Front)

1. Incorrect fork oil level (too high).
2. Incorrect weight fork oil.
3. Plugged fork oil passage.
4. Incorrectly adjusted fork.
5. Excessive tire pressure.
6. Damaged steering head bearings.
7. Incorrect steering head bearing adjustment.

8. Bent fork tubes.
9. Binding slider.
10. Plugged fork oil passage.
11. Worn or damaged fork tube bushing or slider bushing.
12. Damaged damper rod.

Hard Suspension (Rear)

1. Excessive rear tire pressure.
2. Poorly lubricated suspension components.
3. Bent or damaged shock absorber.
4. Incorrect shock adjustment.
5. Damaged shock absorber bushing(s).
6. Damaged shock absorber collar(s).
7. Damaged swing arm or suspension linkage bearings.
8. Damaged swing arm or suspension linkage component.

Soft Suspension (Front)

1. Incorrectly adjusted fork.
2. Insufficient tire pressure.
3. Insufficient fork oil level.
4. Incorrect fork oil viscosity.
5. Weak or damaged fork springs.

Soft Suspension (Rear)

1. Incorrectly adjusted rear shock.
2. Insufficient rear tire pressure.
3. Weak or damaged shock absorber spring.
4. Damaged shock absorber.
5. Leaking damper unit.

BRAKES

Inspect the front and rear brakes frequently. Repair any problem immediately. When adding or changing the brake fluid, use only DOT 4 brake fluid from a sealed container.

Brake Drag

Brakes drag occurs when the brake pads cannot move away from the brake disc once the brake lever or pedal is released. Any of the following can prevent correct brake pad movement and cause brake drag.
1. Warped or damaged brake disc.
2. Brake caliper not sliding correctly on slide pins.
3. Sticking or damaged brake caliper pistons.
4. Contaminated brake pads and disc.
5. Plugged master cylinder port.

6. Contaminated brake fluid and hydraulic passages.
7. Restricted brake hose joint.
8. Loose brake disc mounting bolts.
9. Damaged or misaligned wheel.
10. Incorrect wheel alignment.
11. Incorrectly installed brake caliper.
12. Poorly lubricated brake-lever or brake-pedal.

Brake Grab

1. Damaged brake pad pin. Look for steps or cracks along the pad pin surface.
2. Contaminated brake pads and disc.
3. Incorrect wheel alignment.
4. Warped brake disc.
5. Loose brake disc mounting bolts.
6. Brake caliper not sliding correctly.
7. Mismatched brake pads.
8. Damaged wheel bearings.

Brake Squeal or Chatter

1. Contaminated brake pads and disc.
2. Incorrectly installed brake caliper.
3. Warped brake disc.
4. Incorrect wheel alignment.
5. Mismatched brake pads.
6. Incorrectly installed brake pads.
7. Contaminated brake fluid.
8. Clogged master cylinder return port.

Soft or Spongy Brake Lever or Pedal

Air in the hydraulic system results in a soft or spongy brake lever or pedal action. If air has entered the hydraulic system, bleed the brakes as described in Chapter Fourteen.
1. Air in brake hydraulic system.
2. Low brake fluid level.
3. Leaking brake hydraulic system.
4. Clogged brake hydraulic system.
5. Worn brake caliper seals.
6. Worn master cylinder seals.
7. Sticking caliper piston.
8. Sticking master cylinder piston.
9. Damaged front brake lever.
10. Damaged rear brake pedal.
11. Contaminated brake pads and disc.
12. Excessively worn brake disc or pad.
13. Warped brake disc.

Hard Brake Lever or Pedal Operation

1. Clogged brake hydraulic system.

2. Sticking caliper piston.
3. Sticking master cylinder piston.
4. Glazed or worn brake pads.
5. Mismatched brake pads.
6. Damaged front brake lever.
7. Damaged rear brake pedal.
8. Brake caliper not sliding correctly.
9. Worn or damaged brake caliper seals.

Brake Caliper Leaks

1. Damaged dust and piston seals.
2. Damaged cylinder bore.
3. Loose caliper body bolts.
4. Loose banjo bolt.

5. Damaged banjo bolt sealing washer.
6. Damaged banjo bolt threads in the caliper body.
7. Loose brake bleed valve.

Master Cylinder Leaks

1. Damaged piston secondary seal.
2. Damaged piston ring snap ring or snap ring groove.
3. Worn or damaged master cylinder bore.
4. Loose banjo bolt.
5. Damaged banjo bolt sealing washer.
6. Damaged banjo bolt threads in the caliper body.
7. Loose or damaged reservoir cap.

CHAPTER THREE

LUBRICATION, MAINTENANCE AND TUNE-UP

The cylinder firing order is $1 - 2 - 4 - 3$.

Normal engine rotation is *clockwise* when viewed from the right side (the cam chain side). Use the starter clutch bolt to rotate the crankshaft manually, and always turn the crankshaft *clockwise*.

TUNE-UP

Perform the engine tune-up procedures at the intervals specified in **Table 1**. Inspect and service the following items as described in this chapter:
1. Air filter.
2. Spark plugs.
3. Engine compression.
4. Engine oil and filter.
5. Valve clearance.
6. Throttle valve synchronization.
7. Brake system.
8. Suspension components.
9. Tires and Wheels.
10. Drive chain.
11. Fasteners.

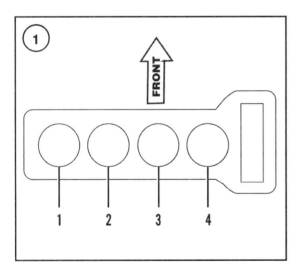

This chapter covers lubrication, maintenance and tune-up procedures. **Tables 1-5** are at the end of this chapter. Refer to **Table 1** for the recommended maintenance schedule. Refer to **Tables 2-5** for specifications.

Refer to Chapter One for general shop information, including fluids and lubricants.

CYLINDER NUMBERING AND FIRING ORDER

The cylinders in this engine are numbered one through four, counting from left to right (**Figure 1**).

AIR FILTER

The air filter removes dust and abrasive particles from the incoming air before it enters the engine. Without an air filter, very fine particles would rapidly wear the piston rings, cylinders and bearings. Never run the engine without a properly installed air filter.

Remove, clean and inspect at the interval specified in **Table 1**. Replace the air filter if it is soiled, severely clogged or broken in any area.

Removal/Installation

1. Lift and support the fuel tank or remove the fuel tank as described in Chapter Eight.
2A. On 2006-2007 models, perform the following:
   a. Disconnect the IAT sensor (A, **Figure 2**), the fuel pump relay (B) and cooling fan relay (C) electrical connectors from the cover.
   b. Disconnect the PCV hose (**Figure 3**) from the cover fitting.
2B. On 2008-2009 models, disconnect the PCV hose (**Figure 4**) from the cover fitting.
3. Remove the cover screws and lift the cover (A, **Figure 5**) from the air filter housing. Do not forget the screw in the deep center recess (B, **Figure 5**).
4. Remove the air filter element assembly (A, **Figure 6**) from the housing.
5. Place a clean shop cloth into throttle body intake horns to keep foreign matter out of the engine.
6. Gently tap the air filter to loosen the trapped dirt and dust.

> *CAUTION*
> *Do not apply compressed air toward the lower side (air filter housing side) of the filter. Air directed at this side will force the dirt and dust into the pores of the element thus restricting air flow.*

7. Apply compressed air to the *top* or *outside* of the air filter element (the side with the UP mark), and remove all loosened dirt and dust.
8. Thoroughly and carefully inspect the filter element. If it is torn or broken in any area, replace the air filter. Do not run the motorcycle with a damaged air filter element. It may admit dirt into the engine. If the element is okay, it can be used until the indicated time for replacement listed in **Table 1**.

> *NOTE*
> *Figure 7 is shown with the air filter housing removed for photo clarity.*

9. Remove the drain plug (**Figure 7**) from the rear of the housing, and drain away any accumulated moisture. Wipe out the interior of the air filter housing (**Figure 8**) and the outside of the cover with a shop cloth dampened in cleaning solvent.
10. Installation is the reverse of removal. Note the following:
   a. Install the air filter element (A, **Figure 6**) so the side with the UP mark faces up.

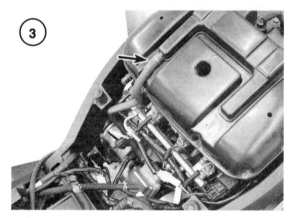

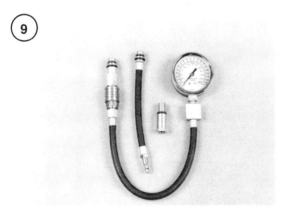

b. On 2006-2007 models, position the fuel pump relay (B, **Figure 6**) and fuel relay (C) outboard of the housing prior to installing the cover.

c. Make sure the air filter components are properly installed and that the housing seals.

COMPERSSION TEST

An engine compression test is performed to evaluate the condition of the piston rings, head gasket, pistons and cylinders. Check the compression at each tune-up, and record the readings in the maintenance log at the end of the manual. Compare the readings with those from earlier tune-ups. The comparison may reveal any developing problems.

Use a screw-in type compression gauge with a flexible adapter (**Figure 9**) when performing this test. Check the rubber gasket on the end of the adapter before each use. This gasket seals the cylinder to ensure accurate compression readings.

1. Before starting this test, confirm that:
   a. The cylinder head bolts are tightened to specification (Chapter Four).
   b. The valves are properly adjusted as described in this chapter.
   c. The battery is fully charged to ensure proper cranking speed (Chapter Nine).
2. Warm the engine to normal operating temperature, and turn the engine off.
3. Raise and support the fuel tank (**Figure 10**) (Chapter Eight).
4. Remove the spark plugs as described in this chapter.

WARNING
Perform Step 5 to disable the fuel system. Otherwise, fuel will enter the cylinders when the engine is turned over during the compression test, flooding the cylinders and creating explosive fuel vapors.

5. Disconnect the fuel pump connector (**Figure 11**) from its harness mate.

6. Turn the compression gauge into one cylinder following the manufacturer's instructions (**Figure 12**). Be sure the gauge is properly seated.

7. Make sure the engine stop switch is in the run position. Turn the main switch on and open the throttle completely. Use the starter button to crank the engine until there is no further rise in pressure. Maximum pressure is usually reached within several seconds of engine cranking. Record the reading and the cylinder number.

8. Repeat Step 7 and Step 8 for the remaining cylinders.

9. Standard compression pressure is specified in **Table 4**. When interpreting the results, actual readings are not as important as the differences between the cylinders. Large differences indicate worn or broken rings, leaky or sticky valves, blown head gasket or a combination of these items.

    a. If the difference in the cylinder's reading is less than the service limit (**Table 4**), it indicates valve or ring trouble. To determine which, pour about a teaspoon of engine oil through the spark plug hole onto the piston crown. Take another compression test and record the reading. If the compression returns to normal, the rings are worn or defective. If compression does not increase, the valves are leaking.

    b. If the difference in the cylinder's reading is the same as listed (**Table 4**), the rings and valves are in good condition.

10. Connect the 2-pin fuel pump connector (**Figure 11**) to its harness mate.

11. Install the spark plugs as described in this chapter.

12. Lower the fuel tank and secure it as described in Chapter Eight.

IGNITION TIMING

The ignition timing is not adjustable.

VALVE CLEARANCE

Measurement

Refer to **Table 4** for intake and exhaust valve clearance specifications. Perform valve clearance measurement and adjustment with the engine cool, at room temperature (below 35° C[95°F]).

In this procedure, the engine is shown removed from the frame for photo clarity. Valve clearance can be checked while the engine is in the frame.

CAUTION
For this procedure, the camshaft lobes must point away from the tappets as

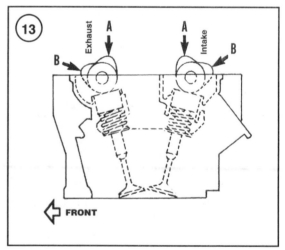

*shown in either position A or B, **Figure** 13). Clearance dimensions taken with the camshaft in any other position yields a false reading leading to incorrect valve clearance adjustment and possible engine damage.*

1. Remove the seat and the both fairing side panels as described in Chapter Fifteen.

2. Remove the cylinder head cover (Chapter Four).

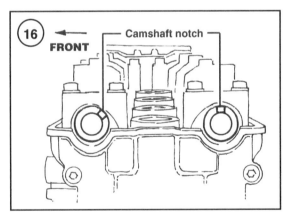

FRONT — Camshaft notch

3. Remove all four spark plugs as described in this chapter so the engine can easily be turned by hand.

4. Remove the timing inspection cap (**Figure 14**) from the clutch cover.

NOTE
In Step 5, both the index line on the starter clutch and the camshaft notches on the left side must be correctly aligned and positioned. Several complete engine revolutions may be necessary to achieve this alignment.

NOTE
If the engine is mounted in the frame, use a mirror to see the camshaft notches on the left side, if necessary.

5. Correctly position the camshafts as follows:
   a. Use the starter clutch bolt (A, **Figure 15**) to rotate the engine clockwise, as viewed from the right side, until the index line (B, **Figure 15**) on the crankshaft position sensor (CKP) rotor starter clutch aligns with the index rib (C) on the on the clutch cover.
   b. At the same time, this brings the camshaft notches, on the left side of each camshaft, to the position shown in **Figure 16**. If the camshaft notches are not positioned as shown, rotate the engine clockwise 360° (one full revolution) until the camshaft notches are positioned correctly.
   c. If it was necessary to rotate the engine an additional revolution, recheck that the index line (B, **Figure 15**) on the CKP sensor once again aligns with the index rib (C) on the clutch cover. Realign this mark if necessary.

6. With the engine in this position, check the valve clearance on the following valves (A, **Figure 17**):
   a. No. 2 cylinder: Intake valves.
   b. No. 3 cylinder: Exhaust valves.
   c. No. 4 cylinder: Intake and exhaust valves.

7. Check the clearance by inserting a flat metric feeler gauge between the lifter and the camshaft lobe (**Figure 18**). The clearance is correct if a slight resistance is felt on the feeler gauge when the gauge is inserted and withdrawn. Write down the clearance for each valve. Identify each valve by its cylinder number and by intake or exhaust valve. The measured valve clearance is needed when selecting the new shim.

8. To measuring the remaining valves, perform the following:
   a. Use the starter clutch bolt (A, **Figure 15**) and rotate the engine 360° (one full revolution) *clockwise*, when viewed from the right side of the motorcycle. Rotate the engine until the index line on the CKP sensor (B, **Figure 15**) once again aligns with the index rib (C) on the clutch cover.
   b. At the same time, this brings the notches on the left side of the camshafts to the position shown in **Figure 19**.

9. With the engine in this position, repeat the procedure described in Step 9, and check the valve clearance on the following valves (B, **Figure 20**):
   a. No. 1 cylinder: Intake and exhaust valves.
   b. No. 2 cylinder: Exhaust valves.
   c. No. 3 cylinder: Intake valves.

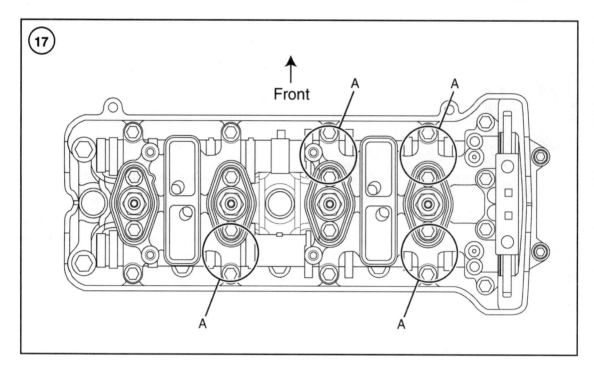

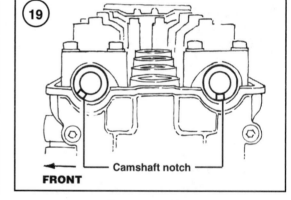

Camshaft notch

FRONT

10. If any valve is out of specification, adjust the clearance as described in this chapter.

Adjustment

To adjust the valve clearance, the shim located under the lifter must be replaced with a shim of different thickness. The camshaft(s) must be removed to gain access to the shims. The shims are available from Suzuki dealerships in increments of 0.05 mm that range from 1.20 to 2.20 mm in thickness.

1. Remove the camshaft(s) as described in Chapter Four.

2. To avoid confusion adjust one valve at a time.

3. Remove the valve lifter (**Figure 21**) for the valve requiring adjustment.

4. Use needlenose pliers or tweezers to remove the shim (**Figure 22**) from the top of the valve spring retainer.

5. Check the number on the shim. This number indicates the shim thickness (**Figure 23**). If the number is no longer legible, measure the shim with a micrometer (**Figure 24**).

6. Use the number on the installed shim and the measured valve clearance to select the new shim by performing the following:

   a. Refer to the appropriate chart for the valve being serviced. Use the chart in **Figure 25** to select new shims for intake valves; refer to **Figure 26** for exhaust valves.

   b. The correct number for a new shim is listed at the intersection of the installed shim number column and the measured clearance row in each chart.

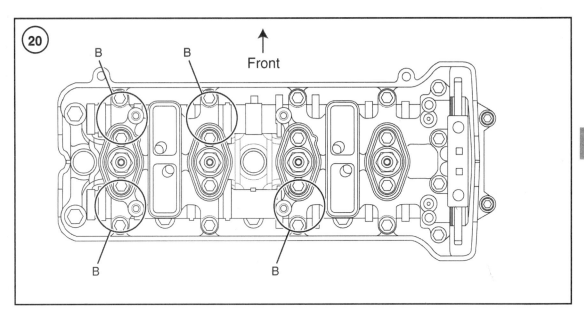

3

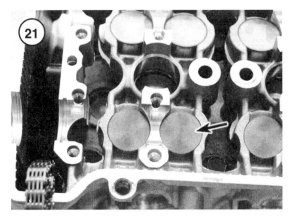

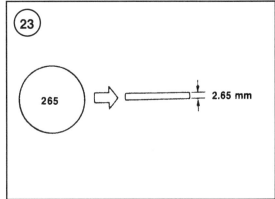

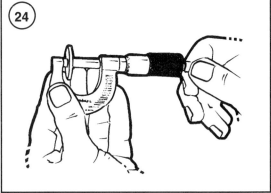

NOTE
The following numbers are examples only. Use the actual measured clearance, and the existing shim number from your engine.

c. For example, if the measured clearance for an intake valve is 0.23 mm and the installed shim number is 170 (1.70 mm), locate the 170 column and the 0.21-0.25 mm row on the intake valve chart (**Figure 25**). Run a finger across the row and down the column to the point where they intersect. The new shim number is listed at that intersection. In this example, install a new No. 180 shim (1.80 mm).

(25) INTAKE VALVE SHIM SELECTION

VALVE CLEARANCE SPECIFICATION*

*Valve clearance specification (cold): 0.10-0.20 mm (0.004-0.008 in.)

Installed shim No. / Shim size (mm)

Measured valve clearance (mm)	120	125	130	135	140	145	150	155	160	165	170	175	180	185	190	195	200	205	210	215	220
0.00-0.04			1.20	1.25	1.30	1.35	1.40	1.45	1.50	1.55	1.60	1.65	1.70	1.75	1.80	1.85	1.90	1.95	2.00	2.05	2.10
0.05-0.09		1.20	1.25	1.30	1.35	1.40	1.45	1.50	1.55	1.60	1.65	1.70	1.75	1.80	1.85	1.90	1.95	2.00	2.05	2.10	2.15
0.10-0.20																					
0.21-0.25	1.30	1.35	1.40	1.45	1.50	1.55	1.60	1.65	1.70	1.75	1.80	1.85	1.90	1.95	2.00	2.05	2.10	2.15	2.20		
0.26-0.30	1.35	1.40	1.45	1.50	1.55	1.60	1.65	1.70	1.75	1.80	1.85	1.90	1.95	2.00	2.05	2.10	2.15	2.20			
0.31-0.35	1.40	1.45	1.50	1.55	1.60	1.65	1.70	1.75	1.80	1.85	1.90	1.95	2.00	2.05	2.10	2.15	2.20				
0.36-0.40	1.45	1.50	1.55	1.60	1.65	1.70	1.75	1.80	1.85	1.90	1.95	2.00	2.05	2.10	2.15	2.20					
0.41-0.45	1.50	1.55	1.60	1.65	1.70	1.75	1.80	1.85	1.90	1.95	2.00	2.05	2.10	2.15	2.20						
0.46-0.50	1.55	1.60	1.65	1.70	1.75	1.80	1.85	1.90	1.95	2.00	2.05	2.10	2.15	2.20							
0.51-0.55	1.60	1.65	1.70	1.75	1.80	1.85	1.90	1.95	2.00	2.05	2.10	2.15	2.20								
0.56-0.60	1.65	1.70	1.75	1.80	1.85	1.90	1.95	2.00	2.05	2.10	2.15	2.20									
0.61-0.65	1.70	1.75	1.80	1.85	1.90	1.95	2.00	2.05	2.10	2.15	2.20										
0.66-0.70	1.75	1.80	1.85	1.90	1.95	2.00	2.05	2.10	2.15	2.20											
0.71-0.75	1.80	1.85	1.90	1.95	2.00	2.05	2.10	2.15	2.20												
0.76-0.80	1.85	1.90	1.95	2.00	2.05	2.10	2.15	2.20													
0.81-0.85	1.90	1.95	2.00	2.05	2.10	2.15	2.20														
0.86-0.90	1.95	2.00	2.05	2.10	2.15	2.20															
0.91-0.95	2.00	2.05	2.10	2.15	2.20																
0.96-1.00	2.05	2.10	2.15	2.20																	
1.01-1.05	2.10	2.15	2.20																		
1.06-1.10	2.15	2.20																			
1.11-1.15	2.20																				

㉖ EXHAUST VALVE SHIM SELECTION

VALVE CLEARANCE SPECIFICATION*

*Valve clearance specification (cold): 0.20–0.30 mm (0.008–0.012 in.)

Measured valve clearance (mm) / Installed shim No. (Shim size mm)	120	125	130	135	140	145	150	155	160	165	170	175	180	185	190	195	200	205	210	215	220
	1.20	1.25	1.30	1.35	1.40	1.45	1.50	1.55	1.60	1.65	1.70	1.75	1.80	1.85	1.90	1.95	2.00	2.05	2.10	2.15	2.20
0.05–0.09	1.20	1.25	1.30	1.35	1.40	1.45	1.50	1.55	1.60	1.65	1.70	1.75	1.80	1.85	1.90	1.95	2.00	2.05	2.10	2.15	2.20
0.10–0.14			1.20	1.25	1.30	1.35	1.40	1.45	1.50	1.55	1.60	1.65	1.70	1.75	1.80	1.85	1.90	1.95	2.00	2.05	2.10
0.15–0.19		1.20	1.25	1.30	1.35	1.40	1.45	1.50	1.55	1.60	1.65	1.70	1.75	1.80	1.85	1.90	1.95	2.00	2.05	2.10	2.15
0.20–0.30																					
0.31–0.35	1.30	1.35	1.40	1.45	1.50	1.55	1.60	1.65	1.70	1.75	1.80	1.85	1.90	1.95	2.00	2.05	2.10	2.15	2.20		
0.36–0.40	1.35	1.40	1.45	1.50	1.55	1.60	1.65	1.70	1.75	1.80	1.85	1.90	1.95	2.00	2.05	2.10	2.15	2.20			
0.41–0.45	1.40	1.45	1.50	1.55	1.60	1.65	1.70	1.75	1.80	1.85	1.90	1.95	2.00	2.05	2.10	2.15	2.20				
0.46–0.50	1.45	1.50	1.55	1.60	1.65	1.70	1.75	1.80	1.85	1.90	1.95	2.00	2.05	2.10	2.15	2.20					
0.51–0.55	1.50	1.55	1.60	1.65	1.70	1.75	1.80	1.85	1.90	1.95	2.00	2.05	2.10	2.15	2.20						
0.56–0.60	1.55	1.60	1.65	1.70	1.75	1.80	1.85	1.90	1.95	2.00	2.05	2.10	2.15	2.20							
0.61–0.65	1.60	1.65	1.70	1.75	1.80	1.85	1.90	1.95	2.00	2.05	2.10	2.15	2.20								
0.66–0.70	1.65	1.70	1.75	1.80	1.85	1.90	1.95	2.00	2.05	2.10	2.15	2.20									
0.71–0.75	1.70	1.75	1.80	1.85	1.90	1.95	2.00	2.05	2.10	2.15	2.20										
0.76–0.80	1.75	1.80	1.85	1.90	1.95	2.00	2.05	2.10	2.15	2.20											
0.81–0.85	1.80	1.85	1.90	1.95	2.00	2.05	2.10	2.15	2.20												
0.86–0.90	1.85	1.90	1.95	2.00	2.05	2.10	2.15	2.20													
0.91–0.95	1.90	1.95	2.00	2.05	2.10	2.15	2.20														
0.96–1.00	1.95	2.00	2.05	2.10	2.15	2.20															
1.01–1.05	2.00	2.05	2.10	2.15	2.20																
1.06–1.10	2.05	2.10	2.15	2.20																	
1.11–1.15	2.10	2.15	2.20																		
1.16–1.20	2.15	2.20																			
1.21–1.25	2.20																				

d. Replacing a 170 shim with a 180 shim increases shim thickness by 0.10 mm. This decreases the clearance from 0.23 mm to 0.13 mm, which is within specification.

7. Apply clean engine oil to both sides of the *new* shim and to the receptacle on top of the valve spring retainer. Position the shim so the side with the printed number faces up, and install the shim (**Figure 22**) into the recess in the valve spring retainer. Make sure it is correctly seated (**Figure 27**).

8. Install the lifter (**Figure 28**) into the cylinder head receptacle. Push it down until it bottoms (**Figure 21**).

9. Repeat this procedure for all valve assemblies that are out of specification.

10. Install the camshaft(s) as described in Chapter Four.

11. Use the starter clutch bolt (A, **Figure 15**) and rotate the engine several complete revolutions clockwise, when viewed from the right side of the motorcycle. This seats the new shims and squeezes any excess oil from between the shims, spring retainers and the lifters.

12. Recheck all valve clearances. If any clearance is outside the specified range, repeat this procedure until all clearances are correct.

13. Install the cylinder head cover (Chapter Four).

14. Install the spark plugs as described in this chapter.

15. Lubricate a *new* inspection cap O-ring with engine oil, install it onto the timing inspection cap (**Figure 14**). Install the cap into the clutch cover and tighten securely.

16. Install the fairing side panels and seat (Chapter Fifteen).

SPARK PLUGS

Removal

1. Raise and support the fuel tank as described in Chapter Eight.

2. Remove the air filter housing (Chapter Eight).

> *CAUTION*
> *Whenever a spark plug is removed, debris around it can fall into the plug hole causing serious engine damage. Remove all loose debris that could fall into the spark plug opening.*

3. Blow away all loose dirt, and then wipe off the top surface of the cylinder head cover.

> *CAUTION*
> *Do not remove the ignition coil/plug cap with the electrical coupler attached.*

4. Disconnect the 2-pin connector (A, **Figure 29**) from each the ignition coil/plug cap (B). If necessary, label the connector so it can be reinstalled onto the correct coil/plug cap.

> *CAUTION*
> *Remove the ignition coil/plug cap assembly from the spark plug only by hand. Handle the ignition coil/plug cap assembly carefully.*

5. The ignition coil/plug caps form a tight seal on the cylinder head cover as well as the spark plugs. Grasp the ignition coil/plug cap (B, **Figure 29**) and pull it straight up and off the spark plug.

6. Label each ignition coil/plug cap with its cylinder number so it will be reinstalled onto the same spark plug.

7. Use compressed air to blow debris from the spark plug tunnels.

> *NOTE*
> *Use a spark plug socket equipped with a rubber insert that grabs the side of*

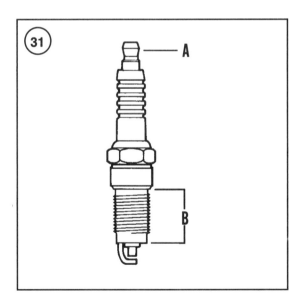

ed on the plug before installing the socket handle. Remove the spark plug about halfway from its hole in the cylinder head. Do not remove it.

9. Use compressed air to blow out the spark plug tunnels, and remove any debris that was trapped below the spark plug hex fitting.

10. Remove the spark plug. Mark the spark plug with its cylinder number.

11. Repeat Steps 7-10 for the remaining spark plugs.

12. Inspect the plugs carefully. Refer to *Reading* in this section. Look for a broken center porcelain insulator, excessively eroded electrodes, and excessive carbon or oil fouling.

13. Inspect the ignition coil/plug caps (**Figure 30**) for damage. If visually damaged, test the assembly as described in Chapter Nine.

14. Inspect each electrical connector and wiring for corrosion and /or damage. The wiring and electrical connectors are part of the main wiring harness and cannot be replaced separately.

15. Measure the spark plug gap. Adjust the gap as described in this section.

Installation

1. Apply a light coat of antiseize compound to the threads of the spark plug prior to installation, do not use engine oil on the plug threads.

2. Screw the spark plug into the cylinder head by hand until the plug bottoms in the spark plug hole. Tighten the plug to 11 N•m (97 in.-lb.). Do not overtighten the plug.

3. Refer to the marks made during removal and install each ignition coil/plug cap (B, **Figure 29**) onto the correct spark plug. Press ignition coil/plug cap into the spark plug tunnel and onto the spark plug. Rotate the assembly slightly in both directions and make sure it is attached to the spark plug.

4. Position the connector fitting on the ignition coil/plug cap so the fitting faces rearward.

5. Carefully connect the electrical connector (A, **Figure 29**) onto the correct ignition coil/plug cap (B).

6. Make sure the electrical connectors are free of corrosion and are on tight.

7. Install the air filter housing and fuel tank as described in Chapter Eight.

Gap

Refer to **Table 4** for specifications.

1. A new spark plug may be equipped with a terminal nut (A, **Figure 31**). This nut is *not* used.

the spark plug. This type of socket is necessary for both removal and installation since the spark plugs are located down deep in the cylinder head tunnels. Fingers cannot be used to remove or install the spark plugs.

8. Install the spark plug socket with a rubber insert onto the spark plug. Make sure it is correctly seat-

2. Insert a wire feeler gauge between the center and side electrodes of the plug (**Figure 32**). If the gap is correct, a slight drag will be felt as the wire is pulled through the gap. If there is no drag or if the gauge will not pass through, bend the side electrode with a gaping tool (**Figure 33**) and set the gap to specification.

Heat Range

The manufacturer provides three spark plug heat ranges. If necessary, select a different a heat range from the standard recommendation to accommodate for load and temperature conditions under which the motorcycle is being operated.

In general, use a hot plug for low speeds and low temperatures. Use a cold plug for high speeds, high engine loads and high temperatures. Refer to **Figure 34**. Do not change the spark plug heat range to compensate for adverse engine or fuel conditions.

A plug should operate hot enough to burn off unwanted deposits but not so hot that it is damaged or causes preignition. To determine if plug heat range is correct, remove each spark plug and examine the insulator.

When replacing plugs, make sure the reach (B, **Figure 31**) is correct. A plug with incorrect reach could interfere with the piston and cause engine damage.

Reading

Reading the spark plugs can provide information about spark plug operation, air/fuel mixture composition and engine conditions (such as oil consumption or pistons). Before checking the spark plugs, operate the motorcycle under a medium load for approximately 6 miles (10 km). Avoid prolonged idling before shutting off the engine. Remove the spark plugs as described in this chapter. Examine each plug and compare it to those shown in **Figure 35**.

Normal condition

Light tan- or gray-colored deposit on the firing tip, and no abnormal gap wear or erosion indicates good engine, ignition and air/fuel mixture conditions. A plug with the proper heat range is being used. It may be serviced and returned to use.

Carbon fouled

Soft, dry, sooty deposits covering the entire firing end of the plug are evidence of incomplete combustion. Even though the firing end of the plug is dry, the

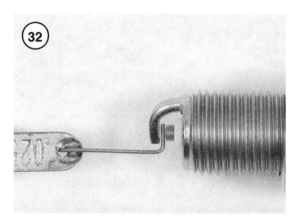

deposits decrease the plug's insulation. The carbon forms an electrical path that bypasses the electrodes resulting in a misfire. One or more of the following conditions can cause carbon fouling:

1. Rich air/fuel mixture.
2. Spark plug heat range too cold.
3. Clogged air filter.
4. Improperly operating ignition component.
5. Ignition component failure.
6. Low engine compression.
7. Prolonged idling.

Oil fouled

An oil fouled plug has a black insulator tip, a damp oily film over the firing end and a carbon layer over the entire nose. The electrodes are not worn. Oil fouled plugs can be cleaned in an emergency, but it is better to replace them. Correct the cause of the fouling before returning the engine to service. Common causes for this condition are:

1. Incorrect air/fuel mixture.
2. Faulty fuel injection system.
3. Low idle speed or prolonged idling.
4. Ignition component failure.
5. Spark plug heat range too cold.
6. Engine still being broken in.

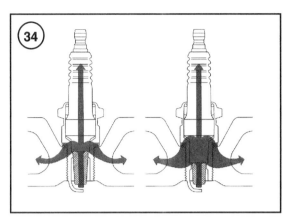

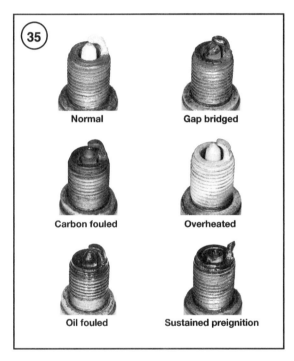

7. Valve guides worn.

8. Piston rings worn or broken.

Gap bridging

Plugs with this condition have deposits building up between the electrodes. The deposits reduce the gap and eventually close it entirely. If this condition is encountered, check for excessive carbon or oil in the combustion chamber. Be sure to locate and correct the cause of this condition.

Overheating

Badly worn electrodes and premature gap wear are signs of overheating, along with a gray or white blistered porcelain insulator surface. This condition is commonly caused by a spark plug with a heat range

that is too hot. If the spark plug heat range is correct, consider the following causes:

1. Lean air/fuel mixture.
2. Faulty fuel injection operation.
3. Improperly operating ignition component.
4. Engine lubrication system malfunction.
5. Cooling system malfunction.
6. Engine air leak.
7. Improper spark plug installation (overtightening).
8. No spark plug gasket.

Worn out

Corrosive gases formed by combustion and high voltage sparks have eroded the electrodes. A spark plug in this condition requires more voltage to fire under hard acceleration. Install a new spark plug.

Preignition

If the electrodes are melted, preignition is almost certainly the cause. Check for throttle body mounting or intake manifold leaks and advanced ignition timing. The plug heat range may also be too hot. Find the cause of the preignition before returning the engine into service. For additional information on preignition, refer to Chapter Two.

ENGINE OIL

The recommended oil and filter change interval is listed in **Table 1**. This assumes that the motorcycle is operated in moderate climates. If it is operated in dusty conditions, the oil gets dirty more quickly and should be changed more frequently than recommended.

Use oil with an API classification of SF, SG or API SH/SJ with MA in JASO. Do not use engine oil classified as Energy Conserving. These types of oil are designed specifically for automotive applications. The additives added to these oils may cause engine an/or clutch damage in motorcycle applications. SAE 10W/40 is recommended viscosity. If possible, use the same brand of oil at each oil change.

Engine Oil Level Check

1. Securely support the motorcycle in an upright position on a level surface.

2. Start the engine and warm it up for several minutes.

3. Shut off the engine and let the oil to settle for approximately three minutes.

CAUTION
Do not take this oil level reading with the motorcycle on the sidestand. The oil will flow away from the window giving a false reading.

4. Have an assistant sit on the bike to hold it vertically.

5. Check the engine oil level in the oil inspection window (A, **Figure 36**). The oil level must be between the full and low lines on the clutch cover.

6. If the oil level is low, unscrew the oil filler cap (**Figure 37**). Insert a small funnel into the filler neck. Add the recommended oil listed in **Table 3** to correct the level.

7. If the oil level is too high, remove the oil filler cap and draw out the excess oil with a syringe or suitable pump.

8. Inspect the O-ring seal on the oil filler cap. Replace the O-ring if it is starting to deteriorate or harden.

9. Install the oil filler cap, and tighten it securely.

10. Recheck the oil level, and adjust if necessary.

Engine Oil and Filter Change

NOTE
Do not discard oil in the household trash or pour it onto the ground. Some service stations and oil retailers accept used engine oil for recycling.

1. Remove the fairing side panels as described in Chapter Fifteen.

2. Start the engine and let it reach normal operating temperature.

3. Shut off the engine. Support the motorcycle in an upright position on a level surface.

4. Place a drain pan under the oil drain bolt (**Figure 38**).

5. Remove the drain bolt and gasket from the bottom of the oil pan.

6. Loosen the oil filler cap (**Figure 37**). This speeds up the flow of oil.

7. Allow the oil to completely drain.

WARNING
The hot oil cooler and exhaust system surround the oil filter, and the working area is very small. Protect your hands accordingly.

8. To replace the oil filter, perform the following:
   a. Move the drain pan under the oil filter so it will catch oil that drains from the filter.
   b. Install a socket-type oil filter wrench onto the oil filter (**Figure 39**), and turn the filter *counterclockwise* until oil begins to run out. Wait

until the oil stops, and then loosen the filter until it is easy to turn.
   c. Due to limited space, remove the oil filter wrench from the end of the filter then completely unscrew and remove the filter. Hold it with the open end facing up.
   d. Hold the filter over the drain pan and pour out any remaining oil. Place the old filter in a reclosable plastic bag. Discard the old filter properly.
   e. Thoroughly clean the sealing surface of the crankcase.
   f. Apply a light coat of clean engine oil to the rubber seal on the new filter.
   g. Install a new oil filter onto the threaded stud.
   h. Tighten the filter by hand until the rubber gasket contacts the crankcase surface, and then tighten it an additional two full turns.

9. Inspect the drain bolt gasket for damage. Replace the gasket if necessary.

10. Install the drain bolt (**Figure 38**) and its gasket. Tighten the oil drain bolt to 23 N•m (17 ft.-lb.).

11. Insert a funnel into the oil filler hole, and add the quantity of oil specified in **Table 3**.

12. Remove the funnel and screw in the oil filler cap securely.

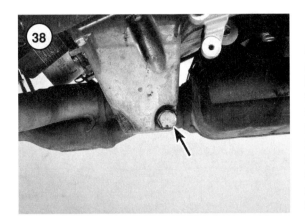

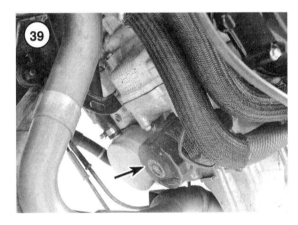

13. Usually some oil finds its way onto the exhaust pipes during this procedure. Wipe off as much as possible with a shop rag, and then spray some aerosol electrical contact cleaner onto the pipes.

14. Start the engine, and let it idle.

15. Check the oil filter and drain plug for leaks. Tighten either if necessary.

16. Turn off the engine, and check the engine oil level as described in this chapter. Adjust the oil level if necessary.

17. Install the fairing side panels (Chapter Fifteen).

Engine Strainer

The oil strainer in the sump can be removed for cleaning while the engine is in the frame. Refer to *Oil Pan and Strainer* in Chapter Five.

ENGINE OIL PRESSURE TEST

1. The following Suzuki special tools, or equivalent tools, are required to check the oil pressure:
    a. Oil pressure gauge hose part No. 09915-74521.
    b. Oil pressure gauge attachment: part No. 09915-74540.

    c. Meter (for high pressure), part No. 09915-77331.

2. Remove the fairing right side panel from the right side (Chapter Fifteen).

3. Check the engine oil level described in this chapter. Add oil if necessary.

4. Place a drain pan under the main oil gallery plug to catch the oil that drains out during the test.

5. Unscrew and remove the main oil gallery plug (B, **Figure 36**) from the crankcase.

6. Install the adapter, and then the gauge into the main oil gallery (B, **Figure 36**). Make sure the fitting is tight to avoid oil loss.

> *CAUTION*
> *Keep the gauge hose away from the exhaust pipe during this test. If it hits an exhaust pipe, the hose could melt and spray hot oil onto the hot exhaust pipe, resulting in a possible fire.*

7. Start the engine and warm it up. During summer months, run the engine at 2000 rpm for 10 minutes. During the winter, run it at 2000 rpm for 20 minutes.

8. Increase engine speed to 3000 rpm. The specified oil pressure when the oil temperature is approximately at 60° C (140° F) is listed in **Table 4**,

9. If the oil pressure is lower than specified, check the following:
    a. Clogged oil filter.
    b. Oil leaking from an oil passageway.
    c. Damaged oil seal(s).
    d. Defective oil pump.
    e. Combination of the above.

10. If the oil pressure is higher than specified check the following:
    a. Oil viscosity too high (drain oil and install lighter weight oil).
    b. Clogged oil passageway.
    c. Combination of the above.

11. Shut off the engine and remove the test equipment.

12. Apply a light coat of gasket sealer to the main oil gallery M16 plug, and then install the plug (B, **Figure 36**) onto the crankcase. Tighten it to 35 N•m (25.5 ft.-lb.).

13. Check oil level and adjust if necessary.

14. Install the fairing right side panel as described in Chapter Fifteen.

THROTTLE CABLE FREE PLAY

> *WARNING*
> *With the engine running at idle speed, turn the handlebars from side to side.*

If the idle speed increases during this movement, either the throttle cables need adjusting or they be incorrectly routed through the frame. Correct his problem immediately. Do not ride the motorcycle in this unsafe condition.

Measure the throttle cable free play at the throttle grip. Make sure it is within specification (**Table 4**)

Adjustment

1. On 2007-2008 models, slide the boot (**Figure 40**) off the pull cable.
2. Loosen the locknut (A, **Figure 41**) on the pull cable.
3. Turn the pull cable adjuster (B, **Figure 41**) until the free play is within the range specified in **Table 4**.
4. Hold the pull cable adjuster (B, **Figure 41**) and tighten the locknut (A).
5. Start the engine and let it idle. Turn the handlebar from side to side and listen to the engine speed. Make sure the idle speed does not increase. If it does, the throttle cables are incorrectly adjusted or improperly routed. Correct the source of the problem before riding.

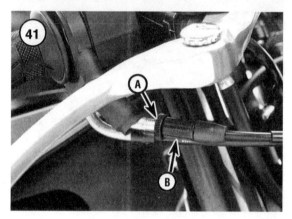

IDLE SPEED ADJUSTMENT (2006-2007 MODELS)

NOTE
Idle speed is controlled by the ECM on 2008-2009 models.

WARNING
With the engine running at idle speed, turn the handlebars from side to side. If the idle speed increases during this movement, either the throttle cables need adjusting or they may be incorrectly routed through the frame. Correct this problem immediately. Do not ride the motorcycle in this unsafe condition.

Before adjusting idle speed, clean or replace the air filter, test the engine compression and synchronize the throttle valves as described in this chapter. Idle speed cannot be properly adjusted if these items are not within specification. Refer to the procedures described in this chapter.
1. Securely support the motorcycle on a level surface.
2. Make sure the throttle cable free play is adjusted correctly as described in this chapter.

3. Start the engine and warm it to normal operating temperature. Turn off the engine.
4. Raise and support the fuel tank (Chapter Eight).

NOTE
Figure 42 *is shown with the throttle body assembly removed for photo clarity. Do not remove the assembly for this procedure.*

5. Start the engine and let it idle. Turn the throttle stop screw on the left side of the throttle bodies (**Figure 42**) until engine idle speed is within specification (**Table 4**).

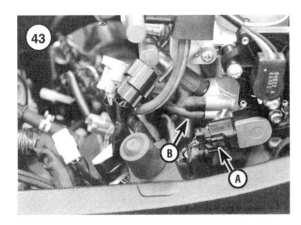

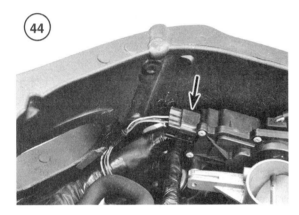

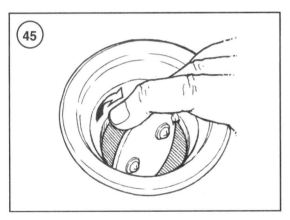

6. Rev the engine a couple of times to see if it settles down to the set speed. Readjust, if necessary.

7. Shut off the engine, and lower the fuel tank.

FAST IDLE SPEED ADJUSTMENT (2006-2007 MODELS)

NOTE
Fast idle speed is controlled by the ECM on 2008-2009 models.

The fast idle system is similar to a starter system. This system operates the fast idle cam, which opens the throttle valve to increase idle speed until the engine warms up.

The Suzuki test harness (part No. 09900-28630) is needed to adjust the fast idle speed on these models. A voltmeter is also required.

1. Support the motorcycle in an upright position.

2. Raise and support the fuel tank (Chapter Eight).

3. Start the engine. Let it idle until the coolant temperature rises to 80-90° C (176-194° F). Turn off the engine.

4. Turn the throttle stop screw (**Figure 42**) on the left side of the throttle bodies until engine idle speed is within specification (**Table 4**).

5. Raise and support the fuel tank (Chapter Eight).

6A. If the special Suzuki test harness (Suzuki part No, 09900-28630) is available, perform the following:

a. Disconnect the 3-pin connector (A, **Figure 43**) from the TP position sensor and connect the test harness.

b. Start the engine and let it idle.

c. Connect a voltmeter positive test probe to the red terminal in the test harness; connect the negative test probe to the black terminal in the test harness.

6B. If the special Suzuki test harness is not available, perform the following:

a. Make sure the TP sensor connector securely engages the TP sensor.

b. Use 0.5 mm (0.02 in.) back probe pins to back probe the harness side of the TP sensor terminals pink/black and black/brown (A, **Figure 43**).

c. Connect the voltmeter's positive test probe to the pink/black terminal connector; connect the negative test probe to the connector's black/brown terminal.

7. Start the engine. Measure the output voltage of the sensor with the engine at idle. Record the TP sensor output voltage listed in **Table 4**.

8. Turn off the engine, and remove the air filter housing (Chapter Eight).

9. Disconnect the connector from the secondary throttle valve actuator (STVA) (**Figure 44**) and measure the TP sensor output voltage at STVA open as follows:

a. Turn the ignition switch on.

b. Manually move the secondary throttle valve to its fully open position (**Figure 45**).

c. Record this reading.

10. Subtract the idle reading (Step 7) from the STV open reading (Step 9). The difference is the TP sensor output voltage variance. The variance should be within the range in **Table 4**.

11A. If the special test harness was used, disconnect the test harness and reconnect the 3-pin connector (A, **Figure 43**) onto the TP position sensor.

11B. If the special test harness was not used, remove the back probe pins from the harness side of the TP sensor.

> *NOTE*
> *Figure 46 is shown with the throttle body removed and partially disassembled for photo clarity. Do not remove the assembly for this procedure.*

12. If the variance is out of specification, adjust the fast idle speed by performing the following:
   a. Loosen the fast idle screw locknut (A, **Figure 46**).
   b. Turn the fast idle screw (B, **Figure 46**) and remeasure the TP sensor output voltage at idle, and recalculate the voltage variance.
   c. Repeat substeps a and b until the variance is within the specified range.

13. Let the engine cool to ambient temperature.

14. Start the engine and note the idle speed. The engine should idle within the specified fast idle speed range (**Table 4**). If fast idle speed is out of range, a short may exists in the engine coolant temperature sensor, the STV actuator or the wiring harness.

15. Turn off the engine, install the air filter housing, and lower the fuel tank (Chapter Eight).

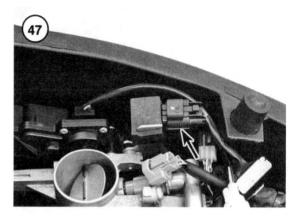

THROTTLE VALVE SYNCHRONIZATION (2006-2007 MODELS)

> *NOTE*
> *The throttle valve synchronization on 2008-2009 models can only be adjusted with the following Suzuki special tools: SDS set (Suzuki part No. 09904-41010) and CD-ROM Ver.15 at a dealership.*

Throttle valve synchronization ensures that each cylinder receives the same air/fuel mixture by synchronizing the vacuum in each throttle intake port. Synchronization is necessary correct, the engine performance.

Before synchronizing the throttle valves, make sure the valve clearances are correct.

> *NOTE*
> *Label the vacuum hoses before removal. Each hose must be reconnected to the correct throttle body once synchronization is completed.*

1. Start the engine and warm it up to normal operating temperature.

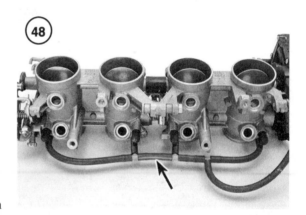

2. Set the idle speed to the specification in **Table 4** with the throttle stop screw (Figure 42). Shut off the engine.

3. Remove the air filter assembly (Chapter Eight).

> *CAUTION*
> *Avoid dirt from entering the throttle bodies while the engine is running.*

4. Disconnect the electrical connector (**Figure 47**) from the intake air pressure (IAP) sensor on the air filter housing.

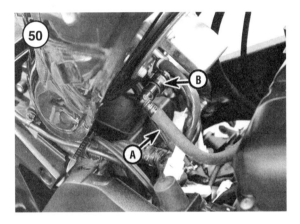

5. Synchronize the vacuum gauge following the tool manufacturer's instructions.

6. Disconnect the vacuum hose from the vacuum fitting on each throttle body. Refer to B, **Figure 43** and **Figure 48**.

7. Connect the vacuum gauge to the vacuum fitting on each throttle body.

8. Connect a portable tachometer following the manufacturer's instructions.

9. Start the engine and let it idle. If necessary, use the throttle stop screw (**Figure 42**) on the left side of the throttle bodies until engine idle speed is within specification (**Table 4**).

10. With the engine running at the idle, check the gauge readings. The throttle valves are balanced if the gauge readings are the same for all cylinders.

NOTE
Figure 49 is shown with the throttle body removed for photo clarity. Do not remove the assembly for this procedure.

11. If necessary, turn the idle air screw (**Figure 49**) to synchronize the left pair of bodies to the right pair.

12. If the bodies are still not synchronized, slowly turn in the idle air screw (**Figure 49**) on each throttle

body until it lightly bottoms. Count and record the number of turns needed to bottom each screw.

13. Check the vacuum gauge for differences between the No. 1 and No. 2 cylinders. Slowly unscrew the idle air screw on the throttle body with the higher vacuum rearing until the readings for the No. 1 and No. 2 cylinders are the same.

14. Repeat Steps 12 and 13 for the No. 3 and No. 4 throttle bodies.

15. If the throttle valves are still not synchronized, shut off the engine, and remove each idle air screw. Clean each screw with an aerosol carburetor cleaner. Blow each screw dry with compressed air.

16. Install the idle air screws. Lightly bottom each screw, and back it out the number of turns noted in Step 12. Repeat Steps 8-13.

17. Start the engine, and snap the throttle a few times and recheck the synchronization readings after all throttle bodies have been adjusted. Readjust synchronization if required.

18. Check the idle speed. If necessary, adjust it as described in this chapter.

19. Stop the engine and detach the equipment.

20. Reconnect the vacuum lines and install the air filter assembly (Chapter Eight).

21. Restart the engine and check the engine idle speed.

22. If necessary, adjust the throttle cable free play as described in this chapter.

FUEL LINE INSPECTION

Inspect the fuel hose at the intervals specified in **Table 1**.

1. Raise and support the fuel tank (Chapter Eight).

2. Inspect the fuel supply hose (A, **Figure 50**) from the fuel pump to the throttle body for leaks, hardness, deterioration or other damage.

3. Make sure the hose is securely attached to their respective fittings.

4. Check that the fuel supply hose is correctly attached to its fittings (B, **Figure 50**) and that the safety clip is securely in place.

5. Replace a damaged fuel hose as needed.

6. Lower the fuel tank (Chapter Eight).

EMISSION CONTROL SYSTEMS

PAIR System

The PAIR (air supply) system injects fresh air into the cylinder exhaust port, reducing the amount of unburned hydrocarbons in the exhaust.

Inspect all PAIR hoses (**Figure 51**) for deterioration, damage or loose connections. Replace any parts

or hoses as required. Check the tightness of the fittings and clamps and fittings.

Remove and inspect the PAIR control valve and the reed valves (Chapter Eight).

Evaporative Emission Control (EVAP) System (California Models)

All models sold in California are equipped with the evaporative emission control system. The vacuum hose routing appears on the vacuum hose routing label in the compartment beneath the passenger seat.

At the service intervals in **Table 1**, check all of the emission control lines (A, **Figure 52**) and the EVAP canister (B) for loose connections or damage. Also check the EVAP canister housing for damage. Replace any parts or hoses as required. Refer to Chapter Eight for additional information.

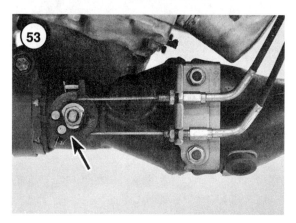

EXHAUST CONTROL VALVE (EXCV)

Check the operation of the exhaust control valve (EXCV) at the intervals in **Table 1**. Turn the ignition switch on, and check the movement of the exhaust control valve (**Figure 53**).

The actuator should operate when the ignition switch is turned on. If it does not, inspect exhaust control valve and the exhaust control valve actuator as described in Chapter Eight. If necessary, adjust the control cables as described in Chapter Eight.

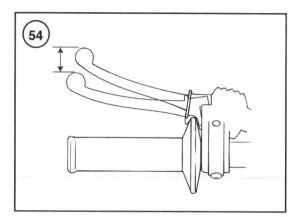

CLUTCH

Clutch Cable Free Play

Clutch cable free play is the amount of clutch lever movement before the clutch begins to disengage. Make sure the cable is adjusted to specification (**Table 4**). Too much free play prevents clutch disengagement and causes clutch drag. Too little free

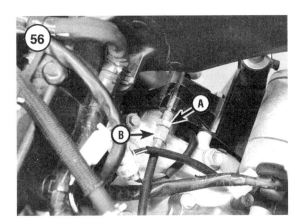

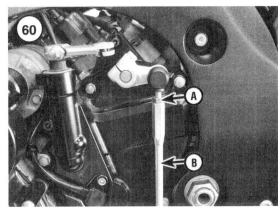

3

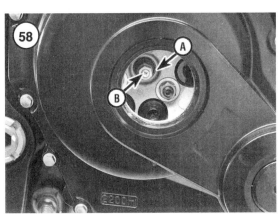

play inhibits full clutch engagement and cause clutch slipping. Adjust the free play regularly to compensate for cable stretch.

1. Clutch cable free play is measured at the end of the clutch lever (**Figure 54**).

2. Raise and support the fuel tank (Chapter Eight).

3. Turn the handlebar adjuster (**Figure 55**) all the way onto the clutch lever bracket.

4. Loosen the clutch cable locknut (A, **Figure 56**) and turn the adjuster (B) until the correct amount of cable free play is achieved.

5. Remove the clutch release cover (**Figure 57**) from the clutch cover.

6. Loosen the clutch release locknut (A, **Figure 58**).

7. Hold the locknut and loosen the clutch release screw (B, **Figure 58**) two or three turns.

8. From that position, secure the locknut. Slowly turn in the screw until resistance is felt.

9. Back out the clutch release screw (B, **Figure 58**) ½ turn, and tighten the locknut (A) securely while holding the release screw.

10. Turn the clutch cable adjuster (B, **Figure 56**) until the free play at the lever is within specification.

11. Tighten the locknut (A, **Figure 56**) securely.

12. Lower the fuel tank (Chapter Eight).

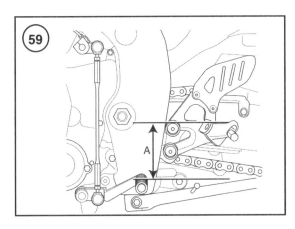

SHIFT PEDAL HEIGHT ADJUSTMENT

1. Support the motorcycle on a level surface.

2. Measure the distance (A, **Figure 59**) from the top of the footpeg to the top of the shift pedal. The specified shift pedal height is listed in **Table 4**.

3. Loosen the locknuts (A, **Figure 60**) at each end of the shift rod.

4. Turn the shift rod (B, **Figure 60**) until the shift pedal moves to the desired height.

5. Tighten each locknut (A, **Figure 60**) securely.

COOLING SYSTEM

> *WARNING*
> *Coolant is toxic and must never be discharged into storm sewers, septic systems, waterways, or onto the ground. Pour used coolant into the original container, and dispose of it according to local regulations. Do not store coolant where it is accessible to children or pets.*

> *CAUTION*
> *Be careful not so spill coolant onto painted surfaces. It will damage the surface. Wash immediately with soapy water and rinse thoroughly.*

> *CAUTION*
> *Many coolant solutions contain silicate inhibitors to protect aluminum parts from corrosion damage. However, silicate inhibitors cause premature wear of water pump seals. Do not use coolant solutions that contain silicate inhibitors.*

Coolant Selection

> *CAUTION*
> *Many coolant solutions contain silicate inhibitors to protect aluminum parts from corrosion damage. However, silicate inhibitors cause premature wear of water pump seals. Do not use coolant solutions that contain silicate inhibitors.*

Use only a high quality, ethylene-glycol based coolant specifically designed for aluminum engines. Mix coolant with distilled water in a 50:50 ratio. *Never* use tap water or salt water when mixing coolant with water. The minerals in them will damage engine parts.

Cooling system capacities are listed in **Table 3**.

Coolant Level Check

The coolant level should be checked when the engine is cold.

1. Securely support the motorcycle on a level surface.

2. Remove the right side fairing panel (Chapter Fifteen).

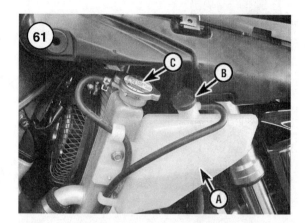

3. Check the coolant level in the coolant reservoir. It should be between the upper and lower level lines on the reservoir (A, **Figure 61**).

4. If necessary, remove the reservoir cap (B, **Figure 61**) and add coolant into the reservoir (not the radiator) to bring the level to the upper mark.

5. Reinstall the reservoir tank cap (B, **Figure 61**).

6. Install the right side fairing panel (Chapter Fifteen).

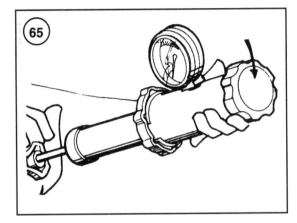

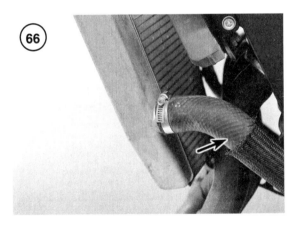

Cooling System Inspection

The coolant level inspection should be checked when the engine is cold.

1. Securely support the motorcycle on a level surface.

2. Remove the side fairing panel from each side (Chapter Fifteen).

3. Check all cooling system hoses for damage or deterioration. Refer to **Figure 62** and **Figure 63**. Replace any hose that is questionable. Make sure all hose clamps are tight.

4. Clean any debris from the radiator core. Use a whiskbroom, compressed air or low-pressure water. Carefully straighten any bent radiator fins with a flat-blade screwdriver.

5. Pressure test the radiator cap by performing the following:

    a. Remove the cap (**Figure 64**) from the radiator.

    b. Use a cooling system tester to pressure test the radiator cap (**Figure 65**) following the tester manufacturer's instructions. Slowly pressurize the cap and stop when the pressure is within the radiator cap opening pressure specified in **Table 4**. Replace the radiator cap if it does not hold pressure or if relief pressure is outside the specified range.

6. Install the radiator cap. Turn the radiator cap clockwise to the first stop. Then, push the cap down and turn it *clockwise* until it stops.

Coolant Change and Air Bleeding

Drain and refill the cooling system at the interval listed in **Table 1**.

Perform the following procedure when the engine is cold.

1. Support the motorcycle on a level surface.

2. Remove the fairing side panel from the each side (Chapter Fifteen).

3. Remove the coolant reservoir (Chapter Ten), and pour out its contents.

4. Place a drain pan under the water pump.

5. Release the clamp and disconnect the water pump outlet hose (**Figure 66**) from the input fitting.

6. Remove the radiator cap (**Figure 64**) and let the coolant completely drain from the system.

7. Reinstall the outlet hose (**Figure 66**) onto the pump outlet fitting. Tighten the clamp securely.

8. Place a funnel into the radiator filler neck and slowly refill the radiator and engine with the specified coolant (**Table 3**). Add the mixture slowly so it will expel as much air as possible from the cooling system.

9. Sit on the motorcycle and slowly rock it from side to side to help expel air bubbles from the engine, radiator and coolant hoses.

10. Top off the radiator as necessary.

11. After filling the radiator, leave the radiator cap off and bleed the cooling system by performing the following:

    a. Start the engine and let it to idle for two to three minutes.

    b. Snap the throttle a few times to bleed air from the cooling system. When the coolant level drops in the radiator, add coolant and raise the level to the bottom of the filler neck.

c. When the radiator coolant level has stabilized, loosen the bleed bolt (**Figure 67**) on the water pump cover. Engine coolant should flow from the bolt.

d. Turn off the engine, and tighten the cooling system bleed bolt (**Figure 67**) securely.

12. Install the radiator cap (**Figure 64**). Turn the radiator cap clockwise to the first stop. Then push the cap down and turn it *clockwise* until it stops.

13. Add coolant to the reservoir (B, **Figure 61**) until the level rises to the upper level line.

14. Start the engine and let it run at idle speed until the engine reaches normal operating temperature. Snap the throttle several times, and turn off the engine.

15. Wait several minutes so the coolant can settle, and check the coolant level in the reservoir (Figure A, **Figure 61**). If necessary, add coolant to the reservoir not to the radiator.

16. Install both fairing side panels (Chapter Fifteen).

17. Test ride the motorcycle and readjust the coolant level in the reservoir as required.

TIRES AND WHEELS

Tire Inspection

Refer to Chapter Eleven for tire changing and repair information.

1. Check and adjust the tire pressure (**Table 2**) to maintain tire profile, good traction and handling, and to get the maximum life out of the tire. Check tire pressure when the tires are cold. Never release air pressure from a warm or hot tire to match the recommended tire pressure. Doing so causes an under-inflated tire. Use an accurate tire pressure gauge to measure tire pressure, and reinstall the air valve cap.

2. Periodically inspect the tires for the following:

a. Deep cuts and imbedded objects, such as nails and stones. If a nail or other object is in a tire, mark its location with a light crayon before removing it. This helps to locate the hole for repair.

b. Flat spots.

c. Cracks.

d. Separating plies.

e. Sidewall damage.

Wear analysis

Analyze abnormal tire wear to determine the cause. Common causes are:

1. Incorrect tire pressure. Check the tire pressure and examine the tire tread. Compare the wear. Compare the wear in the center of the contact patch with the wear at the edge of the contact patch. Note the following:

a. If the tire shows excessive wear at the edge of the contact patch but the wear at the center of the contact patch is normal, the tire has been under-inflated. Under-inflated tires result in higher tire temperatures, hard or imprecise steering and abnormal wear.

b. If the tire shows excessive wear in the center of the contact patch but wear at the edge of the contact patch is normal, the tire has been over-inflated. Large amount of freeway riding will cause the tire to exhibit a similar wear pattern. Over-inflated tires result in a hard ride and abnormal wear.

2. Overloading.

3. Incorrect wheel alignment.

4. Incorrect wheel balance. Balance the tire/wheel assembly when installing a new tire, and then rebalance each time the tire is removed.

5. Worn or damaged wheel bearings.

Tread depth

Measure the tread depth in the center of the tire using a small ruler or a tread depth gauge (**Figure 68**). Replace the original equipment tires before the center tread depth has worn to minimum tread depth listed in **Table 2**. The tires have tread wear indicators that appear when the tires are worn out. When these are visible, the tires are no longer safe.

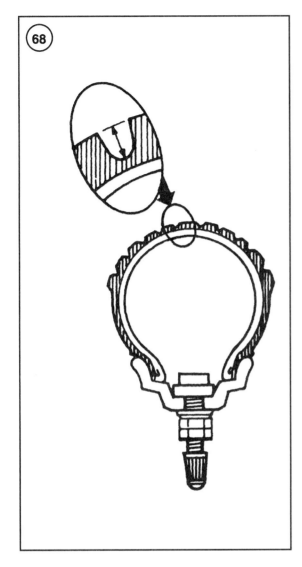

Wheel Inspection

Frequently inspect the wheel for cracks, warp or dents. A damaged wheel may cause an air leak or steering vibration. If the rim portion of an alloy wheel is damaged, the wheel must be replaced. It cannot be serviced or repaired. Check the wheel runout with the wheels on the motorcycle. Refer to *Wheels* in Chapter Eleven.

FRONT SUSPENSION

Fork Oil Change

The manufacturer does not provide an oil change interval for the front fork. However, it is a good practice to change the fork oil once a year. If the fork oil becomes contaminated with dirt or water, change it immediately.

Changing the fork oil requires the fork leg disassembly. Refer to the procedure in Chapter Twelve.

Front Fork Inspection

Inspect the front fork operation at the intervals specified in **Table 1**.

1. Use a soft wet cloth to wipe the fork tubes to remove any dirt and debris. As this debris moves against the fork seals, it eventually damages the seals and causes an oil leak.
2. Check the fork sliders for any oil seal leaks or damage.
3. Apply the front brake and pump the fork up and down as vigorously as possible. Check for smooth operation.
4. Refer to the specifications in **Table 5**, and check the torque of the following items:
   a. Lower fork bridge clamp bolt.
   b. Upper fork bridge clamp bolt.
   c. Handlebar clamp bolt.
   d. Front axle.
   e. Front axle pinch bolts.
5. Adjust the front fork settings as described in this section.

Front Fork Adjustments

> *WARNING*
> *The spring preload, rebound damping and compression damping settings on the left fork leg must match the respective settings on the right fork leg. If they do not, the motorcycle's handling will be adversely affected, which could lead to loss of steering control.*

Spring preload

Adjust the spring preload by turning the preload adjuster (A, **Figure 69**) on the top of each fork cap to one of the eight positions. Position 0 provides the minimum spring preload; position 7 provides the maximum.

Turn the preload adjuster (A, **Figure 69**) counterclockwise to the softest position. To increase preload, turn the adjuster *clockwise* to the desired setting. Make sure to set both forks to the exact same setting.

Rebound damping

Rebound damping affects the speed at which the front suspension returns to the fully extended position after compression.

Each front fork is equipped with a rebound damping adjuster (B, **Figure 69**) in the middle of the spring preload adjuster. The top of the adjuster is marked with a directional arrow and an S (soft) and *H* (hard) designations.

CAUTION
Do not turn the rebound damping adjuster past the point where it stops at its full clockwise or counterclockwise positions. Doing so will damage the adjuster screw.

1. To set the rebound damping to the standard setting, perform the following:
    a. Turn the rebound damping adjuster clockwise until it stops. This is the hardest setting.
    b. Turn the adjuster *counterclockwise*, and back it the number of turns specified in **Table 4**.
2. To further adjust the rebound damping, perform the following:
    a. To reduce rebound damping, turn the adjuster counterclockwise toward the *S*.
    b. To increase rebound damping, turn the adjuster clockwise toward the *H*.
3. Make sure the rebound damping is adjusted to the same setting on both fork legs.

Compression damping

Compression damping affects the speed at which the front suspension compresses when riding hard, riding on rough roads and when the wheel hits a bump. The compression damping adjuster **Figure 70** is marked with a directional arrow and an S (soft) and *H* (hard) designations.

CAUTION
Do not turn the compression damping adjuster past the point where it stops at its full clockwise or counterclockwise positions. Doing so will damage the adjuster screw.

1. To set the compression damping to the standard setting, perform the following:
    a. Turn the compression damping adjuster clockwise until it stops. This is the hardest setting.
    b. Turn the adjuster counterclockwise, and back it out the specified number of turns (**Table 4**). The compression damping is now adjusted to the standard setting.

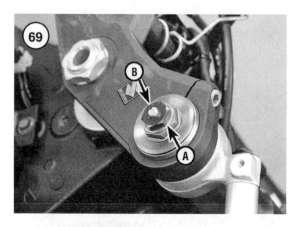

2. To further adjust the compression damping, perform the following:
    a. To reduce compression damping, turn the adjuster *counterclockwise* toward the S.
    b. To increase rebound damping, turn the adjuster *clockwise* toward the H.
3. Make sure the compression damping is adjusted to the same setting on both fork legs.

Steering Tension Inspection

1. Support the motorcycle on a level surface with the front wheel 20-30 mm (0.8-1.2 in.) off the floor.
2. Remove the steering damper (Chapter Twelve).
3. Check that the control cables and wiring harness are properly routed.
4. Connect a spring scale (Suzuki part No. 09946-92720, or equivalent) to the end of the handlebar grip. Position the spring scale so it forms a right angle with the handlebar (**Figure 71**).
5. Position the front wheel so it points straight ahead.
6. Pull the spring scale rearward, and note the reading on the scale when the handlebar first begins to move.
7. Repeat Step 4-6 on the other handlebar.

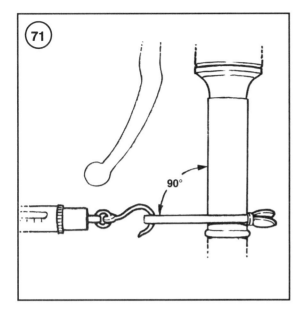

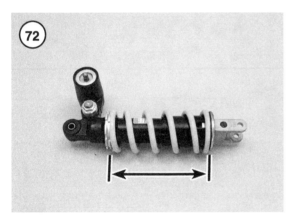

steering head bearings (Chapter Twelve) if excessive movement is noted.

REAR SUSPENSION

Inspection

1. Support the motorcycle with both wheels on the ground. Check the shock absorber by bouncing on the seat several times.
2. Support the motorcycle with the rear wheel off the ground.
3. While an assistant steadies the motorcycle, push hard on the rear wheel (sideways) to check for side play in the swing arm bearings.
4. Check the shock absorber for oil leaks or other damage.
5. Check the shock absorber, suspension linkage, rear axle and swing arm hardware. Make sure all fasteners are tight.

Shock Absorber Adjustment

The shock absorber can be adjusted to suit the load and rider preference. The spring preload, rebound damping and compression damping can be adjusted on the shock absorber.

Spring preload

Set the spring preload by adjusting the spring installed length (**Figure 72**). A longer spring length provides a softer ride; a shorter spring length provides a stiffer ride. There must be preload on the spring at all times. Never ride the motorcycle without some spring preload. Doing so could cause loss of control. The standard, maximum and minimum preload specifications appear in **Table 4**.

> *NOTE*
> *A pair of ring nut wrenches is required for this procedure.*

1. Support the motorcycle on a level surface.
2. Loosen the locknut (A, **Figure 73**).
3. Turn the adjust nut (B, **Figure 73**) *clockwise* to increase preload, counterclockwise to reduce preload.
4. Hold the adjust nut, and tighten the locknut securely.
5. Measure the spring length (**Figure 72**). It must be between the minimum and maximum length specified in **Table 4**.

8. Each reading should be within the steering tension range specified in **Table 4**.
9. If either reading is outside the specified range, adjust the steering head bearings as described in Chapter Twelve.
10. Grasp the lower end both fork legs, and try to rock the steering head back and forth. Adjust the

Compression damping

Compression damping affects the rate at which the shock compresses when the rear wheel hits a bump. This adjustment does not affect the action of the shock absorber on rebound.

1. To adjust the *low speed* compression damping to the standard setting, perform the following:
   a. Turn the low speed compression damping adjuster (A, **Figure 74**) clockwise until it stops. This is the hardest setting.
   b. Back the adjuster out (*counterclockwise* the specified number of turns (**Table 4**). The compression damping is set to the standard setting for an average built rider.

2. To adjust the high speed compression damping to the standard setting, perform the following:
   a. Turn the low speed compression damping adjuster (B, **Figure 74**) *clockwise* until it stops. This is the hardest setting.
   b. Back the adjuster out (counterclockwise the specified number of turns (**Table 4**). The compression damping is set to the standard setting for an average built rider.

3. To fine tune the rebound damping, set the damping to the standard setting and then perform the following:

> *NOTE*
> *When fine tuning the suspension, do so gradually. Turn the rebound damping adjuster in 1/8-turn increments and then test ride the motorcycle.*

   a. To reduce the rebound damping, turn the adjuster *counterclockwise* toward the S (soft) marked on the shock housing.
   b. To increase the rebound damping, turn the adjuster *clockwise* toward the H (hard) mark on the shock housing.

Rebound damping

Rebound damping affects the rate at which the shock absorber returns to its extended position after compression. Rebound damping does not affect the action of the shock on compression.

> *NOTE*
> *When turning the adjuster, make sure it clicks into one of the detent positions. Otherwise the adjuster will automatically be set to the stiffest position.*

1. To adjust the rebound damping to the standard setting, perform the following:

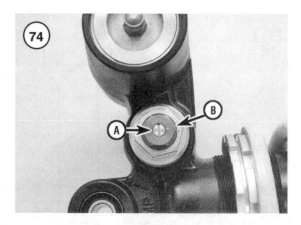

   a. Turn the rebound adjuster (**Figure 75**) *clockwise* until it stops. This is the hardest setting.
   b. Back the adjuster out counterclockwise the specified number of turns indicated in **Table 4**. The rebound damper is set to the standard setting for an average built rider.

2. To fine tune the rebound damping, set the damping to the standard setting and then perform the following:

> *NOTE*
> *When fine tuning the suspension, do so gradually. Turn the rebound damping adjuster in 1/8-turn increments and then test ride the motorcycle.*

   a. To reduce the rebound damping, turn the adjuster *counterclockwise* toward the S (soft) marked on the shock housing.
   b. To increase the rebound damping, turn the adjuster *clockwise* toward the H (hard) mark on the shock housing.

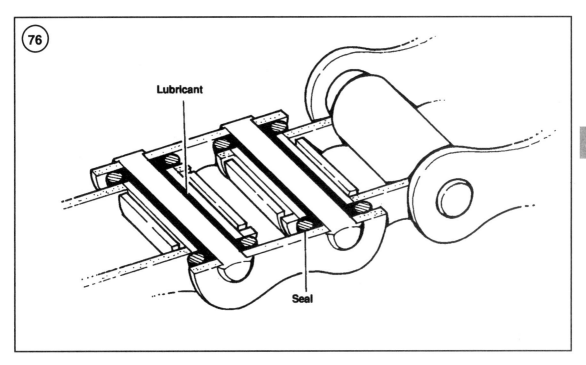

DRIVE CHAIN

Lubrication

Lubricate the drive chain every 600 miles (1000 km) or every month to prevent the side plates and rollers from rusting. The actual chain lubrication is enclosed within the chain by the O-rings (**Figure 76**). A properly maintained drive chain will provide maximum service life and reliability.

> *CAUTION*
> *Not all commercial chain lubricants are recommended for use on O-ring drive chains. Use a chain lube formulated for O-ring chains.*

1. Ride the motorcycle a few miles to warm up the drive chain. A warm chain increases lubricant penetration.
2. Support the motorcycle on a level surface with the rear wheel off the ground.
3. Oil the bottom chain run with a chain lubricant recommended for use on O-ring drive chains. Concentrate on getting the oil down between the side plates on both sides of the chain. Do not over lubricate.
4. Rotate the wheel and continue lubricating the chain until the entire chain has been lubricated.
5. Turn the rear wheel slowly and wipe off excess oil from the chain with a shop cloth. Also wipe off any lubricant from the rear hub, wheel and tire.

Cleaning

Clean the drive chain after riding over dusty or sandy conditions. A properly maintained chain provides maximum service life and reliability.

> *CAUTION*
> *Clean the chain only with kerosene. Solvents and gasoline cause swelling of the O-rings. The drive chain then becomes so stiff it cannot move or flex. If this happens, the drive chain must be replaced. High-pressure washers, steam cleaning and coarse brushes will also damage the O-rings.*

This section describes how to clean the drive chain while it is installed mounted. It is not practical to break the chain in order to clean it.
1. Ride the motorcycle a few miles to warm up the drive chain.
2. Support the motorcycle on a level surface with the rear wheel off the ground.
3. Place some stiff cardboard and a drain pan beneath the drive chain.

> *CAUTION*
> *Wear protective gloves when cleaning the drive chain. To avoid catching your fingers and rag between the chain and the sprocket, do not rotate the rear wheel when cleaning the chain. Clean one section of the chain at a time.*

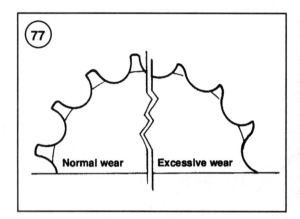

Normal wear   Excessive wear

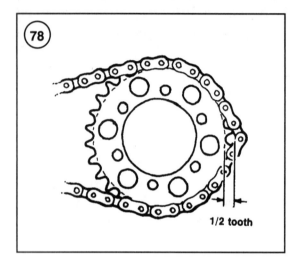

1/2 tooth

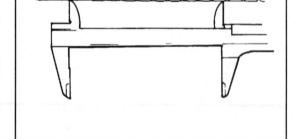

1 2 3   19 20 21 Pins

4. Soak a thick rag in kerosene, and then wipe it against the exposed section of the lower chain run. When this section of the chain is clean, rotate the rear wheel to expose the next section of chain and clean it. Repeat this process until the entire chain is clean. Remove stubborn dirt by scrubbing the rollers and side plates with a soft brush.

5. Turn the rear wheel slowly and wipe the drive chain dry with a thick shop cloth.

6. Clean the rear swing arm, wheel sprocket, chain guard, wheel and tire of all kerosene residues.

7. Lubricate the drive chain as described earlier in this section.

Drive Chain and Sprocket Inspection

1. Clean the drive chain as described in this section.

2. Support the motorcycle on a level surface with the rear wheel off the ground.

3. Turn the rear wheel and inspect both sides of the chain for missing or damaged O-rings.

4. Inspect the inner plate chain faces. They should be polished on both sides. If they show consider-

able uneven wear on one side, the sprockets are not aligned properly.

5. Inspect the engine and rear sprockets for the following defects:

    a. Undercutting or sharp teeth (**Figure 77**).

    b. Broken teeth.

6. Check the engine sprocket nut and the rear sprocket nuts for looseness. If loose, tighten them to the specification in **Table 5**.

7. If excessive chain or sprocket wear is evident, replace the drive chain and both sprockets as a complete set. If only the drive chain is replaced, the worn sprockets will cause rapid chain wear.

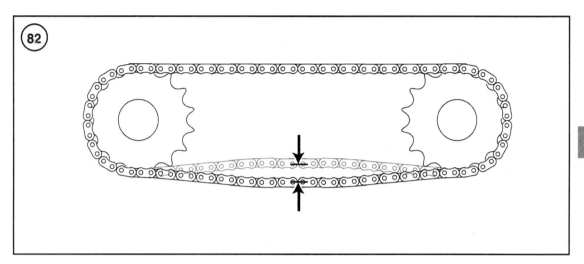

8. At the rear sprocket, pull one of the links away from the sprocket. If the link pulls away more than 1/2 the height of the sprocket tooth (**Figure 78**), the chain is excessively worn. Confirm this by performing Step 9.

9. Measure the drive chain 21-pin length by performing the following:

   a. Remove the cotter pin (**Figure 79**) from the rear axle nut on models so equipped.

   b. Loosen the rear axle nut (A, **Figure 80**).

   c. Loosen chain adjuster locknut (B, **Figure 80**) on each side of the swing arm.

   d. Turn both adjuster bolts (C, **Figure 80**) an equal number of turns until the lower chain run is straight. Check that each chain adjuster aligns with the same index mark (D, **Figure 80**) on the swing arm.

   e. Use a vernier caliper to measure the distance between 21 pins on the lower chain run (**Figure 81**). If this distance exceeds the specification in **Table 4**, the chain is excessively worn and must be replaced.

10. Tighten the rear axle nut (A, **Figure 80**) to 100 N•m (74 ft.-lb.).

11. On models so equipped, install a *new* cotter pin (**Figure 79**) and bend the ends over completely.

Drive Chain Adjustment

Check and adjust the drive chain at the intervals specified in **Table 1**. If the motorcycle is operated at sustained high speeds or if it is repeatedly accelerated very hard, inspect the drive chain adjustment more often. A properly lubricated and adjusted drive chain will provide maximum service life and reliability.

When adjusting the chain, check the slack at several places along its length by rotating the rear wheel. The chain will rarely wear uniformly and as a result will be tighter at some places than others. Measure the chain slack halfway between the sprockets (**Figure 82**). The chain slack at the tightest place on the chain must be within the range specified in **Table 4**.

1. Turn the engine off, and shift the transmission into neutral.

2. Support the motorcycle on a level surface with the rear wheel off the ground.

NOTE
As the drive chain stretches with in use, the chain will become tighter at one point. The chain must be checked and adjusted at this point.

3. Turn the rear wheel slowly, then stop it, and check the chain tightness. Continue until the tightest point is located. Mark this spot with chalk and turn the wheel so that the mark is located on the lower chain run, midway between both drive sprockets. Check the chain slack at this point. If it is outside the specified range (**Table 4**), adjust the drive chain as follows.

4. Remove the cotter pin (**Figure 79**) from the rear axle nut on models so equipped.

5. Loosen the rear axle nut (A, **Figure 80**).

6. Loosen chain adjuster locknut (B, **Figure 80**) on each side of the swing arm. Turn both adjuster bolts (C, **Figure 80**) an equal number of turns to obtain the correct drive chain slack. Check that each chain adjuster aligns with the same index mark (D, **Figure 80**) on the swing arm.

7. Recheck chain slack in the middle of the lower run (**Figure 82**).

8. To verify the swing arm adjuster marks, remove the drive chain guard. Check rear wheel alignment by sighting along the drive chain as it runs over the rear sprocket. It should leave the rear sprocket in a straight line heading toward the engine sprocket as shown in A, **Figure 83**. If the chain veers to one side or the other (B or C), perform the following:

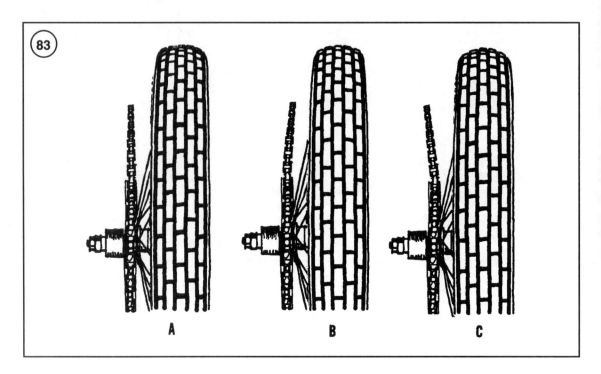

a. Check that the chain adjusters are set to the same index mark on each side of the swing arm.

b. If not, readjust the drive chain to achieve the same position on both sides as well as maintaining the correct free play. Tighten each drive chain adjuster locknut (B, **Figure 80**) securely

9. Tighten the rear axle nut (A, **Figure 80**) to 100 N•m (74 ft.-lb.).

10. On models so equipped, install a new cotter pin and bend the ends over completely.

Drive Chain Slider Inspection

A slider is installed on the left side of the swing arm (**Figure 84**) to protect the swing arm from chain damage. Inspect the slider frequently for advanced wear that would let the chain rub across and damage the swing arm. Replace the slider if it is worn to the limit line. Replace the slider after removing the swing arm (Chapter Thirteen).

BRAKE SYSTEM

Brake Pad and Disc Inspection

Refer to Chapter Fourteen.

Brake Hoses

Check the brake hoses between the master cylinder and each brake caliper. If there is any leakage, tight-en the connections and bleed the brakes as described in Chapter Fourteen. If this does not stop the leak or if a line is obviously damaged, cracked, or chafed, replace the hose(s) and then bleed the brakes.

Brake Fluid Change

Over time, the brake fluid absorbs moisture from the atmosphere. Contaminated brake fluid can impact brake performance and eventually cause internal damage to the brake system.

Replace the brake fluid every two years.

Refer to the brake bleeding procedure in Chapter Fourteen.

Checking Brake Fluid Level

> *WARNING*
> *Use DOT 4 brake fluid. Others may vaporize and cause brake failure. Do not mix different brands or types of brake fluid as they may not be compatible.*

Keep the fluid level above the lower mark on the reservoir. If the fluid level reaches the lower mark (A, **Figure 85**) on the front or (A, **Figure 86**) on the rear, add brake fluid to correct the fluid level.

1. Support the motorcycle on level ground.

2. Clean any dirt from the area around the top cover prior to removing the cover.

3A. Add fluid to the front master cylinder as follows:

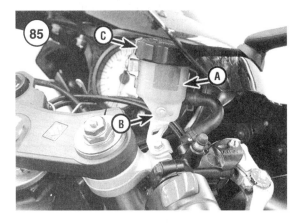

a. Position the handlebars so the master cylinder reservoir is level.

b. Remove the mounting screw (B, **Figure 85**) from the front master cylinder.

c. Remove the top cover, diaphragm plate and diaphragm (C, **Figure 85**)

3B. Add fluid to the rear master cylinder as follows:

a. Remove the mounting bolt (B, **Figure 86**) and move the master cylinder away from the frame to access the top.

b. Make sure the top of the reservoir is level.

c. Remove the screws, top cover, and diaphragm (C, **Figure 86**).

CAUTION
Be careful when handling brake fluid. Do not spill it on painted, plated surfaces or plastic parts. It will destroy the surfaces. Wash the area immediately with soapy water and thoroughly rinse.

4. Add DOT 4 brake fluid to correct fluid level.

5A. On the front master cylinder, perform the following:

a. Reinstall the diaphragm, diaphragm plate and the top cover. Tighten the top cover securely.

b. Install the clamp and tighten the screw securely.

5B. On the rear master cylinder, perform the following:

a. Install the diaphragm and top cover and tighten the screws securely.

b. Move the master cylinder back into position and tighten the mounting bolt securely.

Front Lever Position

The distance between the front brake lever and the hand grip can be adjusted to suit the rider preference.

1. Push the brake lever forward away from the handle grip.

2. Rotate the adjusting dial (A, **Figure 87**) until the desired setting is opposite the arrow (B) on the bracket Position No. 1 sets the lever to the furthest position away from the hand grip; position No. 6 sets the lever to the position closest to the grip.

3. Make sure the stop on the brake lever holder engages the detent in the adjusting dial.

4. After adjusting the lever position, spin the wheel and check for any brake drag. Readjust as necessary.

Brake Pedal Height Adjustment

The pedal height is the distance from the top of the brake pedal to the top of the footpeg. The brake pedal height changes as the brake pads wear. If the brake pedal height is outside the range specified in **Table 4**, adjust the height by performing the following.

1. Support the motorcycle on a level surface.
2. Make sure the brake pedal is in the at-rest position.
3. Loosen the rear brake master cylinder locknut (A, **Figure 88**) and turn the pushrod (B) in either direction until the brake pedal height (C) is within the specified range (**Table 4**).
4. Tighten the rear brake master cylinder locknut (A, **Figure 88**) to 18 N•m (13 ft.-lb.).

Rear Brake Light Switch Adjustment

1. Turn the ignition switch on.
2. Depress the brake pedal and watch the brake light. The brake light should come on just before pressure is felt at the brake pedal. If necessary, adjust the rear brake light switch as follows:

NOTE
Figure 89 is shown with the rear brake pedal mounting bracket assembly removed for photo clarity.

a. To adjust the brake light switch, hold the switch body (A, **Figure 89**) and turn the adjusting locknut (B).
b. To make the light come on earlier, turn the adjusting locknut and move the switch body *up*. Move the switch body down to delay the light coming on.
c. Check that the brake light comes on when the pedal is depressed and goes off when the pedal is released. Readjust if necessary.
3. Turn the ignition switch off.

GENERAL LUBRICATION

Steering Head Bearing Lubrication

Remove, clean and lubricate the steering head bearings with Suzuki Super Grease A as necessary, or when the steering becomes stiff. Refer to the procedure in Chapter Twelve.

Wheel Bearings

Worn wheel bearings cause excessive wheel play results in vibration and other steering troubles.

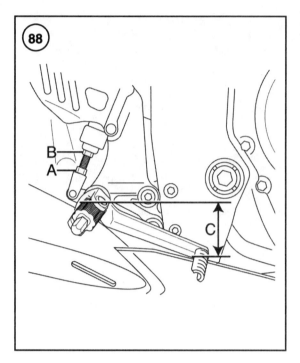

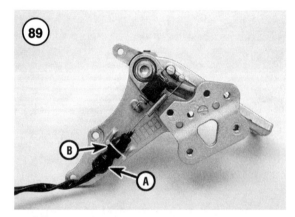

Inspect and lubricate the wheel bearings regularly. Refer to the procedures in Chapter Eleven.

Control Cables

CAUTION
Most nylon lined cables do not require lubrication. If servicing nylon-lined and other aftermarket cables, follow the cable manufacturer's instructions.

Lubricate non-nylon lined control cables with a cable lubricant and lubricant lubricator (**Figure 90**) during cable adjustment or if a cable becomes stiff or sluggish. Periodic lubrication helps ensure a longer service life. During cable lubrication, inspect each cable for fraying and cable sheath damage. Replace any defective cables immediately.

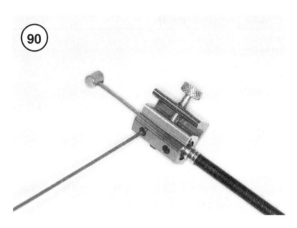

1. Disconnect the cable ends (Chapter Six or Eight).

2. Attach a lubricator tool to the cable following its manufacturer's instructions (**Figure 90**).

3. Insert the lubricant nozzle tube into the lubricator, press the button on the can and hold it down until the lubricant begins to flow out of the other end of the cable. If the lubricant squirts out from around the lubricator, the lubricator is not clamped it to the cable properly.

Loosen and reposition the cable lubricator. It may have to be installed a few times before it seals properly. Place a rag t the end of the cable(s) to catch excess lubricant that flows out.

NOTE
If the lubricant does not flow out of the other end of the cable, check the cable for fraying, bending or other damage.

4. Remove the lubricator tool and wipe off both ends of the cable. Place a dab of grease onto the end before installing it.

5. Install cable(s) (Chapter Six or Eight).

6. Adjust the cable as described in this chapter.

Miscellaneous

Unless otherwise indicated, lubricate the following items with engine oil: shift pedal pivot, brake pedal pivot, footrest pivot, clutch lever pivot, front brake lever pivot, sidestand pivot and control cable ends.

FASTENER INSPECTION

Check the tightness of all fasteners, especially those on:

1. Engine mounting hardware.
2. Engine crankcase and covers.
3. Handlebar and front fork.
4. Gearshift lever.
5. Drive chain components.
6. Brake pedal and lever.
7. Exhaust system.
8. Lighting equipment.
9. Wheel and suspension components.

Table 1 MAINTENANCE SCHEDULE

Initial 600 miles (1,000 km) or 1 month
 Inspect the exhaust control valve; adjust as necessary.
 Change engine oil and replace oil filter.
 Check idle speed; adjust if necessary (2006–2007 models).
 Check throttle cable free play; adjust if necessary.
 Clean and lubricate drive chain.
 Check drive chain slack; adjust if necessary.
 Check drive chain and sprockets for wear or damage.
 Check brake pads for wear.
 Check brake discs thickness; replace if necessary.
 Check brake discs for rust and corrosion; clean if necessary.
 Check steering play; adjust if necessary.
 Check and tighten all nuts, bolts and fasteners on exhaust system.
 Check tightness of all chassis bolts and nuts; tighten if necessary.
 On California models, inspect the throttle body synchronization.
Every 4000 miles (6000 km) or 6 months
 Check air filter element for contamination; clean or replace if necessary.
 Check spark plugs; replace if necessary.
 Change engine oil.
 Check drive chain slack; adjust if necessary.

(continued)

Table 1 MAINTENANCE SCHEDULE (continued)

Every 4000 miles (6000 km) or 6 months (continued)
Check all fuel system hoses for leakage; repair or replace if necessary.
Check idle speed; adjust if necessary (2006–2007 models).
Check throttle cable free play; adjust if necessary.
Check clutch lever free play; adjustment; adjust if necessary.
Check radiator and all coolant hoses for leakage.
Check coolant level, add coolant if necessary.
Check drive chain and sprockets for wear or damage.
Check drive chain slack; adjust if necessary.
Check brake pads for wear.
Check brake discs thickness; replace if necessary.
Check brake discs for rust and corrosion; clean if necessary.
Check brake system for leakage; repair if necessary.
Check brake fluid level in both reservoirs; add fluid if necessary.
Check tire and wheel rim condition.
Lubricate all pivot points.
Check and tighten all chassis fasteners.
Every 7500 miles (12,000 km) or 12 months
Check air filter element for contamination; clean or replace if necessary.
Replace all four spark plugs.
Check all fuel system hoses for leakage; repair or replace if necessary.
Check idle speed; adjust if necessary.
Synchronize the throttle bodies.
Check EVAP hoses (California models).
Check PAIR (air supply) hoses.
Inspect the exhaust control valve; adjust as necessary.
Check throttle cable free play; adjust if necessary.
Check clutch lever free play; adjustment; adjust if necessary.
Check radiator and all coolant hoses for leakage.
Check drive chain and sprockets for wear or damage.
Check drive chain slack; adjust if necessary.
Check brake pads for wear.
Check brake discs thickness; replace if necessary.
Check brake discs for rust and corrosion; clean if necessary.
Check brake system for leakage; repair if necessary.
Check brake fluid level in both reservoirs; add fluid if necessary.
Check tire and wheel rim condition.
Check front fork operation and for leaks.
Check steering play; adjust if necessary.
Check the operation of the rear suspension. Inspect the shock absorber for leaks.
Lubricate control cables.
Every 11,000 miles (18,000 km) or 18 months
All 40000 miles (6000 km) or 6 month interval, plus the following
Replace air filter element.
Replace the engine oil and oil filter.
Every 15,000 miles (24,000 km) or 24 months
All 7,500 miles (12,000 km) or 12 month interval, and plus the following
Check valve clearance; adjust if necessary.
Every year
Change fork oil.
Every 2 years
Replace the coolant.
Replace the brake fluid.
Every 4 years
Replace all brake hoses*
Replace all fuel hoses.
Replace all coolant hoses.
Replace the EVAP hoses (California models)

* Manufacturer's recommendations.

Table 2 TIRE SPECIFICATIONS

Item	Front	Rear
Tire type	Tubeless	Tubeless
Size	120/70 ZR17 M/C (58W)	180/50 ZR17 M/C (73W)
Minimum tread depth	1.6 mm (0.06 in.)	2.0 mm (0.08 in.)
Inflation pressure (cold)*		
Solo	250 kPa (36 psi])	290 kPa (42 psi])
Rider and passenger	250 kPa (36 psi])	250 kPa (36 psi])

*Tire inflation pressure is for original equipment tires. Aftermarket tires may require different inflation pressure. The use of tires other than those specified by Suzuki may cause instability.

Table 3 RECOMMENDED LUBRICANTS AND FLUIDS

Fuel	Regular unleaded
USA, California and Canada models	
Pump octane: (R/2 + M/2)	87 or higher
Research octane	90 or higher
All models except USA, California and	
Canada models	95 or higher
Fuel tank capacity (including reserve)	
2006–2007 modes	
California models	15.5 liter (4.1 US gal. [3.4 Imp gal.])
All models except California	16.5 liter (4.4 US gal. [3.6 Imp gal.])
2007–2008 models	
California models	16.0 liter (4.2 US gal. [3.6 Imp gal.])
All models except California	17.0 liter (4.5 US gal [3.7 Imp gal.])
Engine oil	
Grade	API SF or SG or API SH/SJ with MA in JASO
Viscosity	SAE 10W/40
Capacity	
Oil change only	2.2 liters (2.3 U.S. qt. [1.9 Imp qt.])
Oil and filter change	2.5 liters (2.6 U.S. qt., [2.2 Imp qt.])
Overhaul (completely dry)	2.9 liters (3.1 U.S. qt., [2.6 Imp qt.])
Brake fluid	DOT 4
Fork oil	
Type	Suzuki SS–05 fork oil or equivalent
Capacity per leg	
2006–2007 models	
GSX-R600 models	413 ml (14.0 U.S. oz.)
GSX-R750 models	408 ml (13.8 U.S. oz)
2008–2009 models	
GSX-R600 models	410 ml (13.9 U.S. oz.)
GSX-R750 models	418 ml (14.1 U.S. oz)
Engine coolant	
Type	Anti–freeze/coolant that is compatible with an aluminum radiator.
Mixing Ratio	50–50 with distilled water
Coolant capacity (system total)	
2006–2007 models	2.7 liters (2.9 US. qt. [2.4 Imp qt.])
2008–2009 models	2.65 liters (2.8 US qt. [2.3 Imp qt.])

Table 4 MAINTENANCE AND TUNE-UP SPECIFICATIONS

Item	Specification
Battery	
Type	YT12A–BS Maintenance free (sealed)
Capacity	
GSX-R600	12 volt 36.0 kC (8 amp hour)/10 HR
GSX-R750	12 volt 36.0 kC (10 amp hour)/10 HR
Brake pedal height	65–75 (2.56–2.95) below the footrest

(continued)

Table 4 MAINTENANCE AND TUNE-UP SPECIFICATIONS (continued)

Item	Specification
Compression pressure (at sea level)	
GSX–R600 models	
Standard	1,200–1,600 kPa (12–16 kg/cm2 [(171–228 psi])
Service limit	900 kPa (9 kg/cm2 [128 psi])
Maximum difference between cylinders	200 kPa (2 kg/cm2 [28 psi])
GSX–R750 models	
Standard	1,300–1,700 kPa (13–17 kg/cm2 [(185–242 psi])
Service limit	1000 kPa (10 kg/cm2 [148 psi])
Maximum difference between cylinders	200 kPa (2 kg/cm2 [28 psi])
Clutch cable free play	10–15 mm (0.4–0.6 in.)
Drive chain 21–pin length	319.4 mm (12.6 in.)
Drive chain slack	20–30 mm (0.8–1.2 in.)
Idle speed (2006–2007 models)	
600 cc models	1200–1400 rpm
750 cc models	1100–1300 rpm
Front fork adjustments	
2006–2007 models (standard positions)	
Spring preload	7th turn from softest position
Rebound damping	1 3/4 turns out
Compression damping	1 3/4 turns out
2008–2009 models (standard position)	
Spring preload	7th turn from softest position
Rebound damping	1 ¾ turns out
Compression damping	
GSX–R600	1 ¾ turns out
GSX–R750	
Low speed	2 turn out
High speed	2 ½ turns out
Ignition timing	
GSX–R600 models	6° B.T.D.C. @ 1300 rpm
GSX–R750 models	
2006–2007 models	8° B.T.D.C. @ 1200 rpm
2008–2009 models	5° B.T.D.C. @ 1200 rpm
Oil pressure	100–400 kPa (1.0–4.0 kgf/cm2 [14–57 psi])
Radiator cap opening pressure	108–137 kPa (1.1–1.4 kgf/cm2 [14–19.5 psi])
Shift pedal height	65–75 mm (2.6–3.0 in.) below the footrest
Shock absorber	
2006–2007 models	
Spring preload	
Standard preload (spring length)	181.4 mm (7.14 in.)
Max preload (min spring length)	186.4 mm (7.34 in.
Min preload (max spring length)	176.4 mm (6.94 in.)
Rebound damping	
Standard	1 ½ turns out
Low speed	1 ¾ turns out
High speed	3 turns out
Compression damping	
Low speed	2 turns out
High speed	3 turns out
2008–2009 models	
GSX–R600	
Spring preload	
Standard preload (spring length)	181.4 mm (7.14 in.)
Max preload (min spring length)	186.4 mm (7.34 in.
Min preload (max spring length)	176.4 mm (6.94 in.)
Rebound damping	2 turns out
Compression damping	
Low speed	2 turns out
High speed	3 turns out
GSX–R750	
Spring preload	
Standard preload (spring length)	182.3 mm (7.18 in.)
Max preload (min spring length)	186.4 mm (7.34 in.

(continued)

Table 4 MAINTENANCE AND TUNE-UP SPECIFICATIONS (continued)

Item	Specification
Shock absorber (continued)	
2008–2009 models (continued)	
GSX–R750 (continued)	
Spring preload (continued)	
Min preload (max spring length)	176.4 mm (6.94 in.)
Rebound damping	2 turns out
Compression damping	
Low speed	2 turns out
High speed	3 turns out
Spark plug	
Gap	
2006–2007 models	0.7–0.8 mm (0.028–0.031 in.)
2008–2009 models	0.8–0.9 mm (0.031–0.035 in.)
Type	
2006–2007 models	
Standard	NGK: CR9E, Denso: U27ESR–N
Hot type	NGK: CR8E, Denso: U24ESR–N
Cold type	NGK: CR10E, Denso: U31ESR–N
2008–2009 models	
Standard	NGK: CR9EIA–9, Denso: IUD27D
Hot type	NGK: CR8EIA–9, Denso: IU24D
Cold type	NGK: CR10EIA–9, Denso: IU31D
Steering tension range	200–500 grams (7.05–17.66 oz.)
Throttle cable freeplay	2.0-4.0 mm (0.08-0.16 in.)
Throttle position (TP) sensor (2006-2007 models)	
Input voltage	4.5–5.5 volts
Output voltage	
Fully closed	Approx. 1.1 volts
Fully open	Approx. 4.3 volts
	200–500 grams (7.05–17.66 oz.)
Valve clearance*	
Intake	0–08–0.18 mm (0.003–0.007 in.)
Exhaust	0.18–0.28 mm (0.007–0.011 in.)
Wheel rim runout limit	
Axial	2.0 mm (0.08 in.)
Radial	2.0 mm (0.08 in.)

* Below 35° C (95° F)

Table 5 MAINTENANCE AND TUNE UP TORQUE SPECIFICATIONS

Item	N•m	in.–lb.	ft.–lb.
Brake bleed valve			
Front master cylinder	6.0	53	–
Front caliper	7.5	66	–
Rear caliper	7.5	66	–
Cylinder head cover bolt	14	–	10
Engine sprocket nut	115	–	85
Exhaust header bolt	23	–	17
Exhaust pipe hanger bolt	23	–	17
Fork bridge clamp bolt			
Upper and lower	23	–	17
Front axle	100	–	74
Front axle pinch bolt	23	–	17
Handlebar clamp bolt	23	–	16.5
Muffler connecting bolt	23	–	17
Muffler mounting bolt	23	–	17
Oil drain bolt	23	–	17
Oil gallery plug			
M6	10	89	–
M10	18	–	13
M12	15	–	11
M16 (main)	35	–	25.5

(continued)

Table 5 MAINTENANCE AND TUNE UP TORQUE SPECIFICATIONS

Item	N•m	in.–lb.	ft.–lb.
Oil pan bolt	10	89	–
Rear axle nut	100	–	74
Rear brake master cylinder locknut	18	–	13
Rear sprocket nut	60	–	44
Spark plug	11	97	–
Timing inspection cap	11	97	–
Water pump air bleed bolt	13	115	–

ENGINE TOP END

4

This chapter covers the engine top end. This includes the camshafts, valves and cylinder head. Valve adjustment procedures are located in Chapter Three. The cylinders are an integral part of the upper crankcase half. Refer to Chapter Five when servicing the crankcase/cylinders, pistons and rings.

Tables 1-3 are at the end of this chapter.

The Suzuki GSX-R600 and GSX-R750 features a liquid-cooled, four-valve, in-line four cylinder engine. All valves are operated by dual camshafts driven by a single cam chain. Cam chain tension is maintained by an automatic, spring–loaded tensioner that bears against the rear run of the cam chain.

The engine and transmission share a common case and the same wet-sump oil supply. The flywheel is on the left side of the crankshaft. The wet-plate clutch, timing rotor and crankshaft position sensors are on the right.

CYLINDER HEAD COVER

The cylinder head cover can be removed with the engine installed in the frame. The procedure is shown with the engine removed for photographic clarity.

Removal

1. Support the motorcycle on a level surface.
2. Remove the seats and the fairing side panels (Chapter Fifteen).
3. Disconnect the cable from the battery negative terminal (Chapter Nine).
4. Remove the fuel tank and air filter housing (Chapter Eight).
5. Disconnect the PAIR hose (A, **Figure 1**) from each reed valve port on the cylinder head cover.
6. Disconnect the two-pin connector (B, **Figure 1**) from the camshaft position sensor.
7. Disconnect the two-pin connector (C, **Figure 1**) from each ignition coil/plug cap. Label the connector wire and ignition coil/ plug cap so they can be reinstalled in their original locations.

NOTE
Before removing an ignition coil/ plug
caps, twist it to break the mating seal.

8. Pull straight up and remove the ignition coil/ plug cap from each spark plug.

9. Using a crisscross pattern, evenly loosen and then remove the cylinder head cover bolts (**Figure 2**). Discard the cover bolt gaskets. They must be replaced to prevent an oil leak.

10. Pull the cover straight up and off the cylinder head.

11. The cylinder head cover gasket usually remains attached to the cylinder head cover. Remove and discard gasket. It must be replaced.

12. Remove each reed valve/PAIR gasket assembly (**Figure 3**) from its housing on the camshaft holder.

Installation

1. Fill the voids in the cylinder head with clean engine oil.

2. Install each reed valve/PAIR gasket assembly (**Figure 3**) so the reeds face down into the housing. Make sure the entire gasket sits within the cutout in each camshaft holder.

3. Install a *new* cylinder head cover gasket into the groove in the cover. Make sure the gasket (A, **Figure 4**) is completely seated in the groove.

4. Apply a light coat of Suzuki Bond No. 1207B, to the crescent-shaped portions (B, **Figure 4**) of the gasket. This ensures an oil-tight seal between the cylinder head cover and the cylinder head.

5. Set the cylinder head cover onto the cylinder head so the four crescent-shaped portions of the cover gasket properly engage the crescent-shaped areas of the cylinder head.

6. Install new gaskets (A, **Figure 5**) onto the cylinder head cover bolts (B).

7. Evenly tighten the cylinder head cover bolts (**Figure 2**) in a crisscross pattern. Initially tighten the bolts to 10 N•m (89 in.-lb.), and then tighten to 14 N•m (10. ft.-lb.).

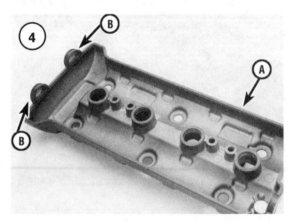

8 Push straight down and install the ignition coil/ plug cap onto each spark plug. Push down until it bottoms.

9. Connect the two-pin connector (C, **Figure 1**) onto each ignition coil/plug cap.

10. Connect the two-pin connector (B, **Figure 1**) onto the camshaft position sensor.

11. Connect the PAIR hose (A, **Figure 1**) onto each reed valve port on the cylinder head cover.

12. Install the air filter housing and fuel tank (Chapter Eight).

13. Connect the cable onto the battery negative terminal (Chapter Nine).

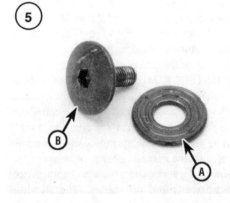

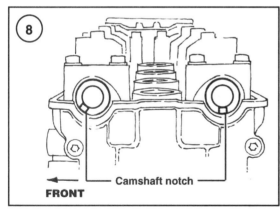

FRONT — Camshaft notch

14. Install the fairing side panels and seats (Chapter Fifteen).

Inspection

1. Remove any old gasket material from the cylinder head or cover.

2. Remove any gasket sealant residue from the gasket sealing surface around the perimeter of the cylinder head. Be sure to clean all old sealant from the crescent-shaped surfaces at each end of the cylinder head.

3. Make sure the gasket groove in the cylinder head cover is clean and free of any oil buildup from a pre-

viously leaking gasket. This surface must be clean and smooth to provide an oil-tight seal.

4. Check the cylinder head cover for warp, cracks or damage. Replace the cover if necessary.

5. Inspect the cover bolts (B, **Figure 5**) thread damage. Replace as necessary.

CAMSHAFT

CAUTION
If the crankshaft must be rotated while the camshafts are removed, pull up on the cam chain so it properly engages the timing rotor. Hold the chain taut on the timing rotor while rotating the crankshaft. If this is not done, the cam chain could become kinked, which could cause damage to the chain, timing rotor and surrounding crankcase.

NOTE
The camshafts can be removed and installed with the engine in the frame. However, timing the camshafts is very difficult because the frame restricts your vision. It is recommended that the engine be removed. The following procedure is shown with the engine removed from the frame for clarity.

Removal

1. Remove the engine (Chapter Five).
2. Remove the cylinder head cover (this chapter).
3. Remove all four spark plugs (Chapter Three). This makes it easier to rotate the engine by hand.
4. Remove the timing inspection cap (**Figure 6**) from the starter clutch cover.
5. Set the No. 1 cylinder to top dead center on the compression stroke by performing the following:
   a. Use the starter clutch bolt (A, **Figure 7**) and rotate the engine 360° (one full revolution) *clockwise*, when viewed from the right side of the motorcycle. Rotate the engine until the index line on the CKP sensor (B, **Figure 7**) once again aligns with the index rib (C) on the clutch cover.
   b. At the same time, this brings the notches on the left side of the camshafts to the position shown in **Figure 8**.
   c. Check the timing mark on the exhaust camshaft sprocket. The No. 1 arrow (**Figure 9**) on the exhaust sprocket should point forward and align with the top edge of the cylinder head.

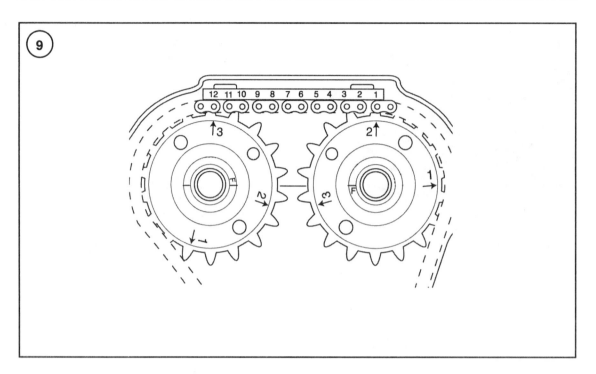

d. If the No. 1 arrow is not positioned as shown, rotate the engine one full revolution clockwise until the index line (B, **Figure 7**) on the starter clutch once again aligns with the pointer (C) on the cover. The No. 1 arrow on the exhaust cam sprocket should now point forward and align with the cylinder head.

6. Remove the cam chain tensioner (this chapter).

7. Remove each reed valve/PAIR gasket assembly (**Figure 3**) from its housing on the camshaft holder.

8. Remove the bolts (A, **Figure 10**) securing the upper cam chain guide (B) and remove the guide.

9. Secure the camshafts to the cam chain with cable ties (A, **Figure 11**).

10. Reverse the tightening sequence stamped on the camshaft holders (**Figure 12**), and evenly loosen remaining camshaft holder bolts. Remove the camshaft holder bolts, pull the camshaft holders (B, **Figure 11**) straight up, and remove them from the cylinder head. Account for the dowels beneath the camshaft holders.

11. Account for the dowels (A, **Figure 13**) that may stay with the camshaft holders or in the cylinder head.

12. Remove and discard the O-rings (B, **Figure 13**) from the camshaft holders.

13. Remove the cable ties (A, **Figure 14**) from the camshafts.

14. Disengage the cam chain from the camshaft sprockets and remove the intake (B, **Figure 14**) and the exhaust camshafts (C) from the cylinder head one at a time.

15. Secure the camshaft chain to the exterior of the engine with safety wire (**Figure 15**).

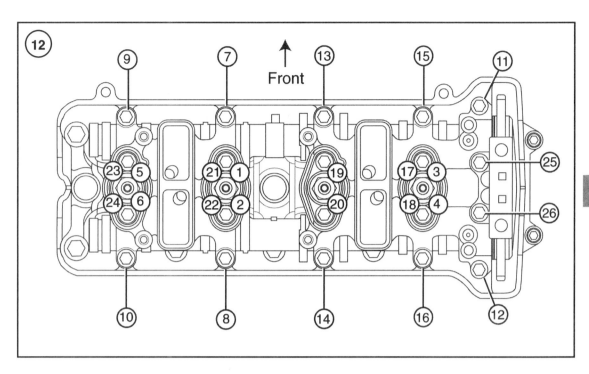

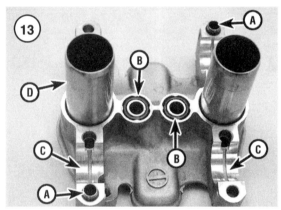

alignment. Recheck the work several times to assure correct alignment.

NOTE
The camshafts are identified by an IN (intake) (A, Figure 16) or EX (exhaust) (B). Install each camshaft in the correct side of the cylinder head.

1. Pull up on the cam chain so it properly meshes with the timing rotor.

2. If necessary, use the starter clutch bolt (A, **Figure 17**) and rotate the engine 360° (one full revolution) *clockwise*, when viewed from the right side of the motorcycle. Rotate the engine until the index line on the CKP sensor (B, **Figure 17**) once again aligns with the index rib (C) on the clutch cover.

Installation

CAUTION
Damage can result from improper cam chain to camshaft installation and

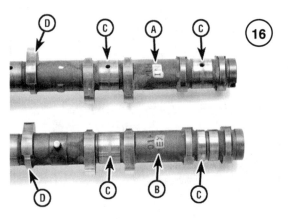

3. Lubricate all bearing surfaces in the cylinder head (**Figure 18**) and camshaft holders (C, **Figure 13**) with molybdenum disulfide oil.

4. Apply molybdenum disulfide oil to the camshaft journals (C, **Figure 16**) and the cam lobes (D).

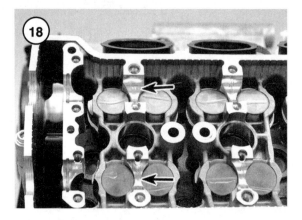

5. Properly mesh the exhaust camshaft into the cam chain (A, **Figure 19**), and lower the camshaft onto the cylinder head bearing surfaces (B) on the exhaust side of the head.

6. Lift the chain and rotate the exhaust camshaft until the No. 1 arrow point forward and aligns with the top surface of the cylinder head (**Figure 20**). The No. 2 arrow (**Figure 21**) should point straight up.

7. Insert the intake camshaft through the cam chain and lower the camshaft into the cylinder head.

8. Properly mesh the cam chain with the sprocket, and secure the cam chain to the cam sprocket with a cable tie (**Figure 22**).

9. Note that the No. 2 arrow on the exhaust cam sprocket points to the No. 1 pin (**Figure 22**) on the cam chain. Mark this first pin as it will be used when setting the timing.

10. Insert the intake camshaft through the cam chain (A, **Figure 23**), and lower the camshaft (B) into the cylinder head.

11. Start at the first pin directly above the arrow marked No. 2, count back to the 12th pin (from the exhaust camshaft side going toward the intake camshaft)

12. Properly mesh the cam chain onto the intake cam sprocket so the marked pin (**Figure 24**) sits opposite the No. 3 arrow on the sprocket. Ensure that the cam chain is secured to both sprockets with a cable tie (A, **Figure 14**).

CAUTION
*The cam chain is now meshed with the timing rotor, the exhaust camshaft sprocket and the intake camshaft sprocket (**Figure 25**). Do not disturb the crankshaft or camshafts until the*

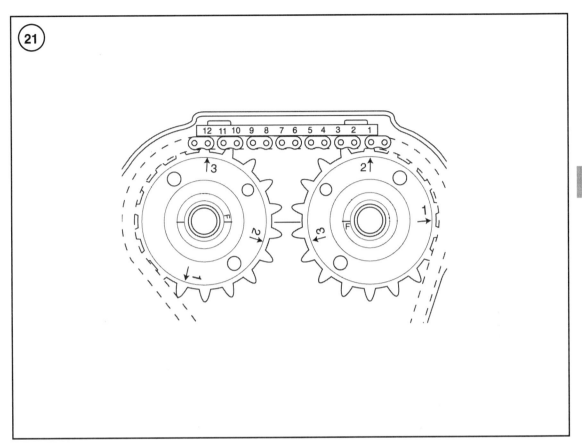

4

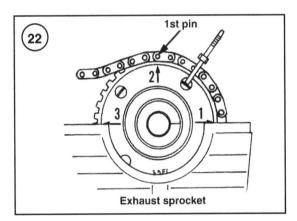

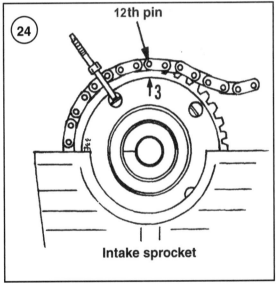

camshaft holders and cam chain tensioner are properly installed.

13. Install new O-rings(A, **Figure 26**) into the camshaft holders.

14. Install the camshaft holder dowels (B **Figure 26**) into the camshaft holders
or cylinder head.

15. Install the camshaft holders (C **Figure 26**) onto the correct location (B, **Figure 11**). Press them down until they bottom.

16. Remove the cable tie (A, **Figure 11**) from each camshaft sprocket.

CAUTION
If the camshaft holder bolts require replacement, do not substitute another type of bolt. The use of a substitute bolt will lead to costly engine damage.

CAUTION
Failure to tighten the bolts in the specified order will result in damage to the bearing surfaces in the cylinder head and camshaft holders.

17. Install the cam chain guide (B, **Figure 10**) and bolts.

18. Install the camshaft holder bolts. Following the sequence embossed on the camshaft holders (**Figure 12**), evenly tighten the bolts in two-three stages to slowly pull the camshaft holders down. Make several passes on each bolt in the specified sequence.

19. Tighten the camshaft holder and chain guide bolts on the final pass to 10 N•m (89 in.-lb.).

20. Install each reed valve/PAIR gasket assembly (**Figure 3**) onto its housing on the camshaft holder.

21. Install the cam chain tensioner (this chapter).

22. Recheck the timing marks. All marks must still be properly aligned as shown in **Figure 21**. If incorrect, reposition the cam chain on the sprockets.

CAUTION
*If there is any binding while rotating the crankshaft, **stop**. Determine the cause before proceeding.*

23. Use the starter clutch bolt (A, **Figure 17**) to rotate the engine *clockwise*, as viewed from the right side of the motorcycle. Rotate the crankshaft through several complete revolutions, and check the operation of the upper end moving parts.

24. Adjust the valves as described in Chapter Three. Lubricate a new O-ring with engine oil, install the O-ring onto the timing inspection cap, and tighten the cap securely.

25. Install the spark plugs (Chapter Three).

26. Install the cylinder head cover (this chapter).

27. Install the engine (Chapter Five).

Inspection

1. Check the camshaft lobes (A, **Figure 27**) for wear. The lobes should not be scored and the edges should be square.

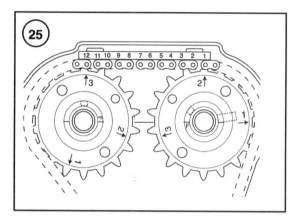

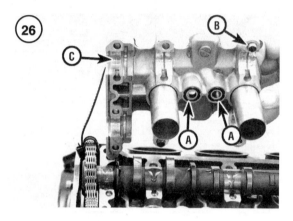

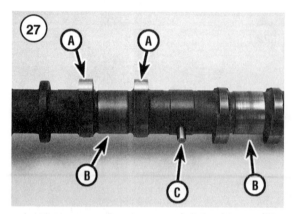

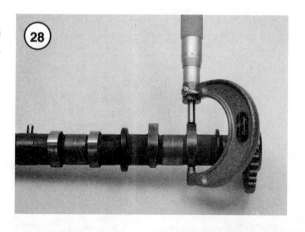

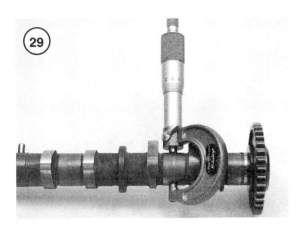

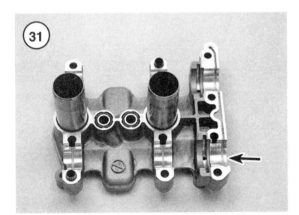

2. Measure the height of each lobe (**Figure 28**) with a micrometer. Replace the camshaft if any lobe is out of specification (**Table 2**).

3. Check each camshaft journal (B, **Figure 27**) for wear and scoring.

4. Measure the outside diameter of each camshaft journal (**Figure 29**) with a micrometer. Record each measurement for use when checking camshaft oil clearance. Replace the camshaft if any journal diameter is out of specification (**Table 2**).

5. If the journals are severely worn or damaged, check the bearing surfaces in the cylinder head (**Figure 30**) and in the camshaft holders (**Figure 31**). They should not be scored or excessively worn. If any of the bearing surfaces are worn or scored, the cylinder head assembly and camshaft holders must be replaced as a set.

6. Place each camshaft on a set of V-blocks and check its runout with a dial indicator. Replace the camshaft if its runout exceeds the specified service limit (**Table 2**).

7. Inspect the camshaft sprocket (**Figure 32**) for broken or chipped teeth. Also check the teeth for cracking or rounding. If the camshaft sprocket(s) is damaged or severely worn, replace the camshaft. Also, inspect the timing rotor as described in this chapter.

NOTE
If the camshaft sprockets are worn, check the cam chain, chain guides and chain tensioner for damage.

8. Ensure that the camshaft position sensor pin (C, **Figure 27**) on the exhaust camshaft is secure.

9. Inspect the sliding surface of upper cam chain guide (**Figure 33**) for wear or damage. Replace the upper guide as necessary.

10. Inspect the camshaft holders (**Figure 34**) for wear or damage. Ensure that the locating pins (A, **Figure 13**), and spark plug channels (D) are secure. The O-rings (B, **Figure 13**) must be replaced every time the camshaft holder is removed.

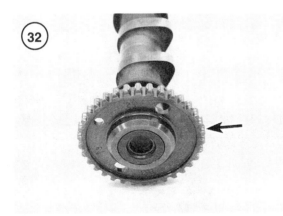

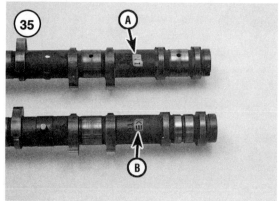

Oil Clearance

Before installing the camshafts, wipe all oil residue from each camshaft journal and from the bearing surfaces of the cylinder head and camshaft holders.

1. Do not install the cam chain onto the camshafts for this procedure.

2. Refer to the IN (intake) (A, **Figure 35**), or EX (exhaust) (B) marks on the camshafts, and install each camshaft in the correct side of the cylinder head.

3. Place a strip of Plastigage onto each camshaft journal so the Plastigage parallels the camshaft (**Figure 36**).

4. Install the camshaft holder dowels (B **Figure 26**) into the camshaft holders
or cylinder head.

5. Install the camshaft holders (C **Figure 26**) onto the correct location (**Figure 37**). Press them down until they bottom.

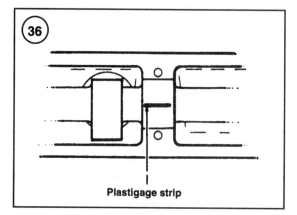

Plastigage strip

CAUTION
Failure to tighten the bolts in the specified order will result in damage to the bearing surfaces in the cylinder head and camshaft holders.

6. Install the cam chain guide (A, **Figure 38**) and (B).

7. Following the sequence embossed on the camshaft holders (**Figure 39**), evenly tighten the bolts in two-three stages to slowly pull the camshaft holders down. Make several passes on each bolt in the specified sequence.

8. Tighten the camshaft holder and chain guide bolts No. 2 on the final pass to 10 N•m (89 in.-lb.).

CAUTION
Do not rotate the camshafts with the Plastigage in place.

9. Reverse the order of the tightening sequence in Step 4, and evenly loosen the camshaft holder bolts in several stages.

10. Pull straight up and carefully remove each camshaft holders.

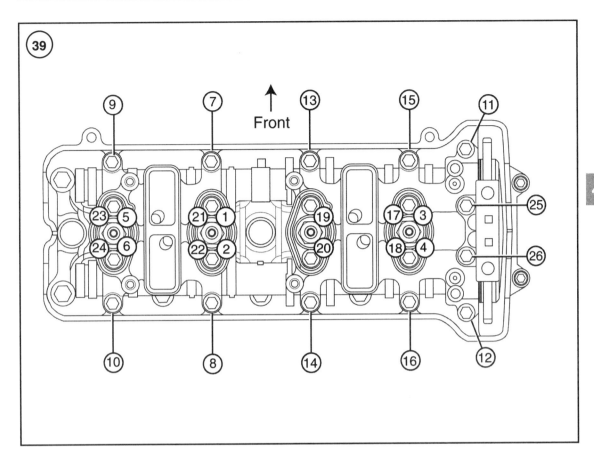

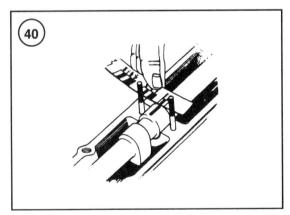

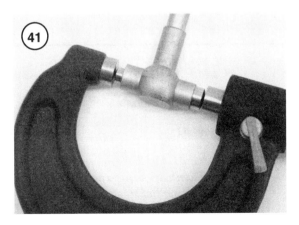

11. Measure the flattened Plastigage (**Figure 40**) at its widest point according to the manufacturer's instructions.

> *CAUTION*
> *Be sure to remove all traces of Plastigage from the camshaft holders and from the camshaft journals. If any Plastigage is left in the engine, it can plug an oil control orifice and cause engine damage.*

12. Remove all Plastigage from the camshaft and camshaft holders.

13. If the camshaft oil clearance is greater than the service limit (**Table 2**), perform the following to determine which component requires replacement:

    a. Remove both camshafts as described in this section. Install the camshaft holders.

    b. Follow the tightening sequence embossed on the holders, and evenly tighten the camshaft holder bolts in several stages listed in **Table 2**.

    c. Use a telescoping gauge to measure the inside diameter of the each bearing surface in the camshaft holders, and measure the telescoping gauge (**Figure 41**). Record the readings.

    d. Measure the outside diameter of each camshaft journal (**Figure 29**). Record the readings.

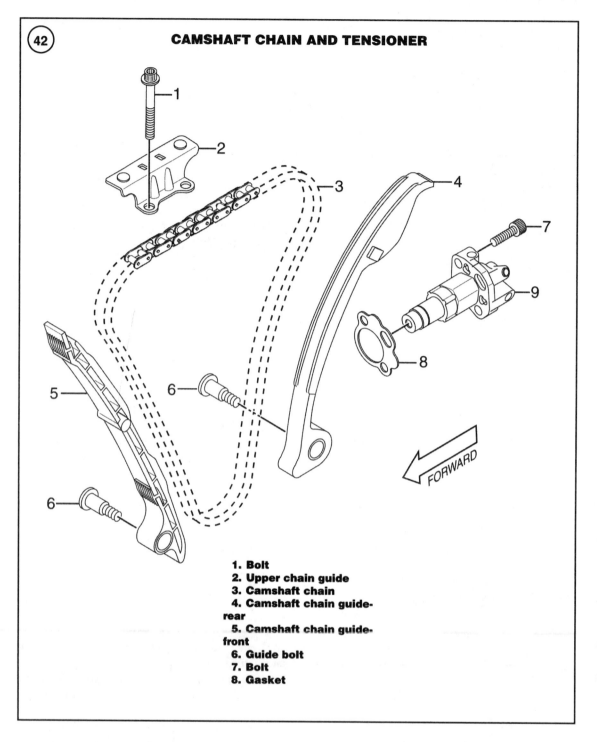

CAMSHAFT CHAIN AND TENSIONER

42

1. Bolt
2. Upper chain guide
3. Camshaft chain
4. Camshaft chain guide-rear
5. Camshaft chain guide-front
6. Guide bolt
7. Bolt
8. Gasket

FORWARD

e. Compare each individual camshaft journal outside diameter to its related camshaft holder inside diameter. If the inside diameter of the camshaft holder exceeds specification, replace the cylinder head and camshaft holders as a set. If the camshaft journal outside diameter exceeds specification, replace the camshaft.

CAM CHAIN TENSIONER

Removal/Inspection/Installation

Refer to **Figure 42**.

CAUTION
The cam chain tensioner is a non-return type. After the tensioner mounting bolts are loosened, the tensioner assembly

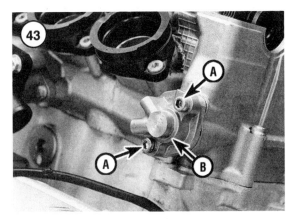

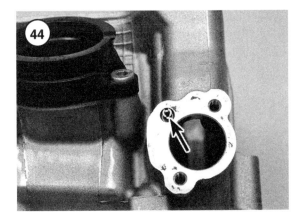

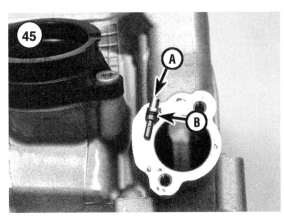

*must be **completely removed** and the plunger reset. If the mounting bolts are loosened, do not simply retighten them. The plunger has already moved out to an extended position and will exert too much pressure on the cam chain leading to engine damage.*

1. Remove the fuel tank and air filter housing (Chapter Eight).

2. Remove the mounting bolts (A, **Figure 43**), and withdraw the cam chain tensioner (B) and its gasket from the cylinder head.

3. Remove the oil jet (**Figure 44**) from the oil gallery in the cylinder head. Make sure the oil jet (A, **Figure 45**) is clear. If necessary, blow out with compressed air. Install a *new* O-ring (B, **Figure 45**).

NOTE
Do not disassembly the tensioner as replacement parts are not available.

4. Inspect the tensioner body (A, **Figure 46**) for cracks or other damage. Replace the tensioner assembly if necessary.

5A. On 2006-2007 models, press in and retract the plunger (B, **Figure 47**) into the tensioner body.

5B. On 2008-2009 models, perform the following:

   a. Hold the tensioner between thumb and finger. Turn the adjuster body clockwise and compress the plunger until the outer circlip groove (A, **Figure 47**) reaches the outer circlip (B). Secure the outer circlip into the outer circlip groove (C, **Figure 47**).

   b. Turn the plunger *clockwise* (D, **Figure 47**) more than 90° to ensure there is a little play in the inner thread mechanism.

6. Install a new gasket (**Figure 48**) onto the tensioner body

7. Tighten the cam chain tensioner mounting bolts to 10 N•m (89 in.-lb.).

8. On 2008-2009 models, perform the following:

   a. On the side of the cylinder head, remove the tensioner adjuster service cap and gasket (**Figure 49**).

   b. Place a small flat blade screwdriver on the plunger head ridge (A, **Figure 50**). Press inward on the plunger head and unhook the outer circlip (B, **Figure 50**) from its groove in the plunger (**Figure 51**).

   c. Rotate the engine *clockwise* several complete revolutions and recheck the camshaft timing marks are still correctly aligned (**Figure 52**).

   d. Check that there is no slack between camshaft chain pins No. 5 and No. 6 (**Figure 53**) to ensure that the adjuster works properly. This

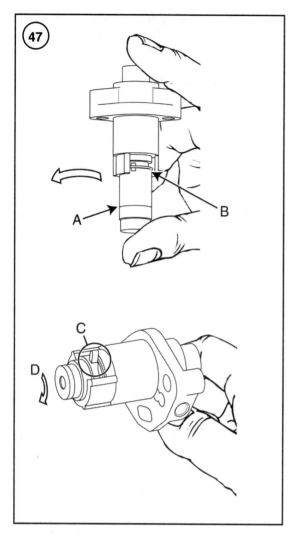

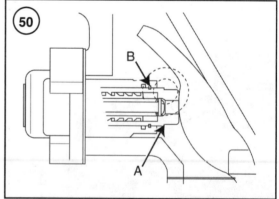

will reseat the outer circlip into the plunger groove.

   e. Install a new gasket and the tensioner adjuster service cap (**Figure 49**). Tighten the cap to 23 N•m (17 ft.-lb.).

9. Install the air filter housing, and the fuel tank (Chapter Eight).

CAM CHAIN, CHAIN GUIDES AND TIMING ROTOR

A continuous cam chain is used on all models. Do not cut the chain; replacement links are not available.

Refer to **Figure 42**.

Removal

NOTE
This procedure is shown with the clutch assembly removed for photo clarity.

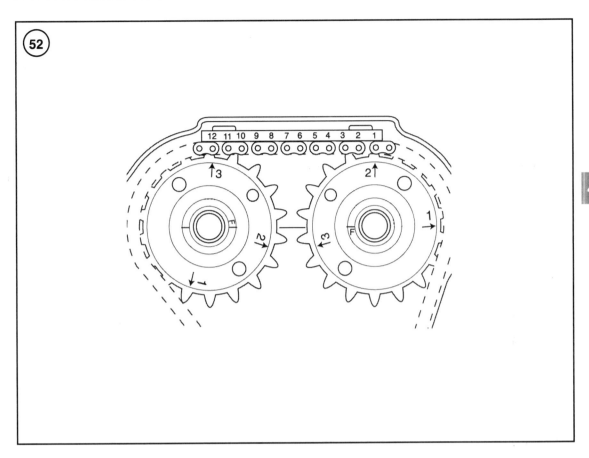

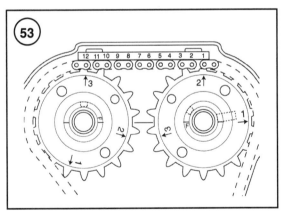

1. Remove the cylinder head (this chapter).

2. Remove the clutch cover (Chapter Six).

3. Remove the alternator cover (Chapter Nine).

4. Remove the rear guide bolt (A, **Figure 54**) and pull the rear guide (B) straight out from the chain tunnel.

5. Secure the alternator rotor bolt (**Figure 55**) to keep the crankshaft from rotating in the next step.

6. Remove the mounting bolt and washer (C, **Figure 54**) and remove the crankshaft position sensor (CKP) (D) from the crankshaft.

7. Remove the front guide bolt (A, **Figure 56**) and pull the front guide (B) straight out from the chain tunnel.

8. Disengage the cam chain (**Figure 57**) from the timing rotor, and lift the chain from the cam chain tunnel.

9. Inspect the cam chain, guides and timing rotor (this chapter).

Installation

1. Insert the cam chain down through the cam chain tunnel.

2. Remove the timing inspection cap (**Figure 58**) from the clutch cover.

3. Engage the cam chain (**Figure 57**) onto the timing rotor and make sure it is properly engaged.

4. Use the starter clutch bolt and rotate the engine *clockwise*, as viewed from the right side, until the index line (A, **Figure 59**) on the crankshaft position sensor (CKP) rotor starter clutch aligns with the index rib (B) on the on the clutch cover.

5. Install the front cam chain guide into the cam chain tunnel (B, **Figure 56**).

6. Apply threadlock (Suzuki Thread Lock 1342 or equivalent) to the threads of the cam chain guide bolts.

7. Install the front guide bolt No. 1 (A, **Figure 56**) and tighten to 23 N•m (17 ft.-lb.).

8. Align the master spline on the CKP sensor with the master spline on the crankshaft, and install the crankshaft position sensor (CKP) (**Figure 60**) onto the crankshaft.

9. Install the rear guide (A, **Figure 61**) into the cam chain tunnel.

10. Install the rear guide bolt No. 1 (B, **Figure 61**) tighten to 23 N•m (17 ft.-lb.).

11. Secure the alternator rotor bolt (**Figure 55**) to keep the crankshaft from rotating in the next step.

12. Install the mounting bolt (C, **Figure 54**) and tighten to 54 N•m (39.0 ft.-lb.).

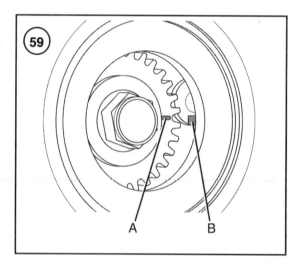

13. Install the clutch cover (Chapter Six).

14. Install the cylinder head (this chapter).

Inspection

If the cam chain is severely worn or damaged, the automatic chain tensioner may not be tensioning the chain properly. Refer to Cam Chain Tensioner Inspection (this chapter).

4

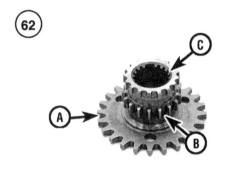

1. Clean the cam chain in solvent. Blow it dry with compressed air.
2. Check the cam chain for:
   a. Worn or damaged pins and rollers.
   b. Cracked or damaged side plates.

CAUTION
If the cam chain, timing rotor or either camshaft sprocket requires replacement, replace them all as a set. The old parts will quickly wear out the new one.

3. If the cam chain is severely worn or damaged, inspect both camshaft sprockets and the CKP timing rotor for the same wear condition. If either camshaft sprocket shows signs of wear or damage, replace them both. If the timing rotor is worn, replace it.
4. Inspect the CKP timing rotor sprocket (A, **Figure 62**), and cam chain (B) for worn or damaged teeth.
5. Inspect the CKP timing rotor's internal splines (C, **Figure 62**) for wear or damage. If damage is found, check the splines on the end of the crankshaft.
6. Inspect the sliding surfaces of the front and rear cam chain guides (**Figure 63**) and the upper cam chain guide (**Figure 64**). Replace the guides as needed.

CYLINDER HEAD

Removal

1. Remove the engine (Chapter Five).
2. Remove the cylinder head cover, both camshafts and the cam chain tensioner (this chapter).
3. Tie one end of a safety wire to the cam chain and secure the other end to the outside of the engine (**Figure 65**).
4. Unscrew and remove the two cylinder head side bolts (**Figure 66**).
5. Remove the tour O-rings (A, **Figure 67**) from the spark plug tunnels.

6. If the cylinder head is going to be inspected and/or serviced, remove the valve lifters and shims before removing the head. Refer to *Valve Lifter and Shim* (this chapter).

NOTE
Make a cardboard template of the cylinder head. Punch a hole in the template for each bolt location, and then mark the bolt number next to the hole. As the bolt is removed, place it into its proper hole.

7. Reverse the tightening sequence shown in **Figure 68**, and loosen the ten 10 mm cylinder head bolts (B, **Figure 67**) in 2-3 stages.

8. Remove the bolts and washers. Note that the cylinder head bolt washers are directional. The rounded side of the washer faces the bolt head (**Figure 69**).

9. Tap around the perimeter of the cylinder head with a rubber or soft faced mallet in order to break the cylinder head free from the head gasket. If necessary, gently pry the cylinder head loose with a broad tipped screwdriver. Do not damage the cylinder or cylinder block mating surfaces or leaks will occur.

10. Lift the cylinder head straight up and off the cylinder block. Guide the cam chain through the tunnel in the cylinder head, and retie the safety wire to the outside of the engine.

11. Remove and discard the cylinder head gasket (A, **Figure 70**). Account the locating dowels (B, **Figure 70**) in the cylinder block.

12. Place a clean shop cloth into the cam chain tunnel, and then cover the cylinder block with another clean shop rag.

13. If necessary, remove the thermostat cover and the thermostat (A, **Figure 71**) (Chapter Ten), and the coolant temperature (CTS) sensor (B) (Chapter Eight).

Installation

1. If removed, install the thermostat cover and the thermostat (A, **Figure 71**) (Chapter Ten), and the CTS sensor (B) (Chapter Eight).

2. Make sure the cylinder head and cylinder block mating surfaces are clean of all gasket residue. Clean them again if necessary.

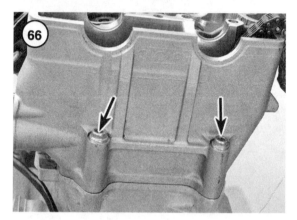

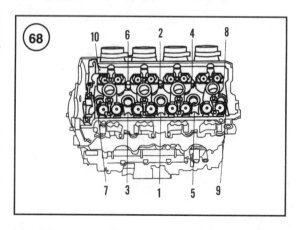

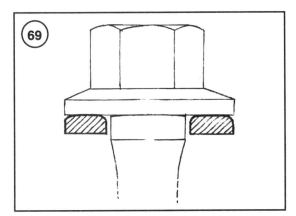

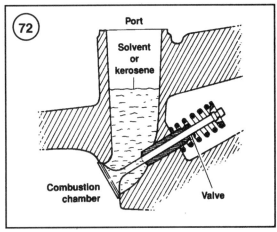

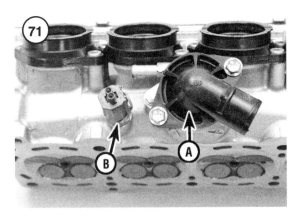

continuing. Tie the cam chain's safety wire to the outside of the engine (**Figure 65**).

8. Correctly install the washers onto the bolts with the round side facing the bolt head as shown in **Figure 69**).

9. Apply clean engine oil to bolt threads and to the bottom side of the washers. Install the ten 10mm cylinder head bolts (B, **Figure 67**) into the correct location in the cylinder head. Start each bolt by hand to avoid cross-threading.

10. Following the tightening sequence shown in **Figure 68**, evenly tighten the ten 10mm cylinder head bolts in several stages, to 31 N•m (23 ft.-lb.).

   a. Reverse the tightening sequence and evenly loosen the 10mm cylinder head bolts.

   b. Retighten the 10mm cylinder head bolts, in sequence, to 31 N•m (23 ft.-lb.).

   c. Using a torque angle gauge, tighten the 10mm cylinder head bolts an additional 60°.

   d. Lubricate each O-ring with Suzuki Super Grease A. Install the O-rings into the spark plug tunnels (A, **Figure 67**).

11. On the right side, install the 6mm cylinder head bolts (B, **Figure 66**), and tighten to 10 N•m (89 in.-lb.).

12. If the valve lifters and shims were removed, install them as described in the Valve Lifter and Shim in this chapter.

13. Install both camshafts and the cam chain tensioner and cylinder head cover (this chapter).

14. Install the engine (Chapter Five).

Inspection

1. Before removing the valves or cleaning the cylinder head, perform the cylinder head leakage test:

   a. Position the cylinder head so the exhaust ports faces up. Pour solvent or kerosene into each exhaust port opening (**Figure 72**).

3. If removed, install the locating dowels (B, **Figure 70**) into the cylinder block.

4. Install a new *cylinder head gasket (A,* **Figure 70**). Make sure all the holes in the gasket align with those in the cylinder block.

5. Position the cylinder head over the cylinder block and run the cam chain and its safety wire up through the cam chain tunnel.

6. Lower the cylinder head onto the engine, and seat the cylinder head onto the cylinder block. Make sure the locating dowels engage the cylinder head.

7. Pull up on the cam chain and make sure it properly engages the sprocket on the timing rotor before

b. Turn the head over slightly, and check each exhaust valve area on the combustion chamber side. If the valves and seats are in good condition, no leakage past the valve seats will be found. If any area is wet, the valve seat is not sealing correctly. This can be caused by a damaged valve seat and/or valve face, a bent or a damaged valve. Remove the valve, and inspect the valve and seat for wear or damage.

c. Pour solvent into the intake ports, and check the intake valves.

2. Remove all traces of gasket residue from the cylinder head (**Figure 73**) and cylinder block mating surfaces. Do not scratch the gasket surfaces.

CAUTION
Cleaning the combustion chamber with the valves removed can damage the valve seat surfaces. A damaged or even slightly scratched valve seat will cause poor valve seating.

3. *Without removing the valves*, remove all carbon deposits from the combustion chamber (A, **Figure 74**). Use a fine wire brush dipped in solvent, or make a scraper from hardwood. Do not damage the head, valves or spark plug threads.

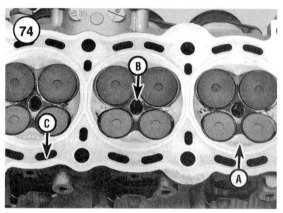

4. Examine the spark plug threads (B, **Figure 74**) in the cylinder head for damage. If damage is minor or if the threads are dirty or clogged with carbon, use a spark plug thread tap (**Figure 75**) and kerosene to clean the threads. If thread damage is severe, the threads can be restored by installing a steel thread insert.

5. Clean the entire head in solvent. Blow it dry with compressed air.

6. Examine the crown on each piston (C, **Figure 70**). A crown should show no signs of wear or damage. If a crown appears pecked or spongy-looking, also check the spark plug, valves and combustion chamber for aluminum deposits. If these deposits are found, the cylinder is overheating.

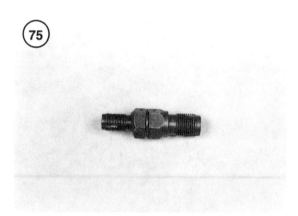

7. Inspect the intake manifolds (A, **Figure 76**) for cracks or other damage that would allow unfiltered air into the engine. If necessary, remove the intake manifolds and discard the O-rings (**Figure 77**).

8. Check for cracks in the combustion chambers, the intake ports (B, **Figure 76**) and the exhaust ports (A, **Figure 78**).

9. Inspect the threads on the exhaust header mounting bosses (B, **Figure 78**) for damage. Clean them with an appropriate size metric tap if damaged.

10. Make sure all coolant passageways (C, **Figure 74**) are clear. If necessary, blow them clear with compressed air.

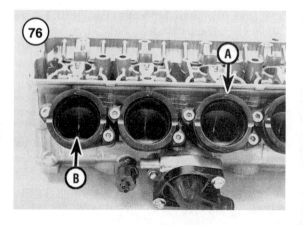

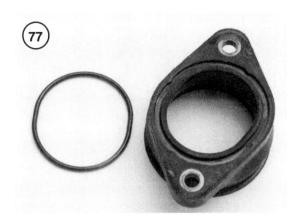

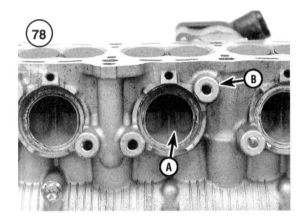

NOTE
If the cylinder head is bead-blasted, clean the head thoroughly with solvent and then with hot soapy water. Chase each exposed thread with a tap to remove grit between the threads so they will not be damaged later. Grit left in the engine will contaminate the oil and cause premature wear.

11. After the head has been thoroughly cleaned, place a straightedge across the gasket surface at several points. Measure the warp by attempting to insert a feeler gauge between the straightedge and cylinder head at each location (**Figure 79**). Warp or nicks in the cylinder head surface could cause an air leak and result in overheating. If warp exceeds the maximum allowable warp limit (**Table 2**), the cylinder head must be resurfaced or replaced. Consult a dealership or machine shop experienced in this type of work.

12. Make sure all engine mounting bolt holes are in good condition. Clean them out with an appropriate size metric tap if necessary.

13. If removed, install the intake manifolds. To prevent a vacuum leak install a new *intake manifold O-ring. Lubricate each O-ring with grease (Suzuki Super Grease A or equivalent). Install each intake manifold in its original location. Position each manifold so the* UP on the manifold face faces the top of the cylinder head. Apply threadlock (Suzuki Thread Lock 1342 or equivalent) to the threads of the manifold screws, and tighten securely.

VALVE LIFTER AND SHIMS

Removal/Installation

Refer to **Figure 80**.

If the cylinder head is going to be inspected and/or serviced, remove the valve lifters and shims before removing the head. To avoid mixing up the parts, work with the lifters from one cylinder at a time.

1. Make a holder for the valve lifters and shims. Mark it with the cylinder number and the intake and exhaust side. The cylinders are numbered one through four counting left to right. The No.1 cylinder sits on the left side of the motorcycle. *Left* refers to the rider's point of view while sitting on the motorcycle and facing forward.

2. Remove the valve lifter (**Figure 81**).

3. Use needlenose pliers or tweezers to remove the shim (**Figure 82**) from the top of the valve spring retainer. Place them in the correct location in the holder. Keep each shim together with its lifter. Shims and lifters must be reinstalled in their original locations.

4. Repeat this for all of the valve lifters and shims in the cylinder head.

5. Repeat this process for the remaining three cylinders.

6. Inspect the valve lifters and shims (**Figure 83**) for wear or heat damage. Service specifications for the outer diameter of the lifter and the inside diameter of the lifter bore in the cylinder head are not available. The lifter (with clean oil applied to its sides) should move up and down in the cylinder head bore with no binding or chatter. If the side of the lifter is scuffed or scratched, replace it.

NOTE
To avoid mixing up the parts, work on one cylinder at a time. Position the holder containing the valve lifters and shims with the same orientation as the cylinder head. Make sure the lifter and shims for the No. 1 cylinder faces on the left side of the engine.

7. Working with one cylinder at a time, first install the shim (**Figure 82**) on the top of the valve keepers. Make sure it is seated correctly (**Figure 84**). The side of the shim with the size stamp must face up.
8. Apply clean engine oil to the sides of the valve lifter, and install it (**Figure 81**).
9. After the valve lifter (**Figure 85**) has been installed, rotate the lifter with a finger. The lifter rotates freely if it is properly seated.
10. Install all shims and lifters into that cylinder, and then continue with the next cylinder.

VALVES AND VALVE COMPONENTS

Refer to **Figure 80**.

Valve Removal

1. Remove the cylinder head, valve lifters and shims (this chapter).
2. Protect the walls of the valve bore during valve removal by performing the following:
    a. Make a small plastic sleeve from flexible plastic.
    b. Insert the plastic sleeve between the valve assembly and the valve bore (**Figure 86**) during valve spring removal and installation.
3. Install a valve spring compressor (**Figure 87**) squarely over the valve spring retainer, and place the other end of tool against the valve head (**Figure 88**).

CAUTION
To avoid loss of spring tension, do not compress the spring any more than necessary to remove the valve keepers.

4. Tighten valve spring compressor until the valve keepers separate from the valve stem. Lift the valve keepers (**Figure 89**) out through the valve spring compressor with a magnet or needlenose pliers.
5. Gradually loosen the valve spring compressor, and remove it from the cylinder head.
6. Remove the spring retainer (**Figure 90**) and the valve spring (**Figure 91**).
7. Remove the plastic sleeve from the valve bore.

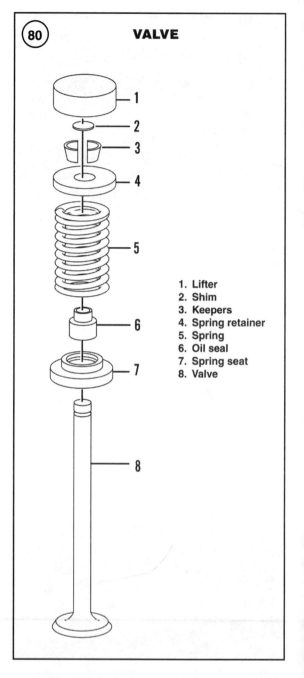

VALVE

1. Lifter
2. Shim
3. Keepers
4. Spring retainer
5. Spring
6. Oil seal
7. Spring seat
8. Valve

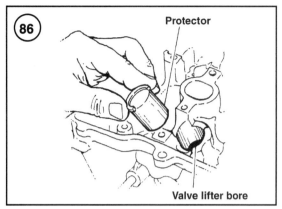

Protector

Valve lifter bore

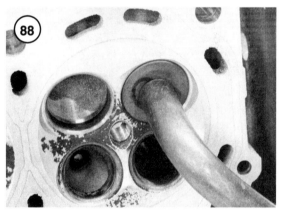

> *CAUTION*
> *Remove any burrs (**Figure 92**) from the valve stem groove before removing the valve. Burrs will damage the valve guide during valve removal.*

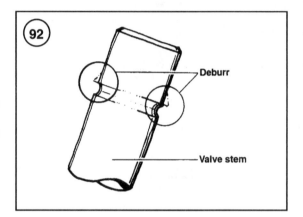

8. Rotate the valve (**Figure 93**), and remove it from the combustion chamber side of the head.

9. Pull the valve seal (**Figure 94**) from the valve guide. Discard the seal.

10. Remove the spring seat (**Figure 95**).

> *CAUTION*
> *All components of each valve assembly must be kept together (**Figure 96**). Place each set in a divided carton, into separate small boxes or into small reclosable plastic bags. Label each valve set. Identify a valve set by its cylinder number and either intake or exhaust valve.*

11. Repeat Steps 3-9 and remove the remaining valves. Keep all valve sets separate.

Valve Installation

1. Clean the end of the valve guide.

2. Install the spring seat (**Figure 95**) over the valve guide.

3. Apply molybdenum disulfide oil to a new oil seal (**Figure 94**), and seat the seal onto the end of the valve guide (**Figure 97**).

4. Coat the valve stem with molybdenum disulfide oil. Install the valve part way into the guide (**Figure 93**). Slowly turn the valve as it enters the oil seal and continue turning it until the valve is completely installed.

5. Position the valve spring (**Figure 91**) with its *closer* wound coils facing down into the cylinder head, and install the spring. If the paint mark is still visible on the spring, the end with the paint should face up out of the head.

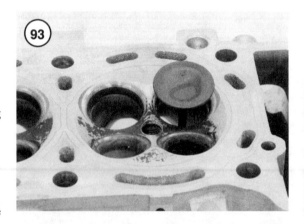

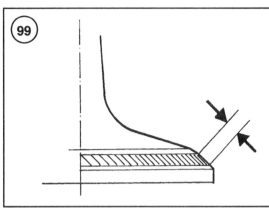

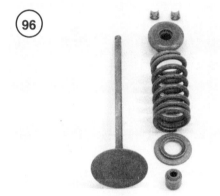

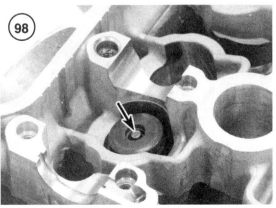

6. Install the spring retainer (**Figure 90**), and seat it onto the valve spring (**Figure 89**).

7. Protect the bore with the plastic sleeve as used during removal (**Figure 86**).

> *CAUTION*
> *To avoid loss of spring tension, do not compress the springs any more than necessary to install the valve keepers.*

8. Compress the valve spring with a valve spring compressor (**Figure 87**), and install the valve keepers (**Figure 89**).

9. Make sure both keepers are seated around the valve stem prior to releasing the compressor.

10. Slowly release the compressor and remove it. Inspect the valve keepers to make sure they are properly seated. Tap the end of the valve stem with a drift and hammer (**Figure 98**). This ensures that the keepers are properly seated.

11. Remove the plastic sleeve from the valve bore.

12. Repeat Steps 1-11 for the remaining valves, as required.

13. Install the shims and valve lifters as described in this chapter.

14. Install the cylinder head as described in this chapter.

15. Adjust the valve clearance as described in Chapter Three.

Valve Inspection

When measuring the valves and valve components in this section, compare any measurements to the specifications listed in **Table 2**. Replace parts that are worn, damaged or out of specification.

1. Clean valves in solvent. Do not damage the valve seating surface.

2. Inspect the valve face (**Figure 99**). Minor roughness and pitting can be removed by lapping the valve as described in this chapter. Excessive unevenness to

the contact surface is an indication that the valve is not serviceable.

3. Inspect the valve stem for wear and roughness. Measure the valve stem outside diameter with a micrometer (**Figure 100**).

4. Remove all carbon and varnish from the valve guides with a stiff spiral wire brush.

5. Measure the valve guide inside diameter with a small hole gauge (**Figure 101**). Measure the guide at the top, center and bottom positions.

6. Subtract the valve stem outside diameter (the Step 3 measurement) from the valve guide inside diameter (the Step 5 measurement). The difference is the valve stem-to-guide clearance. If the clearance is out of specification, examine both measurements. If the valve stem outside diameter is out of specification, replace the valve; valve guide inside diameter out of spec, replace the valve guide.

7. If the valve guide inside diameter cannot be measured, measure the valve stem deflection by performing the following:

   a. Hold the valve approximately 10 mm (0.39 in.) off its seat.

   b. Attach a dial indicator to the valve head (**Figure 102**).

   c. Rock the valve sideways in two directions 90° to each other.

   d. If the valve stem deflection in either direction exceeds the service limit, examine the valve stem outside diameter measurement taken earlier.

   e. If the outside diameter is out of specification, replace the valve. If the outside diameter is within specification, replace the valve guide. However, as a final check, take the cylinder head to a dealership or machine shop and have the valve guides measured.

8. Check each valve spring by performing the following:

   a. Inspect the valve spring for visual damage.

   b. Measure the valve spring free length (**Figure 103**).

   c. Use a square and check the spring for distortion or tilt (**Figure 104**), and spring tension (**Figure 105**).

   d. Repeat for each valve spring.

9. Check the valve spring seats and valve keepers for cracks or other damage.

10. Check the valve stem runout with a V-block and dial indicator as shown in **Figure 106**.

11. Measure valve head radial runout with a dial indicator as shown in **Figure 107**.

12. Measure the valve head thickness with a vernier caliper (**Figure 108**). Replace the valve if valve head thickness is less than the service limit.

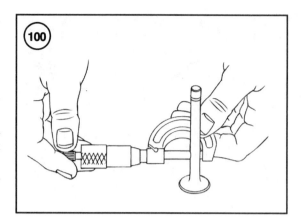

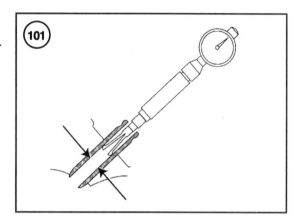

Dial Indicator

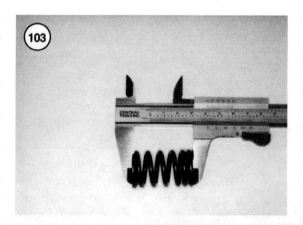

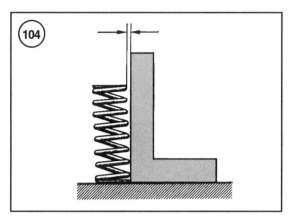

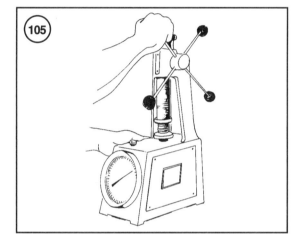

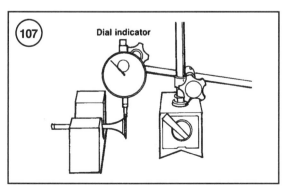

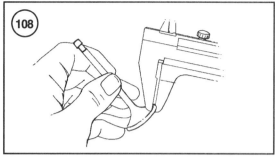

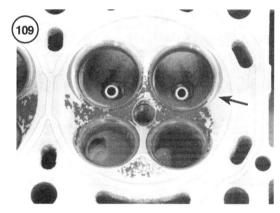

13. Measure the valve head outer diameter with a vernier caliper.

14. Visually inspect the valve seats (**Figure 109**) in the cylinder head. If worn or burned, they may be reconditioned as described in this chapter. Seats and valves in near-perfect condition can be reconditioned by lapping with fine carborundum paste. Check the valve seats as described in *Valve Seat Inspection* later in this chapter.

Valve Guide Removal/Installation

Tools

The following Suzuki special tools, or equivalents, are required to perform this task.

1. Valve guide remover/installer: part No. 09916-43211.
2. Attachment:
   a. 2006-2007 models: part No. 09916-44930, or part No. 09916-53330.
   b. 2008-2009 models: part No. 09916-43240.
3. Valve guide reamer (for reaming the valve guide bores): part No. 09916-33320.
4. Valve guide reamer (for reaming the new valve guides): part No. 09916-33210.
5. Valve guide reamer handle: part No. 09916-34542.

Procedure

1. Place the new valve guides in a freezer.
2. Remove the intake manifolds (this chapter) and engine coolant (ECT) sensor (Chapter Eight) from the cylinder head.

> *CAUTION*
> *Do not heat the cylinder head with a torch. Never bring a flame into contact with the cylinder head. Direct flame can warp the cylinder head.*

3. Place the cylinder head in a shop oven, or hot plate, and warm it to 100° C (212° F). To check the temperature of the cylinder head, flick tiny drops of water onto the head. The cylinder head is heated to the proper temperature if the drops sizzle and evaporate immediately.

> *WARNING*
> *Wear heavy gloves when performing this procedure. The cylinder head will be very hot.*

4. Remove the cylinder head form the oven and place it onto wooden blocks with the combustion chamber facing up.
5. From the combustion side of the head, drive the old valve guide out of the cylinder head with the valve guide installer/remover (**Figure 110**) and a hammer.
6. Remove and discard the valve guide. *Never* reinstall a valve guide.

> *NOTE*
> *Oversized valve guides are available from Suzuki.*

7. After the cylinder head has cooled, ream the valve guide bore as follows:
   a. Apply cutting oil to both the valve guide bore and to the valve guide reamer.

> *CAUTION*
> *Always rotate the valve guide reamer clockwise. The valve guide will be damaged if the reamer is rotated counterclockwise.*

   b. Insert the valve guide reamer from the combustion chamber side (**Figure 111**), and rotate the reamer clockwise. Continue to rotate the reamer and work it down through the entire length of the valve guide bore Continue to apply additional cutting oil during this procedure.
   c. Rotate the reamer clockwise until it has traveled all the way through the bore.
   d. Rotate the reamer clockwise, and completely withdraw the reamer from the valve guide.

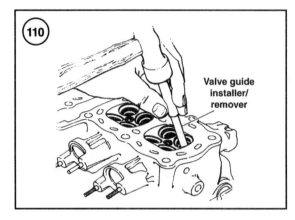

Valve guide installer/remover

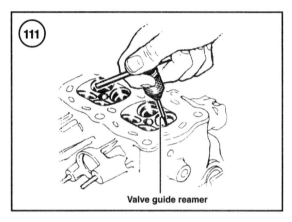

Valve guide reamer

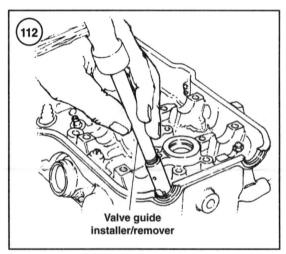

Valve guide installer/remover

8. Reheat the cylinder head as described in Step 3.
9. Remove the cylinder head form the oven and place it onto wooden blocks with the combustion chamber facing down.
10. Remove one valve guide from the freezer.

> *CAUTION*
> *Failure to lubricate the new valve guide and guide bore will result in damage to the cylinder head and/or valve guide.*

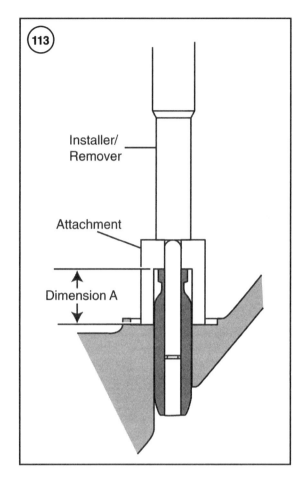

Installer/Remover

Attachment

Dimension A

11. Apply clean engine oil to the new valve guide and to the valve guide bore in the cylinder head.

12. From the top side of the cylinder head (camshaft side), drive the new valve guide into the cylinder head with the valve guide installer/remover, the valve guide attachment and hammer (**Figure 112**). Drive the valve guide into the bore until the attachment bottoms in the cylinder head, which set the guide to the specified set height (**Figure 113**) listed in **Table 1**.

13. After the cylinder head has cooled, ream the new valve guides as follows:

 a. Apply cutting oil to both the new valve guide and to the valve guide reamer.

CAUTION
Always rotate the valve guide reamer clockwise. The valve guide will be damaged if the reamer is rotated counterclockwise.

 b. Insert the valve guide reamer from the combustion chamber side (**Figure 111**) and rotate the reamer clockwise. Continue to rotate the reamer and work it down through the entire length of the new valve guide. Continue to

apply additional cutting oil during this procedure.

 c. Rotate the reamer clockwise *until it has traveled all the way through the new valve guide.*

 d. Rotate the reamer clockwise, *and completely withdraw the reamer from the valve guide.*

 e. Measure the inside diameter of the valve guide with a small hole gauge. Measure the gauge with a micrometer, and compare the measurement to the specification. Replace the valve guide if it is not within specification.

14. If necessary, repeat Steps 1-13 for any other valve guide.

15. Thoroughly clean the cylinder head and valve guides with solvent to wash out all metal particles. Dry the head with compressed air.

16. Lightly oil the valve guides to prevent rust.

17. Lap the valve seats as described in this chapter.

18. Install the intake manifolds (this chapter) and engine coolant sensor (Chapter Eight) from the cylinder head.

Valve Seat Inspection

The most accurate means for inspecting the valve seal involves the use of marking compound, which is available from auto parts stores or machine shops.

1. Remove the valves as described in this section.

2. Thoroughly clean all carbon deposits from the valve face with solvent or detergent. Completely dry the valve face.

3. Spread a thin layer of marking compound evenly on the valve face, and insert the valve into its guide.

4. Support the valve by hand (**Figure 114**), and tap the valve up and down in the cylinder head. Do not rotate the valve; a false impression will result.

5. Remove the valve and examine the impression left by the marking compound. The impression left on the valve or in the cylinder head should be even and continuous, and the valve seat width (**Figure 115**) should be within specification.

6. Closely examine the valve seat in the cylinder head (**Figure 109**). It should be smooth, even, and have a polished seating surface.

7. Measure the valve seat width (**Figure 115**) with a vernier caliper.

8. If the valve seat is within specification, install the valves as described in this chapter.

9. If the valve seat is not correct, recondition the valve seat in the cylinder head as described in this section.

Valve Seat Reconditioning

NOTE
*Suzuki no longer lists the special tools for valve seat reconditioning. Refer to aftermarket suppliers for the required special tools with the various required angles shown in **Figure 116** and **Figure 117**.*

Procedure

1. Carefully rotate and insert the solid pilot into the valve guide. Make sure the pilot is correctly seated.
2. Install the 45° cutter onto the solid pilot. Descale and clean the valve seat with one or two turns (**Figure 118**).

CAUTION
Measure the valve seat contact area in the cylinder head after each cut to make sure the contact area is correct and to prevent removing too much material. If too much material is removed, the cylinder head must be replaced.

3. If the seat is still pitted or burned, turn the 45° cutter additional turns until the surface is clean. Avoid removing too much material from the cylinder head.
4. Measure the valve seat with a vernier caliper (**Figure 115**). Record the measurement to use a reference point.
5. Install the 15° cutter (exhaust valve) or the 30° cutter (intake valve) onto the solid pilot, and lightly cut the seat to remove 1/4 of the existing valve seat (**Figure 119**).
6. Install the 60° degree cutter onto the solid pilot, and lightly cut the seat to remove 1/4 of the existing valve seat (**Figure 120**).
7. Measure the valve seat width with a vernier caliper. Fit the 45° degrees cutter onto the solid pilot, and cut the valve seat to the specified width specified in **Table 2**.
8. Measure the valve seat width as described in *Valve Seat Inspection* earlier in this section.
9. If the contact area is too wide or too high on the valve face (**Figure 121**), use the 15° cutter (for an exhaust valve) or the 30° cutter (for an intake valve) to lower and narrow the contact area.
10. If the contact area is too wide or too low on the valve face, use the 60° cutter to raise and narrow the contact area.
11. If the contact area is too narrow or too low on the valve face (**Figure 122**), use the 45° cutter to remove a portion of the valve seat material and increase the contact area.

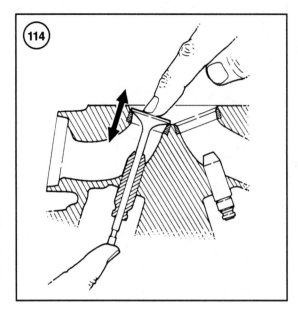

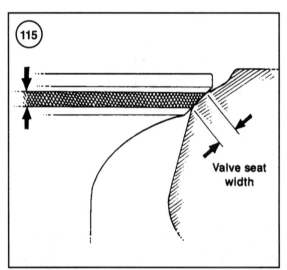

Valve seat width

12. After the desired valve seat position and width is obtained, use the 45° cutter and very lightly clean away any burrs that may have been caused by the previous cuts. Remove only enough material as necessary.
13. Check that the finish has a smooth and velvety surface, it should *not* be shiny or highly polished. The final seating takes place when the engine is first run.
14. Repeat Steps 1-12 for all remaining valve seats.

CAUTION
Do not lap the titanium valves as the oxidized membrane on the valve surface will be removed and the valve must be replaced.

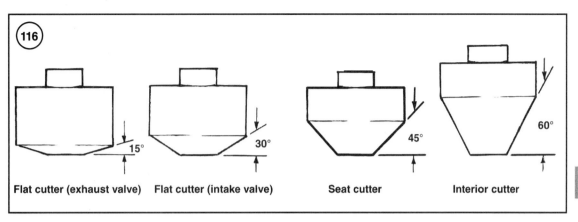

116

15° — Flat cutter (exhaust valve)

30° — Flat cutter (intake valve)

45° — Seat cutter

60° — Interior cutter

4

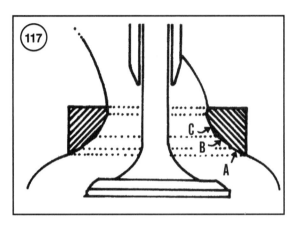

117

C
B
A

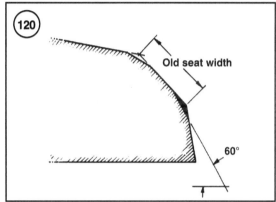

120

Old seat width

60°

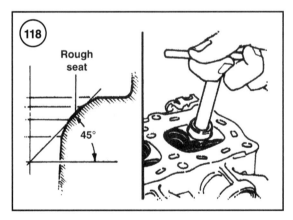

118

Rough seat

45°

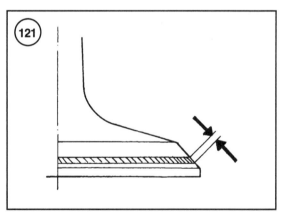

121

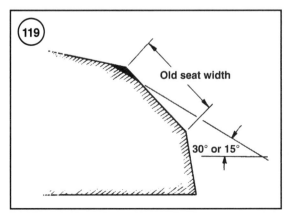

119

Old seat width

30° or 15°

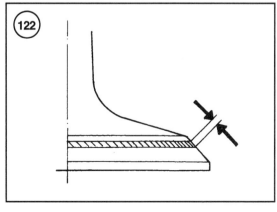

122

Table 1 GENERAL ENGINE SPECIFICATIONS

Item	Specification
Engine type	4–stroke, DOHC, 4–valve head, 4 inline cylinder
Bore x stroke	
GSX–R600 models	67.0 x 42.5 mm (2.638 x 1.673 in.)
GSX–R750 models	79.0 x 48.7 mm (2.756 x 1.917 in.)
Displacement	
GSX–R600 models	599cc (36.5 cu. in.)
GSX–R750 models	750cc (45.8 cu. in.)
Compression ratio	12.5 – 1
Ignition type	Electronic (Transistorized)
Ignition timing (Not adjustable)	
GSX–R600 models	6° B.T.D.C. @ 1300 rpm
GSX–R750 models	
2006–2007 models	8° B.T.D.C. @ 1200 rpm
2008–2009 models	5° B.T.D.C. @ 1200 rpm
Firing order	1–2–4–3
Engine forward rotation	Clockwise, viewed from the right side
Cooling system	Liquid
Lubrication system	Wet sump

Table 2 ENGINE TOP END SPECIFICATIONS

Item	Standard mm (in.)	Service limit mm (in.)
Camshaft		
Cam lobe height		
GSX–R600 models		
Intake	36.58–36.63 (1.440–1.442)	36.28 (1.428)
Exhaust	35.98–36.03 (1.417–1.419)	35.68 (1.405)
GSX–R750 models		
Intake	36.78–36.83 (1.448–1.450)	35.48 (1.397)
Exhaust	35.38–35.43 (1.393–1.395)	35.08 (1.381)
Journal outside diameter	23.959–23.980 (0.9433–0.9441)	–
Camshaft holder inside diameter		24.012–24.025 (0.9454–0.9459)
	–	
Camshaft runout	–	0.10 (0.004)
Camshaft oil clearance	0.032–0.066 (0.0013–0.0026)	0.150 (0.0059)
Cylinder head warp	–	0.20 (0.008)
Valves and valve springs		
Valve clearance (cold)		
Intake	0–08–0.18 mm (0.003–0.007 in.)	–
Exhaust	0.18–0.28 mm (0.007–0.011 in.)	–
Valve stem outside diameter		
Intake	4.475–4.490 (0.1762–0.1768)	–
Exhaust	4.455–4.470 (0.1754–0.1760)	–
Valve stem deflection	–	0.25 (0.010)
Valve stem runout	–	0.05 (0.002)
Valve guide inside diameter	4.500–4.512 (0.1772–0.1776)	–
Valve stem–to–guide clearance		
Intake	0.010–0.037 (0.0004–0.0015)	–
Exhaust	0.030–0.057 (0.0012–0.0022)	–
Valve diameter		
2006–2007 models		
Intake	27.2 (1.07)	–
Exhaust	22.0 (0.87)	–
2008–2009 models		
Intake	29.0 (1.14)	–
Exhaust	23.0 (0.91)	–
Valve head radial runout	–	0.03 (0.001)
Valve seat width	0.9–1.1 (0.035–0.043)	–
Valve seat cutter angle		
Intake	30, 45, 60°	

(continued)

Exhaust   15, 45, 60°

Table 2 ENGINE TOP END SPECIFICATIONS (continued)

Item	Standard mm (in.)	Service limit mm (in.)
Valves and valve springs (continued)		
Valve spring free length		
2006–2007 models	—	37.1 (1.46)
2008–2009 models	—	39.4 (1.55)
Valve spring tension		
GSX–R600 models		
2006–2007 models	203–233 N @ 33.55 mm	
	(20.7–23.8 kgf @ 33.55 mm [45.6–52.4 lbs @ 1.32 in.])	
2008–2009 models	Approx. 231N @ 33.55 mm	
	(23.6 kgf @33.55 mm [51.9 lbs @ 1.32 in.])	
GSX–R750 models		
2006–2007 models	Approx. 147N @ 33.55 mm	
	(15.0 kgf @33.55 mm [33.1 lbs @ 1.32 in.])	
2008–2009	142–157 N @33.55 mm	
	(14.5–16.0 kgf @ 33.55 mm [31.9–35.3 lbs @ 1.32 in.])	

Table 3 ENGINE TOP END TORQUE SPECIFICATIONS

Item	N•m	in.–lb.	ft.–lb.
Camshaft holder bolt	10	89	–
Camshaft timing rotor bolt	54	–	39
Camshaft chain guide bolt			
2006–2007 models	10	89	–
2008–2009 models	10	89	–
No. 1 bolt	23	–	17
No. 2 bolt	10	89	–
Camshaft chain tensioner			
Mounting bolt	10	89	–
Tensioner cap bolt	23	–	17
Cylinder head cover bolt	14	–	10
Cylinder head bolt			
6mm	10	89	–
10mm			
Initial	31	–	23
Final	additional 60°	–	–
Spark plug	11	97	–
Timing inspection cap	11	97	–

4

Notes

CHAPTER FIVE

ENGINE LOWER END

This chapter covers the engine lower end. Components covered include:
1. Crankcase assembly.
2. Crankshaft.
3. Connecting rods and pistons.
4. Balancer (750 cc models).
5. Oil pan, oil pump and oil cooler.
6. Transmission shaft assemblies (removal and installation only).
7. Starter Clutch and Gears.
8. Flywheel.
Table 1-10 are at the end of this chapter.

ENGINE REMOVAL/INSTALLATION

The following components can be serviced while the engine in the frame:
1. External shift mechanism.
2. Clutch.
3. Flywheel.
4. Coolant pump.
5. Oil pump.
6. Starter motor and gears.
7. Throttle bodies.
8. Oil cooler.
9. Exhaust system.
10. Primary driven gear.
11. Cam chain tensioner.

Service Notes

Note the following when removing or installing the engine.
1. A hydraulic floor jack is needed to support the engine.
2. Engine removal and installation requires at least two people.
3. Cover the O-ring chain before degreasing the engine. The chemicals in the degreaser cause O-ring swelling, which permanently damages the chain.
4. Electrical connectors and hoses must be reinstalled in their original locations. Use tape and a permanent marking pen to label them during disconnecting and disassembly.
5. Study the engine mounts closely. Make notes or take photographs of the mounting bolts, clamp bolts and adjusters. Note their positions on the motorcycle, and keep the various components separate.
6. An engine mounting thrust adjuster socket wrench (Suzuki part No. 09940-14980, or its equivalent) (**Figure 1**), is needed to tighten the thrust adjuster locknuts.

Removal

1. Make sure the motorcycle is on level ground, and securely support it on a swing arm stand. Block both sides of the front wheel so it cannot roll in either direction.

2. Remove the seats and the fairing side panels (Chapter Fifteen).

3. Disconnect the negative cable from the battery (Chapter Nine).

4. Drain the engine oil, remove the oil filter and drain the coolant (Chapter Three)

5. Remove the radiator assembly and the coolant reservoir (Chapter Ten).

6. Remove the fuel tank, air filter housing, throttle bodies, and exhaust system (Chapter Eight).

7. Remove the radiator bracket from the front of the engine (Chapter Ten).

8. Remove the front engine cover from the top of the frame (Chapter Fifteen).

9. Disconnect the PAIR hose (A, **Figure 2**) from each reed valve port in the cylinder head cover (Chapter Eight).

10. Remove the engine sprocket cover and the engine sprocket (Chapter Seven).

11. Remove the left clutch push rod from the mainshaft so it will not be damaged.

12. Pull back the rubber boot (A, **Figure 3**) from the starter motor terminal. Remove the nut (B, **Figure 3**), and disconnect the starter cable.

13. Disconnect the 2-pin connector (C, **Figure 3**) from the engine coolant temperature (ECT) sensor.

14. Disconnect the following electrical connectors from their harness mates. Follow each wire and release it from any holder or clamp securing it to the engine or frame.

15. Disconnect the 2-pin connector (**Figure 4**) from the camshaft position (CMP) sensor, and disconnect the 2-pin connector (B, **Figure 2**) from each ignition coil/plug cap.

   a. The 2-pin crankshaft position (CKP) sensor connector (A, **Figure 5**).

   b. The 3-pin gear position (GP) sensor connector (B, **Figure 5**).

   c. Ground wire (C, **Figure 5**).

   d. If still connected, disconnect the 3-pin speed (SP) sensor connector (**Figure 6**).

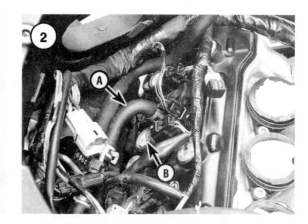

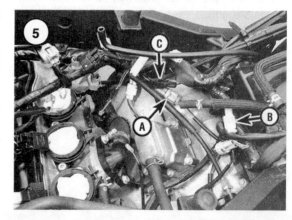

16. If the engine will be disassembled, remove the following subassemblies:

   a. Flywheel (this chapter).

   b. Clutch (Chapter Six).

   c. Starter motor (Chapter Nine).

17. Move all electrical wires, harnesses and hoses out of the way.

18. Support the engine with a hydraulic or scissor jack. Place wood between the jack and the oil pan. Refer to **Figure 7** and **Figure 8**. Raise the jack and place tension against the engine to ease mounting bolt removal.

19. On the left side, remove the front mounting bolt (**Figure 9**).

20. On the right side, perform the following:

   a. Loosen the mounting clamp bolt (A, **Figure 10**).

   b. Remove the front mounting bolt (B, **Figure 10**).

   c. Remove the rear upper mounting nut (**Figure 11**).

   d. Use the special tool, and remove the rear upper thrust adjuster locknut (**Figure 12**).

21. Perform the following on the lower rear engine mount:

a. Remove the engine mounting lock-nut (**Figure 13**). Discard the locknut as it cannot be reused.

b. Use the special tool and loosen and remove thrust adjuster locknut (**Figure 14**). Discard the locknut as it cannot be reused.

22. Make sure the floor jack is still positioned correctly against the engine.

NOTE
The mounting bolts are of a different length. The lower bolt is 10 X 205mm (0.394 X 8.07 in.), the upper bolt is 10 X 215mm (0.394 X 8.46 in).

23. Slowly withdraw the lower mounting bolt from the left side.

24. Slowly withdraw the upper mounting bolt from the left side.

25. Lower the jack and the engine from the frame. Make sure drive chain clears the countershaft.

26. Roll the jack and engine from the frame. Carefully remove the engine from the jack, and support the engine on wooden blocks.

27. Perform the checks described in *Cleaning and Inspection* in this section.

Installation

1. Check that the upper and lower thrust adjusters are in place in the right side of the frame mount.

2. With the help of an assistant, set the engine on a hydraulic floor jack.

3. Center the engine directly beneath the frame.

4. Slowly raise the engine and align the rear engine mounts between their mates in the frame. Set the drive chain onto the countershaft.

5. Install the upper (long bolt) and lower (shorter bolt) mounting bolts from the left side. Make sure each bolt emerges from its thrust adjuster on the right side.

6. On the right side, perform the following:

a. Install the front mounting bolt (B, **Figure 10**), and finger-tighten at this time.

b. Install the mounting clamp bolt (A, **Figure 10**), and finger-tighten at this time.

7. On the left side, install the front mounting bolt (**Figure 9**), and finger-tighten at this time.

8. Install the thrust adjuster onto the upper and lower mounting bolts. Tighten each thrust adjuster to 23 N•m (17 ft.-lb.).

9. Install a new self-locking nut onto each upper and lower engine mounting 10mm bolts.

10. Use the special tool (**Figure 1**) to tighten the thrust adjuster locknuts as follows:

a. Lower self-locking nut (**Figure 14**) to 45 N•m (33 ft.-lb.).

b. Upper self-locking nut (**Figure 12**) to 45 N•m (33 ft.-lb.).

11. On the right side, tighten the front engine mounting 10mm bolt (**Figure 9**) to 55 N•m (40 ft.-lb.).

12. On the left side, perform the following:

a. Tighten the front engine mounting 10mm bolt (B, **Figure 10**) to 55 N•m (40 ft.-lb.).

b. Tighten the clamp 10mm bolt (A, **Figure 10**) to 23 N•m (17 ft.-lb.).

13. Install the following sub-assemblies:

a. Flywheel (this chapter).

b. Clutch (Chapter Six).

c. Starter motor (Chapter Nine).

14. Connect the following electrical connectors to their harness mates. Secure each wire to any holder noted during removal.

a. The 2-pin crankshaft position (CKP) sensor connector (A, **Figure 5**).

b. The 3-pin gear position (GP) sensor connector (B, **Figure 5**).

c. Ground wire (C, **Figure 5**).

d. If still connected, disconnect the 3-pin speed (SP) sensor connector (**Figure 6**).

15. Connect the 2-pin connector (**Figure 4**) onto the camshaft position sensor (CMP), and connect the

2-pin connector (B, **Figure 2**) on to each ignition coil/plug cap.

16. Install cable onto the starter and install the nut (B, **Figure 3**). Push the rubber boot (A, **Figure 3**) back onto the starter motor terminal.

17. Connect the 2-pin connector (C, **Figure 3**) onto the engine coolant temperature (ECT) sensor.

18. Connect the 2-pin connector (**Figure 4**) onto the camshaft position sensor (CMP).

19 Connect the 2-pin connector (B, **Figure 2**) onto each ignition coil/plug cap.

20. Install the left clutch push rod into the mainshaft.

21. Install the engine sprocket and he engine sprocket cover (Chapter Seven).

22. Connect the PAIR hose (A, **Figure 2**) onto each reed valve port in the cylinder head cover (Chapter Eight).

23. Install the front engine cover from the top of the frame (Chapter Fifteen).

24. Install the radiator bracket onto the front of the engine (Chapter Ten).

25. Install the throttle bodies, air filter housing, fuel tank and exhaust system (Chapter Eight).

26. Install the radiator assembly and the coolant reservoir (Chapter Ten).

27. Install a new oil filter and add engine oil (Chapter Three).

28. Add engine coolant (Chapter Three).

29. Connect the negative cable to the battery (Chapter Nine).

30. Start the engine, and check for oil and coolant leaks. Bleed the coolant as described in Chapter Three.

31. Operate the clutch lever. Adjust it as necessary (Chapter Three).

32. Shift the transmission through each gear, and check the operation of the clutch and transmission.

33. Connect the negative cable onto the battery (Chapter Nine).

34. Install the fairing side panels and install the seats (Chapter Fifteen).

35. Slowly test ride the motorcycle to ensure that all systems operate properly.

Cleaning/Inspection

1. Check the mounting hardware for thread damage or wear. Remove any corrosion from the engine mounting bolts.

2. Clean and dry the engine mounting bolts, nuts, and thrust adjusters.

3. Clean the thrust adjuster's mating threads in the frame.

4. Replace all damaged fasteners.

5. Check the coolant hoses for cracks, leaks or other damage. Replace any hose as needed.

6. Check the wiring harness for chafing or other damage. Replace any wire holders or clamps as needed.

7. Clean the electrical connectors with contact cleaner.

8. Check the engine and frame mounts for cracks or other damage.

9. Inspect the exposed portion of the frame for cracks or wear.

STARTER CLUTCH AND GEARS

The flywheel rotor holder (Suzuki part No. 09930-44520), or an equivalent holder, is needed to remove and install the starter clutch.

Refer to **Figure 15**.

Removal

NOTE
This procedure is shown with the engine removed for photo clarity.

1. Remove the right side fairing panel (Chapter Fifteen).

2. Remove the mounting bolts (**Figure 16**) and remove the starter idler cover and O-ring.

3. Remove the wave washer (**Figure 17**) and the flat washer (**Figure 18**) from idler shaft No. 1.

4. Remove starter idler gear No. 1 (**Figure 19**).

5. Remove the needle bearing (**Figure 20**) and thrust washer (**Figure 21**) from idler shaft No. 1.

6. Remove the shaft (**Figure 22**).

7. Remove the alternator cover (this chapter).

8. Remove idler shaft No. 2 (A, **Figure 23**) from its boss in the crankcase.

9. Remove idler gear No. 2 (B, **Figure 23**) from behind the flywheel.

10. Remove the flywheel (C, **Figure 23**) (this Chapter).

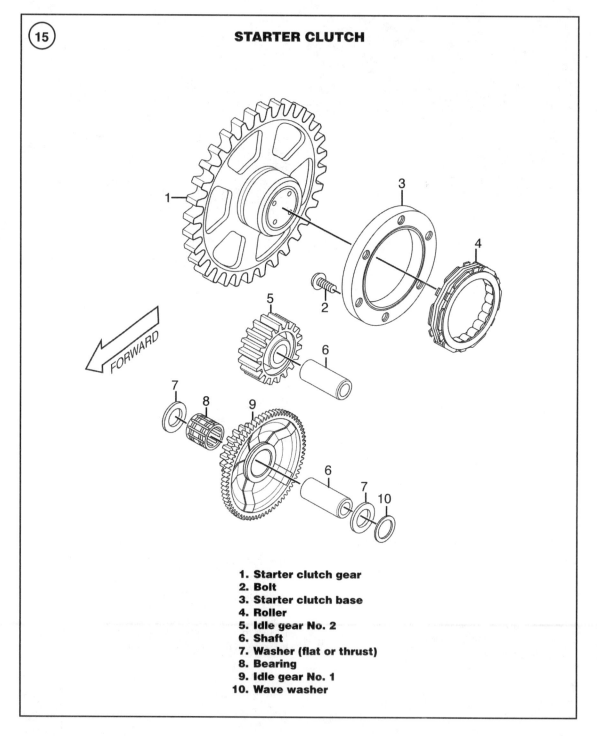

15 **STARTER CLUTCH**

1. Starter clutch gear
2. Bolt
3. Starter clutch base
4. Roller
5. Idle gear No. 2
6. Shaft
7. Washer (flat or thrust)
8. Bearing
9. Idle gear No. 1
10. Wave washer

FORWARD

11. Set the starter clutch on the bench so the starter clutch gear faces up.

Installation

1. Install the flywheel (C, **Figure 23**) (this Chapter).

2. Lubricate idler gear shaft No. 2 with clean engine oil.

3. Install idler gear No. 2 (B, **Figure 23**) into position behind the flywheel, and install the idler shaft No. 2 (A) through the gear and into its boss in the crankcase.

4. Install the alternator cover (this chapter).

5. Install the idle gear shaft No. 1 (**Figure 22**) into the crankcase receptacle. Push it in until it bottoms.

6. Install the thrust washer (**Figure 21**) onto the idle shaft No. 1.

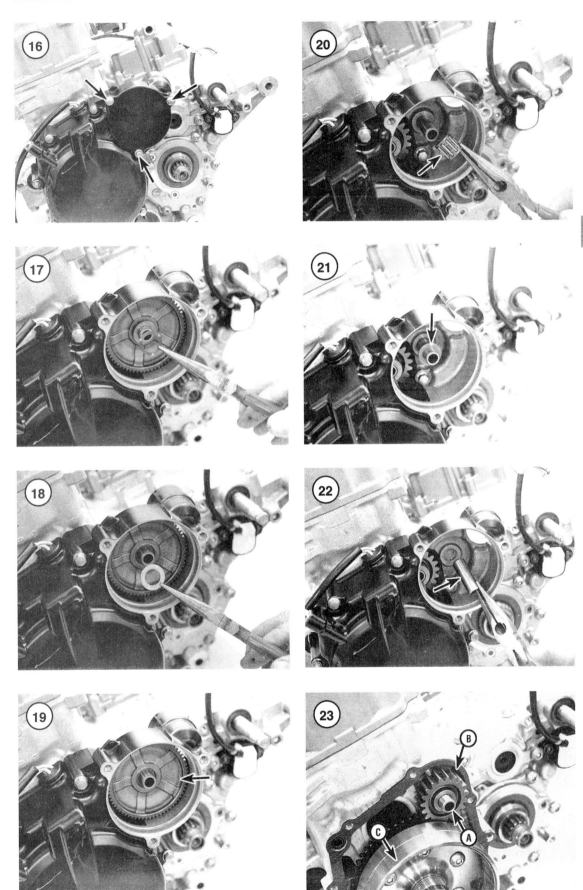

5

7. Install the needle bearing (**Figure 20**) onto the idle shaft No. 1.

8. Position the idle gear as shown in **Figure 24** and install the gear onto the idle shaft No. 1 (**Figure 19**). Properly mesh it with the idle gear No. 2.

9. Install the flat washer (**Figure 18**) and wave washer (**Figure 17**).

10. Install a *new* O-ring onto the cover, and apply a coat of grease to the O-ring.

11. Install the cover and tighten the bolts (**Figure 16**) to 10 N•m (89 in.-lb.).

12. Install the right side fairing panel (Chapter Fifteen).

Inspection

1. Hold the flywheel housing and rotate the starter clutch gear. It should rotate freely when turned clockwise (**Figure 25**) but lock when turned *counter-clockwise*. Replace the starter clutch if it fails either portion of this test.

2. Remove the starter clutch gear by rotating the gear clockwise (**Figure 25**) and simultaneously lifting it from the flywheel.

3. Clean all parts in solvent and dry them with compressed air.

4. Inspect the starter clutch gear (A, **Figure 26**), for worn, chipped or cracked teeth.

5. Inspect the bearing surface (B, **Figure 26**) of the starter clutch gear for scoring or other signs of wear.

6. Inspect the starter idle gear No. 1 gear (**Figure 27**), and idle gear No. 2 (**Figure 28**) for worn, chipped or cracked teeth. Replace any gear as necessary.

7. Inspect each idler shaft for scoring or other signs of wear.

8. Inspect the idler gear No. 1 needle bearing (A, **Figure 29**) and shaft (B) for scoring or other signs of wear.

9. Inspect the rollers (A, **Figure 30**) of the starter clutch for burrs, wear or damage. Replace if necessary.

10. Inspect the shaft bosses in the right crankcase, starter idler cover and in the starter clutch cover for wear or damage.

11. Assemble the starter clutch as follows:

   a. Place the flywheel face down on the bench tip.

   b. Place the starter clutch gear onto the flywheel and rotate the gear *clockwise* (**Figure 25**) and simultaneously press the gear onto the flywheel until the gear bottoms.

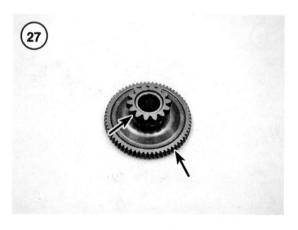

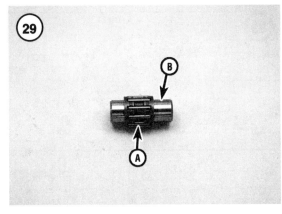

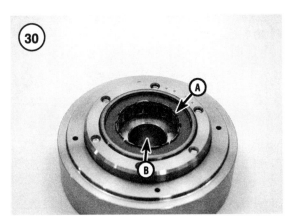

ALTERNATOR COVER

Removal/Installation

NOTE
This procedure is shown with the engine removed for photo clarity.

1. Disconnect the electrical cable from the negative battery terminal (Chapter Nine).
2. Remove the fairing side panel from the left side (Chapter Fifteen).
3. Remove the starter clutch and gears (this chapter).
4. Follow the wiring harness from the alternator cover and disconnect the 3-pin stator connector from its harness mate.
5. Place an oil pan beneath the alternator cover to catch residual oil from the crankcase.
6. Remove the starter clutch cover bolts (A, **Figure 31**).
7. Remove the starter clutch cover (B, **Figure 31**) from the crankcase. Account for the dowels behind the cover.
8. Remove the dowels and the gasket (D, **Figure 23**) from the crankcase. Discard the gasket.
9. Installation is the reverse of removal. Note to the following:
   a. Clean all gasket residues from the mating surfaces of the crankcase and cover.
   b. Apply Suzuki Bond 1207B to the seams formed by the mating surfaces of the crankcases.
   c. If removed, install the dowels in the crankcase, and install a new *cover gasket (B,* **Figure 31**).
   d. Install the starter clutch cover (B, **Figure 31**) onto the crankcase, and tighten the bolts (A) to 10 N•m (89 in.-lb.).

FLYWHEEL

Tools

The following tools are needed to remove the flywheel.
1. The rotor holder (Suzuki part No. 09930-44520), a sheave holder, or a 26 mm wrench.
2. The rotor remover (Suzuki part No. 09930-34980) or an equivalent puller.
3. A 12 mm bolt that is 28-38mm (1.10-1.5 in.) long.

Removal/Installation

1. Remove the alternator cover as described in this chapter.

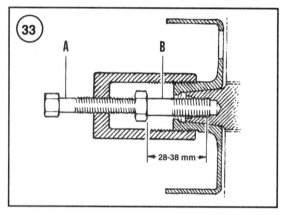

2. Secure the flats of the flywheel, and remove the flywheel bolt (**Figure 32**) from the crankshaft.

3. Install a 12 mm bolt (28-38 mm long) into the end of the crankshaft, and install the rotor remover, or an equivalent, so the center screw (A, **Figure 33**) presses against the 12 mm bolt (B).

4. Hold the flywheel rotor with the rotor holder (A, **Figure 34**), and remove the rotor bolt. Remove the rotor/starter clutch assembly (B, **Figure 34**) from the crankshaft.

5. Hold the remover and turn the center screw until the rotor releases from the crankshaft taper.

6. Remove the rotor remover and the 12 mm bolt from the crankshaft.

7. Remove the flywheel from the taper.

8. Installation is the reverse of removal. Note the following:

    a. Use contact cleaner and clean the crankshaft taper and the flywheel tapered bore (B, **Figure 30**) so they are free of oil and contaminants.

    b. Secure the flywheel with the special tool (A, **Figure 35**) and tighten the bolt (B) to 120 N•m (88 ft.-lb.). Remove the tools.

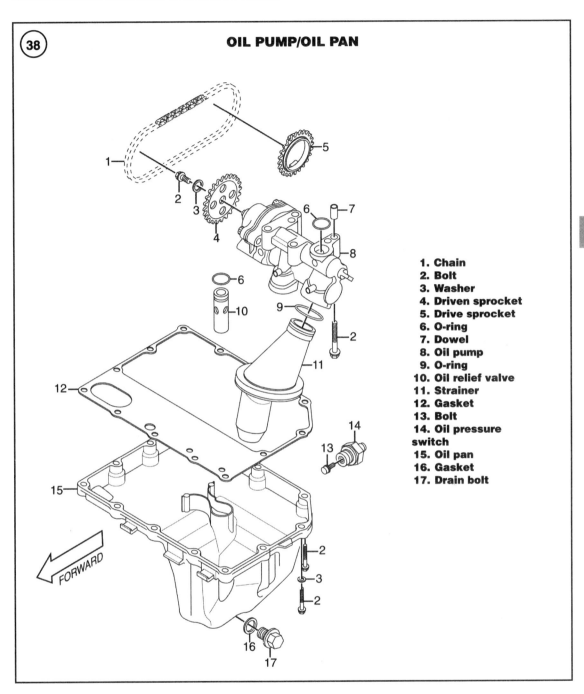

38 **OIL PUMP/OIL PAN**

1. Chain
2. Bolt
3. Washer
4. Driven sprocket
5. Drive sprocket
6. O-ring
7. Dowel
8. Oil pump
9. O-ring
10. Oil relief valve
11. Strainer
12. Gasket
13. Bolt
14. Oil pressure switch
15. Oil pan
16. Gasket
17. Drain bolt

FORWARD

Inspection

WARNING
Replace a cracked or chipped flywheel. A damaged flywheel can fly apart at high engine speeds. Do not attempt to repair a damaged flywheel.

1. Clean the flywheel in solvent, and dry it with compressed air.
2. Check the flywheel for cracks or other signs of damage.

3. Check the flywheel tapered bore (**Figure 36**) and the crankshaft taper for damage.
4. Inspect the flywheel magnet (**Figure 37**) for metal debris it may have attracted. Remove all debris.

OIL PUMP

The oil pump is secured to the base of the crankcase. Replace the oil pump as an assembly if any part is worn or damaged. The only replacement parts available are the O-rings and oil pump gear.

Refer to **Figure 38**.

Removal

1. Remove the engine from the frame (this chapter).

2. Remove the clutch assembly (Chapter Six).

3. Slide the spacer (A, **Figure 39**) away from the oil pump drive sprocket and remove it from the mainshaft.

4A. On 2006-2007 models, disengage the oil pump drive chain and remove the oil pump drive sprocket (B, **Figure 39**).

4B. On 2008-2009 models, disengage the oil pump drive chain and remove the bearing and the oil pump drive sprocket.

5. Rest the oil pump drive chain on the mainshaft (A, **Figure 40**).

6. Disengage the oil pump drive chain from the oil pump driven sprocket (B, **Figure 40**).

7. Leave the clutch thrust washer (C, **Figure 40**) in place behind the oil pump drive chain.

8. Turn the engine on its side on the workbench and remove the oil pan (this chapter).

9. Remove the oil strainer (A, **Figure 41**) from the oil pump.

10. If necessary, pull the oil pressure relief valve (B, **Figure 41**) from its port on the oil pump.

11. Remove the mounting bolts (A, **Figure 42**), pull straight up, and remove the oil pump (B).

12. Remove the dowels (A, **Figure 43**) and O-ring (B). Discard the O-ring.

13. Inspect the oil pump (this section).

Installation

1. Install the dowels (A, **Figure 43**) and new O-ring (B). Apply grease (Suzuki Super Grease A or equivalent) to a *new* O-ring.

2. Install the oil pump straight down on the dowels and make sure the O-ring is still in place. Push the oil pump down until it bottoms.

3. Install the mounting bolts (A, **Figure 42**), and tighten to to10 N•m (84 in.-lb.).

4. Apply a light coat of engine oil or grease to the oil strainer O-ring.

5. Align the notch on the oil strainer with the oil pump boss, and install the oil strainer (A, **Figure 41**) onto the oil pump. Push it down until it bottoms.

6. If removed, install the oil pressure relief valve (B, **Figure 41**) as follows:

    a. Lubricate the O-ring (A, **Figure 44**) with grease (Suzuki Super grease A or equivalent).

    b. Press the relief valve into its port on the oil pump.

7. Install the oil pan (this chapter).

8. Engage the oil pump drive chain onto the oil pump driven sprocket (B, **Figure 40**).

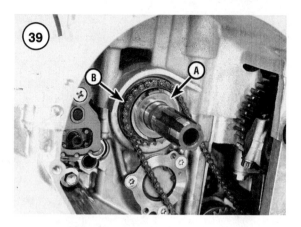

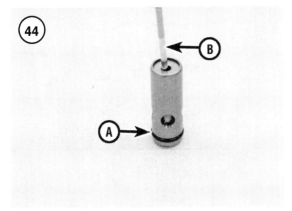

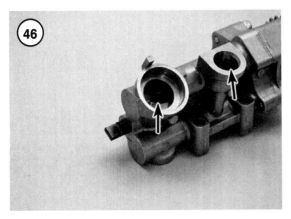

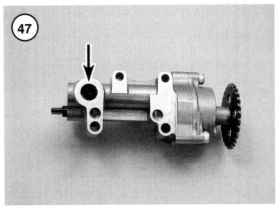

9. Ensure that the clutch thrust washer (C, **Figure 40**) is still in place behind the oil pump drive chain.

10A. On 2006-2007 models, install the oil pump drive sprocket (B, **Figure 39**), and engage the oil pump drive chain. Install the spacer onto the transmission mainshaft and insert it into the sprocket.

10B. On 2008-2009 models, install the oil pump drive sprocket and bearing, and engage the oil pump drive chain. Install the spacer onto the transmission mainshaft and insert it into the sprocket.

11. Install the clutch assembly (Chapter Six).

12. Install the engine into the frame (this chapter).

Inspection

1. Inspect the oil pump housing (**Figure 45**) for cracks or damage.

2. Check that all openings are clear (**Figure 46**) and (**Figure 47**) and free of any sludge.

3. Rotate the oil pump with the driven sprocket by hand and check for smooth operation with no binding. If there is any binding, replace the oil pump as it cannot be serviced.

4. Thoroughly clean the strainer in solvent and dry with compressed air.

5. Use wooden rod to check the operation of the relief valve. Insert the rod into the relief valve (B, **Figure 44**), and press the piston into the valve. The piston must slide smoothly and return to the full closed position when released. If operation is not smooth, clean the relief valve in solvent and dry with compressed air.

OIL COOLER

The oil cooler service is described in Chapter Ten.

OIL PAN AND STRAINER

Removal

1. Remove the engine from the frame (this chapter).
2. Remove the mounting bolts and remove the plate (A, **Figure 48**).
3. Evenly loosen the oil pan bolts (B, **Figure 48**), in a crisscross pattern and several passes. Remove the bolts.
4. Remove the oil pan (C, **Figure 48**) from the crankcase.
5. Remove the oil pan gasket (**Figure 49**).
6. Remove the oil strainer (A, **Figure 41**) from the crankcase.
7. If necessary, pull the oil pressure relief valve (B, **Figure 41**) from its port on the oil pump.

Installation

1. Thoroughly clean the mating surfaces of the crankcase and oil pan with an aerosol electrical contact cleaner.
2. Apply a light coat of engine oil or grease to the oil strainer O-ring.
3. If removed, install the oil pressure relief valve (B, **Figure 41**) into its port on the oil pump.
4. Align the notch on the oil strainer with the oil pump boss, and install the oil strainer (A, **Figure 41**) onto the oil pump. Push it down until it bottoms.
5. Install a new oil pan gasket (**Figure 49**). Make sure it is seated correctly against the crankcase.
6. Set the oil pan (C, **Figure 48**) into place onto the crankcase.
7. Install a *new* gasket washer onto oil pan bolt (D, **Figure 48**).
8. Install plate (A, **Figure 48**), and apply thread-locking compound (Suzuki Thread Lock 1303, or it equivalent), to the threads of the three mounting bolts. Install the bolts.
9. Install the remaining bolts (B, **Figure 48**), and evenly tighten the bolts (A) to 10 N•m (89 in.-lb.).

Inspection

1. Clean all parts in solvent, and dry them with compressed air.
2. Visually inspect the oil pan for cracks or other signs of damage.
3. Inspect the oil strainer for signs of wear or damage. Clean any debris from the strainer as necessary.

CRANKCASE

The two-piece crankcase is made of thin-walled, precision-cast aluminum alloy and is assembled

without gaskets. Only sealant is used during assembly. The upper and lower crankcases are only available as a matched set.

To avoid damage, do not hammer or pry on any of the interior or exterior projected walls. Excessive force will damage these areas.

The procedure that follows describes a complete lower end overhaul. The terms right and *left* refer to the engine as it sits in the frame not as it sits on the bench. Keep this in mind when the crankcase is sitting upside down on the workbench.

Draw an outline of each crankcase section onto a piece of cardboard. Number and punch holes into this template that correspond with each bolt location. As the bolts are removed insert them into the appropriate holes in the template. Leave any cable holder(s) on its respective bolt.

Crankcase Disassembly

1. While the engine is still in the frame, refer to the appropriate chapter and remove the following assemblies:
   a. Flywheel (this chapter).
   b. Starter, crankshaft position sensor and gear position sensor (Chapter Nine).
   c. Starter clutch and gears (this chapter).
   d. Clutch (Chapter Six).
   e. Coolant pump, thermostat and engine coolant temperature sensor (Chapter Ten).
   f. External shift mechanism (Chapter Seven)
2. Remove the engine (this Chapter).
3. Remove the cylinder head, cam chain and chain guides (Chapter Four).
4. Remove the oil cooler (Chapter Ten).
5. Remove the oil pan, and strainer, and oil pump (this chapter).
6. Remove the crankcase breather reed valve cover bolts (A, **Figure 50**), and remove the cover (B). Remove and reed valve assembly (**Figure 51**).
7. Remove the crankcase breather cover bolts (A, **Figure 52**), and remove the cover (B) from the upper crankcase. Remove and discard the cover gasket (**Figure 53**).
8. Remove the mounting bolts (A, **Figure 54**) and remove the clutch pushrod oil seal cover (B).
9. Set the engine right side up on the workbench with the upper crankcase facing up. Support the engine on wooden blocks.
10. Loosen or remove the bolts from the upper crankcase as follows:
    a. Insert each bolt into its place in the upper crankcase template as it is removed from the upper crankcase.
    b. Remove the front two bolts (**Figure 55**).

c. Following a crisscross pattern, evenly loosen all the upper rear crankcase bolts (A, B **Figure 56**). Loosen the bolts in two-three stages, but leave them snug in the crankcase.

11. Turn the engine over so the lower crankcase faces up. Support the engine on wooden blocks.

12. Loosen or remove the bolts from the lower crankcase as follows:

a. Insert each bolt into its place in the lower crankcase template as it is removed from the upper crankcase.

b. Remove the eight 6 mm bolts (A, **Figure 57**). Discard the bolt (B, **Figure 57**) and **Figure 58** and washer. A new bolt must be installed in this location during assembly.

c. Following a crisscross pattern, evenly loosen all the 9 mm crankshaft journal bolts (A, **Figure 59**). Note the location of the gasket washer (B, **Figure 59**) on the four outer bolts. Loosen the bolts in two-three stages, and then remove the bolts.

13. Turn the engine over so the upper crankcase faces up. Support the engine on wooden blocks.

14. Remove the bolts loosened in Step 12. Check that all the upper crankcase bolts have been removed.

15. Turn the engine over so the lower crankcase faces up. Support the engine on wooden blocks.

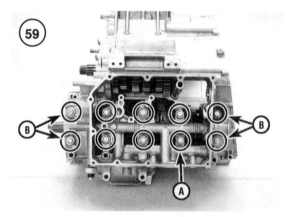

16. Tap around the perimeter of the sealing surfaces of the crankcase with a soft-faced mallet, and separate the lower crankcase from the upper crankcase.

17. Lift the lower crankcase off the upper crankcase. Account for the O-ring (A, **Figure 60**) and the two dowels (B) in the upper crankcase. Remove and discard the O-rings.

18. Account for any loose main bearing inserts from the lower crankcase. If a bearing insert falls, immediately reinstall it into it original boss in the lower crankcase.

19. Remove the internal gearshift mechanism (Chapter Seven).

20. Remove the transmission countershaft from the upper crankcase as follows:

    a. Remove the oil seal (**Figure 61**) from the end of the mainshaft.

    b. Pull straight up and remove the mainshaft assembly (**Figure 62**) from the upper crankcase.

    c. Remove the C-ring (A, **Figure 63**) and bearing location dowel (B).

21. Remove the transmission mainshaft from the lower crankcase as follows:

    a. Remove the screws (A, **Figure 64**) securing the oil seal (B) and remove the oil seal from the left-hand bearing retainer.

    b. Remove the spacer (**Figure 65**) from the countershaft.

    c. Remove the bolts (A, **Figure 66**) securing the left-hand bearing retainer (B).

    d. Secure the countershaft (A, **Figure 67**) and remove the bearing retainer (B) from the crankcase and transmission shaft.

    e. Account for the locating dowel (**Figure 68**) on the crankcase.

    f. Withdraw the countershaft (**Figure 69**) from, the crankcase.

    g. Remove the right side bearing housing mounting bolts and remove the housing (**Figure 70**).

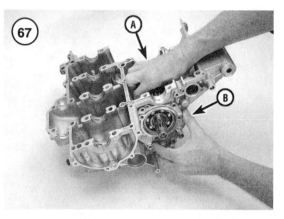

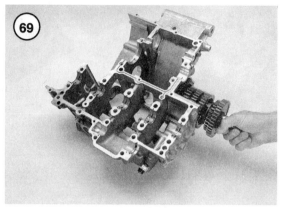

22. If still installed, remove the two dowels (**Figure 71**), (A, **Figure 72**) and the O-ring (B) from the upper crankcase. Discard the O-ring.

23. On 750 cc models, perform the following:

    a. Remove the seal (**Figure 73**) from balancer shaft.

    b. Lift the balancer shaft and both thrust washers (**Figure 74**) from the upper crankcase. If the bearing inserts comes out, immediately reinstall the inserts in its original location in the upper crankcase.

24. Refer to *Crankshaft* in this chapter and measure the crankshaft thrust clearance.

25. Measure the big end side clearance of each connecting rod as follows:

    a. Starting with the No. 1 connecting rod, insert a flat feeler gauge between the connecting rod big end and the machined surface of the crankweb (**Figure 75**).

    b. Record the big end side clearance.

    c. Repeat this for each remaining connecting rod. These measurements will be used during connecting rod inspection.

NOTE
Before proceeding, mark the connecting rods and caps with their cylinder No. (1, 2, 3 or 4) counting from the left to right (Figure 76). Remember, left to

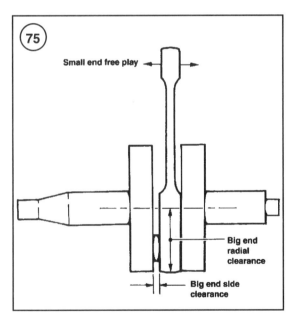

Small end free play

Big end
radial
clearance

Big end side
clearance

*right refers to the engine as it sits in the
frame not on the bench.*

26. Remove the cap from each connecting rod as
follows:

    a. Use a 10 mm 12-point socket to remove the con-
necting rod cap bolts from one connecting rod.

    b. Remove the cap from the connecting rod. If the
bearing inserts falls from the cap, immediately
reinsert into the cap. Note the cylinder number
of the connecting rod. Each rod cap is mated
to its specific connecting rod and must be reinstalled onto the correct rod during assembly.

    c. Repeat substeps a-c for each remaining rod cap.

27. Carefully lift the crankshaft assembly (**Figure
77**) from the upper crankcase as described in this
chapter. Immediately reinsert a loose insert into its
original bearing boss.

28. Remove the two thrust bearings from the upper
crankcase. Refer to **Figure 78** and **Figure 79**. The

right bearing (**Figure 78**) is identified by green paint. If this mark is illegible, label the back of each bearing (left or right) so each can be reinstalled in its original location.

29. Remove each connecting rod/piston assembly from the upper crankcase as described in the *Connecting Rod* section of this chapter.

30. Remove the mounting bolt (A, **Figure 80**) and lift each oil nozzle (B) from the upper crankcase. Discard the O-ring (**Figure 81**) installed with each oil nozzle.

31. Inspect the crankcases (this chapter).

Crankcase Assembly

1. Place the upper crankcase on the work bench with the cylinder head surface facing down.

2. Install the new O-ring (A, **Figure 60**) and the two dowels (B) in the lower crankcase.

3. If removed, install the main bearing inserts in to the upper crankcase (this section)

4. Apply a light coat of molybdenum disulfide oil to the bearing surfaces of all bearing inserts.

5. Install a *new* O-ring onto the fitting on the oil nozzle (**Figure 81**).

6. Install the oil nozzle (B, **Figure 80**) so its nozzle points into the cylinder (**Figure 82**). Apply thread-locking compound (Suzuki Thread Lock 1342, or it equivalent), to the threads of the mounting bolt (A, **Figure 80**), and tighten the bolt to 10 N•m (89 in.-lb.). Repeat for the remaining oil nozzles.

7. Install each connecting rod/piston assembly from the upper crankcase as described in the Connecting Rod section of this chapter.

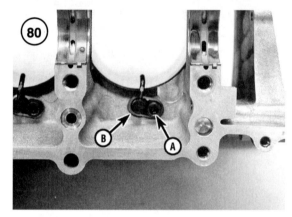

> *CAUTION*
> *Install both right and left thrust bearings with their oil grooves facing out toward the crankshaft web.*

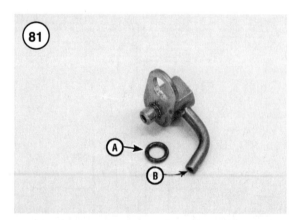

8. Apply a light coat of cold grease to backside of each thrust bearing and install them onto the upper crankcase bearing boss. Install both the left (**Figure 79**) and right (**Figure 78**) thrust bearings so the side with their grooves faces out. The right bearing (**Figure 78**) is identified by green paint.

9. Reinsert any loose inserts into its original bearing location in the crankcase.

10. Make sure the weight mark (**Figure 83**) on each connecting rod faces the intake (rear) side. If it does not, the connecting rod/piston assembly has been installed backwards.

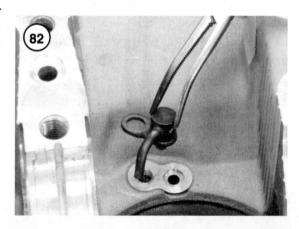

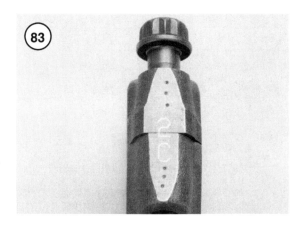

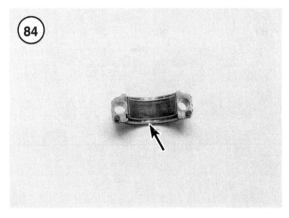

11. Apply molybdenum disulfide oil to the connecting rod bearings, the crankshaft journals and the crankpins.

12. Position the crankshaft so the two outside crankpins (No. 1 and No. 4) face down. Carefully lower the crankshaft onto the crankcase so each journal rests on its main bearing and the No. 1 and No. 4 crankpins rest on the No. 1 and No. 4 connecting rod bearing (**Figure 77**).

NOTE
The connecting rod and rod cap are mated. When installed on its mate, the weight mark on the rod cap aligns with the weight mark on the connecting rod as shown in **Figure 83**. *Refer to the cylinder numbers marked during removal to identify the correct cap for each connecting rod.*

13. Install the No. 1 rod cap onto the No. 1 connecting rod by performing the following:
   a. Make sure the bearing insert (**Figure 84**) is properly seated in the No. 1 connecting rod cap.
   b. Apply molybdenum disulfide oil to the bearing insert in the rod cap.
   c. Align the weight mark on the end of the cap with the mark on the rod and install the cap onto the rod. Push the cap until it bottoms on the connecting rod.
   d. Make sure the weight marks on the cap and connecting rod properly align as shown in **Figure 83**. If they do not, the cap has been installed on the wrong rod.
   e. Apply engine oil to the threads of the cap bolts, and install the bolts into the No. 1 connecting rod.
   f. Use a 10 mm, 12-point socket to evenly tighten the cap bolts, and then tighten both bolts to initial torque of 15 N•m (133 in.-lb.).

14. Repeat Step 13 and install the cap onto the No. 4 connecting rod.

15. Lean the crankcase back. Manually push the No. 2 piston up into the cylinder so the connecting rod sits against the crankpin. Guide the connecting rod so it does not scratch the crankpin.

16. Repeat this Step 15 for the No. 3 connecting rod.

17. Repeat Step 16 and install the rod cap onto the No. 2 connecting rod and then onto the No. 3 connecting rod.

18. Use a torque angle gauge (**Figure 85**) to tighten each connecting rod cap bolt an additional 90° (1/4 turn).

19. Rotate the crankshaft and check that the connecting rods move smoothly around the crankpins. Make sure there is no binding.

20. On 750 cc models, perform the following:
   a. Rotate the crankshaft until the alignment mark (**Figure 86**) faces toward the balancer shaft receptacle, and is flush with the top surface of the crankcase.
   b. Apply molybdenum disulfide grease to the balancer shaft inserts and to the balancer shaft journals.

5

c. Install a thrust washer (A, **Figure 87**) on each side of the balancer shaft.

d. Align the balancer shaft alignment mark with that of the crankshaft (B, **Figure 87**) and install the balancer (**Figure 74**).

e. Install the seal (**Figure 73**) onto the balancer shaft.

21. Install the transmission countershaft into the upper crankcase as follows:

a. Install the C-ring (A, **Figure 63**) into the groove in the crankcase, and install bearing location dowel (B) onto the hole in the crankcase.

b. Lower the mainshaft assembly (**Figure 62**) into the crankcase so the groove in the ball bearing properly engages the C-ring (**Figure 88**), and so the locating hole in the needle bearing engages the locating pin.

c. Seat the mainshaft oil seal (**Figure 61**) between the end of the mainshaft and inside lip in the crankcase.

22. Install the transmission mainshaft into the lower crankcase as follows:

a. Install the countershaft (**Figure 69**) into the crankcase.

b. If removed, install the right-side bearing housing (**Figure 70**). Apply threadlocking compound (Suzuki Thread Lock 1342, or it equivalent), to the bolts threads, and tighten to 12 N•m (144 in.-lb.).

c. If removed, install the locating dowel (**Figure 68**) on the crankcase.

d. Move the right side of the countershaft into the right side bearing housing and secure it in this position (A, **Figure 67**).

e. Install a *new* O-ring (**Figure 89**) onto the left side bearing retainer, and apply Suzuki super grease A, or equivalent to it.

f. Install the left side bearing retainer (B, **Figure 67**) onto the countershaft and crankcase engaging the locating dowel (**Figure 68**).

g. Apply thread lock (Suzuki Thread Lock 1342, or it equivalent), to the threads of the mounting bolts, and tighten the bolt to 12 N•m (144 in.-lb.).

h. Apply Suzuki super grease A, or equivalent, to the lips of the oil seal (**Figure 90**) and O-ring and install the oil seal (B, **Figure 64**). Apply thread lock (Suzuki Thread Lock 1342, or it equivalent), to the threads of the mounting screws (A, **Figure 64**), and tighten to 12 N•m (144 in.-lb.).

i. Apply Suzuki super grease A, or equivalent, to the O-ring (**Figure 91**) and install the spacer (**Figure 65**) onto the countershaft.

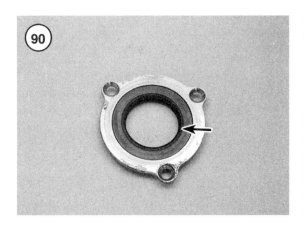

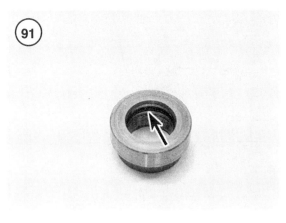

NOTE
*There will be a little lateral play (**Figure 92**) on the mainshaft after both bearing housings have been correctly installed. This amount of play is okay at this time as it will be taken up after the drive sprocket is installed.*

23. Install the internal gearshift mechanism as described in Chapter Seven.
24. Ensure that all main bearing inserts are in place in the lower crankcase.

25. Make sure the sealing surfaces of both crankcases are free of old sealant or other residue.

CAUTION
Keep sealant away from oil hole, oil groove or bearing.

26. Apply a thin coat of Suzuki Bond 1207B sealant, or equivalent, to the portions of the lower crankcase shown in **Figure 93**. Make the coating as thin as possible, but be sure the sealant completely covers the entire mating surface. Note where the sealant is applied to either inside or outside of the bolt hole locations.

CAUTION
When properly aligned, the lower crankcase half slides over the crankshaft, transmission shaft and balancer (750 cc model), and seat against the upper crankcase. If the crankcases do not fit together completely, do not attempt to pull them together with the crankcase bolts. Separate the crankcases and investigate the cause of the interference. Check the gears for proper installation.

27. Tap the halves together lightly with a soft-faced mallet. Do not use a metal hammer.
28. Slowly spin the countershaft and shift the transmission through all of the gears. Make sure the transmission operates properly before proceeding.

NOTE
Before tightening the crankcase bolts, set all bolts into place. Make sure all the bolt heads are the same distance up from the bolt boss on the crankcase. If any bolt is higher or lower that the others, switch the bolts around until all are the same height, indicating that the bolts are in their correct locations.

29. Apply engine oil to the bolt threads and install the 9 mm crankshaft journal bolts onto the lower crankcase as follows:
    a. Install the gasket washer (B, **Figure 59**) on the four outer bolts.
    b. Install the six remaining bolts (A, **Figure 59**).
30. Following a crisscross pattern, evenly tighten the crankshaft journal bolts in two-three stages until all the bolts are snug. Tighten the bolts as follows:
    a. Initial: 18 N•m (13 ft.-lb.).
    b. Final: 50° (**Figure 94**).
31. Turn the engine over so the lower crankcase faces up. Support the engine on wooden blocks.
32. Remove the bolts from the lower crankcase cardboard template, and install the 6 mm and 8 mm bolts

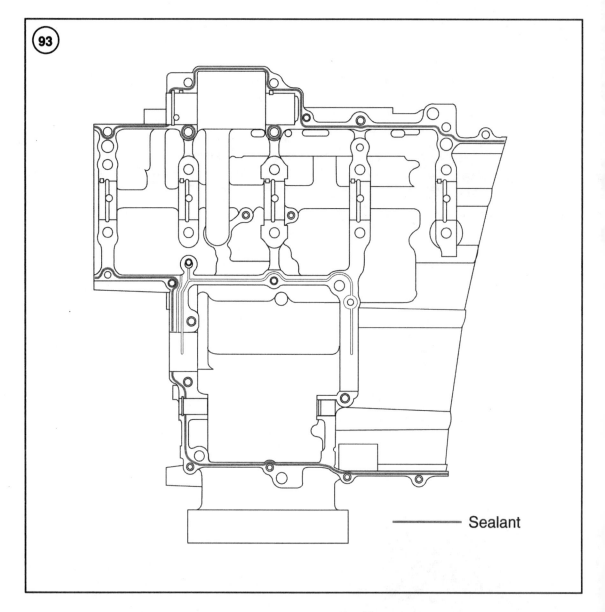

93

Sealant

into correct location in the lower crankcase. Apply engine oil to the bolt threads.

    a. Install a new 8 mm bolt and washer. Refer to (B, **Figure 57**) and **Figure 58**.

    b. Install the remaining 6 mm bolts (A, **Figure 57**).

    c. Tighten all bolts finger-tight at this time.

33. Following a crisscross pattern, evenly tighten the 6 mm and 8 mm lower crankcase bolts in two-three stages until all the bolts are snug. Tighten the 6 mm and 8 mm lower crankcase bolts as follows:

    a. 6 mm bolts: initial torque setting of 6 N•m (53 in.-lb.); final torque setting of 11 N•m (96 in.-lb.);

    b. 8 mm bolts: initial torque setting of 15 N•m (133 ft.-lb.); final torque setting of 26 N•m (19 ft.-lb.).

34. Turn the engine over so the upper crankcase faces up. Support the engine on wooden blocks.

35. Remove the bolts from the upper crankcase cardboard template, and install the 6 mm and 8 mm bolts into correct location in the upper crankcase. Apply engine oil to the bolt threads.

    a. Install the front two bolts (**Figure 55**).

    b. Install a *new* gasket washer under the four bolts (B, **Figure 56**).

    c. Install the remaining 6 mm and 8 mm bolts (A, **Figure 56**).

    d. Tighten all bolts finger-tight at this time.

36. Following a crisscross pattern, evenly tighten the 6 mm and 8 mm upper crankcase bolts in two-three stages as follows:

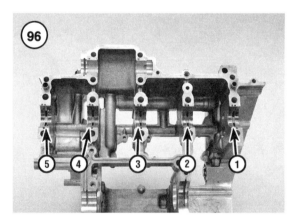

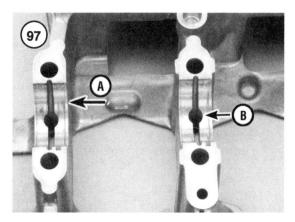

a. 6 mm bolts: initial torque setting of 6 N•m (53 in.-lb.); final torque setting of 11 N•m (96 in.-lb.);

b. 8 mm bolts: initial torque setting of 15 N•m (133 in.-lb.); final torque setting of 26 N•m (19 ft.-lb.).

37. Install the clutch pushrod oil seal cover (B, **Figure 54**) and bolts (A). Tighten the bolts securely.

38. Install a new crankcase breather cover gasket (**Figure 53**).

39. Install the crankcase breather cover (B, **Figure 52**), and bolts (A). Tighten the bolts to of 10 N•m (89 in.-lb.).

40. Install the reed valve assembly (**Figure 51**).

41. Install crankcase breather reed valve cover (B, **Figure 50**), and bolts (A). Tighten the bolts to of 10 N•m (89 in.-lb.).

42. Install the oil pan, and strainer, and oil pump (this chapter).

43. Install the oil cooler (Chapter Ten).

44. Install the cylinder head, cam chain and chain guides (Chapter Four).

45. Install the engine (this Chapter).

46. Install all components removed in Step 1 *Crankcase Disassembly*.

Bearing Insert Removal/Installation

If the crankshaft main bearing inserts will be re-used, they must be reinstalled into their original locations in the upper crankcase and lower crankcase. The crankshaft main bearing bosses are identified as Nos. 1-5 counting from left-to-right as the crankcase sits in the frame.

1. Separate the crankcase (this section), and remove the crankshaft (this chapter).

2. Remove the main bearing inserts from the upper and lower crankcases as follows:

a. Remove the leftmost bearing (alternator side) from one crankcase.

b. Use a permanent marker to label the backside of the insert. Mark them with either a U1 (upper crankcase) (**Figure 95**) or an L1 (lower crankcase) (**Figure 96**).

c. Systematically work left-to-right across the crankcase until each insert is removed and properly labeled.

d. Repeat substeps a-c for the other crankcase.

3. Install the crankshaft main bearing inserts as follows:

a. Make sure each bearing boss (A, **Figure 97**) in the upper and lower crankcase is clean, and its oil control hole (B) is clear.

b. Wipe both sides of the bearing insert with a lint-free cloth.

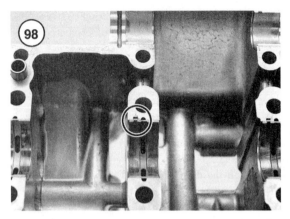

c. If reusing the old bearing inserts, refer to the marks made during removal. Used bearings must be reinstalled in their original locations.

d. Starting with the left most bearing boss in a crankcase (alternator side), insert the No. 1 main bearing insert into the No. 1 bearing boss, the No. 2 main bearing insert into the No. 2 bearing boss, and so on. Refer to (**Figure 95**) or an L1 (lower crankcase) (**Figure 96**).

e. Install an insert into its correct location. Start with the tab end of the insert and carefully press the insert into position with a finger or thumb. Continue across the insert making sure the tab locks into place in the bearing boss (**Figure 98**).

NOTE
All four balancer shaft bearings are symmetrical, but they should be reinstalled in their original location.

4. On 750 cc models, remove the balancer bearing inserts from the upper and lower crankcases as follows:

a. Remove the balancer shaft bearings inserts (**Figure 99**) from the upper and lower crankcases. All four bearings are symmetrical, but they should be reinstalled in the same location.

b. Use a permanent marker to label the backside of the insert. Mark them with either a UR (upper right side) or an UL (upper left side), or an LR (lower right side) or an LR (lower left side).

5. On 750 cc models, install the balancer bearing inserts into the upper and lower crankcases as follows:

a. Make sure each bearing boss in the upper and lower crankcase is clean.

b. Wipe both sides of the bearing insert with a lint-free cloth.

c. If reusing the old bearing inserts, refer to the marks made during removal. Used bearings must be reinstalled in their original locations.

d. Install an insert into its correct location. Start with the tab end of the insert and carefully press the insert into position with a finger or thumb. Continue across the insert making sure the tab locks into place in the bearing boss (**Figure 99**).

Crankcase Inspection

1. Remove the crankshaft main bearing inserts from the upper and middle crankcases as described in Bearing Insert Removal in this section.

2. Pry the shift shaft oil seal from the lower crankcase.

3. Remove the transmission oil jet (**Figure 100**) in the lower crankcase.

NOTE
Step 4 and 5 are shown with the engine partially assembled.

4. Remove the two oil gallery plugs (**Figure 101**) from the right side of the lower crankcase.

5. Remove the oil gallery plug (**Figure 102**) from the left side of upper crankcase.

6. Remove the oil gallery plug (**Figure 103**) from the lower crankcase.

7. Remove the water jacket plugs and O-rings from the upper crankcase. Refer to **Figure 104** and **Figure 105**.

8. Remove the oil pressure switch (**Figure 106**) from the lower crankcase.

9. Clean both crankcases, inside and out, and clean all crankcase bearing inserts with cleaning solvent. Thoroughly dry all components with compressed air. Make sure no solvent residue remains in the cases. It will contaminate the engine oil.

10. Check the crankcase breather opening (**Figure 107**) in the upper crankcase. Clean out all old oil res-

idues and dry with compressed air. Check the breather hose for cracks or damage; replace as necessary.

11. Apply compressed air to the oil galleries and blow out any accumulated residue. If necessary, rinse out the gallery with solvent, and once again apply compressed air to thoroughly dry the gallery.

12. Using a scraper, *carefully* remove any sealer residues from all crankcase mating surfaces.

13. Thoroughly check the mating surfaces of both crankcase components. Check for gouges or nicks that may lead to an oil leak.

14. Inspect the threads on the oil filter union (**Figure 108**) for damage. Repair the threads or replace the union as necessary.

15. Install new O-rings onto the water jacket plugs. Install all three plugs and tighten to 10 N•m (89 in.-lb). Refer to **Figure 104** and **Figure 105**).

16. Install the M12 oil gallery plug (**Figure 103**) into the lower crankcase, and tighten to 15 N•m (133 in.-lb).

> *CAUTION*
> *After tightening the oil gallery plug, make sure the plug end if flush with the crankcase making surface (B, **Figure 103**).*

17. Apply threadlocking compound (Suzuki Thread Lock 1342, or equivalent) to this plug only. Install the M6 oil gallery plug (**Figure 102**) onto the left side of upper crankcase, and tighten to 10 N•m (89 in.-lb).

18. Install the two M16 oil gallery plugs (**Figure 101**) onto the right side of the lower crankcase, and tighten to 35 N•m (26.5 ft.-lb).

19. Install the oil pressure switch (**Figure 106**) onto the lower crankcase, and tighten to 14 N•m (122 in.-lb).

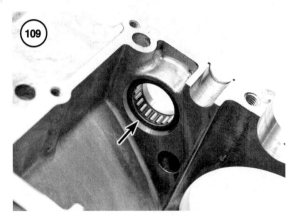

20. Clean the oil jet and oil nozzles (B, **Figure 81**) with compressed air.

21. Inspect the upper and lower crankcases for cracks and fractures. Check the areas around the stiffening ribs, bearing bosses and threaded holes for damage. Replace as necessary.

22. Check the threaded holes for thread damage, dirt or oil buildup. If necessary, clean or repair the threads with a suitable size metric tap. Coat the tap threads with kerosene or an aluminum tap fluid before use.

23. Rotate the shift drum bearing (**Figure 109**) and shift shaft bearing (**Figure 110**) by hand. Each bearing should turn smoothly and quietly. Replace any worn or damaged bearing as necessary.

   a. Use a blind bearing puller (**Figure 111**) to remove a bearing from the crankcase.

   b. Position a *new* bearing so the side with the manufacturer's marks face the outside of the lower crankcase.

   c. Lubricate the bearing and bearing bore with clean engine oil.

   d. Use a bearing driver that matches the outside diameter of the bearing to drive the new bearing into place.

24. Install a new shift shaft oil seal into the crankcase.

   a. Pack the lips of the new oil seal with waterproof grease.

   b. Position the seal so the manufacturer's marks face out.

   c. Install the seal with a driver or socket.

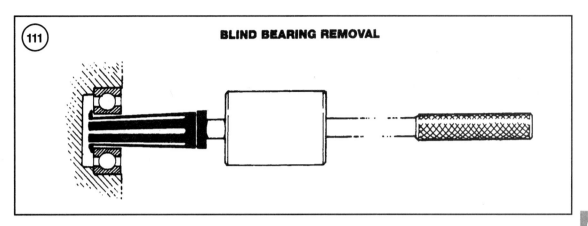

BLIND BEARING REMOVAL

5

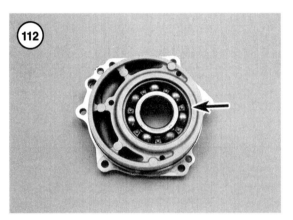

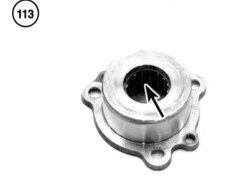

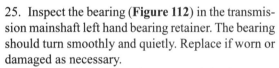

25. Inspect the bearing (**Figure 112**) in the transmission mainshaft left hand bearing retainer. The bearing should turn smoothly and quietly. Replace if worn or damaged as necessary.

26. Inspect the bearing (**Figure 113**) in the transmission mainshaft right hand bearing retainer. The bearing should turn smoothly and quietly. Replace if worn or damaged as necessary.

Cylinder Block Inspection

The cylinder block is an integral part of the upper crankcase. When inspecting the cylinder block, compare measurements to the specifications in **Table 1**.

1. Check the mating surface (**Figure 114**) on the cylinder block for cracks or damage.

2. Check the water jacket passage ways (**Figure 115**). Clean out any noted debris or residues.

3. Check the cylinder walls (**Figure 116**) for deep scratches and for signs of seizure or other damage.

4. Use a straightedge and flat feeler gauge (**Figure 117**) to check the top of the cylinder block for warp. Check this at several places across the cylinder block.

5. Measure each cylinder bore with a cylinder bore gauge (**Figure 118**). Measure the bore at the top, middle and bottom of a cylinder as shown in **Figure**

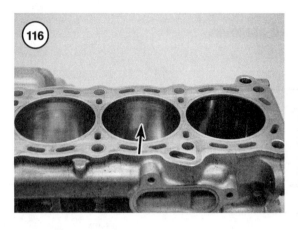

119. At each height, measure the bore across two axes: one parallel to the crankshaft and the other 90° to the crankshaft. Replace the crankcases if a cylinder is out of specification (**Table 1** or **Table 2**). The cylinders cannot be bored or honed.

6. Lubricate the cylinder walls with clean engine oil so they will not rust.

CRANKSHAFT

Removal/Installation

Remove and install the crankshaft as described in Crankcase in this chapter.

Inspection

1. Clean the crankshaft thoroughly with solvent. Clean each crankshaft oil passageway with compressed air. If necessary, clean them with rifle cleaning brushes, and then flush the passageways with solvent. Dry the crankshaft with compressed air. Lubricate all bearing surfaces with a light coat of engine oil.

2. Inspect each crankshaft main journal (A, **Figure 120**) and each crankpin (B) for scratches, ridges, scoring, nicks or heat discoloration. Replace the crankshaft if any journal is scored or pitted.

3. Measure crankshaft runout as follows:
   a. Set the crankshaft on V-blocks so the two outside journals rest on the blocks (**Figure 121**).
   b. Position a dial indicator so that its stem rests against the near-center journal (A, **Figure 122**. Then zero the dial gauge.
   c. Slowly turn the crankshaft while reading the dial gauge. Record the runout limit.
   d. If the runout exceeds the service limit (**Table 1**), replace the crankshaft.

4. Inspect the crankshaft flywheel taper (**Figure 123**) for scoring or signs of heat damage. If the taper

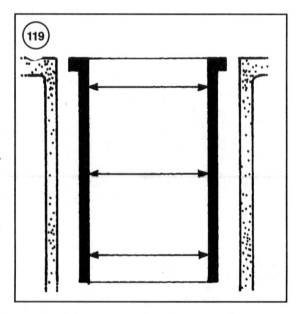

shows damage, also inspect the inside taper on the flywheel.

5. Inspect the crankshaft splines (**Figure 124**). If damaged, the crankshaft must be replaced. If the crankshaft splines are damaged, also inspect the inner splines on the timing rotor and starter clutch. They will probably be damaged also.

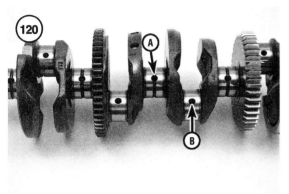

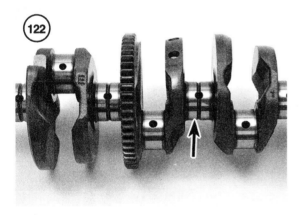

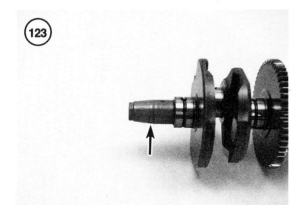

6. Inspect the teeth on primary drive gear (**Figure 125**). If the primary drive gear is damaged, replace the crankshaft and inspect the clutch outer housing gear.

7. On 750 cc models, inspect the teeth on balancer drive gear (**Figure 126**). If the primary drive gear is damaged, replace the crankshaft and inspect the balancer driven gear.

8. Check the tightness of the Torx bolts (**Figure 127**) securing the attached counterweight to the crankshaft. The manufacturer does not provide torque specifications for these fasteners, but they must be tightened securely. If the bolts are loose, remove them and

clean off any old thread lock. Apply threadlocking compound (Suzuki Thread Lock Super 1360 or an equivalent) to the bolt threads before installation, and tighten the bolts securely.

Crankshaft Main Bearing Oil Clearance

NOTE
Whenever checking the crankshaft main bearing oil clearance, also check the balancer shaft bearing oil clearance.

1. Check each crankshaft main bearing insert for evidence of wear, abrasion and scoring. If the bearing inserts are good, they may be reused. If any insert is questionable, replace the entire set.
2. Clean the bearing surfaces of the crankshaft journals and of the main bearing inserts.
3. Place the upper and lower crankcases on the workbench with the bearing boss sides facing up.
4. If removed, install an insert into its correct locations upper and lower crankcases. Start with the tab end of the insert and carefully press the insert into position with a finger or thumb. Continue across the insert making sure the tab locks into place in the bearing boss (**Figure 128**).

5. Install the crankshaft (**Figure 129**) into place in the upper crankcase.
6. Place a piece of Plastigage along each crankshaft journal. The Plastigage must parallel to the crankshaft as shown in **Figure 130**. Make sure Plastigage does not rest on a crankshaft oil hole.

CAUTION
Do not rotate the crankshaft while the Plastigage is in place.

7. Make sure the two dowels are installed in the upper crankcase. Refer to **Figure 131** and **Figure 132**.

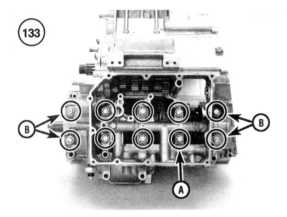

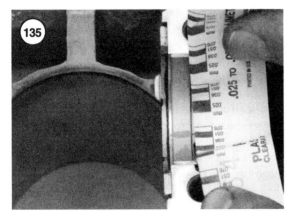

CAUTION
When properly lined up, the lower crankcase slides over the crankshaft assembly and seats against the upper crankcase. If the halves do not fit together completely, do not attempt to pull them together with the crankcase bolts. Separate the crankcases and investigate the cause of the interference.

8. Lower the lower crankcase onto the upper crankcase, and tap them together lightly with a soft-faced mallet. Do not use a metal hammer.

9. Apply engine oil to the bolt threads and install the 9 mm crankshaft journal bolts onto the lower crankcase as follows:

    a. Install the gasket washer (A, **Figure 133**) on the four outer bolts.

    b. Install the six remaining bolts (B, **Figure 133**).

10. Following a crisscross pattern, evenly tighten the crankshaft journal bolts in two-three stages until all the bolts are snug. Tighten the bolts as follows:

    a. Initial: 18 N•m (13 ft.-lb.).

    b. Final: 50° (**Figure 134**).

11. Reverse the tightening sequence. Loosen the crankshaft journal bolts evenly in several stages, and then, remove the bolts.

12. Lift the lower crankcase off the upper crankcase. Turn the lower crankcase over so the crankcase main bearing inserts do not fall out. If any does, immediately reinstall it into its original position if possible.

13. Measure the width of the flattened Plastigage according to the manufacturer's instructions (**Figure 135**). Measure both ends of the Plastigage strip. A difference of 0.025 mm (0.001 in.) or more indicates a tapered journal. Confirm this by measuring the journal outside diameter (**Figure 136**) with a micrometer.

14. If the widest part of the Plastigage on any journal exceeds the crankshaft journal oil clearance (**Table**

1, or **Table 2**), refer to *Main Bearing Selection* and install a new set of crankshaft main bearings.

15. Remove all Plastigage material from the bearing inserts, crankshaft journals and balancer shaft journals.

Crankshaft Main Bearing Selection

1. The crankshaft outside diameter codes (A, B, & C) are stamped onto the outside crank web (**Figure 137**) at the flywheel end of the crankshaft. These codes correspond to the outside diameter of the main bearing journals as shown in **Figure 138**.

2. The bearing boss inside diameter codes (A or B) are stamped on the rear edge of the upper crankcase (**Figure 139**). These codes correspond to the inside diameter of the main bearing bosses in the crankcase (**Figure 140**).

3. Identify the code for each crankshaft journal and its related bearing boss.

4. Select new bearings by cross-referencing the crankshaft outside diameter code in the top row of **Table 2** with the bearing boss inside diameter code in the left column of the table. The intersection of the appropriate row and column indicates the color of the new bearing insert. **Table 3** lists bearing color, part number and thickness for the inserts. Always replace all ten crankshaft bearing inserts as a set.

5. After new bearing inserts have been installed, recheck the clearance by measuring the crankshaft main bearing oil clearance as described in this section. If the oil clearance is still out of specification, measure the journal outside diameter (**Figure 136**) with a micrometer. Identify each journal's outside diameter code (**Figure 138**) and compare the measurement to the specification for the indicated code (**Table 3**). Replace the crankshaft if a journal's outside diameter is less than the range specified. If the journals are within specification, replace the crankcase.

Balancer Shaft Bearing Oil Clearance (750cc Models)

1. Check each balancer bearing insert for evidence of wear, abrasion and scoring. If the bearing inserts are good, they may be reused. If any insert is questionable, replace the entire set.

2. Clean the bearing surfaces of the balancer journals and of the balancer inserts.

3. Place the upper and lower crankcases on the workbench with the bearing boss sides facing up.

4. Make sure each bearing boss in the upper and lower crankcase is clean.

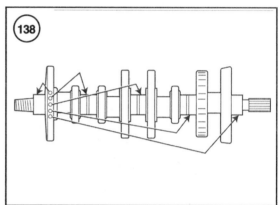

5. Wipe both sides of the bearing insert with a lint-free cloth.

6. If reusing the old bearing inserts, refer to the marks made during removal in *Crankcase Bearing Insert Removal/Installation*. Used bearings must be reinstalled in their original locations.

7. Install an insert into its correct location. Start with the tab end of the insert and carefully press the insert into position with a finger or thumb. Continue across the insert making sure the tab locks into place in the bearing boss (**Figure 99**).

8. Install the balancer shaft (**Figure 74**) into place in the upper crankcase.

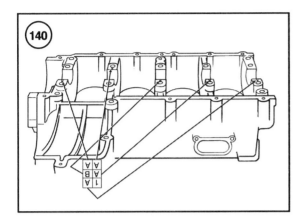

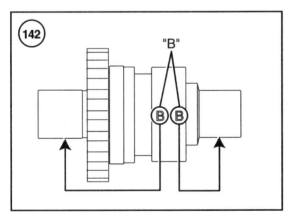

9. Place a piece of Plastigage along each balancer shaft journal. The Plastigage must parallel to the balancer shaft.

CAUTION
Do not rotate the balancer shaft while the Plastigage is in place.

10. Make sure the two dowels are installed in the upper crankcase. Refer to **Figure 131** and **Figure 132**.

CAUTION
When properly lined up, the lower crankcase slides over the balancer

shaft, and crankshaft assembly if in place, and seats against the upper crankcase. If the halves do not fit together completely, do not attempt to pull them together with the crankcase bolts. Separate the crankcases and investigate the cause of the interference.

11. Apply engine oil to the bolt threads and install the 9 mm crankshaft journal bolts onto the lower crankcase as follows:
   a. Install the gasket washer (B, **Figure 133**) on the four outer bolts.
   b. Install the six remaining bolts (A, **Figure 133**).

12. Following a crisscross pattern, evenly tighten the crankshaft journal bolts in two-three stages until all the bolts are snug. Tighten the bolts as follows:
   a. Initial: 18 N•m (13 ft.-lb.).
   b. Final: 50° (**Figure 134**).

13. Install the 8 mm bolts crankcase (A, **Figure 133**) along with a gasket washer under the one 8 mm bolt (B). Tighten the bolts as follows:
   a. Initial torque setting of 15 N•m (133 in.-lb.).
   b. Final torque setting of 26 N•m (19 ft.-lb.).

14. Reverse the tightening sequence. Loosen the crankcase and crankshaft journal bolts evenly in several stages, and then, remove the bolts.

15. Lift the lower crankcase off the upper crankcase. Turn the lower crankcase over so the balancer shaft bearing inserts do not fall out. If any does, immediately reinstall it into its original position if possible.

16. Measure the width of the flattened Plastigage according to the manufacturer's instructions. Measure both ends of the Plastigage strip. A difference of 0.025 mm (0.001 in.) or more indicates a tapered journal. Confirm this by measuring the journal outside diameter with a micrometer.

17. If the widest part of the Plastigage on any journal exceeds the crankshaft journal oil clearance (**Table 2**), refer to Balancer Shaft Bearing Selection and install a new set of balancer shaft bearings.

18. Remove all Plastigage material from the bearing inserts, crankshaft journals and balancer shaft journals.

Balancer Shaft Bearing Selection (750cc Models)

1. The balancer shaft outside diameter codes (A or B) are stamped into the balancer shaft (**Figure 141**). The codes coincide with the outside diameter of the balancer shaft journals (**Figure 142**).

2. The crankcase inside diameter codes (A or B) are stamped on the rear side of the upper crankcase (**Figure 139**). The codes coincide with the inside di-

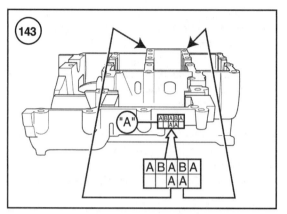

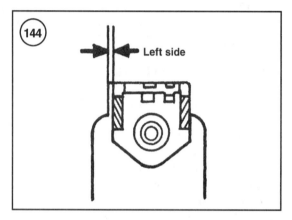

ameter of the balancer shaft bosses in the crankcase (**Figure 143**).

3. Select new bearing by cross-referencing the balancer shaft outside diameter codes in the horizontal row of **Table 7** with the crankcase inside diameter codes in the vertical column. The intersection of the appropriate row and column indicates the color of the new bearing insert. **Table 8** lists bearing color, part number and thickness for the inserts. Always replace all four bearing shaft inserts as a set.

4. After the new bearing inserts have been installed, recheck the clearance by repeating *Crankshaft Journal Oil Clearance* in this section. If the balancer shaft clearance is till out of specification, measure the outside diameter of the balancer shaft journals. Identify each journal's outside diameter code (**Figure 141**) and compare the measurement to the specification of the indicated code (**Table 7**).Replace the balancer shaft if a journal's outside diameter is less than the specified range. If the journals are within specification, replace the crankcase.

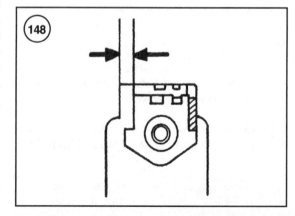

Thrust Clearance Inspection

1. Remove the lower crankcase as described in this chapter.

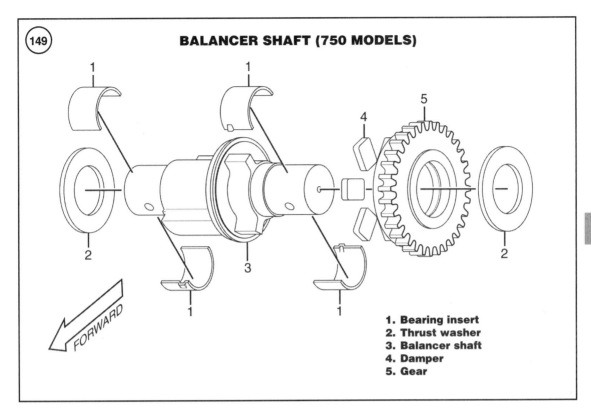

BALANCER SHAFT (750 MODELS)

FORWARD

1. Bearing insert
2. Thrust washer
3. Balancer shaft
4. Damper
5. Gear

2. Push the crankshaft assembly all the way toward the left side until there is no clearance between the crankshaft and the right thrust bearing.

3. Measure the thrust clearance (**Figure 144**) by inserting a flat feeler gauge between the crankshaft web thrust surface and the left thrust bearing as shown in **Figure 145**. Compare the reading to the crankshaft thrust clearance listed in **Table 1**, or **Table 2**.

4. If the thrust clearance is outside the specified range, perform the following.

    a. Remove the right thrust bearing Figure (**Figure 146**), and measure its thickness (**Figure 147**). Compare the reading to the bearing thickness specified in **Table 1** or **Table 2**.

    b. If the thickness is within the specified range, reinstall the right thrust bearing and proceed to Step 5.

    c. If the thickness is less than specified, install a new right thrust bearing and then repeat Step 2 and Step 3.

5. Remove the left thrust bearing.

6. Measure the left thrust clearance by inserting a flat feeler gauge between left surface of the crankcase and the machined surface of the crankshaft (**Figure 148**).

7. Refer to **Table 9** and use the clearance measured in Step 6 to select the correct left thrust bearing. Thrust bearings are identified by color painted on the end of the bearing.

8. Install the *new* left thrust bearing. Measure the thrust clearance by repeating Step 2 and Step 3.

9. If the clearance cannot be brought into specification with the new thrust bearings, replace the crankshaft.

10. After the clearance has been correctly adjusted; remove both thrust bearings and apply a coat of molybdenum disulfide grease to each side of both bearings. Install both bearings into the crankcase with their oil grooves facing out toward the crankshaft web.

11. Install the lower crankcase as described in this chapter.

BALANCER SHAFT (750 CC MODELS)

Removal/Installation

Remove and install the balancer shaft as described in *Crankcase Disassembly* in this chapter.

Inspection

Refer to **Figure 149**.

1. Remove the thrust washer (A, **Figure 150**) from each side of the balancer shaft. Remove the balancer shaft driven gear (B, **Figure 150**).

2. Inspect the dampers (**Figure 151**).

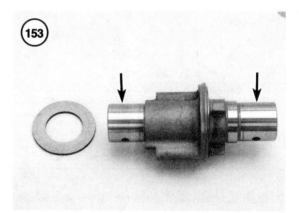

3. Clean the balancer driven gear in solvent and dry with compressed air. Check the damper locating bosses (**Figure 152**) for wear or damage.

4. Inspect the balancer shaft bearing journals (**Figure 153**) scoring or signs of abrasion.

5. Inspect the teeth of the balancer driven gear (A, **Figure 154**) for cracked or broken teeth. If damage it found, replace the driven gear and inspect the crankshaft balancer drive gear for damage.

6. Install the dampers (**Figure 155**) into the receptacles in the balancer driven gear.

7. Install the balancer driven gear (A, **Figure 154**) onto the balancer shaft. Align the indexing dot (B, **Figure 154**) on the gear with the indexing line on the end of the balancer shaft (C). Refer to **Figure 156**. Press the gear into place so the dogs (**Figure 157**) on the shaft sit between the gear dampers (**Figure 155**).

8. Install the trust washer (D, **Figure 154**) onto each end of the balancer shaft.

9. Refer to *Balancer Shaft Oil Clearance* in this chapter and measure the balancer shaft oil clearance.

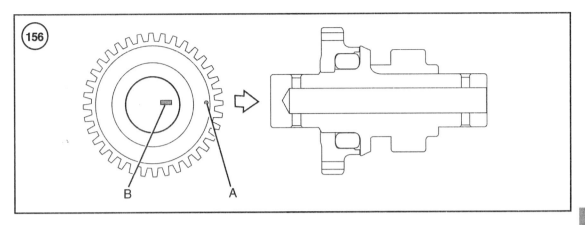

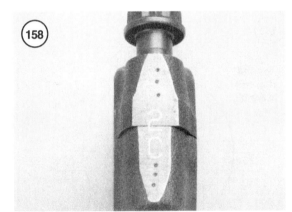

CONNECTING ROD/PISTON

Removal

1. Remove the lower crankcase as described in this chapter.

2. Measure the big end side clearance of each connecting rod as described in Step 25 of *Crankcase Disassembly* in this chapter.

NOTE
*The connecting rod weight mark (**Figure 158**) faces rearward toward the **intake side** of the engine. The rods must be reinstalled with this orientation.*

3. Remove the crankshaft as described in *Crankcase* in this chapter.

4. Set the upper crankcase upright on the bench.

NOTE
*Before proceeding, mark the top of the pistons with their cylinder No. (1, 2, 3 or 4) counting from the left to right (**Figure 159**). Remember, left to right refers to the engine as it sits in the frame not on the bench.*

CAUTION
Carefully push the connecting rod up through the cylinder bore so the rod does not scratch the cylinder walls.

5. Lean the upper crankcase back and push the connecting rod up into its cylinder. Remove the connecting rod/piston assembly from the top of the cylinder block.

6. Install the correct rod cap onto the connecting rod (**Figure 160**) so the parts will not be mixed during assembly. The weight mark on the end of the cap should align with the mark on its connecting rod (**Figure 159**).

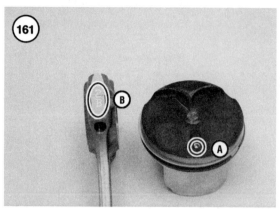

7. Repeat Step 5 and Step 6 for each remaining connecting rods.

> *NOTE*
> *Keep each bearing insert in its original place in the connecting rod and cap. If bearing inserts will be reused, they must be reinstalled in their original locations.*

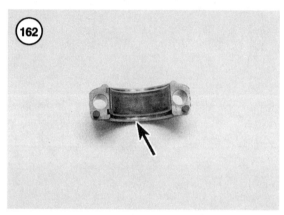

8. Inspect the connecting rods and bearings as described in this section.

9. Measure the connecting rod bearing oil clearance as described in this chapter.

Installation

> *CAUTION*
> *The index dot on the piston crown (A, **Figure 161**) indicates the exhaust side of the piston. The weight mark on the connecting rod (B, **Figure 161**) indicates the intake side of the rod. The piston must be installed so the index dot on the piston crown faces the side of the connecting rod without weight mark.*

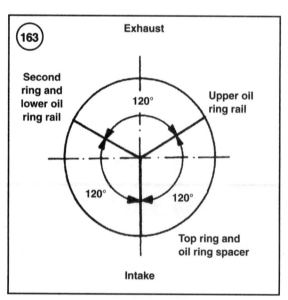

1A. If removed, install the piston onto each connecting rod as described in the Piston Installations in this chapter.

1B. If the pistons are installed, check that the index dot (A, **Figure 161**) on the piston crown faces the side of the connecting rod without the weight mark (B).

2. Make sure the inserts are locked into place in the rod cap (**Figure 162**) and connecting rod.

3. Check that the piston ring end gaps are not lined up with each other. They must be staggered as shown in **Figure 163**.

4. Set the upper crankcase upright on the bench

5. Apply molybdenum disulfide oil to the connecting rod bearing inserts.

6. Lubricate the piston rings with clean engine oil.

> *CAUTION*
> *Carefully lower a connecting rod down the cylinder bore so the rod does not scratch the cylinder walls.*

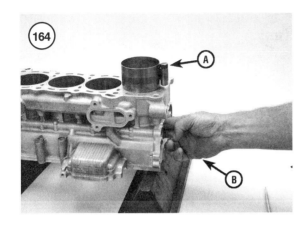

7. Lower a connecting rod/piston assembly into its original cylinder. Make sure the index dot (A, **Figure 161**) on the piston crown faces the exhaust side (front) of the engine.

NOTE
The top of each cylinder bore has a slight lead-in taper so the piston may be installed without a piston ring compressor.

8A. Install a piston ring compressor onto the piston (A, **Figure 164**). Place a hand under the connecting rod (B, **Figure 164**) and guide the connecting rod down the cylinder wall avoid any scratches. With the ring compressor flush against the cylinder block, gently tap the piston crown with a wooden handle until the piston sits flush with the top surface of the cylinder bore (**Figure 165**).

8B. If a piston ring compressor is unavailable, gently press the piston into the cylinder. Manually compress each piston ring (**Figure 166**) as it enters the cylinder.

9. Repeat Steps 4-6 for each remaining connecting rod/piston assembly and install them into the correct cylinder (**Figure 159**).

10. Turn the upper crankcase over so the crankcase bearing bosses face up.

11. Check that the weight mark (**Figure 167**) on each connecting rod faces the intake side (rear) of the engine. If one does not, the piston has been installed backwards on that connecting rod. Remove the connecting rod/piston assembly and reinstall the piston correctly.

12. Install the crankshaft as described in Crankcase as described in this chapter.

Inspection

1. Remove the piston from the connecting rod as described later in this chapter.

2. Check each connecting rod assembly (**Figure 160**) for obvious damage such as cracks or burns.

3. Make sure the small end oil hole (**Figure 168**) is open. Clean it out if necessary.

4. Measure the small end inside diameter (**Figure 169**). Replace the connecting rod if the small end inside diameter is worn to the service limit in **Table 1** or **Table 2**.

5. Check the piston pin for chrome flaking or cracks. Replace the pin if necessary.

6. Check the piston pin contact surface (**Figure 170**) in the small end for wear or abrasion.

7. Oil the piston pin and install it into the connecting rod small end. Slowly rotate the piston pin and check for radial play.

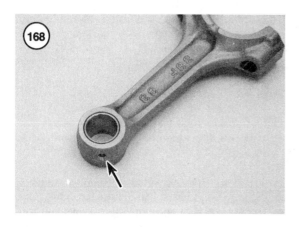

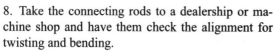

8. Take the connecting rods to a dealership or machine shop and have them check the alignment for twisting and bending.

9. Examine the bearing inserts (**Figure 171**) for wear, scoring or burned surfaces. They are reusable if in good condition. Make a note of the bearing color identification on the side of the insert if the bearing is to be discarded.

10. Compare the connecting rod big end side clearance measurement taken during crankshaft removal to the specification in **Table 1**, or **Table 2**. If the side clearance exceeds the service limit, perform the following:

    a. Measure the width of the connecting rod big end (**Figure 172**). If the width is less than the value specified in **Table 1**, or **Table 2**, replace the connecting rod assembly.

    b. Measure the crankpin width (**Figure 173**) and compare the measurement to the dimension listed in **Table 1** or **Table 2**. If the width is greater than specified, replace the crankshaft.

Oil Clearance

1. Check each connecting rod bearing insert (**Figure 171**) for evidence of wear, abrasion and scoring. If the bearing inserts are good they may be reused. If any insert is questionable, replace both inserts – cap and connecting rod – as a set.

2. Clean the crankpins on the crankshaft (**Figure 174**) and check for signs of scoring or abrasion.

3. If removed, install the existing bearing inserts into the connecting rod and cap. Each insert must be locked into place (**Figure 175**).

4. Install the connecting rod/piston assemblies into their cylinders as described in this section.

5. Set the upper crankcase upside down on the bench. Press each rod into the cylinder so the piston bottoms against the bench (**Figure 167**).

6. Check that the weight mark (**Figure 176**) on each connecting rod faces the intake side (rear) of

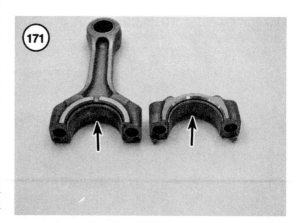

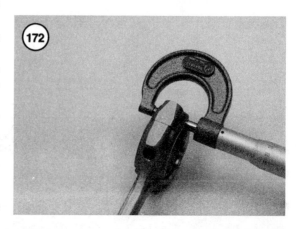

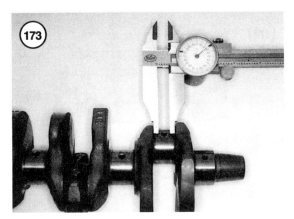

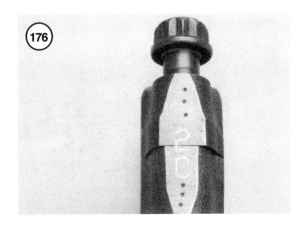

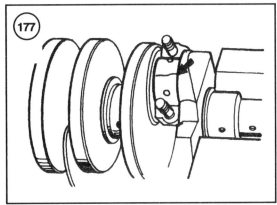

the engine. If it does not, the piston has been incorrectly installed on the connecting rod or connecting rod/piston assembly has been installed backwards. Remove the connecting rod/piston assemblies and correct the problem.

7. Position the crankshaft so the two outside crankpins (No. 1 and No. 4) face down. Lower the crankshaft onto the crankcase so each journal rests on its main bearing and the No. 1 and No. 4 crankpins rest on the No. 1 and No. 4 connecting rod bearing.

8. Place a piece Plastigage across the No. 1 and No. 4 crankpins (**Figure 177**). Do not place Plastigage across an oil hole. Make sure the Plastigage parallels the crankpin.

> *CAUTION*
> *The connecting rod and rod cap are mated. When correctly installed on its mate, the weight mark on the rod cap aligns with the weight mark on the connecting rod as shown in B, **Figure 161**. Use the cylinder numbers marked during removal to identify the correct cap for each connecting rod.*

9. Install the No. 1 rod cap onto the No. 1 connecting rod as follows:

   a. Check the bearing insert (**Figure 171**) is properly seated in the No. 1 connecting rod cap.

   b. Align the weight mark on the end of the cap with the mark on the rod and install the cap onto the rod. Push the cap until it bottoms on the connecting rod.

   c. Check that the weight marks on the cap and connecting rod properly align. If they do not, the cap has been installed on the wrong rod.

   d. Apply engine oil to the threads of the cap bolts, and install the bolts in the No. 1 connecting rod (1, **Figure 178**).

   e. Use a 10 mm, 12-point socket to evenly tighten the cap bolts, and then tighten both bolts to 15 N•m (133 in.-lb.).

10. Repeat Step 9 and install the cap onto the No. 4 connecting rod (4, **Figure 178**).

11. Lean the crankcase back. Manually push the No. 2 piston up into the cylinder so the connecting rod sits against the crankpin. Guide the connecting rod so it does not scratch the crankpin.

12. Repeat Step 11 for the No. 2 and No. 3 connecting rod (2, 3, **Figure 178**).

13. Install a piece Plastigage across the No. 2 and No. 3 crankpins so the Plastigage parallels the crankpin. Do not place the Plastigage across an oil hole.

14. Repeat Step 9 and install the rod cap onto the No. 2 connecting rod and then onto the No. 3 connecting rod.

15. Use a torque angle gauge (**Figure 179**). Tighten each cap bolt an additional 90° (1/4 turn).

16. Loosen the cap bolts. Carefully lift each cap straight up and off the connecting rod.

17. Measure the width of the flattened Plastigage according to the manufacturer's instructions (**Figure 180**). Measure both ends of the Plastigage strip.

   a. A difference of 0.025 mm (0.001 in.) or more indicates a tapered journal. Confirm this by measuring the crankpin outside diameter with a micrometer as shown in **Figure 181**).

   b. If the connecting rod big end oil clearance is greater than the service limit specified in **Table 1**, or **Table 2**, select new bearings as described in this chapter.

18. Remove all of the Plastigage from the crankpins or rod caps.

Bearing Selection

1. A numeric code (1, 2 or 3) stamped into the counterbalance web (**Figure 182**) coincides with the crankpin outside diameter as shown in **Figure 181**.

2. A numeric weight code (1 or 2) marked on the side of the connecting rod (**Figure 176**) coincides with the inside diameter of the connecting rod big end.

3. Select new bearings by cross-referencing the crankpin outside diameter code in the top row of **Table 5** with the connecting rod inside diameter code in the left column of the table. The intersection of the appropriate row and column indicates the color of the new bearing insert. **Table 6** lists the bearing color, part number and thickness. Always replace all connecting rod bearing inserts as a set.

4. After new bearing inserts have been installed, recheck the clearance as described in this section. If the clearance is still out of specification, either the crankshaft or the connecting rod(s) is worn to the service limit and requires replacement. Measure the inside diameter of the connecting rod big end and measure the outside diameter of the crankpin.

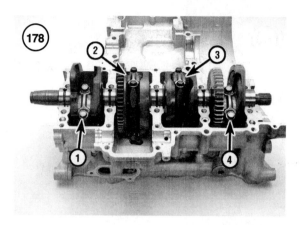

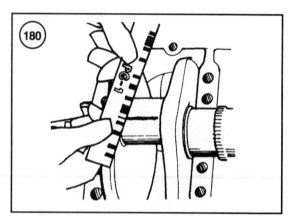

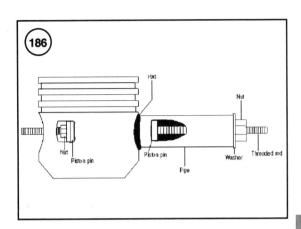

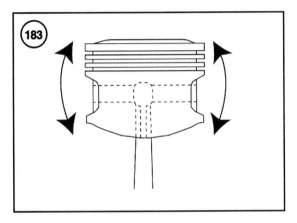

Compare the measurements to the specifications in **Table 1** or **Table 2**. Replace the component that is out of specification.

PISTON AND PISTON RINGS

The pistons are made of an aluminum alloy. The piston pin is made of steel and is a precision fit in the pistons. The piston pins are held in place by a clip at each end.

Piston Removal

1. Remove the lower crankcase as described in this chapter.

2. Make sure that each piston and its connecting rod is marked with its cylinder number (**Figure 159**). These marks help assure that the pistons are reinstalled onto the correct connecting rods and into the correct cylinders.

3. Remove the connecting rod/piston assembly as described in *Connecting Rod/Piston* in this chapter.

4. Before removing the piston, hold the rod tightly and rock the piston (**Figure 183**). Any rocking motion (do not confuse with the normal sliding motion) indicates wear on the piston pin, rod bushing, pin bore, or more likely, a combination of all three.

5. Remove the circlip (**Figure 184**) from one side of the piston pin bore.

6. From the other side, push the piston pin (**Figure 185**) out of the piston by hand. If the pin is tight, use a homemade tool (**Figure 186**) to pull the pin from the piston. Do not drive out the piston pin. This action could damage the pin, connecting rod or piston.

7. Lift the piston off the connecting rod.

8. Repeat for the remaining three pistons.

9. Inspect the pistons as described in this section.

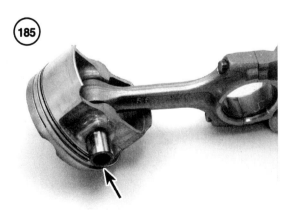

Piston Installation

> **CAUTION**
> *Each piston must be reinstalled onto its original connecting rod. Refer to the cylinder number place on each piston and connecting rod during removal.*

1. Select the No. 1 piston and the No. 1 connecting rod.
2. Apply molybdenum disulfide oil to the piston pin bore in the piston, to the piston pin and to the connecting rod bushing.
3. Install a new circlip into one side of the piston. Make sure the circlip end gap is not seated in the piston's notch (**Figure 187**).
4. Slide the piston pin (**Figure 188**) into the piston until the pin is flush with the inside of the piston pin boss.

> **NOTE**
> *The dot on the piston crown indicates the exhaust side of the piston. The weight mark on the connecting rod indicates the intake side of the connecting rod. The piston must be installed so the index dot on its crown faces the side of the connecting rod **without** the weight mark.*

5. Set the piston onto the connecting rod so that the index dot (**Figure 189**) on the piston crown faces the side of the connecting rod *without* the weight mark.
6. Align the piston pin with the hole in the connecting rod (**Figure 185**). Push the piston pin through the connecting rod until the pin lightly bottoms against the piston pin clip in the opposite side.
7. Install a new piston pin circlip (**Figure 184**) into the piston. Make sure the circlip is properly seated in the piston groove (**Figure 190**). The clip end gap must **not** sit in the piston cutout (Figure (**Figure 187**).
8. Check the installation of the piston.
9. Repeat Steps 1-8 for each remaining piston.

Piston Inspection

1. If necessary, remove the piston rings as described in this section.

> **CAUTION**
> *Be careful not to gouge or otherwise damage the piston when removing carbon. Never use a wire brush to clean the piston skirt or ring grooves. Do not attempt to remove carbon from the sides of the piston above the top ring or from the cylinder bore near the top. Removal of carbon from these two areas may cause increased oil consumption.*

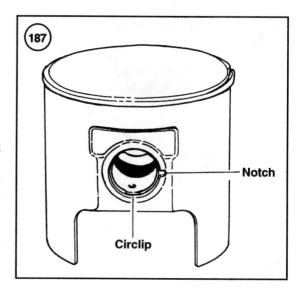

Notch
Circlip

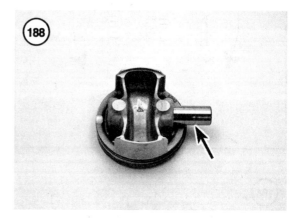

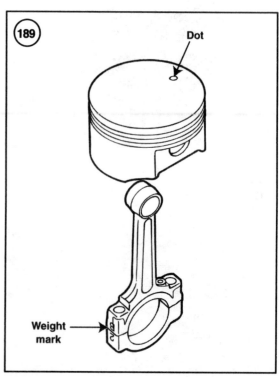

Dot
Weight mark

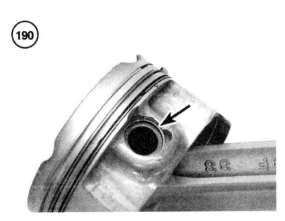

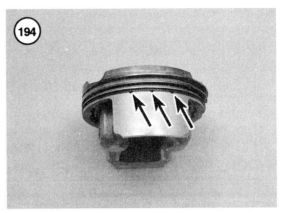

5

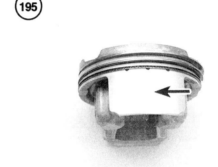

2. Clean the carbon from the piston crown (A, **Figure 191**) with a soft scraper. Re-number the piston as soon as it is cleaned.

3. After cleaning the piston, examine the crown (**Figure 192**). The crown should show no signs of wear or damage. If the crown appears pecked or spongy-looking, also check the spark plug, valves and combustion chamber for aluminum deposits. If these deposits are found, the engine is overheating.

4. Examine each ring groove for burrs, dented edges or other damage. Pay particular attention to the top compression ring groove. It usually wears more than the others. Oil rings and grooves wear little compared to compression rings and their grooves. If there is evidence of oil ring groove wear or if the oil ring assembly is tight and difficult to remove, the piston skirt may have collapsed due to excessive heat and is permanently deformed. Replace the piston.

5. Check the oil control holes in the piston for carbon or oil sludge buildup. Refer to **Figure 193** and **Figure 194**. Clean the holes with wire and blow them clear with compressed air.

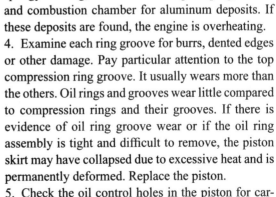

6. Check the piston skirt (**Figure 195**) for cracks or other damage. If a piston shows signs of partial seizure (bits of aluminum build-up on the piston skirt),

the piston should be replaced to reduce the possibility of engine noise and further piston seizure.

NOTE
If the piston skirt is worn or scuffed unevenly from side-to-side, the connecting rod may be bent or twisted.

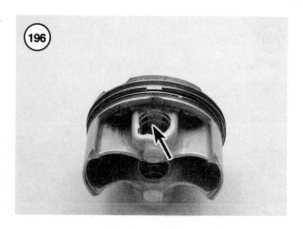

7. Check the circlip groove (**Figure 196**) on each side for wear, cracks or other damage. If the grooves are questionable, check the circlip fit by installing a new circlip into each groove and then attempt to move the circlip from side-to-side. If the circlip has any side play, the groove is worn and the piston must be replaced.

8. Measure the piston outside diameter (**Figure 197**) at a point 15 mm (0.6 in.) from the bottom of the skirt. If the diameter is worn to the service limit (**Table 1** or **2**) replace the piston.

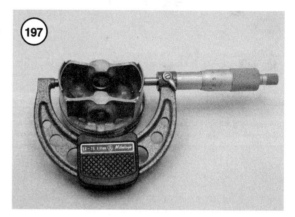

9. Measure piston-to-cylinder clearance as described in *Piston Clearance* in this section.

10. If damage or wear indicate piston replacement, select a new piston as described in Piston Clearance in this section. If the piston, rings and cylinder are not damaged and are dimensionally correct, they can be reused.

Piston Pin Inspection

1. Clean the piston pin in solvent, and dry it thoroughly.

2. Inspect the piston pin (B, **Figure 191**) for chrome flaking or cracks. Replace if necessary.

3. Oil the piston pin and install it into the connecting rod. Slowly rotate the piston pin and check for radial play.

4. Oil the piston pin and partially install it into the piston. Check the piston pin for excessive play (**Figure 198**).

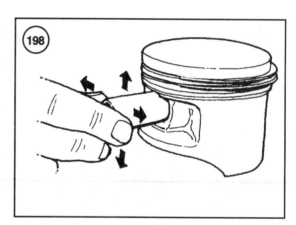

5. Measure the piston pin outside diameter (**Figure 199**). Measure the diameter at three places along the piston pin. If any measurement is less than the service limit specified in **Table 1** or **Table 2**, replace the piston pin.

6. Measure the inside diameter of the piston pin bore (**Figure 200**). If the measurement exceeds the service limit specified in **Table 1** or **Table 2** replace the piston.

7. Replace the piston pin and/or piston or connecting rod if necessary.

Piston Clearance

1. Make sure the piston skirt and cylinder wall are clean and dry.

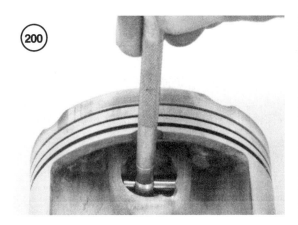

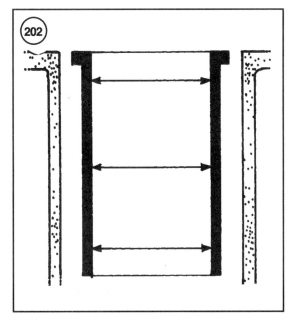

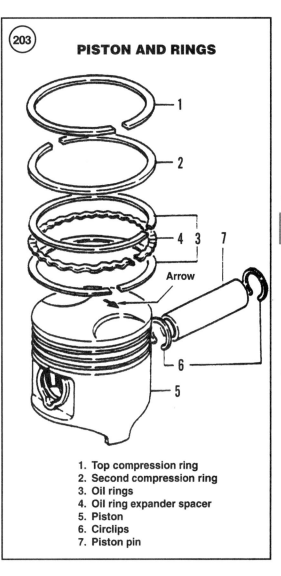

PISTON AND RINGS

Arrow

1. Top compression ring
2. Second compression ring
3. Oil rings
4. Oil ring expander spacer
5. Piston
6. Circlips
7. Piston pin

3. Measure the piston outside diameter (**Figure 197**) at a point 15 mm (0.6 in.) from the bottom of the skirt.

4. Subtract the piston outside diameter from the largest bore inside diameter; the difference is piston-to-cylinder clearance. If clearance exceeds the service limit specified in **Table 1** or **Table 2**, replace the pistons and crankcases. The cylinders in this engine cannot be bored or honed.

Piston Ring Removal/Inspection

When measuring the piston rings (**Figure 203**) and piston in this section, compare the measurements to specifications in **Table 1** or **Table 2**. Replace parts that are out of specification or show damage.

WARNING
The edges of all piston rings are very sharp. Be careful when handling them.

2. Measure the cylinder bore with a cylinder bore gauge (**Figure 201**). Measure the bore at the top, middle and bottom of a cylinder as shown in **Figure 202**. At each height, measure the bore across two axes: one parallel to the crankshaft and the other 90° to the crankshaft.

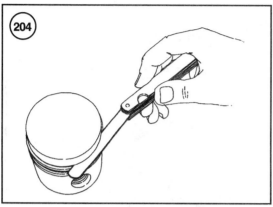

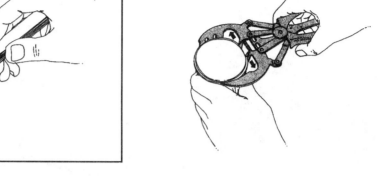

1. Measure the side clearance of each compression ring in its groove with a flat feeler gauge (**Figure 204**). If the clearance is greater than specified, the rings must be replaced. If the clearance is still excessive with the new rings installed, replace the piston.

NOTE
Store the old rings in the order in which they are removed.

2. Remove the compression rings with a ring expander tool (**Figure 205**) or by spreading the ring ends with your thumbs and lifting the rings up evenly (**Figure 206**).
3. Remove the oil ring assembly by first removing the upper and then the lower ring rails. Then remove the expander spacer.
4. Using a broken piston ring, carefully remove carbon and oil residue from the piston ring grooves (**Figure 207**). Do not remove aluminum material from the ring grooves. This will increase ring side clearance.
5. Measure each ring groove width with a vernier caliper. Measure each groove at several points around the piston. Replace the piston if any groove width is outside the specified range.
6. Inspect the ring grooves carefully for burrs, nicks or for broken or cracked lands. Replace the piston if necessary.
7. Measure the thickness of each compression ring (**Figure 208**) the thickness is less than specified, replace the ring(s).
8. Measure the free end gap (**Figure 209**). If the free end gap exceeds the service limit specified in **Table 1** or **Table 2**, the ring(s) must be replaced.
9. Insert the ring into the bottom of the cylinder bore and square it with the cylinder wall by tapping it with the piston. Measure the end gap with a feeler gauge (**Figure 210**). Replace the rings if the end gap equals or exceeds service limit specified in **Table 1** or **Table 2**. Also measure the end gap when installing new piston rings. If the gap on a new compression ring is

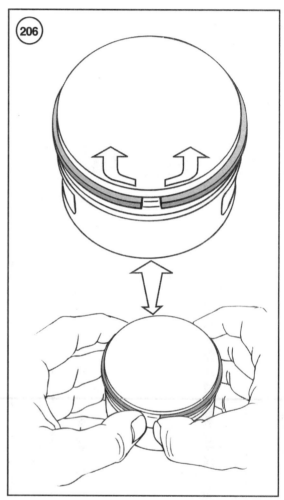

smaller than specified, hold a small file in a vise, grip the ends of the ring with your fingers and enlarge the gap (**Figure 211**).

Piston Ring Installation

1. Clean the piston and rings. Dry them with compressed air.

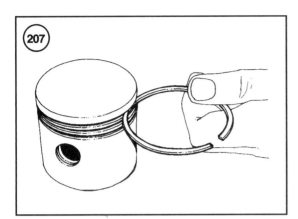

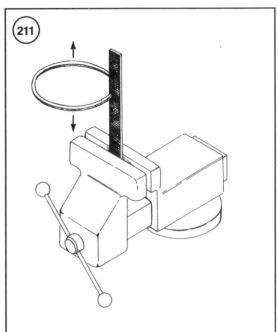

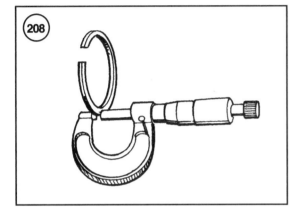

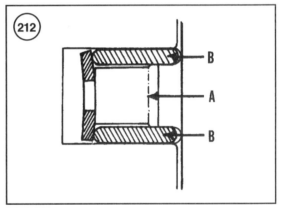

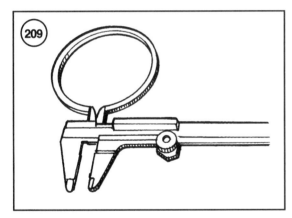

2. Install piston rings as follows:

NOTE
Install the piston rings -- first the bottom, then the middle, then the top ring--by carefully spreading the ends by hand and slipping the rings over the top of the piston. Remember that the piston rings must be installed with the manufacturer's marks facing up toward piston crown. Incorrectly installed piston rings can wear rapidly and/or allow oil to escape past them.

a. Install the oil control ring assembly into the bottom ring groove. Install the oil ring expander spacer first (A, **Figure 212**), and then install each ring rail (B). Be sure the ends of the expander spacer butt together (**Figure 213**). They

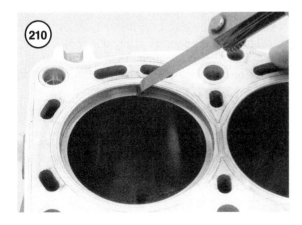

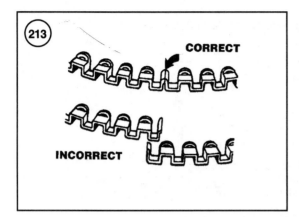

should not overlap. If reassembling used parts, install the ring rails as they were removed.

NOTE
Follow the ring manufacturer's directions when installing aftermarket piston rings.

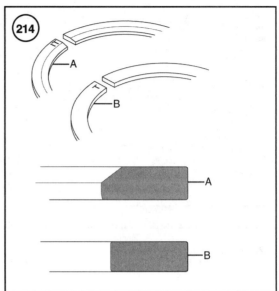

b. Install the 2nd or middle compression ring with the manufacturer's mark facing up. Refer to **Figure 214** or **Figure 215**. The second ring has a slight taper.

c. Install the top compression ring with the manufacturer's mark facing up. Refer to **Figure 214** or **Figure 215**.

3. Make sure the rings are seated completely in their grooves all the way around the piston and that the end gaps are distributed around the piston as shown in **Figure 203**. The ring gaps must not align with each other. This prevents compression pressure from escaping past them.

4. If new parts were installed, the engine should be broken-in just as though it were new. Refer to *Engine Break-In* in this chapter.

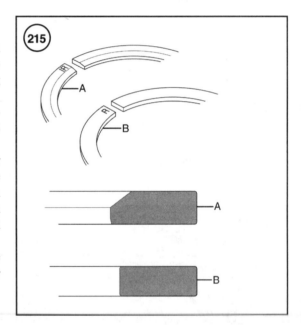

ENGINE BREAK-IN

During break-in, oil consumption will be higher than normal. It is important to check and correct the oil level frequently (Chapter Three). Never allow the oil level to drop below the minimum level.

The manufacturer designates the first 1,600 km (1000 miles) of vehicle operation as the break-in period. During the first 800 km (500 miles) of opera-

tion, do not exceed 7000 rpm. In the period between 800-1,600 km (500 and 1000 miles) of operation, do not exceed 10,0000 rpm.

Vary the engine speed during the break-in period. Avoid prolonged operation at any one engine speed, which can cause overheating in some parts.

After the break-in period, change the engine oil and filter as described in Chapter Three.

Table 1 ENGINE LOWER END SPECIFICATIONS (GSX–R600 MODELS)

Item	Standard mm (in.)	Service limit mm (in.)
Cylinder bore	67.000–67.015 (2.6378–2.6384)	Nicks or scratches
Cylinder warp	–	0.20 (0.008)
Compression pressure (at sea level)		
Standard	1,200–1,600 kPa (12–16 kg/cm² [(171–228 psi])	
Service limit	900 kPa (9 kg/cm² [128 psi])	
Maximum difference between cylinders	200 kPa (2 kg/cm² [28 psi])	
Piston outside diameter*	66.965–66.980 (2.6364–2.6370)	66.880 (2.6331)
Piston–to–cylinder clearance	0.030–0.040 (0.0011–0.0015)	
Piston–pin bore inside diameter	14.002–14.008 (0.5513–0.5515)	14.030 (0.5524)
Piston pin outside diameter	13.995–14.000 (0.5510–0.5512)	13.980 (0.5504)
Piston rings		
Ring-to-groove clearance		
Top	–	0.180 (0.0071)
Second	–	0.150 (0.0059)
Ring thickness		
Top	0.97–0.99 (0.0382–0.0390)	–
Second	0.77–0.79 (0.0303–0.0311)	–
Piston ring groove width		
Top	1.01–1.03 (0.0398–0.0406)	–
Second	0.81–0.83 (0.0319–0.0327)	–
Oil ring	1.51–1.53 (0.0594–0.0602)	–
Ring end gap (installed)		
Top	0.06–0.21 (0.002–0.008)	0.5 (0.02)
Second	0.06–0.21 (0.002–0.008)	0.5 (0.02)
Ring free gap		
First	Approx 5.5 (0.22)	4.4 (0.17)
Second	Approx 8.5 (0.33)	6.8 (0.27)
Connecting rod		
Small end inside diameter	14.010–14.018 (0.5516–0.5519)	14.040 (0.5228)
Big end side clearance	0.10–0.20 (0.004–0.008)	0.30 (0.012)
Big end width	19.95–20.00 (0.7854–0.7874)	–
Big end inside diameter		
Code 1	34.000–34.008 (1.3386–1.3389)	
Code 2	34.008–34.016 (1.3389–1.3392)	–
Big end oil clearance	0.032–0.056 (0.0013–0.0022)	0.080 (0.0031)
Crankshaft		
Crankpin width	20.10–20.15 (0.7913–0.7933)	–
Crankpin outside diameter		–
Standard	30.976–31.000 (1.2195–1.2205)	–
Code 1	30.992–31.000 (1.2202–1.2205)	–
Code 2	30.984–30.992 (1.2198–1.2202)	–
Code 3	30.976–30.984 (1.2195–1.2198)	–
Crankshaft journal outside diameter		
Standard	29.982–30.000 (1.18039–1.18110)	–

(continued)

Table 1 ENGINE LOWER END SPECIFICATIONS (GSX–R600 MODELS) (continued)

Item	Standard mm (in.)	Service limit mm (in.)
Crankshaft (continued)		
Crankshaft journal outside diameter (continued)		
Code A	29.994–30.000 (1.18086–1.18110)	–
Code B	29.988–29.994 (1.18062–1.18086)	–
Code C	29.982–29.988 (1.18039–1.1802)	–
Crankcase main bearing boss inside diameter		
Code A	33.000–33.006 (1.29921–1.29945)	–
Code B	33.007–33.012 (1.29949–1.29968)	–
Code C	33.013–33.018 (1.29972–1.29992)	–
Crankshaft journal oil clearance	0.010–0.028 (0.0004–0.0011)	0.080 (0.0031)
Crankshaft runout	–	0.05 (0.002)
Crankshaft thrust clearance	0.055–0.110 (0.0022–0.0043)	–
Crankshaft thrust bearing thickness		
Right side	2.425–2.450 (0.0955–0.0965)	–
Left side	2.350–2.500 (0.0925–0.0984)	–
Oil pressure @ 60° C (140° F)	100–400 kPa (14–57 psi]) @ 3,000 rpm	

*Measured 15 mm (0.6 in.) from skirt bottom

Table 2 ENGINE LOWER END SPECIFICATIONS (GSX–R750 MODELS)

Item	Standard mm (in.)	Service limit mm (in.)
Cylinder bore	70.000–70.015 (2.7559–2.7565)	Nicks or scratches
Cylinder warp	–	0.20 (0.008)
Compression pressure (at sea level)		
Standard	1,300–1,700 kPa (13–17 kg/cm2 [(185–242 psi])	
Service limit	1000 kPa (10 kg/cm2 [148 psi])	
Maximum difference between cylinders	200 kPa (2 kg/cm2 [28 psi])	
Piston		
Outside diameter*	69.965–69.980 (2.7545–2.7551)	69.880 (2.7512)
Piston–to–cylinder clearance	0.030–0.040 (0.0011–0.0015)	
Piston–pin bore inside diameter 15.030 (0.5917)		15.002–15.008 (0.5906–0.5909)
Piston pin outside diameter	14.995–15.000 (0.5903–0.5905)	14.980 (0.5898)
Piston rings		
Ring–to–groove clearance		
Top	–	0.180 (0.0071)
Second	–	0.150 (0.0059)
Ring thickness		
Top	0.97–0.99 (0.0382–0.0390)	–
Second	0.77–0.79 (0.0303–0.0311)	–
Piston ring groove width		
Top	1.01–1.03 (0.0398–0.0406)	–
Second	0.81–0.83 (0.0319–0.0327)	–
Oil ring	1.51–1.53 (0.0594–0.0602)	–
Ring end gap (installed)		
Top	0.06–0.21 (0.002–0.008)	0.5 (0.02)
Second	0.06–0.18 (0.002–0.007)	0.5 (0.02)
Ring free gap		
First	Approx 9.2 (0.36)	7.3 (0.29)
Second	Approx 7.3 (0.29)	5.8 (0.23)

(continued)

Table 2 ENGINE LOWER END SPECIFICATIONS (GSX–R750 MODELS)

Item	Standard mm (in.)	Service limit mm (in.)
Connecting rod		
Small end inside diameter	15.010–15.018 (0.5910–0.5913)	15.040 (0.5921)
Big end side clearance	0.10–0.20 (0.004–0.008)	0.30 (0.012)
Big end width	20.10–20.15 (0.7913–0.7933)	–
Big end inside diameter		
Code1	36.000–36.008 (1.4173–1.4176)	
Code 2	36.008–36.016 (1.4176–1.4179)	–
Big end oil clearance	0.032–0.056 (0.0013–0.0022)	0.080 (0.0031)
Crankshaft		
Crankpin width	20.10–20.15 (0.7913–0.7933)	–
Crankpin outside diameter		–
Standard	32.976–33.000 (1.2983–1.2992)	–
Code 1	32.992–33.000 (1.2989–1.2992)	–
Code 2	32.984–32.992 (1.2986–1.2989)	–
Code 3	32.976–32.984 (1.2983–1.2986)	–
Crankshaft journal outside diameter		
Standard	31.982–32.000 (1.2591–1.2598)	–
Code A	31.994–32.000 (1.2596–1.2598)	–
Code B	31.988–31.994 (1.2594–1.2596)	–
Code C	31.982–31.988 (1.2591–1.2594)	–
Crankcase main bearing boss inside diameter		
Code A	35.000–35.006 (1.3780–1.3782)	–
Code B	35.006–35.012 (1.3782–1.3784)	–
Code C	35.012–35.018 (1.3784–1.3787)	–
Crankshaft journal oil clearance	0.010–0.028 (0.0004–0.0011)	0.080 (0.0031)
Crankshaft runout	–	0.05 (0.002)
Crankshaft thrust clearance	0.055–0.110 (0.0022–0.0043)	–
Crankshaft thrust bearing thickness		
Right side	2.425–2.450 (0.0955–0.0965)	–
Left side	2.350–2.500 (0.0925–0.0984)	–
Balancer shaft journal		
Outside diameter	22.976–22.992 (0.9046–0.9052)	–
Oil clearance	0.028–0.052 (0.0011–0.0020)	
Oil pressure @ 60° C (140° F)	100–400 kPa (14–57 psi]) @ 3,000 rpm	

*Measured 15 mm (0.6 in.) from skirt bottom

Table 3 CRANKSHAFT MAIN BEARING INSERT SELECTION

Crankcase bearing boss Inside diameter code	Crankshaft journal outside diameter code		
	A	B	C
A	Green	Black	Brown
B	Black	Brown	Yellow
C	Brown	Yellow	Blue

Table 4 CRANKSHAFT MAIN BEARING INSERT DIMENSIONS

Color	Part No.	Specification mm (in.)
Green	12229–02H00–0A0	1.492–1.495 (0.0587–0.0589)
Black	12229–02H00–0B0	1.495–1.498 (0.0589–0.0590)
Brown	12229–02H00–0C0	1.498–1.501 (0.0590–0.0591)
Yellow	12229–02F00–0D0	1.501–1.504 (0.0591–0.0592)
Blue	12229–02H00–0E0	1.504–1.507 (0.0592–0.0593)

5

Table 5 CONNECTING ROD BEARING INSERT SELECTION

Connecting rod inside diameter code	Crankpin journal outside diameter code		
	1	2	3
1	Green	Black	Brown
2	Black	Brown	Yellow

Table 6 CONNECTING ROD BEARING INSERT DIMENSIONS)

Color	Part No.	Specification mm (in.)
Green	12164–30G00–0A0	1.480–1.484 (0.0583–0.0584)
Black	12164–30G00–0B0	1.484–1.488 (0.0584–0.0586)
Brown	12164–30G00–0C0	1.488–1.492 (0.0586–0.0587)
Yellow	12164–30G00–0D0	1.492–1.496 (0.0587–0.0589)

Table 7 BALACER SHAFT BEARING INSERT SELECTION

Bearing boss inside diameter code	Balancer shaft journal outside diameter code	
	A	B
A	Green	Black
B	Black	Brown

Table 8 BALACER SHAFT BEARING INSERT DIMENSION

Color (Part No.)	Specification mm (in.)
Green (12229-40F50-0A0)	1.486-1.490 (0.0585-0.0587)
Black (12229-40F50-0B0)	1.490-1.494 (0.0587-0.0588)
Brown (12229-40F50-0C0)	1.494-1.498 (0.0588-0.0590)

Table 9 THRUST BEARING SELECTION

Clearance without left thrust bearing	Color (part number)	Thrust bearing thickness mm (in.)	Thrust clearance mm (in.)
2.430–2.460 (0.0957–0.0969)	Red (12228–17E00–0A0)	2.350–2.375 (0.0925–0.0935)	0.055–0.110 (0.0022–0.0043)
2.460–2.485 (0.0969–0.0978)	Black (12228–17E00–0B0)	2.375–2.400 (0.0935– 0.0945)	0.060–0.110 (0.0024–0.0043)
2.485–2.510 (0.0978–0.0988)	Blue (12228–17E00–0C0)	2.400–2.425 (0.0945–0.0955)	0.060–0.110 (0.0024–0.0043)
2.510–2.535 (0.0988–0.0998)	Green (12228–17E00–0D0)	2.425–2.450 (0.0955–0.0965)	0.060–0.110 (0.0024–0.0043)
2.535–2.560 (0.0998–0.1008)	Yellow (12228–17E00–0E0)	2.450–2.475 (0.0965–0.0974)	0.060–0.110 (0.0024–0.0043)
2.560–2.585 (0.1008–0.1018)	White (12228–17E00–0F0)	2.475–2.500 (0.0974–0.0984)	0.060–0.110 (0.0024–0.0043)

Table 10 ENGINE LOWER END TORQUE SPECIFICATIONS

Item	N•m	in.-lb.	ft.-lb.
Alternator cover bolt	10	89	–
Connecting rod cap bolt			
Initial	15	133	–
Final	additional 90° (1/4 turn)		
Crankcase breather reed valve cover bolt	10	89	–
Crankcase bolt			
Initial torque			
6 mm	6	53	–
8 mm	15	133	–
Final torque			
6 mm	11	97	–
8 mm	26	•	19
Crankshaft journal bolt 9 mm			
Initial torque	18	159	–
Final torque	additional 50°		
Front engine mounting			
M10 Bolt	55	–	40
Clamp bolt	23	–	17
Engine mounting thrust adjuster	23	–	17
Engine mounting thrust adjuster locknut	45	–	33
Engine sprocket nut	115	–	85
Flywheel bolt	120	–	88
Oil cooler mounting bolt	10	89	–
Oil drain bolt	23	–	17
Oil gallery plug			
M6	10	89	–
M12	15	133	–
M16	35	–	26.5
Oil nozzle mounting bolt	10	89	–
Oil pan bolt	10	89	–
Oil pump mounting bolt	10	89	–
Oil pressure switch	14	124	–
Speed sensor rotor bolt	25	–	18
Starter clutch bolt	13	115	–
Starter clutch cover bolt	10	89	–
Timing inspection cap	11	97	–
Transmission mainshaft			
Bearing housing bolts right and left side	12	106	–
Oil seal screws	12	144	–
Water jacket plugs	10	89	–

5

Notes

CHAPTER SIX

CLUTCH

This chapter covers the clutch and the clutch release mechanism.

Tables 1-3 are at the end if this chapter.

CLUTCH COVER

Refer to **Figure 1**.

Removal

> *NOTE*
> *This procedure is shown with the engine removed and partially dissembled for photo clarity.*

1. Securely support the motorcycle on a level surface.
2. Remove the lower fairing and the right side fairing panel (Chapter Fifteen).
3. Drain the engine oil (Chapter Three).

> *NOTE*
> *Mark the location of the clutch cover bolt (*Figure 2*) with a gasket washer beneath it. The gasket washer must be installed behind this bolt during assembly. Also mark the location of the bolt(s) with cable clamp(s) beneath them.*

4. Evenly loosen and remove the clutch cover bolts.
5. Remove the clutch cover (**Figure 3**) from the crankcase
6. Remove and discard the clutch cover gasket (A, **Figure 4**).
7. Account for the locating dowels (B, **Figure 4**) behind the cover.

Installation

1. Apply Suzuki Bond 1270B to the seams (**Figure 5**) formed by the mating surfaces of the crankcases.
2. Install the dowels. Refer to **Figure 6** and **Figure 7**.
3. Install a *new* gasket (A, **Figure 4**).
4. Install the clutch cover (**Figure 3**).
5. Install gasket washer behind the bolt (**Figure 2**) noted during removal; install the cable holders behind the indicated bolt(s).
6. Tighten the clutch cover bolts to 10 N•m (89 in.-lb.).
7. Add engine oil (Chapter Three). Start the engine and check for oil leaks.
8. Install the lower fairing and the right side fairing panel (Chapter Fifteen).

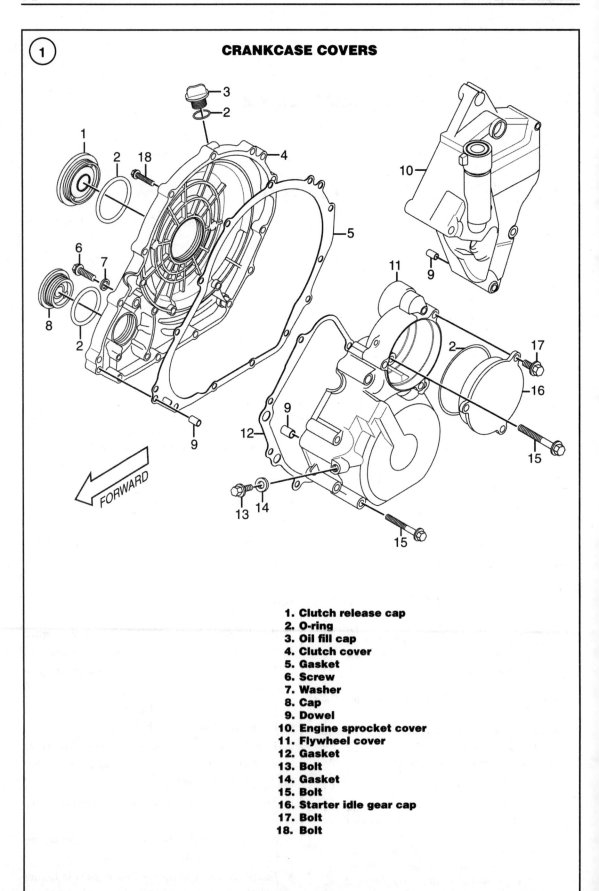

CRANKCASE COVERS

1. Clutch release cap
2. O-ring
3. Oil fill cap
4. Clutch cover
5. Gasket
6. Screw
7. Washer
8. Cap
9. Dowel
10. Engine sprocket cover
11. Flywheel cover
12. Gasket
13. Bolt
14. Gasket
15. Bolt
16. Starter idle gear cap
17. Bolt
18. Bolt

CLUTCH

Removal/Disassembly

Refer to **Figure 8** or **Figure 9**.

1. Remove clutch cover, gasket and locating dowels as described in this chapter.

2. Evenly loosen the clutch spring bolts (**Figure 10**) in a crisscross pattern. Once all the bolts are loose, remove each bolt and the clutch spring (**Figure 11**).

3. Remove the pressure plate (**Figure 12**) from the clutch.

4. Remove the thrust washer (**Figure 13**) and the bearing (**Figure 14**) from the clutch push piece.

5. Remove the clutch push piece (**Figure 15**) and the right clutch push rod (**Figure 16**) from the mainshaft if necessary.

NOTE
Three different types of friction discs and two different types of plain plates are used in this clutch. If the friction discs and clutch plates will be reused, they must be reinstalled in their original locations. During disassembly, stack the plates and discs in the order of their removal (Figure 17). A friction disc is identified by its inside diameter and by the number of friction

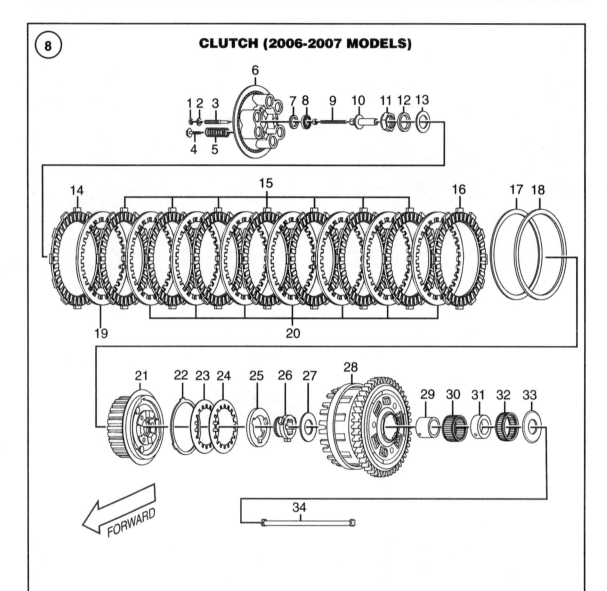

CLUTCH (2006-2007 MODELS)

1. Locknut
2. Washer
3. Clutch lifter adjuster
4. Clutch spring bolt
5. Clutch spring
6. Pressure plate
7. Thrust washer
8. Bearing
9. Nut and clutch release screw
10. Push piece
11. Clutch nut
12. Spring washer
13. Flat washer
14. Friction disc No. 2
15. Friction disc No. 1
16. Friction disc No. 3
17. Spring seat

18. Hub spring
19. Plain plate No. 2
20. Plain plate No. 1
21. Clutch hub
22. Washer
23. Cam reaction spring
24. Cam reaction spring
25. Clutch lifter driven cam
26. Clutch lifter drive cam
27. Thrust washer-outboard
28. Clutch housing
29. Bushing
30. Needle bearing
31. Oil pump drive spacer
32. Bearing
33. Thrust washer-inboard
34. Clutch pushrod

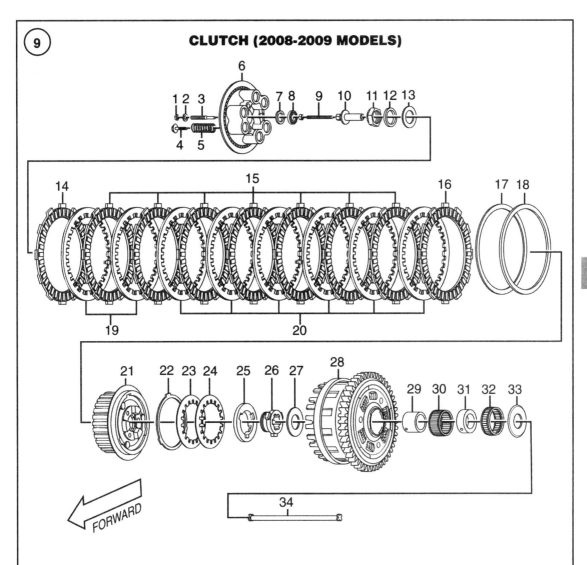

⑨ **CLUTCH (2008-2009 MODELS)**

FORWARD

1. Locknut
2. Washer
3. Clutch lifter adjuster
4. Clutch spring bolt
5. Clutch spring
6. Pressure plate
7. Thrust washer
8. Bearing
9. Nut and clutch release screw
10. Push piece
11. Clutch nut
12. Spring washer
13. Flat washer
14. Friction disc No. 2
15. Friction disc No. 1
16. Friction disc No. 3
17. Spring seat

18. Hub spring
19. Plain plate No. 2
20. Plain plate No. 1
21. Clutch hub
22. Washer
23. Cam reaction spring
24. Cam reaction spring
25. Clutch lifter driven cam
26. Clutch lifter drive cam
27. Thrust washer-outboard
28. Clutch housing
29. Bushing
30. Needle bearing
31. Oil pump drive spacer
32. Needle bearing
33. Thrust washer-inboard
34. Clutch pushrod

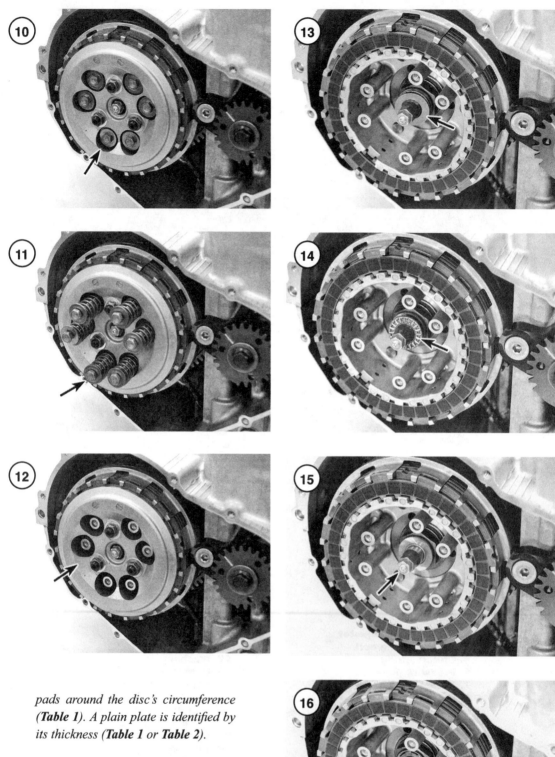

pads around the disc's circumference (**Table 1**). A plain plate is identified by its thickness (**Table 1** or **Table 2**).

6. Remove the outside friction disc, and set it on the bench. Note that the tabs of this outermost friction disc sit in the shallow slots (A, **Figure 18**) of the clutch housing. Also note that the remaining friction discs fit into the deep slots (B, **Figure 18**) of the housing. Each friction disc must be installed in the correct slots during assembly.

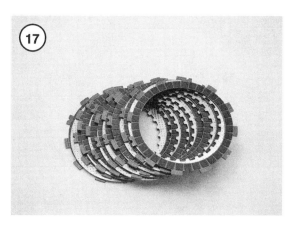

6

7. Remove the outside plain plate (**Figure 19**), and set it on the outside friction disc.

8. Continue to remove a friction disc and then a plain plate. Place each part atop the stack as it is removed. The last part removed is friction disc No. 3.

9. Remove the spring and spring seat (**Figure 20**) from the clutch hub. Note that the concave side of the spring faces out.

10. Unstake the clutch nut (**Figure 21**). Hold the clutch hub with a clutch holder, and remove the clutch nut from the mainshaft.

11. Remove the spring washer (**Figure 22**) and the flat washer (**Figure 23**) from the mainshaft.

12. Remove the clutch hub (**Figure 24**) and out-board thrust washer (**Figure 25**).

13. If the clutch lifter drive cam (A, **Figure 26**), clutch lifter driven cam (B), cam reaction spring (C), and spring seat did not come out with the clutch hub, remove them now.

14. Remove the bushing (**Figure 27**), and needle bearing (**Figure 28**) from the mainshaft.

15. Remove the clutch housing (**Figure 29**) from the mainshaft. If necessary, rotate the crankshaft so the primary driven gear on the clutch housing does not strike the crankshaft web during removal.

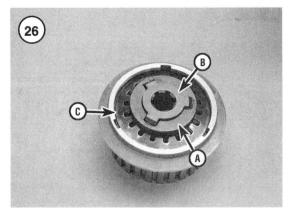

16. Remove the inboard thrust washer (A, **Figure 30**). Note that the chamfered side of the thrust washer faces in toward the mainshaft bearing.

Installation/Assembly

> *NOTE*
> *If installing new friction discs, soak them in clean engine oil for at least 20 minutes before installation.*

1. Install the inboard thrust washer (**Figure 30**) onto the mainshaft so the chamfered side (**Figure 31**) faces the crankcase.

2. Install the clutch housing into the mainshaft (**Figure 29**). Position the housing so the clutch housing primary driven gear (A, **Figure 32**) aligns the primary drive gear (B, **Figure 30**) on the crankshaft. Also align the oil pump sprocket (B, **Figure 32**) with the oil pump drive sprocket (C, **Figure 30**). Rotate the crankshaft or the oil pump gear as necessary to align the gears, and then press the clutch housing onto the mainshaft until the housing bottoms.

3. Support the housing, and install the needle bearing (**Figure 28**) and the bushing (**Figure 27**). Apply clean engine oil to each part, and seat them within the housing.

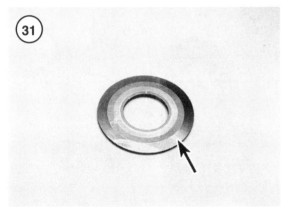

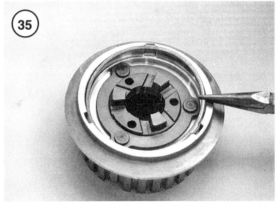

4. Use a screwdriver to make sure the oil pump driven gear (**Figure 33**) still engages the oil pump spur gear on the back of the clutch housing.

5. Install the outboard thrust washer (**Figure 34**) and push it on until it seats (**Figure 25**) on the clutch housing.

6. Install the spring seat (**Figure 35**), and install the cam reaction springs (**Figure 36**) so the slots in the springs all align.

7. Apply molybdenum disulfide oil to the mating surfaces of the clutch lifter drive and driven cams, and install the driven cam (**Figure 37**) onto the clutch hub.

8. Install the drive cam (B, **Figure 26**) onto the driven cam.

9. Partially install the hub (**Figure 38**) onto the mainshaft.

10. Secure the mainshaft with snap ring pliers (**Figure 39**) to keep it from rotating, and align the splines of the clutch hub with those of the mainshaft. Press the clutch hub on until it bottoms (**Figure 24**).

11. Install the flat washer (**Figure 23**) and the spring washer (**Figure 22**) onto the mainshaft. The concave side of the spring washer must face in toward the crankcase.

12. Install a new clutch nut (**Figure 40**) onto the mainshaft.

13. Hold the clutch hub with a clutch holder (A, **Figure 41**), and tighten the clutch nut (B) to 95 N•m (68.7 ft.-lb.).

14. Stake the clutch nut (**Figure 21**) to lock it into place.

15. Install the spring seat (**Figure 42**) onto the clutch hub.

16. Position the spring with the concave side facing away from the spring seat, and install the spring (**Figure 43**) onto the spring seat until it bottoms.

> *NOTE*
> *If reinstalling used friction discs and plain plates, install them in the reverse of their removal order. Used discs and plates must be reinstalled in their original locations within the clutch housing.*

> *NOTE*
> *There two different plain plate thicknesses and they must be installed in the correct sequence. Refer to **Table 1** or table 2 for thickness specification.*

> *NOTE*
> *There are three different friction discs as indicated in **Figure 8** and **Figure 9**. Each is identified by the number of pads on the disc and the inside diameter as listed in **Table 1** and **Table 2**.*

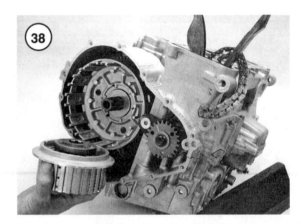

17. Refer to **Figure 44** and **Figure 45** for correct sequence of friction discs and plain plates, and install the following:

a. Install the first friction disc (No. 3) into the clutch housing so the tabs of the disc fit into the deep slots (**Figure 46**) in the clutch housing as noted during removal.

b. Install a plain plate (No. 1) so its splines engage those in the clutch hub (**Figure 47**).

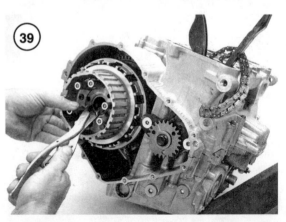

c. Install a friction disc (No. 1) into the deep slots (**Figure 46**), and then a plain plate (No. 1).

d. Repeatedly install a friction disc (No. 1) into the deep slots, and then another plain plate(s) (No.2) until you have installed all but the last friction disc.

e. End by installing the last friction disc (No. 2) (**Figure 48**). This disc must be staggered. The tabs of this last disc must engage the shallow slot in the housing as shown in A, **Figure 18**.

18. Install the right clutch push rod (**Figure 49**) and then the push piece (**Figure 50**) into the mainshaft.

19. Install the bearing (**Figure 51**) and thrust washer (**Figure 52**) onto the clutch piece.

20. Align the raised tab (A, **Figure 53**) on the pressure plate with the cutout in the clutch hub (B). This is necessary to properly align the cam lifter adjusters (C, **Figure 53**) with the holes in the hub.

21. Install the pressure plate (**Figure 54**).

22. Install a spring (**Figure 55**) over each post in the clutch hub, and install the bolts (**Figure 56**).

23. Evenly tighten the clutch spring bolts in a criss-cross pattern. Tighten the clutch spring bolts to 9.5 N•m (84 in.-lb.).

24. Install a *new* clutch cover gasket and clutch cover as described in this chapter.

Inspection

Refer to **Table 1** or **Table 2** for specifications.

1. Clean all clutch parts in a petroleum-based solvent such as kerosene. Thoroughly dry them with compressed air.

2. Measure the thickness of each friction disc at several places around the disc as shown in **Figure 57**. If any measurement reaches the service limit, replace all friction discs.

3. Measure the width of all claws **Figure 58**) on each friction disc. If any claw width is worn to the service limit specified in **Table 1** or **Table 2**, replace all friction discs.

4. Visually inspect the frictions discs and plain plates for damage from heat or lack of oil. If any damage is noted, replace all the clutch plates as a set.

5. Check the plain plates for warp with a flat feeler gauge on a surface plate such as a piece of plate glass (**Figure 59**). If any warp meets or exceeds the service limit in **Table 1**, replace all of the plain plates.

6. Inspect the slots in the clutch housing for cracks, nicks or galling where they come in contact with the friction disc tabs. Inspect both the deep (A, **Figure 60**) and the shallow slots (B) in the housing. If severe damage is evident on any slot the housing must be replaced.

7. Inspect the teeth of the primary driven gear (A, **Figure 61**) and the oil pump sprocket (B) on the

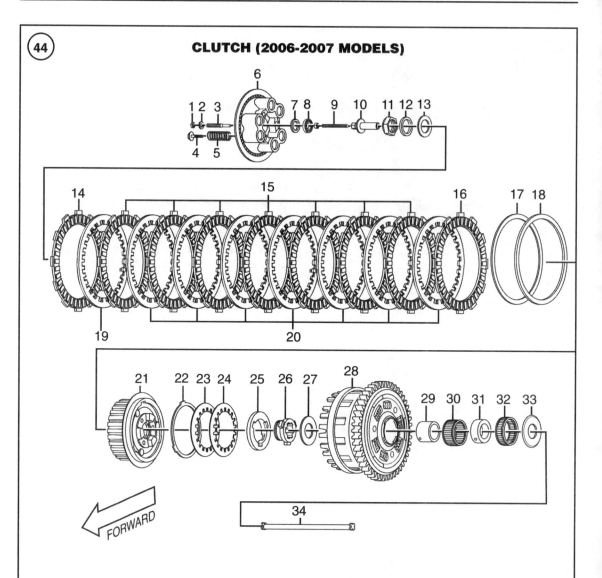

CLUTCH (2006-2007 MODELS)

1. Locknut
2. Washer
3. Clutch lifter adjuster
4. Clutch spring bolt
5. Clutch spring
6. Pressure plate
7. Thrust washer
8. Bearing
9. Nut and clutch release screw
10. Push piece
11. Clutch nut
12. Spring washer
13. Flat washer
14. Friction disc No. 2
15. Friction disc No. 1
16. Friction disc No. 3
17. Spring seat

18. Hub spring
19. Plain plate No. 2
20. Plain plate No. 1
21. Clutch hub
22. Washer
23. Cam reaction spring
24. Cam reaction spring
25. Clutch lifter driven cam
26. Clutch lifter drive cam
27. Thrust washer-outboard
28. Clutch housing
29. Bushing
30. Needle bearing
31. Oil pump drive spacer
32. Bearing
33. Thrust washer-inboard
34. Clutch pushrod

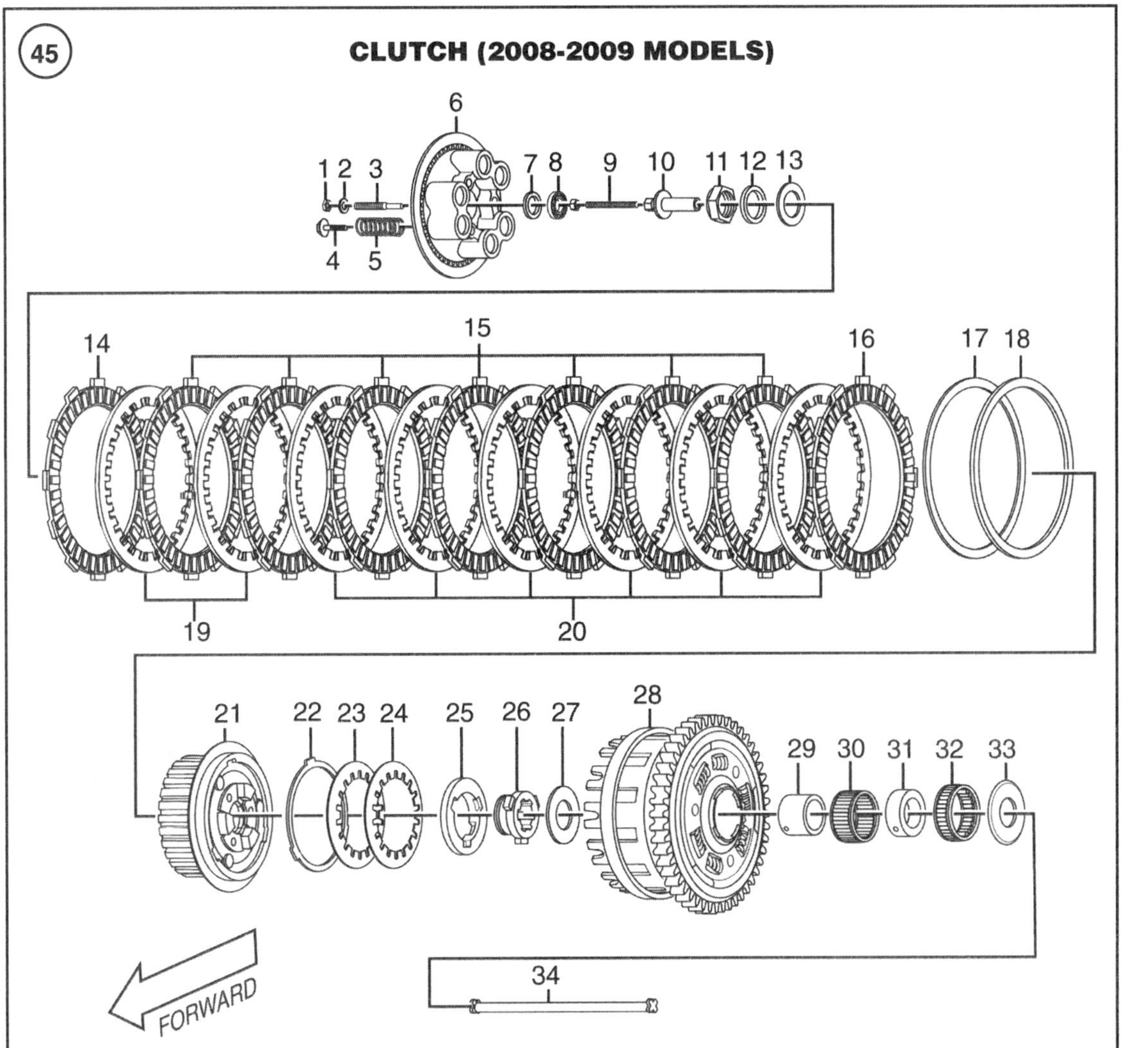

CLUTCH (2008-2009 MODELS)

45

1. Locknut
2. Washer
3. Clutch lifter adjuster
4. Clutch spring bolt
5. Clutch spring
6. Pressure plate
7. Thrust washer
8. Bearing
9. Nut and clutch release screw
10. Push piece
11. Clutch nut
12. Spring washer
13. Flat washer
14. Friction disc No. 2
15. Friction disc No. 1
16. Friction disc No. 3
17. Spring seat

18. Hub spring
19. Plain plate No. 2
20. Plain plate No. 1
21. Clutch hub
22. Washer
23. Cam reaction spring
24. Cam reaction spring
25. Clutch lifter driven cam
26. Clutch lifter drive cam
27. Thrust washer-outboard
28. Clutch housing
29. Bushing
30. Needle bearing
31. Oil pump drive spacer
32. Needle bearing
33. Thrust washer-inboard
34. Clutch pushrod

FORWARD

6

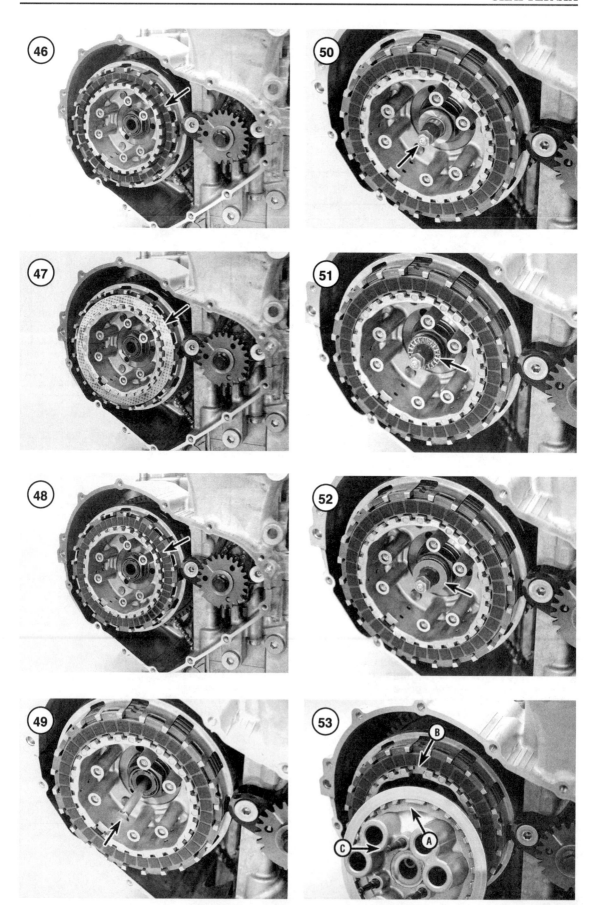

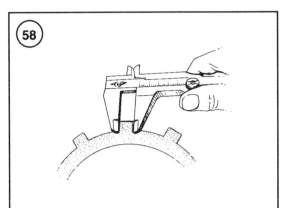

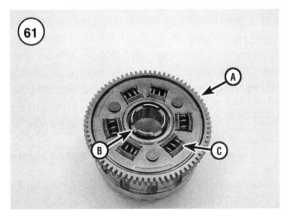

clutch housing for damage. Remove any small nicks with an oilstone. If damage is severe, replace the gear.

8. Inspect the damper springs (C, **Figure 61**). Replace the clutch housing if they are sagged or broken.

9. Check the bearing surface (**Figure 62**) of the clutch housing for signs of wear or damage. Replace the clutch housing if necessary.

10. Inspect the outer splines (**Figure 63**) and spring posts (**Figure 64**) in the clutch hub. If any shows signs of wear or galling, replace the clutch hub.

11. Inspect the clutch lifter driven cam engagement dogs (**Figure 65**) in the clutch hub. If any shows signs of wear or galling, replace the clutch hub.

12. Inspect the inner splines (A, **Figure 66**) and engagement dogs (B) on the clutch lifter drive cam. Inspect the engagement slots (**Figure 67**) on both sides of the clutch lifter driven cam. If excessive wear is found, replace the drive and driven cams as a set.

13. Check the cam retention springs (**Figure 68**) for cracks or other damage.

14. Visually inspect the needle bearing (A, **Figure 69**) for signs of wear or damage.

15. Check the inner and outer surfaces of the bushing (B, **Figure 69**) for signs of wear or damage.

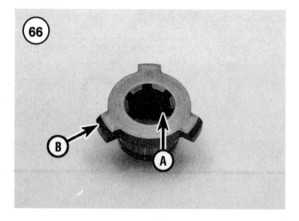

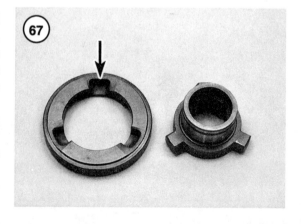

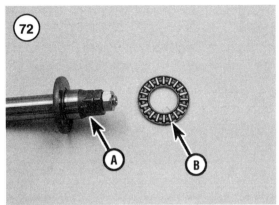

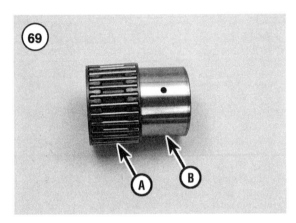

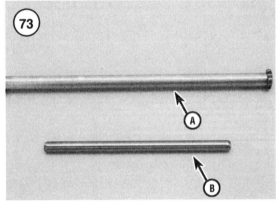

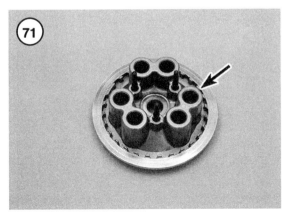

16. Install the bushing into the needle bearing. Rotate the bushing and check for wear. The parts must turn smoothly without excessive play or noise. Replace either/or both parts if necessary.

17. Inspect the pressure plate (**Figure 70**) and the spring towers (**Figure 71**) for wear or damage.

18. Check the clutch push piece (A, **Figure 72**) for wear or damage. Pay particular attention to the end that rides against the clutch right push rod.

19. Check the clutch push piece bearing (B, **Figure 72**). Make sure it rotates smoothly.

20. Install the bearing and washer onto the push piece, and rotate them by hand. Make sure all parts rotate smoothly. Replace any worn part.

21. Inspect the right (A, **Figure 73**) and left (B) clutch push rod for bending. Roll the rod along a surface plate or piece of plate glass. If the rod is bent or deformed in any way, it must be replaced. Otherwise it may hang up within the mainshaft tunnel, causing erratic clutch operation.

22. Inspect the clutch spring, and bolt for wear or damage.

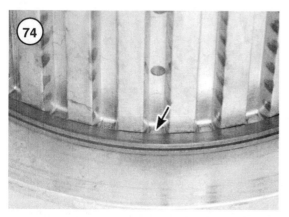

CLUTCH LIFTER ADJUSTER HEIGHT

Two 0.3 mm (0.012 in.) flat feeler gauges and a small flat plate are needed to adjust the clutch lifter height.

Adjustment

1. Set the clutch housing on the bench, and set the clutch hub into the housing.

2. Install the spring seat and spring onto the clutch hub. The concave side of the spring must face away from spring seat as shown in **Figure 74**.

3. Install the friction discs and plain plates by performing Step 16 of *Clutch Installation/Assembly* in this chapter.

4. Install the pressure plate, clutch springs, and the clutch spring bolts.

5. Evenly tighten the clutch spring bolts in a crisscross pattern. Tighten the clutch spring bolts to 9.5 N•m (84 in.-lb.).

6. Slide the pressure plate/hub assembly from the clutch housing, and set the assembly upright on the bench (**Figure 75**).

7. Set the clutch lifter driven cam into place on the clutch hub (**Figure 76**). Hold the driven cam against the adjusters, and use a feeler gauge to measure the height of each adjuster (**Figure 77**). The height of each clutch lifter adjuster should be within specification (**Table 1**). The height of each adjuster should be as close to the others as possible.

8. Perform the following to adjust the lifter height:
   a. Loosen the adjuster locknut (A, **Figure 78**), and turn out the adjuster (B).
   b. Set a 3 mm (0.012 in.) flat feeler gauge on each side of the adjuster.
   c. Set a flat plate over the feeler gauges, and press the gauges against the clutch hub (**Figure 79**).
   d. Slowly turn the adjuster screw (B, **Figure 78**) until slight resistance is felt.

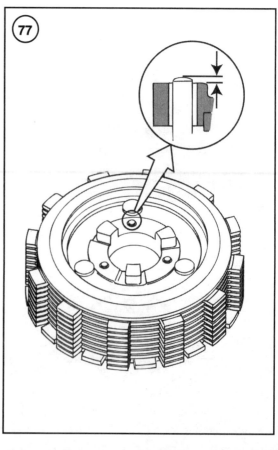

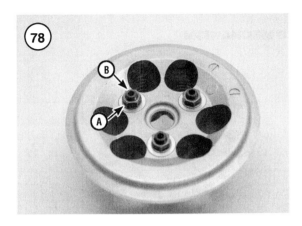

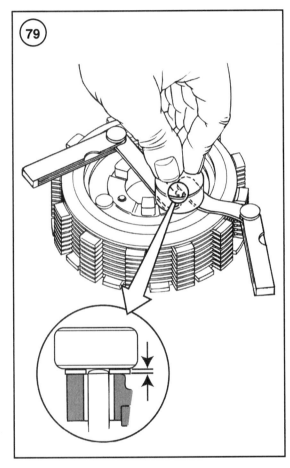

e. Tighten the clutch lifter adjuster locknut to 23 N•m (17 ft.-lb.).

f. Repeat for the other adjusters.

CLUTCH RELEASE MECHANISM

The clutch release mechanism sits is located within the engine sprocket cover on the left side of the engine. The hand lever on the left handlebar operates the cable-controlled clutch.

Removal/Installation

Refer to **Figure 80**.

1. Remove the engine sprocket cover (Chapter Seven).

2. Turn the engine sprocket cover over to gain access to the backside of the cover.

3. Check the operation of the clutch release arm (**Figure 81**). It should move smoothly. Continue with Step 4 and replace the release mechanism as necessary.

4. Bend the lock tab on the clutch release arm, and disconnect the clutch cable end from the arm.

5. Disengage the spring from the release arm, and remove the washer.

6. If necessary, remove the oil seal, upper bearing and the release camshaft from the engine sprocket cover.

7. Installation is the reverse of removal. Adjust the clutch cable (Chapter Three).

CLUTCH CABLE

Removal/Installation

1. Note how the clutch cable is routed through the frame and where the cable is secured with cable holders. The new cable must follow the same path as the old one.

2. If necessary lubricate the new clutch cable (on non-nylon lined cables).

3. Remove both front side fairing panels and front fairing (Chapter Fifteen).

4. Remove the fuel tank (Chapter Eight).

5. At the clutch lever, rotate the cable adjuster (A, **Figure 82**) to achieve maximum slack in the cable.

6. Disconnect the cable end from the clutch lever, and pass the cable out of the slots in the lever (B, **Figure 82**) and adjuster.

7. Disconnect the clutch cable end from the release arm (**Figure 83**).

8. At the inline adjuster, loosen the locknut (A, **Figure 84**), loosen the adjuster (B), and disconnect the cable from the bracket (C).

9. Unhook the cable from any brackets (**Figure 85**) or clamps on the frame.

10. Pull the old cable from the frame, and route the new cable along the same path.

11. Inspect the entire length of the clutch cable as it runs through the frame and engine. Make sure there are no kinks or sharp bends.

12. Apply grease to the upper cable end, and connect the cable end to the clutch lever. Pass the cable through the slot in the clutch lever and the adjuster. Turn the handlebar adjuster so its slot no longer aligns with the slot in the clutch lever.

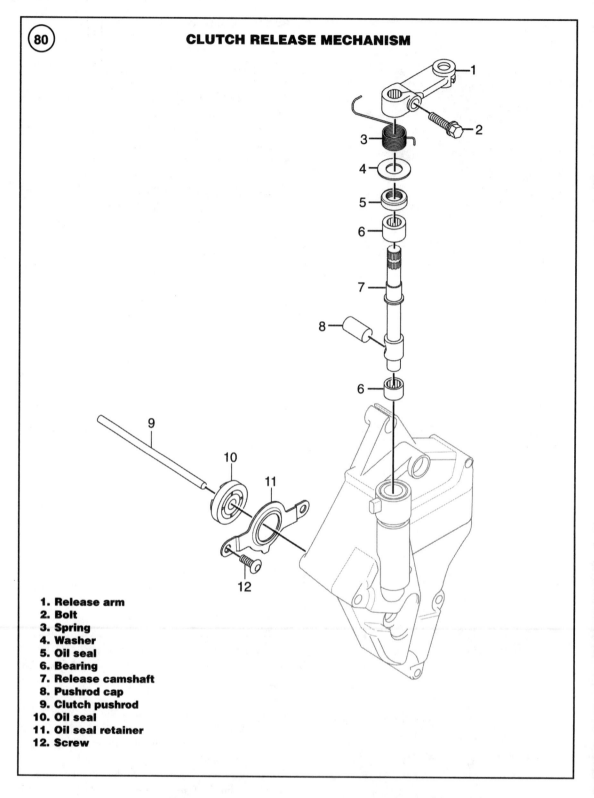

CLUTCH RELEASE MECHANISM

80

1. Release arm
2. Bolt
3. Spring
4. Washer
5. Oil seal
6. Bearing
7. Release camshaft
8. Pushrod cap
9. Clutch pushrod
10. Oil seal
11. Oil seal retainer
12. Screw

13. Apply grease to the lower cable end, and connect the cable (**Figure 83**) onto the release arm.

14. Adjust the clutch cable (Chapter Three).

15. Install the fuel tank (Chapter Eight).

16. Install both front side fairing panels and front fairing (Chapter Fifteen).

CLUTCH LEVER ASSEMBLY

Removal/Installation

1. Securely support the motorcycle on a level surface.

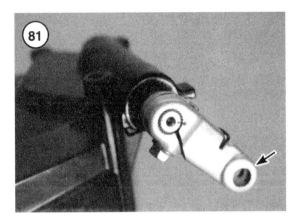

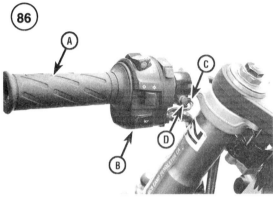

6

2. Remove the handlebar grip (A, **Figure 86**) (Chapter Thirteen).

3. Remove the left handlebar switch (B, **Figure 86**) (Chapter Nine).

4. Disconnect the clutch interlock switch (C, **Figure 86**).

5. At the clutch lever, rotate the cable adjuster (A, **Figure 82**) until its slot aligns with the slot (B) in the clutch lever.

6. Disconnect the cable end from the clutch lever, and pass the cable out of the slots in the lever and adjuster.

7. Loosen the clamp bolt (D, **Figure 86**) on the clutch lever assembly, and slide the clutch lever off the handlebar.

8. Installation is the reverse of removal.

   a. Align the gap in the clutch lever assembly clamp with the alignment dot on the handlebar.

   b. Tighten the clutch lever clamp bolt (D, **Figure 86**) to 10 N•m (89 in.-lb.).

   c. Adjust the clutch cable (Chapter Three).

Table 1 CLUTCH SPECIFICATIONS (2006–2007 MODELS)

Item	Standard mm (in.)	Service limit mm (in.)
Friction disc		
Total quantity (Nos. 1, 2, and 3)	9	
Thickness (Nos. 1, 2 and 3)	2.72–2.88 (0.107–0.113)	2.42 (0.095)
Claw width (Nos. 1, 2 and 3)	13.85–14.04 (0.5453–0.5528)	13.05 (0.5138)
Number of surface pads		
Friction disc No. 1	48 pads	–
Friction disc No. 2 and No 3	36 pads	–
Inside diameter		
Friction disc No. 1 and No. 3	111 (4.4)	–
Friction disc No. 2	118 (4.6)	–
Plain plates		
Total quantity (No. 1 plus No. 2)	7	
Plain plate No. 1	6	–
Plain Plate No. 2	1	–
Plain plate warp (No. 1 and No. 2)	–	0.10 (0.004)
Clutch lifter height	0.2–0.4 (0.008–0.016)	–

Table 2 CLUTCH SPECIFICATIONS (2008–2009 MODELS)

Item	Standard mm (in.)	Service limit mm (in.)
Friction disc		
Total quantity (Nos. 1, 2, and 3)	9	
Thickness (Nos. 1, 2 and 3)	2.72–2.88 (0.107–0.113)	2.42 (0.095)
Claw width (Nos. 1, 2 and 3)	13.85–14.04 (0.5453–0.5528)	13.05 (0.5138)
Number of surface pads		
Friction disc No. 1	48 pads	–
Friction disc No. 2 and No 3	36 pads	–
Inside diameter		
Friction disc No. 1 and No. 3	111 (4.4)	–
Friction disc No. 2	118 (4.6)	–
Plain plates		
Total quantity (No. 1 plus No. 2)	8	
Plain plate No. 1	6–8	–
Plain Plate No. 2	0–2	–
Plain plate thickness		
Plain plate No. 1	2.0 (0.08)	–
Plain Plate No. 2	1.6 (0.06)	–
Plain plate warp (No. 1 and No. 2)	–	0.10 (0.004)
Clutch lifter height	0.2–0.4 (0.008–0.016)	–

Table 3 CLUTCH TORQUE SPECIFICATIONS

Item	N•m	in.–lb.	ft.–lb.
Clutch nut	95	–	68.7
Clutch cover bolt	10	89	–
Clutch release screw locknut	11	97	–
Clutch lifter adjuster locknut	23	–	17
Clutch spring bolts	9.5	84	–
Clutch lever clamp bolt	10	89	–

CHAPTER SEVEN

TRANSMISSION, SHIFT MECHANISM AND ENGINE SPROCKET

This chapter covers transmission shaft and shift mechanism service. Refer to Chapter Five for shaft removal and installation.

Tables 1-3 are at the end if this chapter.

ENGINE SPROCKET COVER

Removal/Installation

1. Support the motorcycle on a level surface.
2. Remove the fuel tank (Chapter Eight).
3. Remove the lower fairing and the left side fairing panel (Chapter Fifteen).
4. At the clutch lever, rotate the cable adjuster (**Figure 1**) to achieve maximum slack in the cable.
5. Disconnect the clutch cable (**Figure 2**) from the release lever.
6. Remove the external shift lever assembly (**Figure 3**) as described at the end of this chapter.
7. Remove the engine sprocket cover bolts, and lift the cover (**Figure 4**) from the crankcase. Account for the two dowels behind the cover.
8. Remove the left side clutch push rod (**Figure 5**) from the mainshaft so it will not be damaged.
9. Installation is the reverse of removal. Note the following:
   a. Lubricate the left clutch push rod (**Figure 5**) with grease (Suzuki Super Grease A or equivalent), and install the rod into the mainshaft.
   b. Align the hole in the clutch release cylinder with the end of the clutch push rod, and install the engine sprocket cover. Tighten the bolts securely.
   c. If necessary, adjust the shift pedal height and clutch cable (Chapter Three).

ENGINE SPROCKET

Removal/Installation

> *NOTE*
> *This procedure is shown with the engine removed from the frame and partially disassembled for photo clarity.*

1. Support the motorcycle on a level surface with the rear wheel off the ground. Shift the transmission into gear.
2. Remove the engine sprocket cover as described in this chapter.
3. Remove the speed sensor rotor bolt (A, **Figure 6**) and remove the speed sensor rotor (B).
4. Remove the engine sprocket nut (**Figure 7**) and its washer (**Figure 8**).
5. Remove the cotter pin (**Figure 9**) from the rear axle nut, on models so equipped.
6. Loosen the rear axle nut (**Figure 10**).

7. Loosen the chain adjuster locknut (A, **Figure 11**) and loosen the adjuster (B) on each side of the swing arm.

8. Slide the wheel forward to slacken the chain.

9. Slide the engine sprocket (**Figure 12**) off the countershaft, and remove the sprocket from between the chain runs. Set the chain onto the countershaft.

10. Installation is the reverse of removal. Note the following:

    a. Install the engine sprocket into the chain, and then slide the sprocket onto the countershaft.

    b. Apply Threadlocker (Suzuki Thread Lock 1342) to the threads of the countershaft, and

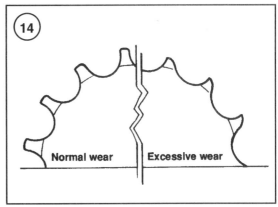

Normal wear   Excessive wear

tighten the engine sprocket nut (**Figure 7**) to 115 N•m (85 ft.-lb.).

  c. Tighten the speed sensor rotor bolt (A, **Figure 6**) to 25 N•m (18 ft.-lb.).

  d. Adjust the drive chain (Chapter Three).

Inspection

1. Inspect the teeth (A, **Figure 13**) of the engine sprocket for any worn, chipped or missing teeth (**Figure 14**). Replace the engine sprocket if wear is noted.

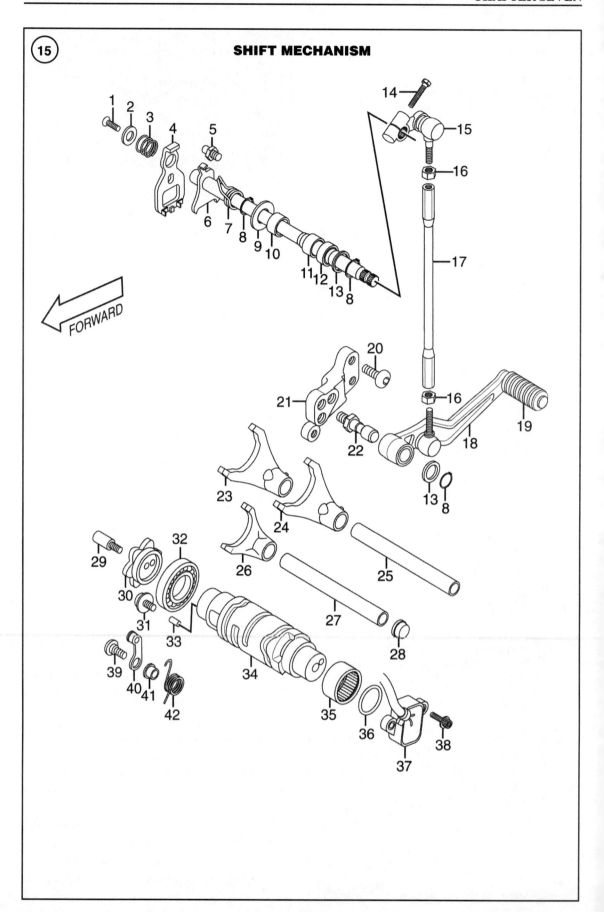

SHIFT MECHANISM

FORWARD

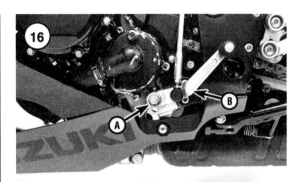

1. Screw
2. Washer
3. Spring
4. Shift plate
5. Retainer bolt
6. Shift shaft
7. Shift shaft return spring
8. Snap ring
9. Washer
10. Bearing
11. Bearing
12. Oil seal
13. Washer
14. Bolt
15. Shift lever--upper
16. Locknut
17. Shift rod
18. Shift lever--lower
19. Cover
20. Bolt
21. Mounting bracket
22. Pivot post
23. Shift fork--countershaft
24. Shift fork--countershaft
25. Shift shaft
26. Shift fork--mainshaft
27. Shift shaft
28. Plug
29. Shift cam bolt
30. Shift cam
31. Screw
32. Bearing
33. Pin
34. Shift drum
35. Needle bearing
36. O-ring
37. Gear position sensor
38. Screw
39. Bolt
40. Stopper lever
41. Spacer
42. Stopper lever return spring

CAUTION
If the engine sprocket is replaced, also replace the driven sprocket and the drive chain. Never install a new drive chain over worn sprockets or a worn chain over new sprockets. The old parts prematurely wear out the new ones.

2. If the engine sprocket requires replacement, also inspect the drive chain and the driven sprocket (Chapter Eleven).

3. Inspect the inner splines (B, **Figure 13**) of the engine sprocket for excessive wear. If wear is noted, also inspect the splines on the countershaft.

EXTERNAL SHIFT MECHANISM

Removal/Installation

Refer to **Figure 15**.

1. Remove the fairing side panel from the each side (Chapter Fifteen).

2. Remove the engine sprocket cover as described in this chapter.

3. Remove the clutch cover and the clutch (Chapter Six).

4. Remove the snap ring and the washer (A, **Figure 16**) and remove the shift lever (B) from the mounting bracket pivot post.

5. Place an alignment dot on the shift lever opposite the dot on the shift shaft so the lever can be reinstalled in its original position.

6. Loosen the clamp bolt (A, **Figure 17**) on the shift lever. Slide the shift lever (B, **Figure 17**) from the shift shaft.

7. Remove the shift lever and shift rod assembly (C, **Figure 17**).

NOTE
The following steps are shown with the engine removed for photo clarity.

8. Remove the snap ring (A, **Figure 18**) and washer (B) from the shift shaft.

9. On the right side of the engine, pull the shift shaft assembly (**Figure 19**) from the crankcase. Note that the arms of the shift shaft spring straddle the shift fork retainer bolt (A, **Figure 20**).

10. Account for the washer as it may come out with the shift shaft.

11. Installation is the reverse of removal. Note the following:

   a. Ensure the washer (A, **Figure 21**) is in place on the shift shaft.

   b. Slide the shift shaft into the shift shaft bearing in the right side of the upper crankcase and out through the bearing and oil seal on the left side.

   c. Ensure the shift shaft spring straddles the shift fork shaft retainer bolt (A, **Figure 20**).

   d. Rotate the shift cam as necessary so the shift pawls engage the shift cam (B, **Figure 20**).

   e. Install the washer (B, **Figure 18**) and snap ring (A) onto the end of the shift shaft. Completely seat the snap ring in its groove on the shift shaft.

Inspection

1. Clean all parts in solvent, and dry them with compressed air.

2. Inspect the return spring (B, **Figure 21**) on the shift shaft assembly. If the spring is broken or weak, replace it as follows:

   a. Remove the washer and snap ring from the shift shaft. Slide the return spring from the shaft.

   b. Install the *new* shift shaft return spring so its arms straddle the tang (C, **Figure 21**) on the shift plate.

   c. Seat a new snap ring into the groove in the shift shaft.

3. Inspect the shift pawls (D, **Figure 21**) on the pawl plate for excessive wear or damage. If necessary, replace the pawl plate as follows:

   a. Remove the screw (A, **Figure 22**) and washer from the end of the shift shaft.

   b. Remove the pawl plate spring (B, **Figure 22**) and the pawl plate (C).

   c. Install the new pawl plate so its hole (D, **Figure 22**) engages the post on the shift plate. Install the pawl plate so the shift pawls face the shift plate.

   d. Install the spring (B, **Figure 22**) and washer.

   e. Apply threadlock (Suzuki Thread Lock 1342 or equivalent) to the threads of the screw (A, **Figure 22**) and tighten securely.

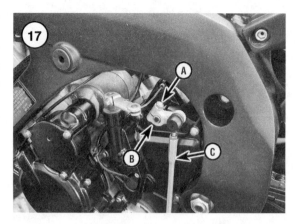

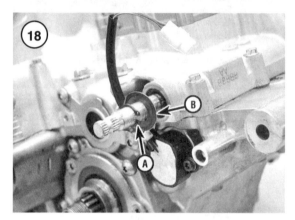

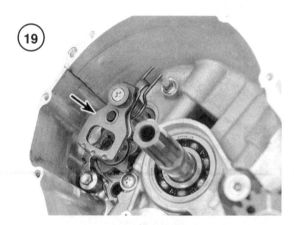

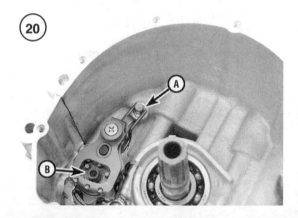

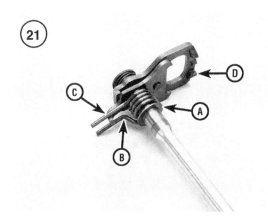

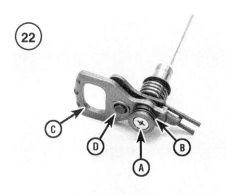

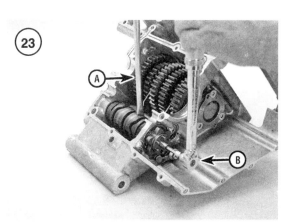

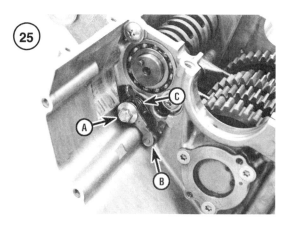

4. Inspect the shift shaft for bending, wear or other damage.

5. Inspect the splines on the end of the shift shaft for damage.

6. Replace any worn or damaged part.

INTERNAL SHIFT MECHANISM

The internal shift mechanism includes the shift drum, shift forks and stopper lever. These assemblies reside in the lower crankcase.

Refer to **Figure 15**.

Removal

1. Remove the external shift mechanism as described in this chapter and the gear position sensor (Chapter Nine).

2. Remove the engine from the frame, and separate the crankcase (Chapter Five).

3. Set the lower crankcase upright on the bench.

> *CAUTION*
> *Step 4 is necessary to avoid damage to the shift forks during shift cam bolt removal.*

4. Insert a flat bladed screwdriver (A, **Figure 23**) between the shift drum and the crankcase to keep the shift drum from rotating in Step 5.

5. Loosen the shift cam mounting bolt (B, **Figure 23**), and remove the screwdriver.

6. Use a screwdriver and press the stopper lever down and away from the shift cam to relieve pressure on the shift cam.

7. Remove the shift cam mounting bolt (A, **Figure 24**) and shift cam (B) from the shift drum.

8. Remove the stopper lever bolt (A, **Figure 25**).

9. Remove the stopper lever (B, **Figure 25**), spring and spacer (C).

10. Remove both shift drum and shift fork retainer bolts (**Figure 26**).

NOTE
The countershaft shift forks are identi-
cal in appearance. Mark the shift forks
during removal so they can be identi-
fied during assembly.

11. Note the position of the countershaft shift forks
(A, **Figure 27**) on the shift fork shaft (B). Each shift
fork must be reinstalled with the same orientation.

12. Partially remove the countershaft shift fork shaft
(A, **Figure 28**) from the right side of the crankcase.
Mark this shift fork (B, **Figure 28**) *L*.

13. Pull the countershaft shift fork shaft (A, **Figure
29**) from the crankcase from the right shift fork (B).
Mark this shift fork *R*.

14. Remove both shift forks (A, **Figure 30**), and
slide the shift drum (B) from the upper crankcase.

15. Set the upper crankcase upside down on the
bench.

16. Remove the washer and plug (**Figure 31**) from
the end of the shift shaft.

17. Remove the shift fork (A, **Figure 32**) and shaft
(B) from the upper crankcase.

18. Inspect the components as described in this section.

Installation

1. Set the upper crankcase upside down on the
bench.

2. Install the shift fork (A, **Figure 32**) and shaft (B)
onto the upper crankcase.

3. Install the washer and plug (**Figure 31**) onto the
end of the shift shaft. Make sure the washer is seated
correctly in the crankcase groove.

4. Set the upper crankcase upright on the bench.

5. Install the shift fork *R* (A, **Figure 33**) and shift
fork *L* (B) onto the correct location on the countershaft gears.

6. Insert the shift drum (A, **Figure 34**) through the
right side of the lower crankcase, and seat it in the
needle bearing (B) in the opposite side of the case.

Push it in until it bottoms in the crankcase (B, **Figure 30**).

7. Lubricate the countershaft shift fork shaft with engine oil.

8. Insert the countershaft shift fork shaft (A, **Figure 29**) partially into the crankcase and through the right shift fork (B).

9. Continue to slide shift fork shaft (A, **Figure 28**) through the left shift fork (B), and seat the shaft in its crankcase boss (C, **Figure 27**). Position each shift fork as noted during removal. Correctly seat each shift fork guide pin (D, **Figure 27**) into its slot in the shift drum.

10. Apply threadlock (Suzuki Thread Lock 1342 or equivalent) to the threads of the shift drum and shift fork retainer bolts (**Figure 26**). Install both bolts and tighten to 10 N•m (89 in.-lb.).

11. Install the spacer (C, **Figure 25**), stopper lever (B), and spring.

12. Apply threadlock (Suzuki Thread Lock 1342 or equivalent) to the threads of the stopper lever bolt (A, **Figure 25**). Install the bolt and tighten the bolt to 10 N•m (89 in.-lb.).

13. Make sure the arm of the stopper lever spring engages the cutout in the stopper lever.

14. Use a screwdriver and press the stopper lever down (**Figure 35**) to allow room for shift cam.

15. Insert a flat bladed screwdriver (A, **Figure 23**) between the shift drum and the crankcase to keep the shift drum from rotating in Step 5.

16. Install the shift cam (B, **Figure 24**) and mounting bolt (A), and tighten the bolt to 13 N•m (115 in.-lb.). Remove the screwdriver and index the stopper lever onto the shift cam.

17. Assembly the crankcase (Chapter Five) and install the engine into the frame (Chapter Five).

Inspection

During inspection, replace any part that is worn, damaged or out of specification.

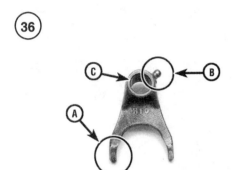

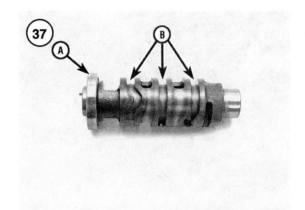

1. Clean all parts in solvent, and thoroughly dry them with compressed air.

2. Inspect each shift fork for signs of wear or cracking. Check for any burned marks on the fingers of the shift forks (A, **Figure 36**).

3. Check the guide pin (B, **Figure 36**) on each shift fork for wear or damage.

4. Check the bore (C, **Figure 36**) of each shift fork and check the shift fork shaft for burrs, wear or pitting.

5. Install each shift fork onto its shaft, slide it back and forth, and check its movement. Each fork should move freely on its shaft with no binding.

6. Roll each shift fork shaft over a flat surface such as a surface plate or a piece of plate glass. If a shaft is bent, it must be replaced.

7. Rotate the shift drum bearing (A, **Figure 37**). Make sure it operates smoothly with no signs of wear or damage. Slide the bearing off the shift drum, and install a new one.

8. Check the grooves in the shift drum (B, **Figure 37**) for wear or roughness. If any of the groove profiles have excessive wear or damage, replace the shift drum.

9. Inspect the shift cam ramps and posts on the shift cam. If wear is noted, replace the shift cam.

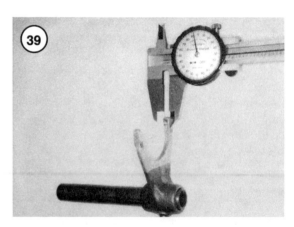

CAUTION
Replace marginally worn shift forks. Worn forks can cause the transmission to slip out of gear, leading to more serious and expensive damage.

10. Install each shift fork into the groove in its respective gear. Use a flat feeler gauge and measure the clearance between the fork and the groove as shown in **Figure 38**. If the shift fork-to-groove clearance exceeds the wear limit specified in **Table 2**, perform the following:

    a. Measure the thickness of the shift fork fingers (**Figure 39**). Replace the shift fork if the thickness is outside the range specified in **Table 2**.

    b. Measure the width of the shift fork groove in the gear (**Figure 40**). Replace the gear if the groove width is outside the range specified in **Table 2**.

11. Inspect the stopper lever (A, **Figure 41**), and spring (B) for cracks or fatigue.

TRANSMISSION

During the following procedures, the term *mainshaft* refers to the transmission input shaft. The mainshaft is splined to the clutch hub. When the clutch is

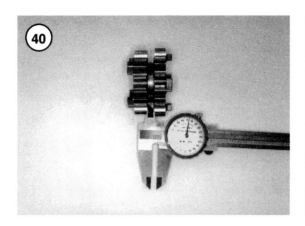

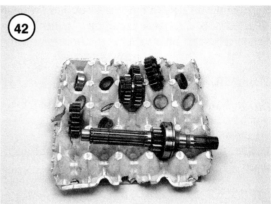

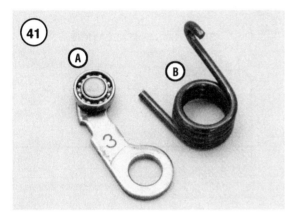

engaged, the hub is driven by the clutch housing via the crankshaft primary drive gear.

The term countershaft refers to the transmission output shaft. The countershaft drives the engine sprocket.

The manufacturer parts information calls the input shaft the countershaft and the output shaft the driveshaft. Note this terminology differences if replacement parts are required.

Removal/Installation

Remove and install the transmission mainshaft and countershaft assemblies as described in *Crankcase* in Chapter Five.

Preliminary Inspection

1. Place an assembled shaft into a large can or plastic bucket, and thoroughly clean the assembly with a petroleum-based solvent such as kerosene and a stiff brush. Dry the assembly with compressed air or let it sit on rags to drip dry. Do this for the other shaft assembly.
2. Inspect the components for excessive wear. Any burrs, pitting or roughness on the teeth of a gear will

cause wear on its mated gear. Minor roughness can be cleaned up with an oilstone but there is little point in attempting to remove deep scars.
3. Carefully check the engagement dogs. If any is chipped, worn, rounded or missing, replace the affected gear.
4. Rotate the transmission bearings by hand. Check for roughness, noise and radial play. Replace any worn or damaged bearing.
5. Slide the clutch pushrods into the mainshaft, and check for binding. If binding occurs, check the pushrods for bending or damage. Also inspect the mainshaft tunnel for debris. Clean out the tunnel if necessary.
6. If the transmission shafts are satisfactory and will not be disassembled, apply clean engine oil to all components, and reinstall them into the crankcase (Chapter Five).

Service Notes

1. As a part is removed from a shaft, set it into an egg crate **Figure 42** in the exact order of removal and with the same orientation the part had when installed on the shaft. Note any additional shims that may have been installed during a previous repair.
2. The snap rings fit tightly on the transmission shafts. All snap rings must be replaced during assembly.
3. Snap rings will turn and fold over making removal and installation difficult. To ease replacement, open a snap ring with snap ring pliers while at the same time holding the back of the snap ring with conventional pliers.
4. When installing a snap ring, align the gap in the snap ring with a groove in the shaft as shown in **Figure 43**.
5. Snap rings have one flat edge and one rounded edge (**Figure 44**). Install a snap ring so the sharp edge faces away from the gear producing the thrust.

6. Align the oil hole in the gear or bushing with an oil holes in the shaft when installing a splined gear or a splined bushing onto a shaft.

Mainshaft

Disassembly

Refer to **Figure 45** and **Figure 46**.
1. Slide the needle bearing and oil seal off the mainshaft.

> *NOTE*
> *The snap ring (**Figure 47**) at the end of the mainshaft sits beneath sixth gear. The sixth gear snap ring must be removed from its groove so sixth and second gears can be moved to provide access to this snap ring.*

2. Slide the second and sixth gears toward the end of the shaft to expose the snap ring. Release the snap ring (**Figure 47**) from its groove, and move the snap ring (**Figure 48**) down the shaft toward the third/fourth combination gear.
3. Slide the sixth and second gears toward the third/fourth combination gear.
4. Use a scribe to pry one end of the snap ring (**Figure 49**) from the outmost groove on the mainshaft. Grasp this end with needlenose pliers. Work around the shaft with the scribe, pry the snap ring from the groove and remove it. Discard the snap ring.
5. Slide second gear from the mainshaft.
6. Slide the sixth gear and the sixth gear splined bushing from the mainshaft.
7. Remove the splined washer and the snap ring.
8. Slide off the third/fourth combination gear.
9. Remove the snap ring and washer.
10. Slide off fifth gear and the fifth gear bushing.
11. Keep the parts in the exact order of removal and with the same orientation they had while installed on the mainshaft (**Figure 42**).
12. Inspect the mainshaft components as described in this chapter.

Assembly

1. Apply a light coat of clean engine oil to all sliding surfaces before installing any part.
2. Slide the fifth gear bushing (A, **Figure 50**) onto the mainshaft and seat it against the first gear.
3. Position the fifth gear (B, **Figure 50**) so its engagement dogs face out away from first gear, and slide the fifth gear onto the mainshaft. Seat the gear over its bushing.

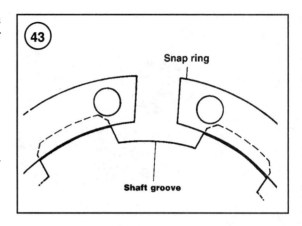

Snap ring

Shaft groove

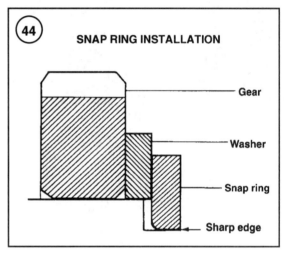

SNAP RING INSTALLATION

Gear

Washer

Snap ring

Sharp edge

4. Install the washer (A, **Figure 51**).
5. Install a new snap ring (B, **Figure 51**) so its flat side faces out away from the washer. Make sure the snap ring (**Figure 52**) is properly seated in the mainshaft groove.
6. Position the third/fourth combination gear so the larger fourth gear (A, **Figure 53**) goes on first toward fifth gear. Align the oil hole (B, **Figure 53**) in the gear with a hole in the mainshaft (C), slide the combination gear onto the shaft and seat the gear up against fifth gear.

> *NOTE*
> *The snap ring installed in Step 7 must be positioned down on the shaft so the snap ring can be installed in Step 10.*

7. Slide a *new* snap ring (A, **Figure 54**) and washer (B) onto the mainshaft. Do not install the snap ring into its groove at this time. Instead, slide the snap ring toward the third/fourth combination gear (C, **Figure 54**). The flat side of this snap ring must face in toward third/fourth combination gear.
8. Position the splined bushing so its oil hole (A, **Figure 55**) aligns with the oil hole (B) in the mainshaft and install the splined bushing.

TRANSMISSION

45

FORWARD

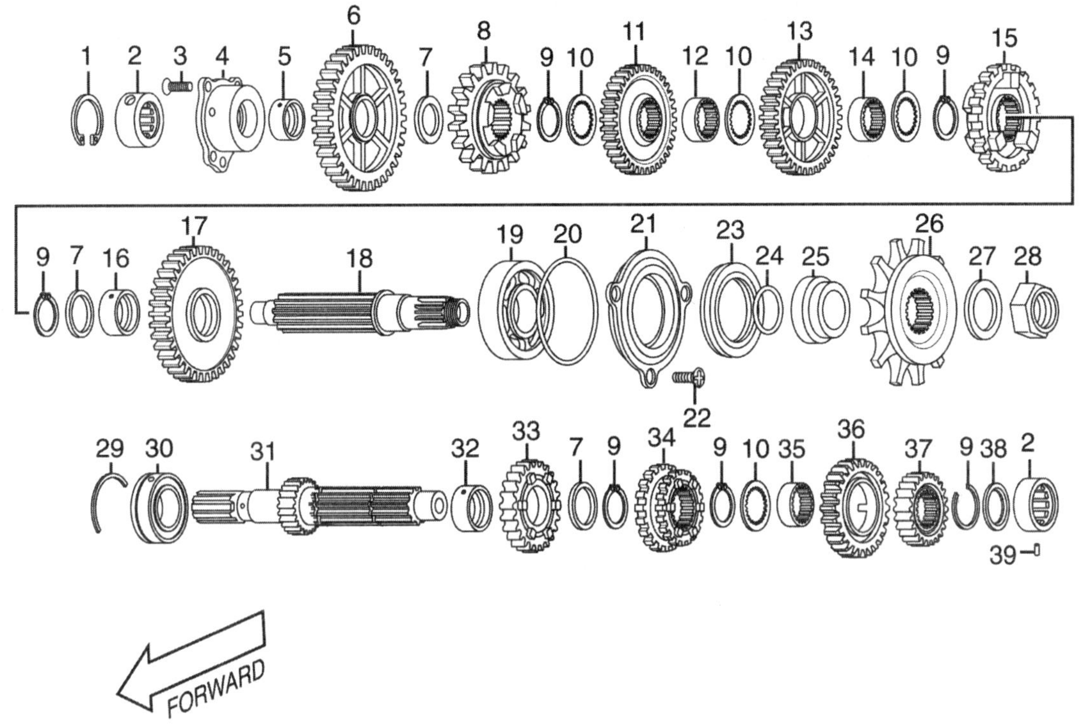

1. Snap ring
2. Needle bearing
   (2006-2007 models only)
3. Bolt
4. Bearing housing–right side
5. Bushing
6. First gear
7. Washer
8. Fifth gear
9. Snap ring
10. Washer
11. Forth gear
12. Splined bushing
13. Third gear
14. Splined bushing
15. Sixth gear
16. Bushing
17. Second gear
18. Countershaft
19. Ball bearing

20. O-ring
21. Bearing retainer—left side
22. Bolt
23. Oil seal
24. O-ring
25. Spacer
26. Drive sprocket
27. Washer
28. Nut
29. C-clip
30. Ball bearing
31. Mainshaft
32. Bushing
33. Fifth gear
34. Third/forth gear
35. Splined bushing
36. Sixth gear
37. Second gear
38. Oil seal
39. Pin

7

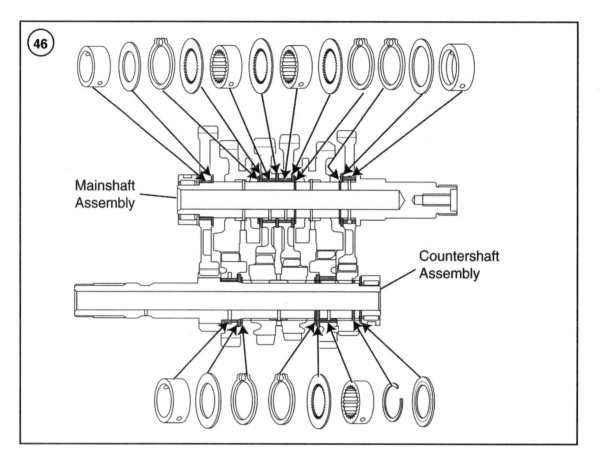

Mainshaft Assembly

Countershaft Assembly

9. Position the sixth gear so its engagement dogs (**Figure 56**) go on first toward the third/fourth combination gear, and install the sixth gear. Seat the sixth gear onto the sixth gear bushing.

10. Position second gear so its recessed side (**Figure 57**) faces in toward sixth gear, and install the second gear (**Figure 58**).

11. Install a *new* snap ring and seat it in the groove in the end of the mainshaft (**Figure 49**).

12. Push sixth and second gears toward the end of the mainshaft.

13. Move the snap ring (**Figure 48**), installed on Step 7, into its correct groove next to sixth gear (**Figure 47**). Make sure the snap ring is completely seated in the groove.

14. Position the new oil seal onto the mainshaft so its concave side faces out (**Figure 59**), and push the seal up against the snap ring.

15. Install the needle bearing (**Figure 60**).

16. Refer to **Figure 61** for correct placement of all gears. Make sure all snap rings are completely seated in their respective grooves.

17. After both transmission shafts have been assembled, mesh the two assemblies together in the correct position (**Figure 62**). Confirm that each gear properly engages its adjoining gear, where applicable. Check

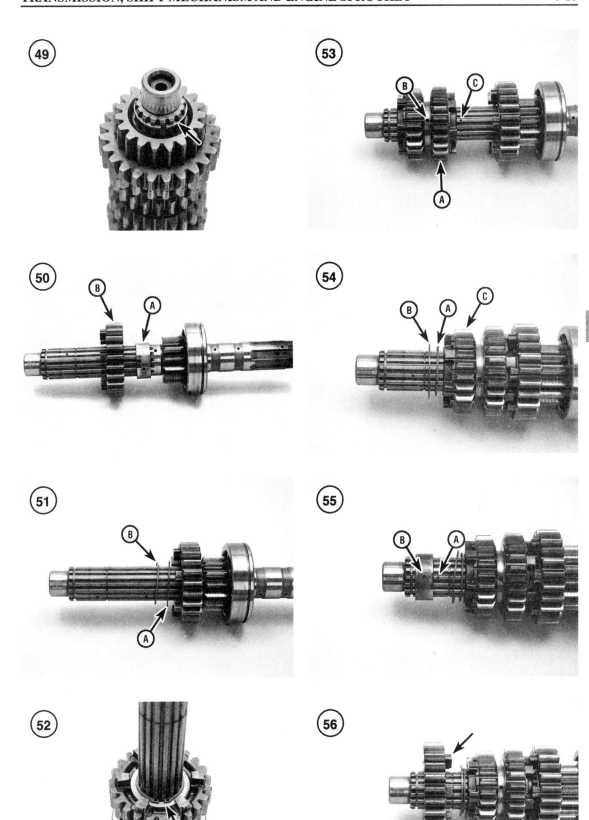

the shaft assemblies now before installing them into the crankcase.

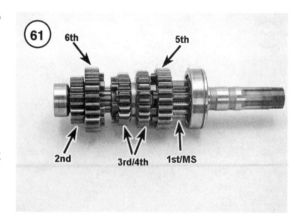

Countershaft

Disassembly

Refer to **Figure 45** and **Figure 46**.

1. Slide off the first gear and the first gear bushing from the countershaft.

2. Remove the washer and fifth gear.

3. Remove the snap ring and the splined washer.

4. Slide off the forth gear and the forth gear splined bushing from the countershaft.

5. Remove the splined washer, third gear, splined bushing, and second splined washer.

6. Remove the snap ring and sixth gear.

7. Remove the snap ring, washer, second gear, and the second gear bushing.

8. Keep the parts in the exact order of removal and with the same orientation they had while installed on the countershaft (**Figure 63**).

9. Inspect the countershaft components as described in this chapter.

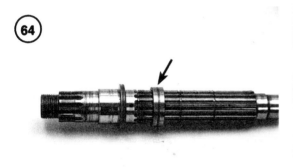

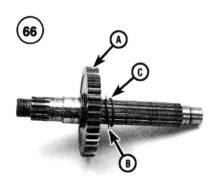

Assembly

1. Apply a light coat of clean engine oil to all sliding surfaces prior to installing any part.

2. Slide the second gear bushing (**Figure 64**) onto the countershaft, and seat it against the shoulder on the shaft.

3. Position the second gear so its engagement slots (**Figure 65**) go on last, and install the second gear (A, **Figure 66**).

4. Slide the washer (B, **Figure 66**) onto the countershaft, and then install a *new* snap ring (C) with its flat side facing out away from the washer. Seat the snap ring (**Figure 67**) in the groove next to second gear.

5. Position the sixth gear so its shift dogs and shift fork groove faces out (**Figure 68**) away from second gear, and install the sixth gear.

6. Install the new snap ring (A, **Figure 69**) so its flat side face in toward sixth gear. Seat the snap ring in the countershaft groove, and install a splined washer (B, **Figure 69**).

7. Position the splined bushing onto the countershaft so the oil hole (A, **Figure 70**) in the bushing aligns with oil holes (B) in the countershaft, and install the splined bushing.

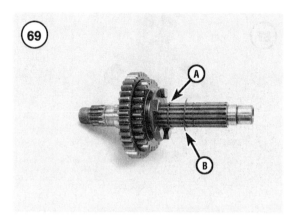

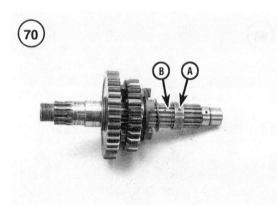

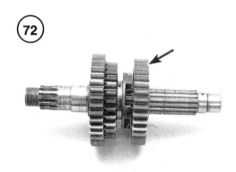

8. Position the third gear so flat side (**Figure 71**) goes on last and faces out. Seat the gear on the splined bushing (**Figure 72**).

9. Install a splined washer (A, **Figure 73**), and seat it next to third gear.

10. Position the splined bushing so its oil hole (B, **Figure 73**) aligns with the oil holes (C) in the countershaft, and install the splined washer.

11. Position the fourth gear so its engagement slot side (**Figure 74**) goes on last facing out away from third gear, and install the forth gear (A, **Figure 75**).

12. Install a splined washer (B, **Figure 75**) and *new* snap ring (C). Position the snap ring so its flat side faces out away from the washer, and seat the snap ring in the groove (**Figure 76**) next to fourth gear.

13. Position the fifth gear so the side with the shift fork groove (A, **Figure 77**) goes on first facing in toward fourth gear. Align the oil hole in the gear (B, **Figure 77**) with the hole in the countershaft (C).

14. Install the fifth gear (A, **Figure 78**) and the washer (B) onto the shaft.

15. Install the first gear bushing (**Figure 79**) onto the shaft.

16. Position the first gear so its flat side going on last (**Figure 80**) facing out away from fifth gear, and install the first gear (**Figure 81**) next to fifth gear.

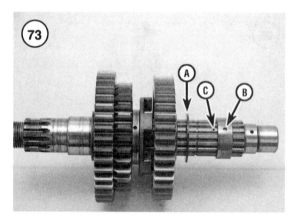

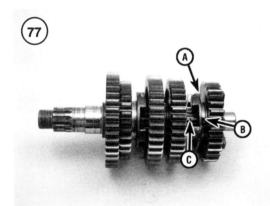

17. Refer to **Figure 82** for correct placement of all gears. Make sure all snap rings are completely seated in their respective grooves.

18. After both transmission shafts have been assembled, mesh the two assemblies together in the correct position (**Figure 62**). Confirm that each gear properly engages its adjoining gear, where applicable. Make sure they are correctly assembled.

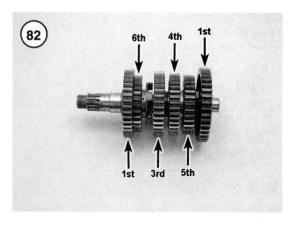

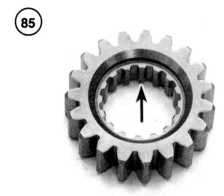

Inspection (Both Shafts)

Replace any part that is worn, damaged or out of specification. When replacing a defective gear, also replace its mate on the opposite shaft even through the mate may not show as much damage or wear. The old gear will rapidly wear down the new gear.

1. Check each gear for excessive wear, burrs, pitting, and chipped or missing teeth (A, **Figure 83**).

2. Inspect the engagement dogs (B, **Figure 83**) and the engagement slots (**Figure 84**) for wear or damage.

3. Check the inner splines on sliding gears (**Figure 85**), on splined bushings (A, **Figure 86**), splined washers. Replace any part with excessive wear or damage.

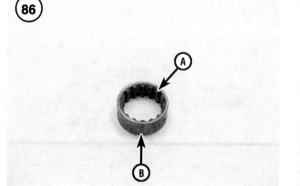

4. Inspect the bearing surfaces on rotating gears (**Figure 87**) and bushings (B, **Figure 86**) for wear, pitting or damage.

5. Check the shift fork groove (A, **Figure 88**) for wear, pitting or damage.

6. Check all oil holes (B, **Figure 88**) on the gears and bushings. Blow them clear with compressed air as necessary.

7. Inspect the washers for bending wear or damage. Replace if necessary.

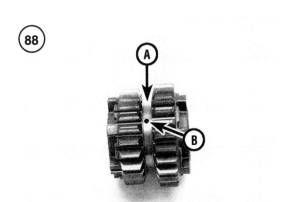

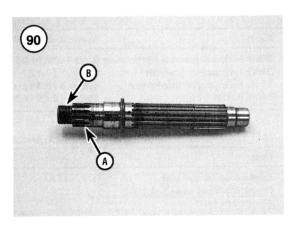

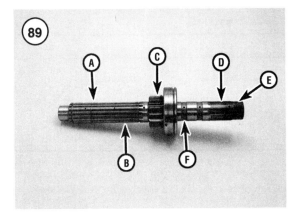

10 Inspect the teeth of first gear (C, **Figure 89**) on the mainshaft.

11. Inspect the clutch hub splines (D, **Figure 89**) and clutch nut threads (E) on the mainshaft.

12. Inspect the engine sprocket splines (A, **Figure 90**) and engine sprocket nut threads (B) on the countershaft.

13. Check all oil holes (F, **Figure 89**) on both shafts. Blow them clear with compressed air as necessary.

14. If any spline is damaged, the shaft must be replaced. If the threads have burrs or have minor damage, clean them with a proper size metric thread die. If the threads are excessively worn, replace the shaft.

15. Make sure that all gears and bushings slide smoothly on their respective shaft splines.

8. Measure the shift fork-to-gear clearance as described in *Internal Gearshift Mechanism* this chapter.

9. Inspect the snap ring grooves (A, **Figure 89**) and the shaft splines (B) on each shaft.

Table 1 TRANSMISSION SPECIFICATIONS

Item	Standard
Transmission gear ratios	
First gear	2.785 (39/14)
Second gear	2.052 (39/19)
Third gear	1.714 (36/21)
Fourth gear	1.500 (36/24)
Fifth gear	1.347 (31/23)
Sixth gear	1.208 (29/24)
Primary reduction ratio	
GSX-R600 models	1.974 (77/39)
GSX-R750 models	1.761 (74/42)
Secondary reduction ratio	
GSX-R600 models	2.687 (43/16)
GSX-R750 models	2.647 (45/17)
Drive chain	
GSX-R600	
2006-2007 models	**RK 525 SMOZ7Y, 114 links**
2008-2009 models	**RK 525 SMOZ8, 114 links**
GSX-R750	**RK 525 R0Z5Y, 116 links**

7

Table 2 SHIFT MECHANISM SPECIFICATIONS

Item	Standard mm (in.)	Service limit mm (in.)
Shift fork–to–groove clearance	0.10–0.30 (0.004–0.012)	0.50 (0/020)
Shift fork groove width	5.0–5.1 (0.197–0.201)	–
Shift fork finger thickness	4.8–4.9 (0.189–0.193)	–
Shift pedal height	65–75 (2.56–2.95)	–

Table 3 SHIFT MECHANISM TORQUE SPECIFICATIONS

Item	N•m	in.-lb.	ft.-lb.
Engine sprocket nut	115	–	85
Front footrest bracket bolt	23	–	17
Shift cam bolt	10	98	–
Shift cam retainer bolt*	13	115	–
Shift drum bearing retainer bolt*	10	89	–
Speed sensor rotor bolt	25	–	18
Stopper lever bolt*	10	97	–
*Apply threading locking compound.			

CHAPTER EIGHT

AIR, FUEL INJECTION, EMISSIONS AND EXHAUST SYSTEMS

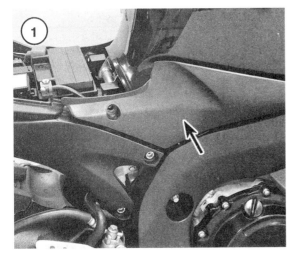

This chapter covers the air and fuel delivery systems, emissions systems, and the exhaust system.

Tables 1-3 are at the end of the chapter.

FUEL TANK

Supporting the Fuel Tank

1. Securely support the motorcycle on a level surface.
2. Remove the rider and passenger seats (Chapter Fifteen)
3. Remove the seat side covers (**Figure 1**) (Chapter Fifteen).
4. Remove the tank prop from the storage compartment.
5. Remove the fuel tank mounting bolt and washer (**Figure 2**). Account for the collar and damper installed on the tank mount.
6. Lift the front of the fuel tank, and support the tank with the prop rod (**Figure 3**).

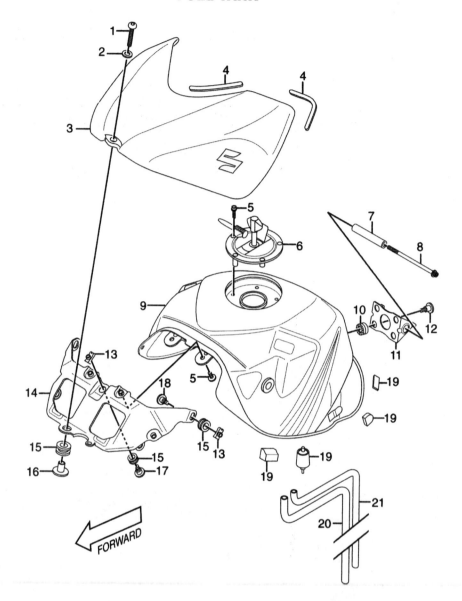

FUEL TANK

1. Bolt
2. Washer
3. Fuel tank cushion
4. Trim
5. Screw
6. Filler cap
7. Spacer
8. Bolt
9. Fuel tank
10. Grommet
11. Mounting bracket--rear
12. Shoulder bolt
13. Tinnerman clip
14. Mounting bracket--front
15. Cushion
16. Collar
17. Shoulder bolt
18. Shoulder bolt
19. Cushion
20. Drain hose
21. Breather

FORWARD

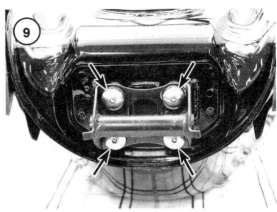

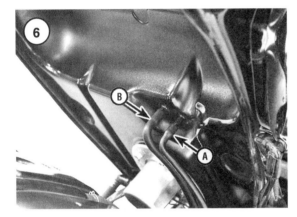

7. Reverse the procedure to lower and install the fuel tank. Make sure the washer and collar are installed in the tank mount. Tighten the bolt securely.

Removal/Installation

Refer to **Figure 4**.

1. Disconnect the battery negative cable (Chapter Nine).

2. Raise and support the fuel tank as described in this chapter.

NOTE
As a hose or electrical connector is removed, label each hose and its fitting. Hoses and connectors must be reconnected to their original locations.

3. Disconnect the fuel pump electrical connector (**Figure 5**) from its harness mate.

4. Label and disconnect the drain hose (A, **Figure 6**), and breather hose (B) from their respective fittings on the tank.

5. Disconnect the fuel supply hose (A, **Figure 7**) from the output port on the fuel pump. Be prepared to catch residual gasoline dribbling from the hose.

6. On California models, disconnect the EVAP hose from the fitting on the fuel tank.

7. Lower the fuel tank. Do not damage any of the disconnected hoses.

8. Remove the fuel tank through bolt (**Figure 8**), and remove the fuel tank from the motorcycle. Account for the spacer in the fuel tank mounting bracket pivot.

9. Check the tightness of the fuel tank mounting bracket bolts (**Figure 9**). Tighten if necessary.

10. Installation is the reverse of removal. Note the following:

    a. Ensure the spacer is in place in the fuel tank pivot, and tighten the through bolt securely.

    b. Ensure the hose is securely attached to their respective fittings.

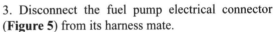

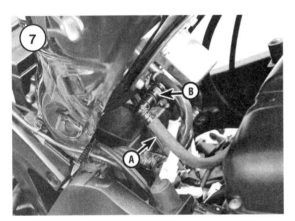

8

c. Check that the fuel supply hose is correctly attached to its fittings (B, **Figure 7**) and that the safety clip is in place.

FUEL PUMP (2006-2007 MODELS)

The fuel pump is inside the fuel tank and operates whenever the ignition switch is on. The pressure regulator, which is an integral art of the fuel pump, maintains fuel line pressure at 300 kPa (43 psi). If fuel pressure becomes excessive, a check valve in the regulator opens so fuel flows back into the fuel tank. This negates the need for a fuel return line.

Removal/Installation

1. Remove the fuel tank as described in this chapter. Drain the fuel into a suitable container.
2. Set the fuel tank upside down on towels or a blanket on the workbench.
3. Evenly loosen the fuel pump bolts (**Figure 10**) in a crisscross pattern.
4. Remove the fuel pump bolts, and slowly withdraw the fuel pump (A, **Figure 11**) from the tank. Do not bend the float arm (B, **Figure 11**).
5. Remove and discard the fuel pump O-ring (**Figure 12**).
6. Installation is the reverse of removal.
   a. Apply grease (Suzuki Super Grease A or equivalent) to a *new* O-ring, and install the O-ring into the channel in the tank (**Figure 12**).
   b. Apply threadlocking compound (Suzuki Thread Lock 1342 or equivalent) to the threads of the fuel pump bolts and install the bolts (**Figure 10**).
   c. Evenly tighten the bolts in a crisscross pattern. Tighten the fuel pump bolts to 10 N•m (89 in.-lb.).

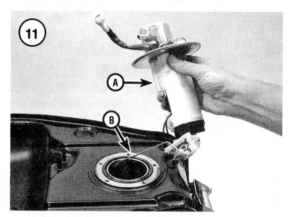

Disassembly

Refer to **Figure 13**.
1. Remove the fuel pump as described in this chapter.
2. Disconnect the electrical lead from each terminal by performing the following:
   a. Label each wire and its terminal. Each wire must be reconnected to the correct terminal during assembly. The thick wire in located on the right side and the thin wire on the left side.
   b. Remove the terminal nut (**Figure 14**), lockwasher, wire ring terminal and star washer (**Figure 15**) from each terminal.

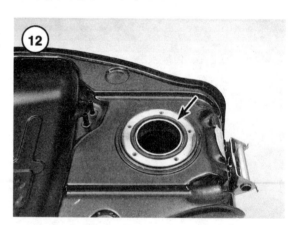

3. Remove the lead wire screw (**Figure 16**) and the remaining screw and wire on the other side (**Figure 17**). Account for the special nut installed on each mounting arm.
4. Remove the fuel level gauge mounting screws (A, **Figure 18**), and remove the gauge (B) from the fuel pump.
5. Slide up and remove the fuel pump (A, **Figure 19**) from the pump plate (B).
6. Slip the fuel pump holder and cushion (**Figure 20**) off the fuel pump, and remove it.
7. Withdraw the strainer (**Figure 21**) from the end of the fuel pump.

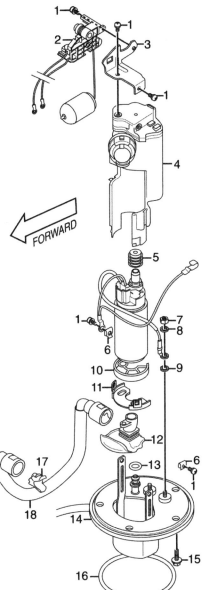

**FUEL PUMP
(2006-2007 MODELS)**

FORWARD

1. Screws
2. Fuel level gauge
3. Bracket
4. Fuel pump case/filter
5. Bushing
6. Clip
7. Nut
8. Lockwasher
9. Star washer
10. Cushion
11. Holder
12. Strainer
13. O-ring

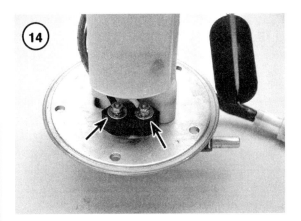

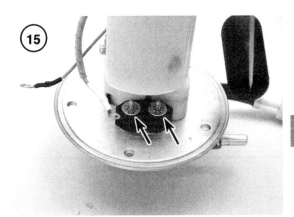

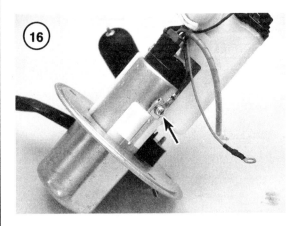

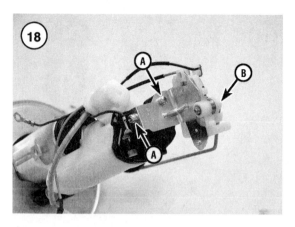

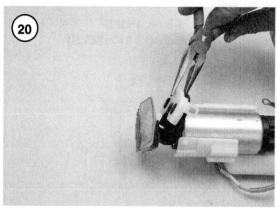

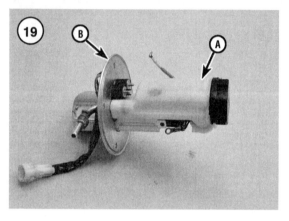

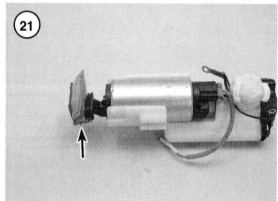

8. Remove the fuel pump (A, **Figure 22**) from the fuel pump case/filter assembly (B).

9. Inspect the components as described in this chapter.

Assembly

1. Apply a light coat of engine oil to the new bushing, and press the bushing (A, **Figure 23**) into the fuel pump port (B).

2. Align the fuel pump with the thick pink wire as shown in **Figure 24**, and slide it into place on the fuel pump case/filter assembly. Push the fuel pump in until it bottoms.

3. Install the strainer (**Figure 21**) onto the end of the fuel pump.

4. Install the cushion onto the fuel pump holder and slip the fuel pump holder and cushion (**Figure 20**) onto the fuel pump until it locks into place.

5. Lubricate a *new* O-ring (A, **Figure 25**) with clean engine oil, and install it onto the fitting on the pump base (B).

6. Correctly locate the fuel pump (A, **Figure 26**) to the pump plate (B), and install the fuel pump (A, **Figure 19**) onto the pump plate (B). Press it on until the bushing is correctly seated in the fuel pump case/filter assembly

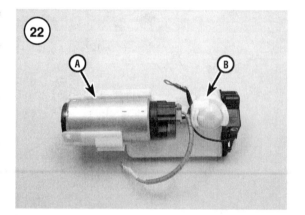

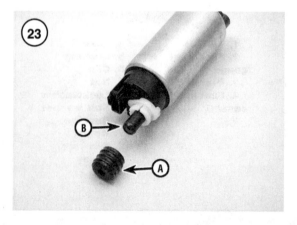

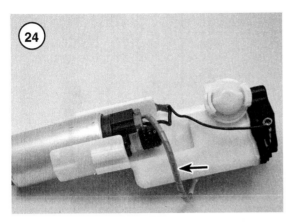

8

7. Install the fuel level gauge (B, **Figure 18**) onto the fuel pump. Tighten the mounting screws (A, **Figure 18**) securely.

8. Make sure the pump wires are located as shown in **Figure 27**. The thick wire in located on the right side and the thin wire on the left side.

9. Ensure that the special nut installed on each mounting arm. Refer to **Figure 28** and **Figure 29**.

10. Install the lead wire screw (**Figure 16**) and the remaining screw and wire on the other side (**Figure 17**). Tighten the screws securely.

11. Install the star washer and wire ring terminal (**Figure 15**) onto each terminal.

12. Install the wires onto the terminal. Install the lockwasher and the terminal nut (**Figure 14**) onto each terminal. Tighten the terminal nut securely.

13. Install the fuel pump as described in this chapter.

Inspection

1. Clean any sediment from the fuel pump base (B, **Figure 25**).

2. Clear the ports (**Figure 30**) in the fuel pump assembly.

3. Inspect the fuel pump case/filter (**Figure 31**) for damage.

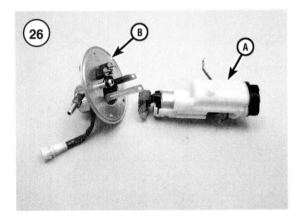

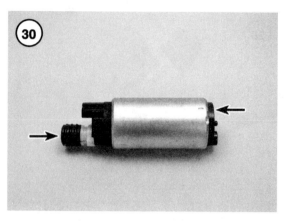

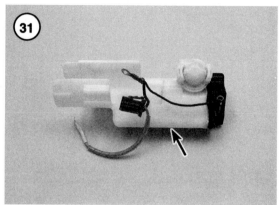

4. Blow the filter strainer element (**Figure 32**) clear with low-pressure compressed air. Replace the element if it remains clogged.

5. Inspect the cushion (A, **Figure 33**) and holder (B) for damage.

6. Inspect the float level gauge (A, **Figure 34**) for damage. Check for ease of movement of the float level arm (B, **Figure 34**). Make sure it is not bent.

FUEL PUMP (2008-2009 MODELS)

The fuel pump is inside the fuel tank and operates whenever the ignition switch is on. The pressure regulator, which is an integral art of the fuel pump, maintains fuel line pressure at 300 kPa (43 psi). If fuel pressure becomes excessive, a check valve in the regulator opens so fuel flows back into the fuel tank. This negates the need for a fuel return line.

Removal/Installation

1. Remove the fuel tank as described in this chapter. Drain the fuel into a suitable container.

2. Set the fuel tank upside down on towels or a blanket on the workbench.

3. Evenly loosen the fuel pump bolts (**Figure 35**) in a crisscross pattern.

4. Remove the fuel pump bolts, and slowly withdraw the fuel pump (**Figure 36**) from the tank. Do not bend the float arm (**Figure 37**).

5. Remove and discard the fuel pump O-ring (**Figure 38**).

6. Installation is the reverse of removal.
   a. Apply grease (Suzuki Super Grease A or equivalent) to a new O-ring, and install the O-ring into the channel in the tank (**Figure 38**).
   b. Apply threadlocking compound (Suzuki Thread Lock 1342 or equivalent) to the threads of the fuel pump bolts and install the bolts (**Figure 35**).

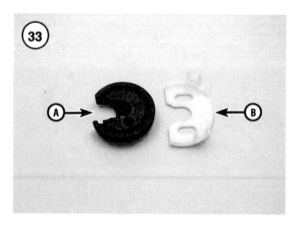

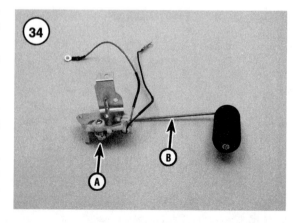

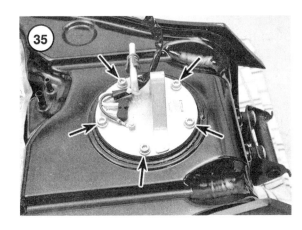

c. Evenly tighten the bolts in a crisscross pattern. Tighten the fuel pump bolts to 10 N•m (89 in.-lb.).

Disassembly

Refer to **Figure 39**.

1. Remove the fuel pump as described in this chapter.

2. Label each wire and its terminal on the pump plate. Each wire must be reconnected to the correct terminal during assembly. The thick red wire (A, **Figure 40**) is located on the right side and the thin black wire (B) on the left side.

3. Disconnect the thick red wire (A, **Figure 40**) and the thin black wire (B) from the terminals.

4. Remove the fuel level gauge mounting screw (**Figure 41**) on the left side.

5. Remove the fuel level gauge mounting screw (A, **Figure 42**) on the right side. Account for the wire (B, **Figure 42**) under the screw, and remove the gauge from the assembly.

6. Unhook the thick red wire (A, **Figure 43**) and remove the fuel filter cartridge (B) from the fuel pump case.

7. Slide up and remove the fuel pump (A, **Figure 44**) from the fuel pump case (B).

8. Slide the fuel pump case (A, **Figure 45**) off of the fuel pump plate (B), and remove it.

9. Withdraw the strainer (**Figure 46**) from the end of the fuel pump.

10. Inspect the components as described in this chapter.

Assembly

1. Install the strainer (**Figure 46**) onto the end of the fuel pump. Push it down until it bottoms.

2. Install the fuel pump (A, **Figure 47**) into the fuel pump case (B).

3. Install the fuel pump case (A, **Figure 45**) onto of the fuel pump plate (B). Push it down until it bottoms (**Figure 48**).

4. Install *new* O-ring (A, **Figure 49**) onto the fuel pump plate, and onto the fuel pump (B).

5. Install the fuel filter cartridge (B, **Figure 43**) onto the fuel pump.

6. Hook the thick red wire onto the fuel filter cartridge groove (A, **Figure 43**).

7. Connect the thick red wire (A, **Figure 40**) onto the terminal on the pump plate.

8. Install the fuel level gauge (**Figure 50**) onto the assembly.

8

**FUEL PUMP
(2008-2009 MODELS)**

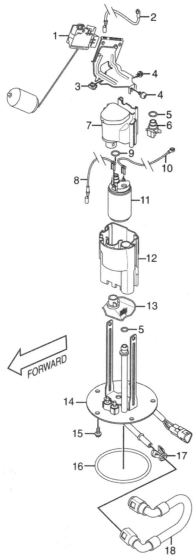

FORWARD

1. Fuel level gauge
2. Wire
3. Bracket and Tinnerman clip
4. Screw
5. O-ring
6. Joint
7. Fuel filter cartridge
8. Wire—thick red
9. O-ring
10. Wire—thin black
11. Fuel pump
12. Fuel pump case
13. Strainer
14. Fuel pump plate
15. Screw
16. O-ring
17. Connector

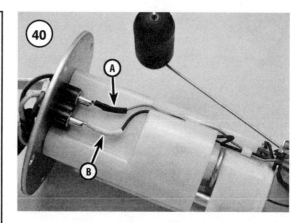

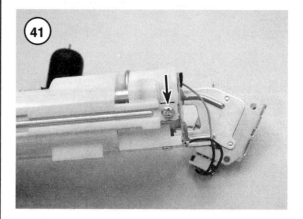

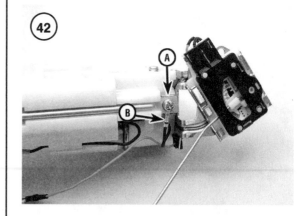

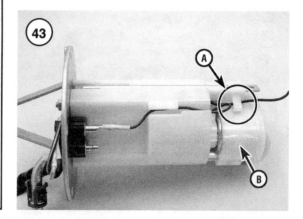

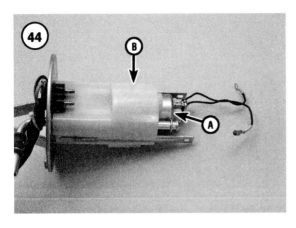

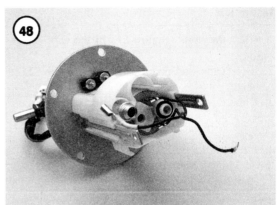

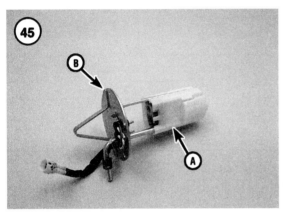

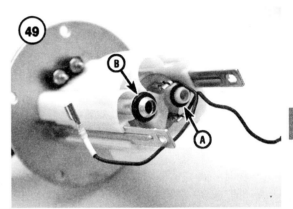

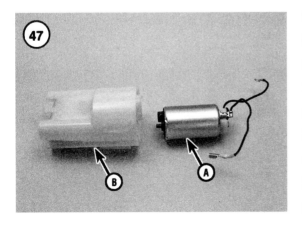

8

9. Install the fuel level gauge mounting screw (**Figure 41**) on the left side. Tighten the screw securely.

10. Position the wire (B, **Figure 42**) under the screw, and install the fuel level gauge mounting screw (A, **Figure 42**) on the right side. Tighten the screw securely.

11. Connect the thin black wire (B, **Figure 40**) onto the terminal on the pump plate.

Inspection

1. Clear the ports (**Figure 51**) in the cartridge assembly.

2. Inspect the fuel pump cartridge (**Figure 52**) for damage.

3. Blow the strainer clear with low-pressure compressed air. Replace the strainer if it remains clogged.

4. If removed, install a new O-ring (A, **Figure 53**) in the fuel filter cartridge and install the joint (B).

5. The check valve (C, **Figure 53**) is an integral part of the fuel filter cartridge, and is not replaceable.

6. Inspect the pump plate (**Figure 54**) for damage.

7. Inspect the float level gauge (A, **Figure 55**) for damage. Check for ease of movement of the float level arm (B, **Figure 55**). Make sure it is not bent.

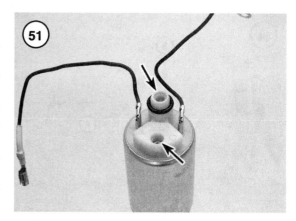

FUEL PUMP TESTS

Fuel Pressure Test

1. The following tools are needed to perform this test:

   a. Fuel pressure gauge adapter (Suzuki part No. 09940-40211).

   b. Fuel pressure gauge hose attachment (Suzuki part No. 09940-40220).

   c. Oil pressure gauge (Suzuki part No. 09915-77331).

   d. Oil pressure gauge hose (Suzuki part No. 09915-74521).

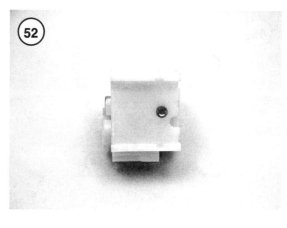

2. Raise and support the fuel tank as described in this chapter.

3. Disconnect the fuel hose (A, **Figure 56**) from the output port on the fuel pump. Be prepared to catch residual gasoline dribbling from the hose.

4. Use the adapters to install the gauge inline between the fuel pump and the fuel rail (**Figure 57**). Follow the manufacturer's instructions.

5. Turn the ignition switch on, and read the fuel pressure. It should equal the fuel pump output pressure specified in **Table 1**.

6. If fuel pressure is less than specified, check for a leak in the fuel system, a clogged fuel filter, faulty pressure regulator or faulty fuel pump.

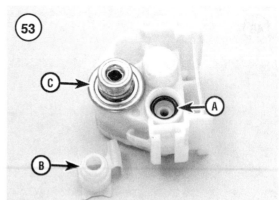

7. If fuel pressure exceeds specification, check the fuel pump check valve or the pressure regulator.

8. Disassemble the fuel pump and visually inspect the components. Replace any part as needed. The check valve is an integral part of the fuel pump and cannot be replaced separately.

9. Connect the fuel hose (A, **Figure 56**) onto the output port on the fuel pump. Check that the fuel supply hose is correctly attached to its fittings (B, **Figure 56**) and that the safety clip is in place.

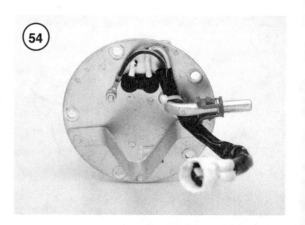

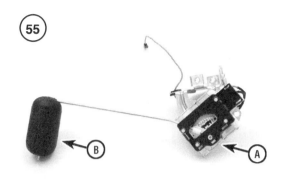

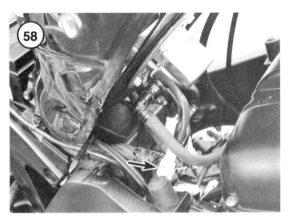

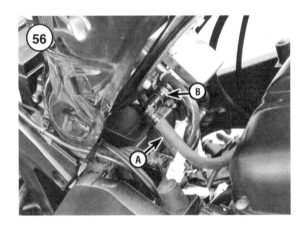

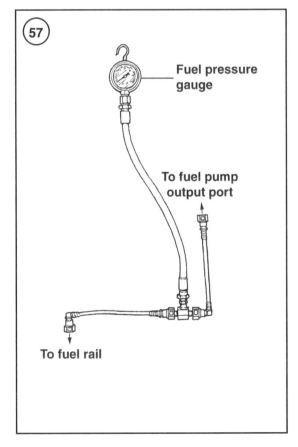

Fuel pressure gauge

To fuel pump output port

To fuel rail

10. Lower and secure the fuel tank as described in this chapter.

Fuel Pump Operation Test

1. Turn the ignition switch on and listen for the operation of the fuel pump.
2. If no sound is heard, test the fuel pump relay and the tip over sensor as described in this chapter. If both of these components are within specification, replace the fuel pump.

Fuel Pump Discharge Test

A fuel-safe container and jumper wire are needed for this test.
1. Raise and support the fuel tank as described in this chapter.
2. Disconnect the fuel pump electrical connector (**Figure 58**) from its harness mate.
3. Disconnect the fuel hose (A, **Figure 56**) from the output port on the fuel pump. Be prepared to catch residual gasoline from the hose.
4. Connect a suitable hose to the fuel pump output port, and feed the opposite end of the hose into a container.
5. Apply battery voltage directly to the fuel pump by performing the following:
   a. Use a jumper to connect the battery positive terminal to the yellow/red wire in the pump side of the fuel pump connector. Connect the negative battery terminal to the black/white terminal in the pump side of the connector.
   b. When performing this test, apply battery voltage to the fuel pump for 10 seconds.
   c. Keep the jumpers connect to the terminals for the specified time. Disconnect the jumpers from the fuel pump connector and from the battery terminals.

6. Measure the amount of fuel in the container. The fuel pump is faulty if the volume is significantly less than fuel pump output volume specified in **Table 1**.

7. Connect the fuel hose (A, **Figure 56**) onto the output port on the fuel pump. Check that the fuel supply hose is correctly attached to its fittings (B, **Figure 56**) and that the safety clip is in place.

8. Lower and secure the fuel tank as described in this chapter.

Fuel Level Sensor Test

Refer to **Figure 59** and **Figure 60**.

1. Remove the fuel pump as described in this chapter.
2. Secure the fuel pump assembly in a vertical position.
3. Connect an ohmmeter to the fuel pump black/white and black/light green fuel pump 3-pin electrical connector.
4. Lower the float and arm to the indicated empty position and observe the reading.
5. Raise the float and arm to the indicated full position and observe the reading.
6. Replace the fuel level sensor assembly if the readings fail the specifications listed in **Table 2**.
7. Install the fuel pump as described in this chapter.

FUEL PUMP RELAY

Removal/Installation

1. Disconnect the battery negative cable (Chapter Nine).
2. Remove the rider and passenger seats (Chapter Fifteen).
3. Lift and support the fuel tank as described in this chapter.
4A. On 2006-2007 models, pull the fuel pump relay (**Figure 61**) straight up, and remove its rubber mount.
4B. On 2008-2009 models, pull the fuel pump relay (**Figure 62**) straight up, and remove its rubber mount.
5. Installation is the reverse of removal. Make sure the rubber mount securely engages its mounting tang.

Test

1. Remove the relay (this section).
2. Check the continuity between the A and B terminals on the relay (**Figure 63**). The relay should be no continuity.
3. Use jumpers to connect the positive terminal of a 12 volt battery to the C terminal on the relay (**Figure**

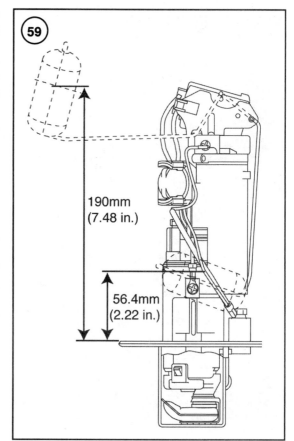

59

190mm
(7.48 in.)

56.4mm
(2.22 in.)

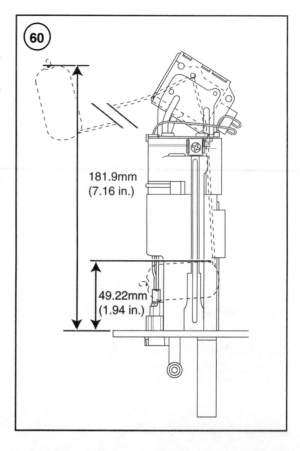

60

181.9mm
(7.16 in.)

49.22mm
(1.94 in.)

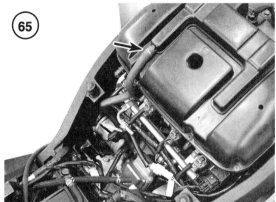

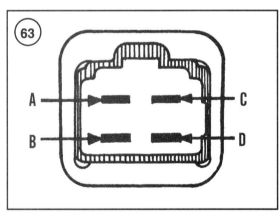

63); connect the negative battery terminal to the D relay terminal.

4. Check the continuity between the relay's A & B terminals. The relay should have continuity while voltage is applied.

5. Replace the relay if it fails either portion of this test.

AIR FILTER HOUSING

Removal/Installation

1. Lift and support the fuel tank or remove the fuel tank as described in this chapter.

2. On 2006-2007 models, disconnect the IAT sensor (A, **Figure 64**), the fuel pump relay (B) and cooling fan relay (C) electrical connectors from the cover.

3. Disconnect the PCV hose (**Figure 65**) from the cover fitting.

4. Remove the cover screws and lift the cover (A, **Figure 66**) from the air filter housing. Do not forget the screw in the deep center recess (B, **Figure 66**).

5. Remove the air filter element assembly (A, **Figure 67**) from the housing.

6. On 2008-2009 models, perform the following:

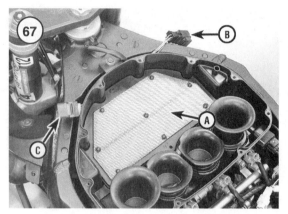

a. Disconnect the IAT sensor (**Figure 68**) and the ISC valve (**Figure 69**) electrical connectors from the cover.

b. Disconnect the idle speed control (ISC) valve hose (**Figure 70**).

7. On the right side, disconnect the PAIR hose (**Figure 71**) from the lower housing.

8A. On 2006-2007 models, insert a long screwdriver (**Figure 72**) through the frame opening, and loosen clamp screw on the throttle body clamp. Repeat for the other side.

8B. On 2008-2009 models, perform the following:

a. Remove the plug (**Figure 73**) from the frame opening.

b. Insert a 3mm Allen wrench (**Figure 74**) through the frame opening, and loosen clamp screw on the throttle body clamp. Repeat for the other side.

9. Remove the air filter lower housing bolt (**Figure 75**).

10. Disengage each air filter housing port from its respective throttle body, and remove the lower housing from the motorcycle.

11. Stuff clean rags (**Figure 76**) into each throttle body inlet to keep contaminants out of the throttle bodies.

12. Inspect the air filter lower housing and cover as described in this section.

13. Install the air filter lower housing by reversing the removal steps. Note the following:

a. On 2006-2007 models, position the fuel pump relay (B, **Figure 67**) and cooling fuel relay (C) outboard of the lower housing prior to installing the cover.

b. Make sure each air filter housing port securely engages its throttle body intake.

c. The foam seal on each intake must seal against the frame duct.

Inspection

Refer to **Figure 77**.

1. If still in place, remove the cover screws and lift the cover from the housing.

2. If still in place, remove the air filter element.

3. Inspect the air filter element as described in Chapter Three.

4. Wipe out the interior of the lower housing (A, **Figure 78**) and cover.

5. Inspect the air filter housing and its intake ports (B, **Figure 78**) for cracks, wear or damage. If any damage is noted, replace the housing to avoid the possibility of unfiltered air entering the engine.

6. Inspect the foam seal (A, **Figure 79**) on each housing inlet. Replace the seals if they are worn broken or starting to deteriorate.

7. Inspect the throttle body fittings (B, **Figure 79**) for hardness, deterioration or damage. Replace them as necessary.

8. Remove the drain plug (**Figure 80**), and clean out all residues from the plug and air box. Reinstall the drain plug.

9. Inspect the cover for damage (**Figure 81**).

10. Inspect the base (C, **Figure 78**) for damage.

THROTTLE BODY
(2006-2007 MODELS)

The throttle bodies include a secondary throttle valve installed above the throttle valve. The secondary throttle valve is operated by the secondary throttle valve (STV) actuator located on the right side of the throttle valve assembly.

During operation, the ECM opens and closes the secondary throttle valve to control the volume and speed of incoming air, which improves the output at particular throttle settings.

NOTE
The hoses and electrical connectors
must be reinstalled onto their original

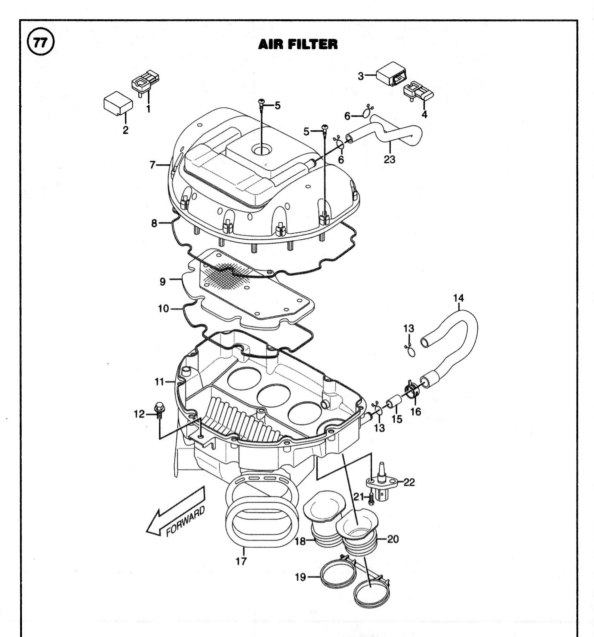

AIR FILTER

1. Intake air pressure (IAP) sensor
   (2006-2007 models)
2. Cover
3. Cover
4. Intake air pressure (IAP) sensor
   (2008-2009 models)
5. Bolt
6. Hose clamp
7. Cover
8. Gasket
9. Air filter
10. Gasket
11. Lower housing
12. Bolt
13. Hose clamp

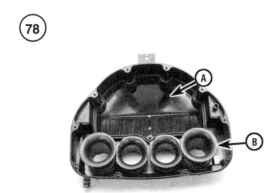

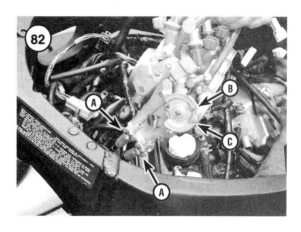

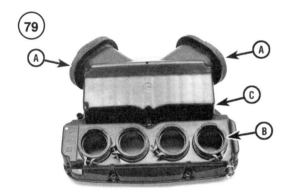

locations. Mark each hose and connector as well as the location where they are connected as each is removed.

Removal/Installation

1. Remove the fuel tank and air filter housing as described in this chapter.

NOTE
A single clamp screw loosens the two outside intake manifold clamps on each side of the motorcycle.

2. Loosen the intake manifold clamp screw on each side.

3. Lift the throttle body assembly and disengage each throttle body from its intake manifolds. Raise the assembly sufficiently to access the throttle wheel, and lower the assembly.

4. Loosen the locknut (A, **Figure 82**) on both throttle cables. Turn the adjuster to create sufficient slack, and disconnect the throttle pull cable end (B, **Figure 82**) from the top slot in the throttle wheel.

5. Repeat Step 4 and disconnect the return cable end (C, **Figure 82**) from the bottom slot of the throttle wheel.

6. Disconnect the fuel feed hose.

7. Disconnect the following electrical connectors:
   a. STVA 4-pin electrical connector (A, **Figure 83**).
   b. TP 3-pin electrical connector (B, **Figure 83**).
   c. IAP 3-pin electrical connector (C, **Figure 83**).
   d. Fuel injector 2-pin electrical connector (D, **Figure 83**) from each fuel injector.

8. Lift the throttle body assembly straight up and remove from engine.

9. Place a clean cloth into each intake manifold (**Figure 76**) to prevent the entry of foreign matter.

10. Installation is the reverse of removal. Note the following:

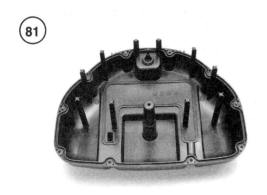

a. Lubricate the inner surface of each intake manifold with a soap solution to ease installation.
b. Remove the cloths from the intake manifolds.
c. Fully seat each throttle body into its intake manifold. A solid bottoming will be felt when a throttle body is correctly seated.
d. Tighten the intake manifold clamp screws securely.
e. Add fuel, start the engine and check for fuel leaks.
f. Adjust the throttle cable free play, idle speed, and fast idle speed (Chapter Three).

Disassembly

Refer to **Figure 84**.
1. Remove each fuel rail screw from the fuel rail. Refer to A, **Figure 85** and A, **Figure 86**.
2. Pull the fuel delivery pipe (B, **Figure 85**) and (B, **Figure 86**) until it disengages from the throttle body.
3. Remove and discard the cushion seal in each fuel-rail receptacle (A, **Figure 87**) in the throttle body assembly.
4. If necessary, disconnect the vacuum hose (B, **Figure 87**) from the fitting on each throttle body. On California models, also disconnect the EVAP hoses from their respective fittings. Label each hose and its fitting to ease assembly.
5. Pull each fuel injector (**Figure 88**) from the fuel delivery pipe. Remove and discard the O-ring seal from each fuel injector.
6. Further disassembly is not recommended.

Assembly

1. Lubricate a *new* O-ring (A, **Figure 89**) and new cushion (B) with clean engine oil, and install each onto the fuel injector (C).
2. Repeat Step 1 for each fuel injector.
3. Press an injector (**Figure 90**) into it port on the fuel delivery pipe until the injector bottoms. Do not rotate the injectors during installation. Repeat for any other removed injectors. Make sure each injector is completely seated in its fuel delivery pipe receptacle.
4. Position the fuel delivery pipe so the fuel injectors align with the ports in the throttle body. Gently press the fuel delivery pipe straight into the throttle body until the fuel injector bottom.
5. Install each fuel delivery pipe screws onto the fuel rail. Refer to A, **Figure 85** and A, **Figure 86**, and tighten to 5 N•m (44 in.-lb.).
6. If removed, connect the vacuum hose (B, **Figure 87**) onto the fitting on each throttle body. On

California models, also connect the EVAP hoses onto their respective fittings.

Throttle Body Inspection

CAUTION
Do not use tools to clean passages in the throttle bodies.

1. Clean the throttle bodies with an aerosol carburetor cleaner. Dry the bodies and all passages with compressed air.
2. Visually inspect the throttle bodies for crack or other damage that could admit unfiltered air.
3. Manually operate the throttle valves (**Figure 91**) and secondary throttle valves (**Figure 92**). They must move smoothly. Never remove the primary throttle and the secondary throttle valves.
4. Check the operation of the throttle wheel (**Figure 93**). It must operate smoothly.
5. Check all return springs for weakness and/or breakage. Refer to **Figure 94** and A, **Figure 95**.
6. Check the assembly bolt nuts (**Figure 96**) for tightness.
7. Inspect the hoses (B, **Figure 95**) for cracks or other signs of damage. Replace any hose that is becoming brittle.
8. Inspect the fuel rail and injectors as described in *Fuel Injector Inspection* in this chapter).
9. Do not disassemble the throttle body.

THROTTLE BODY
(2008-2009 MODELS)

The throttle bodies include a secondary throttle valve installed above the throttle valve. The secondary throttle valve is operated by the secondary throttle valve (STV) actuator located on the right side of the throttle valve assembly.

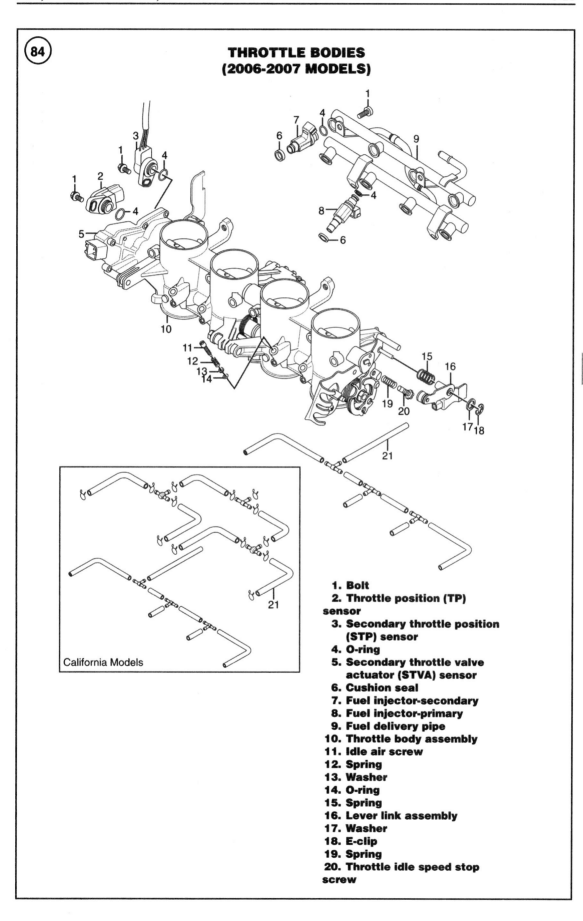

(84)

THROTTLE BODIES
(2006-2007 MODELS)

California Models

1. Bolt
2. Throttle position (TP) sensor
3. Secondary throttle position (STP) sensor
4. O-ring
5. Secondary throttle valve actuator (STVA) sensor
6. Cushion seal
7. Fuel injector-secondary
8. Fuel injector-primary
9. Fuel delivery pipe
10. Throttle body assembly
11. Idle air screw
12. Spring
13. Washer
14. O-ring
15. Spring
16. Lever link assembly
17. Washer
18. E-clip
19. Spring
20. Throttle idle speed stop screw

8

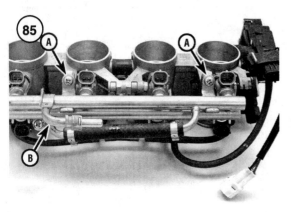

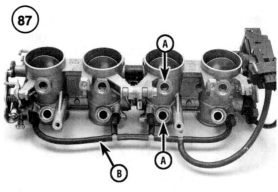

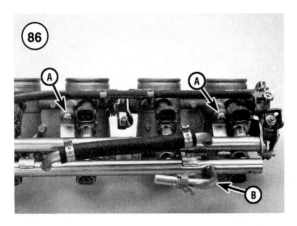

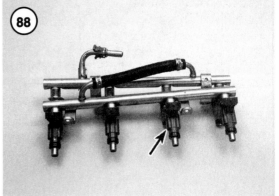

During operation, the ECM opens and closes the secondary throttle valve to control the volume and speed of incoming air, which improves the output at particular throttle settings.

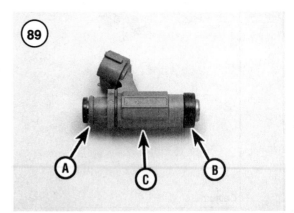

> *NOTE*
> *The hoses and electrical connectors must be reinstalled onto their original locations. Mark each hose and connector as well as the location where they are connected as each is removed.*

Removal/Installation

1. Remove the fuel tank and air filter housing as described in this chapter.

> *NOTE*
> *A single clamp screw loosens the two outside intake manifold clamps on each side of the motorcycle.*

2. Use a long Allen wrench (**Figure 97**), and loosen the intake manifold clamp screw on each side.
3. Lift the throttle body assembly and disengage each throttle body from its intake manifolds. Raise

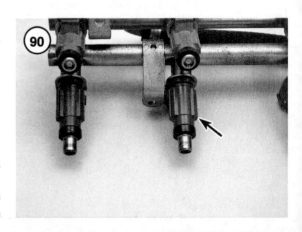

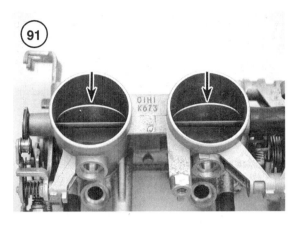

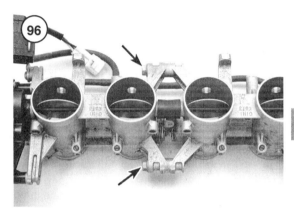

8

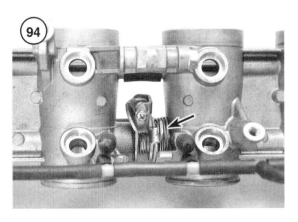

the assembly sufficiently to access the throttle wheel, and lower the assembly.

4. Loosen the locknut (A, **Figure 98**) on both throttle cables. Turn the adjuster to create sufficient slack, and disconnect the throttle pull cable end (B, **Figure 98**) from the top slot in the throttle wheel.

5. Repeat Step 4 and disconnect the return cable end (C, **Figure 98**) from the bottom slot of the throttle wheel.

6. Disconnect the fuel feed hose.

7. Disconnect the following electrical connectors:

    a. STVA 4-pin electrical connector (A, **Figure 99**).

b. TP 3-pin electrical connector (B, **Figure 99**).

c. IAP 3-pin electrical connector (**Figure 100**).

d. STP 3-pin electrical connector (**Figure 101**).

e. IAC 3-pin electrical connector (**Figure 102**).

f. Fuel injector 2-pin electrical connector from each primary (**Figure 103**) fuel injector.

8. Disconnect the hose (**Figure 104**) from the purge control solenoid valve (California models only).

9. Lift the throttle body assembly partially straight up and disconnect the 2-pin electrical connector from each secondary fuel injector.

10. Remove the throttle body from the engine.

11. Place a clean cloth into each intake manifold to prevent the entry of foreign matter.

12. Installation is the reverse of removal. Note the following:

a. Lubricate the inner surface of each intake manifold with a soap solution to ease installation.

b. Remove the cloths from the intake manifolds.

c. Fully seat each throttle body into its intake manifold. A solid bottoming will be felt when a throttle body is correctly seated.

d. Tighten the intake manifold clamp screws securely.

e. Add fuel, start the engine and check for fuel leaks.

f. Adjust the throttle cable free play, and idle speed (Chapter Three).

Disassembly

Refer to **Figure 105**.

1. Remove the fuel rail mounting screws (A, **Figure 106**).

CAUTION
Do not twist the fuel delivery pipe during removal to avoid damage to the T-joint that

connects the fuel deliver pipes.

2. Pull the fuel delivery pipe (B, **Figure 106**) straight out until it disengages from the throttle body.

3. If necessary, disconnect the vacuum hose (A, **Figure 107**) from the fitting on each throttle body. On California models, also disconnect the EVAP hoses (B, **Figure 107**) from their respective fittings. Label each hose and its fitting to ease assembly.

4. Pull each fuel injector (**Figure 108**) from the fuel delivery pipe.

5. Remove and discard the cushion seals (**Figure 109**) from the throttle body, or fuel injector.

6. Remove and discard the O-ring seal (**Figure 110**) from each fuel injector.

7. Further disassembly is not recommended except for the STVA assembly as described in this chapter.

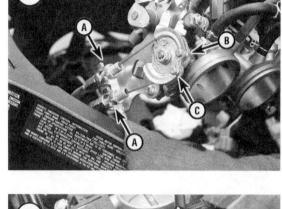

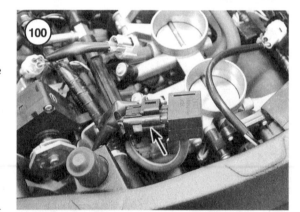

4. Position the fuel delivery pipe so the fuel injectors align with the ports in the throttle body. Gently press the fuel delivery pipe (B, **Figure 106**) straight into the throttle body until it bottoms.

5. Install each fuel delivery pipe screws (A, **Figure 106**) onto the fuel rail, and tighten to 3.5 N•m (31 in.-lb.).

6. If removed, connect the vacuum hose (A, **Figure 107**) onto the fitting on each throttle body. On California models, also connect the EVAP hoses (B, **Figure 107**) onto their respective fittings as noted during disassembly.

Throttle Body Inspection

CAUTION
Do not use tools to clean passages in the throttle bodies.

1. Clean the throttle bodies with an aerosol carburetor cleaner. Dry the bodies and all passages with compressed air.

2. Visually inspect the throttle bodies for crack or other damage that could admit unfiltered air.

3. Manually operate the primary throttle valves (**Figure 112**) and secondary throttle valves (**Figure 113**). They must move smoothly. Never remove the primary throttle and the secondary throttle valves.

4. Check the operation of the throttle wheel (**Figure 114**). It must operate smoothly.

5. Check all return springs for weakness and/or breakage. Refer to **Figure 115** and **Figure 116**.

6. Check the assembly bolt (**Figure 117**) for tightness.

7. Inspect, the vacuum hoses (A, **Figure 107**), and on California models, also check the EVAP hoses (B, **Figure 107**) for cracks or other signs of damage. Replace any hose that is becoming brittle.

8. Inspect the fuel rail (A, **Figure 118**) and fuel inlet hose (B) for damage. Check the quick-disconnect fitting (C, **Figure 118**) for cracks or damage.

9. Do not disassemble the throttle body.

Assembly

1. Lubricate a new O-ring (**Figure 110**) and *new* cushion (**Figure 109**) with clean engine oil.

2. Install the primary fuel injectors (A, **Figure 111**) and secondary (B) fuel injectors.

3. Press the fuel injectors (**Figure 108**) into it port on the fuel delivery pipe until the injector bottoms. Do not rotate the injectors during installation. Repeat for any other removed injectors. Make sure each injector is completely seated in its fuel delivery pipe receptacle.

FUEL INJECTOR

Removal/Installation

Remove and install the fuel injectors as described in *Throttle Body* in this chapter.

Inspection

1. Inspect the fuel injectors for damage. Inspect the injector nozzle (**Figure 119**) for carbon buildup or damage.

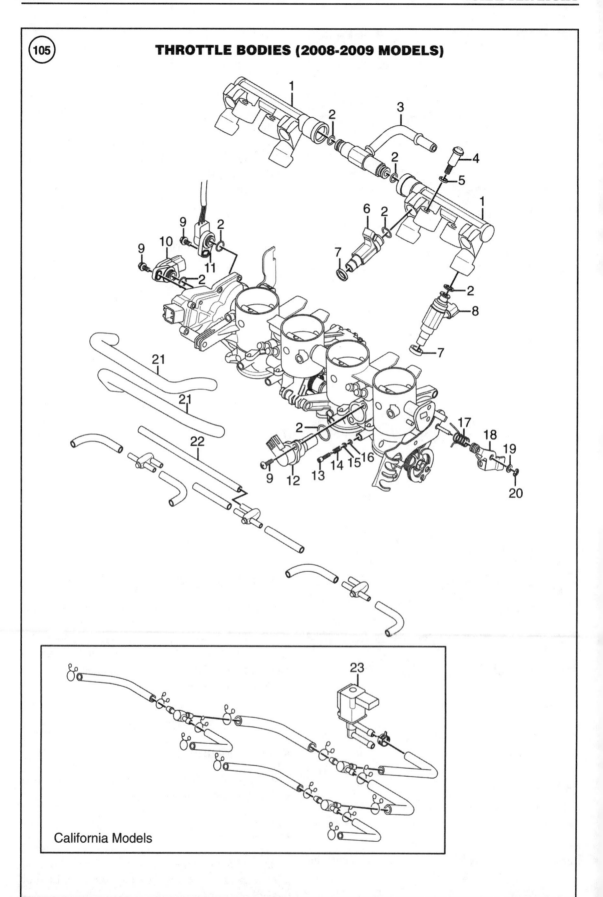

105

THROTTLE BODIES (2008-2009 MODELS)

California Models

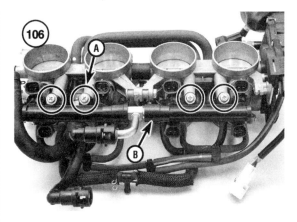

1. Fuel delivery pipe
2. O-ring
3. Fuel delivery pipe T-joint
4. Shoulder bolt
5. Washer
6. Fuel injector-secondary
7. Cushion seal
8. Fuel injector-primary
9. Screw
10. Throttle position (TP) sensor
11. Secondary throttle position (STP)
    sensor
12. ISC valve
13. Idle air screw
14. Spring
15. Washer
16. O-ring
17. Spring
18. Lever link assembly
19. Washer
20. E-clip
21. Hose
22. Hose assembly
23. Evaporation purge control solenoid

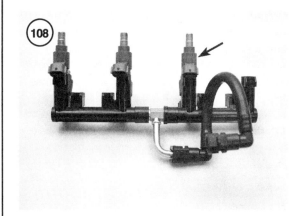

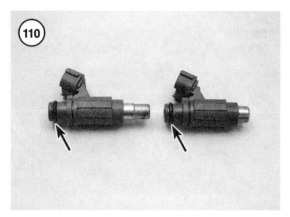

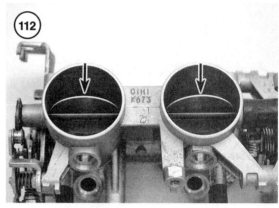

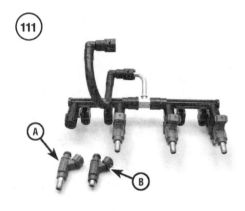

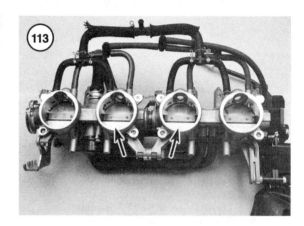

2. Check for corrosion or damage in the terminals of each fuel injector connector (**Figure 120**) and each subharness connector.

3. Clean the fuel injection ports in the fuel delivery pipe. Clear the pipe if necessary with compressed air.

4. Inspect the injector ports (**Figure 109**) in the throttle body for contamination.

5. Replace any worn or damaged part.

Resistance Test

1. Turn the ignition switch off.

2. Raise and support the fuel tank as described in this chapter.

3. Remove the air filter housing as described in this chapter.

4. Disconnect the connector from the primary (**Figure 121**) and secondary (A, **Figure 122**) fuel injectors.

5. Use an ohmmeter to measure the resistance between the two terminals in the fuel injector (B, **Figure 122**). The resistance should be within the range specified in **Table 2**.

6. Repeat this test for each of the remaining fuel injectors.

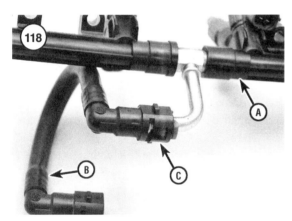

7. Lower and secure the fuel tank as described in this chapter.

Continuity Test

1. Perform Steps 1-3 of the injector resistance test.

2. Check the continuity between each terminal (B, **Figure 122**) in the injector and ground. No continuity (infinity) should be indicated.

3. Repeat this test for each remaining fuel injector.

Voltage Test

1. Perform Steps 1-3 of the injector resistance test.
2. Connect a voltmeter positive test probe to the yellow/red wire in the injector connector; connect the negative test probe to a good ground.

NOTE
Injector voltage will be present for only three seconds after the ignition switch is turned off. If necessary, turn the switch off and then back on.

3. Turn the ignition switch on and measure the voltage. It should equal battery voltage.
4. Repeat this test for each of the remaining fuel injectors.

THROTTLE POSITION (TP) SENSOR

Tools

The following Suzuki tools, or equivalent tools, are needed to test and service the TP sensor.
1. The Suzuki Torx wrench (part No. 09930-11950) is needed to remove, install and adjust the TP sensor.
2. The Suzuki mode select switch (part No. 09930-82720) is needed to adjust the TP sensor.
3. The Suzuki needle pointed test probe (part No. 09900-25009) to test the TP sensor.

Removal/Installation

2006-2007 Models

NOTE
The TPS and STPS are very similar in appearance. Make sure to check both the sensors and the electrical connector colors prior to removal of the sensor.

1. Disconnect the electrical lead from the negative battery terminal (Chapter Nine).
2. Remove the throttle body assembly as described in his chapter.
3. Scribe an index line across the TP sensor and throttle body so the sensor can be reinstalled in the same position.
4. Use the Torx wrench and remove the single mounting screw (A, **Figure 123**).
5. Pull the TP sensor (B, **Figure 123**) from the throttle shaft, and remove the sensor. Note how the throttle position sensor engages the throttle shaft.
6. Installation is the reverse of removal.

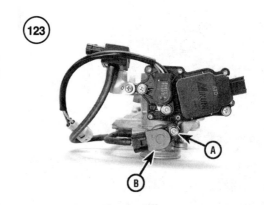

a. Apply grease (Suzuki Super Grease A, or equivalent) to the end of the throttle shaft.
b. Align the groove in the TP sensor with end of the throttle shaft, and slide the sensor (C) onto the shaft.
c. Position the TP sensor so the index mark made on the sensor aligns with the mark on throttle body.
d. Install the TP sensor mounting screw (A, **Figure 123**), and tighten to 3.5 N•m (31 in.-lb.).

2008-2009 Models

NOTE
The TPS and STPS are very similar in appearance. Make sure to check both the sensors and the electrical connector colors prior to removal of the sensor.

1. Disconnect the electrical lead from the negative battery terminal (Chapter Nine).
2. Remove the throttle body assembly as described in this chapter.

3. Scribe an index line across the TP sensor and throttle body so the sensor can be reinstalled in the same position.

4. Use the Torx wrench and remove the single mounting screw (A, **Figure 124**).

5. Pull the TP sensor (B, **Figure 124**) from the throttle shaft, and remove the sensor. Note how the throttle position sensor engages the throttle shaft.

6. Installation is the reverse of removal.

   a. Apply grease (Suzuki Super Grease A, or equivalent) to the end of the throttle shaft.

   b. Align the groove in the TP sensor with end of the throttle shaft, and slide the sensor (C) onto the shaft.

   c. Position the TP sensor so the index mark made on the sensor aligns with the mark on throttle body.

   d. Install the TP sensor mounting screw (A, **Figure 124**), and tighten to 3.5 N•m (31 in.-lb.).

Adjustment

2006-2007 Models

CAUTION
Do not attempt this procedure without the mode select switch. Shorting the terminals in the dealer model connector could damage the ECM.

1. Start the engine and check the idle speed. If necessary, adjust the idle to specification (Chapter Three).

2. Stop the engine.

3. Remove the rider seat and the passenger seat/tail cover (Chapter Fifteen).

4. Remove the cover (**Figure 125**), and connect the mode select switch to the dealer mode connector.

5. Turn the model select switch to on.

6. The malfunction code *c00* should appear in the meter display. The dash before the code indicates the

state of the TP sensor adjustment. The dash should be in the middle position as shown in **Figure 126**. If the dash is in the upper or lower position, adjust the sensor by performing the following:

   a. Raise and support the fuel tank as described in this chapter.

NOTE
The following photographs show the throttle bodies removed for photographic clarity. The bodies do not need to be removed to adjust the TP sensor.

   b. Loosen the throttle position sensor screw (A, **Figure 123**).

   c. Rotate the throttle position sensor (B, **Figure 123**) until the dash moves to the center position.

   d. Tighten the TP sensor screw to 3.5 N•m (31 in.-lb.).

7. Disconnect the mode select switch and install the cover.

8. Install the rider seat and the passenger seat/tail cover (Chapter Fifteen).

2008-2009 Models

CAUTION
Do not attempt this procedure without the mode select switch. Shorting the terminals in the dealer model connector could damage the ECM.

1. Start the engine and check the idle speed. If necessary, adjust the idle to specification (Chapter Three).

2. Stop the engine.

3. Remove the rider seat and the passenger seat/tail cover (Chapter Fifteen).

4. Remove the cover (**Figure 125**), and connect the mode select switch to the dealer mode connector.

5. Turn the model select switch to on.

6. The malfunction code c00 should appear in the meter display. The dash before the code indicates the state of the TP sensor adjustment. The dash should be in the middle position as shown in **Figure 126**. If the dash is in the upper or lower position, adjust the sensor by performing the following:

   a. Raise and support the fuel tank as described in this chapter.

NOTE
The following photographs show the throttle bodies removed for photographic clarity. The bodies do not need to be removed to adjust the TP sensor.

b. Loosen the throttle position sensor screw (A, **Figure 123**).

c. Rotate the throttle position sensor (B, **Figure 123**) until the dash moves to the center position.

d. Tighten the TP sensor screw to 3.5 N•m (31 in.-lb.).

7. Disconnect the mode select switch and install the cover.

8. Install the rider seat and the passenger seat/tail cover (Chapter Fifteen).

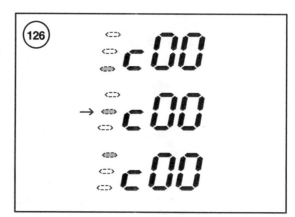

Continuity Test (All Models)

1. Turn the ignition switch off.

2. Raise and support the fuel tank as described in this chapter.

3. Disconnect the 3-pin throttle position sensor connector (**Figure 127**, typical) from its subharness mate.

4. Check the continuity between the pink/black wire (A, **Figure 128**) and red wire (C) in the sensor side of the connector and a good ground.

5. Reverse the test probes, and check the continuity in the opposite direction.

6. Both readings should indicate no continuity (infinity).

Resistance Test (2006-2007 Models Only)

NOTE
The manufacturer does not provide resistance procedure or specifications for the 2008-2009 models.

1. Perform Steps 1-3 of the TP sensor continuity test as described in this chapter

2. Check the resistance between the pink/black and red wire in the sensor side of the connector.

3. Read the resistance when the throttle is fully closed and fully open. Record each reading.

4. The fully open and fully closed resistance should be within the ranges specified in **Table 2**.

Input Voltage Test (All Models)

1. Perform Steps 1-2 of the TP sensor continuity test.

2. Connect a voltmeter's positive test probe to the red terminal (A, **Figure 129**) in the harness side of the TP sensor connector; connect the voltmeter's negative probe to ground.

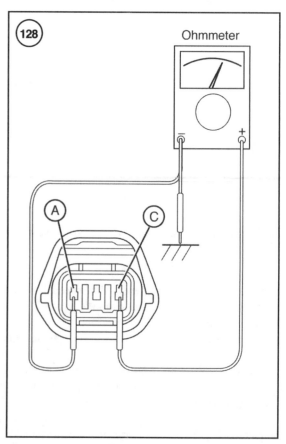

Ohmmeter

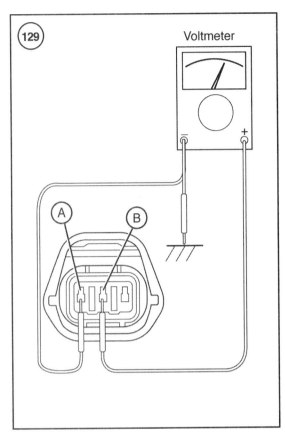

Voltmeter

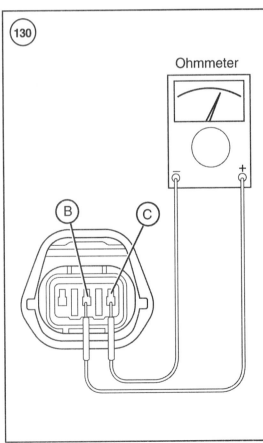

Ohmmeter

3. Turn the ignition switch on, and measure the input voltage. It should be within the range specified in **Table 2**.

4. Connect the voltmeter's positive test probe to the red terminal (A, **Figure 129**) in the harness side of the TP sensor connector; connect the negative test probe to the black/brown terminal (B, **Figure 129**) in the harness side of the connector.

5. The input voltage should be within the range specified in **Table 2**.

Output Voltage Test
(All Models)

1. Raise and support the fuel tank as described in this chapter.

2. Make sure the 3-pin connector (**Figure 127**, typical) securely engages the TP sensor.

3. Connect the positive end of the test probe to the pink/black wire (B, **Figure 130**) at the TP sensor.

4. Connect the negative end of the test probe to the black/brown wire (C, **Figure 130**) at the TP sensor.

5. Turn the ignition switch on.

6. Measure the output voltage when the throttle is fully closed and fully opened. Each measurement should be within the range specified in **Table 2**.

7. Lower and secure the fuel tank as described in this chapter.

SECONDARY THROTTLE POSITION
(STP) SENSOR

Tools

The following Suzuki tools, or equivalent tools, are needed to test and service the TP sensor.

1. The Suzuki Torx wrench (part No. 09930-11950) is needed to remove, install and adjust the STP sensor.

2. The Suzuki mode select switch (part No. 09930-82720) is needed to adjust the STP sensor.

3. The Suzuki needle pointed test probe (part No. 09900-25009) to test the STP sensor.

Removal/Installation
(All Models)

NOTE
The TPS and STPS are very similar in appearance. Make sure to check both the sensors and the electrical connector colors prior to removal of the sensor.

1. Disconnect the electrical lead from the negative battery terminal (Chapter Nine).

2. Remove the throttle body assembly as described in this chapter.

3. Scribe an index line across the STP sensor and throttle body so the sensor can be reinstalled in the same position.

4A. On 2006-2007 models, use the Torx wrench and remove the single mounting screw (A, **Figure 131**), and pull the STP sensor (B) from the secondary throttle valve shaft.

4B. On 2008-2009 models, use the Torx wrench and remove the single mounting screw (A, **Figure 132**), and pull the STP sensor (B) from the secondary throttle valve shaft.

5. Installation is the reverse of removal.

   a. Apply grease (Suzuki Super Grease A, or equivalent) to the end of the secondary throttle valve shaft.

   b. Align the STP slot with the secondary throttle shaft, and install the sensor onto the shaft.

   c. Position the secondary throttle position sensor on the actuator so the index line on the sensor aligns with the mark on the actuator or throttle body.

   d. Install the STP sensor screw, and tighten 3.5 N•m (31 in.-lb.). Refer to A, **Figure 131** or A, **Figure 132**.

6. Install the throttle body as described in this chapter.

7. Connect the electrical lead onto the negative battery terminal (Chapter Nine).

Adjustment and Output Voltage Test (2006-2007 Models)

1. Remove the fuel tank and air filter housing as described in this chapter.

NOTE
A single clamp screw loosens the two outside intake manifold clamps on each side of the motorcycle.

2. Loosen the intake manifold clamp screw on each side.

3. Lift the throttle body assembly and disengage each throttle body from its intake manifolds. Raise the assembly sufficiently to access the throttle wheel, and lower the assembly.

4. Loosen the locknut (A, **Figure 133**) on both throttle cables. Turn the adjuster to create sufficient slack, and disconnect the throttle pull cable end (B, **Figure 133**) from the top slot in the throttle wheel.

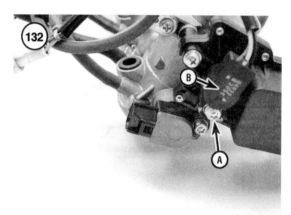

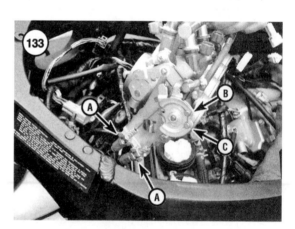

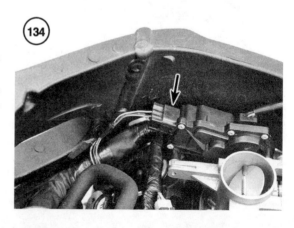

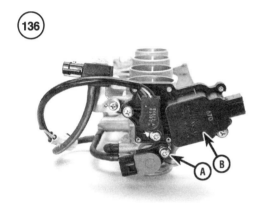

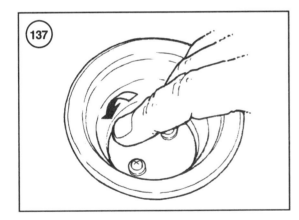

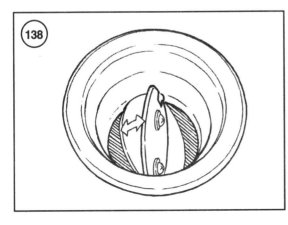

5. Repeat Step 4 and disconnect the return cable end (C, **Figure 133**) from the bottom slot in the throttle wheel.

6. Disconnect the STVA 4-pin electrical connector (**Figure 134**).

7. Disconnect the STP 3-pin electrical connector (**Figure 135**).

8. Connect a voltmeter's positive test probe to the yellow terminal in the harness side of the STP sensor connector; connect the voltmeter's negative probe to black terminal.

9. Manually move the secondary throttle valve to its fully closed position, and measure the STP output voltage. The voltage should equal the fully-closed resistance specified in **Table 2**.

10. If the voltage is out of specification, loosen the STP sensor screw (A, **Figure 136**) and rotate the sensor (B) around the screw until the voltage is within specification.

11. Tighten the STP sensor screw to 3.5 Nm (31 in.-lb.).

12. Disconnect the test probe from the STP sensor connector.

13. Lubricate the inner surface of each intake manifold with a soap solution to ease installation.

14. Fully seat each throttle body into its intake manifold. A solid bottoming will be felt when a throttle body is correctly seated.

15. Tighten the intake manifold clamp screws securely.

16. Install the fuel tank and air filter housing as described in this chapter.

17. Adjust the throttle cable free play, idle speed, and fast idle speed (Chapter Three).

**Output Voltage Test
(2008-2009 Models)**

1. Raise and support the fuel tank as described in this chapter.

2. Disconnect the STVA 4-pin electrical connector (A, **Figure 99**).

3. Connect a voltmeter's positive test probe to the yellow terminal in the harness side of the STP sensor 3-pin connector (**Figure 101**);connect the voltmeter's negative probe to black terminal.

4. Manually move the secondary throttle valve to its fully closed position (**Figure 137**), and measure the STP output voltage. The voltage should equal the fully-closed resistance specified in **Table 2**.

5. Manually move the secondary throttle valve to its fully open position (**Figure 138**), and measure the STP output voltage. The voltage should equal the fully-closed resistance specified in **Table 2**.

6. Lower and secure the fuel tank as described in this chapter.

8

Input Voltage Test
(All Models)

1. Raise and support the fuel tank as described in this chapter.
2. Connect a voltmeter positive test probe to the red terminal (A, **Figure 139**) in the harness side of the connector; connect the negative test probe to a good ground.
3. Turn the ignition switch on, and measure the voltage. It should be within the input voltage range specified in **Table 2**.
4. Turn the ignition switch off.
5. With the voltmeter positive test probe still connected to the red terminal (A, **Figure 139**), connect the negative test probe to the black/brown terminal (C, **Figure 139**) in the harness side of the connector.
6. Turn the ignition switch on and measure the voltage. It should also be within the specified input voltage range.
7. Connect the 3-pin STP sensor connector.
8. Lower and secure the fuel tank as described in this chapter.

Continuity Test
(All Models)

1. Remove the air filter housing as described in this chapter.
2. Make sure the ignition switch is off.
3. Make sure the 3-pin connector securely engages the STP sensor.
4A. On 2006-2007 models, disconnect the 3-pin connector (**Figure 135**) from the STP sensor.
4B. On 2007-2008 models, disconnect the 3-pin connector (**Figure 101**) from the STP sensor.
5. Connect an ohmmeter positive test probe to the connector white/yellow wire (B, **Figure 140**); connect the negative test probe the connector red wire (A) on the harness side of the connector.
6. There should be continuity.
7. Install the air filter housing as described in this chapter.

Resistance Test
(All Models)

1. Perform Step 1 and Step 2 of the STP sensor continuity test.
2A. On 2006-2007 models, disconnect the 3-pin connector (**Figure 135**) from the STP sensor.
2B. On 2008-2009 models, disconnect the 3-pin connector (**Figure 101**) from the STP sensor.

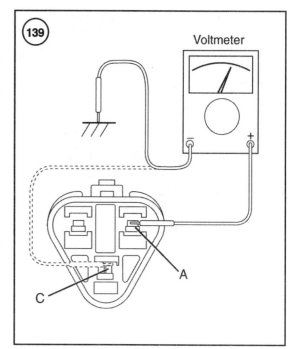

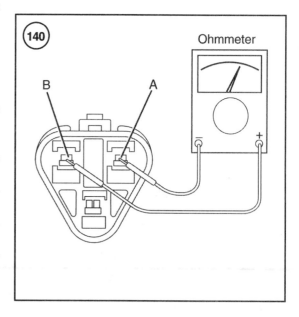

3. Check for continuity between each terminal and ground. Each measurement should indicate no continuity.
4. Connect an ohmmeter positive test probe to the yellow terminal (B, **Figure 141**) in the sensor side of the connector; connect the negative test probe to the black terminal (C) in the sensor side of the connector.
5. Manually move the secondary throttle valve to its fully closed position (**Figure 137**), and measure the resistance. It should equal the fully closed resistance specified in **Table 2**.

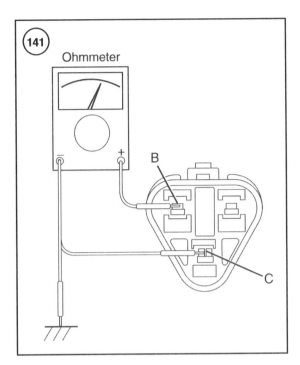

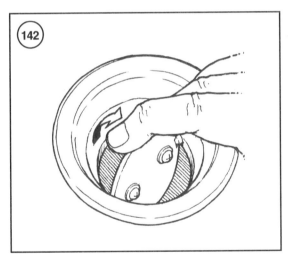

6. Manually move the secondary throttle valve to its fully open position (**Figure 142**), and measure the resistance. It should equal the specified fully open resistance specified in **Table 2**.

SECONDARY THROTTLE VALVE (STV) ACTUATOR

CAUTION
Do not remove the secondary throttle valve actuator from the throttle body. Replace the throttle body if the STCA requires replacement.

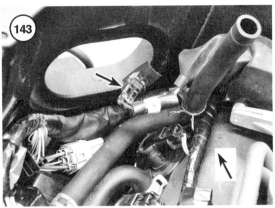

Operation Test

1. Remove the air filter housing as described in this chapter.
2. Turn the ignition switch on, and watch the movement of secondary throttle valves (**Figure 138**).
3. Each valve should move from its fully open position to its 95% open position.
4. Install the air filter housing as described in this chapter.

Continuity Test

1. Remove the air filter housing as described in this chapter.
2A. On 2006-2007 models, disconnect the 4-pin electrical connector (**Figure 134**) from the secondary throttle valve actuator.
2B. On 2008-2009 models, disconnect the 4-pin electrical connector (**Figure 143**) from the secondary throttle valve actuator.
3. Check the continuity between each terminal in the actuator and a good ground (**Figure 144**). Take a total of four readings.
4. Each measurement should indicate no continuity (infinite resistance).
5. Install the air filter housing as described in this chapter.

Resistance Test

1. Turn the ignition switch off, and support the fuel tank.
2A. On 2006-2007 models, disconnect the 4-pin electrical connector (**Figure 134**) from the secondary throttle valve actuator.
2B. On 2008-2009 models, disconnect the 4-pin electrical connector (**Figure 143**) from the secondary throttle valve actuator.

3. Connect an ohmmeter negative test probe to the A terminal shown in **Figure 145**; connect the positive test probe to the B terminal. Record the resistance.

4. Connect an ohmmeter negative test probe to the C terminal as shown in **Figure 145**; connect the positive test probe to the D terminal. Record the resistance.

5. Each reading should equal the specified value (**Table 2**).

6. Lower and secure the fuel tank as described in this chapter.

ATMOSPHERIC PRESSURE (AP) SENSOR

Removal/Installation

1. Remove the rider's and passenger seat (Chapter Fifteen).

2. Disconnect the electrical lead from the negative battery terminal (Chapter Nine).

3A. On 2006-2007 models, perform the following:
   a. Lift the AP sensor (A, **Figure 146**) from its mounting tang.
   b. Disconnect the 3-pin connector (B, **Figure 146**), and remove the sensor from the damper.

3B. On 2008-2009 models, perform the following:
   a. Lift the AP sensor (A, **Figure 147**) from its mounting tang.
   b. Disconnect the 3-pin connector (B, **Figure 147**), and remove the sensor from the damper.

4. Installation is the reverse of removal.

Input Voltage Test

1. Remove the rider and passenger seat (Chapter Fifteen).

2. Make sure the ignition switch is off.

3. Make sure the 3-pin connector securely engages the AP sensor.

4A. On 2006-2007 models, perform the following:
   a. Lift the AP sensor (A, **Figure 146**) from its mounting tang.
   b. Disconnect the 3-pin connector (B, **Figure 146**), and remove the sensor from the damper.

4B. On 2008-2009 models, perform the following:
   a. Lift the AP sensor (A, **Figure 147**) from its mounting tang.
   b. Disconnect the 3-pin connector (B, **Figure 147**), and remove the sensor from the damper.

5. Connect a voltmeter's positive test probe to the red terminal (A, **Figure 148**) in the sensor's connector; connect the negative test probe (B) to ground.

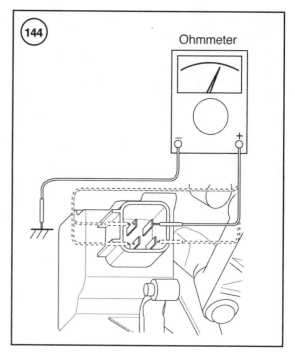

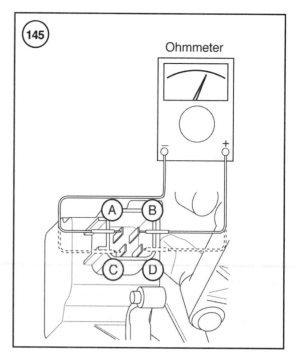

6. Turn the ignition switch on, and measure the voltage. It should be within the input voltage range specified in **Table 2**.

7. Turn the ignition switch off.

8. Connect the voltmeter's positive test probe to the red terminal (A, **Figure 148**) in the sensor's connector; connect the negative test probe to the black/brown terminal (B) in the sensor's connector.

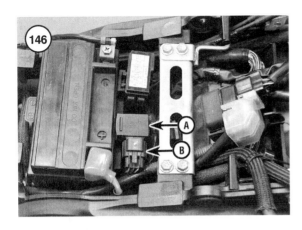

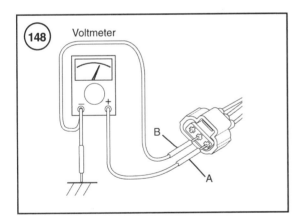

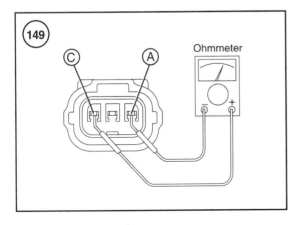

9. Turn the ignition switch on, and measure the voltage. It should be within the input voltage range specified in **Table 2**.

10. Reconnect the 3-pin electrical connector.

11. Install the rider's and passenger seat (Chapter Fifteen).

Resistance Test

1. Perform Step 1-5 of the AP sensor input voltage test.

2. Connect the ohmmeter negative test probe to the gray/yellow terminal (A, **Figure 149**); connect the positive test probe to the red wire terminal (B).

3. The measurement should indicate no continuity (infinite resistance).

Vacuum Test

Refer to **Figure 150**.

1. Remove the atmospheric pressure sensor as described this section.

2. Make sure the sensor's air passage is clear, and connect a vacuum pump and gauge to the air passage.

3. Connect three new 1.5 volt batteries in series. Measure the total voltage of the batteries. The voltage must be 4.5-5 volts. Replace the batteries if necessary.

4. Connect the battery positive terminal to the Vcc terminal in the sensor; connect the battery negative terminal to the ground terminal in the sensor.

5. Connect the voltmeter's positive test probe to the Vout terminal in the sensor; connect the negative test probe to the battery negative terminal.

6. Note the voltage reading. It should be within the Vout voltage range specified in **Table 2**.

7. Use the vacuum pump to apply vacuum to the sensor's air passage, and note the changes in the voltage reading. The voltage should decrease as vacuum increases up to 53 kPa (400 mm Hg).

8. Install the atmospheric pressure sensor (this section).

INTAKE AIR PRESSURE (IAP) SENSOR

Removal/Installation

1. Disconnect the electrical cable from the negative battery terminal.

2. Raise and support the fuel tank as described in this chapter.

3. Disconnect the electrical connector (**Figure 151**) from the intake air pressure (IAP) sensor on the air filter housing.

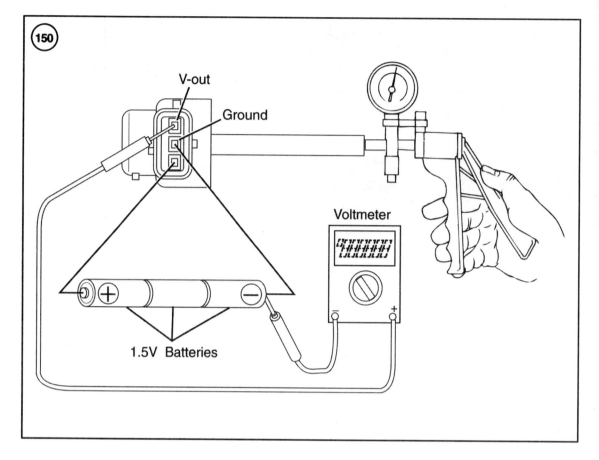

Input Voltage Test

1. Turn the ignition switch off, and disconnect the 3-pin connector from the IAP sensor.

2. Connect a voltmeter's positive test probe to the red terminal (in the sensor's connector; connect the negative test probe to ground.

3. Turn the ignition switch on, and measure the voltage. It should be within the input voltage range specified in **Table 2**.

4. Turn the ignition switch off.

5. Connect the voltmeter's positive test probe to the red terminal (A, **Figure 148**) in the sensor's connector; connect the negative test probe to the black/brown terminal (B) in the sensor's connector.

6. Turn the ignition switch on, and measure the voltage. It should be within the input voltage specified range (**Table 2**).

7. Turn the ignition switch off.

4. Withdraw the IAP from the air filter lower housing.

5. Installation is the reverse of removal.

Output Voltage Test

1. Make sure the IAP sensor connector is securely mated to the IAP sensor.

2. Connect a voltmeter's positive test probe to the red terminal (A, **Figure 149**) in the connector; connect the negative test probe to the black/brown terminal (C). Use 0.5 mm (0.02 in.) wires to back probe the IAP connector during this test.

3. Start the engine and run it at idle, and measure the voltage. It should equal the output voltage specified in **Table 2**.

Vacuum Test

1. Remove the intake air pressure sensor as described in this chapter.

2. Make sure the sensor's air passage is clear, and connect a vacuum pump and gauge to the air passage.

3. Connect three new 1.5 volt batteries in series. Measure the total voltage of the batteries. The voltage must be 4.5-5 volts. Replace the batteries if necessary.

4. Connect the battery positive terminal to the Vcc terminal in the sensor; connect the battery negative terminal to the ground terminal in the sensor.

5. Connect the voltmeter's positive test probe to the Vout terminal in the sensor; connect the negative test probe to the battery negative terminal.

6. Note the voltage reading. It should be within the Vout voltage range specified in **Table 2**.

7. Use the vacuum pump to apply vacuum to the sensor's air passage, and note the changes in the voltage reading. The voltage should decrease as vacuum increases up to 53 kPa (400 mm Hg).

8. Install the intake air pressure sensor as described in this chapter.

INTAKE AIR TEMPERATURE (IAT) SENSOR

Removal/Installation

1. Disconnect the electrical lead from the negative battery terminal.

2. Raise and support the fuel tank as described in this chapter.

3A. On 2006-2007 models, perform the following:

    a. Disconnect the 2-pin connector (A, **Figure 152**) from the IAT sensor.

    b. Unscrew and remove the sensor (B, **Figure 152**) from the air filter housing. Discard the sensor's O-ring.

3B. On 2008-2009 models, perform the following:

    a. Remove the air filter housing mounting screw, and raise the left side of the housing.

    b. Disconnect the 2-pin connector (**Figure 153**) from the IAT sensor.

    c. Unscrew and remove the sensor from the air filter housing. Discard the sensor's O-ring.

4. Installation is the reverse of removal. Install a *new* O-ring onto the sensor and tighten securely.

Input Voltage Test

1. Turn the ignition switch off, and perform Step 2 and Step 3 of the IAT sensor removal procedure.

2. Connect the voltmeter positive test probe to the dark green terminal (A, **Figure 154**) in the connector; connect the negative test probe to a good ground.

3. Turn on the ignition switch and measure the voltage. It should be within the range specified in **Table 2**.

4. Connect the voltmeter positive test probe to the dark green terminal (A, **Figure 154**) in the connector; connect the negative test probe to the black/brown terminal (B) in the connector.

5. Turn the ignition switch on. The voltage should be within the range specified in **Table 2**.

6. Turn the ignition switch off.

Output Voltage Test

1. Turn the ignition switch off, and perform Step 2 and Step 3 of the IAT sensor removal procedure.

2. Connect the voltmeter positive test probe to the dark green terminal (**Figure 155**) in the connector; connect the negative test probe to a good ground.

3. Turn on the ignition switch and measure the voltage. It should be within the range specified in **Table 2**.

4. Turn the ignition switch off.

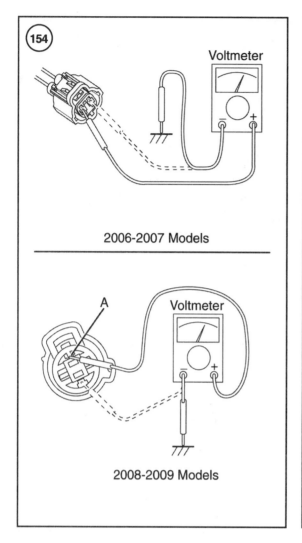

2006-2007 Models

2008-2009 Models

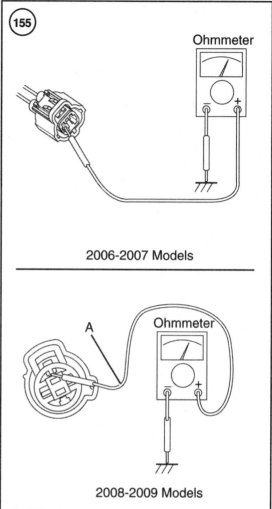

2006-2007 Models

2008-2009 Models

Resistance Test

1. Turn the ignition switch off, and perform Step 2 and Step 3 of the IAT sensor removal procedure.

2. Connect the ohmmeter negative test probe to the dark green terminal (A, **Figure 156**) in the sensor; connect the positive test probe to the sensor's black/brown terminal (B).

3. Measure the resistance. It should be within the range specified in **Table 2**.

ENGINE COOLANT TEMPERATURE (ECT) SENSOR

Removal/Installation

1. Disconnect the electrical lead from the negative battery terminal.

2. Drain the coolant as described in Chapter Three.

3. Remove the air filter housing as described in this chapter.and the throttle bodies (if necessary).

4. Disconnect the two-pin connector (**Figure 157**) from the ECT sensor.

CAUTION
The ETC sensor is sensitive to shock. Use caution when handling the sensor.

5. Remove the ECT sensor from the back of the cylinder head. Account for the sealing washer installed with the sensor.

6. Installation is the reverse of removal. Install the *new* sealing washer, and tighten the engine coolant temperature sensor to 18 N•m (13 ft.-lb.).

Bench Test

1. Remove the ECT sensor (this section).

2. Fill a beaker or pan with clean oil, and place it on a stove or hot plate.

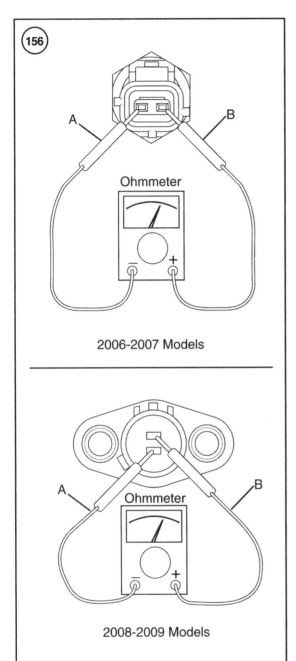

2006-2007 Models

2008-2009 Models

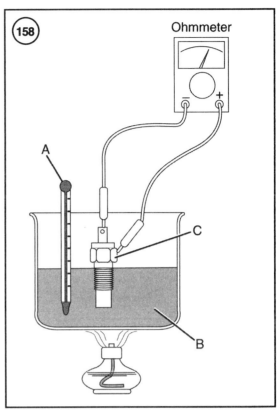

NOTE
The thermometer and the sensor must not touch the container sides or bottom. If either does, test readings will be inaccurate.

3. Place a thermometer (A, **Figure 158**) in the pan (use a cooking or candy thermometer that is rated higher than the test temperature).

4. Mount the ECT sensor so that the temperature sensing tip and the threaded portion of the body are submerged (B, **Figure 158**)

5. Attach an ohmmeter to the sensor terminals as shown in C, **Figure 158**. Check the resistance as follows:

    a. Gradually heat the oil to the temperatures specified in **Table 2**. Note the resistance of the sensor when the oil temperature reaches the specified values.

    b. Replace the ECT sensor if any reading equals infinity or is considerably different than the specified resistance at a given temperature in **Table 2**.

6. Install the ECT sensor (this section).

Input Voltage Test

1. Turn the ignition switch off, and perform Step 2-4 of the ECT sensor removal procedure.

2. Connect the voltmeter positive test probe to the black/blue terminal (A, **Figure 154**) in the connector; connect the negative test probe to a good ground.

3. Turn the ignition switch on, and measure the voltage. It should be within the range specified in **Table 2**.

4. Connect the voltmeter positive test probe to the black/blue terminal (A, **Figure 154**) in the connector; connect the negative test probe to the black/brown terminal (B) in the connector.

5. Turn the ignition switch on. The voltage should be within the specified range in **Table 2**.

Output Voltage Test

1. Turn the ignition switch off, and perform Step 2-3 of the ECT sensor removal procedure.

2. Connect the two-pin connector (**Figure 157**) onto the ECT sensor.

3. Connect the voltmeter positive test probe to the black/blue terminal on the connector; connect the negative test probe to a good ground.

4. Turn on the ignition switch and measure the voltage. It should be within the range specified in **Table 2**.

5. Turn the ignition switch off.

Resistance Test

1. Turn the ignition switch off, and perform Step 2 and Step 3 of the IAT sensor removal procedure.

2. Connect the ohmmeter between the two sensor terminals.

3. Measure the resistance. It should be within the range specified in **Table 2**.

CAMSHAFT POSITION (CMP) SENSOR

Removal/Installation

1. Disconnect the battery negative cable as described in Chapter Nine.

2. Remove the fuel tank as described in this chapter.

3. Remove the air filter housing as described in this chapter.

4A. On 2006-2007 models, disconnect the 3-pin connector (**Figure 159**) from the CMP sensor.

4B. On 2008-2009 models, disconnect the 3-pin connector (**Figure 160**) from the CMP sensor.

NOTE
***Figure 161** is shown with the cylinder head cover removed for photo clarity.*

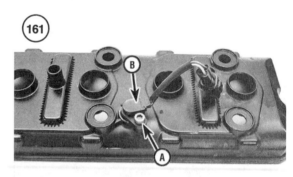

5. Remove the CMP bolt (A, **Figure 161**), and lift the sensor (B) from the cylinder head cover. Watch for the oil seal behind the sensor

6. Installation is the reverse of removal.

    a. Install a new oil seal with the sensor.

    b. Tighten the camshaft position sensor bolt (B, **Figure 161**) to 10 N•m (89 in.-lb.).

Voltage Test

1. Remove the CMP sensor as described in this section.

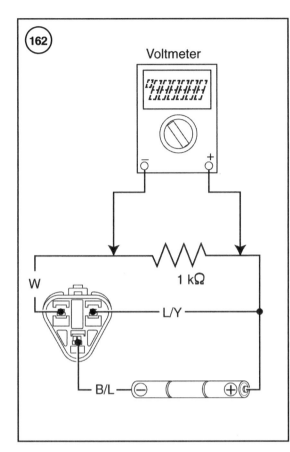

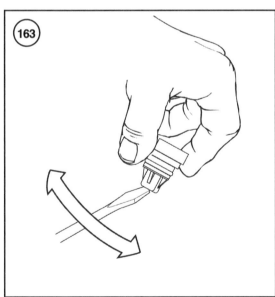

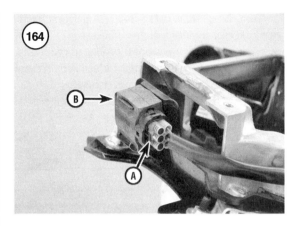

4. The voltage should be within the range specified in **Table 2**.

5. Install the CMP sensor (this section).

CRANKSHAFT POSITION (CKP) SENSOR

Refer to *Ignition System* in Chapter Nine for crankshaft position sensor removal and test procedures.

TIP OVER (TO) SENSOR

Whenever the tip over sensor is activated, the ECM cuts off power to the fuel pump, ignition coils and fuel injectors.

Removal/Installation

1. Disconnect the electrical cable from the negative battery terminal.

2A. On 2006-2007 models, perform the following:

    a. Remove the seat/tail cover (Chapter Fifteen).

    b. Disconnect the 3-pin connector (A, **Figure 164**) from the tip over sensor.

    c. Disengage the tip over sensor (B, **Figure 164**) from the mounting tabs on the frame, and remove it.

2B. On 2008-2009 models, perform the following:

    a. Remove the rider seat (Chapter Fifteen).

    b. Disconnect the 3-pin connector (A, **Figure 165**) from the tip over sensor.

    c. Disengage the tip over sensor (B, **Figure 165**) from the mounting tabs on the frame, and remove it.

3. Installation is the reverse of removal.

Resistance Test

1. Disconnect the electrical cable from the negative battery terminal.

2. Connect three new 1.5 volt batteries in series, and a 1 K resistor. Connect a voltmeter on each side of the resistor as shown in **Figure 162**.

3. Touch the surface of the sensor with a flat-blade screwdriver, and move it back and forth as shown in **Figure 163**.

2. Turn the ignition switch off, and perform Step 2 of the TO sensor removal procedure.

3. Connect the ohmmeter test probes to the red terminal (A, **Figure 166**) and to the black/brown terminal (C) in the sensor. Read the resistance.

4. The resistance should be within the range specified in **Table 2**.

Continuity Test

1. Disconnect the electrical cable from the negative battery terminal.

2. Turn the ignition switch off, and perform Step 2 of the TO sensor removal procedure.

3. Connect the ohmmeter positive test probe to the black terminal (B, **Figure 167**) in the connector; connect the negative test probe to a good ground. There should be continuity.

4. Connect the ohmmeter positive test probe to the black terminal (B, **Figure 167**) in the connector; connect the negative test probe to the black/brown terminal (C). There should be continuity.

5. Connect the ohmmeter positive test probe to the red terminal (A, **Figure 168**) in the connector; connect the negative test probe to the black terminal (B). There should be continuity.

Voltage Test

1A. On 2006-2007 models, remove the seat/tail cover (Chapter Fifteen).

1B. On 2008-2009 models, remove the rider seat (Chapter Fifteen).

2. Position the motorcycle in the upright position.

3. Connect the voltmeter positive test probe to black terminal in the harness side of the connector; connect the negative test probe to the black/brown terminal (harness side). Use 0.5 mm (0.02 in.) wires to back probe the connector during this test.

4. Turn the ignition switch on, and read the voltage.

5. Disengage the tip over sensor from the mounting tabs on the frame, and remove it.

6. Measure the voltage while tilting the sensor 65° and more from the horizontal position to the left and right side. Read the voltage.

7. Each reading should be within the range specified in **Table 2**.

8. Install the tip over sensor as described in this section.

9A. On 2006-2007 models, install the seat/tail cover (Chapter Fifteen).

9B. On 2008-2009 models, install the rider seat (Chapter Fifteen).

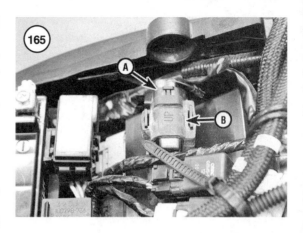

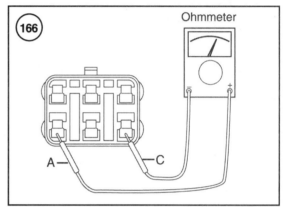

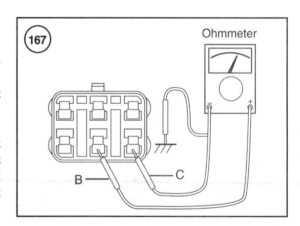

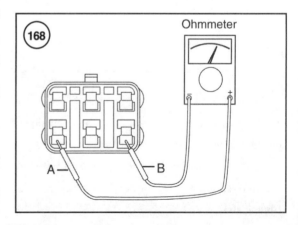

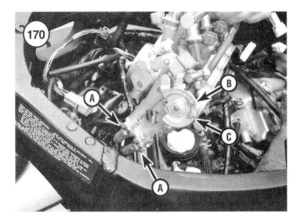

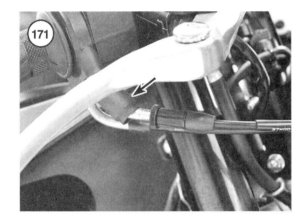

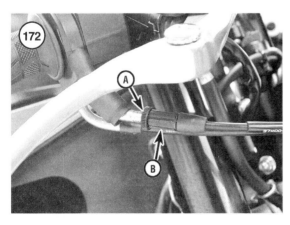

THROTTLE CABLE

All models are equipped with two throttle cables: the pull (or accelerator) cable and the return (or decelerator) cable. These cables are not identical. Label the old cables before removing them. Replace both cables as a set.

Removal/Installation

1. Disconnect the electrical cable from the negative battery terminal (Chapter Nine).
2. Remove the fuel tank and the air filter housing as described in this chapter.
3. Note how the throttle cables are routed from the right handlebar switch housing, through the holder adjacent to the ignition switch (A, **Figure 169**), and past the fork leg and steering stem (B). Make a drawing so the new cables can be rerouted along the same path followed by the old cables. Also note where the cables are secured to the motorcycle. The new cables must pass through the same holders/cable ties as the originals.

> *NOTE*
> *A single clamp screw loosens the two outside intake manifold clamps on each side of the motorcycle.*

4. Loosen the intake manifold clamp screw on each side.
5. Lift the throttle body assembly and disengage each throttle body from its intake manifolds. Raise the assembly sufficiently to access the throttle wheel, and lower the assembly.
6. Loosen the locknut (A, **Figure 170**, typical) on both throttle cables. Turn the adjuster to create sufficient slack, and disconnect the throttle pull cable end (B, **Figure 170**) from the top slot in the throttle wheel.
7. Repeat Step 6 and disconnect the return cable end (C, **Figure 170**) from the bottom slot of the throttle wheel.
8. On 2007-2008 models, slide the boot (**Figure 171**) off the pull cable.
9. At the throttle grip, loosen the pull cable locknut (A, **Figure 172**) and turn the adjuster (B) all the way into the switch assembly to allow maximum slack in the cable.
10. Remove the screw, and move the clamp away from the handlebar switch housing.
11. At the right handlebar switch, remove the screw and lower the return cable clamp from the switch housing.
12. Remove the switch housing screws and separate the housing halves.

13. Disconnect each cable end (A, **Figure 173**) from the throttle drum, and feed the cables through the housing half.

CAUTION
Do not lubricate nylon-lined cables. Nylon-lined cables are generally used dry. Oil and most cable lubricants will cause liner expansion, pinching the liner against the cable. Follow the cable manufacturer's instructions when installing nylon-lined and other aftermarket cables.

14. Lubricate the new cables as described in Chapter Three. Do not lubricate cable with nylon liners.

15. Route the new cables along the same path as the old cables.

16. Feed the pull cable through the upper port in the upper switch half. Feed the return cable through the lower port.

17. Move the cable clamp onto the switch housing, and install the securing screw.

18. Apply grease to the cable ends, and connect each cable end to the throttle drum (A, **Figure 173**). Make sure each cable is seated in the throttle drum channel.

19. Install the upper switch half over the throttle drum. Make sure its index pin (B, **Figure 173**) engages the hole in the handlebar, and install the switch housing screws. Tighten the screws securely.

20. At the throttle bodies, apply grease to the ends of the throttle cables, connect the return cable end (C, **Figure 170**) to the top slot in the throttle wheel, and fit the cable onto the bracket. Make sure a locknut sits on each side of the bracket.

21. Repeat Step 20 and connect the pull cable end (C, **Figure 170**) to the bottom slot of the throttle wheel. Make sure a locknut sits on each side of the bracket.

22. At the throttle body assembly, loosen the locknuts (A, **Figure 170**) on the both cables.

23. Turn each cable adjuster fully into the cable to create maximum amount of cable slack. Turn the forward locknut on each cable up against the cable adjuster so there is zero clearance between the nut and the adjuster (**Figure 174**).

24. Tighten the rear locknut on each cable against the cable bracket.

25. Operate the throttle drum on the handlebar and make sure the throttle wheel move smoothly. If any drag or binding is noted, check that the cables are attached correctly and there are no tight bends in either cable.

26. Adjust the cable free play (Chapter Three).

27. Install the air filter housing and fuel tank and the air filter housing as described in this chapter.

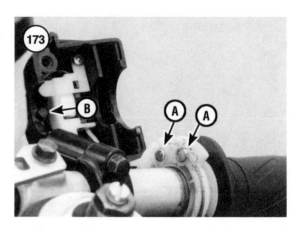

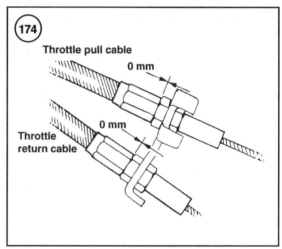

Throttle pull cable
0 mm
Throttle return cable
0 mm

WARNING
An improperly adjusted or incorrectly routed throttle cable can cause the throttle to hang open and lead to a crash. Do not ride the motorcycle until the throttle cable operation is correct.

28. Start the engine and let it idle. Turn the handlebar from side to side and listen to the engine speed. Make sure the idle speed does not increase. If it does, the throttle cables are incorrectly adjusted or improperly routed. Find and correct the source of the problem before riding. Turn off the engine.

EXHAUST SYSTEM (2006-2007 MODELS)

Refer to **Figure 175**.

Muffler Removal/Installation

1. Remove the lower faring (Chapter Fifteen).

2. Loosen the left-side mounting bolts (**Figure 176**).

3. Loosen the right-side mounting flange bolt (A, **Figure 177**).

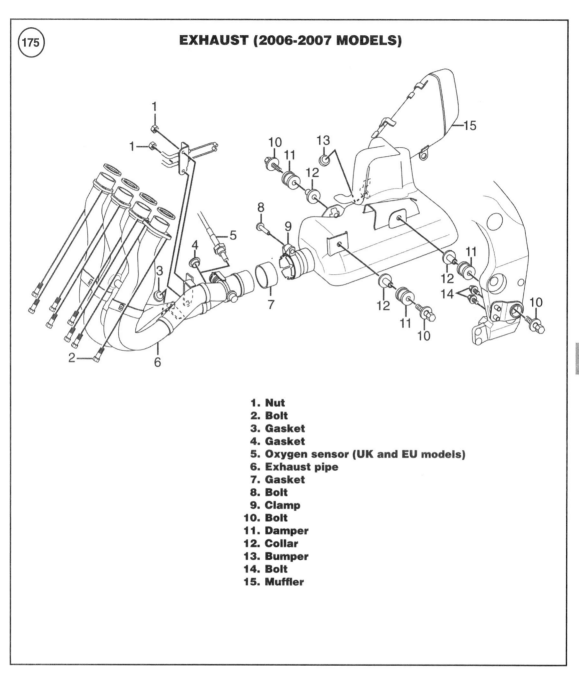

EXHAUST (2006-2007 MODELS)

1. Nut
2. Bolt
3. Gasket
4. Gasket
5. Oxygen sensor (UK and EU models)
6. Exhaust pipe
7. Gasket
8. Bolt
9. Clamp
10. Bolt
11. Damper
12. Collar
13. Bumper
14. Bolt
15. Muffler

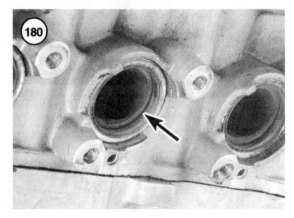

4. Loosen the muffler-to-exhaust pipe clamp bolt (B, **Figure 177**).

5. Remove the right and left side mounting flange bolts.

6. Pull the muffler (**Figure 178**) straight back and withdraw it from the exhaust pipe.

7. Observe the grommet and collar on each mounting tab.

8. Remove the gasket from the muffler, and discard it.

9. Installation is the reverse of removal. Note the following:

    a. Seat a *new* gasket into the muffler.

    b. Tighten the muffler mounting and clamp bolts to 23 N•m (17 ft.-lb.) on 2006-2007 models, or 25 N•m (18 ft-lbs.) on 2008-2009 models.

Exhaust Pipe Removal/Installation

1. Remove the front and both side fairing side panels (Chapter Fifteen).

2. Remove the radiator (Chapter Ten).

3. Remove the muffler (this section).

4. Lift and support the fuel tank as described in this chapter.

5. On models so equipped, disconnect the HO2 sensor connector from the harness connector.

6. Remove the EXCV cables and mounting bracket from the exhaust pipe as described in this chapter.

7. Remove the exhaust header bolts (A, **Figure 179**), and lower each header pipe clamp (B) from the cylinder head.

8. Disengage the header pipes from the cylinder head ports. Pull the exhaust header pipe forward, and remove the exhaust pipe assembly from the motorcycle.

9. Remove the exhaust gasket (**Figure 180**) from each exhaust port, and remove the gasket from the muffler pipe fitting.

10. Installation is the reverse of removal. Note the following:

    a. Position *new* exhaust gaskets with the tabs facing the exhaust pipe. Install a new exhaust gas-

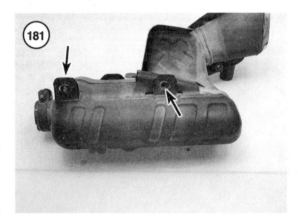

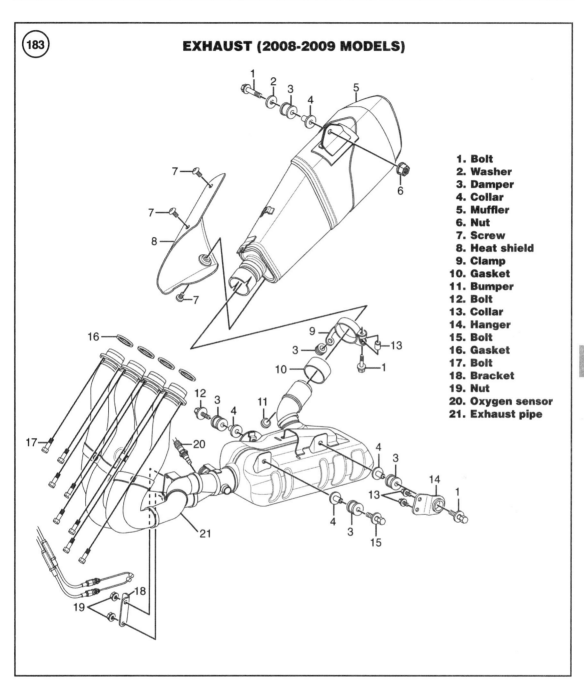

EXHAUST (2008-2009 MODELS)

1. Bolt
2. Washer
3. Damper
4. Collar
5. Muffler
6. Nut
7. Screw
8. Heat shield
9. Clamp
10. Gasket
11. Bumper
12. Bolt
13. Collar
14. Hanger
15. Bolt
16. Gasket
17. Bolt
18. Bracket
19. Nut
20. Oxygen sensor
21. Exhaust pipe

ket (**Figure 180**) into each exhaust port in the cylinder head.

   b. Tighten the exhaust header bolts to 23 N•m (17 ft.-lb.).

Inspection

1. Inspect all muffler hanger brackets (**Figure 181**), dampers, and collars for wear, cracks or damage.

2. Inspect the exhaust pipe-to-cylinder head fittings for corrosion, burned areas or damage.

3. Inspect the fitting on the exhaust pipe-to-muffler fitting in the muffler (**Figure 182**) for corrosion or damage.

4. Inspect all welds for leakage or corrosion.

EXHAUST SYSTEM (2008-2009 MODELS)

   Refer to **Figure 183**.

Muffler Removal/Installation

1. Remove the lower faring (Chapter Fifteen).

2. Remove the mounting screws and remove the chrome shield (**Figure 184**) from the muffler.

3. Loosen the muffler-to-exhaust pipe clamp bolt (**Figure 185**).

4. Remove the mounting bolt and nut (A, **Figure 186**).

5. Pull the muffler (B, **Figure 186**) straight back from the exhaust pipe.

6. Installation is the reverse of removal. Note the following:

   a. Apply engine oil to the new muffler stud O-rings, and install an O-ring onto each stud.

   b. Seat a new gasket into the muffler.

   c. Tighten the muffler mounting bolt/nut (A, **Figure 186**) to 25 N•m (18 ft.-lb.).

   d. Tighten the muffler clamp bolt (**Figure 185**) to 23 N•m (17 ft.-lb.).

Exhaust Pipe Removal/Installation

1. Remove the front and both side fairing side panels (Chapter Fifteen).

2. Remove the radiator (Chapter Ten).

3. Remove the muffler (this section).

4. Lift and support the fuel tank as described in this chapter.

5. Disconnect the HO2 sensor connector from the harness connector.

6. Remove the EXCV cables and mounting bracket from the exhaust pipe as described in this chapter.

7. Remove the exhaust header bolts (A, **Figure 179**), and lower each header pipe clamp (B) from the cylinder head.

8. Disengage the header pipes from the cylinder head ports. Pull the exhaust header pipe forward, and remove the exhaust pipe assembly from the motorcycle.

9. Remove the exhaust gasket (**Figure 180**) from each exhaust port, and remove the gasket from the muffler pipe fitting.

10. Remove the three exhaust pipe mounting bolts on each side.

11. Installation is the reverse of removal. Note the following:

   a. Position *new* exhaust gaskets with the tabs facing the exhaust pipe. Install a new exhaust gasket (**Figure 180**) into each exhaust port in the cylinder head.

   b. Tighten the exhaust header bolts, and the exhaust pipe mounting bolts to 23 N•m (17 ft.-lb.).

Inspection

1. Inspect all muffler mounting brackets, dampers, and collars for wear, cracks or damage.

2. Inspect the exhaust pipe-to-cylinder head fittings for corrosion, burned areas or damage.

3. Inspect the fitting on the exhaust pipe-to-muffler fitting in the muffler for corrosion or damage.

4. Inspect all welds for leakage or corrosion.

EXHAUST CONTROL VALVE ACTUATOR (EXCV) (2006-2007 MODELS)

The exhaust control valve actuator (**Figure 187**) opens and closes the exhaust control via a pulley and cables. The actuator/exhaust control valve sys-

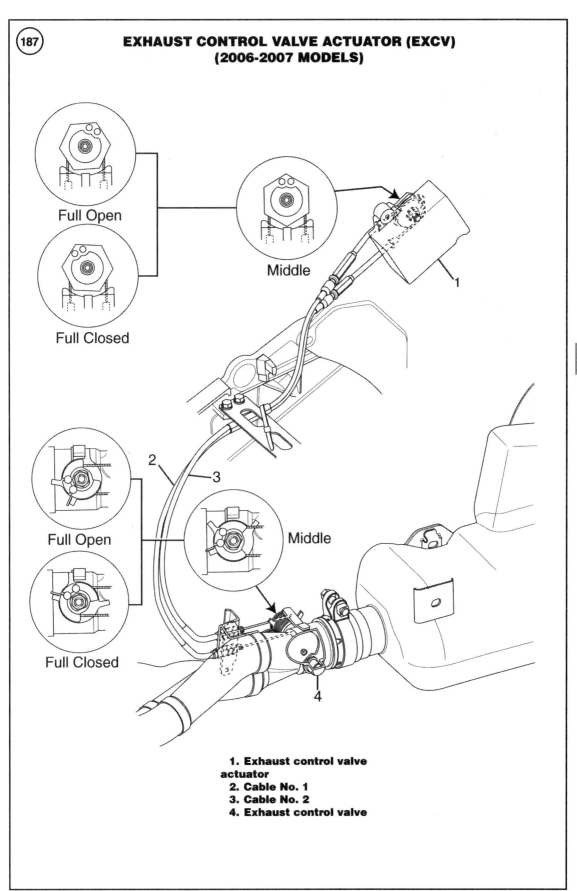

EXHAUST CONTROL VALVE ACTUATOR (EXCV)
(2006-2007 MODELS)

Full Open

Full Closed

Middle

Full Open

Middle

Full Closed

1. Exhaust control valve
actuator
2. Cable No. 1
3. Cable No. 2
4. Exhaust control valve

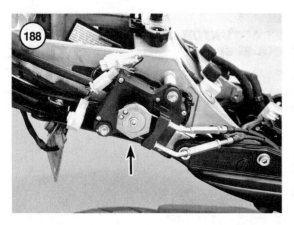

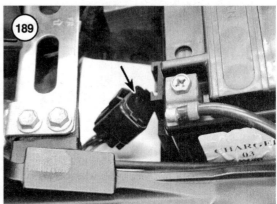

tem improves engine torque at low engine speeds. During operation, the ECM determines the control valve's optimum opening angle based upon engine speed and gear selection.

Whenever the ignition switch is turned on, the exhaust control valve actuator moves the exhaust control valve to its fully open position, to its fully closed position and then sets the exhaust control valve to the middle position.

The EXCVA mounts on the outboard side of the right side seat rail (**Figure 188**).

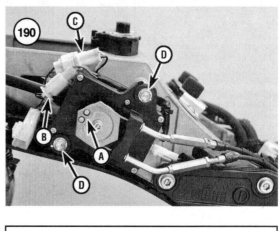

Removal

1. Remove the rider seat, and the seat/tail cover (Chapter Fifteen).
2. Turn the ignition switch off.
3. Remove the cover (**Figure 189**), and connect the mode select switch to the dealer mode connector.
4. Turn the model select switch on, turn the ignition switch on.
5. Check that the EXCVA pulley control cable slots are facing rearward in the correct adjusted position (A, **Figure 190**).
6. Turn the ignition switch off.
7. Disconnect the mode select switch and install the cover.
8. Disconnect the 2-pin (B, **Figure 190**), and 3-pin (C) electrical connectors from the EXCVA.
9. Measure the exposed thread lengths as shown in A and B, **Figure 191**, and note the dimensions prior to disconnecting the cables.
10. Identify the cables by their ID part numbers as follows:
    a. No. 1 cable (A, **Figure 192**) is numbers O1HOCL located in the upper slot.
    b. No. 2 cable (B, **Figure 192**) is numbers O1HOOP located in the lower slot.
11. Loosen the locknut (C, **Figure 192**) on the No. 1 cable (A), and turn in the adjuster (D) fully to provide slack.

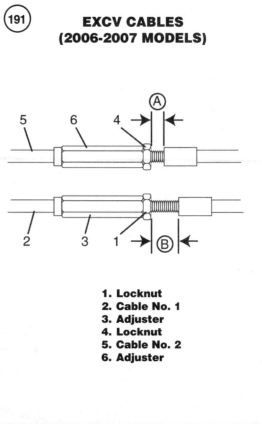

EXCV CABLES (2006-2007 MODELS)

1. Locknut
2. Cable No. 1
3. Adjuster
4. Locknut
5. Cable No. 2
6. Adjuster

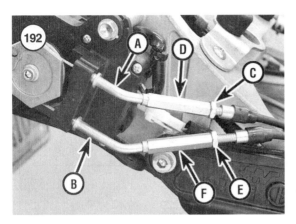

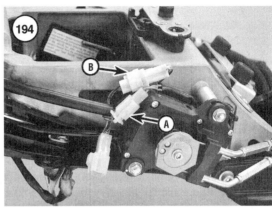

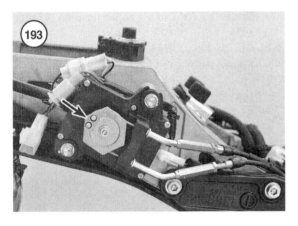

until the exposed thread length is the same as noted in Step 9. Tighten the locknut securely.

9. Loosen the cable locknut (E, **Figure 192**) on the No. 2 cable (A), and turn in the adjuster (F) in or out until the exposed thread length is the same as noted in Step 9. Tighten the locknut securely.

10. Connect the 2-pin (B, **Figure 190**), and 3-pin (C) electrical connectors onto the EXCVA.

11. Check that the EXCVA pulley control cable slots are facing rearward in the correct adjusted position (A, **Figure 190**).

12. Adjust the cables (this section).

13. Install the rider seat, and the seat/tail cover (Chapter Fifteen).

EXCVA Cable Adjustment

1. Remove the rider seat, the seat/tail cover, and the lower fairing (Chapter Fifteen).

2. Check that the EXCVA pulley control cable slots are facing rearward in the correct adjusted position (**Figure 193**).

3. Ensure the No. 1 and No. 2 cables are secure within the clamp at the exhaust pipe.

4. Remove the cover (**Figure 189**), and connect the mode select switch to the dealer mode connector.

5. Turn the model select switch off, turn the ignition switch on, and check the EXCVA operation.

6. Turn the model select switch on, and observe the meter display. Cable adjustment is correct if malfunction code C46 is *not* shown. If the code 46 is shown, proceed to Step 7.

7. Turn ignition switch off.

8. Use 0.5 mm (0.02 in.) wires to back probe the connector during this test. Insert the back probe wires into the EXAVC position sensor 3-pin electrical connector (A, **Figure 194**).

9. Disconnect the EXCVA motor lead wire 2-pin connector (B, **Figure 194**).

12. Loosen the locknut (E, **Figure 192**) on the No. 2 cable (B), and turn in the adjuster (F) fully to provide slack.

13. Disconnect the No. 2 cable (B, **Figure 192**) from the lower slot in the EXCVA pulley.

14. Disconnect the No. 1 cable (**Figure 193**) from the upper slot in the EXCVA pulley.

15. Remove the mounting bolts (D, **Figure 190**), and remove the EXCVA from the seat rail.

Installation

1. Install the EXCVA onto the seat rail in the correct position.

2. Install the mounting bolts (D, **Figure 190**), and tighten to 6 N•m (53 in.-lb.).

3. Turn the two cable adjusters in fully.

4. Make sure both cables are not kinked or excessively bent.

5. Apply clean engine oil to the cable ends.

6. Connect the No. 1 cable (A, **Figure 192**) onto the upper slot in the EXCVA pulley.

7. Connect the No. 2 cable (B, **Figure 192**) onto the lower slot in the EXCVA pulley.

8. Loosen the cable locknut (C, **Figure 192**) on the No. 1 cable (A), and turn in the adjuster (D) in or out

CAUTION
To avoid motor damage, disconnect the
12 volt battery as soon as the EXAVC
reaches the fully closed position.

10. To set the EXAVC to the fully closed position.
Attach the 12 volt battery positive terminal to the
2-pin connector (B, **Figure 194**) pink wire, and the
negative terminal to the gray wire.

11. Connect a voltmeter to the harness side of the
EXAVC position sensor 3-pin electrical connector (A, **Figure 194**); positive test probe to the yellow wire terminal and the negative test probe to the
black/brown wire terminal

12. Turn the ignition switch on, and measure the
position sensor output voltage at the fully closed position. The voltage should be within the range specified in **Table 2**.

CAUTION
Do not adjust the No. 1 cable with the
EXCV in the fully closed position as the
EXCVA will be damaged.

13. If the sensor output voltage is less than specified,
adjust the No. 1 cable as follows:
   a. Set the EXAVC to the adjust position (**Figure
     193**).
   b. On the No. 1 cable, loosen the locknut (A,
     Figure 195).
   c. Slowly turn out the cable adjuster (B, **Figure
     195**) until the voltage is within the range speci-
     fied in **Table 2**.
   d. If the malfunction code C46 is shown on
     the meter display; adjust the cable adjuster
     to achieve 0.9 volt. Tighten the locknut (A,
     Figure 195).

14. To set the EXAVC to the fully open position.
Attach the 12 volt battery positive terminal to the
2-pin connector (B, **Figure 194**) pink wire, and the
negative terminal to the gray wire.

CAUTION
To avoid motor damage, disconnect the
12 volt battery as soon as the EXAVC
reaches the fully open position.

15. Connect a voltmeter to the harness side of the
EXAVC position sensor 3-pin electrical connector (A, **Figure 194**); positive test probe to the yellow wire terminal and the negative test probe to the
black/brown wire terminal

16. Turn the ignition switch on, and measure the
position sensor output voltage at the fully open position. The voltage should be within the range specified in **Table 2**.

17. If the sensor output voltage is less than specified,
adjust the No. 2 cable as follows:

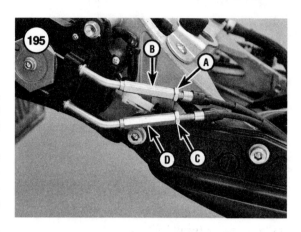

   a. Set the EXAVC to the adjust position (**Figure
     193**).
   b. On the No. 2 cable, loosen the locknut (C,
     Figure 195).
   c. Slowly turn out the cable adjuster (D, **Figure
     195**) until the voltage is within the range speci-
     fied in **Table 2**.
   d. If the malfunction code C46 is not shown on
     the meter display, the cable is adjusted cor-
     rectly.

18. Install the lower fairing, the seat/tail cover, and
rider seat (Chapter Fifteen).

Operation Test

1. Remove the rider seat and the seat/tail cover
(Chapter Fifteen).

2. Check that the 2-pin (A, **Figure 194**), and 3-pin
(B) electrical connectors are connected correctly.

3. Turn ignition on and watch the EXCVA pulley
operate.

4. The pulley should operate and move the EXAVC
valve to its fully closed position, to it fully open position and then set the valve to its adjustment position
(30% open).

5. Install the rider seat, and the seat/tail cover
(Chapter Fifteen).

Battery Test

1. Remove the rider seat and the seat/tail cover
(Chapter Fifteen).

2. Turn the ignition switch off.

3. Disconnect the 2-pin (A, **Figure 194**) EXCVA
electrical connector.

CAUTION
To avoid damage to the EXCVA motor,
disconnect the 12 volt battery from the
motor 2-pin connector as soon as the

valve moves to its fully open or closed position.

4. Use jumpers to apply battery voltage directly to the terminals in the motor side of the 2-pin connector. The EXCVA pulley should turn in one direction.

5. Reverse the jumpers from the battery, and once again apply battery voltage directly to the terminals in the motor side of the 2-pin connector. The EXCVA pulley should turn in the opposite direction.

6. Install the rider seat, and the seat/tail cover (Chapter Fifteen).

Position Sensor Input Voltage Test

1. Remove the rider seat and the seat/tail cover (Chapter Fifteen).

2. Turn the ignition switch off.

3. Disconnect the 3-pin (B, **Figure 194**) EXCVA electrical connector.

4. Connect the voltmeter's positive test probe to the red terminal in the harness side of the connector; connect the negative test probe to the black/brown terminal in the harness side of the connector.

5. Turn the ignition switch on, and measure the voltage.

6. Each voltage measurement should be within the range specified in **Table 2**.

7. Install the rider seat, and the seat/tail cover (Chapter Fifteen).

Position Sensor Input Continuity Test

1. Remove the rider seat and the seat/tail cover (Chapter Fifteen).

2. Turn the ignition switch off.

3. Disconnect the 3-pin (B, **Figure 194**) EXCVA electrical connector.

4. Connect the ohmmeter's positive test probe to the yellow terminal in the sensor side of the connector; connect the negative test probe to a good ground.

5. The sensor should have continuity.

Position Sensor Resistance Test

1. Remove the rider seat and the seat/tail cover (Chapter Fifteen).

2. Check that the 3-pin (B, **Figure 194**) electrical connector is connected correctly.

3. Set the EXCVA to the adjusted position as described in this chapter.

4. Disconnect the 3-pin (B, **Figure 194**) electrical connector.

5. Connect the ohmmeter's positive test probe to the yellow terminal in the sensor side of the connector;

connect the negative test probe to the white terminal in the sensor side, and measure the resistance.

6. The resistance should be within the range specified in **Table 2**.

7. Connect the 3-pin (B, **Figure 194**) electrical connector.

8. Install the rider seat, and the seat/tail cover (Chapter Fifteen).

Position Sensor Output Voltage Test

1. Remove the rider seat and the seat/tail cover (Chapter Fifteen).

2. Check that the 3-pin (B, **Figure 194**) electrical connector is connected correctly.

3. Use 0.5 mm (0.02 in.) wires to back probe pins to back probe the yellow and black/brown terminals in the harness side of the 3-pin EXCVA position sensor connector.

4. Disconnect the 2-pin (A, **Figure 194**) EXCVA motor connector.

CAUTION
To avoid damage to the EXCVA motor, disconnect the 12 volt battery from the motor 2-pin as the EXAVC reaches the fully open position.

5. Move the EXCVA to it fully closed position. Use jumpers and connect the positive battery terminal to the pink terminal in the motor side of the 2-pin connector, and connect the negative battery terminal to the gray terminal on the 2-pin connector. Disconnect the battery jumpers once the EXCVA moves to the fully closed position.

6. Turn the ignition switch on, and measure the voltage across the yellow and black/brown terminals in the 3-pin EXCVA position sensor connector. The voltage should equal the fully-closed output voltage specified in **Table 2**.

7. Move the EXCVA to it fully open position. Use jumpers and connect the positive battery terminal to the gray terminal in the motor side of the 2-pin connector, and connect the negative battery terminal to the pink terminal on the 2-pin connector. Disconnect the battery jumpers once the EXCVA moves to the fully open position.

8. Turn the ignition switch on, and measure the voltage across the yellow and black/brown terminals in the 3-pin EXCVA position sensor connector. The voltage should equal the fully-closed output voltage specified in **Table 2**.

9. Install the seat/tail cover and rider seat (Chapter Fifteen).

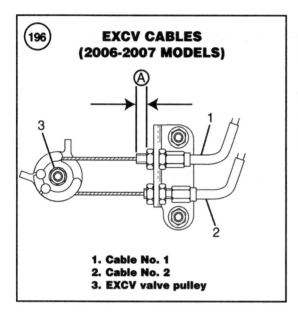

**EXCV CABLES
(2006-2007 MODELS)**

1. Cable No. 1
2. Cable No. 2
3. EXCV valve pulley

Cable Replacement

1. Remove the rider seat, the seat/tail cover, and the lower fairing (Chapter Fifteen).
2. Check that the EXCVA pulley control cable slots are facing rearward in the correct adjusted position (**Figure 193**).
3. Disconnect the cables from the actuator as described in *Removal* (this section).
4. At the exhaust pipe, measure the exposed thread length (**Figure 196**) on cable No. 1 prior to disconnecting the cable. Note this dimension A.
5. Loosen the locknut on the No. 1cable (A, **Figure 197**), and the No. 2 cable (B).
6. Disconnect the No. 1 cable from the upper slot (C, **Figure 197**) in the EXCVA pulley.
7. Disconnect the No. 2 cable from the lower slot (D, **Figure 197**) in the EXCVA pulley.
8. Connect the No. 1 cable onto the upper slot (C, **Figure 197**) in the EXCVA pulley.
9. Connect the No. 2 cable onto the lower slot (D, **Figure 197**) in the EXCVA pulley.
10. Ensure that the cables are secure in the mounting bracket (**Figure 198**).
11. Turn the adjuster (5, **Figure 199**) on the No. 1 cable in or out to achieve the expose thread length noted in Step 4. Tighten the locknut (6, **Figure 199**)
12. On the No. 1 cable, turn the adjuster (5, **Figure 199**) and adjust the inner cable length (B, **Figure 199**) to 41.0-42.0 mm (1.61-1.65 in.). Tighten the locknut
(6, **Figure 199**).
13. Turn the No. 2 cable adjuster (7, **Figure 199**) out fully.
14. Loosen the locknuts (8, **Figure 199**) on the No. 2 cable, and turn the adjuster (9) in or out until

the inner cable length (C, **Figure 199**) to 60.0-61.0 mm (2.36-2.40 in.). Tighten the locknuts (8, **Figure 199**).
15. Connect the No. 1 cable (A, **Figure 192**) onto the upper slot in the EXCVA pulley.
16. Connect the No. 2 cable (B, **Figure 192**) onto the lower slot in the EXCVA pulley.
17. Loosen the locknut (3, **Figure 200**) on the No. 2 cable.
18. Turn the adjuster (4, **Figure 200**) in or out to achieve the expose thread length
to 11.0-12.0 mm (0.43-0.47 in.). Tighten the locknut (3, **Figure 200**).
19. Adjust the cables (this section).
20. Install the lower fairing, seat/tail cover, and rider seat (Chapter Fifteen).

EXCVA PulleyInspection/Removal/Installation

CAUTION
Always secure the pulley with an adjustable wrench to avoid ECTVA internal damage.

1. Check the pulley grooves for wear and damage. Replace the pulley as necessary, as follows.

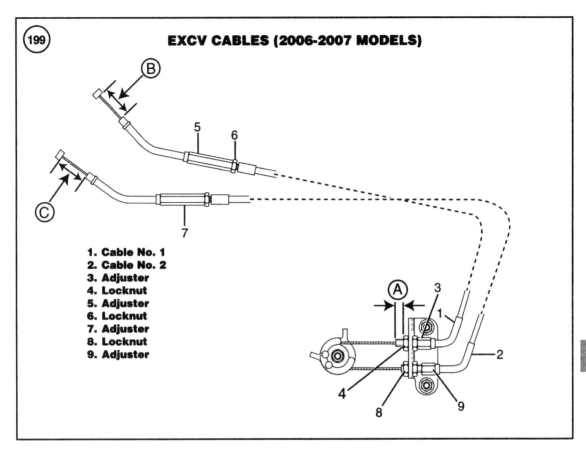

199 **EXCV CABLES (2006-2007 MODELS)**

1. Cable No. 1
2. Cable No. 2
3. Adjuster
4. Locknut
5. Adjuster
6. Locknut
7. Adjuster
8. Locknut
9. Adjuster

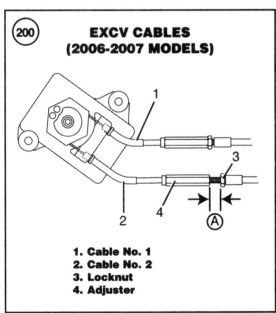

200 **EXCV CABLES
(2006-2007 MODELS)**

1. Cable No. 1
2. Cable No. 2
3. Locknut
4. Adjuster

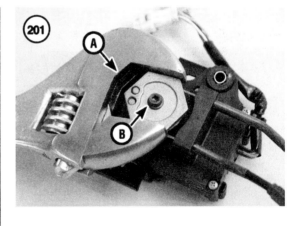

201

5. Install the pulley and secure the pulley with an adjustable wrench (A, **Figure 201**). Tighten the bolt (B, **Figure 201**) to 5 N•m (44 in.-lb.).

EXHAUST CONTROL VALVE ACTUATOR (EXCV) (2008-2009 MODELS)

The exhaust control valve actuator (**Figure 202**) opens and closes the exhaust control via a pulley and cables. The actuator/exhaust control valve system improves engine torque at low engine speeds. During operation, the ECM determines the control

2. Secure the pulley with an adjustable wrench (A, **Figure 201**) and loosen the bolt (B).

3. Remove the pulley from the EXCVA unit.

4. Align the cable slots on the backside of the pulley with the line on the EXCVA shaft, and install the pulley onto the shaft.

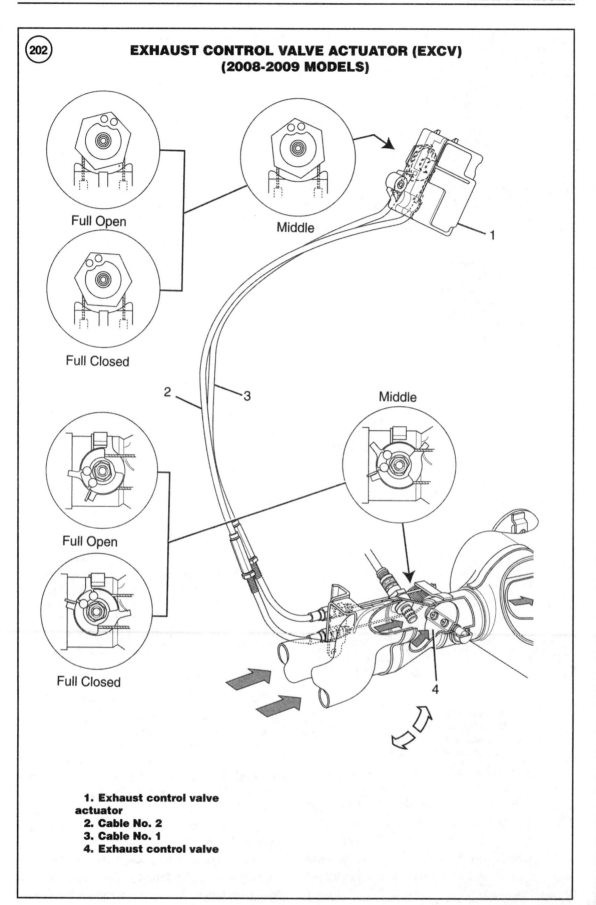

(202)

EXHAUST CONTROL VALVE ACTUATOR (EXCV)
(2008-2009 MODELS)

Full Open

Middle

Full Closed

1

Middle

2   3

Full Open

Full Closed

4

1. Exhaust control valve
actuator
2. Cable No. 2
3. Cable No. 1
4. Exhaust control valve

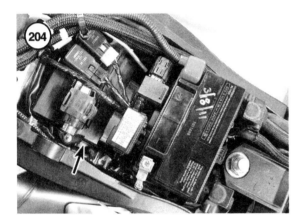

valve's optimum opening angle based upon engine speed and gear selection.

Whenever the ignition switch is turned on, the exhaust control valve actuator moves the exhaust control valve to its fully open position, to its fully closed position and then sets the exhaust control valve to the middle position.

The EXCVA mounts on the inboard right side of the frame rail (**Figure 203**).

Removal

1. Remove the rider's seat, and the right side fairing (Chapter Fifteen).
2. Turn the ignition switch off.

NOTE
***Figure 204** indicates the location of the mode select switch below the fuse panel. The actual switch is not shown.*

3. Remove the cover, and connect the mode select switch (**Figure 204**) to the dealer mode connector.
4. Turn the model select switch on, turn the ignition switch on.
5. Check that the EXCVA pulley control cable slots are facing straight up in the correct adjusted position (**Figure 205**).
6. Turn the ignition switch off.
7. Disconnect the 4-pin motor (A, **Figure 206**), and 3-pin position sensor (B) electrical connectors from the EXCVA.
8. Disconnect the cables (this section).
9. Remove the mounting bolt (C, **Figure 206**), and remove the EXCVA from the mounting bracket.

Installation

1. Install the EXCVA onto the mounting bracket in the correct position.
2. Install the mounting bolt (C, **Figure 206**), and tighten securely.
3. Connect the cables (this section).
4. Connect the 4-pin motor (A, **Figure 206**), and 3-pin position sensor (B) electrical connectors to the EXCVA.
5. Check that the EXCVA pulley control cable slots are facing straight up in the correct adjusted position.
6. Adjust the cables (this section).
7. Install the right side fairing and the rider's seat (Chapter Fifteen).

Cable Adjustment

1. Remove the rider's seat, and the right side fairing (Chapter Fifteen).
2. Check that the EXCVA pulley control cable slots are facing straight up in the correct adjusted position (**Figure 205**).
3. Turn the ignition switch off.

NOTE
***Figure 204** indicates the location of the mode select switch below the fuse panel. The actual switch is not shown.*

4. Remove the cover, and connect the mode select switch (**Figure 204**) to the dealer mode connector.
5. Turn the model select switch off, turn the ignition switch on, and check the EXCVA operation.
6. Turn the model select switch on, and observe the meter display. Cable adjustment is correct if malfunction code C46 is not shown. If code 46 code is shown, proceed to Step 7.
7. Turn ignition switch off.
8. Disconnect the 4-pin motor (A, **Figure 206**) electrical connector from the EXCVA.

CAUTION
To avoid motor damage, disconnect the 12 volt battery as soon as the EXAVC reaches the fully closed position.

9. To set the EXAVC to the *fully closed position*. Attach the 12 volt battery positive terminal to the 4-pin connector pink wire, and the negative terminal to the gray wire.
10. Use 0.5 mm (0.02 in.) wires to back probe the connector during this test. Insert the back probe wires into the EXAVC position sensor 3-pin electrical connector (B, **Figure 206**).
11. Connect a voltmeter to the harness side of the EXAVC position sensor 3-pin electrical connector (B, **Figure 206**); positive test probe to the yellow wire terminal and the negative test probe to the black/brown wire terminal.
12. Turn the ignition switch on, and measure the position sensor output voltage at the fully closed position. The voltage should be within the range specified in **Table 2**.

CAUTION
Do not adjust the No. 1 cable with the EXCV in the fully closed position as the EXCVA will be damaged.

13. If the sensor output voltage is less than specified, adjust the No. 1 cable as follows:
  a. Set the EXAVC to the adjust position (**Figure 205**).

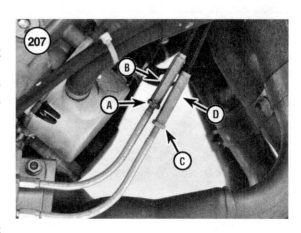

  b. On the No. 1 cable, loosen the locknut (A, **Figure 207**).
  c. Slowly turn out the cable adjuster (B, **Figure 207**) until the voltage is within the range specified in **Table 2**.
  d. If the malfunction code C46 is shown on the meter display; adjust the cable adjuster to achieve 0.9 volt. Tighten the locknut (A, **Figure 207**).

CAUTION
To avoid motor damage, disconnect the 12 volt battery as soon as the EXAVC reaches the fully open position.

14. To set the EXAVC to the fully open position. Attach the 12 volt battery positive terminal to the 4-pin connector (B, **Figure 206**) gray wire, and the negative terminal to the pink wire.
15. Use 0.5 mm (0.02 in.) wires to back probe the connector during this test. Insert the back probe wires into the EXAVC position sensor 3-pin electrical connector (B, **Figure 206**).
16. Connect a voltmeter to the harness side of the EXAVC position sensor 4-pin motor electrical connector (A, **Figure 206**); positive test probe to the yellow wire terminal and the negative test probe to the black/brown wire terminal
17. Turn the ignition switch on, and measure the position sensor output voltage at the fully open position. The voltage should be within the range specified in **Table 2**.
18. If the sensor output voltage is less than specified, adjust the No. 2 cable as follows:
  a. Set the EXAVC to the adjust position (**Figure 205**).
  b. On the No. 2 cable, loosen the locknut (C, **Figure 206**).
  c. Slowly turn out the cable adjuster (D, **Figure 207**) until the voltage is within the range specified in **Table 2**.

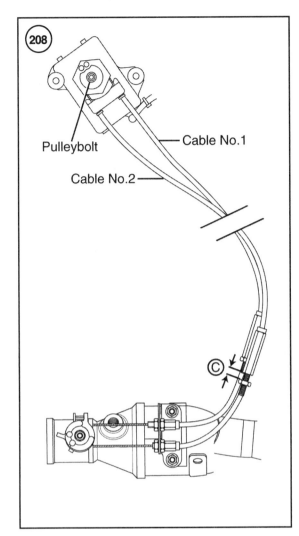

Pulleybolt

Cable No.1

Cable No.2

© ↓↑

Battery Test

1. Remove the rider's seat and the right side fairing (Chapter Fifteen).
2. Turn the ignition switch off.
3. Disconnect the 4-pin motor (A, **Figure 206**) EXCVA electrical connector.

CAUTION
To avoid damage to the EXCVA motor, disconnect the 12 volt battery from the motor 2-pin connector as soon as the valve moves to its fully open or closed position.

4. Use jumpers and apply 12 battery voltage directly to the terminals in the motor side of the 4-pin connector. Connect the positive terminal to the 4-pin connector (B, **Figure 206**) gray wire, and the negative terminal to the pink wire. The EXCVA pulley should turn in one direction.
5. Reverse the jumpers from the battery, and once again apply battery voltage directly to the terminals in the motor side of the 2-pin connector. The EXCVA pulley should turn in the opposite direction.
6. Install the right side fairing and the rider's seat (Chapter Fifteen).

Cable Removal

1. Remove the rider's seat, the right side and the lower fairing (Chapter Fifteen).
2. Turn the ignition switch off.

NOTE
Figure 204 *indicates the location of the mode select switch below the fuse panel. The actual switch is not shown.*

3. Remove the cover, and connect the mode select switch (**Figure 204**) to the dealer mode connector.
4. Turn the model select switch on, turn the ignition switch on.
5. Check that the EXCVA pulley control cable slots are facing straight up in the correct adjusted position (**Figure 205**).
6. Turn the ignition switch off.
7. Identify the cables by their ID part numbers as follows:
   a. No. 1 cable (**Figure 208**) is numbered 37HO-CL and is located in the EXCVA pulley front slot.
   b. No. 2 cable (**Figure 208**) is numbered 37HOOP and is located in the EXCVA pulley rear slot.
8. Loosen the locknut (A, **Figure 207**) on the No. 1 cable, and turn in the adjuster (B) fully to provide slack.

d. If the malfunction code C46 is not shown on the meter display, the cable is adjusted correctly.

Operation Test

1. Remove the rider's seat and the right side fairing (Chapter Fifteen).
2. Check that the 4-pin motor (A, **Figure 206**), and 3-pin position sensor (B) electrical connectors are connected correctly.
3. Turn ignition on and watch the EXAVC pulley operate.
4. The pulley should operate and move the EXAVC valve to its fully closed position, to it fully open position and then set the valve to its adjustment position (30% open).
5. Install the right side fairing and the rider's seat (Chapter Fifteen).

9. Loosen the locknut (C, **Figure 207**) on the No. 2 cable, and turn in the adjuster (D fully to provide slack.

10. At the exhaust pipe, perform the following:

   a. Loosen the locknut (A, **Figure 209**) on the No. 2 cable (B). Disconnect the No. 2 cable from the lower slot (C, **Figure 209**) in the EXCVA pulley.

   b. Loosen the locknut (D, **Figure 209**) on the No. 1 cable (E). Disconnect the No. 1 cable from the upper slot (F, **Figure 209**) in the EXCVA pulley.

11. Remove the EXCVA mounting bolts (**Figure 210**), and move the EXCVA up within the frame.

12. Disconnect the No. 1 cable from the front slot in the EXCVA pulley.

13. Disconnect the No. 2 cable from the rear slot in the EXCVA pulley.

14. Note the path of the cables within the frame and remove both cables from the frame.

Cable Installation

1. Install the cables within the frame path as noted during removal.

2. At the exhaust pipe, perform the following:

   a. Connect the No. 2 cable onto the lower slot (C, **Figure 209**) in the EXCVA pulley.

   b. Connect the No. 1 cable onto the upper slot (F, **Figure 209**) in the EXCVA pulley.

   c. Tighten the locknut (A, **Figure 209**) on the No. 2 cable (B).

   d. Tighten the locknut (D, **Figure 209**) on the No. 1 cable (E).

   e. Turn the adjuster (B, **Figure 209**) in or out to achieve the inner length of the No. 1 cable (A, **Figure 211**) to 44-45 mm (1.73-1.77 in.), and tighten the locknut (A).

   f. On the No. 2 cable, turn the adjuster (D, **Figure 207**) in fully.

   g. Loosen the locknut (A, **Figure 209**) and turn the cable adjuster (G, **Figure 209**) in or out to achieve the inner length of the No. 2 cable (B, **Figure 211**) to 60-61 mm (2.36-2.40 in.), and tighten the locknut (A, **Figure 202**).

3. Connect the No. 1 cable from the front slot in the EXCVA pulley.

4. Connect the No. 2 cable from the rear slot in the EXCVA pulley.

5. Install the EXCVA and the mounting bolts (**Figure 210**). Tighten the bolts securely.

6. Loosen the locknut (C, **Figure 207**), and turn the adjuster in or out to achieve the inner length of the No. 2 cable (C, **Figure 208**) to 11-12 mm (0.43-0.47 in.), and tighten the locknut (C, **Figure 207**) securely.

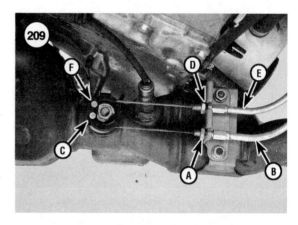

7. Install the lower fairing, right side and lower fairing, and seat (Chapter Fifteen).

EXCVA Pulley Inspection/Replacement

1. Remove the rider's seat, the right side and the lower fairing (Chapter Fifteen).

2. Turn the ignition switch off.

NOTE
Figure 204 indicates the location of the mode select switch below the fuse panel. The actual switch is not shown.

3. Remove the cover, and connect the mode select switch (**Figure 204**) to the dealer mode connector.

4. Turn the model select switch on, turn the ignition switch on.

5. Check that the EXCVA pulley control cable slots are facing straight up in the correct adjusted position (**Figure 205**).

6. Turn the ignition switch off.

7. Disconnect the 4-pin motor (A, **Figure 206**), and 3-pin position sensor (B) electrical connectors from the EXCVA.

8. Disconnect the cables from the EXCVA (this section).

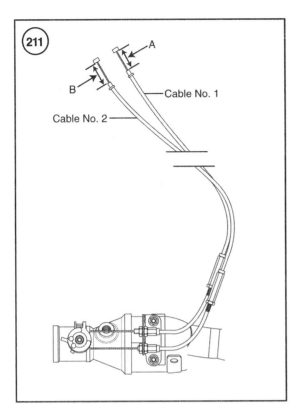

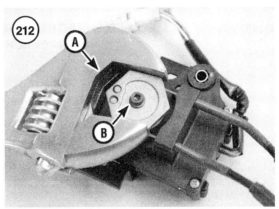

9. Remove the mounting bolts (C, **Figure 206**), and remove the EXCVA from the mounting bracket.

10. Check the pulley grooves for wear and damage. Replace the pulley as follows.

CAUTION
Always secure the pulley with an adjustable wrench to avoid ECTVA internal damage.

11. Secure the pulley with an adjustable wrench (A, **Figure 212**) and loosen the bolt (B).

12. Remove the pulley from the EXCVA unit.

13. Align the cable slots on the backside of the pulley with the line on the EXCVA shaft, and install the pulley onto the shaft.

14. Install the pulley and secure the pulley with an adjustable wrench (A, **Figure 212**). Tighten the bolt (B, **Figure 212**) to 5 N•m (44 in.-lb.).

15. Install the lower fairing, right side and lower fairing, and seat (Chapter Fifteen).

EVAPORATIVE EMISSIONS CONTROL SYSTEM (CALIFORNIA MODELS)

WARNING
Ensure the work area is free of any ignition source (open flames or sparks) before working on the EVAP system.

California models are equipped with an evaporative (EVAP) emission control system, consisting of a charcoal canister, fuel shutoff valve, pressure control valve, assorted hoses and modified throttle bodies and fuel tank.

The EVAP system captures fumes from the fuel tank, and stores them in the charcoal canister. When the motorcycle is ridden, these vapors are routed to the throttle bodies and drawn into the engine where they are burned. The fuel shutoff valve, located between the fuel tank and charcoal canister, assures that the fumes remain in the canister until they can be safely burned.

Refer to the vacuum hose routing label on the frame. Make sure the hoses are correctly routed and attached to the right components. Inspect the hoses and replace any if necessary.

On most models, the hoses and fittings are color coded with labels or bands. If these have deteriorated or are missing, mark the hose and the fittings before removing them. There are very many vacuum hose on these models. Refer to **Figure 213** or **Figure 214**. The canister is mounted on the left side (**Figure 215**) on 2006-2007 models or on the right side (**Figure 216**) on 2008-2009 models.

Maintenance/Service

1. Whenever servicing the evaporative system, make sure the main switch is turned off.

2. Inspect the canister mounting and the routing of the hoses.

3. Check all hoses. They must not be damaged or pinched, and they must be securely attached to their respective fittings.

4. Replace any worn or damaged part immediately.

5. When purchasing replacement parts (throttle bodies and fuel tank) make sure the parts are for California models.

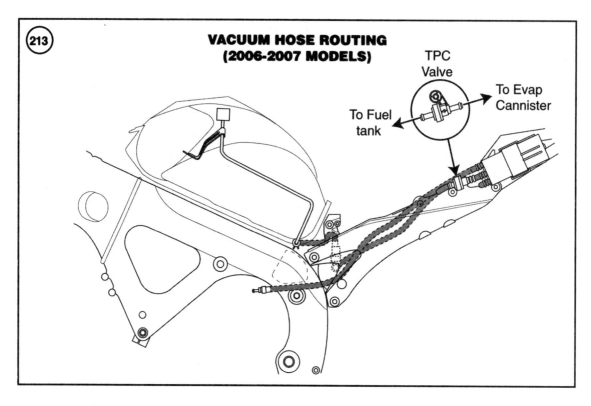

VACUUM HOSE ROUTING (2006-2007 MODELS)

Fuel Shutoff Valve Removal/Installation

The fuel shutoff valve is mounted in front of the battery box.

1. Remove the rider seat, and the seat/tail cover (Chapter Fifteen).

2. Follow the center surge hose (**Figure 217**, typical) from the pressure control valve adjacent to the canister, under the battery, and to the fuel shut off valve.

3. Disconnect the hoses from the fuel shutoff valve. Label the hose and fitting. Hoses must be reinstalled onto the correct fitting.

4. Release any clamps and remove the shutoff valve.

5. Test the fuel shutoff valve as follows:
   a. Blow into the A port as shown in **Figure 218**. Air should flow out of the B port.
   b. Reverse the valve and blow into the B port. Air should not flow from the A port.
   c. Replace the valve if it fails either port of this test.

NOTE
The shutoff valve is directional. Note that the straight fitting goes to the fuel tank and the elbow fitting goes to the surge hose and pressure control valve. The fuel shutoff valve must be reinstalled with this same orientation.

6. Install by reversing these removal steps. Note the following:
   a. Install the shutoff valve so it is positioned as noted during removal.
   b. Connect the surge hose and tank hose to their respective fittings on the valve.
   c. Secure each hose in place.

Canister Removal/Installation

CAUTION
Label each hose and its fitting so they can be identified during assembly. Hoses must be reinstalled onto the correct fittings during assembly.

1. Remove the rider's seat, and the seat/tail cover (Chapter Fifteen).

2. Disconnect the purge hose (A, **Figure 219**, typical) and surge hose (B) from each fitting on the canister.

3. Pull the rubber mount (**Figure 215**, typical) from its mounting tangs, and remove the canister.

4. Install by reversing these removal steps. Note the following:
   a. Connected each hose to the correct fitting on the canister.
   b. Securely mount the canister to the rear frame.

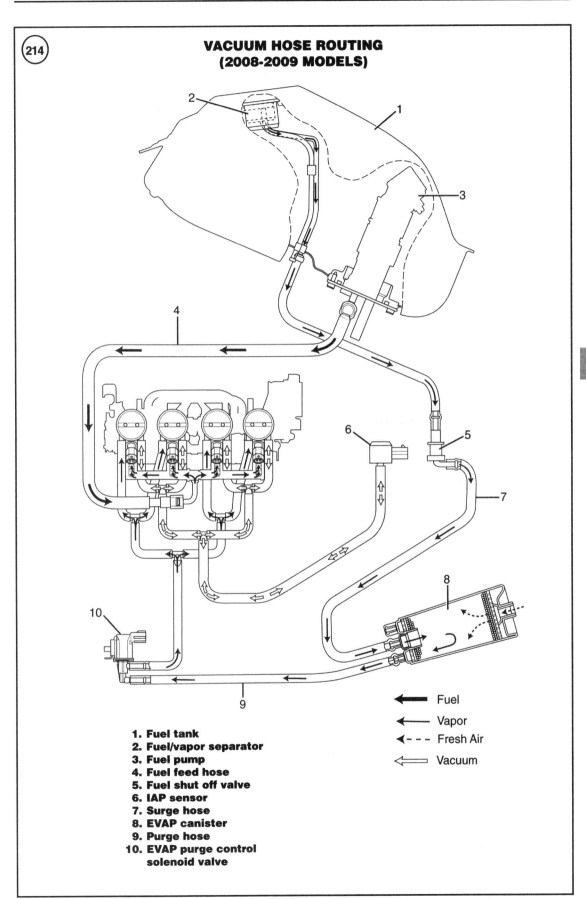

VACUUM HOSE ROUTING (2008-2009 MODELS)

1. Fuel tank
2. Fuel/vapor separator
3. Fuel pump
4. Fuel feed hose
5. Fuel shut off valve
6. IAP sensor
7. Surge hose
8. EVAP canister
9. Purge hose
10. EVAP purge control solenoid valve

Fuel
Vapor
Fresh Air
Vacuum

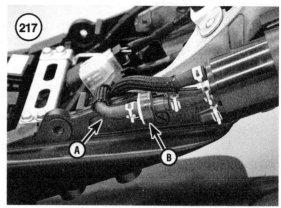

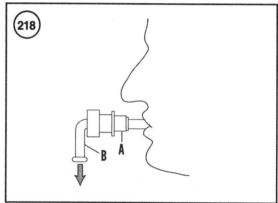

Tank Pressure Control Valve Removal/Inspection/Installation

1. Remove the rider seat, and the seat/tail cover (Chapter Fifteen).

2. Disconnect the surge hose (A, **Figure 217**, typical) from the control valve.

3. Disconnect the control valve (B, **Figure 217**) from the canister, and remove the control valve.

4. Test the pressure control valve by performing the following:

    a. Blow into the A port as shown in **Figure 220**. Air should flow out of the B port.

    b. Reverse the valve and blow into the B port. Air should not flow from the A port.

    c. Replace the valve if it fails either port of this test.

5. Installation is the reverse of removal. Install the valve so the A side faces the canister.

PAIR (AIR SUPPLY) SYSTEM

The PAIR system consists of a PAIR control solenoid valve, two reed valves, and hoses. Refer to **Figure 221** and **Figure 222**.

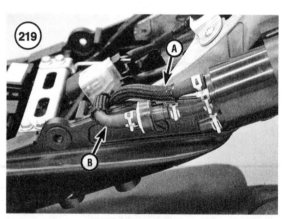

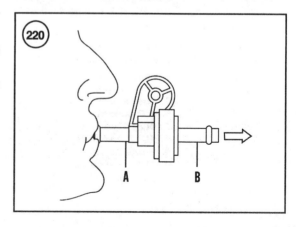

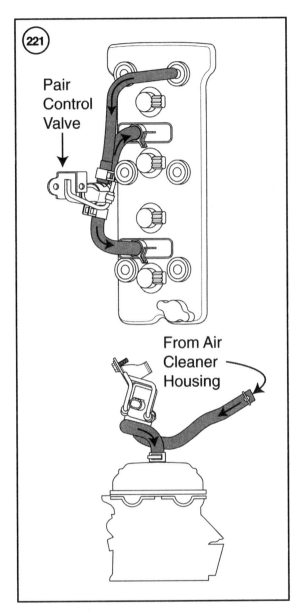

Pair
Control
Valve

From Air
Cleaner
Housing

b. Air should flow from the two solenoid-valve outlet ports.

c. Connect the battery positive terminal to the orange/white terminal in the PAIR control valve; connect the negative terminal to the white/green terminal on the control valve (**Figure 225**).

d. Blow into the control valve inlet port. Air should not flow from the outlet ports when the battery power is applied.

e. Replace the PAIR control solenoid valve if it fails either portion of this test.

6. Inspect all hoses for cracks, damage or deterioration. Replace as necessary.

7. Installation is the reverse of removal. Connect each hose to the proper port as noted during removal. Tighten the bracket bolt securely.

PAIR Control Valve Resistance Test

1. Remove the PAIR control solenoid valve as described in this section.

2. Connect an ohmmeter positive test probe to the orange/white terminal in the PAIR control valve; connect the negative test probe to the white/green terminal in the control valve (**Figure 225**).

3. Measure the resistance. It should be within the range specified in **Table 2**.

PAIR Control Valve Voltage Test

1. Disconnect the 2-pin PAIR connector from the PAIR control solenoid valve.

2. Connect a voltmeter positive test probe to the orange/white terminal in the PAIR connector; connect the negative test probe to a good ground.

3. Turn on the ignition switch, and measure the voltage. It should equal battery voltage.

PAIR Control Valve Removal/Installation

1. Remove the air filter housing as described in this chapter.

2. Disconnect the 2-pin PAIR connector from the PAIR control solenoid valve.

3. Disconnect each hose (A, **Figure 223**) from its port on the PAIR control solenoid valve. Label each hose and its port. Hoses must be reconnected to the correct port during assembly.

4. Remove the bracket bolt, and lift the PAIR control solenoid valve (B, **Figure 223**) and its bracket from the motorcycle.

5. Inspect the PAIR control solenoid valve as follows:

    a. Blow air into the air inlet port on the solenoid valve (**Figure 224**).

Reed Valve Removal/Inspection/Installation

1. Remove the cylinder head cover (Chapter Four).

2. Note that the reeds on the reed valve face down into the housing.

> *NOTE*
> **Figure 226** *is shown with the engine removed from the frame for photo clarity.*

3. Remove each reed valve/PAIR gasket assembly (**Figure 226**) from its housing on the camshaft holders.

4. Remove the reed valve (A, **Figure 227**) from the PAIR gasket.

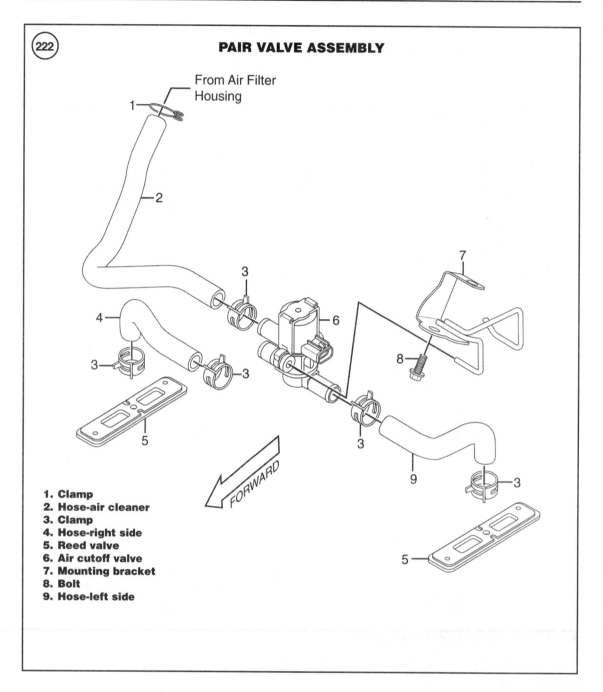

PAIR VALVE ASSEMBLY

From Air Filter Housing

FORWARD

1. Clamp
2. Hose-air cleaner
3. Clamp
4. Hose-right side
5. Reed valve
6. Air cutoff valve
7. Mounting bracket
8. Bolt
9. Hose-left side

5. Inspect the reed valve for carbon deposits. Replace the reed valve if deposits are found.

6. Installation is the reverse of removal. Note the following:

    a. Install the reed valve into the gasket so the reeds will face down with the stopper (A, **Figure 227**) facing up when installed.

    b. Position the reed valve assembly with the gasket projection (B, **Figure 227**) facing the exhaust side of the cylinder head.

    c. Make sure the entire gasket sits within the cutout (**Figure 226**) in the camshaft holder.

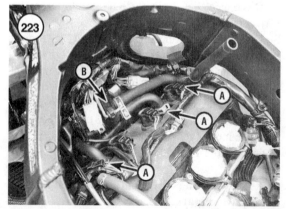

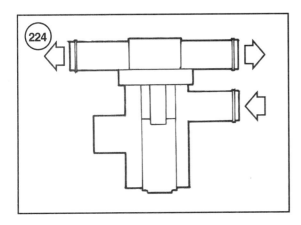

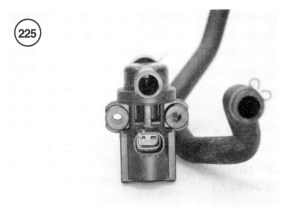

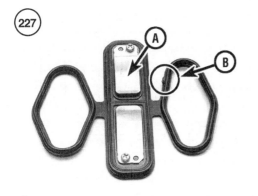

FUEL INJECTION TROUBLESHOOTING

Self-Diagnosis

The electronic control module (ECM) includes a self-diagnostic function that constantly monitors the sensors and actuators in fuel injection system. Whenever an error is detected; the ECM records the malfunction and sets a malfunction code. It also turns on the indicator LED (A, **Figure 228**) in the meter assembly and FI appears in the coolant temperature/ FI portion (B) of the meter display. Any stored malfunction code can be retrieved by entering the dealer mode.

ECM Connectors

Some wiring colors are used more than once in the ECM's connectors. To assure that the correct wire is tested, the test procedures include a wire color and pin location in parentheses. On 2006-2007 models, refer to **Figure 229** to determine where a terminal is located in the relevant ECM connector. On 2008-2009 models, refer to **Figure 230**.

A number of troubleshooting tests also require back probing a connector. Always back probe the harness side of the connector with probe pin that is 0.5 mm (0.02 in.) in diameter or less. Refer to *Electrical Testing* in Chapter Two.

Dealer Mode

CAUTION
Do not perform this procedure without the mode select switch. Shorting the terminals in the dealer model connector could damage the ECM.

NOTE
Record any malfunction code(s) before disconnecting the ECM connectors from the ECM, the ECM ground wire from the harness or engine, or the electrical leads from the battery or before pulling the main fuse. Any of these actions erases the malfunction code(s) from memory.

The meter assembly LCD displays stored malfunction code once the system enters the dealer mode. The Suzuki mode select switch (part No. 09930-82720) is needed to enter the dealer mode.

1. Remove the rider seat and the passenger seat/tail cover (Chapter Fifteen).

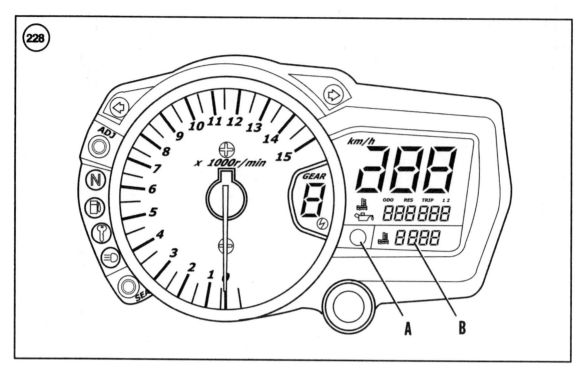

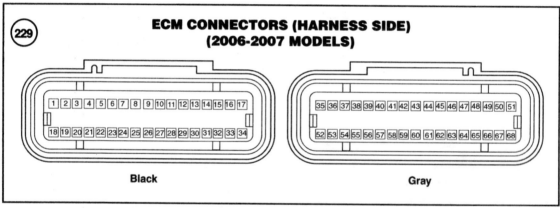

ECM CONNECTORS (HARNESS SIDE)
(2006-2007 MODELS)

Black

Gray

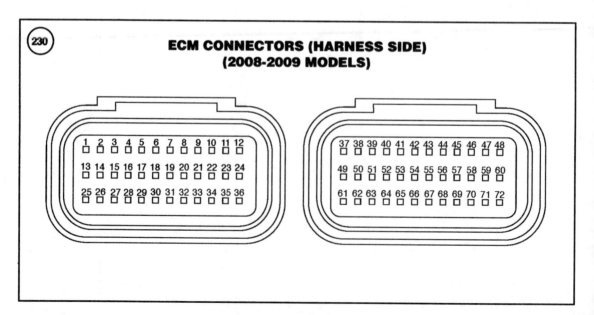

ECM CONNECTORS (HARNESS SIDE)
(2008-2009 MODELS)

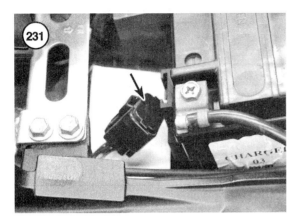

2. Remove the cover (**Figure 231**), and connect the mode select switch to the dealer mode connector.

3. Run the engine for four seconds. If the engine will not start, crank the engine for 4 seconds.

4. After four seconds, turn the mode select switch to on. The system enters the dealer mode, and displays a stored malfunction code in the LCD portion of the meter assembly (B, **Figure 228**). If more than one code is stored, codes are displayed in numeric order starting with the lowest numbered code.

5. Record the codes. The malfunction code table (**Figure 232**) lists the malfunction codes and their likely causes.

6. If no signal is received from the ECM within 5 seconds, the LCD displays CHEC. When this occurs check the wiring between the ECM and the meter connectors. This condition also occurs if the engine stop switch is in the off position, the sidestand/ignition interlock system is malfunctioning, or the ignition fuse is burned out.

7. Install the cover (**Figure 231**) on the mode select switch.

8. Install the rider seat and the passenger seat/tail cover (Chapter Fifteen).

Fail-Safe Operation

For some errors, the ECM sets a preset value for the input so the motorcycle can still operate.

If a detected error is not too severe, the ECM sets the affected component to a preset value so the motorcycle can still operate. This fail-safe operation gives a rider the opportunity to get home or to a service shop. Refer to **Figure 233** to determine if a malfunction code has a fail-safe operation.

If the motorcycle continues to run with a stored malfunction code, troubleshoot the system and eliminate the problem immediately. If the problem cannot be solved, take the motorcycle to a dealership.

Troubleshooting

1. Enter the dealer mode as described earlier in this section.

2. Record any displayed malfunction code(s).

3. Turn to **Figure 234**, and identify the relevant diagnostic flow chart for the malfunction code.

4. Turn to the indicated diagnostic flow chart (**Figures 235-252**). Perform the test procedures in the order listed until the problem is resolved.

5. Once a fault has been corrected, reset the self-diagnostic system as described in this section.

Resetting the Self-diagnostic System

Perform the following to reset the system once a fuel injection system malfunction has been corrected.

1. While in the dealer mode, turn the ignition switch off and then turn it back on.

2. The LCD should display the no fault code: c00.

3. Turn the dealer mode switch to off, and disconnect the switch from the dealer mode connector.

4. Install the rider seat and the passenger seat/tail cover (Chapter Fifteen).

FIGURES 232-252 ARE ON THE FOLLOWING PAGES

MALFUNCTION CODE TABLE

Malfunction Code	Related Item	Detected Failure	Probable Cause
c00	No error	-	-
c11	Camshaft position (CMP) sensor	The ECM has not received a signal from the camshaft position sensor 3, or 4 seconds after it received the start signal.	Faulty CMP sensor, intake cam pin, sensor wiring and/or connector.
c12	Crankshaft position (CKP) sensor	The ECM has not received a signal from the crankshaft position sensor 3, or 4 seconds after it received the start signal.	Faulty CKP sensor, its wiring or connector.
c13	Intake air pressure (IAP) sensor	The sensor's voltage is outside the range 0.5-4.85 volts.	Faulty IAP sensor, its wiring or connector.
c14	Throttle position (TP) sensor	The sensor's voltage is outside the range 0.2-4.80 volts.	Faulty TP sensor, its wiring or connector.
c15	Engine coolant temperature (ECT) sensor	The sensor's voltage is outside the range: 0.15-4.85 volts.	Faulty ETC sensor, its wiring or connector.
c21	Intake air temperature (IAT) sensor	The sensor's voltage is outside the range 0.15-4.85 volts.	Faulty IAT sensor, its wiring or connector.
c22	Atmospheric pressure (AP) sensor	The sensor's voltage is outside the range 0.5-4.85 volts	Faulty AP sensor, its wiring or connector.
c23	Tip-over (TP) sensor	The sensor's voltage is not within the range of 0.2 – 4.80 volts 2 seconds after the ignition switch has been turned on.	Faulty TO sensor, its wiring or connector.
c24 (No. 1) c25 (No. 2) c26 (No. 3) c27 (No. 4)	Ignition system malfunction	The ECM does not receive a proper signal from an ignition coil.	Faulty ignition coil, its wiring or connector. Faulty power supply from the battery.
c28	Secondary throttle valve (STV) actuator	Signal voltage from the ECM is not reaching the actuator, the ECM is not receiving a signal from the actuator, or load voltage is not reaching the actuator motor.	Faulty STV actuator, its wiring or connector.
c29	Secondary throttle position (STP) sensor	The sensor's voltage is outside the range 0.15-4.85 volts.	Faulty STP sensor, its wiring or connector.
c31	Gear position (GP) signal	The gear position sensor's voltage is less than 0.6 volts for 3 or more seconds.	Faulty GP sensor, its wiring, connector or faulty shift cam.
c32 (No. 1) c33 (No.2), c34 (No. 3) c35 (No. 4)	Fuel injector	The ECM does not receive a proper signal from the fuel injector.	Faulty fuel injector, its wiring or connector. Faulty power supply to the injector.

(continued)

MALFUNCTION CODE TABLE (CONTINUED)

Malfunction Code	Related Item	Detected Failure	Probable Cause
c41	Fuel pump relay	No voltage reaches the fuel pump when the relay is energized; or voltage reaches the fuel pump when the relay is not energized.	Faulty fuel pump relay, wiring or connector. Faulty power source to the fuel pump relay or injectors.
c42	Ignition switch	The ECM does not receive a signal from the ignition switch.	Faulty ignition switch, faulty wiring or connector.
c46	Exhaust control valve actuator (EXCVA)	The sensor's voltage is outside the range 0.10-4.90 volts.	Faulty EXCVA, faulty wiring or connector.
c49	PAIR control solenoid valve	The ECM does not receive a signal from the PAIR control solenoid valve.	Faulty PAIR control solenoid valve, its wiring or connector.

8

FAIL-SAFE ACTION

(233)

Failed item	Fail-safe Action	Operation status
Camshaft position (CMP) sensor.	The ECM defaults to the cylinder identification data noted before the failure.	Engine continues operating; cannot restart.
Crankshaft position (CKP) sensor.	The motorcycle stops.	Engine stops operating; cannot restart.
Intake air pressure (IAP) sensor.	Intake air pressure is set to 760 mmHg (29.92 in. Hg).	Engine continues operating; can restart.
Throttle position (TP) sensor.	Throttle valve is set to its fully open position. Ignition timing is set to a present value	Engine continues operating; can restart.
Engine coolant temperature (ECT) sensor.	Engine coolant temperate is set to 80° C (176° F).	Engine continues operating; can restart.
Intake air temperature (IAT) sensor.	Intake air temperature set to 40° C (104° F).	Engine continues operating; can restart.
Atmospheric pressure (AP) sensor.	Atmospheric pressure is set to 760 mmHg (29.92 in. Hg).	Engine continues operating; can restart.
Ignition signal, cylinder No. 1.	No spark at cylinder No. 1.	Cylinder Nos 2, 3 and 4 continue operating; can restart
Ignition signal, cylinder No. 2.	No spark at cylinder No. 2.	Cylinder Nos 1, 3 and 4 continue operating; can restart
Ignition signal, cylinder No. 3.	No spark at cylinder No. 3.	Cylinder Nos 1, 2 and 4 continue operating; can restart
Ignition signal, cylinder No. 4.	No spark at cylinder No. 4.	Cylinder Nos 1, 2, and 3 continue operating; can restart
Fuel injector No. 1.	Fuel cut-off to injector No. 1.	Cylinder Nos 2, 3 and 4 continue operating; can restart

(continued)

FAIL-SAFE ACTION (CONTINUED)

Failed item	Fail-safe Action	Operation status
Fuel injector No. 2.	Fuel cut-off to injector No. 2.	Cylinder Nos 1, 3 and 4 continue operating; can restart
Fuel injector No. 3.	Fuel cut-off to injector No. 3.	Cylinder Nos 1, 2 and 4 continue operating; can restart
Fuel injector No. 4.	Fuel cut-off to injector No. 4.	Cylinder Nos 1, 2 and 3 continue operating; can restart
Secondary throttle valve (STV) actuator.	On 2006-2007 models, secondary throttle valves set to the full open position; 2008-2009 models, they are set to fully closed.	Engine continues operating; can restart.
Secondary throttle position sensor.	Secondary throttle valves set to the fully closed position.	Engine continues operating; can restart.
Gear position signal.	Gear position signal set to sixth gear.	Engine continues operating; can restart.
PAIR control solenoid valve	ECM stops operating the PAIR control solenoid valve.	Engine continuies operating; can restart.

TROUBLESHOOTING CHART

Malfunction Code	Diagnostic Flow Chart
c00	No fault detected
c11	Figure 235
c12	Figure 236
c13	Figure 237
c14	Figure 238
c15	Figure 239
c21	Figure 240
c22	Figure 241
c23	Figure 242
c24, c25, c26 or c27	Figure 243
c28	Figure 244
c29	Figure 245
c31	Figure 246
c32, c33, c34 or c35	Figure 247
c41	Figure 248
c49	Figure 249

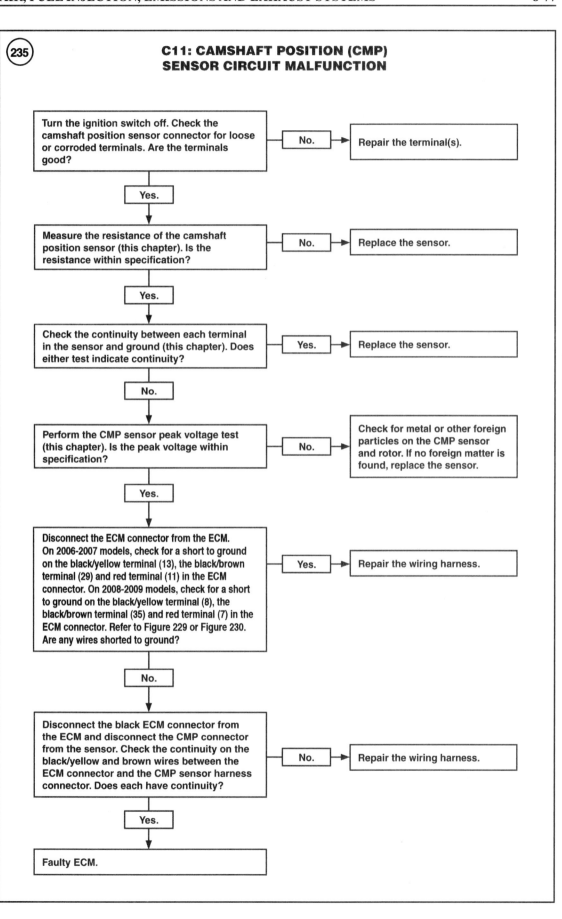

(235)

C11: CAMSHAFT POSITION (CMP) SENSOR CIRCUIT MALFUNCTION

Turn the ignition switch off. Check the camshaft position sensor connector for loose or corroded terminals. Are the terminals good?

→ No. → Repair the terminal(s).

↓ Yes.

Measure the resistance of the camshaft position sensor (this chapter). Is the resistance within specification?

→ No. → Replace the sensor.

↓ Yes.

Check the continuity between each terminal in the sensor and ground (this chapter). Does either test indicate continuity?

→ Yes. → Replace the sensor.

↓ No.

Perform the CMP sensor peak voltage test (this chapter). Is the peak voltage within specification?

→ No. → Check for metal or other foreign particles on the CMP sensor and rotor. If no foreign matter is found, replace the sensor.

↓ Yes.

Disconnect the ECM connector from the ECM. On 2006-2007 models, check for a short to ground on the black/yellow terminal (13), the black/brown terminal (29) and red terminal (11) in the ECM connector. On 2008-2009 models, check for a short to ground on the black/yellow terminal (8), the black/brown terminal (35) and red terminal (7) in the ECM connector. Refer to Figure 229 or Figure 230. Are any wires shorted to ground?

→ Yes. → Repair the wiring harness.

↓ No.

Disconnect the black ECM connector from the ECM and disconnect the CMP connector from the sensor. Check the continuity on the black/yellow and brown wires between the ECM connector and the CMP sensor harness connector. Does each have continuity?

→ No. → Repair the wiring harness.

↓ Yes.

Faulty ECM.

8

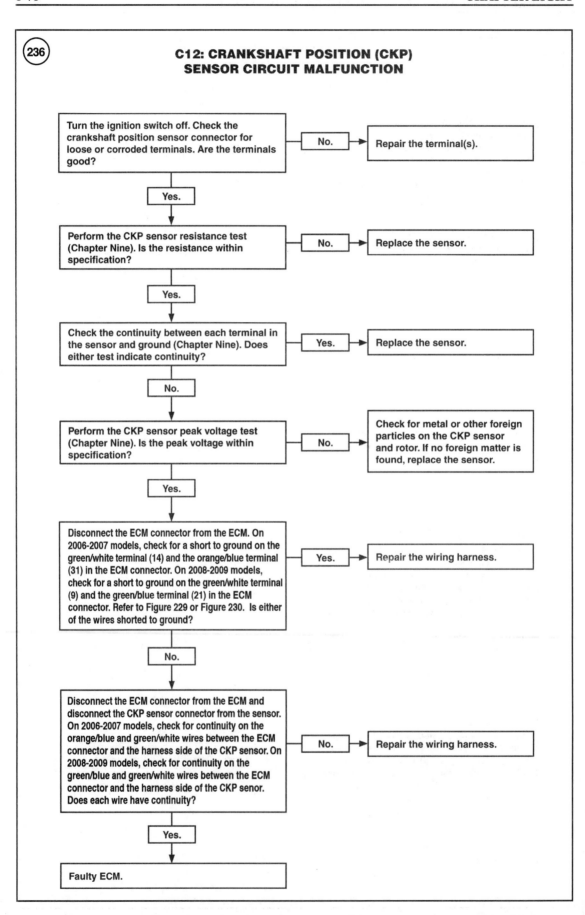

(236)

C12: CRANKSHAFT POSITION (CKP)
SENSOR CIRCUIT MALFUNCTION

Turn the ignition switch off. Check the crankshaft position sensor connector for loose or corroded terminals. Are the terminals good?

No. → Repair the terminal(s).

Yes.

Perform the CKP sensor resistance test (Chapter Nine). Is the resistance within specification?

No. → Replace the sensor.

Yes.

Check the continuity between each terminal in the sensor and ground (Chapter Nine). Does either test indicate continuity?

Yes. → Replace the sensor.

No.

Perform the CKP sensor peak voltage test (Chapter Nine). Is the peak voltage within specification?

No. → Check for metal or other foreign particles on the CKP sensor and rotor. If no foreign matter is found, replace the sensor.

Yes.

Disconnect the ECM connector from the ECM. On 2006-2007 models, check for a short to ground on the green/white terminal (14) and the orange/blue terminal (31) in the ECM connector. On 2008-2009 models, check for a short to ground on the green/white terminal (9) and the green/blue terminal (21) in the ECM connector. Refer to Figure 229 or Figure 230. Is either of the wires shorted to ground?

Yes. → Repair the wiring harness.

No.

Disconnect the ECM connector from the ECM and disconnect the CKP sensor connector from the sensor. On 2006-2007 models, check for continuity on the orange/blue and green/white wires between the ECM connector and the harness side of the CKP sensor. On 2008-2009 models, check for continuity on the green/blue and green/white wires between the ECM connector and the harness side of the CKP senor. Does each wire have continuity?

No. → Repair the wiring harness.

Yes.

Faulty ECM.

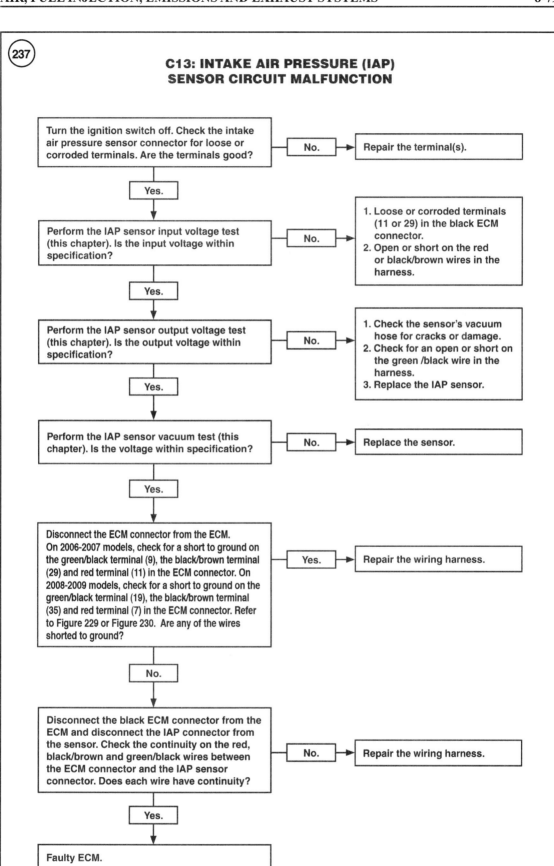

(237)

C13: INTAKE AIR PRESSURE (IAP)
SENSOR CIRCUIT MALFUNCTION

Turn the ignition switch off. Check the intake air pressure sensor connector for loose or corroded terminals. Are the terminals good?

→ No. → Repair the terminal(s).

↓ Yes.

Perform the IAP sensor input voltage test (this chapter). Is the input voltage within specification?

→ No. →
1. Loose or corroded terminals (11 or 29) in the black ECM connector.
2. Open or short on the red or black/brown wires in the harness.

↓ Yes.

Perform the IAP sensor output voltage test (this chapter). Is the output voltage within specification?

→ No. →
1. Check the sensor's vacuum hose for cracks or damage.
2. Check for an open or short on the green /black wire in the harness.
3. Replace the IAP sensor.

↓ Yes.

Perform the IAP sensor vacuum test (this chapter). Is the voltage within specification?

→ No. → Replace the sensor.

↓ Yes.

Disconnect the ECM connector from the ECM. On 2006-2007 models, check for a short to ground on the green/black terminal (9), the black/brown terminal (29) and red terminal (11) in the ECM connector. On 2008-2009 models, check for a short to ground on the green/black terminal (19), the black/brown terminal (35) and red terminal (7) in the ECM connector. Refer to Figure 229 or Figure 230. Are any of the wires shorted to ground?

→ Yes. → Repair the wiring harness.

↓ No.

Disconnect the black ECM connector from the ECM and disconnect the IAP connector from the sensor. Check the continuity on the red, black/brown and green/black wires between the ECM connector and the IAP sensor connector. Does each wire have continuity?

→ No. → Repair the wiring harness.

↓ Yes.

Faulty ECM.

8

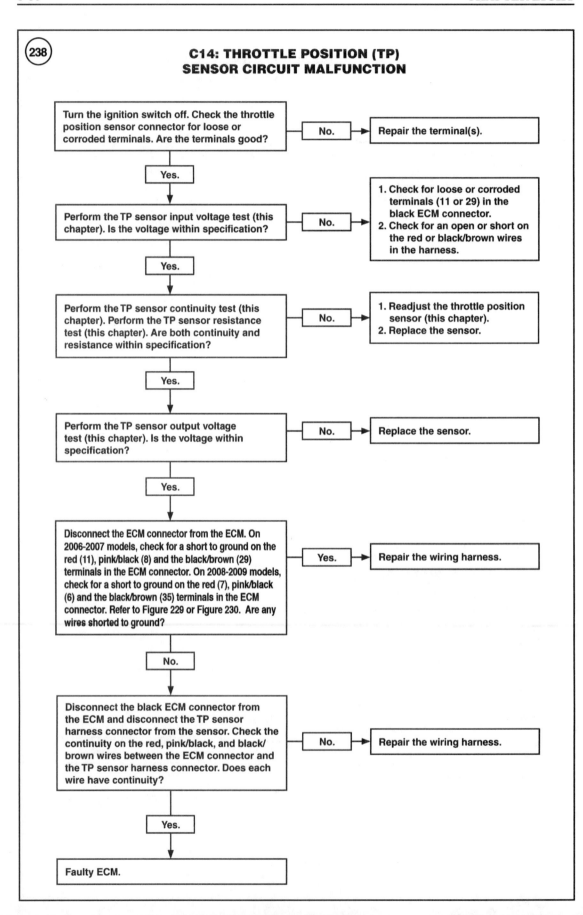

238

C14: THROTTLE POSITION (TP)
SENSOR CIRCUIT MALFUNCTION

Turn the ignition switch off. Check the throttle position sensor connector for loose or corroded terminals. Are the terminals good? — **No.** → Repair the terminal(s).

Yes.

Perform the TP sensor input voltage test (this chapter). Is the voltage within specification? — **No.** → 1. Check for loose or corroded terminals (11 or 29) in the black ECM connector.
2. Check for an open or short on the red or black/brown wires in the harness.

Yes.

Perform the TP sensor continuity test (this chapter). Perform the TP sensor resistance test (this chapter). Are both continuity and resistance within specification? — **No.** → 1. Readjust the throttle position sensor (this chapter).
2. Replace the sensor.

Yes.

Perform the TP sensor output voltage test (this chapter). Is the voltage within specification? — **No.** → Replace the sensor.

Yes.

Disconnect the ECM connector from the ECM. On 2006-2007 models, check for a short to ground on the red (11), pink/black (8) and the black/brown (29) terminals in the ECM connector. On 2008-2009 models, check for a short to ground on the red (7), pink/black (6) and the black/brown (35) terminals in the ECM connector. Refer to Figure 229 or Figure 230. Are any wires shorted to ground? — **Yes.** → Repair the wiring harness.

No.

Disconnect the black ECM connector from the ECM and disconnect the TP sensor harness connector from the sensor. Check the continuity on the red, pink/black, and black/brown wires between the ECM connector and the TP sensor harness connector. Does each wire have continuity? — **No.** → Repair the wiring harness.

Yes.

Faulty ECM.

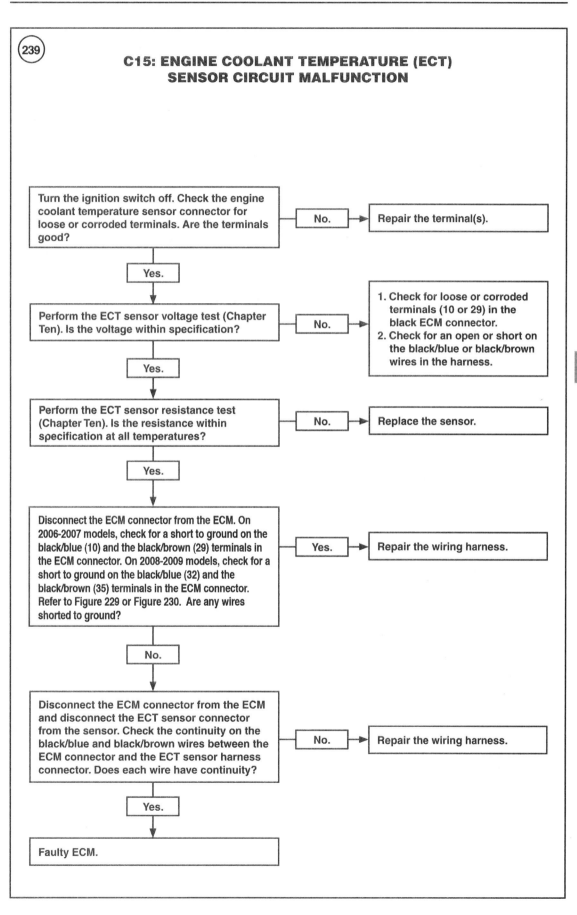

(239)

C15: ENGINE COOLANT TEMPERATURE (ECT) SENSOR CIRCUIT MALFUNCTION

Turn the ignition switch off. Check the engine coolant temperature sensor connector for loose or corroded terminals. Are the terminals good? → **No.** → Repair the terminal(s).

↓ **Yes.**

Perform the ECT sensor voltage test (Chapter Ten). Is the voltage within specification? → **No.** →
1. Check for loose or corroded terminals (10 or 29) in the black ECM connector.
2. Check for an open or short on the black/blue or black/brown wires in the harness.

↓ **Yes.**

Perform the ECT sensor resistance test (Chapter Ten). Is the resistance within specification at all temperatures? → **No.** → Replace the sensor.

↓ **Yes.**

Disconnect the ECM connector from the ECM. On 2006-2007 models, check for a short to ground on the black/blue (10) and the black/brown (29) terminals in the ECM connector. On 2008-2009 models, check for a short to ground on the black/blue (32) and the black/brown (35) terminals in the ECM connector. Refer to Figure 229 or Figure 230. Are any wires shorted to ground? → **Yes.** → Repair the wiring harness.

↓ **No.**

Disconnect the ECM connector from the ECM and disconnect the ECT sensor connector from the sensor. Check the continuity on the black/blue and black/brown wires between the ECM connector and the ECT sensor harness connector. Does each wire have continuity? → **No.** → Repair the wiring harness.

↓ **Yes.**

Faulty ECM.

8

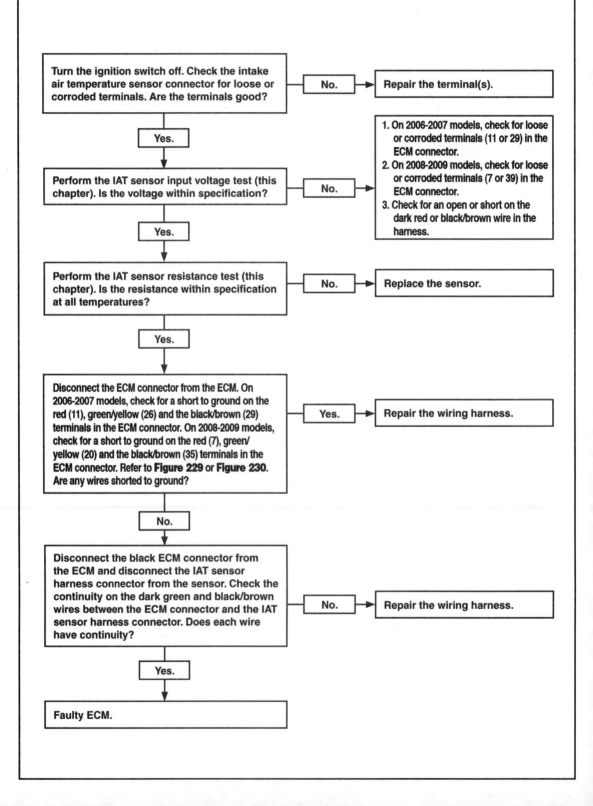

(240)

C21: INTAKE AIR TEMPERATURE (IAT) SENSOR CIRCUIT MALFUNCTION

Turn the ignition switch off. Check the intake air temperature sensor connector for loose or corroded terminals. Are the terminals good?

No. → Repair the terminal(s).

Yes.

Perform the IAT sensor input voltage test (this chapter). Is the voltage within specification?

No. →
1. On 2006-2007 models, check for loose or corroded terminals (11 or 29) in the ECM connector.
2. On 2008-2009 models, check for loose or corroded terminals (7 or 39) in the ECM connector.
3. Check for an open or short on the dark red or black/brown wire in the harness.

Yes.

Perform the IAT sensor resistance test (this chapter). Is the resistance within specification at all temperatures?

No. → Replace the sensor.

Yes.

Disconnect the ECM connector from the ECM. On 2006-2007 models, check for a short to ground on the red (11), green/yellow (26) and the black/brown (29) terminals in the ECM connector. On 2008-2009 models, check for a short to ground on the red (7), green/yellow (20) and the black/brown (35) terminals in the ECM connector. Refer to **Figure 229** or **Figure 230**. Are any wires shorted to ground?

Yes. → Repair the wiring harness.

No.

Disconnect the black ECM connector from the ECM and disconnect the IAT sensor harness connector from the sensor. Check the continuity on the dark green and black/brown wires between the ECM connector and the IAT sensor harness connector. Does each wire have continuity?

No. → Repair the wiring harness.

Yes.

Faulty ECM.

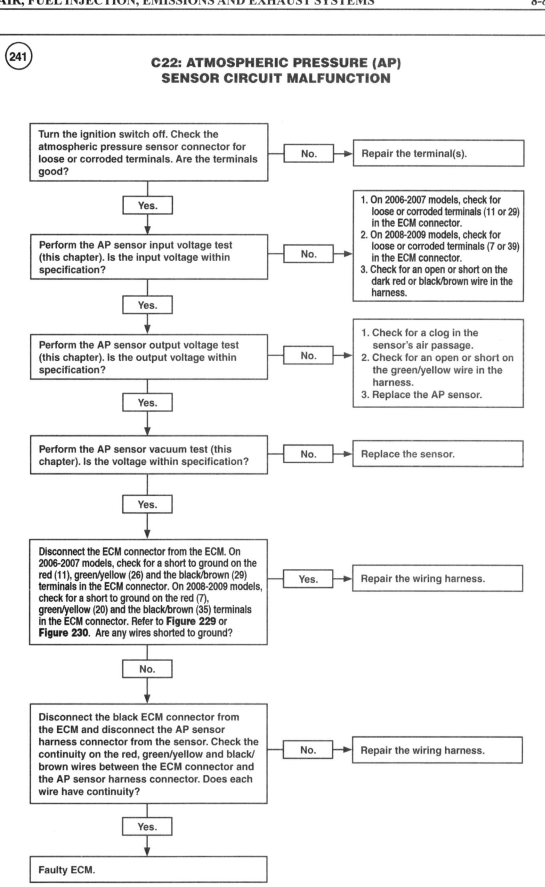

(241)

C22: ATMOSPHERIC PRESSURE (AP) SENSOR CIRCUIT MALFUNCTION

Turn the ignition switch off. Check the atmospheric pressure sensor connector for loose or corroded terminals. Are the terminals good? → No. → Repair the terminal(s).

↓ Yes.

Perform the AP sensor input voltage test (this chapter). Is the input voltage within specification? → No. →
1. On 2006-2007 models, check for loose or corroded terminals (11 or 29) in the ECM connector.
2. On 2008-2009 models, check for loose or corroded terminals (7 or 39) in the ECM connector.
3. Check for an open or short on the dark red or black/brown wire in the harness.

↓ Yes.

Perform the AP sensor output voltage test (this chapter). Is the output voltage within specification? → No. →
1. Check for a clog in the sensor's air passage.
2. Check for an open or short on the green/yellow wire in the harness.
3. Replace the AP sensor.

↓ Yes.

Perform the AP sensor vacuum test (this chapter). Is the voltage within specification? → No. → Replace the sensor.

↓ Yes.

Disconnect the ECM connector from the ECM. On 2006-2007 models, check for a short to ground on the red (11), green/yellow (26) and the black/brown (29) terminals in the ECM connector. On 2008-2009 models, check for a short to ground on the red (7), green/yellow (20) and the black/brown (35) terminals in the ECM connector. Refer to **Figure 229** or **Figure 230**. Are any wires shorted to ground? → Yes. → Repair the wiring harness.

↓ No.

Disconnect the black ECM connector from the ECM and disconnect the AP sensor harness connector from the sensor. Check the continuity on the red, green/yellow and black/brown wires between the ECM connector and the AP sensor harness connector. Does each wire have continuity? → No. → Repair the wiring harness.

↓ Yes.

Faulty ECM.

8

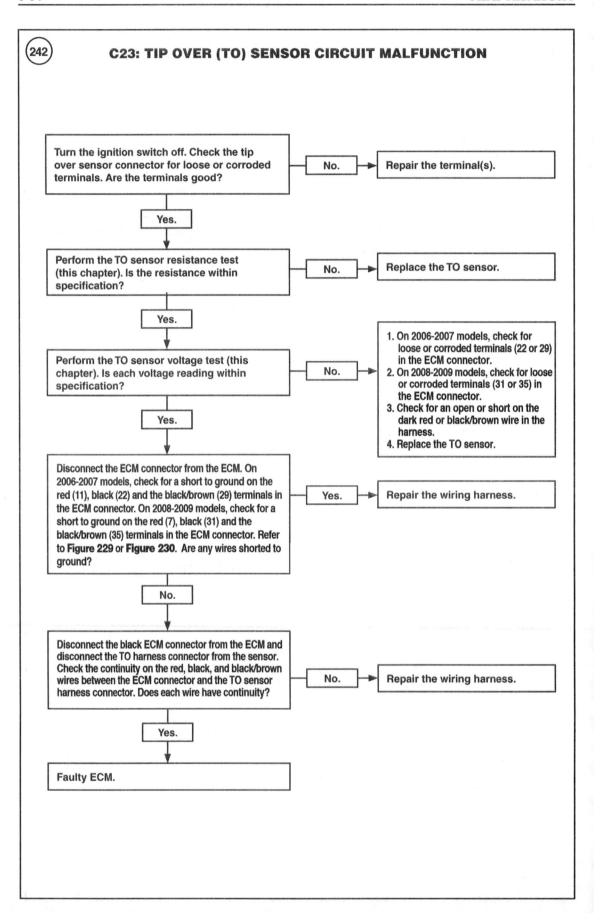

(242)

C23: TIP OVER (TO) SENSOR CIRCUIT MALFUNCTION

Turn the ignition switch off. Check the tip over sensor connector for loose or corroded terminals. Are the terminals good? → No. → Repair the terminal(s).

Yes.

Perform the TO sensor resistance test (this chapter). Is the resistance within specification? → No. → Replace the TO sensor.

Yes.

Perform the TO sensor voltage test (this chapter). Is each voltage reading within specification? → No. →
1. On 2006-2007 models, check for loose or corroded terminals (22 or 29) in the ECM connector.
2. On 2008-2009 models, check for loose or corroded terminals (31 or 35) in the ECM connector.
3. Check for an open or short on the dark red or black/brown wire in the harness.
4. Replace the TO sensor.

Yes.

Disconnect the ECM connector from the ECM. On 2006-2007 models, check for a short to ground on the red (11), black (22) and the black/brown (29) terminals in the ECM connector. On 2008-2009 models, check for a short to ground on the red (7), black (31) and the black/brown (35) terminals in the ECM connector. Refer to **Figure 229** or **Figure 230**. Are any wires shorted to ground? → Yes. → Repair the wiring harness.

No.

Disconnect the black ECM connector from the ECM and disconnect the TO harness connector from the sensor. Check the continuity on the red, black, and black/brown wires between the ECM connector and the TO sensor harness connector. Does each wire have continuity? → No. → Repair the wiring harness.

Yes.

Faulty ECM.

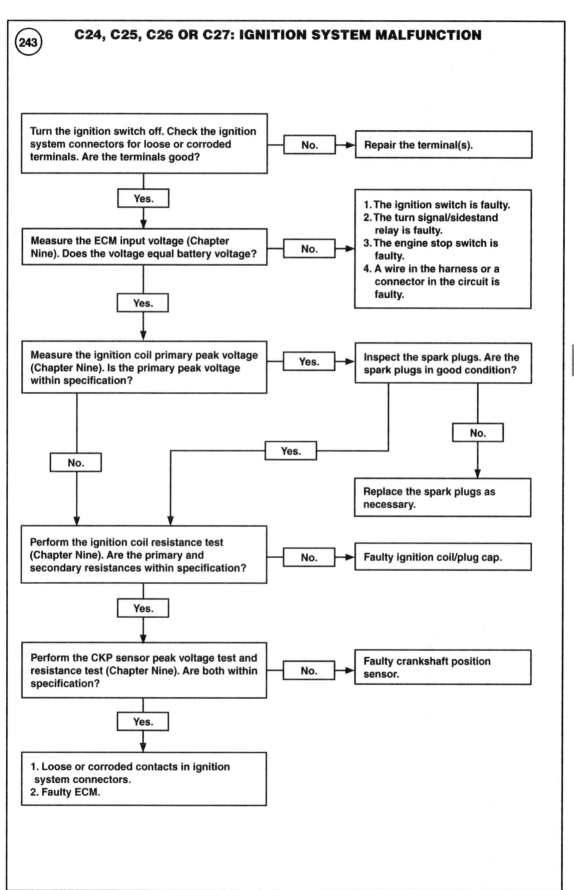

(243) **C24, C25, C26 OR C27: IGNITION SYSTEM MALFUNCTION**

Turn the ignition switch off. Check the ignition system connectors for loose or corroded terminals. Are the terminals good?

→ No. → Repair the terminal(s).

↓ Yes.

Measure the ECM input voltage (Chapter Nine). Does the voltage equal battery voltage?

→ No. →
1. The ignition switch is faulty.
2. The turn signal/sidestand relay is faulty.
3. The engine stop switch is faulty.
4. A wire in the harness or a connector in the circuit is faulty.

↓ Yes.

Measure the ignition coil primary peak voltage (Chapter Nine). Is the primary peak voltage within specification?

→ Yes. → Inspect the spark plugs. Are the spark plugs in good condition?

↓ No.

→ Yes. →

→ No. → Replace the spark plugs as necessary.

Perform the ignition coil resistance test (Chapter Nine). Are the primary and secondary resistances within specification?

→ No. → Faulty ignition coil/plug cap.

↓ Yes.

Perform the CKP sensor peak voltage test and resistance test (Chapter Nine). Are both within specification?

→ No. → Faulty crankshaft position sensor.

↓ Yes.

1. Loose or corroded contacts in ignition system connectors.
2. Faulty ECM.

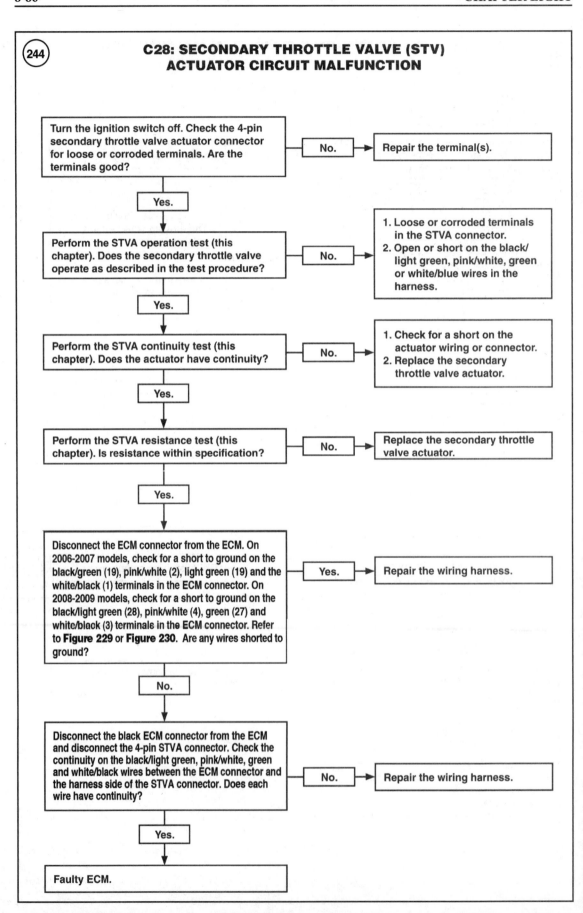

(244)

C28: SECONDARY THROTTLE VALVE (STV)
ACTUATOR CIRCUIT MALFUNCTION

Turn the ignition switch off. Check the 4-pin secondary throttle valve actuator connector for loose or corroded terminals. Are the terminals good? → **No.** → Repair the terminal(s).

↓ Yes.

Perform the STVA operation test (this chapter). Does the secondary throttle valve operate as described in the test procedure? → **No.** →
1. Loose or corroded terminals in the STVA connector.
2. Open or short on the black/light green, pink/white, green or white/blue wires in the harness.

↓ Yes.

Perform the STVA continuity test (this chapter). Does the actuator have continuity? → **No.** →
1. Check for a short on the actuator wiring or connector.
2. Replace the secondary throttle valve actuator.

↓ Yes.

Perform the STVA resistance test (this chapter). Is resistance within specification? → **No.** → Replace the secondary throttle valve actuator.

↓ Yes.

Disconnect the ECM connector from the ECM. On 2006-2007 models, check for a short to ground on the black/green (19), pink/white (2), light green (19) and the white/black (1) terminals in the ECM connector. On 2008-2009 models, check for a short to ground on the black/light green (28), pink/white (4), green (27) and white/black (3) terminals in the ECM connector. Refer to **Figure 229** or **Figure 230**. Are any wires shorted to ground? → **Yes.** → Repair the wiring harness.

↓ No.

Disconnect the black ECM connector from the ECM and disconnect the 4-pin STVA connector. Check the continuity on the black/light green, pink/white, green and white/black wires between the ECM connector and the harness side of the STVA connector. Does each wire have continuity? → **No.** → Repair the wiring harness.

↓ Yes.

Faulty ECM.

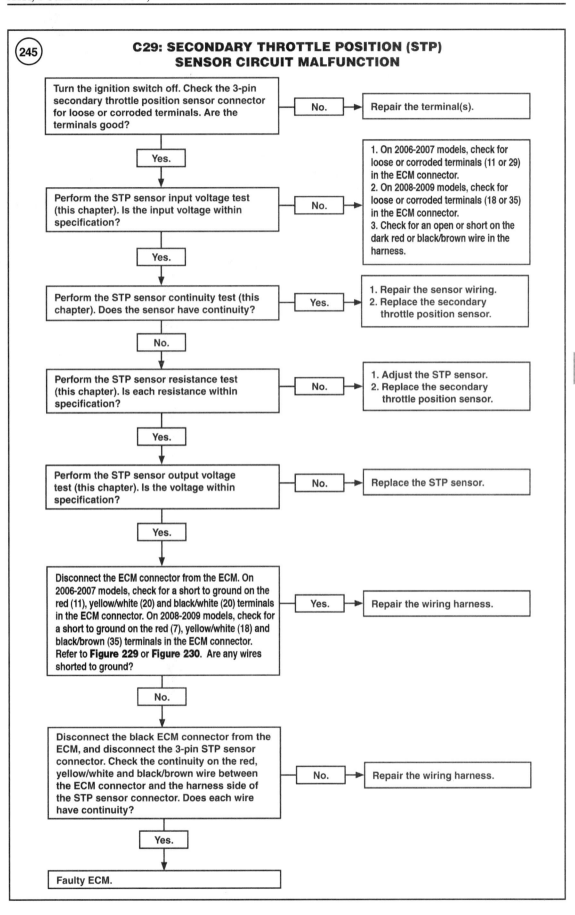

245

C29: SECONDARY THROTTLE POSITION (STP) SENSOR CIRCUIT MALFUNCTION

Turn the ignition switch off. Check the 3-pin secondary throttle position sensor connector for loose or corroded terminals. Are the terminals good?

No. → Repair the terminal(s).

Yes.

Perform the STP sensor input voltage test (this chapter). Is the input voltage within specification?

No. →
1. On 2006-2007 models, check for loose or corroded terminals (11 or 29) in the ECM connector.
2. On 2008-2009 models, check for loose or corroded terminals (18 or 35) in the ECM connector.
3. Check for an open or short on the dark red or black/brown wire in the harness.

Yes.

Perform the STP sensor continuity test (this chapter). Does the sensor have continuity?

Yes. →
1. Repair the sensor wiring.
2. Replace the secondary throttle position sensor.

No.

Perform the STP sensor resistance test (this chapter). Is each resistance within specification?

No. →
1. Adjust the STP sensor.
2. Replace the secondary throttle position sensor.

Yes.

Perform the STP sensor output voltage test (this chapter). Is the voltage within specification?

No. → Replace the STP sensor.

Yes.

Disconnect the ECM connector from the ECM. On 2006-2007 models, check for a short to ground on the red (11), yellow/white (20) and black/white (20) terminals in the ECM connector. On 2008-2009 models, check for a short to ground on the red (7), yellow/white (18) and black/brown (35) terminals in the ECM connector. Refer to **Figure 229** or **Figure 230**. Are any wires shorted to ground?

Yes. → Repair the wiring harness.

No.

Disconnect the black ECM connector from the ECM, and disconnect the 3-pin STP sensor connector. Check the continuity on the red, yellow/white and black/brown wire between the ECM connector and the harness side of the STP sensor connector. Does each wire have continuity?

No. → Repair the wiring harness.

Yes.

Faulty ECM.

8

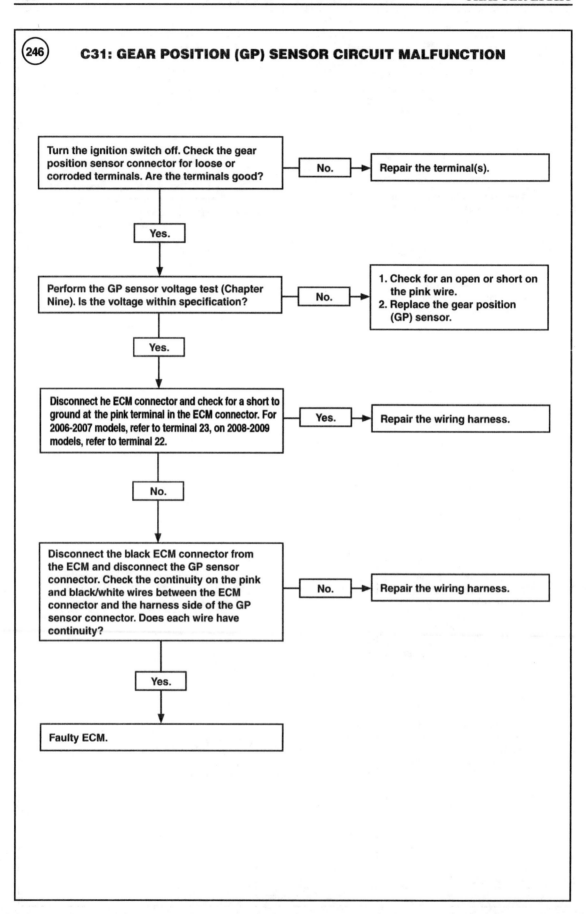

(246)   C31: GEAR POSITION (GP) SENSOR CIRCUIT MALFUNCTION

Turn the ignition switch off. Check the gear position sensor connector for loose or corroded terminals. Are the terminals good?

No. → Repair the terminal(s).

Yes.

Perform the GP sensor voltage test (Chapter Nine). Is the voltage within specification?

No. →
1. Check for an open or short on the pink wire.
2. Replace the gear position (GP) sensor.

Yes.

Disconnect he ECM connector and check for a short to ground at the pink terminal in the ECM connector. For 2006-2007 models, refer to terminal 23, on 2008-2009 models, refer to terminal 22.

Yes. → Repair the wiring harness.

No.

Disconnect the black ECM connector from the ECM and disconnect the GP sensor connector. Check the continuity on the pink and black/white wires between the ECM connector and the harness side of the GP sensor connector. Does each wire have continuity?

No. → Repair the wiring harness.

Yes.

Faulty ECM.

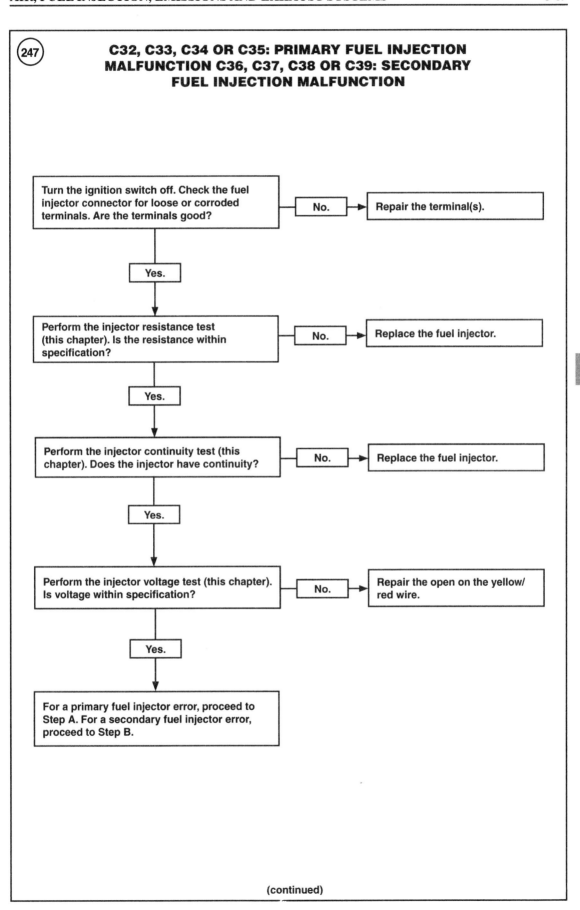

(247) **C32, C33, C34 OR C35: PRIMARY FUEL INJECTION MALFUNCTION C36, C37, C38 OR C39: SECONDARY FUEL INJECTION MALFUNCTION**

Turn the ignition switch off. Check the fuel injector connector for loose or corroded terminals. Are the terminals good? → No. → Repair the terminal(s).

Yes. ↓

Perform the injector resistance test (this chapter). Is the resistance within specification? → No. → Replace the fuel injector.

Yes. ↓

Perform the injector continuity test (this chapter). Does the injector have continuity? → No. → Replace the fuel injector.

Yes. ↓

Perform the injector voltage test (this chapter). Is voltage within specification? → No. → Repair the open on the yellow/red wire.

Yes. ↓

For a primary fuel injector error, proceed to Step A. For a secondary fuel injector error, proceed to Step B.

(continued)

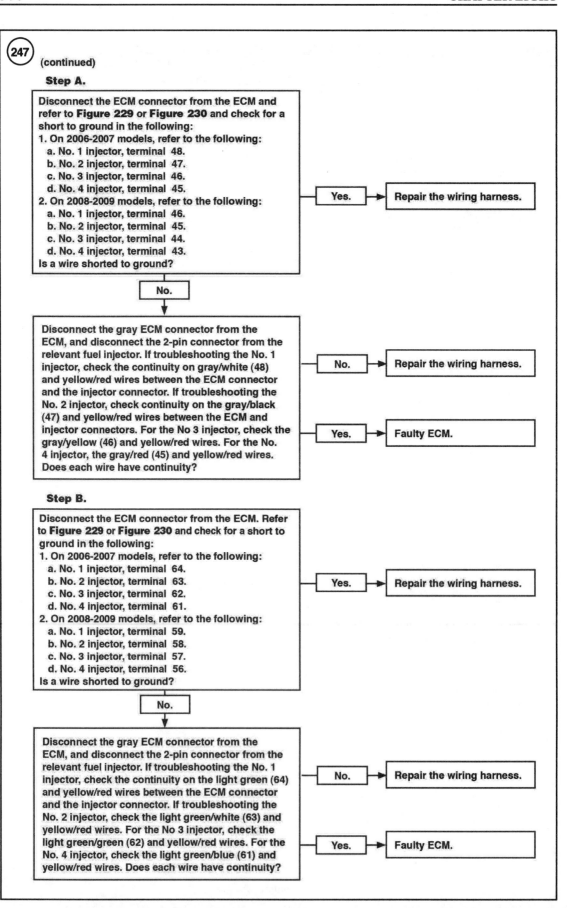

(247) (continued)

Step A.

Disconnect the ECM connector from the ECM and refer to **Figure 229** or **Figure 230** and check for a short to ground in the following:
1. On 2006-2007 models, refer to the following:
   a. No. 1 injector, terminal 48.
   b. No. 2 injector, terminal 47.
   c. No. 3 injector, terminal 46.
   d. No. 4 injector, terminal 45.
2. On 2008-2009 models, refer to the following:
   a. No. 1 injector, terminal 46.
   b. No. 2 injector, terminal 45.
   c. No. 3 injector, terminal 44.
   d. No. 4 injector, terminal 43.
Is a wire shorted to ground?

Yes. → Repair the wiring harness.

No.

Disconnect the gray ECM connector from the ECM, and disconnect the 2-pin connector from the relevant fuel injector. If troubleshooting the No. 1 injector, check the continuity on gray/white (48) and yellow/red wires between the ECM connector and the injector connector. If troubleshooting the No. 2 injector, check continuity on the gray/black (47) and yellow/red wires between the ECM and injector connectors. For the No 3 injector, check the gray/yellow (46) and yellow/red wires. For the No. 4 injector, the gray/red (45) and yellow/red wires. Does each wire have continuity?

No. → Repair the wiring harness.

Yes. → Faulty ECM.

Step B.

Disconnect the ECM connector from the ECM. Refer to **Figure 229** or **Figure 230** and check for a short to ground in the following:
1. On 2006-2007 models, refer to the following:
   a. No. 1 injector, terminal 64.
   b. No. 2 injector, terminal 63.
   c. No. 3 injector, terminal 62.
   d. No. 4 injector, terminal 61.
2. On 2008-2009 models, refer to the following:
   a. No. 1 injector, terminal 59.
   b. No. 2 injector, terminal 58.
   c. No. 3 injector, terminal 57.
   d. No. 4 injector, terminal 56.
Is a wire shorted to ground?

Yes. → Repair the wiring harness.

No.

Disconnect the gray ECM connector from the ECM, and disconnect the 2-pin connector from the relevant fuel injector. If troubleshooting the No. 1 injector, check the continuity on the light green (64) and yellow/red wires between the ECM connector and the injector connector. If troubleshooting the No. 2 injector, check the light green/white (63) and yellow/red wires. For the No 3 injector, check the light green/green (62) and yellow/red wires. For the No. 4 injector, check the light green/blue (61) and yellow/red wires. Does each wire have continuity?

No. → Repair the wiring harness.

Yes. → Faulty ECM.

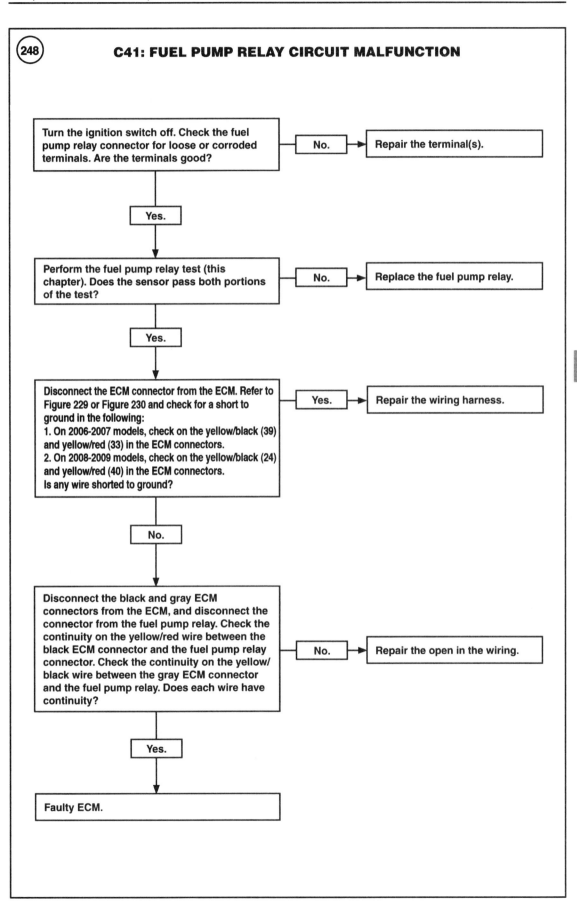

(248)   **C41: FUEL PUMP RELAY CIRCUIT MALFUNCTION**

Turn the ignition switch off. Check the fuel pump relay connector for loose or corroded terminals. Are the terminals good?

No. → Repair the terminal(s).

Yes.

Perform the fuel pump relay test (this chapter). Does the sensor pass both portions of the test?

No. → Replace the fuel pump relay.

Yes.

Disconnect the ECM connector from the ECM. Refer to Figure 229 or Figure 230 and check for a short to ground in the following:
1. On 2006-2007 models, check on the yellow/black (39) and yellow/red (33) in the ECM connectors.
2. On 2008-2009 models, check on the yellow/black (24) and yellow/red (40) in the ECM connectors.
Is any wire shorted to ground?

Yes. → Repair the wiring harness.

No.

Disconnect the black and gray ECM connectors from the ECM, and disconnect the connector from the fuel pump relay. Check the continuity on the yellow/red wire between the black ECM connector and the fuel pump relay connector. Check the continuity on the yellow/black wire between the gray ECM connector and the fuel pump relay. Does each wire have continuity?

No. → Repair the open in the wiring.

Yes.

Faulty ECM.

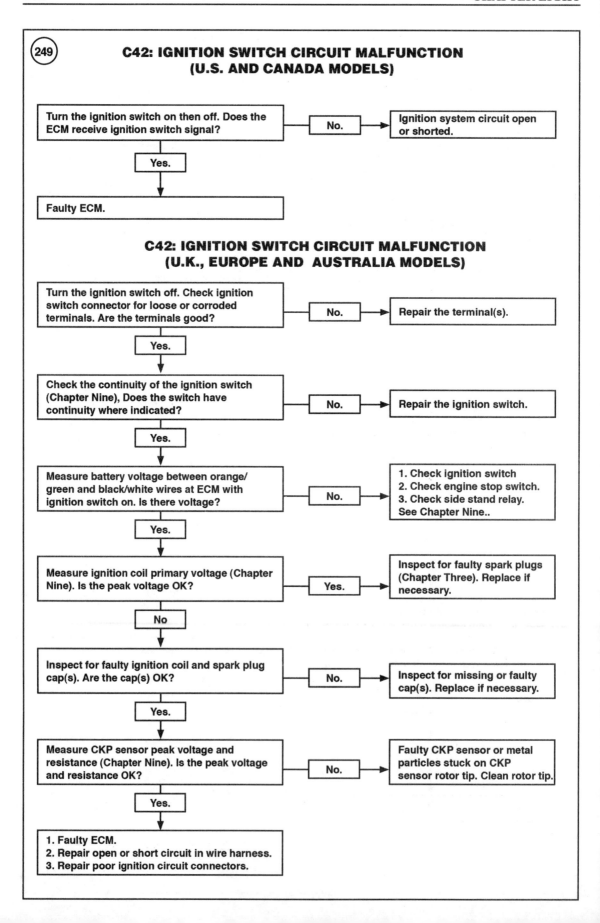

(249)

C42: IGNITION SWITCH CIRCUIT MALFUNCTION
(U.S. AND CANADA MODELS)

Turn the ignition switch on then off. Does the ECM receive ignition switch signal? → **No.** → Ignition system circuit open or shorted.

Yes.

Faulty ECM.

C42: IGNITION SWITCH CIRCUIT MALFUNCTION
(U.K., EUROPE AND AUSTRALIA MODELS)

Turn the ignition switch off. Check ignition switch connector for loose or corroded terminals. Are the terminals good? → **No.** → Repair the terminal(s).

Yes.

Check the continuity of the ignition switch (Chapter Nine), Does the switch have continuity where indicated? → **No.** → Repair the ignition switch.

Yes.

Measure battery voltage between orange/green and black/white wires at ECM with ignition switch on. Is there voltage? → **No.** → 1. Check ignition switch 2. Check engine stop switch. 3. Check side stand relay. See Chapter Nine..

Yes.

Measure ignition coil primary voltage (Chapter Nine). Is the peak voltage OK? → **Yes.** → Inspect for faulty spark plugs (Chapter Three). Replace if necessary.

No

Inspect for faulty ignition coil and spark plug cap(s). Are the cap(s) OK? → **No.** → Inspect for missing or faulty cap(s). Replace if necessary.

Yes.

Measure CKP sensor peak voltage and resistance (Chapter Nine). Is the peak voltage and resistance OK? → **No.** → Faulty CKP sensor or metal particles stuck on CKP sensor rotor tip. Clean rotor tip.

Yes.

1. Faulty ECM.
2. Repair open or short circuit in wire harness.
3. Repair poor ignition circuit connectors.

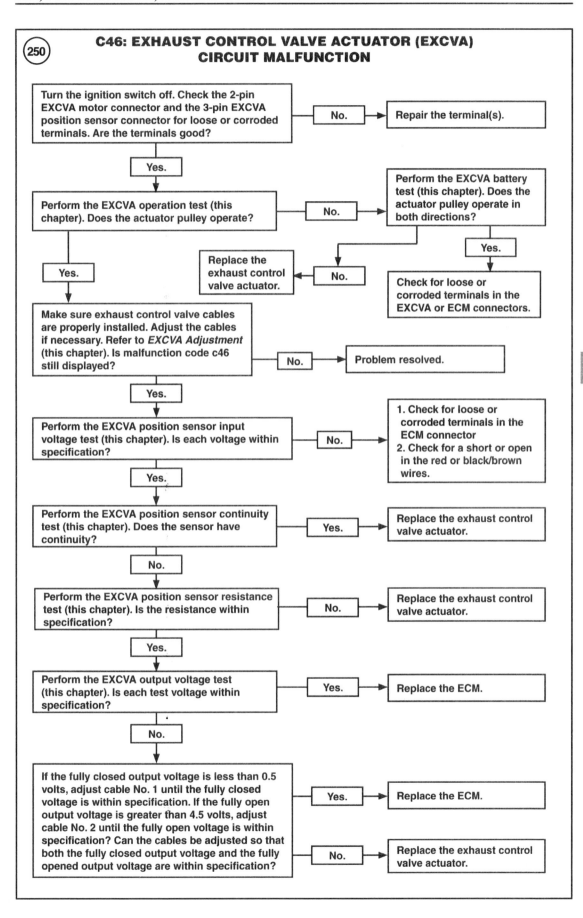

(250) C46: EXHAUST CONTROL VALVE ACTUATOR (EXCVA) CIRCUIT MALFUNCTION

Turn the ignition switch off. Check the 2-pin EXCVA motor connector and the 3-pin EXCVA position sensor connector for loose or corroded terminals. Are the terminals good? — **No.** → Repair the terminal(s).

Yes.

Perform the EXCVA operation test (this chapter). Does the actuator pulley operate? — **No.** → Perform the EXCVA battery test (this chapter). Does the actuator pulley operate in both directions?

Yes. → Check for loose or corroded terminals in the EXCVA or ECM connectors.

No. → Replace the exhaust control valve actuator.

Yes.

Make sure exhaust control valve cables are properly installed. Adjust the cables if necessary. Refer to *EXCVA Adjustment* (this chapter). Is malfunction code c46 still displayed? — **No.** → Problem resolved.

Yes.

Perform the EXCVA position sensor input voltage test (this chapter). Is each voltage within specification? — **No.** →
1. Check for loose or corroded terminals in the ECM connector
2. Check for a short or open in the red or black/brown wires.

Yes.

Perform the EXCVA position sensor continuity test (this chapter). Does the sensor have continuity? — **Yes.** → Replace the exhaust control valve actuator.

No.

Perform the EXCVA position sensor resistance test (this chapter). Is the resistance within specification? — **No.** → Replace the exhaust control valve actuator.

Yes.

Perform the EXCVA output voltage test (this chapter). Is each test voltage within specification? — **Yes.** → Replace the ECM.

No.

If the fully closed output voltage is less than 0.5 volts, adjust cable No. 1 until the fully closed voltage is within specification. If the fully open output voltage is greater than 4.5 volts, adjust cable No. 2 until the fully open voltage is within specification? Can the cables be adjusted so that both the fully closed output voltage and the fully opened output voltage are within specification? — **Yes.** → Replace the ECM.

No. → Replace the exhaust control valve actuator.

8

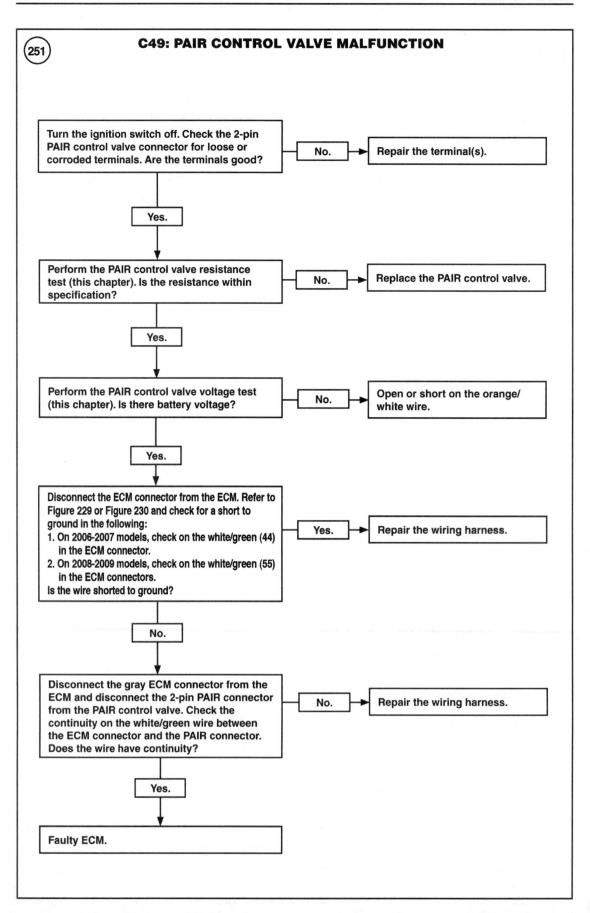

(251) **C49: PAIR CONTROL VALVE MALFUNCTION**

Turn the ignition switch off. Check the 2-pin PAIR control valve connector for loose or corroded terminals. Are the terminals good? → No. → Repair the terminal(s).

Yes.

Perform the PAIR control valve resistance test (this chapter). Is the resistance within specification? → No. → Replace the PAIR control valve.

Yes.

Perform the PAIR control valve voltage test (this chapter). Is there battery voltage? → No. → Open or short on the orange/white wire.

Yes.

Disconnect the ECM connector from the ECM. Refer to Figure 229 or Figure 230 and check for a short to ground in the following:
1. On 2006-2007 models, check on the white/green (44) in the ECM connector.
2. On 2008-2009 models, check on the white/green (55) in the ECM connectors.
Is the wire shorted to ground? → Yes. → Repair the wiring harness.

No.

Disconnect the gray ECM connector from the ECM and disconnect the 2-pin PAIR connector from the PAIR control valve. Check the continuity on the white/green wire between the ECM connector and the PAIR connector. Does the wire have continuity? → No. → Repair the wiring harness.

Yes.

Faulty ECM.

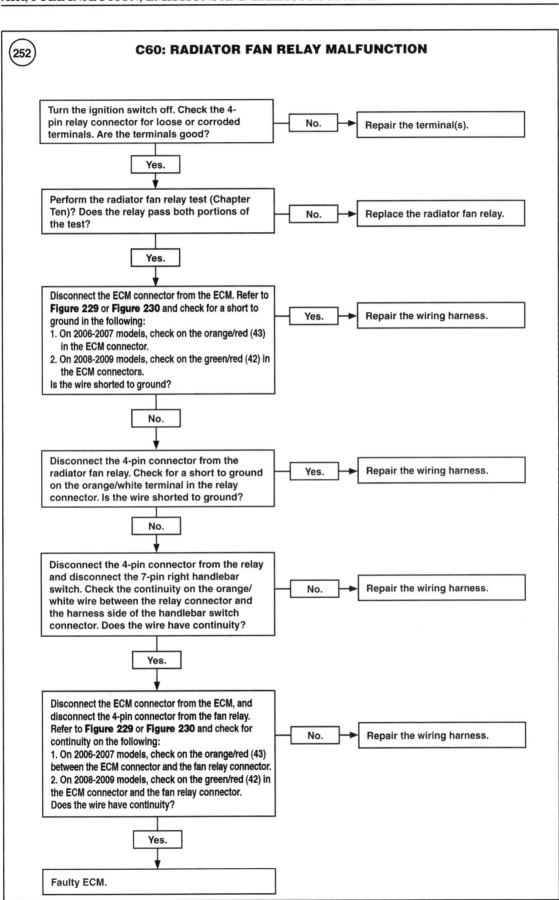

(252)

C60: RADIATOR FAN RELAY MALFUNCTION

Turn the ignition switch off. Check the 4-pin relay connector for loose or corroded terminals. Are the terminals good? → No. → Repair the terminal(s).

Yes.

Perform the radiator fan relay test (Chapter Ten)? Does the relay pass both portions of the test? → No. → Replace the radiator fan relay.

Yes.

Disconnect the ECM connector from the ECM. Refer to **Figure 229** or **Figure 230** and check for a short to ground in the following:
1. On 2006-2007 models, check on the orange/red (43) in the ECM connector.
2. On 2008-2009 models, check on the green/red (42) in the ECM connectors.
Is the wire shorted to ground? → Yes. → Repair the wiring harness.

No.

Disconnect the 4-pin connector from the radiator fan relay. Check for a short to ground on the orange/white terminal in the relay connector. Is the wire shorted to ground? → Yes. → Repair the wiring harness.

No.

Disconnect the 4-pin connector from the relay and disconnect the 7-pin right handlebar switch. Check the continuity on the orange/white wire between the relay connector and the harness side of the handlebar switch connector. Does the wire have continuity? → No. → Repair the wiring harness.

Yes.

Disconnect the ECM connector from the ECM, and disconnect the 4-pin connector from the fan relay. Refer to **Figure 229** or **Figure 230** and check for continuity on the following:
1. On 2006-2007 models, check on the orange/red (43) between the ECM connector and the fan relay connector.
2. On 2008-2009 models, check on the green/red (42) in the ECM connector and the fan relay connector.
Does the wire have continuity? → No. → Repair the wiring harness.

Yes.

Faulty ECM.

8

Table 1 FUEL SYSTEM SPECIFICATIONS

Item	Specification
Throttle body bore size	
GSX-R600 models	40 mm (1.575 in.)
GSX-R750 models	42 mm (1.65 in.)
Throttle body ID No.	
GSXR-600 models	
2006-2007 models	
All models except California	01H0
California models	01H1
2008-2009 models	
All models except California	37H0
California models	37H1
GSXR-750 models	
2006-2007 models	
All models except California	02H0
California models	02H1
2008-2009 models	
All models except California	38H0
California models	38H1
Idle speed	1100-1300rpm
Fast idle speed (with cold engine)	1500-2000
Throttle cable free play	2.0-4.0 mm (0.08-0.16 in.)
Fuel pump output pressure	Approx. 300 kPa (43 psi])
Fuel pump output volume	
2006-2007 models	Approx 168 ml (5.7 US oz.) per 10 seconds
2008-2009 models	Approx 167 ml (5.6 US oz.) per 10 seconds
Fuel tank capacity (including reserve)	
2006-2007 modes	
California models	15.5 liter (4.1 US gal. [3.4 Imp gal.])
All models except California	16.5 liter (4.4 US gal. [3.6 Imp gal.])
2008-2009 models	
California models	16.0 liter (4.2 US gal. [3.6 Imp gal.])
All models except California	17.0 liter (4.5 US gal [3.7 Imp gal.])
Fuel	Regular unleaded
USA, California and Canada models	
Pump octane: (R/2 + M/2)	87 or higher
Research octane	90 or higher
All models except USA, California and	
Canada models	95 or higher

Table 2 FUEL SYSTEM ELECTRICAL SPECIFICATIONS

Item	Specification
Atmospheric pressure (AP) sensor	
Input voltage	4.5-5.5 volts
Output voltage	Approx. 3.6 volts @ 100 kPa(760 mmHg)
VCC out voltage	4.5-5.0 volts @ 20-30° C (68-86° F)
Camshaft position (CMP) sensor	
Voltage	0.8 volts or higher
Engine coolant temperature (ETC) sensor	
Resistance	2.45 k ohms @ 20° C (68° F)
Input voltage	4.5-5.5 volts
Output voltage	0.15-4.85 volts
Bench test resistance	
20° C (68° F)	Approx. 2.45 k ohms
50° C (122° F)	Approx. 0.811 k ohms
80° C (176° F)	Approx. 0.318 k ohms
110° C (230° F)	Approx. 0.142 k ohms
130° C (266° F)	Approx 0.088 k ohms

(continued)

Table 2 FUEL SYSTEM ELECTRICAL SPECIFICATIONS (continued)

Item	Specification
Exhaust control valve actuator (EXCVA) position sensor	
Position sensor output voltage	
2006-2007 models	
Closed position	0.5-1.3 volts
Open position	3.7-4.5 volts
2008-2009 models	
Closed position	0.45-1.4 volts
Open position	3.6-4.55 volts
Position sensor input voltage	
2006-2007 models	4.5-5.5 volts
2008-2009 models	NA
Resistance	3,100 ohms
Fuel injector	
Voltage	Battery voltage
Resistance	11-13 ohms @ 20° C (68° F)
Fuel level sensor gauge resistance	
2006-2007 models	
Lower (empty) position	3-5 ohms
Raised (full) position	179-185 ohms
2008-2009 models	
Lower (empty) position	80-88 ohms
Raised (full) position	4.5-6.5 ohms
HO2 sensor	
Input voltage	
At idle speed	0.4 volts and less
5,000 rpm	0.6 volts
Heater resistance	
2006-2007 models	4.0-5.0 ohms @ 23° C (73° F)
2008-2009 models	6.7-9.5 ohms @ 23° C (73° F)
Intake air pressure (IAP) sensor	
Input voltage	4.5-5.5 volts
Output voltage	Approx. 2.7 volts @ idle
Vout voltage	4.5-5.0 volts @ 20-30° C (68-86° F)
Intake air temperature (IAT) sensor	
Input voltage	4.5-5.5 volts
Output voltage	0.15-4.85 volts
Resistance	
2006-2007 models	Approx. 2.45 k ohms @ 20° C (68° F)
2008-2009 models	Approx. 2.58 k ohms @ 20° C (68 ° F)
Bench test resistance	
20° (68° F)	Approx. 2.45 k ohms
50° C (122° F)	Approx. 0.808 k ohms
80° C (176° F)	Approx. 0.322 k ohms
110° C (230° F)	Approx. 0.148 k ohms
ISC valve resistance	Approx. 20 ohms @ 20° C (68 ° F)
PAIR control valve resistance	
2006-2007 models	18-22 ohms @ 20-30° C (68-86° F)
2008-2009 models	20-24 ohms @ 20-30° C (68-86° F)
Secondary throttle position (STP) sensor	
Input voltage	4.5-5.5 volts
Output voltage	
2006-2007 models	
Fully closed	Approx. 0.57-0.67 volt
Fully open	Approx. 3.9 volt
2008-2009 models	
Fully closed	Approx. 0.6 volt
Fully open	Approx. 3.9 volt
Resistance (2006-2007 models)•	
Fully closed	Approx. 0.5 k ohms
Fully open	Approx. 3.9 k ohms

(continued)

8

Table 2 FUEL SYSTEM ELECTRICAL SPECIFICATIONS (continued)

Item	Specification
Secondary throttle valve (STV) actuator resistance	
2006-2007 models	Approx. 7.0 ohms
2008-2009 models	Approx. 6.5 ohms
Throttle position (TP) sensor	
Input voltage	4.5-5.5 volts
Output voltage	
Fully closed	Approx. 1.1 volts
Fully open	Approx. 4.3 volts
Resistance (2006-2007 models)*	Approx. 4.68 k ohms
Fully closed	Approx. 1.1 k ohms
Fully open	Approx. 4.3 k ohms
Tip over (TO) sensor	
Resistance	16.5-22.3 k ohms
Voltage	Upright: 0.4 volts
	Leaning 43°: 3.7-4.4 volts

* 2008-2009 specifications not available.

Table 3 FUEL AND EXHAUST SYSTEM TORQUE SPECIFICATIONS

Item	N•m	in.-lb.	ft.-lb.	
Camshaft position (CMP) sensor bolt		10	89	–
Crankshaft position (CKP) sensor				
mounting bolt	8	71	–	
Engine coolant temperature (ECT)				
sensor	18	–	13	
EXCVA				
Cable bracket mounting bolt	5.5	48	–	
Mounting bolt	6	53	–	
Pulley mounting bolt	5	44	–	
Exhaust header bolt	23	–	17	
Exhaust pipe mount and clamp bolt	23	–	17	
Exhaust pipe mounting bolt				
(2008–2009 models)	223	–	17	
Fuel delivery pipe mounting screw				
2006–2007 models	5	44	–	
2008–2009 models	3.5	31	–	
Fuel pump bolt	10	89	–	
ISC valve screw (2008–2009 models)		2	17.7	–
Intake air temperature (IAT) sensor				
screw	1.3	11.5	–	
Muffler connecting bolt	23	–	17	
Muffler cover bolt (2008–2009 models)	5.5	48	–	
Muffler mounting bolt				
2006–2007 models	23	–	17	
2008–2009 models	25	–	18	
Oxygen sensor				
2006–2007 models	48	–	35	
2008–2009 models	25	–	18	
Secondary throttle position (STP)				
sensor screw	3.5	31	–	
Throttle position (TP) sensor Torx screw	3.5	31	–	

CHAPTER NINE

ELECTRICAL SYSTEM

This chapter contains service and test procedures for components for the electrical system.

Electrical components in the fuel system and cooling system are addressed in the Chapter Eight and Chapter Ten respectively. Refer to Chapter Three for spark plug information.

Before working on the electrical system, review *Electrical System Fundamentals* in Chapter One and *Electrical Testing* in Chapter Two.

Refer to the appropriate color wiring diagram at the end of this manual when working on the electrical system to ensure that the correct component or corrector is located.

ELECTRICAL COMPONENT REPLACEMENT

Most motorcycle dealerships and parts suppliers will not accept the return of any electrical part. Consider any test results carefully replacing a component that test results are only slightly out of specification, especially resistance. If the exact cause of an electrical system malfunction cannot be determined, have a dealership verify test results. If a new electrical component is installed and the system still does not work, the unit, in all likelihood, cannot be returned for a refund.

ELECTRICAL CONNECTORS

To prevent corrosion, pack electrical connectors with dielectric grease when reconnecting them. Dielectric grease is formulated for sealing and waterproofing electrical connectors, and it will not interfere with current flow. Only use this compound or an equivalent sealant designed for this purpose. Other materials may interfere with the current flow. Do not use silicone sealant.

In addition to packing electrical connectors, also regularly check the ground connections at the various locations on the motorcycle. Loose or dirty ground terminals are often sources of electrical problems.

The position of electrical connectors can vary between model years, and a connector may have been repositioned during a previous repair. Refer to the appropriate wiring diagram, and use the wiring colors to identify the connector. Follow the electrical cable from the specific component to where it connects to the wiring harness or to another electrical component.

BATTERY

All models use a sealed, maintenance-free battery. The battery electrolyte cannot be serviced. Never attempt to remove the sealing bar cap from the top of a maintenance free battery.

When replacing the battery, use a sealed type. Do not install a non-sealed battery.

Precautions

To prevent accidental shorts during electrical service, always disconnect electrical cable from the negative battery terminal (A, **Figure 1**) before beginning work.

1. Always wear safety glasses when servicing the battery.

2. Do not smoke or permit any open flame near a battery being changed or one that has been recently changed.

3. Do not disconnect live circuits at the battery. A spark usually occurs when a live circuit is broken.

4. Always disconnect electrical cable from the negative battery terminal (A, **Figure 1**) before beginning work.

5. Exercise caution when connecting or disconnecting a battery charger. Turn the power switch off before making or breaking connections. Charge the battery with the battery removed from the motorcycle.

6. Keep children and pets away from the charging equipment and the battery.

Removal/Installation

1. Turn the ignition switch off.

2. Remove the rider's seat as described in Chapter Fifteen.

> *CAUTION*
> *When removing the battery, always disconnect the negative battery cable first, and then disconnect the positive cable.*

3. Disconnect the battery negative cable (A, **Figure 1**) as described in this chapter.

4. Move the positive cable cap, and disconnect the cable from the positive battery terminal (B, **Figure 1**).

5. Lift the battery (C, **Figure 1**) from the battery box.

6. Inspect pads in the battery box for wear or deterioration. Replace any if necessary.

7. Install the battery into the battery box with the negative battery terminal (A, **Figure 1**) on the right side of the motorcycle.

> *CAUTION*
> *Make sure each battery cable is connected to the correct battery terminal. Connecting the cables backwards reverses the polarity and damages the rectifier and ignition system.*

8. First connect the positive cable to the positive battery terminal (B, **Figure 1**), and then connect the

negative cable to the negative terminal (A, **Figure 1**).

9. Coat the battery connections with dielectric grease to retard corrosion.

10. Install the positive cable cap.

Inspection/Testing

1. Remove the battery as described in this chapter. Do not clean the battery while it is mounted in the frame.

2. Set the battery on a stack of newspapers or shop cloths to protect the workbench surface.

3. Inspect the battery pads in the battery box for contamination or damage. Clean the pads and compartment with a solution of baking soda and water.

4. Check the entire battery case for cracks or other damage. If the battery case is warped, discolored or has a raised top, the battery has been overcharging or overheating.

5. Check the battery terminals and bolts for corrosion or damage. Clean parts thoroughly with a solution of baking soda and water. Replace severely corroded or damaged parts.

6. If corroded, clean the top of the battery with a stiff bristle brush using the baking soda and water solution.

7. Check the cable terminals for corrosion and damage. If corrosion is minor, clean the cable terminals with a stiff wire brush. Replace severely worn or damaged cables.

> *NOTE*
> *Test the battery temperature at 20°C (68° F).*

8. Connect a digital voltmeter across the battery terminals to check the state of charge.

   a. The battery is fully charged if voltage equals 13.0-13.2 volts.

   b. If the battery voltage is less than 12.5 volts, the battery is undercharged and requires charging.

Charging

A digital voltmeter and a charger with an adjustable amperage output are required when charging a maintenance free battery. If this equipment is not available, have the battery charged by a shop with the proper equipment. Excessive voltage and amperage from an unregulated charger can damage the battery and shorten its service life.

A battery self-discharges approximately one percent of its given capacity each day. If a battery not in use loses its charge within a week after charging, the battery is defective.

If the motorcycle is not used for long periods of time, an automatic battery charger with variable voltage and amperage outputs is recommended for optimum battery service life.

1. Remove the battery from the motorcycle (this section).
2. Set the battery on a stack of newspapers or shop cloths to protect the workbench surface.
3. First, connect the positive charger lead to the positive battery terminal. Next, connect the negative charger lead to the negative battery terminal.
4. Set the charger to 12 volts. Charge the battery at 1/10 its given capacity. **Table 1** lists the battery capacity and recommended charge rate.

> *CAUTION*
> *Never set the battery charger to more than 4 amps. The battery will be damaged if the charge rate exceeds 4 amps.*

5. The charging time depends upon the discharged condition of the battery. Use the charging amperage and length of time suggested on the battery label.
6. Turn the charger on.
7. After the battery has been charged for the predetermined time, turn the charger off and disconnect the leads.
8. Wait 30 minutes, and then measure the battery voltage.
   a. If the battery voltage is greater than 13.0-13.2 volts, the battery is fully charged.
   b. If the battery voltage is less than 12.5 volts, continue charging the battery.
   c. If battery voltage is less than 12.5 volts 30 minutes after the second charging, replace the battery.
9. If the battery remains stable for one hour, the battery is charged.
10. Install the battery into the motorcycle.

Initialization

When replacing the old battery, make sure the new battery has received an initial charge before installing it in the motorcycle. Failure to do so causes permanent battery damage and reduces the service life of the battery. Charging a new battery after it has been used does not bring its charge to. When purchasing a new battery from a dealership or parts store, verify its charge status. If necessary, have the store perform an initial or booster charge to bring the battery up to 100% charge before accepting the battery.

CHARGING SYSTEM

The charging system consists of the battery, alternator and a voltage regulator/rectifier. A 30-amp main fuse protects the circuit.

Alternating current generated by the alternator is rectified to direct current. The voltage regulator maintains constant voltage to the battery and additional electrical loads, like the lights and ignition system, regardless of variations in engine speed and load.

A malfunction in the charging system generally causes the battery to remain undercharged. To prevent damage to the alternator and the regulator/rectifier during charging system service, note the following:

1. Always disconnect the electrical cable from the negative battery terminal (A, **Figure 1**) before removing a component from the charging system.
2. When charging the battery, remove it from the motorcycle and follow the charging procedures as described in this chapter.
3. Inspect the physical condition of the battery. Look for bulges or cracks in the case, leaking electrolyte or corrosion build-up.
4. Check the wiring in the charging system for signs of chafing, deterioration or other damage. Repair any problems with the wiring.
5. Check the wiring for corroded or loose connections. Clean, tighten or reconnect as required.

Current Draw Test

Perform this test before performing the regulated voltage test.
1. Turn the ignition switch off.
2. Remove the rider's seat (Chapter Fifteen).
3. Disconnect the battery negative cable (A, **Figure 1**) as described in this chapter.

> *CAUTION*
> *Before connecting the ammeter, set the meter to its highest amperage scale.*

This prevents a possible large current flow from damaging the meter or blowing the meter's fuse.

4. Connect the ammeter between the battery negative cable and the negative terminal of the battery (**Figure 2**).

5. Switch the ammeter from its highest to lowest amperage scale while reading the meter. The reading must not exceed the maximum current draw specified in **Table 1**.

6. If the current draw is excessive, check the following:

   a. Damaged battery.

   b. Short circuit in the system.

   c. Loose, dirty or faulty electrical system connectors in the charging system wiring harness system.

   d. Aftermarket electrical accessory added to the system.

7. To determine the source of a current dray, disconnect the individual circuits at connectors or fuses and monitor the current draw. When the current draw returns to the specified level, the faulty circuit is indicated. Refer to the wiring diagrams and test the circuit further to isolate the problem.

8. Disconnect the ammeter test leads and reconnect the battery negative lead.

9. Connect the battery negative cable (A, **Figure 1**) as described in this chapter.

10. Install the rider's seat (Chapter Fifteen).

Regulated Voltage Test

Before troubleshooting the charging system, make sure the battery is fully charged and in good condition. Clean and test the battery as described earlier in this chapter. Make sure all electrical connectors are tight and free of corrosion.

1. Start the engine and let it reach normal operating temperature. Turn off the engine.

2. Remove the rider seat (Chapter Fifteen).

3. Turn the headlight dimmer switch to the high position.

4. Restart the engine and let it idle.

5. Connect a voltmeter positive test lead to the positive battery terminal, and connect the negative test probe to the negative battery terminal.

6. Increase engine speed to 5000 rpm. The voltage reading should be within the regulated voltage range specified in **Table 1**. If the voltage is outside the specified range, inspect the alternator and the voltage regulator as described in this chapter.

7. If the charging voltage is too high; the voltage regulator/rectifier is probably at faulty.

8. Install the rider seat (Chapter Fifteen).

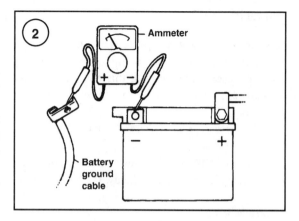

No-Load Voltage Test

1. Remove the fuel tank and air filter assembly (Chapter Eight).

2. Disconnect 3-pin stator connector (3 yellow wires) from its harness mate (**Figure 3**). If necessary, follow the electrical cable from the alternator cover to the connector.

3. Start the engine and let it idle. Begin the test while the engine is cold.

4. Use 0.5 mm (0.02 in.) back probe pins on the voltmeter to back probe the alternator side of the connector.

5. Increase engine speed to 5000 rpm, and check the voltage on the meter. Record the voltage for that pair of terminals.

6. Repeat Step 4 and Step 5 and measure the voltage between each of the remaining terminal pairs. Take a total of three readings. Refer to **Figure 4**.

7. If the voltage in any test is less than the no-load voltage specified in **Table 1**, the alternator is faulty and must be replaced.

8. Install the air filter assembly and the fuel tank.

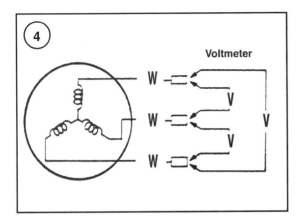

Voltmeter

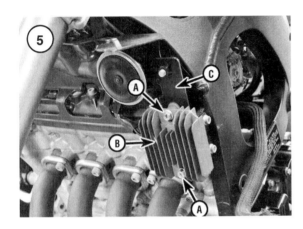

VOLTAGE REGULATOR/RECTIFIER

Removal/Installation

2006-2007 Models

1. Remove the left side fairing (Chapter Fifteen).
2. Disconnect the battery negative cable as described in this chapter.
3. Remove each mounting bolt (A, **Figure 5**) and move the voltage regulator/rectifier (B) away from the frame mounting bracket (C).
4. Follow the electrical cable from the voltage regulator/rectifier through the frame opening to the connectors adjacent to the cylinder head cover.
5. Remove any cable tie(s) from the harness.
6. Disconnect the 4-pin and 2-pin voltage regulator/rectifier connectors from its harness mate.
7. Withdraw the harness from the frame and remove the voltage regulator/rectifier assembly from the frame.
8. Install by reversing the removal steps. Note the following:
    a. Tighten the mounting bolt securely.
    b. Make sure the electrical connectors are tight and free of corrosion.

2008-2009 Models

Refer to **Figure 6**.
1. Remove the left side fairing (Chapter Fifteen)
2. Remove the fuel tank and air filter assembly (Chapter Eight).
3. Disconnect the battery negative cable as described in this chapter.
4. Remove the harness clamp mounting bolt (A, **Figure 7**).

> *NOTE*
> *The 2-pin electrical connector is adjacent to 4-pin (B, **Figure 7**), but not visible.*

5. Disconnect the 4-pin and 2-pin voltage regulator/rectifier connectors from its harness mate.
6. Remove the mounting bolts (A, **Figure 8**) and nuts, and remove the voltage regulator/rectifier (B). Account for the collar within the grommets located on the backside of the mounting bracket.
7. Remove the electrical wiring harness and the voltage regulator/rectifier assembly from the frame.
8. Install by reversing the removal steps. Note the following:
    a. Install the collars must be reinstalled during installation.
    b. Tighten the mounting bolts and nuts to 10 N•m (89 in.-lb.).
    c. Tighten the clamp bolt securely.
    d. Make sure the electrical connectors are tight and free of corrosion.

Voltage Test

2006-2007 Models

The manufacturer specifies the use of a multicircuit tester (Suzuki part No. 09900-25008) for testing the regulator/rectifier unit. If this tester is not available, take the regulator/rectifier to a dealership for testing. Refer to *Electrical Testing* in Chapter Two.

> *NOTE*
> *Prior to making this test, check the condition of the tester's battery.*

1. Perform Steps 1-6 of the voltage regulator/rectifier removal procedures.
2. Set the multicircuit Tester to the diode setting.
3. **Figure 9** identifies the terminals in the regulator/rectifier connector. Connect the tester probes to the terminals indicated in **Figure 10**, and check the voltage across each pair of terminals.
4. If any voltage reading differs from the stated value in **Figure 10**, replace the voltage regulator/rectifier.

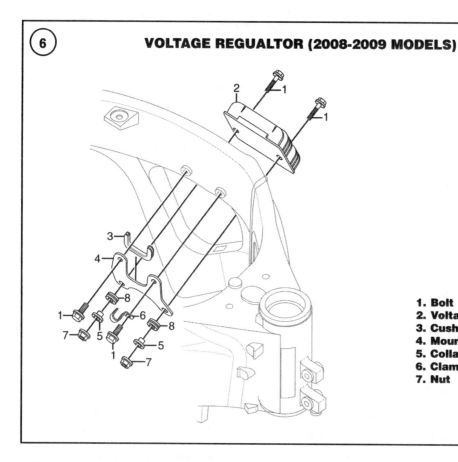

VOLTAGE REGUALTOR (2008-2009 MODELS)

1. Bolt
2. Voltage regulator
3. Cushion
4. Mounting bracket
5. Collar
6. Clamp
7. Nut

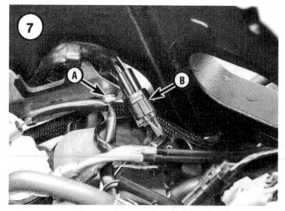

2008-2009 Models

The manufacturer specifies the use of a multicircuit tester (Suzuki part No. 09900-25008) for testing the regulator/rectifier unit. If this tester is not available, take the regulator/rectifier to a dealership for testing.

> *NOTE*
> *Prior to making this test, check the condition of the tester's battery.*

1. Perform Steps 1-4 of the voltage regulator/rectifier removal procedures.

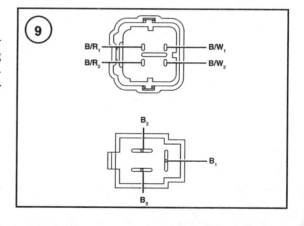

⑩ REGUALTOR/RECTIFIER (2006-2007 MODELS)

		+ Probe of tester to:						
		B/R_1	B/R_2	B_1	B_2	B_3	B/W_1	B/W_2
− Probe of tester to:	B/R_1		0	0.4-0.7V	0.4-0.7V	0.4-0.7V	0.5-1.2V	0.5-1.2V
	B/R_2	0		0.4-0.7V	0.4-0.7V	0.4-0.7V	0.5-1.2V	0.5-1.2V
	B_1	*	*		*	*	0.4-0.7V	0.4-0.7V
	B_2	*	*	*		*	0.4-0.7V	0.4-0.7V
	B_3	*	*	*	*		0.4-0.7V	0.4-0.7V
	B/W_1	*	*	*	*	*		0
	B/W_2	*	*	*	*	*	0	

*1.4 V and more (tester's battery voltage). All units in Volts.

⑪ REGUALTOR/RECTIFIER (2008-2009 MODELS)

		(+) probe of tester to:						
		B/R_1	B/R_2	B_1	B_2	B_3	B/W_1	B/W_2
(−) probe of tester to:	B/R_1	−	0	0.2-0.9	0.2-0.9	0.2-0.9	0.3-1.0	0.3-1.0
	B/R_2	0	−	0.2-0.9	0.2-0.9	0.2-0.9	0.3-1.0	0.3-1.0
	B_1	*	*	−	0.5-1.2	0.5-1.2	0.1-0.8	0.1-0.8
	B_2	*	*	0.5-1.2	−	0.5-1.2	0.1-0.8	0.1-0.8
	B_3	*	*	0.5-1.2	0.5-1.2	−	0.1-0.8	0.1-0.8
	B/W_1	*	*	0.3-1.0	0.3-1.0	0.3-1.0	−	0
	B/W_2	*	*	0.3-1.0	0.3-1.0	0.3-1.0	0	−

*1.4 V and more (tester's battery voltage).All units in Volts

2. Set the multicircuit Tester to the diode setting.

3. **Figure 9** identifies the terminals in the regulator/rectifier connector. Connect the tester probes to the terminals indicated in **Figure 11**, and check the voltage across each pair of terminals.

4. If any voltage reading differs from the stated value in **Figure 11**, replace the voltage regulator/rectifier.

STATOR COIL

Removal/Installation

1. Remove the left side fairing (Chapter Fifteen)

2. Remove the fuel tank and air filter assembly (Chapter Eight).

3. Disconnect the battery negative cable as described in this chapter.

4. Disconnect 3-pin stator connector (3 yellow wires) from its harness mate (**Figure 3**). If necessary, follow the electrical cable from the alternator cover to the connector.

5. Remove the alternator cover (Chapter Five).

6. Place several shop cloths on the workbench and turn the alternator cover upside down on these cloths.

7. Note how the clamp secures the stator wiring to the alternator cover. Remove the clamp bolt and lift out the clamp (A, **Figure 12**).

8. Remove the stator bolts (A, **Figure 13**) from the assembly.

9. Carefully pull the rubber grommet (B, **Figure 13**) from the alternator cover, and remove the stator assembly (C). Note how the stator wire is routed through the cover.

10. Install the stator by reversing these removal steps. Note the following:

   a. Tighten the stator bolts (A, **Figure 13**) to 10 N•m (89 in.-lb.).

   b. Make sure the grommet (B, **Figure 12**) is seated in place.

   c. The small metal clamp (A, **Figure 12**) must be reinstalled in the correct location and tighten securely. This clamp secures the wiring harness to the cover and away from the spinning rotor.

Resistance Test

1. Remove the left side fairing (Chapter Fifteen).

2. Remove the fuel tank and air filter assembly (Chapter Eight).

3. Disconnect the battery negative cable as described in this chapter.

4. Disconnect 3-pin stator connector (3 yellow wires) from its harness mate (**Figure 3**). If necessary, follow the electrical cable from the alternator cover to the connector.

5. Use 0.5 mm (0.02 in.) back probe pins on the voltmeter to back probe the alternator side of the connector.

6. Check the reading on the meter, and record the resistance for that pair of terminals.

7. Repeat Step 5 and Step 6 and measure the resistance between each of the remaining terminal pairs. Take a total of three readings (**Figure 14**).

8. The stator is faulty and must be replaced if any resistance is outside the specified range (**Table 1**).

9. Use the ohmmeter to check the continuity between each terminal in the stator side of the connector and ground. If any reading indicates continuity, one or more of the stator wires is shorted to ground. Replace the stator.

10. Connect the battery negative cable as described in this chapter.

11. Install the fuel tank and air filter assembly (Chapter Eight).

12. Install the left side fairing (Chapter Fifteen).

IGNITION SYSTEM

WARNING
High voltage is present during ignition system operation. Do not touch any ignition component, wire or test leads while cranking or running the engine.

The digital ignition system consists of a crankshaft position (CKP) sensor, camshaft position (CMP) sensor, electronic control module (ECM), and four ignition coil/spark plug caps.

During operation, the ECM uses input from the CKP sensor, CMP sensor, throttle position (TP) sensor, engine coolant temperature (ECT) sensor and gear position (GP) sensor to calculate the best ignition timing for the current operating conditions.

The ECM then sends a signal to the power source, which sends its energy to the primary side of the ignition coil. This induces a high voltage in the coil's secondary windings and fires the spark plug.

The ECM in all models includes an engine over-rev limiter to protect against excessive engine speed.

The ECM controls engine speed through a fuel cutoff circuit. The ECM cuts off fuel to the injectors whenever engine speed reaches 15,100 rpm under load. However, under no load conditions - with

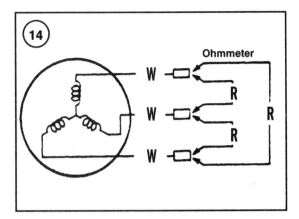

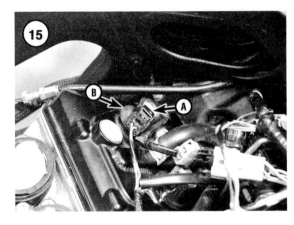

the clutch lever pulled in or with the transmission in neutral - fuel is cut off when engine speed reaches 15,100 rpm.

Under no-load conditions (when the clutch lever is pulled in or when the transmission is in neutral), the ECM limits engine speed to 15,100 rpm.

> *CAUTION*
> *In some instances, the no-load engine speed can exceed 15,500 rpm even if the ignition cutoff circuit is operational. Do not exceed 15,100 rpm without load at any time. Engine damage could occur.*

Troubleshooting

Refer to *Diagnostic System* in Chapter Eight.

IMMOBLIZER SYSTEM (U.K. AND EUROPEAN MODELS)

The immobilizer system disables the ignition system unless the ECM recognizes the ignition key. The ignition key includes a transponder that contains the key's identification code. When the ignition switch is turned on, the ECM communicates with the key

transponder through the antenna in the lock cylinder. The ECM compares the key identification code to the code stored in memory. If these are the same, the ECM enables the ignition system, and the motorcycle is ready to start.

When the system is used for the first time, the immobilizer indicator LED in the meter assembly flashes to indicate the number of registered identification codes stored in the ECM (2, 3 or 4 times for example). After the initial operation the immobilizer indicator LED in the meter assembly turns on for 2 seconds when the key is turned on, then goes off.

A rapid flashing immobilizer indicator LED indicator communications error. Turn the ignition switch off, and then turn on again. If the immobilizer indicator LED indicator remains on or if the LED does not come on at all, a fault exists in the key, key cylinder, wiring or the ECM. Take the motorcycle to a dealership for service.

IGNITION COIL/PLUG CAP

Removal/Installation

1. Raise and support the fuel tank (Chapter Eight).
2. Remove the air filter housing (Chapter Eight).
3. Disconnect the 2-pin connector (A, **Figure 15**) from each the ignition coil/plug cap (B). If necessary, label the connector so it can be reinstalled onto the correct coil/plug cap.

> *CAUTION*
> *Remove the ignition coil/plug cap assembly from the spark plug only by hand. Handle the ignition coil/plug cap assembly carefully.*

4. The ignition coil/plug caps form a tight seal on the cylinder head cover as well as the spark plugs. Grasp the ignition coil/plug cap (B, **Figure 15**) and pull it straight up and off the spark plug.
5. Label each ignition coil/plug cap with its cylinder number so it will be reinstalled onto the same spark plug.
6. Inspect the ignition coil/plug caps (**Figure 16**) for damage. If visually damaged, test the assembly as described in Chapter Nine.
7. Inspect each electrical connector and wiring for corrosion and /or damage. The wiring and electrical connectors are part of the main wiring harness and cannot be replaced separately.
8. Refer to the marks made during removal and install each ignition coil/plug cap (B, **Figure 15**) onto the correct spark plug. Press ignition coil/plug cap into the spark plug tunnel and onto the spark plug. Rotate the assembly slightly in both directions and make sure it is attached to the spark plug.

9

9. Position the connector fitting on the ignition coil/plug cap so the fitting faces rearward.

10. Carefully connect the electrical connector (A, **Figure 15**) onto the correct ignition coil/plug cap (B).

11. Make sure the electrical connectors are free of corrosion and are on tight.

12. Install the air filter housing and fuel tank (Chapter Eight).

13. Lower and secure the fuel tank (Chapter Eight).

Primary Peak Voltage Test

The manufacturer specifies the use of a multicircuit tester (Suzuki part No. 09900-25008) is needed for this test. Refer to *Electrical Testing* in Chapter Two.

1. Connect the peak voltage adapter to the meter according to the manufacturer's instructions.

2. Perform steps 1-3 of removal, and remove each ignition coil/plug cap from its spark plug.

3. Insert a new spark plug into each cap.

CAUTION
Do not ground the spark plugs to the cylinder head cover. An electrical spark will damage the magnesium cover.

4. Connect each 2-pin connector to its respective ignition coil/plug cap, and ground the spark plug against the cylinder head (**Figure 17**).

5. Use 0.5 mm (0.02 in.) back probe pins to back probe the ignition coil connector.

6. Connect the positive test probe to the white/blue terminal of the No. 1 ignition coil/spark plug cap; connect the negative test probe to a good ground (**Figure 18**).

7. Shift the transmission into neutral and turn the ignition switch on.

8. Press the starter button and crank the engine for a few seconds while reading the voltmeter. Note the

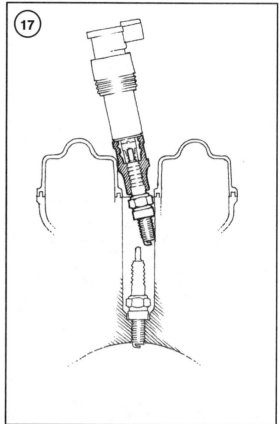

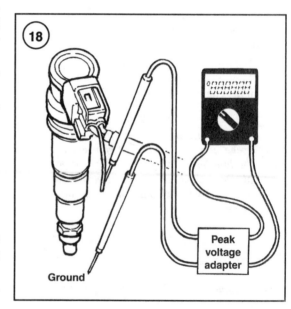

meter's highest reading, and record it for that cylinder.

9. Repeat Steps 5-8 for each of the remaining coils. Connect the positive test probe to back probe in the connector in the terminal to the following:

    a. Cylinder No. 2: black terminal.

    b. Cylinder No. 3: yellow terminal.

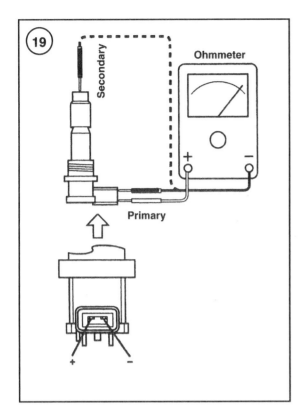

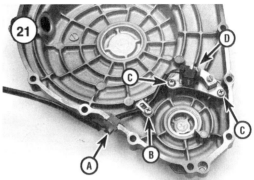

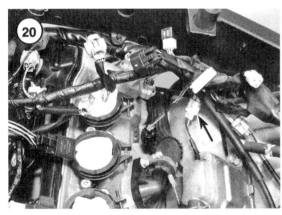

2. Connect the ohmmeter to the two terminals in the ignition coil/plug cap, and measure the primary coil resistance (**Figure 19**). Compare the reading to the primary coil resistance specification in **Table 1**.

3. Move the negative test probe to the spark plug connector in the ignition coil/plug cap, and measure the secondary coil resistance (**Figure 19**). Compare the reading to the secondary coil resistance specification in **Table 1**.

4. Repeat Step 2 and Step 3 for the other three ignition coils.

5. If the resistance values are less than specified, there is most likely a short in the coil windings. Replace the coil.

6. If the resistance values are more than specified, this may indicate corrosion or oxidation of the coil's terminals. Thoroughly clean the terminals, and spray with an aerosol electrical contact cleaner. Repeat Step 2 and Step 3 and if the resistance value is still high, replace the coil.

7. If the coil resistance does not meet (or come close to) either of these specifications, the coil must be replaced. If the coil exhibits visible damage, it should be replaced as described in this chapter.

8. Install the ignition coil as described in this chapter.

c. Cylinder No. 4: green terminal.

10. Compare the reading to the minimum ignition coil primary peak voltage specification in **Table 1**. The individual peak voltage reading for each ignition coil can vary as long as the voltage meets or exceed the specific minimum value.

11. If the ignition coil primary peak voltage at the ignition coil/spark plug is less than the specific value, perform the ignition coil resistance test in this section.

CRANKSHAFT POSITION (CKP) SENSOR

Removal/Installation

1. Turn the ignition switch off.

2. Lift and support the fuel tank as described in this chapter.

3. Disconnect the 2-pin crankshaft position sensor connector (**Figure 20**) from its harness mate.

4. Remove the clutch cover (Chapter Six).

5. Pull the grommet (A, **Figure 21**) from the clutch cover.

Coil resistance Test

1. Perform steps 1-3 of removal, and remove each ignition coil/plug cap from its spark plug.

6. Remove the mounting screw (B, **Figure 21**) and release the sensor wire from its clamp.

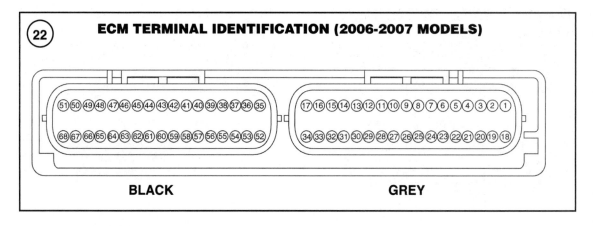

7. Remove the mounting bolts (C, **Figure 21**) and remove the CKP sensor (D) from the clutch cover. Note how the sensor's wire is routed through the motorcycle.

8. Installation is the reverse of removal. Route the sensor's wire along the path noted during removal.

Resistance Test

1. Perform Steps 1-3 of the CKP sensor removal procedure.

2. On the sensor side of the connector, connect the positive test probe to the black terminal in the sensor side of the connector; connect the negative test probe to the green terminal.

3. The resistance should be within the range specified in **Table 1**.

Continuity Test

1. Perform Steps 1-3 of the CKP sensor removal procedure.

2. Check the continuity between the green terminal in the sensor side of the connector and a good ground.

3. Check the continuity between the black terminal in the sensor side of the connector and a good ground.

4. No continuity should be indicated during either test. The sensor is shorted to ground if it has continuity during either portion of this test.

Peak Voltage Test

A multicircuit tester with a peak voltage adapter (Suzuki part No. 09900-25008, or equivalent), is needed to perform this test.

Refer to *Electrical Testing* in Chapter Two.

1. Perform Steps 1-3 of the CKP sensor removal procedure.

2. Connect the peak voltage adapter to the voltmeter following the manufacturer's instructions.

3. Connect the voltmeter positive test probe to the black terminal in the sensor side of the connector; connect the negative test probe to the green terminal in the sensor side.

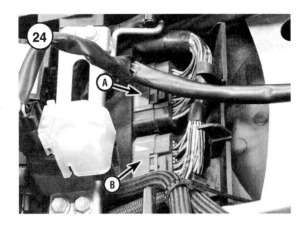

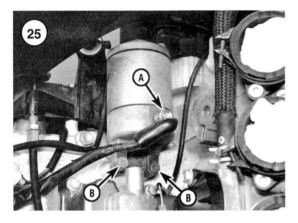

4. Turn the ignition switch on and shift the transmission to neutral.

5. Use the starter motor to crank the engine for a few seconds. Record the highest reading.

6. The peak voltage reading should equal or exceed the value specified (**Table 1**).

If peak voltage is out of specification, check the following:

   a. Check for loose or corroded contacts in the crankshaft position sensor connector. Repair the connector as necessary. If the connectors are good, replace the sensor.

   b. Check for loose or corroded contacts in the ECM connector terminals No. 14 and No. 21. Repair the connector as necessary. If the connectors are good, replace the sensor.

   c. Check for metal particles or foreign material stuck on the CKP sensor and rotor tip. Clean off if necessary.

ENGINE CONTROL MODULE (ECM)

Refer to **Figure 22** or **Figure 23**.

Removal/Installation

1. Remove the rider's seat (Chapter Fifteen).

2. Disconnect the battery negative cable as described in this chapter.

3. Move the starter relay up and out of the way.

4. Depress the latches, and disconnect the black (A, **Figure 24**) and gray (B) terminal from the ECM. Label each connector and its ECM harness mate.

5. Pull straight back and remove the ECM from the chassis channel.

6. Installation is the reverse of removal. Securely connect the black (A, **Figure 24**) and gray (B) connectors. Make sure the connectors latch correctly into place.

STARTING SYSTEM

The starting system consists of the starter motor, starter gears, starter relay, clutch switch, gear position (GP) sensor, sidestand switch, turn signal/sidestand relay and the starter button. When the starter button is pressed, it engages the starter relay and completes the circuit allowing electricity to flow from the battery to the starter motor.

The starting system includes an interlock system that interrupts current flow to the starter relay unless certain conditions are met. The engine will not crank unless the transmission is in neutral and the clutch disengaged, or the transmission is in gear, the clutch disengaged, and the sidestand is up.

> *CAUTION*
> *During starting, do not operate the starter for more than 5 seconds at a time. Let it rest approximately 10 seconds, and then use it again.*

Troubleshooting

Refer to *Electrical Troubleshooting, Starting System* in Chapter Two.

STARTER

Operation Test

1. Securely support the motorcycle on level ground. Make sure the transmission is in neutral.

2. Disconnect the battery negative cable as described in this chapter.

3. Remove the fuel tank (Chapter Eight).

4. Pull back the rubber boot from the starter motor terminal.

> *NOTE*
> ***Figure 25*** *is shown with the throttle body removed for photo clarity.*

5. Remove the starter motor terminal nut (A, **Figure 25**), and disconnect the electrical cable from the starter motor.

WARNING
The test in the next step will probably produce sparks. Be sure no flammable gas or fluids are in the vicinity.

6. Pull back the cover from the positive battery terminal. Apply battery voltage directly to the starter by connecting a jumper from the positive terminal to the starter motor terminal. The motor should operate.

7. If the starter motor does not operate when battery voltage is applied, repair or replace the motor.

8. Install the fuel tank (Chapter Eight).

9. Connect the battery negative cable as described in this chapter.

Removal/Installation

NOTE
Refer to Chapter Five for starter gear service procedures.

1. Support the motorcycle on level ground.

2. Disconnect the battery negative cable as described in this chapter.

3. Remove the fuel tank (Chapter Eight).

4. Pull back the rubber boot from the starter motor terminal.

5. Remove the starter motor terminal nut (A, **Figure 25**), and disconnect the starter motor cable from the motor.

6. Remove the starter motor mounting bolts (B, **Figure 25**). Pull the motor toward the left side, and remove it from the starter gear housing.

7. Thoroughly clean the starter mounting pads on the crankcase and the mounting lugs on the starter motor.

8. Inspect the starter motor O-ring (A, **Figure 26**) in the front cap for hardness or deterioration. Replace the O-ring if necessary. Apply grease (Suzuki Super Grease A, or equivalent) to the O-ring before installing the starter motor.

9. Push the starter motor into the crankcase so the teeth on the armature shaft engage the starter reduction gear.

10. Install the starter motor mounting bolts (B, **Figure 25**), and tighten securely.

11. Secure the starter motor cable to the starter terminal. Tighten the starter motor terminal nut (A, **Figure 25**) to the specification in **Table 3**. Press the rubber boot back into position.

12. Install the fuel tank (Chapter Eight).

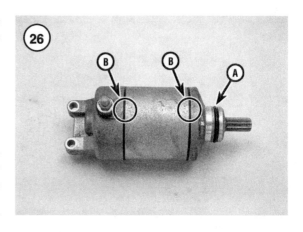

13. Connect the battery negative cable as described in this chapter.

Disassembly

Refer to **Figure 27**.

As the starter motor is disassembled, lay each part out in the order of removal (**Figure 28**). The parts must be reinstalled in their original locations to insulate the brush holder from the armature housing. Pay particular attention to the washers. The number and type of washers may differ.

1. Note that the index mark on each cap aligns with the mark on the armature housing (B, **Figure 26**). Theses marks must be aligned during assembly.

2. Remove both case bolts (**Figure 29**), and slide front cap (**Figure 30**) from the armature housing.

3. Slide the armed washer (A, **Figure 31**) and all the washers (B) from the armature shaft.

4. Remove the end cap (A, **Figure 32**) from the armature housing. Remove the washers from the commutator end of the armature shaft.

5. Press the armature (**Figure 33**) from the housing.

6. Remove the terminal nut (**Figure 34**) from the positive terminal bolt.

7. Remove the washers. Note the type and order of the washers. Each washer must be reinstalled in its original location.

8. Lift the brush holder from the rear cap, press the terminal bolt into the rear cap, and remove the brush holder (**Figure 35**).

9. Inspect all starter components (this section).

Assembly

1. Make sure the insulator (**Figure 36**) and O-ring are in place on the terminal bolt on the brush holder. Install the terminal bolt through the hole in the rear cap, and install the brush holder into the rear cap. Make sure the O-ring (**Figure 37**) is correctly seated in the rear cap receptacle.

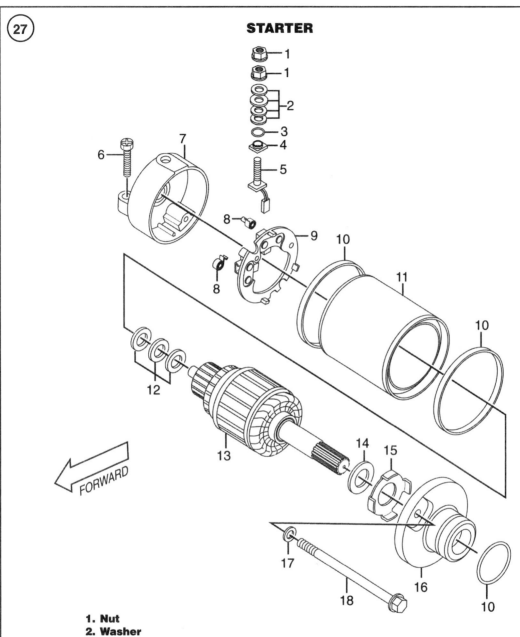

STARTER

1. Nut
2. Washer
3. O-ring
4. Insulator
5. Positive brush
6. Bolt
7. Rear cap
8. Spring
9. Negative brush holder
10. O-ring
11. Armature housing
12. Shim
13. Armature
14. Shim
15. Armed washer
16. Front cap
17. Washer
18. Bolt

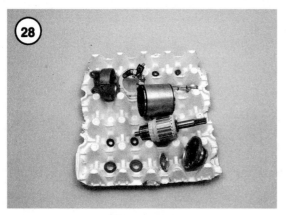

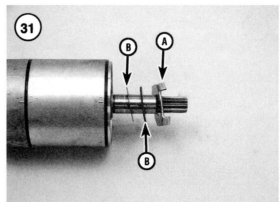

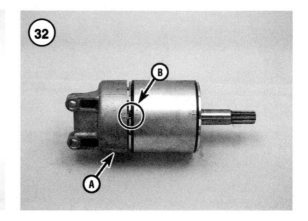

2. Install the washers onto the terminal bolt in the order noted during removal. In this example shown here, two smaller diameter fiber washers (A, **Figure 38**) are installed, followed by a larger diameter fiber washer (B) and a metal washer (C).

3. Install and tighten the terminal nut (**Figure 34**), and tighten securely.

4. Install a *new* O-ring (**Figure 39**) onto each end of the armature housing.

5. Install the washers (A, **Figure 40**) onto the commutator end of the armature shaft. Install the washers in the order noted during removal. Apply Suzuki

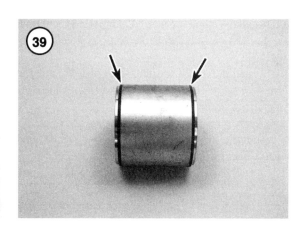

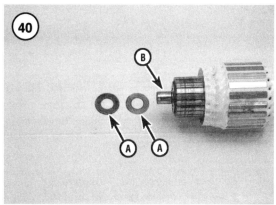

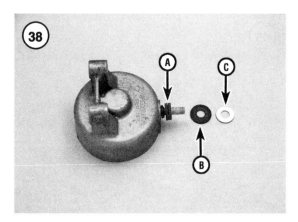

9

Moly Paste to each end of the armature shaft. (B, **Figure 40**).

6. Install the armature (**Figure 33**) into the armature housing so the commutator end of the armature faces the end of the housing with the cutout for the rear cap.

7. Guide the armature into the rear cap past the brushes (**Figure 41**).

8. Align the cutout for the rear cap with the notch in the armature (B, **Figure 32**) with the commutator end of the housing so the cap engages the cutout in the housing. The index mark on the cap must align with the mark on the housing.

9. Install the metal washers (A, **Figure 42**), and fiber washer (B) onto the armature shaft as noted during removal.

10. Install the armed washer (A, **Figure 31**) into the armature shaft so the washer's arms engage the slots in the front end cap.

11. Apply grease (Suzuki Super Grease A, or equivalent) to the lips of the oil seal (A, **Figure 43**) and needle bearing (B) in the front cap.

12. Install the front cap (**Figure 30**) so its index mark aligns with the mark on the armatures housing.

13. Install a *new* O-ring onto each case bolt. Apply threadlocking compound (Suzuki Thread Lock 1322, or equivalent) to the case bolts threads, and tighten the bolts securely (**Figure 29**).

Inspection

The O-rings, washers, brush holder and oil seal can be purchased separately. If the armature, armature housing or either end cap is faulty, replacement, replace the starter assembly.

> *CAUTION*
> *Do not immerse the armature (A, **Figure 44**) in solvent as the insulation may be damaged. Wipe the windings with a cloth lightly moistened with solvent. Dry thoroughly.*

1. Clean all grease, dirt and carbon from all components.

2. Inspect each brush (**Figure 45**) for abnormal wear. Service specifications are not available. Replace the brush holder if any brush is excessively worn.

3. Inspect the bushing (**Figure 46**) in the rear cap for wear or damage. If it is damaged, replace the rear cap.

4. Inspect the armature shaft (B, **Figure 44**) where it rides on the bushing. Check for wear, burrs or damage. If the armature is worn or damaged, replace the starter motor.

5. Check the entire length of the armature assembly (C, **Figure 44**) for straightness or heat damage.

6. Inspect the commutator (D, **Figure 44**). The mica in a good commentator sits below the surface of the copper bars. On a worn commutator, the mica and copper bars may be worn to the same level (**Figure 47**). If necessary, have the commutator serviced by a dealership or electrical repair shop.

7. Inspect the commutator copper bars (D, **Figure 44**) for discoloration. If a pair of bars is discolored, grounded armature coils are indicated.

8. Use an ohmmeter and perform the following:

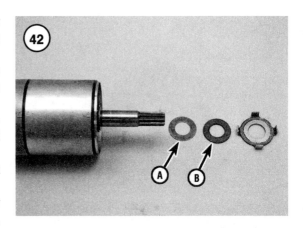

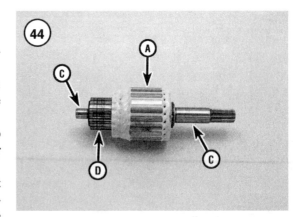

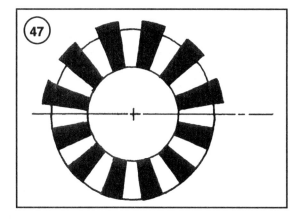

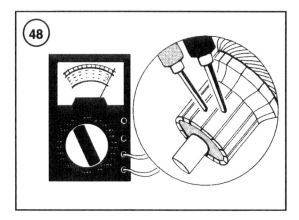

a. Check for continuity between the commutator bars (**Figure 48**); there should be continuity between pairs of bars.

b. Check for continuity between the commutator bars and the shaft (**Figure 49**); there should be no continuity.

c. The armature is faulty if it fails either of these tests.

9. Inspect the O-ring oil seal (A, **Figure 43**) in the front cap for wear, hardness or damage. Replace the O-ring if necessary. Lubricate the new O-ring with Suzuki Super Grease A.

10. Inspect the needle bearing (B, **Figure 43**) in the front cap. It must turn smoothly without excessive play or noise. Replace the starter as necessary.

11. Inspect the magnets (**Figure 50**) within the armature housing assembly. Make sure they have not picked up any small metal particles. If so remove them prior to assembly. Also inspect the armature housing for loose, chipped or damaged magnets.

12. Inspect both front and rear cap for wear or damage. Replace the starter as necessary.

13. Check the long case bolts for thread damage. Clean the threads with the appropriate size metric die if necessary.

STARTER RELAY

Removal/Installation

1. Remove rider's and pillion seat (Chapter Fifteen).

2. Remove the rear left-side cover (Chapter Fifteen).

3. Disconnect the battery negative cable as described in this chapter.

4. Pull the starter relay up, and pull the cover (**Figure 51**) from the relay.

5. Disconnect the 4-pin primary connector (A, **Figure 52**) from the relay.

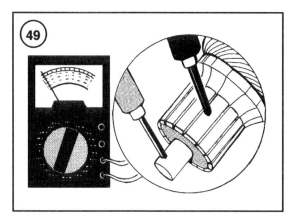

6. Disconnect the black starter motor lead (B, **Figure 52**) and the red battery lead (C) from the starter relay, and remove the relay.

7. Install by reversing these removal steps. Note the following:

    a. Securely install the black (B, **Figure 52**) and red (C) cables to their original terminals.

    b. Make sure the electrical connector (A, **Figure 52**) is tight and that the cover (**Figure 51**) is properly installed to keep out moisture.

Continuity/Resistance Test

1. Perform Steps 1-6 of the starter relay removal procedure in this section.

2. Connect an ohmmeter and a 12 volt battery to the starter relay terminals as shown in **Figure 53**, and check the continuity.

    a. When the battery is connected, there should be continuity (zero or low ohms) across the two load terminals.

    b. When the battery is disconnected, there should be no continuity (infinity) across the load terminals.

3. Disconnect the battery from the starter relay.

4. Connect an ohmmeter to the starter relay terminals as shown in **Figure 54** and measure the resistance. The resistance should be within the range specified in **Table 1**.

5. Install the starter relay.

Input Voltage Test

1. Remove rider's and pillion seat (Chapter Fifteen).

2. Remove the rear left-side cover (Chapter Fifteen).

3. Shift the transmission into neutral and make sure the engine stop switch is in the run position.

4. Pull the starter relay up, and pull the cover (**Figure 51**) from the relay.

5. Disconnect the 4-pin primary connector (A, **Figure 52**) from the relay.

6. Connect a voltmeter's positive test probe to the yellow/green terminal in the primary connector; connect the negative test probe to the black/yellow terminal.

7. Turn the ignition switch on, press the starter button, and measure the voltage. It should equal battery voltage.

8. Install the starter relay.

9. Install the rear left-side cover (Chapter Fifteen).

10. Install the rider's and pillion seat (Chapter Fifteen).

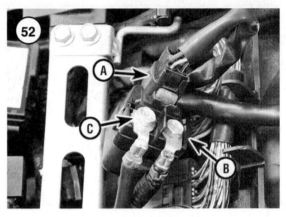

SIDESTAND SWITCH

Removal/Installation

1. Support the motorcycle so the sidestand can move freely.

2. Disconnect the battery negative cable as described in this chapter.

3. Remove the fuel tank (Chapter Eight).

4. Remove the air filter assembly (Chapter Eight).

5. Follow the sidestand switch wiring up the left side of the frame and locate the 2-pin electrical connector adjacent to the fuel rail.

6. Disconnect the 2-pin sidestand switch connector from its harness mate.

7. Lower the sidestand.

8. Remove the sidestand switch mounting bolts (A, **Figure 55**), and remove the switch. Note how the switch wiring is routed through the motorcycle.

9. Install a *new* switch. Apply threadlocking compound (Suzuki Thread Lock 1342, or equivalent) to the mounting bolts, and tighten them securely.

10. Raise the sidestand and make sure the switch plunger moves in.

11. Make sure the electrical connectors are free of corrosion and are tight.

12. Install the air filter assembly (Chapter Eight).

13. Install the fuel tank (Chapter Eight).

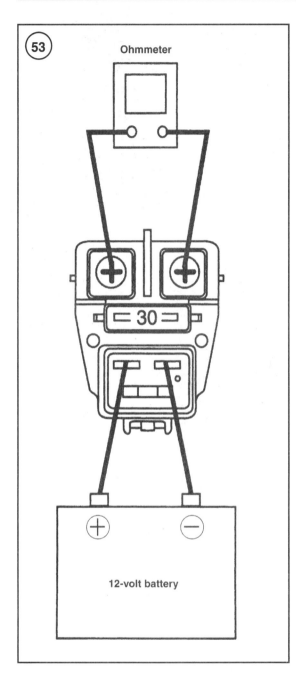

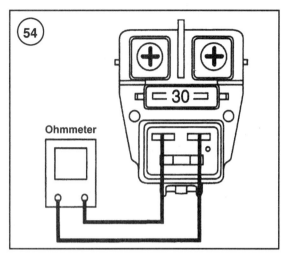

14. Connect the battery negative cable as described in this chapter.

Test

A multicircuit tester (Suzuki part No. 09900-25008, or equivalent), is needed to perform this test.
1. Support the motorcycle so the sidestand can move freely.
2. Perform Steps 2-6 of sidestand switch removal in this section.
3. Turn the test knob on the tester to diode.

4. Connect the tester positive prove to the green terminal in the switch side of the connector; connect the negative test probe to the black/white terminal.
5. Lower the sidestand.
6. Push up on the sidestand switch plunger (B, **Figure 55**) and read the voltage on the meter.
7. Release the sidestand switch plunger and read the voltage on the meter.
8. If either reading is outside the sidestand test voltage range specified in **Table 1**, replace the sidestand switch.
9. If the sidestand switch test cannot be performed, test the continuity of the sidestand switch by performing the following:
   a. Connect an ohmmeter to the terminals in the switch side of the connector.
   b. Raise the sidestand. The meter should indicate continuity.
   c. Lower the sidestand. The meter should indicate no continuity.
   d. If the switch fails either of these tests, it is faulty and must be replaced.

GEAR POSITION (GP) SWITCH

Removal/Installation

1. Remove the engine sprocket cover (Chapter Seven).
2. Disconnect the battery negative cable as described in this chapter.
3. Remove the fuel tank (Chapter Eight).
4. Remove the air filter assembly (Chapter Eight).
5. Follow the gear position switch wire (A, **Figure 56**) and disconnect the 3-pin GP switch connector (B) from its harness mate.
6. Note how the wire is routed through the engine. Release the wire from any holder that secures it in place.
7. Remove the GP switch mounting bolts (A, **Figure 57**).
8. Remove the GP switch (B, **Figure 57**), and discard the O-ring.
9. Lubricate a *new* O-ring with grease (Suzuki Super Grease A, or equivalent), and install the O-ring (A, **Figure 58**) onto the switch.
10. Align the locating pin (B, **Figure 58**) with the shift drum receptacle and install the switch.
11. Install the air filter assembly (Chapter Eight).
12. Install the fuel tank (Chapter Eight).
13. Connect the battery negative cable as described in this chapter.
14. Install the engine sprocket cover (Chapter Seven).

Continuity Test

1. Support the motorcycle so the sidestand can move freely.
2. Perform Steps 2-5 of gear position switch removal in this section.
3. Connect an ohmmeter to blue and black/white terminals in the switch side of the connector.
4. Shift the transmission to neutral, and read the ohmmeter. It should indicate continuity.
5. Shift the transmission into any gear, and read the meter. It should indicated no continuity
6. If the switch fails either of these tests, it is faulty and must be replaced.

Voltage Test

1. Support the motorcycle so the sidestand can move freely.
2. Perform Steps 2-5 of gear position switch removal in this section.
3. Connect a voltmeter positive test probe to the pink terminal in the harness side of the GP sensor connector; connect the negative test probe to the black/

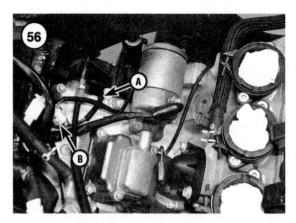

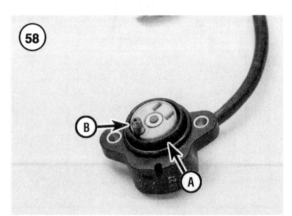

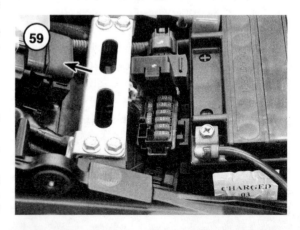

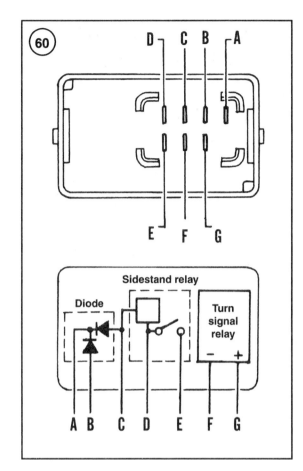

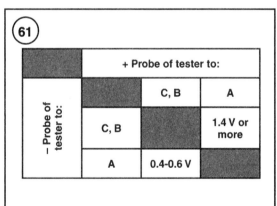

white terminal. Use 0.5 mm (0.02 in.) wires to back probe the harness side of the GP switch connector (B, **Figure 56**). Do not disconnect the connector.

4. Raise the sidestand switch and turn the ignition switch on.

5. Read the voltage with the transmission in neutral.

6. Successively shift the transmission into each gear, first through sixth, and read the voltage. It should equal or exceed the specified GP sensor voltage range specified in **Table 1**, in every gear except neutral.

TURN SIGNAL/SIDESTAND RELAY

Removal/Installation

1. Remove rider's and passenger seat (Chapter Fifteen).
2. Remove the seat/side/tailpiece (Chapter Fifteen).
3. Move the relay (**Figure 59**) from under the frame rear cross member.
4. Disconnect the 8-pin electrical connector and remove the relay.
5. Installation is the reverse of removal.

Sidestand Relay Test

1. Remove the turn signal/sidestand relay as described in this section.
2. Apply 12 volts to the relay by connecting the negative side of the battery to the C terminal in the relay; connect the positive battery terminal to the D terminal (**Figure 60**) in the relay.
3. Use an ohmmeter to check the continuity between terminals D and E on the relay. There should be continuity.
4. Replace the turn signal/sidestand relay if no continuity is found.

Diode Test

A multicircuit tester (Suzuki part No. 09900-25008, or equivalent) is needed to perform this test.

1. Remove the turn signal/sidestand relay as described in this section.
2. Set the Suzuki Multi Circuit Tester to diode test.
3. Refer to **Figure 61**, and connect the tester probes to the indicated terminals. Record the voltage for each test. Also refer to **Figure 60**.
4. Replace the turn signal/sidestand relay if any measurement is outside the range specified in **Figure 61**.

Turn Signal Relay Test

If a turn signal light does not turn on, first inspect the bulbs. If the bulbs are okay, check the turn signal switch as described in this chapter and check all electrical connections within the turn signal circuit.

If all of these items are working, replace the turn signal/sidestand relay.

STEERING DAMPER (2008-2009 MODELS)

Resistance Test

1. Disconnect the battery negative cable as described in this chapter.
2. Remove front firing (Chapter Fifteen).
3. Disconnect the 2-pin electrical connector from the steering damper connector (**Figure 62**).
4. Connect an ohmmeter to the terminals in the damper side of the connector (**Figure 63**).
5. If either reading is outside the steering damper resistance range specified in **Table 1**, replace the steering damper (Chapter Twelve).
6. Connect the 2-pin electrical connector onto the steering damper.
7. Install front firing (Chapter Fifteen).
8. Connect the battery negative cable as described in this chapter.

LIGHTING SYSTEM

The lighting system consists of a headlight, taillight/brake light, license plate light, and turn signals.

Always use the correct bulb wattage (**Table 2**).

Headlight Bulb Replacement (2006-2007 Models)

> *WARNING*
> *If the headlight has just burned out or has just been turned off, it will be **very hot!** Do not touch the bulb until it cools.*

> *CAUTION*
> *All models are equipped with quartz-halogen bulbs. Do not touch the bulb glass with your fingers. Traces of oil will drastically reduce the life of the bulb. Clean the bulb with a cloth moistened in alcohol or lacquer thinner.*

The following photographs are shown with the fairing removed for photographic clarity. The bulbs can be replaced with the fairing on the motorcycle.

Refer to **Figure 64**.

Low beam

1. Remove the combination meter as described in this chapter.

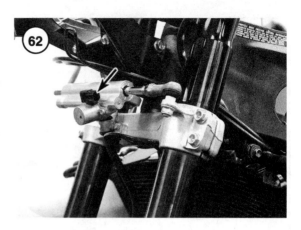

2. Pull straight out and disconnect the electrical connector (**Figure 65**) from the back of the headlight assembly.
3. Pull the tab (A, **Figure 66**) and remove the rubber dust boot (B). Check the boot for tears or deterioration; replace it if necessary.
4. Unhook the light bulb retaining clip (**Figure 67**) and pivot it out of the way.
5. Remove and discard the blown bulb (**Figure 68**).
6. Install the *new* bulb so the bulb tangs engage the notches in the headlight housing.
7. Hook the retaining clip (**Figure 67**) over the bulb to hold it in place.
8. Install the dust boot so the *TOP* on the boots sits at the top of the headlight assembly. Make sure the cover is correctly seated against the lens assembly and the bulb.
9. Align the electrical plug terminals with the bulb and connect it to the bulb. Push the connector (**Figure 65**) until it bottoms on the bulb and the rubber cover.
10. Install the combination meter as described in this chapter.
11. Check headlight operation.
12. Adjust the headlight as described in this chapter.

High beam

1. Remove the combination meter as described in this chapter.
2. Release the clip, pull straight out, and disconnect the electrical connector (**Figure 69**) from the back of the headlight assembly.
3. Rotate the bulb assembly (**Figure 70**) counterclockwise and release the bulb from the headlight assembly (**Figure 71**).
4. Remove and discard the blown bulb.
5. Install a new bulb into the headlight assembly and rotate the bulb assembly (**Figure 70**) clockwise until it is locked into place.

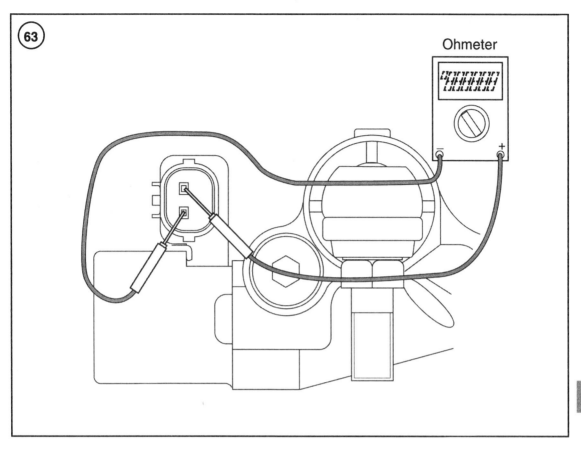

Ohmeter

9

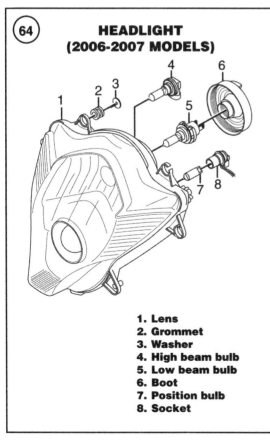

HEADLIGHT
(2006-2007 MODELS)

1. Lens
2. Grommet
3. Washer
4. High beam bulb
5. Low beam bulb
6. Boot
7. Position bulb
8. Socket

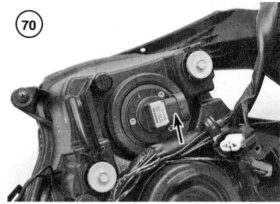

6. Connect the electrical connector (**Figure 69**) onto the back of the headlight assembly and push it until it clicks into place.

7. Install the combination meter as described in this chapter.

8. Check headlight operation.

9. Adjust the headlight as described in this chapter.

Position

1. Remove the combination meter as described in this chapter.

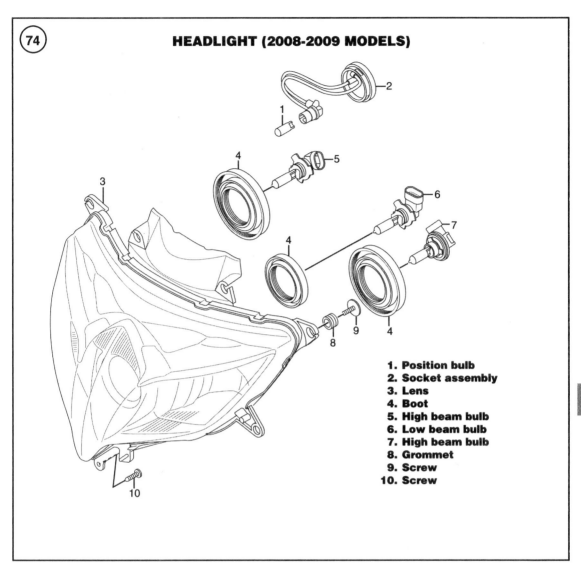

HEADLIGHT (2008-2009 MODELS)

1. Position bulb
2. Socket assembly
3. Lens
4. Boot
5. High beam bulb
6. Low beam bulb
7. High beam bulb
8. Grommet
9. Screw
10. Screw

2. Pull straight out and remove the position bulb socket/harness assembly (**Figure 72**) from the headlight assembly.

3. Pull straight out and remove the bulb (**Figure 73**) from the socket/harness assembly. Discard the blown bulb.

4. Install a *new* bulb into the socket/harness assembly, and press it in until it bottoms.

5. Push the position bulb socket/harness assembly (**Figure 72**) into the headlight assembly, and press it in until it bottoms.

6. Install the combination meter as described in this chapter.

Headlight Bulb Removal/Installation (2008-2009 Models)

WARNING
If the headlight has just burned out or has just been turned off, it will be
very hot! Do not touch the bulb until it cools.

CAUTION
All models are equipped with quartz-halogen bulbs. Do not touch the bulb glass with your fingers. Traces of oil will drastically reduce the life of the bulb. Clean the bulb with a cloth moistened in alcohol or lacquer thinner.

Refer to **Figure 74**.

The following photographs are shown with the fairing removed for photographic clarity. The bulb assemblies can be replaced with the fairing on the motorcycle.

Low beam

1. Remove the combination meter as described in this chapter.

2. Pull straight out and disconnect the low beam electrical connector (**Figure 75**) from the back of the headlight assembly.

3. Rotate the bulb assembly (**Figure 76**) *counterclockwise* and release the bulb assembly from the headlight assembly.

4. Install the *new* bulb assembly and rotate the bulb assembly (**Figure 76**) *clockwise* until it locks into place.

5. Connect the low beam electrical connector (**Figure 75**) onto the headlight assembly.

6. Install the combination meter as described in this chapter.

7. Check headlight operation.

8. Adjust the headlight as described in this chapter.

High beam

1. If the front fairing is still in pace, remove the combination meter as described in this chapter.

2. Rotate the bulb assembly (A, **Figure 77**) *counterclockwise* and release the bulb assembly from the headlight assembly.

3. Pull straight out and disconnect the high beam electrical connector (A, **Figure 78**) from the bulb (B).

4. Install a *new* bulb (**Figure 79**) and connect it to the high beam electrical connector (A, **Figure 78**).

5. Install the *new* bulb assembly and rotate the bulb assembly (A, **Figure 77**) *clockwise* until it locks into place.

6. Repeat for the remaining bulb assembly if necessary.

7. Install the combination meter as described in this chapter.

8. If removed, install the combination meter as described in this chapter.

9. Check headlight operation.

10. Adjust the headlight as described in this chapter.

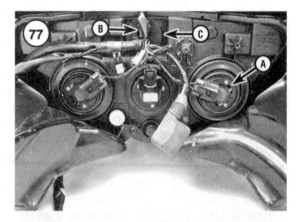

Position

1. Remove the combination meter as described in this chapter.

2. Pull straight out and disconnect the electrical connector (B, **Figure 77**) from the back of the headlight assembly.

3. Rotate the back cover assembly (B, **Figure 77**) *clockwise* and release the back cover assembly from the headlight assembly.

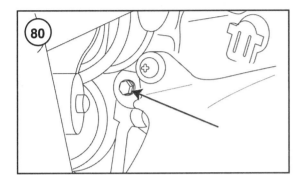

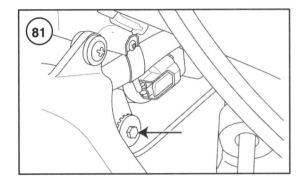

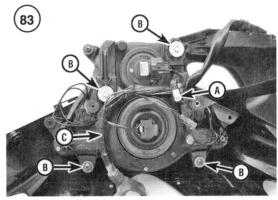

8. Install the back cover assembly onto the headlight assembly (B, **Figure 77**) and rotate it *counterclockwise* until it locks into place.

9. Connect the electrical connector (B, **Figure 77**) onto the back of the headlight assembly.

10. Install the combination meter as described in this chapter.

11. Check position light operation.

Headlight Adjustment

The headlight housing is equipped with a horizontal and vertical adjuster for each beam. When adjusting the headlight beam, first adjust the headlight horizontally and then adjust it vertically.

1. On 2006-2007 models:
   a. Horizontal **Figure 80**.
   b. Vertical **Figure 81**.
2. On 2008-2009 models:
   a. Horizontal A, **Figure 82**.
   b. Vertical B, **Figure 82**.

Headlight Housing
Removal/Installation

2006-2007 models

Refer to **Figure 64**.

1. Remove the front fairing (Chapter Fifteen).

2. Disconnect the electrical connectors from the back of the headlight assembly as (in this section).

3. Release the subharness from the wire clamp (A, **Figure 83**) on the headlight assembly.

4. Remove the headlight assembly mounting screws (B, **Figure 83**) and washers.

5. Remove the assembly (C, **Figure 83**) from the front fairing. Account for the damper in each headlight housing mount.

6. Installation is the reverse of removal. Note the following:

4. Pull straight out and remove the bulb socket/harness assembly.

5. Pull straight out and remove the bulb from the socket/harness assembly. Discard the blown bulb.

6. Install the *new* bulb into socket/harness assembly.

7. Install the bulb socket/harness assembly (C, **Figure 77**) into the headlight assembly.

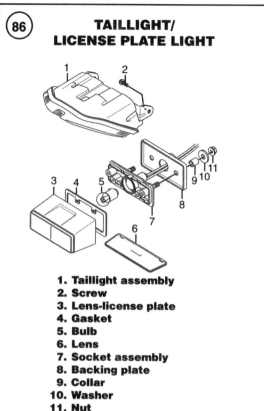

**TAILLIGHT/
LICENSE PLATE LIGHT**

1. Taillight assembly
2. Screw
3. Lens-license plate
4. Gasket
5. Bulb
6. Lens
7. Socket assembly
8. Backing plate
9. Collar
10. Washer
11. Nut

a. Make sure a damper is in place on each mount. Tighten the screws securely.
b. Secure the wire sub-harness to the wire clamp (A, **Figure 83**).
c. Check headlight operation.
d. Adjust the headlight as described in this chapter.

2008-2009 models

Refer to **Figure 74**.

1. Remove the front fairing (Chapter Fifteen).
2. Remove the air intake pipe and cover from each side (Chapter Fifteen).
3. Disconnect the electrical connectors from the back of the headlight assembly as described in this section.
4. Remove the headlight assembly mounting screws (**Figure 84**) and washers.
5. Pull the headlight assembly (**Figure 85**) straight out of the front fairing releasing the assembly from the two Velcro fasteners at the front.
6. Account for the damper in each headlight housing mount.
7. Installation is the reverse of removal. Note the following:

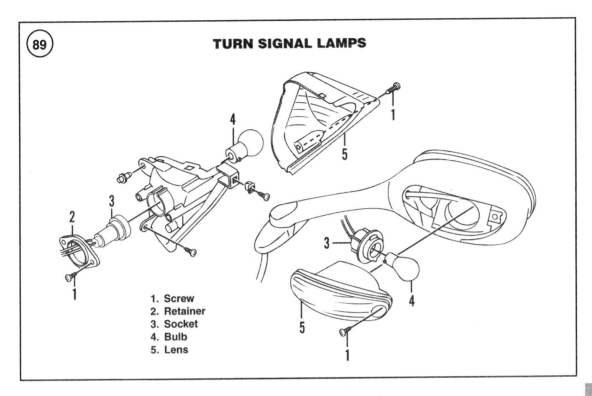

TURN SIGNAL LAMPS

1. Screw
2. Retainer
3. Socket
4. Bulb
5. Lens

a. Make sure a damper is in place on each mount. Tighten the screws securely.
b. Check headlight operation.
c. Adjust the headlight as described in this chapter.

Taillight/Brake Light
Bulb Removal/Installation

On all models, the taillight/brake light is an LED assembly. If any portion burns out, replace the taillight/brake light housing.

Taillight/Brake Light Housing
Removal/Installation

Refer to **Figure 86**.
1. Remove the seat/side cover and tail piece assembly (Chapter Fifteen).
2. Disconnect the 3-pin electrical connector (A, **Figure 87**) and release the harness clamp (B).
3. Remove the mounting bolt (C, **Figure 87**) from each side of the LED taillight/brake light assembly.
4. Slide the assembly (**Figure 88**) from the tail piece.
5. Installation is the reverse of removal. Note the following:
   a. Tighten the mounting bolt to 2.8 N•m (24 in.-lb.)
   b. Check taillight/brake light operation.

License Plate Light
Bulb Removal/Installation

Refer to **Figure 86**.
1. Remove the mounting nuts and washers, and remove the housing from the mounting bracket.
2. Remove the screws and separate the lens from the socket housing.
3. Rotate the bulb *counterclockwise* and remove the bulb from the socket.
4. Installation is the reverse of removal.

License Plate Light Housing
Removal/Installation

Refer to **Figure 86**.
1. Remove the seat/side cover and tail piece assembly (Chapter Fifteen).
2. Disconnect the 2-pin electrical connector.
3. Remove the mounting nuts and washers, and remove the housing from the mounting bracket.
4. Installation is the reverse of removal.

Turn Signal
Bulb Removal/Installation

Refer to **Figure 89**.
1A. Perform the following to replace the front turn signal bulb:
   a. Remove the socket mounting screw (**Figure 90**).

b. Pivot the lens assembly outward until its locating tab (A, **Figure 91**) disengages from the mirror stalk and remove the assembly.

c. Turn the bulb socket (B, **Figure 91**) *counterclockwise*, and remove it from the lens assembly.

d. Press the bulb (A, **Figure 92**) into the socket, turn it *counterclockwise*, and remove it.

1B. Perform the following to replace the rear turn signal bulb:

a. Remove the lens mounting screw and remove the lens from the tailpiece.

b. Press the bulb into the socket, turn it *counterclockwise*, and remove the bulb.

2. Installation is the reverse of removal. Check turn signal light operation.

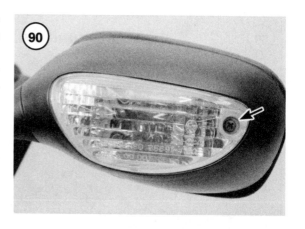

Front Socket Removal/Installation

1. Remove the bulb from the front turn signal assembly.

2. Follow the socket electrical wire (B, **Figure 92**) to the 2-pin turn signal connector within the mirror housing.

3. Disconnect the 2-pin connector, and remove the socket.

4. Installation is the reverse of removal.

Rear Assembly Removal/Installation

The rear turn signal housing mounts inside the wings on either side of the seat/side cover and tail piece assembly.

1. Remove the seat/side cover and tail piece assembly (Chapter Fifteen).

2. Remove the lens mounting screw and remove the lens (A, **Figure 93**) from the tailpiece.

3. Remove the fastener and partially separate the side cover (B, **Figure 93**) from the tail piece (A).

4. Disconnect the 2-pin turn signal electrical connector (C, **Figure 93**).

5. Remove the housing mounting screw (D, **Figure 93**) and remove the turn signal housing (E) from the side cover.

6. Installation is the reverse of removal.

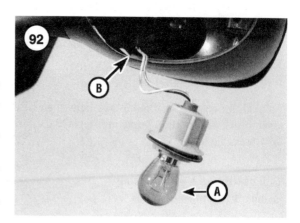

HORN

Removal/Installation

1. Remove the front fairing (Chapter Fifteen).

2A. On 2006-2007 models, perform the following:

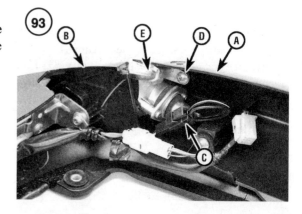

NOTE
This procedure is shown with the radiator assembly removed for photo clarity.

a. Partially remove the radiator to gain access to the horn mount.
b. Disconnect the 2-pin connector (A, Figure 94) from the horn.
c. Remove the mounting bolt on the backside of the voltage regulator/rectifier mounting bracket (B, Figure 94) and remove the horn (C) from the bracket.

2B. On 2008-2009 models, perform the following:
a. Remove the mounting bolts (A, Figure 95), and move the horn and mounting bracket from the frame mount.
b. Disconnect the 2-pin connector and remove the horn (B, Figure 95).

3. Installation is the reverse of removal.

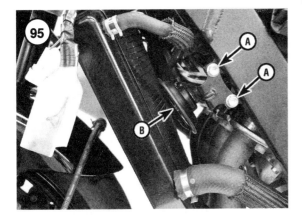

Testing

1. Disconnect the electrical lead from the negative battery terminal as described in this chapter.
2. Remove the front fairing (Chapter Fifteen).
3A. On 2006-2007 models, perform the following:
a. Partially remove the radiator to gain access to the horn mount.
b. Disconnect the 2-pin connector (A, **Figure 94**) from the horn.

3B. On 2008-2009 models, disconnect the 2-pin connector from the horn.
4. Use jumpers to connect a 12 volt battery to the horn terminals. The horn should sound.
5. If it does not, replace the horn.

METER ASSEMBLY

Removal/Installation

NOTE
This procedure is shown with the front fairing removed for photo clarity.

1. Remove the mounting screw (A, **Figure 96**) from the front of the meter.
2. Pull the meter assembly rearward until the meter claws (A, **Figure 97**) disengage from the dampers (B) in the headlight housing.
3. Disconnect the electrical connector (**Figure 98**), and remove the meter assembly (B, **Figure 96**)

4. Installation is the reverse of removal. The meter posts (A, **Figure 97**) or claws must properly engage the fairing dampers.

Disassembly/Assembly

> *NOTE*
> *Check the availability of replacement parts prior to disassembling the meter assembly.*

Refer to **Figure 99**.
1. Remove the meter assembly as described in this chapter.
2. Place the meter upside down on a towel.
3. Remove the attachment screws (**Figure 100**) around the perimeter of the back cover.
4. Separate the back cover and meter unit from the meter case.
5. Assemble the meter assembly by reversing these steps. Do not overtighten the attachments screws as they strip out the mounting bosses in the meter case.

Resetting the Tachometer

Whenever the ignition switch is turned on, the tachometer needle swings to its maximum setting and then returns to zero. This is part of the self-checking operation. If the needle does not return to zero, reset the tachometer by performing the following.
1. Press and hold the meters adjust button (A, **Figure 101**).
2. Turn the ignition switch on.

> *NOTE*
> *The adjust button must be pressed twice within one second after it has been released.*

3. Three to five seconds after turning on the ignition switch, release the adjust button, and then press it twice.
4. The needle should return to zero. Please note that the entire resetting process should be completed within 10 seconds after the ignition switch is turned on.
5. If the needle does not return to zero, replace the meter assembly.

Coolant Temperature Display Test

Before performing this test, check the engine coolant temperature sensor by performing the ECT sensor bench test (Chapter Eight). Replace the sensor

if it is out of specification. If the display is still not working, perform the following test.
1. Lift or remove the fuel tank assembly (Chapter Eight).
2. Disconnect the 2-pin connector (**Figure 102**) from the engine coolant temperature (ECT) sensor.
3. Connect a variable resistor across the two terminals in the harness side of the engine coolant temperature sensor connector.

> *NOTE*
> *If the engine stop switch is off when the ignition switch is turned on, CHECK will appear in the LCD. This is normal. The system is indicating that no signal is reaching the ECM. Turn the engine stop switch on, and retry.*

4. Turn the ignition switch on.
5. Refer to the chart in **Figure 103**. Set the resistor to each resistance listed in the chart, and check the meter. The indicator LED (A, **Figure 101**), the coolant temperature/FI display (B) and the coolant temperature warning LCD (C) should appear as indicated in the chart.
6. Replace the meter if it fails any portion of this test.

Fuel Level Indicator Light Inspection

If the fuel level indicator light does not operate properly, check the wiring and connectors in the fuel level indicator circuit. Test the fuel level sensor (Chapter Eight),

Speedometer Inspection

If either the speedometer, odometer or trip meter fails to operate properly, inspect the wiring and connectors in the speedometer circuit and test the speed sensor as described in this chapter.If the wiring and speed sensor are working properly, replace the meter assembly.

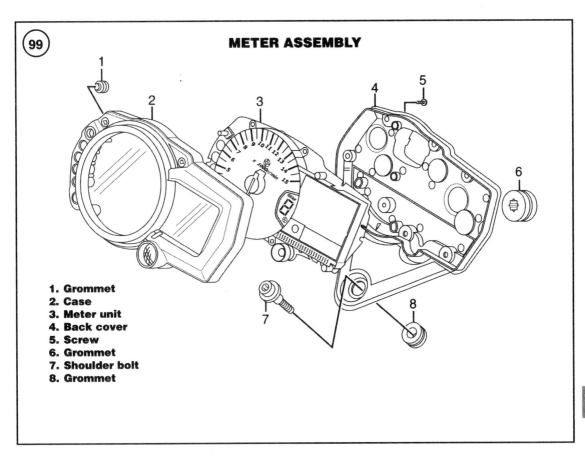

METER ASSEMBLY

99

1. Grommet
2. Case
3. Meter unit
4. Back cover
5. Screw
6. Grommet
7. Shoulder bolt
8. Grommet

9

100

Low Oil Level Indicator Inspection

If the low oil level indicator fails to operate properly, perform the *Oil Pressure Switch Test* described in this chapter. If the switch and wiring are in good working order, replace the meter assembly.

SPEED SENSOR

Removal/Installation

1. Lift and support the fuel tank (Chapter Eight).

2. Follow the speed sensor electrical lead (A, **Figure 104**), locate the 3-pin speed sensor connector and disconnect the connector (**Figure 105**) from its harness mate.

3. Remove the mounting bolt (B, **Figure 104**), and pull the sensor from the engine sprocket cover.

4. Installation is the reverse or removal. Route the cable along the path noted during removal. Tighten the bolt securely.

Test

1. Remove the speed sensor as described in this chapter.

2. Connect the negative battery terminal to the black/white terminal in the sensor side of the connector; connect the positive battery terminal to the sensor's black/red terminal.

3. Connect a 10k ohm resistor to the black/red and black terminals on the sensor side of the connector.

4. Connect the voltmeter the resistor as shown in **Figure 106**.

5. Touch the pick-up surface of the sensor with a screwdriver and watch the voltmeter. The voltage reading should change from 0 to 12 volts or from 12 to 0 volts. If it does not, replace the sensor.

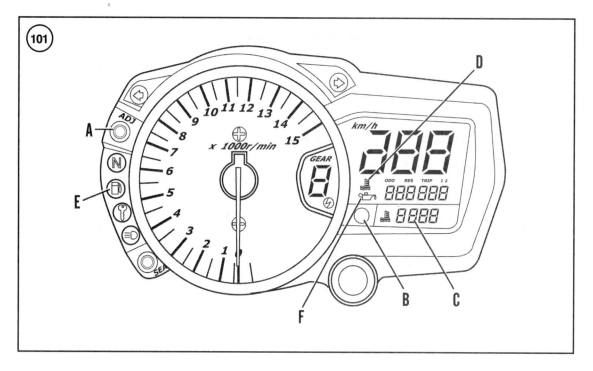

OIL PRESSURE SWITCH

Removal/Installation

The oil pressure switch is mounted onto the right side of the lower crankcase below the starter clutch assembly.

1. Disconnect the battery negative cable as described in this chapter.
2. Remove the right fairing side panel (Chapter Fifteen).
3. Drain the engine oil (Chapter Three).
4. Remove the screw and pull the electrical wire from the oil pressure switch.
5. Unscrew and remove the oil pressure switch (**Figure 107**) from the crankcase.
6. Installation is the reverse of these steps. Note the following:

    a. Apply a light coat of sealant (Suzuki 1207B sealant, or equivalent), to the switch threads where shown in **Figure 108**.

    b. Tighten the oil pressure switch to 14 N•m (124 in.-lb.).

Oil Pressure Switch Test

As soon as the ignition switch is turned ON, the low oil pressure indicator (B, **Figure 101**) in the display should flicker and the indicator LED (C) should turn on. As soon as the engine is started, each should go out. If the oil pressure is less than the normal operating pressure range, the symbol flickers and indicator LED turns on and stays on.

If the warning light is not operating correctly or does not come on when the ignition switch is in the on position with the engine not running, perform the following test.

1. Check the engine oil level (Chapter Three). Add oil if necessary.
2. Remove the fairing side panel from the left side (Chapter Fifteen).
3. Remove the mounting screw, and disconnect the wire from the oil pressure switch.
4. Use a jumper wire to connect the oil pressure switch wire to a good engine ground.
5. Turn the ignition switch on. The indicator LED (C, **Figure 101**) should turn on and the low oil pressure indicator (D) should flicker.
6. If each does not occur, check the wiring and connectors between the oil pressure switch and the meter. If they are good, replace the meter assembly.

103 **COOLANT TEMPERATURE DISPLAY TEST**

Resistance	LED	Coolant Temp Display	Coolant Temp Warning LCD
2.45 ohms or higher	OFF	"— — —"	—
Approx. 0.811 k ohms	OFF	50	—
Approx. 0.1 k ohms	ON	120-139	Flicker
0 ohms (jumper)	ON	HI	Flicker

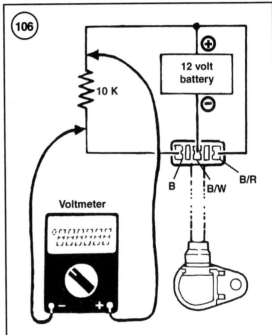

SWITCHES

Testing

Test switches for continuity with an ohmmeter or a test light. The continuity diagrams for various switches are found in the wiring diagrams at the back of this manual.

1. When testing a switch, note the following:

  a. First check the fuse for the related circuit as described in this chapter.

  b. Check the battery as described in this chapter.

  c. Disconnect the battery negative terminal if the switch connectors are not disconnected in the circuit.

  d. When separating two connectors, pull the connector housings and not the wires.

  e. After locating a defective circuit, check the connectors to make sure they are clean and properly connected. Check all wires going into a connector housing to make sure each wire is properly positioned and makes good contact with the connector terminal.

  f. When reconnecting electrical connector halves, push them together until they click or snap into place.

2. To test a particular switch:

  a. Turn to the relevant wiring diagram, and locate the continuity diagram for the switch being tested.

b. Disconnect the switch connector, and check continuity at the terminals on the switch side of the connector.

c. Set the switch to each of its operating positions indicated in the continuity diagram, connect an ohmmeter test leads to the indicated terminals, and compare the results with the appropriate switch continuity diagram.

d. For example, **Figure 109** and **Figure 110** show a continuity diagram for the ignition switch. The horizontal lines indicate which terminals should show continuity when the switch is in a given position. When the ignition switch shown in is in the park position, for example, there should be continuity between the red and brown terminals. An ohmmeter connected between these two terminals should indicate little or no resistance or a test light should light. When the ignition switch is in the *off* position, there should be no continuity between any of the terminals.

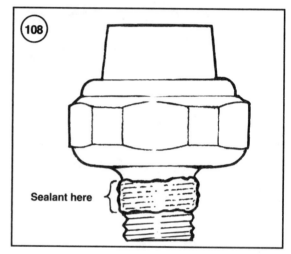

Sealant here

Right Handlebar Switch Removal/Installation

The switches located within the right handlebar switch housing are not available separately. If any switch is damaged, replace the right handlebar switch. The front brake light switch is a separate unit and can be replaced independently.

1. The right handlebar switch includes the following switches:

a. Engine stop switch (A, **Figure 111**).

b. Starter button (B, **Figure 111**).

c. Front brake light switch (electrical connectors only - the switch is separate).

d. Headlight switch (U.K. and Europe models).

e. Driving mode selector switch (2008-2009 models.)

2. If the right handlebar switch is being replaced, perform the following:

a. Disconnect the battery negative cable as described in this chapter.

b. Remove the front fairing (Chapter Fifteen). It is not necessary, but it does allow additional working space.

c. Remove the air filter housing (Chapter Eight).

d. Disconnect the right handlebar switch connector (A, **Figure 112**) from its harness mate.

e. Remove any cable ties securing the switch wiring to the frame. Note how the wire is routed through the frame. New wire must be routed along the same path.

f. Disconnect the connectors (C, **Figure 111**) from the front brake light switch.

3. Remove the clip from the throttle cables.

4. Loosen the pull cable locknut (A, **Figure 113**) and turn the adjuster (B) to create maximum slack.

5. Remove the screw (C, **Figure 113**), and lift the clamp (D) from the switch housing.

6. Remove the switch housing screws and separate the switch halves.

7. Disconnect each cable end (A, **Figure 114**) from the throttle drum, and feed the cables through the housing half.

8. Install by reversing these removal steps. Note the following:

a. Rote the pull cable through the upper port in the upper switch half. Route the return cable through the remaining port.

b. Apply grease to the cable ends, and connect each cable end to the throttle drum (A, **Figure 114**). Make sure each cable is seated in the throttle drum channel.

c. Join the switch halves so its index pin (B, **Figure 114**) engages the hole in the handlebar.

d. Route the electrical cable along the path noted during removal. Make sure the electrical connectors are free of corrosion and are tight.

109

U.K. AND EUROPE MODELS

Position \ Color	R	O	Gr	Br
ON	○—	—○	○—	—○
OFF				
LOCK				
P	○———	———	———	—○

110

U.S., CALIFORNIA AND CANADA MODELS

Position \ Color	R	O	O/Y	Gr	Br
ON	○—	—○—	—○	○—	—○
OFF					
LOCK					
P	○———	———	———	———	—○

9

111

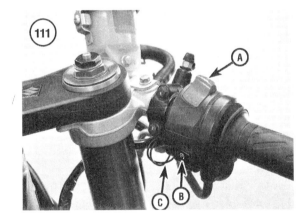

113

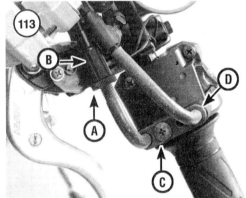

112

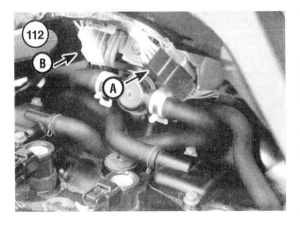

114

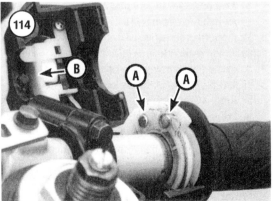

e. Check the operation of each switch mounted in the right handlebar switch housing.

f. Operate the throttle grip and make sure the throttle linkage operates smoothly. If any binding or sluggish operation is noted, carefully check that the cable is attached correctly and there are no tight bends in the cable.

g. Adjust the throttle cable free play (Chapter Three).

Left Handlebar Switch
Removal/Installation

The switches located within the left handlebar switch housing are not available separately. If one switch is damaged, replace the left switch housing assembly. The clutch switch is a separate unit and can be replaced independently.

1. The left handlebar switch housing is equipped with the following switches:

a. Headlight dimmer switch (A, **Figure 115**).

b. Turn signal switch (B, **Figure 115**).

c. Hazard switch (C, **Figure 115**).

d. Horn button (D, **Figure 115**).

e. Clutch switch (electrical connectors only – the switch is separate) (E, **Figure 115**).

f. Passing button (U.K. Australia and Europe models).

2. If the left handlebar switch is being replaced, perform the following:

a. Disconnect the battery negative cable as described in this chapter.

b. Remove the front fairing (Chapter Fifteen). It is not necessary, but it does allow additional working space.

c. Remove the air filter housing (Chapter Eight).

d. Disconnect the left handlebar switch connector (B, **Figure 112**) from its harness mate.

e. Remove any cable ties securing the switch wiring harness to the frame. Note how the wire is routed through the frame. New wire must be routed along the same path.

f. Disconnect the connectors from the clutch switch (A, **Figure 116**).

3. Remove the housing screws (B, **Figure 116**) and separate the switch halves (C).

4. Remove the switch assembly.

5. Install by reversing these removal steps. Note the following:

a. Align the locating pin on the switch housing with the hole in the handlebar. Install the switch onto the handlebar and tighten the housing screws (B, **Figure 116**) securely.

b. Route the electrical cable along the path noted during removal.

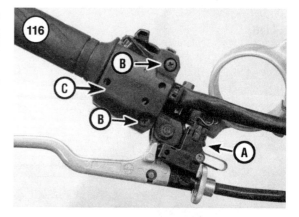

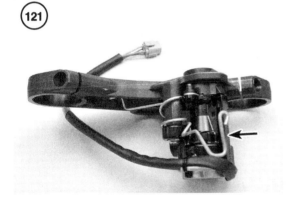

c. Check the operation of each switch mounted in the left switch housing.

Ignition Switch
Removal/Installation

A JT40H Torx bit (Suzuki part number: 09930-11920) and bit holder (Suzuki part number: 09930-11940), or equivalent tools, are needed to perform this procedure.

1. Disconnect the battery negative cable as described in this chapter.
2. Remove the front fairing (Chapter Fifteen).
3. Raise and support the fuel tank (Chapter Eight).
4. Remove the air filter housing (Chapter Eight).
5. Disconnect the ignition switch 3-pin connector (**Figure 117**) from its harness mate. Note how the wire is routed through the frame (**Figure 118**). New wire must be routed along the same path (**Figure 119**).
6. Remove both Torx bolts (**Figure 120**) securing the ignition switch to the bottom of the upper fork bridge.
7. On USA, California and Canada models, apply Suzuki Thread Lock 1342 to the Torx bolt threads. On UK, Europe and Australia models, apply Suzuki Thread Lock Super 1322.
8. Install the *new* ignition switch, and tighten the Torx bolts securely.
9. Install the ignition cable retainer as shown in (**Figure 121**), on models so equipped.
10. Route the ignition switch wire along the path noted during removal. Make sure the connector is tight.

Front Brake Switch
Removal/Installation

1. Disconnect the electrical connector(s) (**Figure 122**) from the front brake switch on the brake lever assembly.
2. Remove the mounting screw, and lower the switch (**Figure 123**) from the lever assembly.
3. Installation is the reverse of removal. Tighten the screw securely.

Rear Brake Switch
Removal/Installation

The rear brake switch is located on the inside of the brake pedal/footpeg assembly. The switch can be removed with the assembly on the motorcycle, but removing the brake pedal/footpeg assembly is recommended.

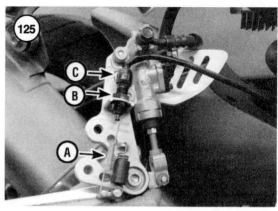

1. Remove the rear footpeg bracket bolts (**Figure 124**) along with their washers. Rotate the brake pedal/footpeg assembly around from the frame.

2. Disconnect the switch spring (A, **Figure 125**) from the boss on the brake pedal.

3. Hold the adjusting nut (B, **Figure 125**). Loosen and remove the switch (C, **Figure 125**).

4. Installation is the reverse of removal. Note the following:

    a. Install a washer with each rear footpeg bracket bolt (**Figure 124**), and tighten the bolts to 23 N•m (17 ft.-lb.).

    b. Adjust the rear brake switch as described in Chapter Three.

Clutch Switch
Removal/Installation

1. Disconnect the electrical connectors from the clutch switch (**Figure 126**).

2. Remove the mounting screw, and lower the switch from the lever assembly.

3. Installation is the reverse of removal.

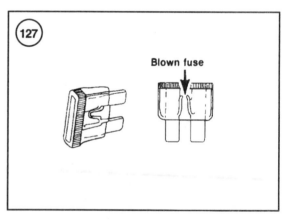

Blown fuse

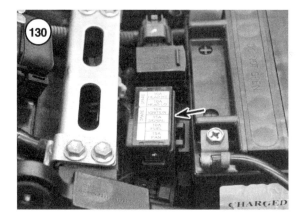

FUSES

When troubleshooting any electrical problem, first check for a blown fuse (**Figure 127**). Before replacing blown a fuse, however, determine the reason for the failure. This may be caused by worn-through insulation or a disconnected wire that is shorted to ground. Check by testing the circuit the fuse protects.

Main Fuse Removal/Installation

All models are equipped with a single 30-amp main fuse.

1. Remove the riders seat (Chapter Fifteen).
2. Remove the starter relay cover (**Figure 128**).
3. Using needlenose pliers, pull the fuse (**Figure 129**) out and inspect it.
4. Install a *new* fuse and push it into place until it bottoms.

Circuit Fuse Removal/Installation

Individual circuit fuses are located in the fuse box located under the seat on the right side (**Figure 130**). The fuse box contains two spare fuses (10A and 15A). Replace the spare fuse as soon as possible.

1. Remove the rider's seat (Chapter Fifteen).
2. Depress the catch, and open the fuse panel cover (A, **Figure 131**).
3. Use needlenose pliers and remove the suspect fuse (B, **Figure 131**).
4. Install a replacement fuse of the same amperage.

COLOR WIRING DIAGRAMS

Color wiring diagrams for all models are located at the end of this manual.

Table 1 ELECTRICAL SYSTEM SPECIFICATIONS

Battery	
Type	YT12A-BS Maintenance free (sealed)
Capacity	
GSX-R600	12 volt 36.0 kC (8 amp hour)/10 HR
GSX-R750	12 volt 36.0 kC (10 amp hour)/10 HR
Maximum current draw	Less than 3 mA
Charge rate	
Normal charge	1.2A for 5-10 hours
Quick charge	5A for 1 hour
Alternator	
Type	Three-phase AC
No-load voltage (when engine is cold)	65 volts or more (AC) @ 5,000 rpm
Regulated voltage (charging voltage)	14.0-15.5 volts @ 5,000 rpm
Stator resistance	0.2-1.0 ohms
Gear position switch (GP) voltage	
(all gears except neutral)	0.6 volts or more
Ignition System	
Type	Electronic ignition (transistorized)
Firing order	1-2-4-3
Ignition timing	
GSX-R600 models	6° B.T.D.C. @ 1300 rpm
GSX-R750 models	
2006-2007 models	8° B.T.D.C. @ 1200 rpm
2008-2009 models	5° B.T.D.C. @ 1200 rpm
Crankshaft position (CKP) sensor	
Resistance	142-194 ohms
Peak voltage (when cranking)	0.28 volts and more
Ignition coil primary peak voltage	80 volts or more
Ignition coil resistance	
Primary	1.1-1.9 ohms
Secondary	
2006-2007 models	10.8-16.2 k ohms
2008-2009 models	7.4-9.6 k ohms
Sidestand switch and relay test voltage	
Raised position	0.4-0.6 volt
Lowered position	more than 1.4 volts
Starter relay resistance	3-6 ohms
Spark plug	
Gap	
2006-2007 models	0.7-0.8 mm (0.028-0.031 in.)
2008-2009 models	0.8-0.9 mm (0.031-0.035 in.)
Type	
2006-2007 models	
Standard	NGK: CR9E, Denso: U27ESR-N
Hot type	NGK: CR8E, Denso: U24ESR-N
Cold type	NGK: CR10E, Denso: U31ESR-N
2008-2009 models	
Standard	NGK: CR9EIA-9, Denso: IUD27D
Hot type	NGK: CR8EIA-9, Denso: IU24D
Cold type	NGK: CR10EIA-9, Denso: IU31D
Steering damper (2008-2009 models)	
Resistance	Approximately 12.5 ohms @ 20°C (68°F)

Table 2 REPLACEMENT BULBS AND FUSES

Item	Voltage/wattage x quantity
Headlight (high/low beam)	
2006-2007 models	
High beam	12 V, 65 W
Low beam	12 V, 55 W
2008-2009 models	
High beam	12 V, 60 W x 2
Low beam	12 V, 55 W

(continued)

Table 2 REPLACEMENT BULBS AND FUSES (continued)

Item	Voltage/wattage x quantity
Position light (2006-2007 UK and Europe models)	12 V, 5 W x 2
Brake light/taillight	LED
License plate light	12 V 5 W
Turn signal	12 V, 18 W x 4
Meter assembly light	LED
Neutral indicator light	LED
High beam indicator light	LED
Turn signal indicator light	LED
Fuel indicator light	LED
Oil pressure, coolant temperature, FI warning lights	LED
Immobilizer light	LED
Headlight fuse	
2006-2007 models	
High	10 amp
Low	10 amp
2008-2009	
High	15 amp
Low	10 amp
Signal fuse	
2006-2007 models	15 amp
2008-2009 models	10 amp
Ignition fuse	
2006-2007 models	10 amp
2008-2009 models	15 amp
Fuel fuse	10 amp
Fan fuse	10 amp
Main fuse	30 amp

Table 3 ELECTRICAL SYSTEM TORQUE SPECIFICATIONS

Item	N•m	in.-lb.	ft.-lb.
Flywheel bolt	120	-	88.5
Rear footpeg bracket bolt	23	–	17
Oil pressure switch	14	124	–
Spark plug	11	97	–
Stator coil bolt	10	89	–
Starter motor terminal nut	6	53	–
Voltage regulator bolts (2008-2009 models)	10	89	–

9

Notes

CHAPTER TEN

COOLING SYSTEM

This chapter covers procedures for the cooling system components. For routine maintenance, refer to Chapter Three.

Tables 1-3 are at the end of this chapter.

TEMPERATURE WARNING SYSTEM

During engine operation, the ECM monitors the engine coolant temperature (ECT) sensor and displays coolant temperature in the meter assembly. When the ignition switch is turned on, a test pattern of assorted numbers appear in the coolant temperature/ FI portion (A, **Figure 1**) of the meter assembly for three seconds. During normal operation, the engine coolant temperature is displayed here. Whenever the coolant temperature is below 20° C (68° F), the display indicates three dashes (- - -).

> *CAUTION*
> *If the temperature exceeds 120° C (248° F), turn off the engine. Do not run the engine until the coolant temperature drops below 120° C (248° F).*

If the temperature exceeds 120° C (248° F), the coolant temperature warning LCD icon (B, **Figure 1**) flickers and the icon (C) turns on. Should the coolant temperature exceed 140° C (284° F), the display (A, **Figure 1**) flashes *HI*, the coolant warning LED icon (B) flickers and the LED icon remains on.

HOSES AND HOSE CLAMPS

Hoses deteriorate with age and should be replaced if they show signs of cracking or leaking. Loss of coolant can also lead to engine overheating and spray from a leaking hose can injure the rider and passenger. Whenever any component of the cooling system is removed, inspect the adjoining hose(s).

1. Make sure the cooling system is cool before removing any coolant hose.
2. Replace the hoses with original equipment hoses. These hoses are formed to a specific shape with a precise length and inner diameter so they fit correctly.
3. Loosen the clamps on the hose that is to be replaced. Slide the clamps back from the component fittings.

> *CAUTION*
> *Do not pry or twist too hard when attempting to remove a stubborn hose from the radiator. The aluminum radiator inlet and outlet fittings are fragile and easily damaged.*

4. Twist the hose to release it from the fitting. If the hose has been on for a long duration, it will probably be difficult to break loose. If so, carefully insert a pick tool or small screwdriver under the hose and pry it loose from the fitting.

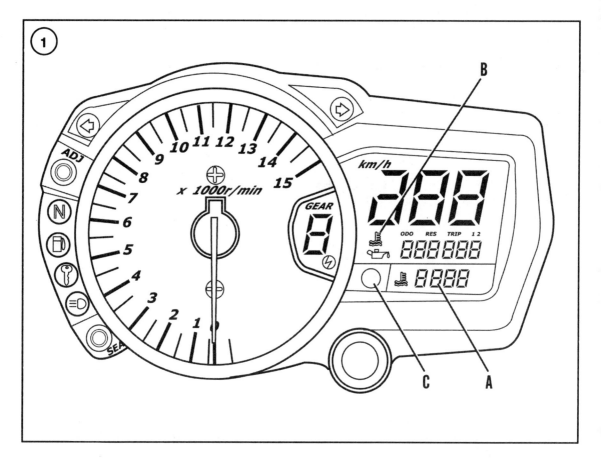

5. Examine the fittings for cracks or other damage. Repair or replace the fitting as necessary. If the fitting is good, use sandpaper and clean off any hose residue, and wipe the fitting clean with a cloth.

6. New hoses can be stiff and are often difficult to install onto their fittings. Before install hoses, soak the ends in hot water to make them more pliable. Do not use any type of lubricant to in the inner surfaces of the hoses. The hose could slip off the fitting when the engine is running even with the hose clamp(s) securely in place.

7. Inspect the hose clamps for rust and corrosion. Replace it if necessary. For best results, always use the screw adjusting type hose clamps.

8. With the hose correctly installed on the each fitting, position the clamp approximately 13 mm (1/2-in.) from the end of the hose. Make sure the hose clamp is still positioned over the fitting and tighten the clamp.

COOLING SYSTEM PRECAUTIONS

Refer to *Cooling System* in Chapter Three.

WARNING
*Do not remove the radiator cap (A, **Figure 2**) when the engine is hot. The*

coolant is very hot and under pressure. Severe scalding could result if the coolant comes in contact with your skin. Let the engine cool before removing any cooling system component.

WARNING
Whenever the engine is warm or hot, the fan may operate even with the ignition switch turned off. Never work around the fan or touch the fan until the engine and coolant are completely cool.

WARNING
Engine coolant is toxic. Place any spent coolant into a suitable container and dispose of it according to EPA or local regulations. Do not store coolant where it is accessible to children or pets.

WARNING
Coolant is very slippery when spilled on concrete or similar surfaces. Wipe up spilled coolant immediately.

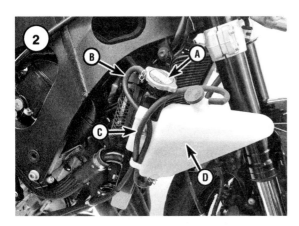

Cooling System Inspection

CAUTION
Drain and flush the cooling system at least every two years. Refill the system with a mixture of ethylene glycol antifreeze (formulated for aluminum radiators and engines) and distilled (or purified) water. Discard old coolant. It deteriorates with use and is unsuitable for reuse. **Do not** *operate the cooling system with only distilled water (even in climates where antifreeze protection is not required). The engine will oxidize internally and have to be replaced. Refer to* **Cooling System** *in Chapter Three.*

1. Start the engine and run it until it reaches operating temperature. While the engine is running, a pressure surge may be felt when the water pump inlet hose (**Figure 3**) is squeezed.
2. If steam is observed at the muffler outlet, the head gasket might be damaged. If enough coolant leaks into a cylinder, it could hydrolock and thus preventing the engine from being cranked. Coolant may also be present in the engine oil. If the oil visible in the oil level window is foamy or milky-looking, there is

coolant in the oil. If so, correct the problem before returning the motorcycle to service.

CAUTION
If the engine oil is contaminated with coolant, change the oil and filter after performing the coolant system repair. Refer to Chapter Three.

3. Check the radiator for clogged or damaged fins. If more than 15 percent of the radiator fin area is damaged, repair or replace the radiator.
4. Check all coolant hoses for cracks or damage. Replace all questionable parts. Make sure all hose clamps are tight, but not so tight that they cut the hoses. Refer to Hoses and Clamps *in this chapter.*
5. Pressure test the cooling system (Chapter Three).

COOLANT RESERVOIR

Removal/Installation

1. Support the motorcycle on a level surface.
2. Remove the left side front fairing (Chapter Fifteen).
3. Disconnect the reservoir inlet hose (B, **Figure 2**) from the fitting on the radiator filler neck.
4. Remove the reservoir mounting bolt (C, **Figure 2**).
5. Pull the coolant reservoir leftward until it disengages from the index post on the radiator, and remove the reservoir (D, **Figure 2**).
6. Remove the filler cap, and drain any residual coolant from the reservoir. Dispose of the coolant properly.
7. If necessary, clean the inside of the reservoir with a liquid detergent. Thoroughly rinse the reservoir with clean water.
8. Install by reversing these removal steps. Make sure the reservoir engages the indexing post.

RADIATOR

Removal/Installation

NOTE
This procedure is shown with the exhaust system for photo clarity only. It is not necessary to remove the exhaust system, but it does allow additional working area.

Refer to **Figure 4** or **Figure 5**.
1. Support the motorcycle on a level surface.
2. Remove both fairing side panels (Chapter Fifteen).

10

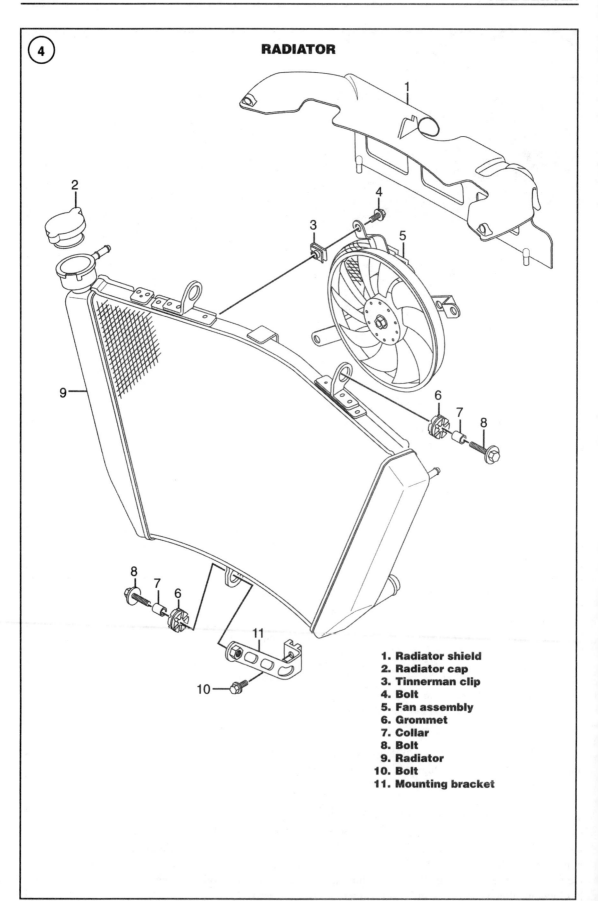

RADIATOR

1. Radiator shield
2. Radiator cap
3. Tinnerman clip
4. Bolt
5. Fan assembly
6. Grommet
7. Collar
8. Bolt
9. Radiator
10. Bolt
11. Mounting bracket

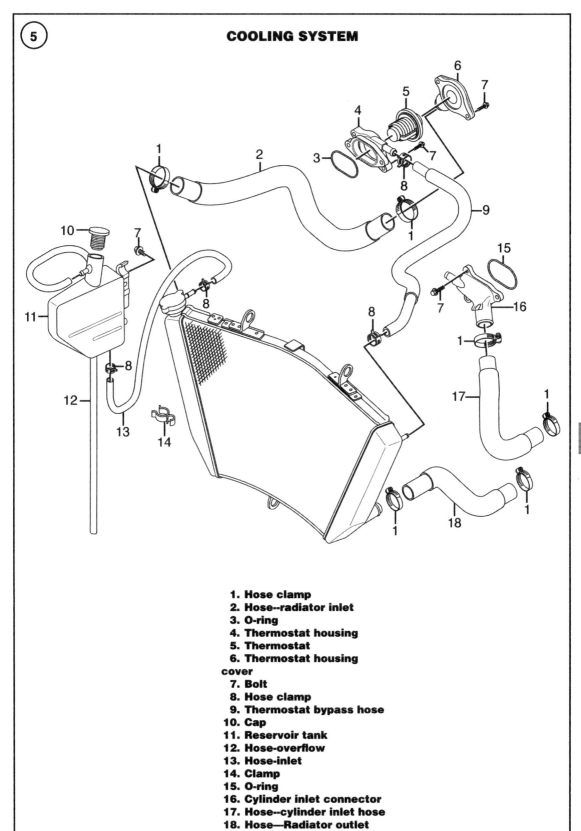

COOLING SYSTEM

1. Hose clamp
2. Hose--radiator inlet
3. O-ring
4. Thermostat housing
5. Thermostat
6. Thermostat housing cover
7. Bolt
8. Hose clamp
9. Thermostat bypass hose
10. Cap
11. Reservoir tank
12. Hose-overflow
13. Hose-inlet
14. Clamp
15. O-ring
16. Cylinder inlet connector
17. Hose--cylinder inlet hose
18. Hose—Radiator outlet

10

3. Remove the fuel tank (Chapter Eight).

4. Drain the coolant from the system (Chapter Three).

5. Disconnect the battery negative cable (Chapter Nine).

6. Disconnect the 2-pin radiator fan electrical connector (**Figure 6**) from its harness mate.

NOTE
Even though the cooling system has been drained, some residual coolant remains in the radiator and hoses. Place a drain pan under each hose as it is removed. Also have shop rags handy to wipe up any spilled coolant.

7. Loosen the clamp on the thermostat bypass hose (A, **Figure 7**). Remove the hose from the radiator upper fitting on the left side, and plug the end of the hose.

8. Loosen the hose clamp on the radiator outlet hose (B, **Figure 7**). Remove the hose from the radiator lower fitting on the left side, and plug the end of the hose.

9. Loosen the hose clamp on the radiator inlet hose (A, **Figure 8**). Remove the hose from the radiator upper fitting on the right side, and plug the end of the hose.

10. Release the hose clamp, and disconnect the oil cooler outlet hose (B, **Figure 8**) from the lower fitting on the right side of the radiator.

11. Remove the lower radiator mounting bolt and collar (**Figure 9**), and disengage the radiator from its mounting bracket. Watch for the collar in radiator damper.

12. Remove the upper radiator-mounting bolt (**Figure 10**) from each side of the radiator. Watch for the collar in radiator dampers, and note the location of the clutch cable bracket on the right side.

13. Carefully remove the radiator assembly from the frame. Do not strike the front fender during removal to avoid damage to either the fender or radiator.

14. Inspect the radiator as described in this section.

15. Install by reversing these removal steps. Note the following:

    a. Replace all radiator hoses if they are starting to deteriorate or are damaged in any way.

    b. Make sure the damper and collar are in place on each radiator and oil cooler mount.

    c. Make sure the radiator fan electrical connector (**Figure 6**) is free of corrosion and is tight.

    d. Refill and bleed the cooling system (Chapter Three).

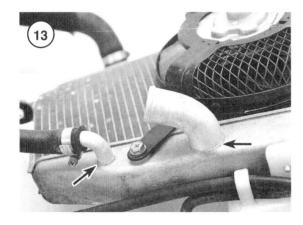

Inspection

1. Inspect the radiator cap top and bottom seals (**Figure 11**) for deterioration or damage. Check the spring for damage. Pressure test the radiator cap (Chapter Three).

2. Remove the radiator fan assembly as described in this chapter. This allows access to the back portion of the radiator for inspection.

3. If compressed air is available, use short spurts of air directed to the backside (**Figure 12**) of the radiator core, and blow out debris.

4. Flush off the exterior of the radiator with a garden hose on low pressure. Spray both the front and the back to remove all debris. Carefully use a whisk broom or stiff paint brush to remove any stubborn dirt from the cooling fins.

> *CAUTION*
> *Do not press too hard or the cooling fins and tubes may be damaged causing a leak.*

5. Carefully straighten out any bent cooling fins with a broad tipped screwdriver or putty knife.

6. Check for cracks or leakage (usually a green colored residue) at all hose fittings (**Figure 13**) and both radiator tank seams (**Figure 14**).

7. To prevent oxidation of the radiator, touch up any areas where the paint is worn off with several *light* coats of spray paint.

8. Inspect the rubber damper (**Figure 15**) in the radiator mount. Replace any that are damaged or starting to deteriorate.

RADIATOR FAN

Removal/Installation

1. Support the motorcycle on a level surface.

2. Remove the radiator as described in this chapter.

3. Place a blanket or large towels on the workbench to protect the radiator.

4. Remove the radiator fan mounting bolts (**Figure 16**), and carefully detach the fan assembly from the radiator.

5. Install by reversing these removal steps. Tighten the radiator fan mounting bolts to 8 N•m (71 in.-lb.).

Radiator Fan Motor Test

1. Remove the front fairing panel from the right side (Chapter Fifteen).

2. Disconnect the 2-pin radiator fan electrical connector (**Figure 6**) from its harness mate.

3. Connect a 12-volt battery directly to the connector with jumper wires. Connect the battery positive terminal to the blue terminal in the motor side of the connector; connect the battery negative terminal to the black terminal on the motor side of the connector.

4. The motor should turn when power is directly applied.

5. Connect an ammeter in line between the motor and the battery as shown in **Figure 17**. Measure the load current. It should not exceed the specification in **Table 2**.

6. Replace the motor if it does not operate with direct power or if current draw is excessive.

7. Disconnect the ammeter and jumper wires.

8. Connect the 2-pin radiator fan electrical connector (**Figure 6**) onto its harness mate.

9. Install the front fairing panel from the right side (Chapter Fifteen).

COOLING FAN RELAY

Removal/Installation

1A. On 2006-2007 model, perform the following:
    a. Raise and support the fuel tank, or remove the tank (Chapter Eight).
    b. Pull the cooling fan relay (**Figure 18**) straight up and remove the damper from the mounting tang.

1B. On 2008-2009 models, perform the following:
    a. Remove the rider's seat (Chapter Fifteen).
    b. Pull the cooling fan relay (**Figure 19**) straight up and remove it from the mounting tang.

2. Disconnect the 4-pin connector from the relay.

3. Installation is the reverse of removal. Make sure the relay's damper engages the mounting tang.

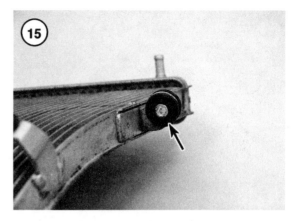

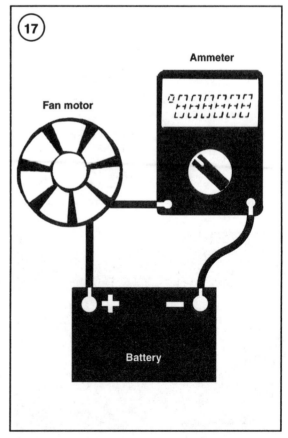

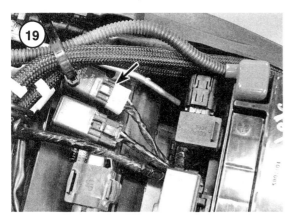

Test

1. Remove the relay (this section).
2. Check for continuity between relay terminals A and B (**Figure 20**).
3. Use jumper wires and a 12-volt battery, connect the positive battery wire to terminal C (**Figure 20**) and the negative to terminal D of the relay. There should continuity between A and B with voltage applied.
4. Replace the relay if it fails either portion of this test.
5. Install the relay (this section).

ENGINE COOLANT TEMPERATURE (ECT) SENSOR

Refer to Chapter Eight.

THERMOSTAT

Removal/Inspection/Installation

The thermostat sits inside the housing on the back of the cylinder head. Refer to **Figure 5**.
1. Support the motorcycle on a level surface.
2. Drain the cooling system (Chapter Three).
3. Remove the fuel tank, air filter housing and throttle bodies (Chapter Eight).
4. Release the hose clamp and disconnect the inlet hose (A, **Figure 21**) and the bypass hose (B) from the thermostat housing.
5. Remove the thermostat housing cover bolts and lower the cover (C, **Figure 21**) from the cylinder head.

> *NOTE*
> *The following steps are shown with the cylinder head removed from the engine for photo clarity.*

6. Remove the thermostat (A, **Figure 22**).

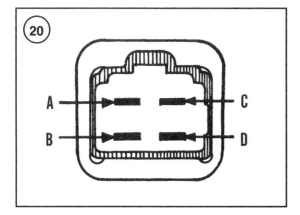

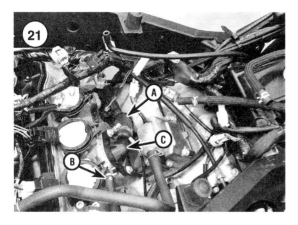

7. If necessary, test the thermostat as described in this chapter.

8. Inspect the thermostat (**Figure 23**) for damage. Make sure the spring has not sagged or broken. Replace the thermostat if necessary.

9. Clean any debris or coolant residue from the thermostat housing. Make sure the ports are clear.

10. Installation is the reverse of removal. Note the following:

   a. Apply grease (Suzuki Super Grease A or equivalent) to the rubber seal on the thermostat.

   b. Seat the thermostat so its air bleed hole (B, **Figure 22**) faces the top of the cylinder head.

   c. Tighten the thermostat housing cover bolts to 10 N•m (89 in.-lb.).

   d. Refill and bleed the cooling system (Chapter Three).

Testing

Test the thermostat to ensure proper operation. The thermostat should be replaced if it remains open at normal room temperature or stays closed after the specified test temperature has been reached.

> *NOTE*
> *The thermometer and the thermostat must not touch the container sides or bottom during the test. If either does, the test readings will be inaccurate.*

1. Suspend the thermostat and thermometer in a pan of water (**Figure 24**). Use a cooking or candy thermometer that is rated higher than the test temperatures.

> *NOTE*
> *It can take 3-5 minutes for the valve to operate properly and to open completely. If the valve fails to open, replace the thermostat. Replace it with one of the same temperature rating.*

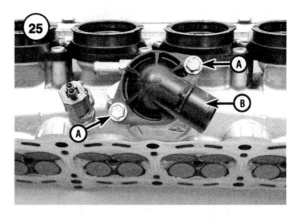

2. Gradually heat and gently stir the water until it reaches the valve opening temperature listed in **Table 1**. At this temperature the thermostat valve should open.

3. Continue heating the water until its temperature equals the valve lift temperature specified in **Table 1**.

4. Measure the valve lift. It should equal or exceed the specification in **Table 1**.

5. Replace the thermostat if it fails either portion of this test.

THERMOSTAT HOUSING FITTING

Removal/Installation

1. Support the motorcycle on a level surface.

2. Drain the cooling system (Chapter Three).

3. Remove the fuel tank, air filter housing and throttle bodies (Chapter Eight).

4. Release the hose clamp and disconnect the inlet hose (A, **Figure 21**) and the bypass hose (B) from the thermostat housing.

NOTE
The following steps are shown with the cylinder head removed from the engine for photo clarity.

5. Remove the thermostat housing cover bolts (A, **Figure 25**), and remove the cover (B) from the cylinder head.

6. Remove the thermostat (A, **Figure 22**).

7. Remove the thermostat housing fitting bolts (**Figure 26**), and pull the fitting from the cylinder block. Discard the O-ring.

8. Installation is the reverse of removal. Install a new O-ring, and tighten the bolts to 10 N•m (89 in.-lb.).

CYLINDER INLET CONNECTOR

Removal/Installation

1. Support the motorcycle on a level surface.

2. Drain the cooling system (Chapter Three).

3. Remove the radiator assembly as described in this chapter.

4. Remove the exhaust pipe assembly (Chapter Eight).

NOTE
The following steps are shown with the engine removed for photo clarity.

5. Release the hose clamp and disconnect the cylinder inlet hose (A, **Figure 27**) and the oil cooler inlet hose (B) from the connector.

6. Remove the cylinder inlet connector bolts, and remove the connector (C, **Figure 27**) from the cylinder head. Discard the O-ring.

7. Installation is the reverse of removal. Install a *new* O-ring, and tighten the bolts to 10 N•m (89 in.-lb.).

WATER PUMP

Removal/Installation

1. Support the motorcycle on a level surface.

2. Remove the front fairing left side panel and under panel (Chapter Fifteen).

3. Drain the coolant and engine oil (Chapter Three).

4. Place a drain pan beneath the water pump to catch residual coolant that will leak from the hoses.

NOTE
The following steps are shown with the engine removed for photo clarity.

5. Release the hose clamp the water pump outlet hose and disconnect the hose from the fitting (A, **Figure 28**).

6. Release the hose clamp the water pump inlet hose (B, **Figure 28**) and disconnect the hose from the fitting.

7. Remove the water pump mounting bolts (C, **Figure 28**), and pull the pump from the crankcase. Discard the water pump O-ring (A, **Figure 29**).

8. Inspect the water pump as described in this chapter.

9. Install a new O-ring (A, **Figure 29**) onto the water pump. Lubricate the O-ring with grease (Suzuki Super Grease A, or equivalent).

10. Align the slot in the water pump shaft (B, **Figure 29**) with the tab on the oil pump shaft (**Figure 30**), and then install the water pump into the crankcase. The water pump shaft must engage the oil pump shaft. Reposition the water pump shaft as necessary, and seat the water pump in the crankcase. Tighten the water pump mounting bolts (C, **Figure 28**) to 10 N•m (89 in.-lb.).

11. Install the inlet hose (B, **Figure 28**) and outlet hose (A) onto their respective pump fitting. Tighten the clamps securely.

12. Refill the cooling system (Chapter Three).

13. Refill the engine oil (Chapter Three).

14. Start the engine and check for leaks before install the fairing side panel.

15. Install the under panel and the front fairing left side panel (Chapter Fifteen).

Disassembly

Refer to **Figure 31**.

A bearing remover set (Suzuki part No. 09921-20240 or equivalent) is needed to remove and install the bearings and mechanical seal in the water pump. Do not attempt to remove the mechanical seal without this tool. The pump housing can be damaged. If the bearings or mechanical seal requires replacement and the special tool is unavailable, take the pump to a dealership for service.

1. Remove the housing screws (A, **Figure 32**), and separate the pump cover (B) from the housing.

2. Thoroughly clean the pump housing and cover in solvent to remove all coolant residues.

3. Inspect the water pump housing (A, **Figure 33**) and cover for wear or damage.

4. Turn the impeller (B, **Figure 33**), and check the bearing for excessive noise or roughness. If the bearing operation is rough, replace the pump.

5. Insert a combination wrench (A, **Figure 34**) into the water pump shaft slot to prevent the shaft from rotating.

6. Remove the impeller bolt (B, **Figure 34**) from the pump shaft.

7. Lift the lockwasher (A, **Figure 35**), gasket (B) and impeller (C) from the pump housing.

8. Remove the shaft (A, **Figure 36**) along with its washer (B) from the pump housing.

9. Inspect the water pump as described in this section.

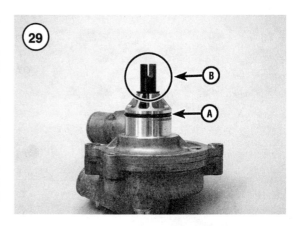

Assembly

1. Install the washer (B, **Figure 36**) onto the shaft.

2. Apply grease (Suzuki Super Grease A, or equivalent) to the pump shaft and install the shaft (A, **Figure 36**) into the housing. Push it in until it bottoms (**Figure 37**).

3. Install impeller (**Figure 38**) so its flats engage those on the shaft.

4. Install a *new* gasket (A, **Figure 39**) and lockwasher (B) onto the bolt (C). Make sure the metal side of the gasket (**Figure 40**) and the convex side of the lockwasher (B) face the bolt head.

5. Insert a combination wrench into the water pump shaft slot (A, **Figure 34**) to prevent the shaft from rotating.

6. Apply threadlocking compound (Suzuki Thread Lock 1342 or equivalent) to the bolt threads. Install the impeller bolt (C, **Figure 33**) and tighten to 8 N•m (71 in.-lb.).

7. Lubricate a new O-ring with coolant, and fit the O-ring into the groove in the pump cover.

8. Install the pump cover (B, **Figure 32**) onto the pump housing, and install the housing screws (A, **Figure 32**). Tighten the water pump housing screw to 5 N•m (44 in.-lb.).

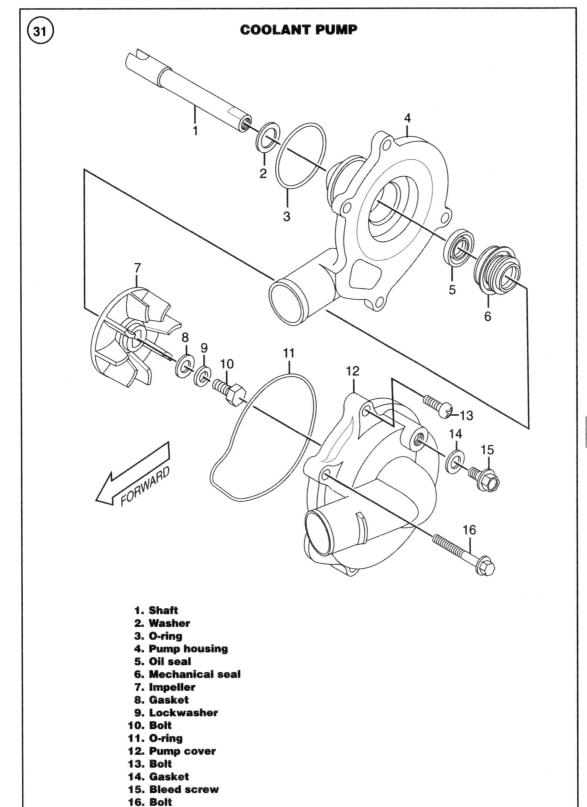

COOLANT PUMP

31

FORWARD

1. Shaft
2. Washer
3. O-ring
4. Pump housing
5. Oil seal
6. Mechanical seal
7. Impeller
8. Gasket
9. Lockwasher
10. Bolt
11. O-ring
12. Pump cover
13. Bolt
14. Gasket
15. Bleed screw
16. Bolt

10

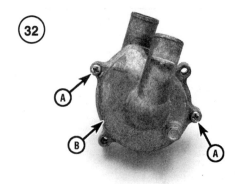

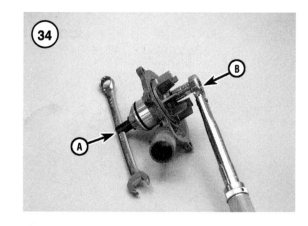

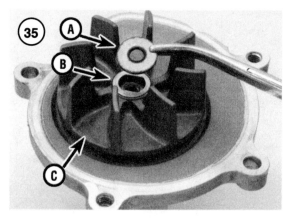

Inspection

1. Inspect the mechanical seal (A, **Figure 41**) and pump housing (B) for corrosion, damage or signs of leaking. Pay particular attention to the sealing face of the mechanical seal. If necessary, replace the mechanical seal as follows:

    a. Remove the mechanical seal with a bearing set remover or an equivalent.

> *NOTE*
> *Do not apply sealant to the new mechanical seal. Sealant has been pre-applied.*

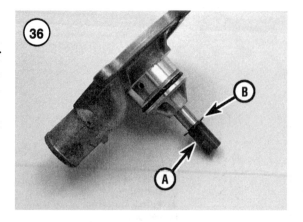

    b. Set the mechanical seal into place in the pump housing.

    c. Drive the seal into place with a driver or socket that matches the seal's outside diameter.

2. Inspect the water pump housing (B, **Figure 41**) for corrosion and damage. Remove any corrosion from the housing. Make sure the inlet fitting and opening (C, **Figure 41**) are clear.

3. Inspect the pump shaft (**Figure 42**) for scoring or other signs of damage.

4. Check the impeller blades (**Figure 43**) for corrosion or damage. If corrosion is minor, clean the

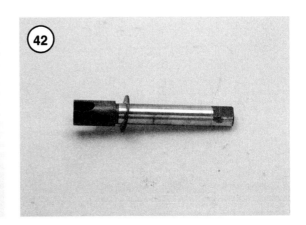

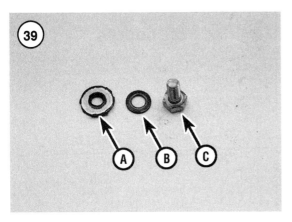

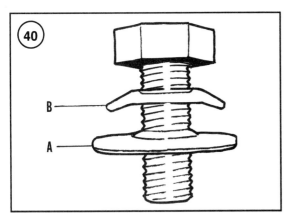

10

blades. Replace the impeller if corrosion is severe or if the blades are cracked or broken.

5. Inspect the impeller oil seal and rubber seal for signs of damage or leaking. If necessary, replace them as follows:

    a. Pry the impeller seal (**Figure 44**) and then the rubber seal from the impeller.

    b. Lubricate a *new* rubber seal with grease (Suzuki Super Grease A or equivalent) and install the seal.

    c. Position the new impeller seal with the marked side faces the rubber seal, and install the impeller seal.

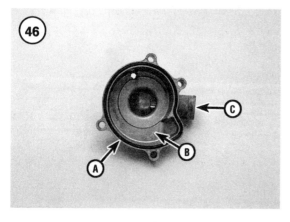

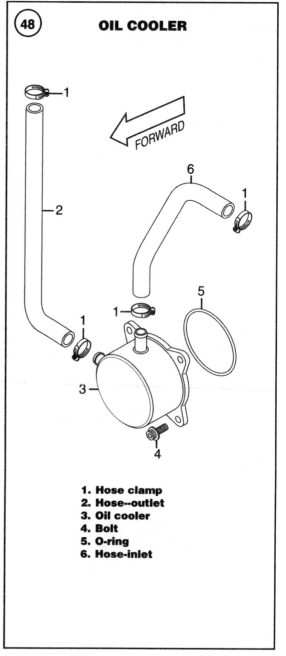

OIL COOLER

1. Hose clamp
2. Hose--outlet
3. Oil cooler
4. Bolt
5. O-ring
6. Hose-inlet

d. Drive the seal into place with a driver or socket that matches the impeller seal's outside diameter (**Figure 45**).

6. Inspect the pump cover oil seal (A, **Figure 46**) for damage or leaking. If necessary, replace them as follows:

    a. Pry the oil from the cover.

    b. Lubricate a *new* rubber seal with grease (Suzuki Super Grease A or equivalent) and install the seal.

    c. Drive the seal into place with a driver or socket that matches the oil seal's outside diameter.

7. Inspect the water pump cover (B, **Figure 46**) for corrosion and damage. Remove any corrosion from the cover. Make sure the outlet fitting (C, **Figure 46**) is clear.

8. Inspect the shaft journal in the housing (**Figure 47**) for scoring or other damage. Replace the water pump if the journal is damaged.

9. Replace any worn or damaged part.

OIL COOLER

Removal/Installation

Refer to **Figure 48**.

1. Support the motorcycle on a level surface.

2. Remove the front fairing right side panel and under panel (Chapter Fifteen).

3. Drain the coolant and engine oil (Chapter Three).

4. Place a drain pan beneath the oil cooler to catch residual coolant that will leak from the hoses.

5. Release the hose clamp the oil cooler inlet hose (A, **Figure 49**) and disconnect the hose from the fitting.

NOTE

Some of the following steps are shown with the engine removed from the frame for photo clarity.

6. Release the hose clamp the oil cooler outlet hose (**Figure 50**) and disconnect the hose from the fitting on the crankcase (B, **Figure 27**).

7. Remove the oil cooler mounting bolts (A, **Figure 51**), and pull the cooler (B) from the crankcase. Do not damage the EXUP control cables (B, **Figure 49**) during removal.

8. Discard the oil cooler O-ring (**Figure 52**).

9. Install a new O-ring (**Figure 52**) onto the groove in the oil cooler. Lubricate the O-ring with grease (Suzuki Super Grease A, or equivalent).

10. Install the oil cooler onto the crankcase. Make sure the O-ring is still in place.

11. Apply threadlocking compound (Suzuki Thread Lock 1342 or equivalent) to the bolt threads. Install the bolts (B, **Figure 51**) and tighten to 10 N•m (89 in.-lb.).

12. Install the inlet hose and outlet hose onto their respective fittings. Tighten the clamps securely.

13. Refill the cooling system (Chapter Three).

14. Refill the engine oil (Chapter Three).

15. Start the engine and check for leaks before install the fairing side panels.

16. Install the front fairing under panel and right side panel (Chapter Fifteen).

Table 1 COOLING SYSTEM SPECIFICATIONS

Item	Specification
Coolant type	Anti-freeze/coolant that is compatible with an aluminum radiator.
Mixing Ratio	50-50 with distilled water
Coolant capacity (system total)	
2006-2007 models	2.7 liters (2.9 US. qt. [2.4 Imp qt.])
2008-2009 models	2.65 liters (2.8 US qt. [2.3 Imp qt.])
Thermostat	
Valve opening temperature	Approx. 82° C (180° F)
Valve lift/temperature	Over 8.0 mm @ 95° C (over 0.31 in. @ 203° F)

Table 2 COOLING SYSTEM ELECTRICAL SPECIFICATIONS

Thermostat operating temperature	
Off-On	Approximately 105° C (221° F)
On-Off	Approximately 100° C (212° F)
Radiator fan load current (maximum)	5 amps

Table 3 COOLING SYSTEM TORQUE SPECIFICATIONS

Item	N•m	in.-lb.	ft.-lb.
Cylinder inlet connector bolt	10	89	–
Engine coolant temperature			
(ECT) sensor	18	–	13
Impeller bolt*	8	71	–
Oil cooler mounting bolt*	10	89	–
Radiator fan mounting bolts	8	71	–
Thermostat housing cover bolt	10	89	–
Water pump			
Air bleed bolt	13	115	–
Housing cover screw	5	44	–
Pump mounting bolt	10	89	–
* Use threadlock (Suzuki Threadlock 1342 or equivalent)			

CHAPTER ELEVEN

WHEELS, TIRES AND DRIVE CHAIN

This chapter describes repair and maintenance procedures for the front and rear wheels, tires and the drive chain.

Table 1 and **Table 2** are at the end of this chapter.

MOTORCYCLE STAND

Many procedures in this chapter require that the motorcycle be supported with a wheel off the ground. A motorcycle front end stand (**Figure 1**) or swing arm stand does this safely and effectively. Before purchasing or using a stand, check the manufacturer's instructions to make sure the stand will work on a particular motorcycle.

An adjustable centerstand can also be used to support the motorcycle with a wheel off the ground. Again, check the manufacturer's instructions and perform any necessary modifications before lifting the motorcycle. Some means to tie down one end of the motorcycle is also needed.

BRAKE ROTOR PROTECTION

Protect the rotor when servicing a wheel. Never set a wheel down on the brake rotor. It may be bent or scratched. When a wheel must be placed on its side, support the wheel on wooden blocks (**Figure 2**). Position the blocks along the outer circumference of the wheel so the rotor lies between the blocks not on them.

WHEEL INSPECTION

During inspection, compare all measurement to the specification in **Table 1**. Replace any part that is damaged, out of specification or worn to the service limit.

1. Remove the wheel (this chapter).
2. If necessary, support the wheel on wooden blocks (**Figure 2**).
3. Inspect the oil seal(s) (A, **Figure 3**) for excessive wear, hardness, cracks or other damage. If necessary, replace the seal(s) as described in the front- or rear-hub sections later in this chapter.
4. Inspect the bearings by performing the following.
   a. Pry the oil seal(s) from the hub (**Figure 4**) or rear coupling. Place a shop cloth under the screwdriver to protect the hub. Discard a removed oil seal.
   b. Remove any applicable collar (**Figure 5**) from, the oil seal.
   c. Turn each bearing inner race (B, **Figure 3**) by hand. Each bearing must turn smoothly with no trace of roughness, binding or excessive noise. Some axial play (side-to-side) is normal, but radial play (up and down) must be negligible. Refer to **Figure 6**.
   d. Check a sealed bearing's outer seal for buckling or other damage that would allow dirt to enter the bearing.

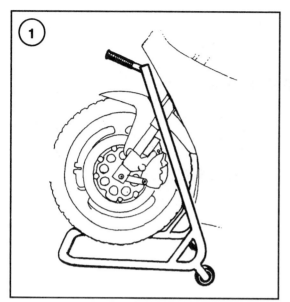

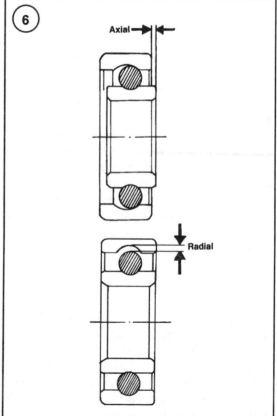

e. On a non-sealed bearing, check the balls for evidence of wear, pitting or excessive heat (bluish tint).

f. Manually try to move the bearing laterally within the hub or rear coupling. The bearing should fit tightly in the bore. Loose bearings allow the wheel to wobble. If a bearing is loose,

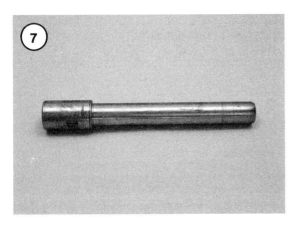

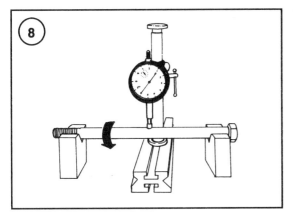

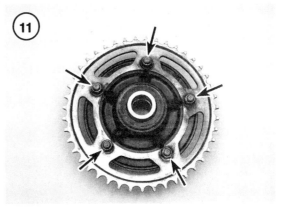

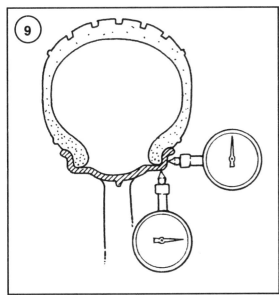

6. Check axle runout with a dial gauge and V-blocks (**Figure 8**). Replace an axle that exceeds its specified runout limit. Do not try to straighten a bent axle.

7. Install the wheel on a truing stand. Measure the radial (up and down) wheel runout and measure the axial (side to side) wheel runout. Use a dial indicator as shown in **Figure 9**.

8. If the wheel runout is out of specification, inspect the wheel bearings as described in this section.

    a. If the wheel bearings are okay, the wheel must be replaced.

    b. If either wheel bearing is worn, disassemble the hub and replace both bearings as a set.

9. Check the tightness of the brake disc bolts (**Figure 10**). If a bolt is loose, remove and reinstall the bolt. Apply threadlocking compound (Suzuki Thread Lock Super 1360 or equivalent) to the threads of the bolt. Tighten front disc brake bolts to 23 N•m (17 ft.-lb.); rear disc bolts to 35 N•m (26 ft.-lb.).

10. Inspect the brake discs and measure the brake disc deflection (Chapter Fourteen). If deflection is excessive, measure the wheel runout. If wheel runout is within specification, replace the brake disc as described in Chapter Fourteen.

11. Check the tightness of the rear sprocket nuts (**Figure 11**). If a nut is loose, tighten it to 60 N•m (44 ft.-lb.).

the bearing bore in the hub is probably worn or damaged.

    g. Replace questionable bearings. Ensure a perfect match by comparing the old bearing to the new one.

5. Use a piece of fine emery cloth to remove any corrosion from the axle (**Figure 7**).

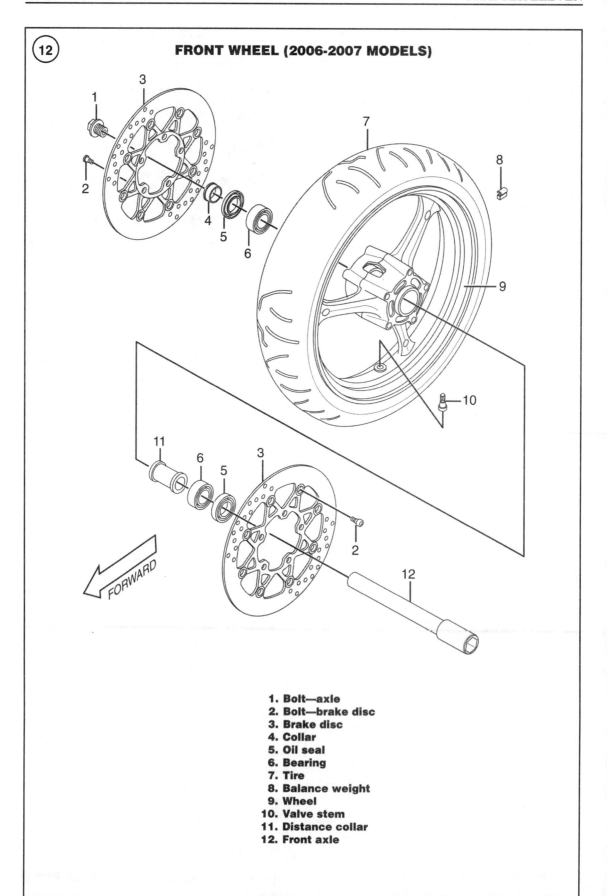

FRONT WHEEL (2006-2007 MODELS)

FORWARD

1. Bolt—axle
2. Bolt—brake disc
3. Brake disc
4. Collar
5. Oil seal
6. Bearing
7. Tire
8. Balance weight
9. Wheel
10. Valve stem
11. Distance collar
12. Front axle

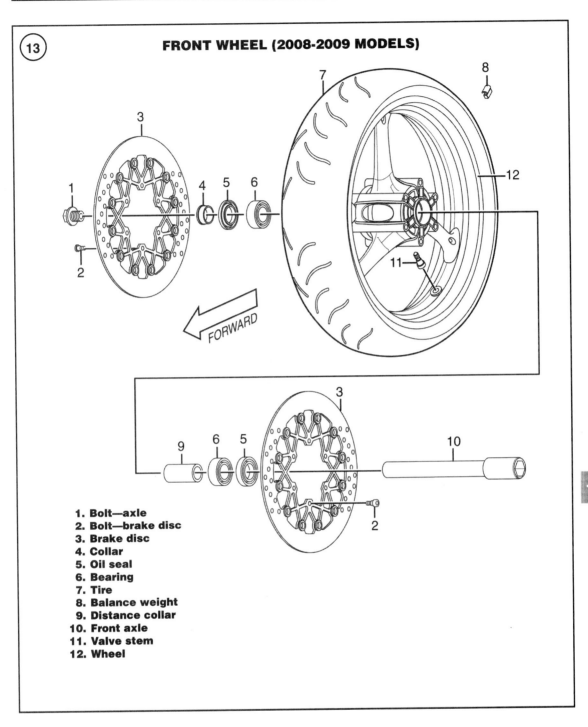

FRONT WHEEL (2008-2009 MODELS)

FORWARD

1. Bolt—axle
2. Bolt—brake disc
3. Brake disc
4. Collar
5. Oil seal
6. Bearing
7. Tire
8. Balance weight
9. Distance collar
10. Front axle
11. Valve stem
12. Wheel

12. Inspect the wheel rim for dents, bending or cracks. Check the rim and rim sealing surface for scratches that are deeper than 0.5 mm (0.01 in.). If any of these conditions are present, replace the wheel.

13. While the caliper(s) are off the disc(s) at this time, check the brake pads for wear (Chapter Fourteen).

14. Install the wheel as described in this chapter.

FRONT WHEEL

Removal

Refer to **Figure 12** or **Figure 13**.

1. Support the motorcycle on level ground.

2. Shift the transmission into gear to prevent the motorcycle from rolling in either direction.

3. Remove the under fairing panels (Chapter Fifteen).

4. Remove each front brake caliper (Chapter Fourteen). Suspend the calipers from the motorcycle. Do not let the caliper hang by the brake hose.

NOTE
Insert a piece of vinyl tubing or wood between the pads of each caliper once the caliper is removed. If the brake lever is inadvertently squeezed, the pistons will not be forced out of the cylinder. If this does happen, the caliper may have to be disassembled to reseat the pistons and the system will have to be bled. By using the wood, bleeding the brake is not necessary when installing the wheel.

NOTE
If a 24 mm Allen socket is unavailable, fashion a pivot shaft holder (Figure 14) from a bolt and two nuts that measure 24 mm across opposite flats.

5. On the right fork leg, loosen both clamp bolts (A, **Figure 15**), and remove the axle bolt (B). Do not remove the axle at this time.
6. On the left fork leg, loosen the clamp bolts (A, **Figure 16**).

CAUTION
If using a jack, place a piece of wood on the jack pad to protect the oil pan.

7. Place a suitable jack, or wooden blocks, under the oil pan and frame. Refer to **Figure 17** and **Figure 18**. Support the motorcycle securely with the front wheel off the ground.
8. Pull the axle (B, **Figure 16**) from the wheel and fork legs.
9. Lower the wheel, and roll it from between the fork legs. Watch for the collar on the right side of the hub. No collar is used on the left side.

CAUTION
Do not set the wheel down on the brake disc. It may get scratched or warped. Set the tire sidewalls on two wood blocks (Figure 2).

10. Inspect the wheel as described in this chapter.

Installation

1. Make sure the bearing surfaces of each fork leg (**Figure 19**), and the axle (**Figure 7**) are free from burrs and nicks.

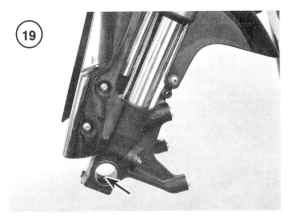

2. Install the collar (**Figure 20**) in right side of the hub.

3 Correctly position the wheel so its directional arrow points in the direction of forward wheel rotation.

4. Apply a light coat of grease to the front axle.

5. Position the wheel between the fork legs, lift the wheel and insert the front axle (B, **Figure 16**) through the left fork leg, and the wheel hub. Push the axle in until it bottoms.

6. On the right side, install the front axle bolt (A, **Figure 5**) and tighten securely.

7. Hold the axle (B, **Figure 16**) with a 24 mm Allen wrench, and tighten the front axle bolt (A, **Figure 15**) to 100 N•m (74 ft.-lb.).

8. Tighten the clamp bolts on the right fork leg (A, **Figure 15**) to 23 N•m (17 ft.-lb.).

9. Remove the jack or wooden block(s) from under the oil pan.

10. Apply the front brake, push down hard on the handlebars and pump the forks four or five times to seat the front axle.

11. Tighten the clamp bolts on the left fork leg (A, **Figure 16**) to 23 N•m (17 ft.-lb.).

12. Install each brake calipers (Chapter Fourteen).

13. Shift the transmission into neutral.

14. Roll the motorcycle back and forth the several times. Apply the front brake as many times as necessary to make sure all brake pads seat against the brake disc correctly.

FRONT HUB

Disassembly

Refer to **Figure 12** or **Figure 13**.

1. Remove the front wheel as described in this chapter.

2. Remove the right side collar (**Figure 5**) from the oil seal.

3. Pry out each oil seal (**Figure 4**) with a large screwdriver. Place a shop cloth under the screwdriver to protect the hub. Discard all removed oil seals. They cannot be reinstalled.

4. If necessary, remove the brake disc bolts (**Figure 10**) and remove the disc.

5. Before proceeding further, inspect the wheel bearings (B, **Figure 3**) as described in *Wheel Inspection* in this chapter. If they must be replaced, perform Step 5.

6A. Remove the bearings with an expandable collet bearing removal tool (**Figure 21**).

    a. Select the correct size remover head tool and insert it into the bearing.

    b. Turn the wheel over and insert the remover shaft into the back of the remover head. Tap the shaft and force it into the slit in the remover head (**Figure 22**). This forces the head against the bearing inner race.

   c. Tap on the end of the shaft with a hammer and drive the bearing out of the hub (**Figure 23**). Remove the bearing and the distance collar.

   d. Repeat for the bearing on the other side.

6B. If bearing removal tools are unavailable, perform the following:

   a. To remove the right and left bearings and distance collar, insert a soft aluminum or brass drift into one side of the hub (**Figure 24**).

   b. Push the distance collar to one side and place the drift on the inner race of the lower bearing.

   c. Tap the bearing out of the hub with a hammer, working around the perimeter of the inner race. Remove the bearing and distance collar.

   d. Repeat for the bearing on the other side.

7. Clean the inside and the outside of the hub with solvent. Dry with compressed air.

Assembly

> *CAUTION*
> *Always install new bearings. The old bearings are damaged during removal and must not be reused. Replace bearings as a set. If any one bearing in the wheel is worn, replace all the bearings in that wheel. On a front wheel, replace both wheel bearings. On a rear wheel replace both wheel bearings as well as the rear coupling bearing.*

1. On non-sealed bearings, pack the bearings with grease (Suzuki Super Grease A or equivalent). To pack the bearings, spread some grease in the palm of your hand and scrape the open side of the bearing across your palm until the bearing is completely packed full of grease. Spin the bearing a few times to determine if there are any open areas. Repack as necessary.

2. Blow any debris out of the hub.

3. Apply a light coat of grease to the bearing seating areas of the hub.

> *CAUTION*
> *Install non-sealed bearings with the single sealed side facing outward. Tap the bearings squarely into place and tap on the outer race only. Do not tap on the inner race or the bearing might be damaged. Be sure that the bearings are completely seated.*

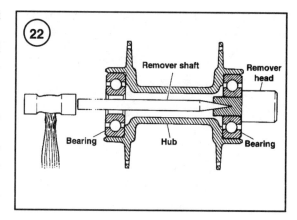

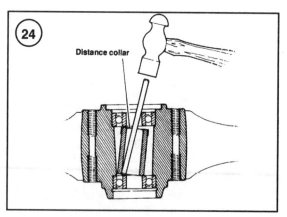

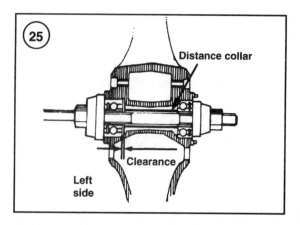

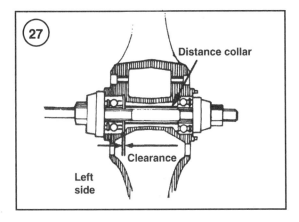

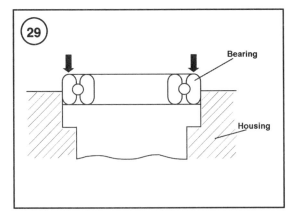

NOTE
When installing the bearings in the front hub, install the right bearing first and then the left bearing.

4A. If using the installer set (Suzuki part No. 09924-84510) to install the front wheel bearings, perform the following:

    a. Set the right bearing into the hub with the sealed side facing out, and install the bearing installer as shown in **Figure 25**.

    b. Tighten the bearing installer (**Figure 26**) and pull the left bearing into the hub until it is completely seated. Remove the bearing installer.

    c. Turn the wheel over (right side up) on the workbench and install the distance collar.

    d. Set the left bearing into the hub with the sealed side facing out, and install the bearing installer as shown in **Figure 27**.

    e. Tighten the bearing installer and pull the right bearing into the hub until there is a slight *clearance between the inner race and the distance collar.*

    f. Remove the bearing installer.

4B. If the special tools are not available, perform the following:

    a. Set the left bearing into place in the hub so its sealed side faces out.

    b. Using a bearing driver or socket (A, **Figure 28**) that matches the diameter of the outer bearing race, tap the first bearing squarely into place in the hub (B). Tap on the outer race only (**Figure 29**). Do not tap on the inner race or the bearing might be damaged. Make sure that the bearing is completely seated.

    c. Turn the wheel over on the workbench and install the distance collar.

    d. Use the same tool set-up and drive the right bearing into the hub until there is a *slight c*learance between the inner race and the distance collar. The races and distance collar must not be pressed together.

5. If the brake disc was removed, perform the following:

    a. Apply a small amount threadlocking compound (Suzuki Thread Lock Super 1360 or equivalent) to the brake disc bolt threads prior to installation.

    b. Install the brake disc. Tighten the brake disc bolts (**Figure 10**) to 23 N•m (17 ft.-lb.).

6. Pack the lips of the new oil seals with grease (Suzuki Super Grease A or equivalent) and install the oil seals. Drive each oil seal into the hub with a seal driver or socket (**Figure 30**) that matches the outside diameter of the seal.

7. Install the right side collar (**Figure 5**) onto the oil seal.

8. Install the front wheel as described in this chapter.

REAR WHEEL

Removal

Refer to **Figure 31**.

1. Support the motorcycle on a level surface. Block the front wheel to prevent the motorcycle from rolling in either direction.

2. Remove the cotter pin (**Figure 32**) from the rear axle nut (models so equipped). Discard the cotter pin. A new one must be installed during installation.

3. Have an assistant apply the rear brake, and then loosen the axle nut (**Figure 33**).

CAUTION
If using a jack, place a piece of wood on the jack pad to protect the oil pan.

4. Place a suitable jack, or wooden blocks, under the oil pan and frame. Refer to **Figure 17** and **Figure 18**. Support the motorcycle securely with the rear wheel off the ground.

5. Remove the rear caliper (Chapter Fourteen).

NOTE
Insert a piece of vinyl tubing, cardboard or wood into the caliper in place of the brake disc. That way if the brake pedal is inadvertently pressed, the pistons will not be forced out of the cylinders. If this does happen, the caliper may have to be disassembled to reseat the pistons and the system will have to be bled. By using the wood, bleeding the brake is not necessary when installing the wheel.

6. Loosen the chain adjuster locknut (A, **Figure 34**), then loosen the adjuster (B) on each side of the swing arm to allow maximum slack in the drive chain.

7. Remove the rear axle nut (**Figure 33**) and the washer (models so equipped).

8. Pull the rear axle (C, **Figure 34**) from the right side of the motorcycle, and lower the wheel. The adjuster block (D, **Figure 34**) on each side comes off when the rear axle is withdrawn. The adjuster blocks are not interchangeable. Mark each block with an R (right) or L (left) so it will be reinstalled on the correct side.

9. Push the wheel forward, and remove the drive chain from the rear sprocket.

10. Hold onto the caliper bracket and pull the wheel rearward. Remove the wheel from the swing arm.

11. Remove the caliper bracket (**Figure 35**) from the swing arm. Note that the bracket indexing block sits within the slot in the swing arm.

12. Remove the collar from each side of the wheel.

CAUTION
Do not set the wheel down on the brake disk. It may get scratched or warped. Set the sidewalls on two wooden blocks (Figure 2).

13. Inspect the wheel as described in this chapter.

Installation

1. Make sure all axle-contact surfaces on the swing arm and collars are free of dirt and small burrs.

2. Apply a light coat of grease (Suzuki Super Grease A or equivalent) to the axle (**Figure 36**), bearings, collars and oil seals.

3. Make sure the collars (A and B, **Figure 37**) are installed on each side of the rear hub.

4. Make sure the rear brake caliper rubber boot (**Figure 38**) is in place on the caliper bracket.

5. Install the caliper bracket (**Figure 35**) onto the swing arm. Make sure the indexing block (**Figure 39**) on the bracket engages the slot in the swing arm.

6. Hold the caliper bracket (A, **Figure 40**) in place.

7. Position the wheel into place and roll it forward (B, **Figure 40**). Install the drive chain onto the rear sprocket.

8. Install the chain adjuster onto the right side of the rear axle.

9. Raise the rear wheel up and into alignment with the swing arm. From the right side of the motorcycle insert the rear axle through swing arm, the caliper bracket, the rear wheel and out through the left side of the swing arm. Push the axle all the way to the left until it bottoms in the chain adjuster (D, **Figure 34**)

10. Install the chain adjuster onto the rear axle.

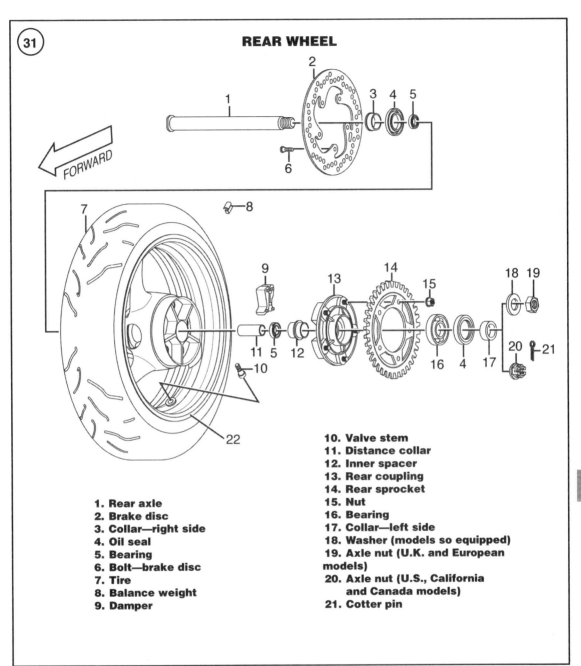

REAR WHEEL

FORWARD

1. Rear axle
2. Brake disc
3. Collar—right side
4. Oil seal
5. Bearing
6. Bolt—brake disc
7. Tire
8. Balance weight
9. Damper
10. Valve stem
11. Distance collar
12. Inner spacer
13. Rear coupling
14. Rear sprocket
15. Nut
16. Bearing
17. Collar—left side
18. Washer (models so equipped)
19. Axle nut (U.K. and European models)
20. Axle nut (U.S., California and Canada models)
21. Cotter pin

11

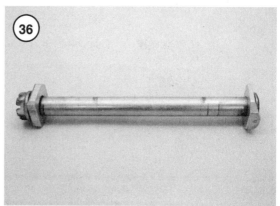

11. Install the washer (models so equipped), and the rear axle nut (**Figure 33**). Tighten the rear axle nut finger-tighten at this time.

12. Adjust the drive chain as described in Chapter Three.

13. Tighten the rear axle nut (**Figure 33**) to100 N•m (74 ft.-lb.).

14. Tighten each chain adjuster locknut (B, **Figure 34**) securely.

15. On models so equipped, install a new *cotter pin* (**Figure 41**) onto the rear axle nut, and bend both ends over completely.

16. Install the rear caliper (Chapter Fourteen).

17. Remove the jack or wooden block(s) from under the oil pan. Remove the blocks from the front wheel.

18. Roll the motorcycle back and forth the several times. Apply the rear brake as many times as necessary to make sure the brake pads are against the brake disc correctly.

**REAR COUPLING AND
REAR SPROCKET**

Removal/Installation

Refer to **Figure 31**.

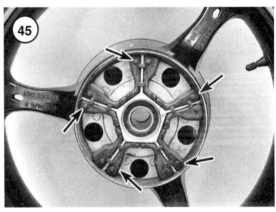

1. Remove the rear wheel as described in this chapter.

2. If the rear sprocket is going to be removed, loosen the rear sprocket nuts (**Figure 42**) at this time.

3. Pull straight up and remove the rear coupling assembly from the rear hub. If the rear coupling assembly is difficult to remove from the hub, tap on the backside of the sprocket (from the opposite side of the wheel through the wheel spokes) with the wooden handle of a hammer.

4. If still in place, remove the collar (A, **Figure 43**) from the left side.

5. If necessary, remove the rear sprocket nuts (B, **Figure 43**) and separate the rear sprocket from the rear coupling.

6. Remove the inner spacer (**Figure 44**) from the rear coupling.

7. Remove the dampers (**Figure 45**) from the rear hub.

8. Install by reversing these removal steps while noting the following:

    a. Install each damper so locks into place (A, **Figure 46**) in the hub.

    b. Align the rear coupling bosses (**Figure 47**) with the cutouts in the rubber dampers (B, **Figure 46**) and press the rear coupling onto the hub.

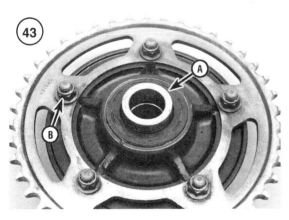

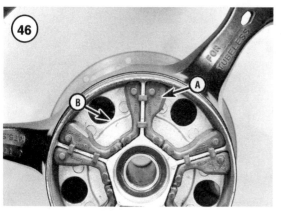

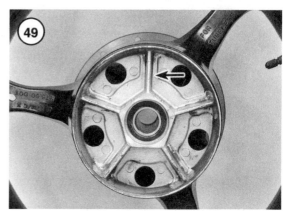

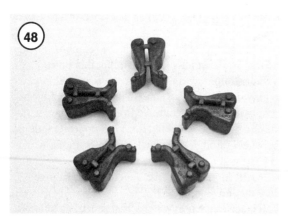

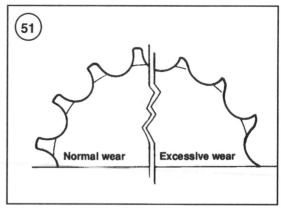

c. If removed, install the rear sprocket, and tighten the rear sprocket nuts (B, **Figure 43**) to 60 N•m (44 ft.-lb.) after the assembly has been reinstalled in the rear wheel. Recheck the tightness of the sprocket nuts after a few rides.

Inspection

1. Inspect the rubber dampers (**Figure 48**) for signs of damage or deterioration. If damaged, replace all the dampers as a set.

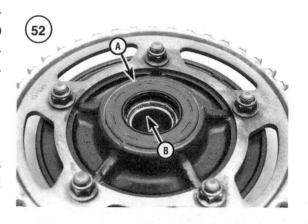

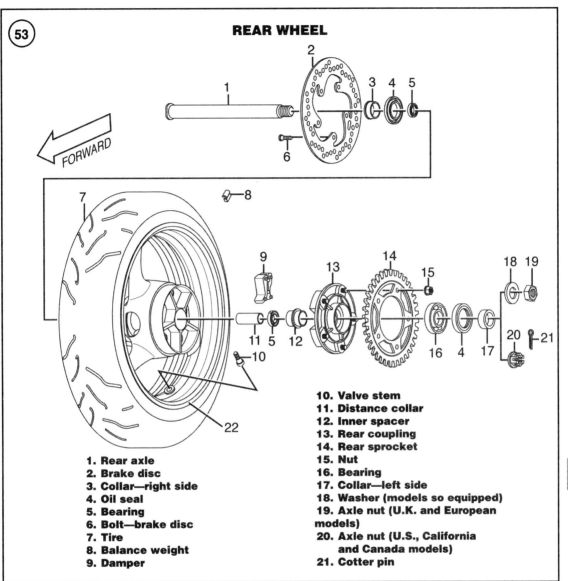

REAR WHEEL

FORWARD

1. Rear axle
2. Brake disc
3. Collar—right side
4. Oil seal
5. Bearing
6. Bolt—brake disc
7. Tire
8. Balance weight
9. Damper
10. Valve stem
11. Distance collar
12. Inner spacer
13. Rear coupling
14. Rear sprocket
15. Nut
16. Bearing
17. Collar—left side
18. Washer (models so equipped)
19. Axle nut (U.K. and European models)
20. Axle nut (U.S., California and Canada models)
21. Cotter pin

11

2. Inspect the raised webs (**Figure 49**) in the rear hub. Check for cracks or wear. If any damage is visible, replace the rear wheel.

3. Inspect the rear coupling assembly for cracks or damage, replace if necessary.

4. Inspect the rear sprocket teeth (**Figure 50**). If the teeth are worn (**Figure 51**), replace the rear sprocket as described in this chapter.

CAUTION
If the rear sprocket requires replacement, also replace the engine sprocket and the drive chain. Never install a new drive chain over worn sprockets or a worn drive chain over new sprockets. The old part will wear out the new part prematurely.

5. If the rear sprocket requires replacement, also inspect the drive chain (Chapter Three) and engine sprocket (Chapter Seven). They also may be worn and need replacing.

6. Inspect the oil seal (A, **Figure 52**) for excessive wear, hardness, cracks or other damage. If necessary, replace the seal as described in the front- or rear-hub sections in this chapter.

7. Inspect the bearings (B, **Figure 52**) as described in this chapter. Ensure a perfect match by comparing the old bearing to the new one.

REAR HUB

Refer to **Figure 53**.

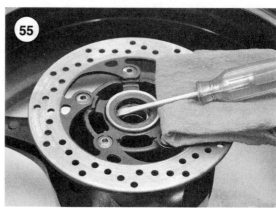

Disassembly

1. Remove the rear wheel as described in this chapter.

2. If still in place, remove the collar (A, **Figure 37**) from the brake disc side of the hub.

3. Remove the rear coupling from the hub as described in this chapter.

4. Pry out the oil seal (A, **Figure 54**) from the brake disc side of the hub. Place a shop cloth under the screwdriver (**Figure 55**) to protect the hub. Discard all removed oil seals. They cannot be reinstalled.

5. If necessary, remove the brake disc bolts (B, **Figure 54**) and remove the disc.

6. Before proceeding further, inspect the wheel bearings as described under *Wheel Inspection* in this chapter. If they must be replaced, remove the bearings from the rear hub and rear coupling by performing Step 6A or 6B in *Front Hub Disassembly* in this chapter.

7. Clean the inside and the outside of the hub with solvent. Dry with compressed air.

Assembly

> *CAUTION*
> *Always reinstall new bearings. The bearings are damaged during removal and must not be reused. If any one bearing in a wheel is worn, replace all the bearings in that wheel. On a front wheel, replace both wheel bearings. On a rear wheel, replace both wheel bearings as well as the rear coupling bearing.*

1. Perform Steps 1-3 of *Front Hub Assembly* in this chapter by performing Step 2A or 2B.

2A. If using a bearing/steering race installer (Suzuki part No. 09941-34513) to install the rear wheel bearings, perform the following:

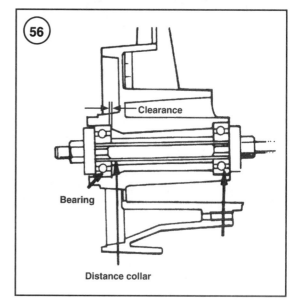

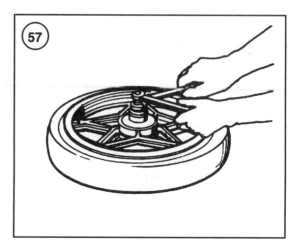

a. Set the right bearing into the hub with its sealed side facing out, and install the bearing installer as shown in **Figure 56**.

b. Tighten the bearing installer (**Figure 57**) and pull the right bearing into the hub until it is completely seated. Remove the bearing installer.

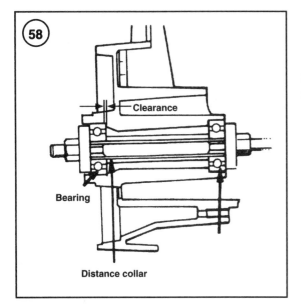

c. Turn the wheel over on the workbench and install the distance collar.

d. Set the left bearing into the hub with the sealed side facing out, and install the bearing installer as shown in **Figure 58**.

e. Tighten the bearing installer and pull the left bearing into the hub until there is a *slight* clear-

ance between the inner race and the distance collar. Do not press the parts completely together.

f. Remove the bearing installer.

2B. If special tools are not used, perform the following:

a. Set the right bearing onto the hub with its sealed side facing out.

b. Use a bearing driver or socket (**Figure 59**) that matches the diameter of the outer bearing race, tap the bearing squarely into place in the hub. Tap on the outer race only. Do not tap on the inner race or the bearing might be damaged. Be sure that the bearing is completely seated.

c. Turn the wheel over on the workbench and install the distance collar.

d. Use the same tool set-up and drive the left bearing into the hub until there is a *slight* clearance between the inner race and the distance collar.

3. Install a new bearing into the rear coupling. Use the bearing installer as described in Step 2A or repeat Step 2B.

4. If the brake disc was removed, perform the following:

a. Apply threadlocking compound (Suzuki Thread Lock Super 1360 or equivalent) to the brake disc bolt threads prior to installation.

b. Install the brake disc. Tighten the brake disc bolts (B, **Figure 54**) to 35 N•m (26 ft.-lb.).

5. Pack the lips of a new oil seal with grease (Suzuki Super Grease A or equivalent). Drive the oil seal into the rear coupling with a seal driver or socket (**Figure 60**) that matches the outside diameter of the seal. Install the collar (A, **Figure 37**) into the oil seal.

6. Install the rear coupling into the hub as described in this chapter.

WHEEL BALANCE

Before balancing the wheel, make sure that the wheel bearings are in good condition and properly lubricated. Also check the brakes for drag. The wheel must rotate freely. When balancing the wheels do so with the brake disc(s) and the rear coupling attached. These components rotate with the wheel and they affect the balance.

1. Remove the front or rear wheel as described in this chapter.

2. Mount the wheel on an inspection stand (**Figure 61**) so the wheel can rotate freely.

3. Give the wheel a spin and let it coast to a stop. Mark the tire at the lowest point with chalk or light colored crayon.

4. Spin the wheel several more times. If the wheel keeps coming to rest at the same point, it is out of balance.

5. Attach a test weight to the upper (or light) side of the wheel.

6. Experiment with different weights until the wheel, when spun, comes to rest at a different position each time.

> *NOTE*
> *Once the balance weight has been determined, divide that weight in half so two balance weights can be installed onto the wheel, one on each side of the rim. This distributes the weight evenly across the wheel. The difference between these two weights must be less than 10 grams (0.0353 oz.).*

7. Remove the test weights, thoroughly clean the rim surface, and install the correct size weight onto each side of the rim. Make sure they are secured in place so they do not fly off when riding.

TIRES

> *WARNING*
> *The original equipped wheels are designed for use with tubeless tires only. Do not install a tube into a tubeless tires. Excessive heat may build up in the tire can cause the tube to burst.*

> *CAUTION*
> *These wheels can easily be damaged during tire removal. Work carefully to avoid damage to the tire beads, inner liner of the tire or the wheel rim sealing surfaces. Insert rim protectors between the tire iron and the rim to protect the rim.*

> *CAUTION*
> *It is easier to replace tires when the wheel is mounted on a raised platform. A metal drum with the edge covered by a length of garden or heater hose, split lengthwise, works well. Whatever method is used, support the brake disc to prevent damage.*

Tire performance is greatly affected by tire pressure. Inspect the pressure frequently. Refer to **Table 1** for original equipment tire specifications. If using another tire brand, follow the manufacturer's recommendations.

Follow the break-in recommendations for new tires. Do not subject the tires to hard cornering or hard braking for the first 160 km (100 miles).

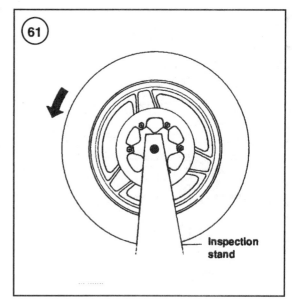

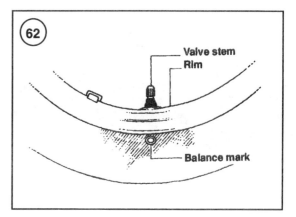

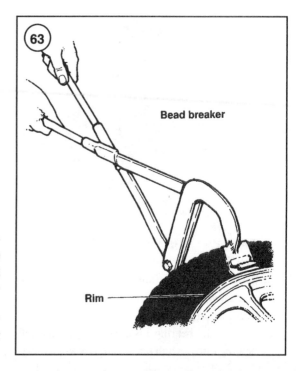

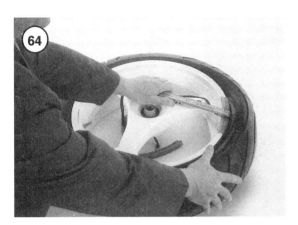

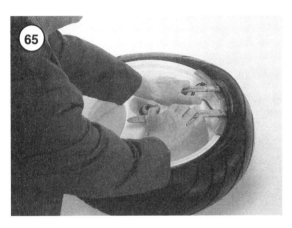

Changing

Due to the size of the tire and tighten bead/rim seal, changing tires can be difficult. Incorrect installation can damage both the tire and/or the wheel. It is recommended the tires be changed by a dealership with tire equipment designed for alloy wheels.

Refer to the following procedures as a guideline.

Removal

1. If reusing the tire, mark the valve stem location on the tire (**Figure 62**) so it can be installed in the same location for easier balancing.
2. Remove the valve core to deflate the tire.
3. Use a bead breaker (**Figure 63**) and break the bead all the way around the tire. Do not try to force the bead with the tire irons. Make sure both beads are clear of the rim beads.
4. Lubricate both beads with soapy water on the side to be installed first.
5. Use rim protectors, insert a tire iron under the top bead (**Figure 64**). Force the bead on the opposite side of the tire into the center of the rim, and pry the bead over the rim with the tire iron.
6. Insert a second tire iron next to the first iron to hold the bead outside the rim. Then work around the

tire with the first tire iron, prying the bead over the rim (**Figure 65**). Work slowly, and take small bites with the tire irons. Taking large bites or using excessive force can damage the tire bead or rim.
7. If the tire is tight and difficult to pry over the rim use a third tire iron and a rim protector. Use one hand on the rim to hold the first two tire irons, and then use the other hand to operate the third tire iron when prying the tire over the rim.
8. Stand the tire upright. Insert a tire iron between the second bead and the side of the rim that the first bead was pried over (**Figure 66**). Force the bead on the opposite side from the tool into the center of the rim. Pry the second bead off the rim working around the wheel with two rim protectors and tire irons.
9. Remove the valve stem and discard it. Remove all rubber residue from the valve stem hole and inspect the hole for cracks or other damage.
10. Remove the old balance weights from the rim.

Inspection

WARNING
Carefully consider whether a tire should be replaced. If there is any doubt about the quality of the existing tire, replace it. Do not take a chance on a tire failure at any speed. If there is any doubt as to wheel/tire condition, take them to a dealership for a thorough inspection.

1. Carefully clean the rim bead with a brush. Do not use excessive force or damage to the rim sealing surface will occur. Inspect the sealing surface for cracks, corrosion or other damage.
2. If any one of the following are observed; replace the tire:
   a. A large puncture or split in the tread area.
   b. A bulge, puncture or split on the side wall.
   c. Any type of ply separation.

d. Tread separation or excessive abnormal wear pattern.

e. Tread depth of less than the minimum in **Table 1** on original equipment tires. Aftermarket tires tread depth minimum may vary.

f. Damage to either sealing bead.

g. The cord is cut in any place.

h. Flat spots in the tread from skidding.

i. Any abnormality in the inner liner.

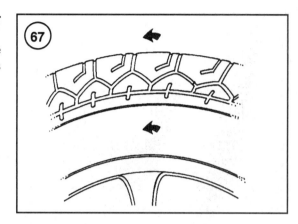

Installation

> *WARNING*
> *After installing new tires, follow the tire manufacturer's instructions for break-in.*

1. Install a *new* air valve.

2A. If installing the original tire, carefully inspect it as described in this section.

2B. If installing a new tire, remove all stickers from the tire tread.

3. Lubricate both beads of the tire with soapy water.

4. Make sure the correct tire, either front or rear, is installed on the correct wheel and that the direction arrow on the tire faces in the same direction as the wheel direction arrow (**Figure 67**).

5. If remounting the old tire, align the mark made during removal to denote the location of the valve stem. If installing new tire, align the balance mark on the bead (indicating the lightest point of the tire) with the valve stem. Refer to **Figure 62**. Place the backside of the tire onto the center of the rim. The lower bead should go into center of the rim and the upper bead outside. Use both hands to push the backside of the tire into the rim (**Figure 68**) as far as possible. Use tire irons when it becomes difficult to install the tire by hand.

6. Press the upper bead into the rim opposite the valve stem. Pry the bead into the rim on both sides of the initial point with the tire tool, working around the rim to the valve stem (**Figure 69**). If the tire wants to pull up on one side, either use another tire iron or your knee to hold the tire in place. The last few inches are usually the most difficult to install. If possible, continue to push the tire into the rim by hand. Relubricate the bead if necessary. If the tire bead wants to pull out from under the rim use both knees to hold the tire in place. If necessary, use a tire iron for the last few inches (**Figure 70**).

7. Check the bead on both side of the tire for an even fit around the rim. Make sure the balance mark aligns with the valve stem.

8. Lubricate both sides of the tire with soapy water.

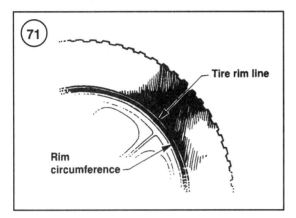

Tire rim line

Rim circumference

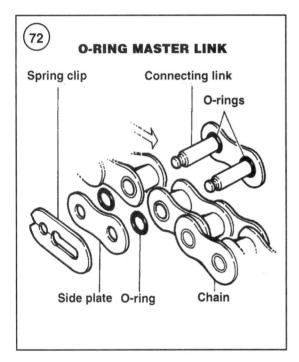

O-RING MASTER LINK

Spring clip   Connecting link

O-rings

Side plate O-ring   Chain

WARNING
In the next step, never exceed 380 kPa (56 psi) inflation pressure as the tire could burst causing injury. Never stand directly over a tire while inflating it.

9. Inflate the tire until the beads swat in to place. A loud pop should be heard as each bead seats against the inside of the rim.

10. After inflating the tire, check to see that the beads are fully seated and that the rim lines are the same distance from the rim all the way around the tire (**Figure 71**). If the beads do not seat, deflate the tire and relubricate the rim and beads with soapy water and reinflate the tire.

11. Inflate the tire to the specified pressure as listed in **Table 1**. Screw on the valve stem cap.

12. Balance the wheel as described in this chapter.

Repairs

Only use the tire plugs for an emergency repair. Refer to the manufacturer's instructions, and note the motorcycle weight and speed restrictions. After performing an emergency tire repair with a plug, consider the repair temporary and replace the tire at the earliest opportunity.

Refer all tire repairs to a dealership.

DRIVE CHAIN

Removal/Installation

All models are originally equipped with an O-ring chain that uses a staked master link (**Figure 72**). On these models, the chain can be replaced with the swing arm mounted on the motorcycle.

Refer to **Table 1** for drive chain specifications. Refer to *Drive Chain* in Chapter Three for routine drive chain inspection and lubrication procedures.

The drive chain tool (Suzuki part No. 09922-22711 or equivalent), is needed to replace the original equipment chain.

The following procedure describes the removal and installation of a drive chain with a typical chain tool. Install and replace a drive chain with the tool recommended by the chain's manufacturer. Use the following steps to supplement the instructions provided with that chain tool.

1. Support the motorcycle on a level surface.

2. Block the front wheel so the motorcycle will not roll in either direction while the rear wheel is off ground.

3. Remove the engine sprocket cover (Chapter Seven).

4. Remove the cotter pin (**Figure 73**) from the rear axle nut, on models so equipped. Discard the cotter pin. A new one must be installed during assembly.

5. Have an assistant apply the rear brake, and loosen the axle nut (**Figure 74**).

CAUTION
If using a jack, place a piece of wood
on the jack pad to protect the oil pan.

6. Place a suitable jack, or wooden blocks, under the oil pan and frame. Refer to **Figure 75** and **Figure 76**. Support the motorcycle securely with the rear wheel off the ground.

7. Loosen the chain adjuster locknut (A, **Figure 77**), then loosen the adjuster (B) on each side of the swing arm to allow maximum slack in the drive chain.

8. Remove the rear axle nut (**Figure 74**) and the washer (models so equipped).

9. Assemble the chain tool, following the manufacturer's instructions.

10. Rotate the wheel and located crimped pins (**Figure 78**). Break the chain at this link.

11. Install the chain tool across the link (**Figure 79**) to be removed. Operate the tool and push the connecting link out of the side plate to break the chain. Remove the side plate, connecting link and O-rings.

WARNING
Never reuse the connecting link, side plate and O-rings. They could break and cause the chain to separate. Reusing a master link may cause the chain to come apart and lock the rear wheel.

12. Remove the drive chain.

13. If installing a new drive chain, count the links of the new chain, and if necessary, cut the chain to length as described in this section. Refer to **Table 1** for the original equipment chain sizes and link length.

NOTE
Always install the drive chain through the swing arm before connecting and staking the master link.

14. Install the drive chain through the swing arm and around the engine sprocket with both link ends located at the top of the rear sprocket.

15. Refer to **Figure 72** and assembly the new connecting link by performing the following:

　a. Install a *new* O-ring onto each connecting link pin. Apply the lubricant supplied with the new master link kit.

　b. Insert the connecting link through the inside of the chain and connect both chain ends together.

　c. Lubricate the remaining two *new* O-rings with additional lubricant, and install them onto the connecting link pins.

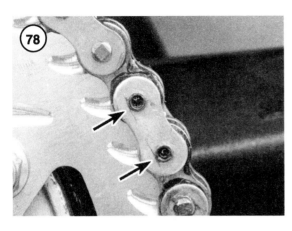

d. Install the side plate (**Figure 80**) with its identi-fication mark facing out (away from the chain) and crimp it into place with needlenose pliers.

e. Use the appropriate size plate holder (**Figure 79**) to press the plate onto the pins until the link width equals the specification in **Table 1**. Link width is the distance between the outside edges of the two chain plates (A, **Figure 81**).

16. Install the flair rivet pin into the chain tool fol-lowing the manufacturer's instructions. Assemble the chain tool onto the connecting link and carefully stake each pin in the connecting link (**Figure 82**) un-til the outside diameter of each pin (B, **Figure 81**) equals the specification in **Table 1**.

17. Remove the chain tool and inspect the link (**Figure 78**) for any cracks or other damage (**Figure 83**). Check the staked area for cracks. Then make sure the connecting link O-rings were not crushed. If there are any cracks on the staked link surfaces or other damage, remove the link and install a new one.

18. If there are no cracks, pivot the chain ends where they hook onto the connecting link. Each chain end must pivot freely. Compare by pivoting other links of the chain. If one or both drive chain ends cannot pivot on the connecting link, the chain is too tight. Remove and install a *new* connecting link assembly.

> *WARNING*
> *An incorrectly installed connect-ing link may cause the chain to come apart and lock the rear wheel, causing an accident. If a proper chain tool is not available, take the motorcycle to a dealership. Do not ride the motorcycle unless absolutely certain the connect-ing link is installed correctly.*

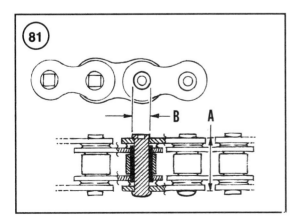

19. Rotate the rear wheel and chain to make sure the chain is traveling over both sprockets without any binding.

20. Reinstall the chain guard onto the swing arm.

21. Install the engine sprocket cover (Chapter Seven).

22. Adjust the drive chain and tighten the rear axle nut (Chapter Three).

Cutting a Drive Chain to Length

Table 1 lists the correct number of chain links required for original equipment gearing. If the replacement drive chain is too long, cut it to length as follows:

1. Stretch the new chain on a workbench.

2. If installing a new chain over original equipment gearing, refer to **Table 1** for the correct number of links for the new chain. If sprocket sizes were changed, install the new chain. If sprocket sizes were changed, install the chain over both sprockets - with the rear wheel moved forward - to determine the correct number of links to remove. Make a chalk mark on the two chain pins to be cut. Count the chain links one more time or check the chain length before cutting.

> **WARNING**
> *Using a grinder as described in Step 3 will cause flying particles. Wear proper eye protection.*

3. Grind the head of two pins flush with the face of the side plate with an angle grinder or suitable grinding tool.

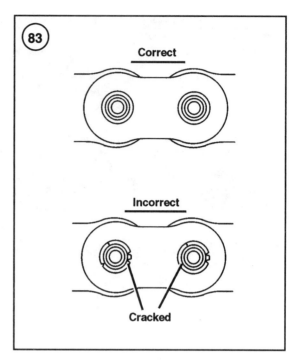

4. Press the side plate out of the chain with a chain breaker; support the chain carefully while doing this. If the pins are still tight, grind more material from the end of the pins and then try again.

5. Remove the side plate and push out the connecting link.

6. Install the new drive chain as described in this chapter.

Table 1 WHEELS, TIRES AND DRIVE CHAIN SPECIFICATIONS

Item	Specification
Axle runout limit	
Front	0.25 mm (0.010 in.)
Rear	0.25 mm (0.010 in.)
Drive Chain	
Type	
GSX-R600 models	
2006-2007 models	RK525SM0Z7Y (114 links)
2008-2009 models	RK525SM0Z8 (114 links)
GSX-R750 models	RK525R0Z5Y (116 links)
20-pin length	319.4 mm (12.6 in.)
Chain slack (motorcycle on side stand)	20-30 mm (0.8-1.2 in.)
Link width	
2006-2007 models	18.6-18.9 mm (0.732-0.744 in.)
2008-2009 models	20.1-20.4 mm (0.79-0.80 in.)
Pin outside diameter	5.45-5.85 mm (0.21-0.23 in.)
Rim runout limit	
Axial	2.0 mm (0.08 in.)
Radial	2.0 mm (0.08 in.)

(continued)

Table 1 WHEELS, TIRES AND DRIVE CHAIN SPECIFICATIONS (continued)

Tire Size	
Front	120/70 ZR17 M/C (58W)
Rear	180/50 ZR17 M/C (73W)
Tire tread minimum depth	
Front	1.6 mm (0.06 in.)
Rear	2.0 mm (0.08 in.)
Tire pressure (cold)*	
Front	
Solo	250 kPa (36 psi)
Rider and passenger	250 kPa (36 psi)
Rear	
Solo	290 kPa (42 psi)
Rider and passenger	250 kPa (36 psi)
Wheel rim size	
Front	17M/C x MT 3.50
Rear	17M/C x MT 5.50

*Tire inflation pressure is for original equipment tires. Aftermarket tires may require different inflation pressure. The use of tires other than those specified by Suzuki may cause instability.

Table 2 WHEELS, TIRES AND DRIVE CHAIN TORQUE SPECIFICATIONS

Item	N•m	in.-lb.	ft.-lb.
Brake disc bolt			
Front	23	–	17
Rear	35	–	26
Engine sprocket nut	115	–	85
Front axle bolt	100	–	74
Front fork clamp bolt	23	–	17
Front caliper mounting bolt			
2006-2007 models	35	–	25.5
2008-2009 models	39	–	29
Rear axle nut	100	–	74
Rear sprocket nut	60	–	44

11

Notes

CHAPTER TWELVE

FRONT SUSPENSION AND STEERING

This chapter covers the front fork and steering components. Wheel removal and hub service are addressed in Chapter Eleven.

When servicing the components described in this chapter, compare any measurements to the specifications in **Table 1**.

Table 1 and **Table 2** are at the end if this chapter.

HANDLEBAR

The individual front handlebars mount onto the fork sliders below the bottom surface of the upper fork bridge. The fork leg must be lowered to remove a particular handlebar. Remove, service and reinstall one handlebar assembly, and repeat for the other assembly.

Removal/Installation

1. Remove the front wheel (Chapter Eleven).
2. Remove the front fender and both fairing side panels (Chapter Fifteen).
3A. If replacing the right handlebar, perform the following:
  a. Remove the right handlebar switch assembly (A, **Figure 1**) (Chapter Nine).
  b. Remove the front brake master cylinder and reservoir (B, **Figure 1**) (Chapter Fourteen).

  c. Secure the master cylinder assembly to the frame, keeping the front brake master cylinder and reservoir in an upright position. This prevents air from entering into the system.
3B. If replacing the left handlebar, perform the following:
  a. Remove the left handlebar switch assembly (A, **Figure 2**) (Chapter Nine).
  b. Remove the left hand grip (B, **Figure 2**) as described in this chapter.
  c. Remove the clutch lever assembly (C, **Figure 2**) (Chapter Six).
4. Remove either handlebar by performing the following:
  a. Loosen the upper fork bridge clamp bolt (A, **Figure 3**) and handlebar clamp bolt (B).
  b. Loosen the lower fork bridge clamp bolts (**Figure 4**).
  c. Lower the fork leg until its top is below the handlebar mounting bracket or completely remove the fork leg.
  d. Remove the handlebar assembly from the motorcycle.
5. Installation is the reverse of removal. Note the following:
  a. Seat the handlebar against the upper fork bridge so the index post (**Figure 5**) on the handlebar bracket engages the slot in the fork bridge.

b. Align the handlebar clamp with the upper fork bridge clamp, and slide the fork leg assembly through the lower fork bridge (if fork was totally removed), the handlebar clamp and the upper fork bridge. Position the fork leg so the distance from the top of the fork leg to the top of the upper fork bridge (**Figure 6**) is 5.0 mm (0.196 in.).

c. Snug the upper and lower fork bridge clamp bolts.

d. Check the height of the fork leg. Adjust it as necessary.

e. Tighten the lower fork bridge clamp bolts (**Figure 4**) to 23 N•m (17 ft.-lb.).

f. Tighten the upper fork bridge clamp bolt (A, **Figure 3**) to 23 N•m (17 ft.-lb.).

g. Tighten the handlebar clamp bolt (B, **Figure 3**) to 23 N•m (17 ft.-lb.).

> *WARNING*
> *After installation is completed, make sure the brake lever does not contact the throttle grip assembly when the brake is fully applied. If it does, the brake fluid may be low in the reservoir; refill it as necessary. Refer to Chapter Fourteen.*

h. Adjust the throttle and clutch cables (Chapter Three).

i. Check the operation of all switch assemblies (Chapter Nine).

Inspection

Check the handlebars bolt holes and the entire mounting bracket for cracks or damage. Replace a bent or damaged handlebar immediately. If the motorcycle has been involved in a crash, thoroughly examine the individual handlebars, the steering stem and front fork for any sign of damage or misalignment. Correct any problem immediately.

HANDLEBAR LEFT GRIP

> *NOTE*
> *The factory equipped right grip is part of the throttle grip assembly and cannot be replaced separately.*

Removal/Installation

1. Remove the screw and weight from the end of the handlebar.

2. Slide a thin screwdriver between the left grip and handlebar. Spray electrical contact cleaner into the opening under the grip.

3. Pull the screwdriver out and quickly twist the grip to break its bond with the handlebar, and then slide the grip off the handlebar.

4. Clean all rubber or sealant residue from the handlebar.

5. Install the new grip following the manufacturer's directions. Apply an adhesive (ThreeBond Griplock), between the grip and handlebar. Follow the adhesive manufacturer's instructions for drying time before operating the motorcycle.

STEERING HEAD AND STEM

A steering stem nut wrench (Suzuki part No. 09940-14911) and socket (Suzuki part No. 09940-14960), or equivalent tools, are needed to service the steering head.

Removal

Refer to **Figure 7**.

1. Remove the fuel tank (Chapter Eight).
2. Remove the front fairing (Chapter Fifteen).

3. Remove the brake hose holder bolt (A, **Figure 8**), and release the brake hose from the lower fork bridge.
4. Remove the steering damper (B, **Figure 8**) as described in this chapter.
5. Protect the steering head nut with several layers of electrical tape (**Figure 9**), and loosen the nut. Do not remove it at this time.
6. Remove the steering head nut (**Figure 10**) and washer (**Figure 11**).
7. Unhook the control cables (**Figure 12**) from the holder on the ignition switch.
8. If necessary, disconnect the ignition switch 4-pin electrical connector (**Figure 13**) from the harness mate.
9. Remove the upper fork bridge (**Figure 14**) from the steering stem and fork tubes.
10. Loosen the handlebar clamp bolt and slide the handlebar off the front fork tube.

Repeat for the remaining handlebar

NOTE
Move the handlebars forward, and suspended them from the front of the frame. Keep the front brake master cylinder upright so air cannot enter the system.

11. Remove each fork leg as described in this chapter.
12. Remove the steering stem locknut (A, **Figure 15**) and washer (B). Note that the tab on the washer engages the slot in the steering stem.

NOTE
Support the weight of the steering stem while removing the adjusting nut or the assembly will drop out of the steering head.

13. Loosen the steering stem adjusting nut (A, **Figure 16**).
14. Hold onto the steering stem (B, **Figure 16**), and remove the adjusting nut (A).
15. Remove the dust seal cover (**Figure 17**) and dust seal (**Figure 18**) from the top of the steering head.
16. Carefully remove the upper bearing inner race (A, **Figure 19**) and the upper bearing (B) from the steering head.
17. Lower the steering stem assembly (**Figure 20**) from the frame steering head.
18. Lift up and remove the lower bearing (**Figure 21**) from the steering stem.
19. Inspect the steering stem as described in this section.

12

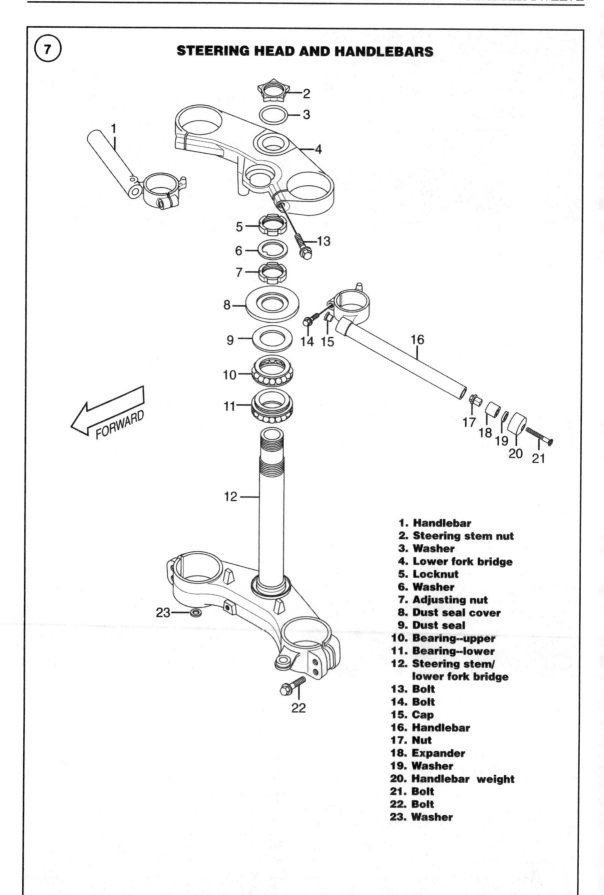

⑦ STEERING HEAD AND HANDLEBARS

1. Handlebar
2. Steering stem nut
3. Washer
4. Lower fork bridge
5. Locknut
6. Washer
7. Adjusting nut
8. Dust seal cover
9. Dust seal
10. Bearing--upper
11. Bearing--lower
12. Steering stem/
    lower fork bridge
13. Bolt
14. Bolt
15. Cap
16. Handlebar
17. Nut
18. Expander
19. Washer
20. Handlebar weight
21. Bolt
22. Bolt
23. Washer

FORWARD

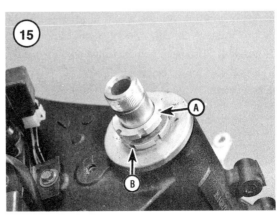

12

CAUTION
Do not attempt to remove the bearing inner race from the steering stem unless the bearing is going to be replaced. The race is pressed onto the steering stem and is damaged during removal.

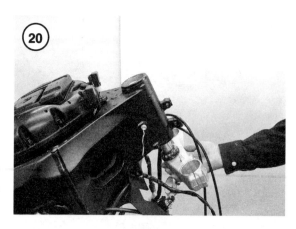

Installation

1. Make sure the upper (**Figure 22**) and lower (**Figure 23**) bearing outer races are clean and properly seated in the steering head.
2. Apply an even, complete coat of grease (Suzuki Super Grease A or equivalent), to the outer races (**Figure 24**). Also pack both bearings with grease.
3. Install the lower bearing (**Figure 21**) onto the steering stem.

NOTE
The fork receptacles in the steering stem are offset and must face forward. This is necessary for proper alignment with the fork receptacles in the upper fork bridge.

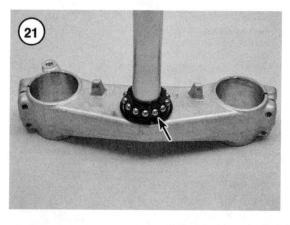

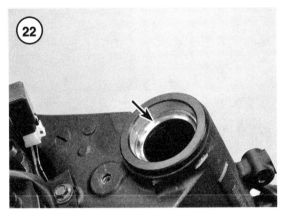

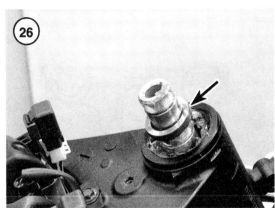

4. Position the steering stem with the fork receptacles facing the front of the motorcycle. Slide the steering stem up into the frame (**Figure 20**).

5. Install the upper bearing (**Figure 25**) into the outer race in the top of the steering head, and install the inner race (**Figure 26**). Press it down until it bottoms (**Figure 27**).

6. Pack the dust seal with grease (Suzuki Super Grease A or equivalent) and seat it onto the steering head (**Figure 18**).

7. Install the dust seal cover (**Figure 17**).

8. Install the adjusting nut (**Figure 28**) and perform the following:

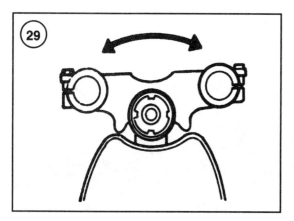

a. Tighten the steering stem adjusting nut (**Figure 28**) to the initial torque of 45 N•m (33 ft.-lb.).

b. Turn the steering stem from side-to-side (**Figure 29**) five-to-six times to help seat the bearings.

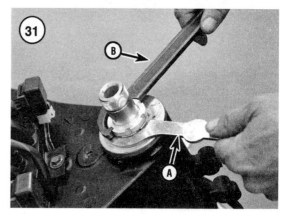

NOTE
The amount of adjustment (substep c) varies for each motorcycle. After the adjusting nut is loosened, there must be no bearing preload detected in the steering stem.

c. Loosen the adjusting nut 1/4 to 1/2 turn.

9. Check the steering head bearing adjustment by performing the following:

a. Check the bearing preload by turning the steering stem from side-to-side five-to-six times (**Figure 29**). It should turn smoothly from lock-to-lock without drag or binding. There should be no preload. If necessary, loosen the adjuster nut in 1/8-turn increments and recheck the preload.

b. Check for bearing free play by grasping one fork clamp area on the lower fork bridge. Try to rock the side of the lower fork bridge up and down. There should be little or no bearing free play in the steering head. If any play is felt, tighten the adjusting nut 1/8 of a turn. Recheck the play.

c. Repeatedly check the bearing free play and preload, and make any necessary adjustments. The steering head bearings are properly adjusted when there is little or no free play and absolutely no preload.

10. Install the washer (**Figure 30**) so its tab engages the slot in the steering stem (B, **Figure 15**).

11. Install the locknut (A, **Figure 15**) onto the steering stem. Hold the adjusting nut with a ring nut wrench (A, **Figure 31**), and tighten the steering stem locknut (B) to 80 N•m (59 ft.-lb.).

12. Slide both fork leg assemblies (A, **Figure 32**) through the lower fork bridge into their approximate height location. Tighten the lower fork bridge clamp bolts securely to hold the fork assemblies in place.

13. Install the handlebar assemblies (B, **Figure 32**) onto the fork tubes. Do not tighten the clamp bolts at this time.

14. Correctly position the cables as shown in **Figure 33**.

15. Install the upper fork bridge (**Figure 14**) onto the steering stem and fork assemblies.

16. Position the washer so its convex side faces the upper fork bridge, and install the washer (**Figure 11**).

17. Thread the steering head nut (**Figure 10**) onto the steering stem. Tighten the head nut finger-tight at this time.

18. Adjust the position of the fork leg until the distance from the top of the fork leg to the top surface of the upper fork bridge equals the fork leg height (**Figure 34**) listed in **Table 1**.

NOTE
Steps 19-24 must be performed in the given order to assure proper fork alignment.

19. Protect the steering head nut with several layers of electrical tape (**Figure 35**).

20. Tighten the steering head nut (**Figure 36**) to 90 N•m (66 ft.-lb.). Remove the electrical tape (**Figure 35**).

21. Move the handlebars into position indexing the locating pin into the slot in the upper fork bridge. Tighten each handlebar mounting bolt (A, **Figure 37**) to 23 N•m (17 ft.-lb.).

22. Tighten the lower fork bridge clamp bolts (**Figure 38**) to 23 N•m (17 ft.-lb.).

23. Tighten upper fork bridge clamp bolts (B, **Figure 37**) to 23 N•m (17 ft.-lb.).

24. Check the movement of the front fork and steering stem assembly. The steering stem must turn

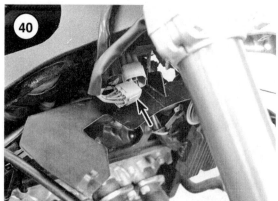

freely from side-to-side but without any binding or without free play when the fork legs are moved fore and aft. Refer to *Steering Tension Inspection* in Chapter Three.

25. Secure the brake hose holder to the lower fork bridge (A, **Figure 39**) and tighten the bolt securely.

26. Install the steering damper (B, **Figure 39**) as described in this chapter.

27. If necessary, connect the ignition switch 4-pin electrical connector (**Figure 40**)
onto the harness mate.

28. On models so equipped with the holder, secure the control cables (**Figure 41**) onto the ignition switch holder.

29. Install the front fairing (Chapter Fifteen).

30. Install the fuel tank (Chapter Eight).

Inspection

1. Clean the upper and lower bearings (**Figure 42**) with a bearing degreaser. Make certain that the bearing degreaser is compatible with the bearing cage. Thoroughly dry the bearings with compressed air. All solvent must be removed from each bearing.

2. Wipe the old grease from each inner race. Clean each race with a rag soaked in solvent. Thoroughly dry the races.

3. Wipe the old grease from both outer races in the steering head, and then clean the outer races with a rag soaked in solvent. Thoroughly dry the races with a lint-free cloth.

4. Check the races (**Figure 22**) and (**Figure 23**) for pitting, galling or corrosion. If any race is worn or damaged, replace the race(s) and bearing as an assembly as described in this chapter.

5. Inspect the seal (**Figure 43**) on the lower fork bridge.

6. Check the welds around the steering head for cracks and fractures. If any damage is found, have the frame repaired at a competent frame or welding shop.

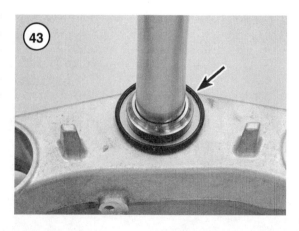

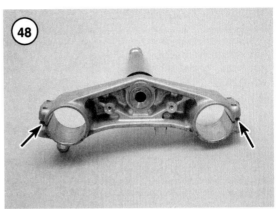

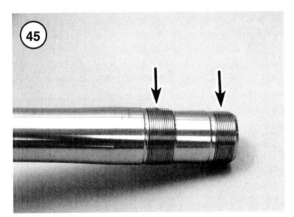

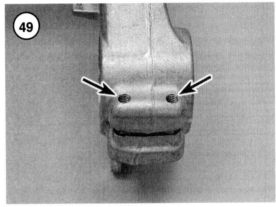

7. Check the balls for pitting, scratches or discoloration indicating wear or corrosion. Replace the bearing if any balls are less than perfect.

8. If the bearings are in good condition, pack them thoroughly with grease (Suzuki Super Grease A or equivalent). Pack both sides of the cage so grease surrounds each ball.

9. Thoroughly clean all mounting parts in solvent. Dry them completely.

10. Inspect the steering stem adjusting nut and locknut (**Figure 44**) for wear or damage. Pay particular attention to the threads. If necessary, clean them with an appropriate size metric tap or replace the nut(s). If the threads are damaged, inspect the appropriate steering stem thread(s) (**Figure 45**) for damage. If necessary, clean the threads with an appropriate size metric die.

11. Inspect the steering stem nut washer for damage, replace if necessary. If damaged, check the underside of the steering stem nut for damage, replace as necessary.

12. Inspect the dust seal lip (**Figure 46**) for rips or deterioration; replace as necessary.

13. Inspect the steering stem and the lower fork bridge (**Figure 47**) for cracks or other damage. Make sure the fork bridge clamping areas (**Figure 48**) are free of burrs and that the bolt holes (**Figure 49**) are in good condition.

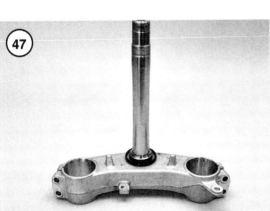

12

14. Inspect the upper fork bridge for cracks or other damage. Check both the upper and lower surface of the fork bridge. Make sure the fork bridge clamping areas (**Figure 50**) are free of burrs and that the bolt holes are in good condition.

15. Make sure the ignition switch mounting bolts (**Figure 51**) are tight.

16. Replace any worn or damaged component. If any bearing or any race is worn or damaged, replace the races and bearing in both bearing sets.

STEERING HEAD BEARING RACE

A bearing race installer set (Suzuki part No. 09941-34513 and part No. 09913-70210, or equivalent) is needed to perform this procedure.

Removal/Installation

1. Remove the steering stem as described in this chapter.

2. Insert an aluminum drift into the steering head and carefully tap the lower race from the frame (**Figure 52**). Repeat for the upper race.

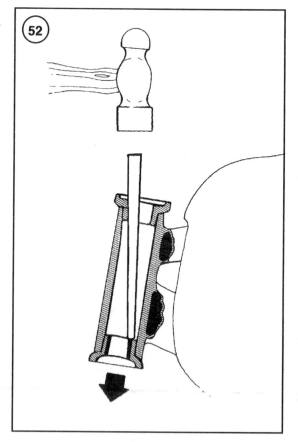

3. Chill the new bearing races (**Figure 53**) in a freezer for a few hours to shrink the outer diameter of the race.

4. Clean the race seats in the steering head. Check for cracks or other damage.

5. Set the new race into the steering head so the larger side of the taper faces out. Square the race with the bore.

CAUTION
When installing the bearing outer races do not let the tool shaft contact the face of the bearing race. The race could be damaged.

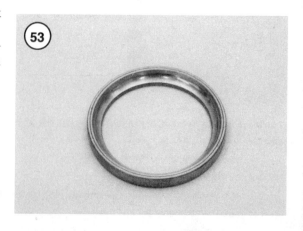

6. Assemble the special tool through the bearing race per the manufacturer's instructions (**Figure 54**).

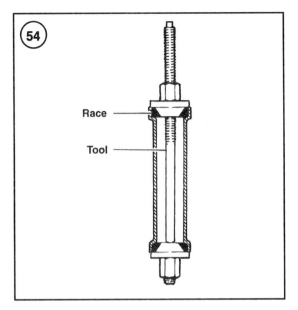

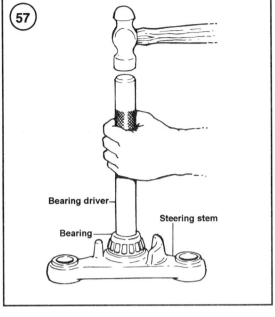

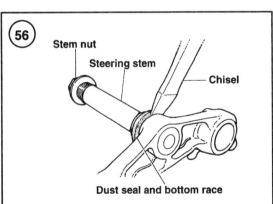

7. Hold the installer shaft and slowly turn the upper nut until the tool and outer race are square with the steering head bore (**Figure 55**).

8. Turn the upper nut, and slowly press the race into the bore until the race bottoms (**Figure 55**).

9. Turn the special tool over and repeat this procedure for the lower bearing race.

10. Install the steering stem as described in this chapter.

STEERING STEM RACE

Do not remove the lower-bearing inner race (**Figure 43**) and seal from the steering stem unless they must be replaced. The race can be difficult to remove. If the race cannot be removed as described here, take the steering stem to a dealership for removal and installation of a new inner race and seal.

Never reinstall a race that has been removed. It is no longer true and will damage the rest of the bearing assembly if reused.

Removal/Installation

1. Install the steering stem nut onto the top of the steering stem to protect the threads.

2. Use a chisel to loosen the lower race from the shoulder at the base of the steering stem (**Figure 56**). Slide the race and seal off the steering stem. Discard them.

3. Clean the steering stem with solvent, and dry thoroughly.

4. Position the new seal with the flange side facing up.

5. Slide the seal and the inner race onto the steering stem until the race stops on the raised shoulder.

6. Align the race with the machined shoulder on the steering stem. Slide the steering bearing installer (Suzuki part No. 09925-18010), or a piece of pipe (**Figure 57**), over the steering stem until it seats

against the inner circumference of the race. Drive the race onto the steering stem until it bottoms.

STEERING DAMPER

Removal/Inspection/Installation

Refer to **Figure 58**.

1. Support the motorcycle on a level surface with the front wheel off the ground.
2. Remove the front fairing (Chapter Fifteen).
3. On 2008-2009 models, disconnect the steering damper electrical connector (**Figure 59**) from the harness mate.
4. Remove the steering damper nut (A, **Figure 60**).
5. Remove the steering damper mounting bolt (B, **Figure 60**) and its dust seal.
6. Disengage the steering damper stud from the mount on the lower fork bridge, and remove the damper (C, **Figure 60**). Account for the dust seal (A, **Figure 61**) that sits on each side of the damper bearing (B).
7. Inspect the steering damper body, bearing and seals for signs of leaks.
8. Move the steering damper rod into and out of the body (**Figure 62**). It should move smoothly.
9. Inspect the locknut (A, **Figure 63**), rubber boot (B) and mounting stud threads (C) for damage.

> *CAUTION*
> *Do not remove the bolt from the damper body.*

10. Replace the steering damper is any defect is found.
11. Installation is the reverse of removal. Note the following:

   a. Lubricate the damper bearing (B, **Figure 61**) and the concave side of each dust seal with grease (Suzuki Super Grease A or equivalent).
   b. Install a dust seal on each side of the bearing so a seal's concave side faces the bearing (**Figure 64**).
   c. Tighten the steering damper nut (A, **Figure 60**) and steering damper bolt (B) to 23 N•m (17 ft.-lb.).

FRONT FORK

Simplify fork service and prevent the mixing of parts by removing, servicing and installing each fork let individually.

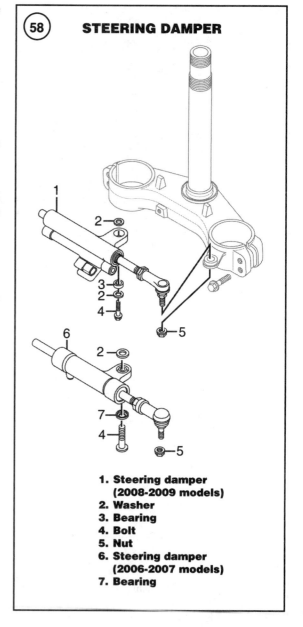

58 **STEERING DAMPER**

1. Steering damper (2008-2009 models)
2. Washer
3. Bearing
4. Bolt
5. Nut
6. Steering damper (2006-2007 models)
7. Bearing

Removal

> *NOTE*
> *For fork assembly removal only, do not perform Step 4. This step is only necessary if the fork is going to be disassembled for service.*

1. Support the motorcycle on a level surface.
2. Remove the front wheel (Chapter Eleven).
3. Remove the front fender, both fairing side panels and the front fairing (Chapter Fifteen).
4. If a fork leg requires service, perform the following:

   a. Place a drain pan under the fork tube.

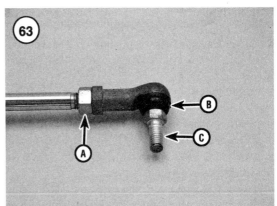

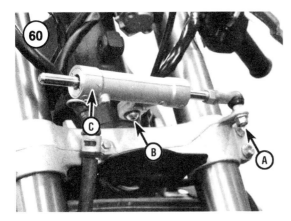

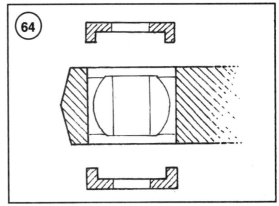

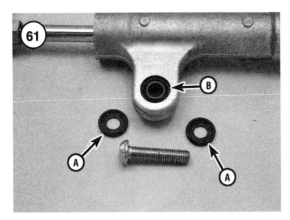

12

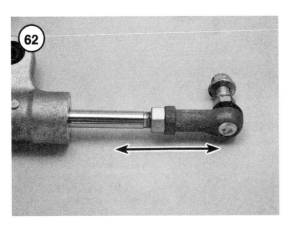

b. Use an impact driver to loosen the Allen bolt in the base of the slider. Remove the Allen bolt, and drain the fork oil. Pump the fork leg several times to expel most of the fork oil.

c. Turn the rebound damping adjuster (A, **Figure 65**) counterclockwise to its softest setting.

d. Loosen the upper fork bridge clamp bolt (A, **Figure 66**).

e. Apply electrical tape over (**Figure 67**) the cap bolt to protect the finish. Loosen the cap bolt (B, **Figure 65**) with a 6-point, 32mm deep socket.

5. If not loosened in Step 4, loosen the upper fork bridge clamp bolt (A, **Figure 66**).

6. Loosen the handlebar clamp bolt (B, **Figure 66**).

7. Loosen the lower fork bridge clamp bolts (**Figure 68**).

8. Carefully lower the fork assembly out of the upper fork bridge, the handlebar clamp and the lower fork bridge. It may be necessary to rotate the fork leg slightly while pulling it down. If the fork is not going to be serviced, warp it in a large towel or blanket to protect the surface from damage.

9. If both fork legs are going to be removed, mark them with an R (right side) and L (left side). Each must be reinstalled on the correct side during assembly.

Installation

1. Slide the fork leg assembly through the lower fork bridge, the handlebar clamp and the upper fork bridge. Adjust the position of the fork leg until the distance from the top of the fork leg to the top surface of the upper fork bridge (**Figure 69**) as specified in **Table 1**.

2. Tighten the lower fork bridge clamp bolts (**Figure 68**) to 23 N•m (17 ft.-lb.).

3. If the fork leg was disassembled for service, Tighten the cap bolt (B, **Figure 65**) to 35 N•m (26 ft.-lb.).

4. Tighten the upper fork bridge clamp bolt (A, **Figure 66**) to 23 N•m (17 ft.-lb.).

5. Hold the handlebar snug against the upper fork bridge so the index post engages the slot in the upper fork bridge. Tighten the handlebar clamp bolt (B, **Figure 66**) to 23 N•m (17 ft.-lb.).

6. If necessary, repeat Steps 1-5 for the other fork leg.

7. Install the front fender (Chapter Fifteen) and front wheel (Chapter Eleven).

8. Install the front fairing and the fairing side panels (Chapter Fifteen).

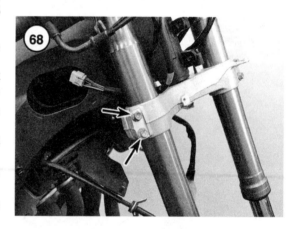

Disassembly

Refer to **Figure 70**.

> *NOTE*
> *The fork spring cannot be compressed sufficiently by hand to remove the cap bolt from the cartridge. A spring compression tool, or tools, is required for this procedure.*

1A. The following Suzuki special tools are needed to service the front fork:

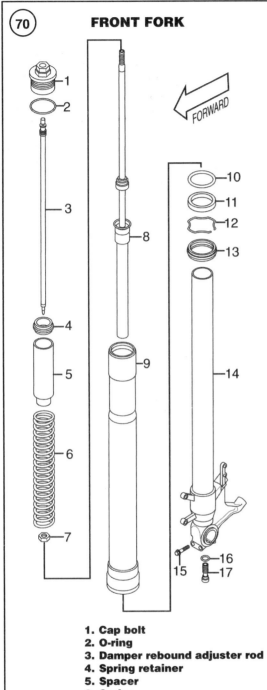

FRONT FORK

70

FORWARD

1. Cap bolt
2. O-ring
3. Damper rebound adjuster rod
4. Spring retainer
5. Spacer
6. Spring
7. Locknut
8. Cartridge
9. Fork tube
10. Seal spacer
11. Oil seal
12. Circlip
13. Dust seal
14. Slider
15. Clamp bolt
16. Washer
17. Allen bolt

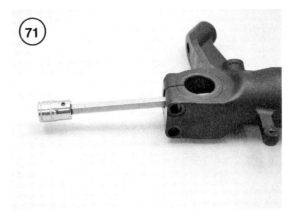

71

a. Front fork oil seal installer (Suzuki part No. 09940-52861, or equivalent).
b. Front fork spacer holder (Suzuki part No. 09940-94930, or equivalent).
c. Stopper plate (Suzuki part No. 09940-94922, or equivalent).
d. Front fork assembling tool (Suzuki part No. 09940-30221, or equivalent).
e. Inner rod holder (Suzuki part No. 09940-50120, or equivalent).
f. Fork oil level gauge (Suzuki part No. 09943-74111, or equivalent).

1B. The following special tool is needed to service the front fork. The fork spring compression tool is available from motorcycle dealerships and motorcycle parts/tool suppliers. The following procedure is shown with this special tool.

2. If the fork slider Allen bolt was not loosened during the fork removal sequence, perform the following:

a. Secure the fork leg horizontally in a vise with soft jaws.
b. Use an Allen socket (**Figure 71**) and impact wrench and loosen the Allen bolt on the bottom of the slider. Do not remove the Allen bolt and gasket at this time. The leg is still full of fork oil.

3. Completely remove the compression damping force adjuster (**Figure 72**) from the base of the slider.

CAUTION
The cap bolt is under spring pressure. Exercise caution when unthreading the cap bolt.

NOTE
Some of the following steps are shown with the fork assembly horizontally for photo clarity.

12

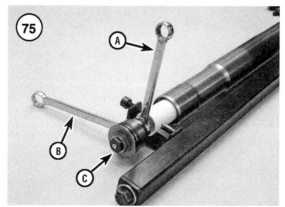

4. Secure the fork leg in a fork spring compressor. Refer to **Figure 73** and **Figure 74**. Compress the spring until the cartridge locknut nut emerges from the washer.

5. Secure the damper adjuster (A, **Figure 75**) and loosen the cartridge locknut (B).

6. Loosen the fork cap bolt (C, **Figure 75**) from the cartridge rod threads.

7. Remove the fork cap bolt (A, **Figure 76**) and spring retainer (B) from the cartridge.

8. Withdraw the rebound adjuster rod (**Figure 77**).

9. Slowly relieve the tension on the spring compressor tool and remove the fork from the compressor tool.

10. Remove the spacer and withdraw the spring (**Figure 78**).

11. Invert the fork leg and pour the oil from the end of the fork slider. Pump the damper rod in and out to expel oil from the cartridge. Dispose of the fork oil properly.

12. Remove the Allen bolt (**Figure 71**) from the end of the fork slider. If the Allen bolt has not been loosened, hold the cartridge with the front fork assembling tool (**Figure 79**) and remove the Allen bolt.

13. Withdraw the cartridge assembly (A, **Figure 80**) from the top of the fork slider (B).

14. Pry the dust seal (**Figure 81**) from the slider.

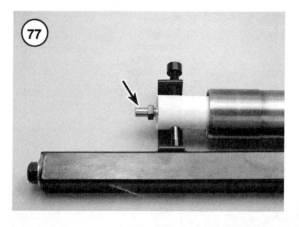

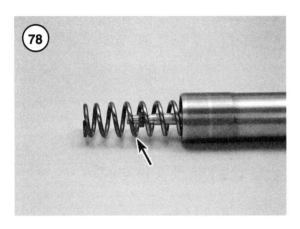

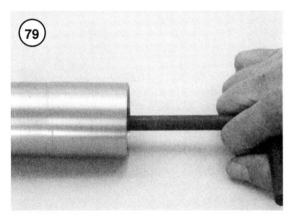

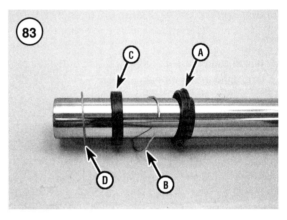

15. Remove the circlip (**Figure 82**) from its seat in the fork tube.
16. Withdraw the fork tube from the slider.
17. Inspect the components (this section).

Assembly

1. Coat all parts with fresh fork oil (Suzuki SS05, or equivalent) before installation.
2. Apply fork oil to both bushings within the fork tube.
3. Apply fork oil to the oil seal.
4. Slide the dust (A, **Figure 83**), circlip (B), *new* oil seal (C) and the oil seal spacer (D) onto the slider.
5. Insert the fork slider into the tube (**Figure 84**), and push the fork seal spacer down into the fork tube until it bottoms.
6. Use a fork seal driver (**Figure 85**) and drive the oil seal into place in the fork tube. Drive the oil seal until the circlip groove in the fork tube is visible above the top of the oil seal.
7. Slide the circlip down the fork slider, and install it into the fork tube. Be sure the circlip is completely seated in the circlip groove in the fork tube (**Figure 82**).
8. Slide the dust seal (**Figure 81**) down the fork slider, and seat it in the tube.

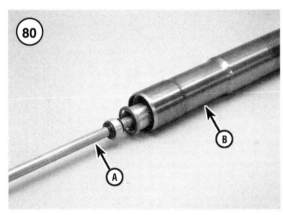

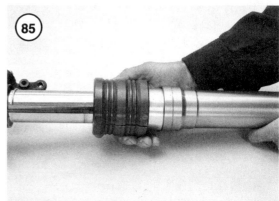

9. Insert the cartridge (A, **Figure 80**) through the top of the fork tube (B) until the cartridge bottoms in the fork slider.

10. Install a new washer onto the Allen bolt and apply threadlocking compound (Suzuki Thread Lock 1342 or equivalent) to the bolt threads.

11. Insert the Allen bolt into the fork slider (**Figure 86**), and turn it into the cartridge. Hold the cartridge with the front fork assembling tool (**Figure 79**), and tighten the cartridge Allen bolt to 35 N•m (26 ft.-lb.).

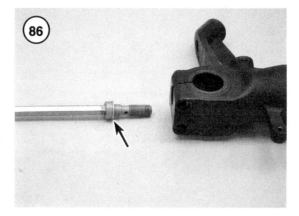

12. Install a *new* O-ring (**Figure 87**) onto compression damping adjuster, and install the adjuster. Tighten the compression damping adjuster (**Figure 88**) to the specification listed in **Table 2**.

13. Fill the fork with oil, set the oil level and complete fork assembly as described in Fork Oil Adjustment as described in this chapter.

14. Install the fork assembly as described in this chapter, and then tighten the cap bolt to 35 N•m (26 ft.-lb.).

15. Adjust the spring preload, compression damping and rebound damping (Chapter Three).

Inspection

CAUTION
Do not clean the cartridge in solvent. It is extremely difficult to remove all the solvent from the cartridge, and solvent will contaminate the fork oil. Instead, wipe the cartridge with a clean cloth, and set it aside for inspection and assembly.

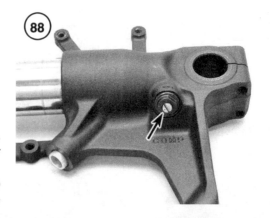

1. Thoroughly clean all parts, except the cartridge, in solvent and dry them. Check the fork slider for signs of wear or scratches.

2. Check the cartridge assembly (A, **Figure 89**) for straightness and damage. Manually move the

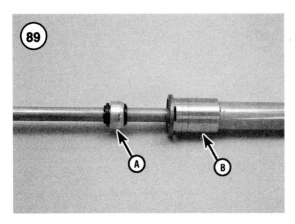

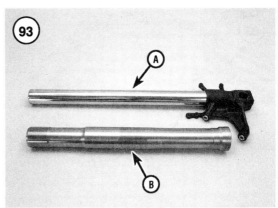

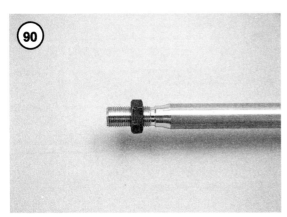

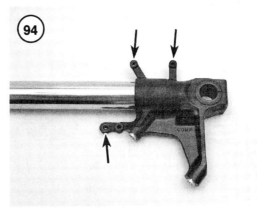

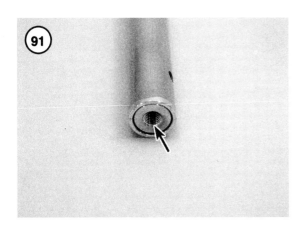

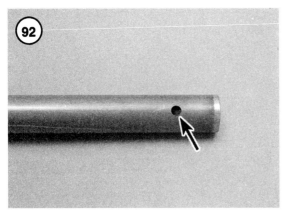

cartridge rod (A, **Figure 89**) into and out of the cartridge (B). It should move smoothly.

3. Check the threads and nut (**Figure 90**) at the top end of the cartridge rod for damage. Clean the threads with an appropriate size metric tap and/or die if necessary.

4. Check the threads (**Figure 91**) for the Allen bolt at the lower end of the cartridge for damage. Clean the threads with an appropriate size metric tap if necessary.

5. Roll the rebound damper adjuster rod along a surface plate or a piece of glass. Replace the rod if it is not straight.

6. Make sure the oil holes (**Figure 92**) in the cartridge are clear. Clean out if necessary.

7. Check the fork slider as follows:
   a. Check for straightness and/or scratches (A, **Figure 93**).
   b. Check for dents or exterior damage that may cause the fork tube to stick.
   c. Inspect the mounting bosses (**Figure 94**) for cracks or other damage.
   d. Make sure the caliper mounting inserts (**Figure 95**) are in place.
   e. Inspect the threads (**Figure 96**) for the damping force adjuster. Clean the threads with the appropriate size metric tap if necessary.

12

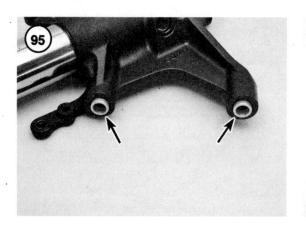

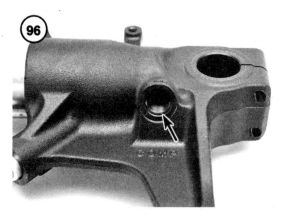

8. Check the fork tube as follows:
   a. Check for straightness and/or scratches (B, **Figure 93**).

> *CAUTION*
> *The oil seal has a very hard stiff plastic insert and is very difficult to remove. Do not use a flat blade screwdriver to remove seal as the fork tube inner surface may be damaged.*

   b. Inspect the oil seal in the fork tube for leakage or damage. If necessary, use a tire iron and carefully work around the perimeter of the oil seal (**Figure 97**) and pry it out.
   c. Inspect the oil seal location surface (A, **Figure 98**) for damage or burrs. Pay particular attention to the circlip groove and the sealing surfaces. Clean the tube if necessary.
   d. Inspect both bushings (B, **Figure 98**) for scratches or scoring. If either is scratched or scored, replace the fork tube as the bushings cannot be replaced on all models.
   e. Inspect the threads (**Figure 99**) in the top for wear or damage. Clean the threads with the appropriate size metric tap if necessary.

9. Inspect the fork cap threads (A, **Figure 100**) for signs of damage. The fork cap cannot be serviced. If

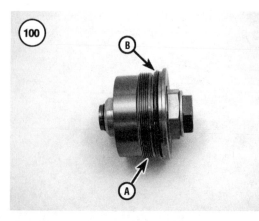

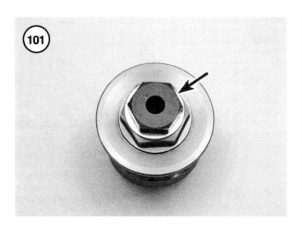

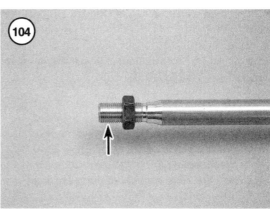

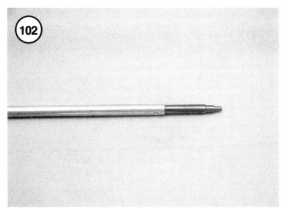

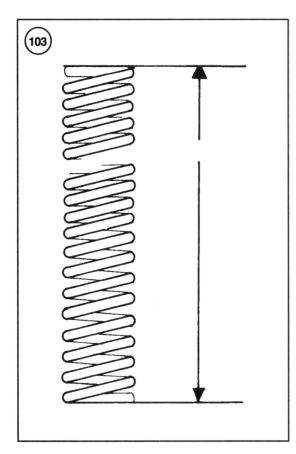

any damaged is noted, replace it. Inspect the cap bolt O-ring (B, **Figure 100**). Replace it as necessary.

10. Inspect the spring preload adjuster (**Figure 101**) and the rebound damper adjuster rod (**Figure 102**) for wear and damage.

11. Inspect the Allen bolt as follows:

    a. Make sure the oil hole is clear. Clean out if necessary.

    b. Inspect for thread damage. Clean the threads with the appropriate size metric tap if necessary.

12. Visually inspect the fork spring for wear, cracks or other damage.

13. Inspect the spring seats, retainer and washer on each respective model.

14. Measure the uncompressed length of the fork spring as shown in **Figure 103**. Replace the spring if it has sagged to less than the wear limit specified in **Table 1**.

12

Fork Oil Adjustment

NOTE
This procedure is shown with the fork assembly horizontal for photo clarity. The assembly must be kept vertical at all times.

1. Thread the cartridge locknut down the cartridge rod to expose approximately 12 mm (0.47 in.) of threads (**Figure 104**).

2. Secure the fork slider vertically in a vise with soft jaws.

3. Push the fork slider down onto fork tube until the slider bottoms.

4. Install a *new* O-ring (**Figure 105**) onto the adjuster rod.

5. Thread the adjuster rod (A, **Figure 106**) into the cap bolt (B) until the adjuster rod protrudes approximately 1.5 mm (0.06 in.) above the cap bolt.

6. Install the inner rod holder (**Figure 107**) onto the cartridge rod.

7. Refer to **Table 1**, for the recommended type of fork oil. Add the fork oil until it almost reaches to the top surface of the fork tube.

NOTE
During the bleeding procedure, the fork oil level must remain above the top of the cartridge assembly. If the oil level drops below this level, air may enter the cartridge nullifying the bleeding procedure.

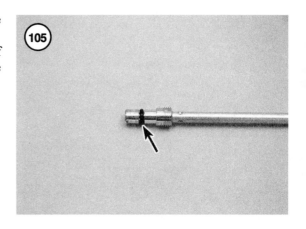

8. Bleed the air from the cartridge as follows:
   a. Keep the fork assembly in a vertical position during bleeding.
   b. Grasp the inner rod holder (**Figure 107**) and slowly move the cartridge rod up and down using full travel strokes.
   c. Repeat this for more than 10 times or until the fork oil is free of bubbles.
   d. If necessary, add additional fork oil.
   e. Hold the fork tube and slowly move the fork slider up and down several stokes until bubbles are no longer emitted from the oil.
   f. Keep the fork assembly in this vertical position for 5-10 minutes to allow any additional trapped air to escape. Tap the fork leg to break away any bubbles adhering to the sides.

9. Set the fork oil level as follows:
   a. Hold the fork assembly vertical and fully compress the fork slider over the tube.
   b. The oil level is the distance from the top of the compressed fork leg to the upper edge of the oil (**Figure 108**).
   c. Use a ruler, or an oil level gauge (**Figure 109**) to set the oil level to the value listed in **Table 1**.
   d. Let the oil to settle completely and recheck the oil level. Adjust the oil level if necessary.

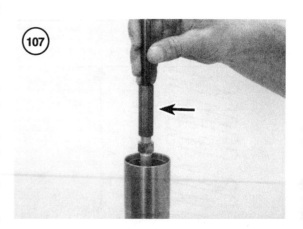

10. If still in place, remove the inner rod holder from the cartridge rod.

11. Position the spring with the larger outer diameter of the coil facing down and install the spring (**Figure 78**).

12. Install the spacer (A, **Figure 110**) onto the fork spring (B).

13. Secure the assembly in a fork spring compressor, and compress the fork spring until the cartridge rod locknut emerges above the spacer (**Figure 111**).

14. Install the retainer (A, **Figure 112**) onto the adjuster rod/cap bolt assembly (B).

15. Release some of the pressure from the spring compressor and allow the cap bolt to move closer to the fork tube.

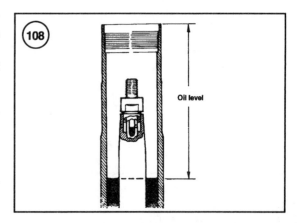

Oil level

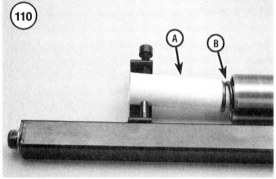

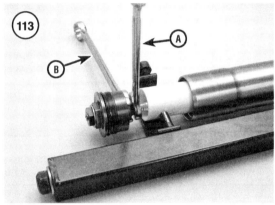

18. Hold the rebound damper adjuster (A, **Figure 113**) and tighten the cartridge locknut (B) to 20 N•m (14.5 ft.-lb.).

19. Pull the fork tube up against the cap bolt and turn the cap bolt into the tube. Tighten the cap bolt securely. It will tightened to specification once the fork leg is installed is installed on the motorcycle as described in this chapter.

20. Install the fork assembly as described in this chapter.

21. Adjust the spring preload, compression damping and rebound damping as described in Chapter Three.

16. Turn the cap bolt (A, **Figure 76**) onto the cartridge until the rebound damper rod lightly bottoms in the cartridge.

17. Turn the cartridge locknut (C, **Figure 76**) until it bottoms against the rebound damper adjuster.

TABLES 1-2 LOCATED ON THE FOLLOWING PAGE

Table 1 FRONT SUSPENSION SPECIFICATIONS

Item	Specification	Service Limit
Fork leg height (above upper fork bridge)		5.0 mm (0.20 in.) –
Front fork stroke	120 mm (4.72 in.)	–
Fork spring free length		
GSX-R600 models	268 mm (10.55 in.)	241.2 mm (9.50 in.)
GSX-R750 models	264.6 mm (10.43 in.)	259.5 mm (10.22 in.)
Front fork oil level	102 mm (4.02 in.)	–
Fork oil		
Type	Suzuki SS-05 fork oil or equivalent	
Capacity per leg		
2006-2007 models		
GSX-R600 models	413 ml (14.0 U.S. oz.)	–
GSX-R750 models	408 ml (13.8 U.S. oz.)	–
2008-2009 models		
GSX-R600 models	410 ml (13.9 U.S. oz.)	–
GSX-R750 models	418 ml (14.1 U.S. oz.)	–
Front fork adjustments		
2006-2007 models (standard positions)		
Spring preload	7th turn from softest position	
Rebound damping	1 3/4 turns out	
Compression damping	1 3/4 turns out	
2008-2009 models (standard positions)		
Spring preload	7th turn from softest position	
Rebound damping	1 ¾ turns out	
Compression damping		
GSX-R600	1 ¾ turns out	
GSX-R750		
Low speed	2 turn out	
High speed	2 ½ turns out	

Table 2 FRONT SUSPENSION AND STEERING TORQUE SPECIFICATIONS

Item	N•m	in.-lb.	ft.-lb.
Front axle	100	–	74
Front axle clamp bolt	23	–	17
Front fork			
Compression damping adjuster			
2006-2007 models	18	–	13
2008-2009 models			
GSX-R600 models	18	–	13
GSX-R750 models	30	–	21.5
Damper rod			
Allen bolt	35	–	26
Locknut	20	–	14.5
Fork bridge clamp bolt			
Upper and lower	23	–	17
Front fork cap bolt	35	–	26
Handlebar clamp bolt	23	–	17
Steering damper			
Mounting bolt	23	–	17
Mounting nut	23	–	17
Steering head nut	90	–	66
Steering stem			
Adjusting nut (initial torque)*	45	–	33
Locknut	80	–	59

* See text for complete tightening procedure.

CHAPTER THIRTEEN

REAR SUSPENSION

This chapter covers the rear suspension components. Rear wheel removal and rear hub service appear in Chapter Eleven.

Table 1 and **Table 2** are at the end of this chapter.

SHOCK ABSORBER

Removal/Installation

Refer to **Figure 1**.

1. Remove the fairing side panel from each side and the lower fairing (Chapter Fifteen).

2. Remove the seat (Chapter Fifteen).

3. Support the motorcycle on a level surface with the rear wheel off the ground.

4. Remove the rear wheel (A, **Figure 2**) (Chapter Eleven).

5. Support the swing arm at the rear to eliminate any load on the shock absorber and suspension linkage.

6. Remove the rear caliper brake hose from the swing arm clamp (B, **Figure 2**).

7. Remove the muffler and the muffler bracket (Chapter Eight).

8. Remove the sidestand (Chapter Fifteen).

9. Remove the rear master cylinder reservoir mounting bolt and move the reservoir out of the way.

NOTE
Note that all lower suspension arm bolts are installed from the left side. Install all bolts from the correct side.

10. Remove the nut (**Figure 3**) from the lower suspension arm bolt, and remove the suspension arm bolt from the left side.

11. Lower the suspension arm (A, **Figure 4**) from the lever.

12. Remove the nut (B, **Figure 4**) from the lower shock absorber bolt, and remove the shock absorber bolt from the left side.

13. Remove the nut (A, **Figure 5**) from the upper shock bolt (B). Pull the bolt (**Figure 6**) from the upper mount.

14. Disengage the shock absorber from the upper mount. Lift the shock absorber up and out of the swing arm (A, **Figure 7**) and remove the shock absorber.

15. Inspect the shock absorber as described in this chapter.

16. Installation is the reverse of removal. Note the following:

   a. Apply a light coat of grease (Suzuki Super Grease A or equivalent) to the bolts and to the shock absorber upper and lower mounts.

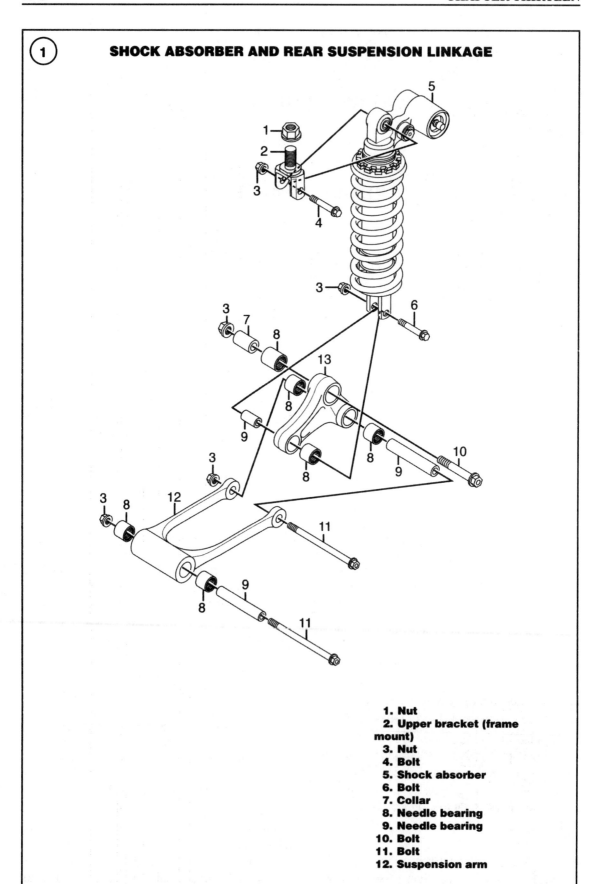

① SHOCK ABSORBER AND REAR SUSPENSION LINKAGE

1. Nut
2. Upper bracket (frame mount)
3. Nut
4. Bolt
5. Shock absorber
6. Bolt
7. Collar
8. Needle bearing
9. Needle bearing
10. Bolt
11. Bolt
12. Suspension arm

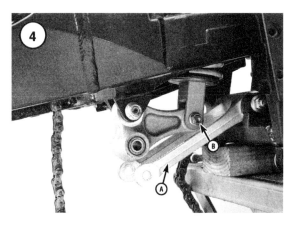

b. Install the shock absorber into place so its compression damping adjuster (B, **Figure 7**) faces the left side.

c. Tighten the shock absorber mounting bolts and nuts to 50 N•m (37 ft.-lb.). Refer to B, **Figure 4**, and A, **Figure 5**.

d. Tighten the suspension arm nut (**Figure 3**) to 78 N•m (57 ft.-lb.).

e. Adjust the shock absorber (Chapter Three).

Inspection

WARNING
The shock absorber contains highly compressed nitrogen gas. Do not tamper with or attempt to open the housing. Do not place it near an open flame or other extreme heat source. Do not weld on the frame near the shock. Take the unit to a dealership where it can be deactivated and disposed of properly.

Replacement parts are unavailable for the original equipment shock absorber. If any part of the shock absorber is faulty, replace it.

1. Inspect the shock absorber housing (A, **Figure 8**) for dents, damage or oil leaks.

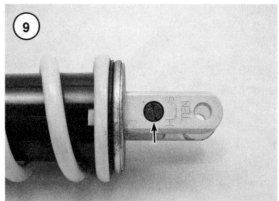

2. Check the spring (B, **Figure 8**) for cracks or other damage.

3. Check the reservoir for leakage or damage.

4. Rotate the rebound damping force adjuster (**Figure 9**) from one stop to another. The adjuster should rotate freely and should engage the detent at each stop.

5. Rotate the low speed compression damping force adjuster (A, **Figure 10**), and high speed compression damping force adjuster (B) from one stop to another. The adjusters should rotate freely and should engage the detent at each stop.

6. Inspect the upper mount (A, **Figure 11**) for wear, or damage, especially check the flexible damper (B) for deterioration.

7. Inspect the lower mount for wear, damage and bolt hole for elongation (**Figure 12**).

8. Inspect the spring length adjust nut and locknut (C, **Figure 8**) to ensure they can be rotated for adjustment.

9. If part is worn or damaged, replace the shock absorber.

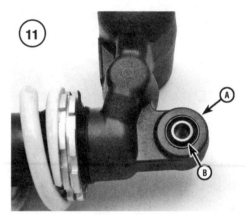

SUSPENSION LINKAGE

Removal

Refer to **Figure 1**.

1. Remove the fairing side panel from each side and the lower fairing (Chapter Fifteen).

2. Remove the seat (Chapter Fifteen).

3. Support the motorcycle on a level surface with the rear wheel off the ground.

4. Remove the rear wheel (Chapter Eleven).

5. Support the swing arm at the rear to eliminate any load on the shock absorber and suspension linkage.

6. Remove the muffler and the muffler bracket (Chapter Eight).

7. Remove the sidestand (Chapter Fifteen).

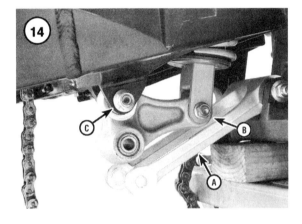

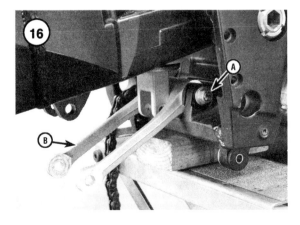

NOTE

Note that all lower suspension arm bolts are installed from the left side. Install all bolts from the correct side.

8. Remove the nut (**Figure 13**) from the lower suspension arm bolt, and remove the suspension arm bolt from the left side.

9. Lower the suspension arm (A, **Figure 14**) from the lever.

10. Loosen the nut (B, **Figure 14**) on the lower shock absorber bolt.

11. Remove the suspension lever nut (C, Figure14) and remove the bolt from the left side.

12. Lower the suspension lever (A, **Figure 15**), and raise the suspension arm (B). Remove the lower shock absorber bolt and nut (C, **Figure 15**), and remove the suspension lever (A).

13. Remove the nut (A, **Figure 16**) from the suspension arm bolt, and remove the bolt from the left side.

14. Remove the suspension arm (B, **Figure 16**) from the frame.

15. Inspect the suspension linkage as described in this chapter.

16. Installation is the reverse of removal. Note the following:

   a. Apply a light coat of grease (Suzuki Super Grease A or equivalent) to the bolts and to the shock absorber upper and lower mounts.

   b. Tighten the suspension arm mounting nuts to 78 N•m (57 ft.-lb.). Refer to **Figure 16**.

   c. Tighten the suspension lever mounting nuts to 98 N•m (71 ft.-lb.). Refer to C, **Figure 14**.

   d. Tighten the shock absorber lower mounting nuts to 50 N•m (37 ft.-lb.). Refer to B, **Figure 14**.

   e. Tighten the suspension arm-to-suspension lever mounting nuts to 78 N•m (57 ft.-lb.). Refer to **Figure 13**.

Inspection

1. Inspection the suspension lever (**Figure 17**) and suspension arm (**Figure 18**) for cracks, wear and damage.

2. Inspect the suspension lever spacers as follows:

   a. Remove each spacer (**Figure 19**) from its pivot in the suspension lever. Note that three different size spacers are used. Each must be reinstalled into the correct location during assembly.

   b. Inspect the spacers for wear and damage.

3. Inspect the suspension lever bearings as follows:

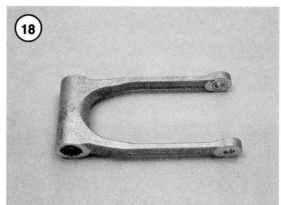

a. Use a clean lint-free rag and wipe off surface grease from each suspension lever needle bearing (**Figure 20**).

b. Turn each bearing by hand. The bearings should turn smoothly without excessive play or noise.

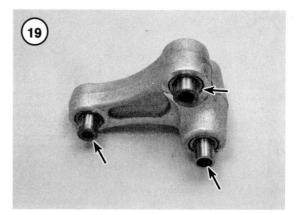

c. Check the rollers for evidence of wear, pitting or rust.

d. Reinstall each spacer (**Figure 19**) into its respective bearing. Slowly rotate the spacer. Each spacer must turn smoothly without excessive play or noise.

e. Replace worn or damaged bearing as described in *Suspension Bearing* in this chapter.

4. Inspect the suspension arm spacers as follows:

a. Remove the spacer (**Figure 21**) from in the suspension arm.

b. Inspect the spacer for wear and damage.

5. Inspect the suspension arm bearing as follows:

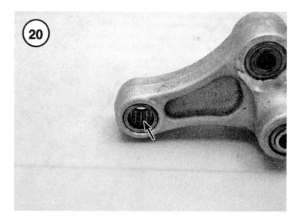

a. Use a clean lint-free rag and wipe off surface grease from the suspension arm needle bearing (**Figure 22**) on each side.

b. Turn each bearing by hand. The bearings should turn smoothly without excessive play or noise.

c. Check the rollers for evidence of wear, pitting or rust.

d. Reinstall the spacer (**Figure 21**) into the bearings. Slowly rotate the spacer. Each spacer must turn smoothly without excessive play or noise.

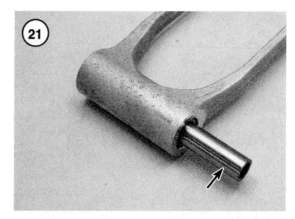

e. Replace worn or damaged bearing as described in *Suspension Bearing* in this chapter.

6. Clean the bolts and nuts in solvent. Check the bolts for straightness. A bent, bolt will restrict linkage movement.

7. Replace any part that is worn or damaged.

8. Lubricate the bearings and spacers with grease (Suzuki Super Grease A or equivalent). Insert each spacer into its original pivot in the suspension lever.

9. Inspect the suspension arm frame mounting bosses (**Figure 23**) for wear, cracks or damage.

SWING ARM

The swing arm pivot thrust adjuster socket wrench (Suzuki part No. 09940-14940, ore equivalent) is needed to remove and install the swing arm. Do not attempt to service the swing arm without this special tool (**Figure 24**), or its equivalent.

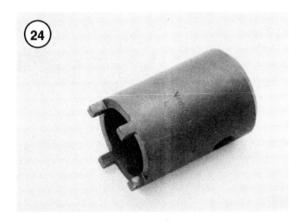

Preliminary Inspection

The swing arm bearings condition will affect the handling of the motorcycle. Worn bearings cause wheel hop, pulling to one side under acceleration and pulling to the other side during braking. Perform the following procedure to check the condition of the swing arm bearings.

1. Remove the rear wheel (Chapter Eleven).
2. Remove the nut (**Figure 13**) from the lower suspension arm bolt, and remove the suspension arm bolt from the left side.
3. Lower the suspension arm (A, **Figure 14**) from the lever.
4. On the right side, make sure the swing arm pivot locknut (A, **Figure 25**) is tight.
5. On the left side, make sure the pivot nut (**Figure 26**) is tight.
6. The swing arm is now free to move under its own weight.

NOTE
Have an assistant steady the motorcycle
when performing Step 6 and Step 7.

7. Grasp both ends of the swing arm and attempt to move it from side to side in a horizontal arc. If more than a slight amount of movement is felt, the swing arm bearings are worn and must be replaced.

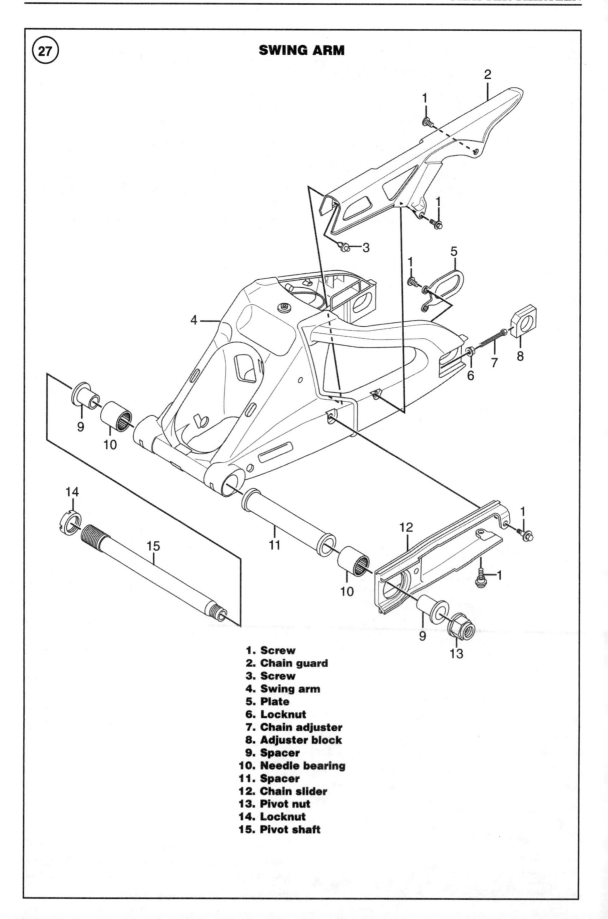

㉗ **SWING ARM**

1. Screw
2. Chain guard
3. Screw
4. Swing arm
5. Plate
6. Locknut
7. Chain adjuster
8. Adjuster block
9. Spacer
10. Needle bearing
11. Spacer
12. Chain slider
13. Pivot nut
14. Locknut
15. Pivot shaft

8. Grasp both ends of the swing arm and move it up and down. The swing arm should move smoothly with no binding or abnormal noise from the bearings. If there is binding or noise, the bearings are worn and must be replaced.

Removal

Refer to **Figure 27**.

1. Remove the fairing side panel from each side and the lower fairing (Chapter Fifteen).

2. Remove the seat (Chapter Fifteen).

3. Support the motorcycle on a level surface with the rear wheel off the ground.

4. Remove the rear brake caliper (Chapter Fourteen).

5. Remove the rear wheel (A, **Figure 2**) (Chapter Eleven).

6. Support the swing arm at the rear to eliminate any load on the shock absorber and suspension linkage.

7. Remove the rear caliper brake hose from the swing arm clamp (B, **Figure 2**).

8. Remove the muffler and the muffler bracket (Chapter Eight).

9. Remove the sidestand (Chapter Fifteen).

10. If replacing the swing arm, break the chain (Chapter Eleven), otherwise it can remain in place as shown in this procedure.

11. If the drive chain is to remain in place, remove the drive sprocket (**Figure 28**) (Chapter Five).

12. If necessary, remove the screws and remove the chain guard from the swing arm.

13. Remove the shock absorber and suspension linkage as described in this chapter.

14. On the right side, use the swing arm pivot thrust adjuster socket wrench, and remove the pivot locknut (A, **Figure 25**).

NOTE
*A 24mm Allen socket is needed to hold, tighten and loosen the pivot shaft. If a 24mm Allen socket is unavailable, make a pivot shaft holder from (**Figure 29**) from a bolt and two nuts that measure 24mm across opposite flats. This tool also works on the front axle.*

15. Hold the pivot shaft (B, **Figure 25**) with the appropriate socket, and loosen the pivot nut (**Figure 26**) on the left side. Remove the pivot nut (**Figure 26**) from the pivot shaft.

16. Lower the swing arm (**Figure 30**).

17. Loosen the pivot shaft and withdraw it from the right side of the frame.

18. Remove the swing arm assembly from the frame

19. If the swing arm bearings will not be serviced, place a strip of duct tape each spacer to keep them in place.

20. Inspect the swing arm as described in this section.

Installation

1. Lubricate the swing arm and suspension linkage bearings, the pivot shaft and spacers with grease (Suzuki Super Grease A or equivalent) before installation.

13

2. Remove the duct tape and make sure the spacer (A, **Figure 31**) is in place each side of the swing arm pivot.

3. Set the swing arm in place under the motorcycle.

4. Raise the swing arm, and fit it between the frame pivots (**Figure 30**).

5. Insert the swing arm pivot shaft through the pivot boss in the right side of the frame, through the swing arm pivots, and out through the pivot boss in the left side.

6. Turn the pivot shaft into the frame pivot boss, and tighten the pivot shaft (B, **Figure 25**) to 15 N•m (11 ft.-lb.).

7. On the left side, loosely install the pivot nut (**Figure 26**) onto the end of the pivot shaft.

8. Set the thrust clearance by tightening the swing arm pivot fasteners in the order described in the following. Tighten each fastener to the specified torque (**Table 2**).

    a. Hold the pivot shaft (**Figure 32**) with the appropriate socket, and tighten the pivot nut (A, **Figure 33**) to 100 N•m (74 ft.-lb.).

    b. Screw the swing arm pivot locknut (A, **Figure 25**) onto the pivot shaft.

    c. Use the swing arm pivot thrust adjuster socket wrench, and tighten the pivot locknut (**Figure 34**) to 90 N•m (66 ft.-lb.).

9. Move the swing arm up and down and check for smooth movement. If the swing arm is tight or loose, the fasteners were either tightened in the wrong sequence or to the incorrect torque specification. Repeat Steps 5-7.

10. Support the swing arm at the rear.

11. Install the shock absorber as described in this chapter.

12. Install the shock absorber and suspension linkage as described in this chapter.

13. If removed, install the chain guard onto the swing arm and tighten screws securely.

14. If the drive chain remained in place, install the drive sprocket (B, **Figure 33**) (Chapter Five).

15. If removed, install a new drive chain (Chapter Eleven).

16. Install the sidestand (Chapter Fifteen).

17. Install the muffler bracket and the muffler (Chapter Eight).

18. Install the rear wheel (Chapter Eleven).

19. Install the brake hose onto the on the swing arm.

20. Install the rear brake caliper, and bleed the rear caliper (Chapter Fourteen).

21. Install the seat (Chapter Fifteen).

22. Install the lower fairing and the fairing side panel onto each side (Chapter Fifteen).

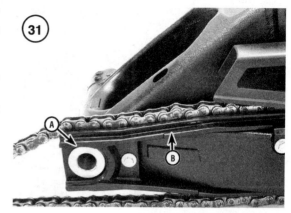

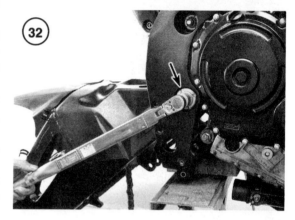

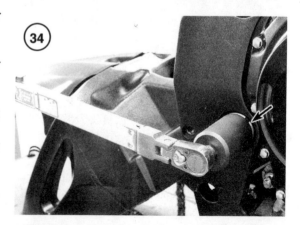

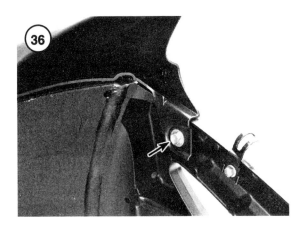

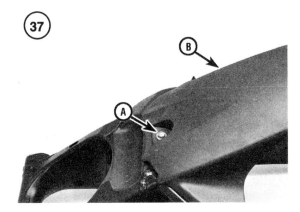

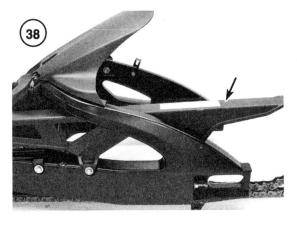

Disassembly

Refer to **Figure 27**.

1. Remove the swing arm assembly as described in this chapter.

2. Remove the spacer (**Figure 35**) from the needle bearing in each side of the swing arm pivot.

3. Remove the lower rear fender mounting bolts. Refer to **Figure 36** and A, **Figure 37** and remove the lower rear fender (B, **Figure 37**).

4. Remove the mounting bolts, and remove the chain guard (**Figure 38**).

5. Inspect the swing arm as described later in this section.

Assembly

1. Lubricate the swing arm pivot bearings (**Figure 39**) and spacers (**Figure 35**) with grease (Suzuki Super Grease A or equivalent):

2. Install the spacer (**Figure 35**) into the needle bearing on each side of the swing arm pivot.

3. Install the chain guard (**Figure 38**).

4. Install the lower rear fender (B, **Figure 37**) and mounting bolts and tighten securely. Refer to **Figure 36** and A, **Figure 37**.

Inspection

1. Wash the bolts and spacers in solvent, and thoroughly dry them.

2. Inspect the spacers (**Figure 35**) for wear, scratches or score marks.

3. Inspect the bearings as follows:

   a. Use a clean lint-free rag and wipe away surface grease from the needle bearings.

   b. Turn each needle bearing (**Figure 39**) by hand. The bearing should turn smoothly without excessive play or noise. Check the rollers for evidence of wear, pitting or rust.

   c. Reinstall each spacer into its bearing, and slowly rotate the spacer. Each must turn smoothly without excessive play or noise.

   d. Remove the spacers.

4. Replace any worn or damaged needle bearing as described in this chapter.

5. Check all welds on the swing arm (**Figure 40**) for cracks or fractures.

6. Inspect the drive chain adjuster block, adjuster (A, **Figure 41**), and the locknut (B) for wear or damage.

7. Check the pivot shaft (A, **Figure 42**) for straightness with V-blocks and a dial indicator (**Figure 43**). Replace the pivot shaft if its runout equals or exceeds the service limit specified in **Table 1**.

13

8. Inspect the threads on the pivot shaft (B, **Figure 42**), pivot nut (C), and pivot shaft locknut (D). If damage is noted, also inspect the threads in the frame pivot (**Figure 44**). Clean minor damage with a tap or die.

9. Inspect the drive chain slider (B, **Figure 31**) for wear or damage.

10. Inspect the suspension lever mounting bosses (**Figure 45**) for wear, cracks or damage.

11. If necessary, repair or replace any damage part(s).

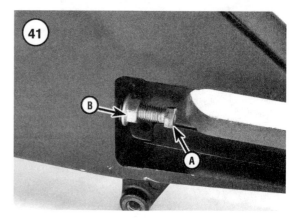

SUSPENSION BEARING

Swing Arm Needle Bearing
Removal/Installation

The 28 mm bearing remover set (Suzuki part No. 09921-20220 or equivalent), is needed to removed the bearings. The bearings can be installed using a homemade tool consisting of a piece of threaded rod, two thick washers and two nuts (**Figure 46**).

Do not remove the swing arm bearings unless they must be replaced. The needle bearings are pressed onto the swing arm and are damaged during removal. Replace the spacers (**Figure 35**) whenever replacing the swing arm pivot bearings (**Figure 39**). These parts should always be replaced as a set.

1. If still installed, remove the spacers from the needle bearings as described in this chapter.

2. Insert the blind bearing puller through the needle bearing, and expand it behind the bearing (**Figure 47**).

3. Using sharp strokes of the slide hammer, withdraw the needle bearing from the pivot boss.

4. Remove the bearing puller and the bearing.

5. Withdraw the distance collar located between the bearings.

6. Repeat for the bearing on the other side.

7. Thoroughly clean out the inside of the pivot bore with solvent, and dry it with compressed air.

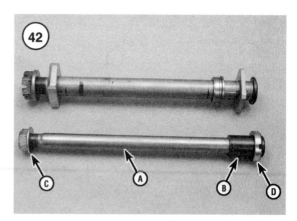

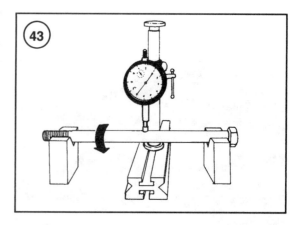

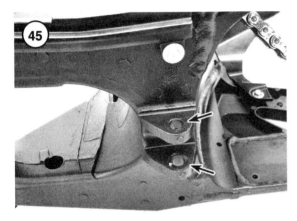

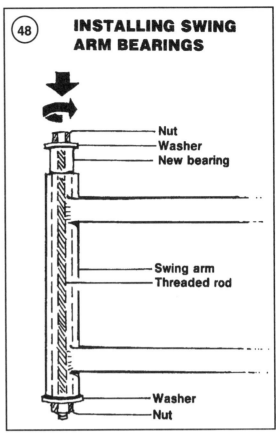

INSTALLING SWING ARM BEARINGS

Nut
Washer
New bearing

Swing arm
Threaded rod

Washer
Nut

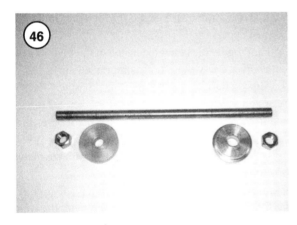

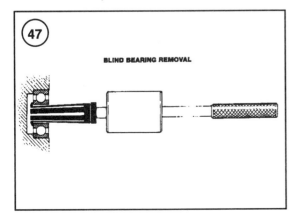

BLIND BEARING REMOVAL

8. Apply a light coat of grease (Suzuki Super Grease A or equivalent) to the exterior of the *new* bearings and to the inner circumference of the pivot bore.

NOTE
Install one needle bearing at a time. Make sure the bearing enters the pivot boss squarely, otherwise the bearing and the pivot boss may be damaged.

9. Position the bearing with the manufacturer's marks facing out.

10. Locate and square the new bearing in the pivot bore. Assemble the homemade tool through the pivot bore so the socket presses against the bearing.

11. Hold the nut at the bearing end of the tool (**Figure 48**).

12. Tighten the nut on the opposite end and pull the bearing into the pivot bore until the bearing sits flush with the outer surface of the pivot boss (**Figure 39**).

13. Install the distance collar.

14. Repeat Steps 9-13 and install the bearing into the opposite side of the pivot bore. Remove tool.

15. Make sure the bearings are properly seated. Turn each bearing by hand. It should turn smoothly.

16. Lubricate the new bearings with grease (Suzuki Super Grease A or equivalent).

13

Suspension Lever
and Suspension Arm Needle Bearing
Removal/Installation

The 17 mm, 20 mm, and 28 mm bearing remover set (Suzuki part No. 09921-20220 or equivalent), is needed to removed the bearings. The bearings can be installed using a homemade tool consisting of a piece of threaded rod, two thick washers and two nuts (**Figure 46**).

Do not remove the needle bearings unless they must be replaced. The needle bearings are pressed onto the lever, or arm, and are damaged during removal. If the needle bearings are replaced, replace the spacers at the same time. These parts should always be replaced as a set.

1. If still installed, remove the spacers from the suspension lever (**Figure 49**) and suspension arm (**Figure 50**).

2A. On the suspension arm, perform the following:
  a. Insert a blind bearing puller through the needle bearing and expand it behind the bearing in the front pivot bore (**Figure 47**).
  b. Using sharp strokes of the slide hammer, withdraw the needle bearing from the front pivot hole.
  c. Remove the special tool and the bearing.
  d. Repeat sub-step a and b for the bearing on the other side of the center pivot bore.

2B. On the suspension lever-to-suspension arm 20 mm bearings, perform the following:
  a. Insert a blind bearing puller through the needle bearing and expand it behind the bearing in the pivot bore (**Figure 47**).
  b. Using sharp strokes of the slide hammer, withdraw the needle bearing from the front pivot hole.

> *NOTE*
> *The bearings are different sizes. Mark the bearings front, center and rear as they are removed. The center two bearings are identical.*

  c. Remove the special tool and the bearing.
  d. Repeat sub-step a, and b for the bearing on the other side of the pivot bore.

2C. On the remaining two 17 mm suspension lever bearings, perform the following:
  a. Support the suspension arm on wooden blocks.
  b. Use a bearing drive or socket that matches the diameter of the bearing outer race.
  c. Carefully tap the bearing out of the suspension arm bore.

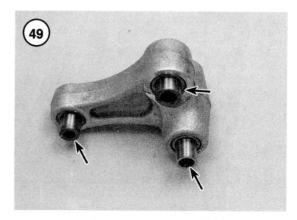

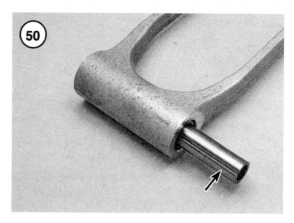

  d. Repeat sub-step b and c for the other bearing, if necessary.

3. Thoroughly clean out the inside of the pivot bores with solvent. Dry them with compressed air.

4. Apply a light coat of grease (Suzuki Super Grease A or equivalent) to the exterior of the *new* bearings and to the inner circumference of the pivot bores.

5. Locate and square the new bearing in the pivot bore. Position the center bore bearings with the manufacturer's marks face out.

6A. Install each bearing with the homemade tool by performing Steps 9-12 of *Swing Arm Needle Bearing Replacement* in this section.

6B. If the homemade tool is unavailable, install the bearings with a hammer and socket that matches the outer race diameter. Tap the bearings into place.

7. Check that each bearing is properly seated in the suspension arm and lever. Turn each bearing by hand. The bearing should turn smoothly.

8. Lubricate the needles of the new bearing with grease (Suzuki Super Grease A or equivalent).

9. Installed the spacers into the suspension lever (**Figure 49**) and suspension arm (**Figure 50**).

Table 1 REAR SUSPENSION SPECIFICATIONS

Item	Specification
Rear wheel travel	130 mm (5.1 in.)
Swing arm pivot-shaft runout wear limit	0.3 mm (0.01 in.)
Shock absorber	
2006-2007 models	
Spring preload	
Standard preload (spring length)	181.4 mm (7.14 in.)
Max preload (min spring length)	186.4 mm (7.34 in.
Min preload (max spring length)	176.4 mm (6.94 in.)
Rebound damping	
Standard	1 ½ turns out
Low speed	1 ¾ turns out
High speed	3 turns out
Compression damping	
Low speed	2 turns out
High speed	3 turns out
2008-2009 models	
GSX-R600	
Spring preload	
Standard preload (spring length)	181.4 mm (7.14 in.)
Max preload (min spring length)	186.4 mm (7.34 in.
Min preload (max spring length)	176.4 mm (6.94 in.)
Rebound damping	2 turns out
Compression damping	
Low speed	2 turns out
High speed	3 turns out
GSX-R750	
Spring preload	
Standard preload (spring length)	182.3 mm (7.18 in.)
Max preload (min spring length)	186.4 mm (7.34 in.
Min preload (max spring length)	176.4 mm (6.94 in.)
Rebound damping	2 turns out
Compression damping	
Low speed	2 turns out
High speed	3 turns out

Table 2 REAR SUSPENSION TORQUE SPECIFICATIONS

Item	N•m	in.-lb.	ft.-lb.
Rear axle nut	100	–	74
Rear sprocket nut	60	–	44
Shock absorber			
Mounting bolt/nut	50	–	37
Suspension arm bolt/nut	78	–	57
Suspension lever bolt/nut	98	–	71
Swing arm			
Pivot nut	100	–	74
Pivot shaft locknut	90	–	66
Pivot shaft	15	–	11

13

Notes

CHAPTER FOURTEEN

BRAKES

This chapter covers all brake components. **Tables 1-3** are at the end of this chapter.

BRAKE SERVICE PRECAUTIONS

CAUTION
Do not use silicone-based DOT 5 brake fluid on the motorcycles covered in this manual. Silicone-based fluid can damage these brake components leading to a brake system failure.

CAUTION
Never reuse brake fluid, like the fluid expelled during brake bleeding. Contaminated brake fluid can cause brake failure. Dispose of used brake fluid properly.

WARNING
When working on the brake system. do not inhale brake dust. It may contain asbestos, which can cause lung injury and cancer. Wear a face mask that meets OSHA requirements for trapping asbestos particles, and wash hands and forearms thoroughly after completing the work. Never use compressed air to

clean any part of the brake system. Use an aerosol brake cleaner.

When working on hydraulic brakes, the work area and all tools must be absolutely clean. Caliper or master cylinder components can be damaged by even tiny particles of grit that enter the brake system. Do not use sharp tools inside the master cylinder, calipers or on the pistons.

Note the following when working on the brake systems:

1. Disc brake components rarely require disassembly. Do not disassemble them unless necessary.
2. When adding brake fluid, only use DOT 4 brake fluid from a sealed container. Other grades of brake fluid may vaporize and cause brake failure.
3. Always use the same brand of brake fluid. One manufacturer's brake fluid may not be compatible with another's. Do not mix different brands of brake fluids.
4. Brake fluid absorbs moisture from the air, which greatly reduces its ability to perform correctly. Purchase brake fluid in small containers, and properly discard any small leftover quantities.
5. Always keep the master cylinder reservoir cover installed. It keeps dust or moisture out of the system.
6. Use only DOT 4 brake fluid or isopropyl alcohol to wash parts. Never use petroleum-based solvents of

14

any kind on the brake system's internal components. The seals will swell and distort.

7. Whenever any brake banjo bolt or brake line nut is loosened, the system is opened and must be bled to remove air. If the brakes feel spongy, this usually means air has entered the system. For safe operation, refer to *Brake Bleeding* in this chapter.

BRAKE BLEEDING

General Bleeding Tips

Bleeding the brakes removes air from the brake system. Air in the brakes increases brake-lever or brake-pedal travel, and it makes the brakes feel soft or spongy. Under extreme circumstances, it can cause complete loss of brake pressure.

The brakes can be bled manually or with the use of a vacuum pump. Both methods are described in this section. Refer to *Brake Service* in this section.

1. Clean the bleed valve and surrounding area before beginning. Make sure the opening in the valve is clear.

2. Use a box end wrench to open and close the bleed valve. This prevents damage to the valve.

3. Replace a bleed valve with damaged threads or a rounded hex head. A damaged valve is difficult to remove, and it cannot be properly tightened.

4. Use a clear catch hose (**Figure 1**) so the fluid can be seen as it leaves the bleed valve. Air bubbles in the catch hose indicate that air may be trapped in the brake system.

5. Open the bleed valve just enough to allow fluid to pass through the valve and into the catch bottle. If a bleed valve is too loose, air can be drawn into the system through the valve threads.

6. If air does enter through the valve threads, apply silicone brake grease around the valve where it emerges from the caliper. The grease should seal the valve and prevent the entry of air. Wipe away the grease once the brakes have been bled.

7. Tapping the banjo bolts at the calipers, master cylinders and any other hose connections in the brake line also helps dislodge trapped air bubbles.

Manual Bleeding

> *NOTE*
> *The setting on the front brake lever adjusters affects bleeding. Initially bleed the front brake first with the adjuster (**Figure 2**) on the No. 6 setting. Check the feel with the lever adjuster in several settings once the brakes feel solid. If the levers feels soft at any setting or*

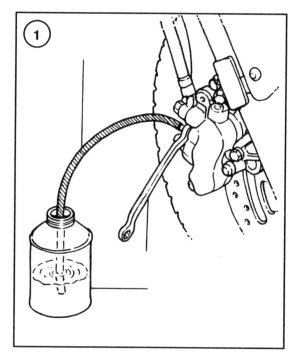

if the lever hits the handlebar, air is still trapped in the system. Continue bleeding.

1. Make sure all banjo bolts in the system are tight.

2. Remove the dust cap from the bleed valve on the caliper assembly.

3. Connect a length of clear tubing to the bleed valve (**Figure 1**, typical). Place the other end of the tube into a clean container. Fill the container with enough fresh DOT 4 brake fluid to keep the end submerged. The tube should be long enough so that its loop is higher than the bleed valve. This prevents air from being drawn into the caliper during bleeding.

NOTE
When bleeding the front brakes, turn the handlebars straight ahead to level the front master cylinder.

4. Clean all dirt or foreign matter from the top of the master cylinder reservoir,

5A. On the front master cylinder perform the following:

   a. Remove the mounting screw (A, **Figure 3**) from the front master cylinder, and keep it upright.

   b. Remove the top cover, diaphragm plate and diaphragm (B, **Figure 3**).

5B. On the rear master cylinder perform the following:

   a. Remove the mounting bolt (**Figure 4**) and move the master cylinder away from the frame to access the top cover, and keep it upright.

   b. Make sure the top of the reservoir is level.

   c. Remove the screws, top cover, and diaphragm (**Figure 5**)

6. Add brake fluid to the reservoir until the fluid level reaches the reservoir upper limit. Loosely install the diaphragm and the cover. Leave them in place during bleeding to keep dirt out of the system and so brake fluid cannot spurt from the reservoir.

7. Pump the brake lever or brake pedal a few times, and then release it.

8. Apply the brake lever or pedal until it stops, and hold it in this position.

9. Open the bleed valve with a wrench. Let the brake lever or pedal move to the limit of its travel, and then close the bleed valve. Do not release the brake lever or pedal while the bleed valve is open.

NOTE
As break fluid enters the system, the level in the reservoir drops. Add brake fluid as necessary to keep the fluid level 10 mm (3/8 in.) below the reservoir top so air will not be drawn into the system.

10. Repeat Steps 6-9 until the brake fluid flowing from the hose is clear and free of air. If the system is difficult to bleed, tap the master cylinder or caliper with a soft mallet to release trapped air bubbles.

11. Test the feel of the brake lever or pedal. It should feel firm and offer the same resistance each time it is operated. If the lever or pedal feels soft, air is still trapped in the system. Continue bleeding.

12. When bleeding is complete, disconnect the hose from the bleed valve. Tighten the bleed valve to specification (**Table 2**).

13A. When bleeding the front brakes, repeat Steps 2-11 on the opposite front caliper. Also repeat Steps 2-11 at the bleed valve (**Figure 6**) on the front brake master cylinder.

14

13B. When bleeding the rear brakes, repeat Steps 2-11 at the bleed valve (**Figure 7**) on the caliper.

14. Add fresh DOT 4 brake fluid to the master cylinder to correct the fluid level.

15. Install the diaphragm, diaphragm plate (front brake) and top cap. Be sure the cap is secured in place. Install the top-cover clamp onto the front master cylinder reservoir.

16. Test ride the motorcycle slowly at first to make sure the brakes are operating properly.

Vacuum Bleeding

1. Make sure all banjo bolts in the system are tight.

2. Remove the dust cap (**Figure 2**) from the bleed valve on the caliper assembly.

> *NOTE*
> *When bleeding the front brakes, turn the handlebars straight ahead to level the front master cylinder.*

3. Clean all dirt or foreign matter from the top of the master cylinder reservoir.

4A. On the front master cylinder perform the following:

    a. Remove the mounting screw (A, **Figure 3**) from the front master cylinder, and keep it upright.

    b. Remove the top cover, diaphragm plate and diaphragm (B, **Figure 3**)

4B. On the rear master cylinder perform the following:

    a. Remove the mounting bolt (**Figure 4**) and move the master cylinder away from the frame to access the top cover, and keep it upright.

    b. Make sure the top of the reservoir is level.

    c. Remove the screws, top cover, and diaphragm (**Figure 5**).

5. Add fresh DOT 4 brake fluid to the reservoir until the fluid level reaches the reservoir upper limit. Loosely install the diaphragm and the cover. Leave them in place during bleeding to keep dirt out of the system and so brake fluid cannot spurt out of the reservoir.

6. Assemble the vacuum tool following the manufacturer's instructions.

7. Connect the vacuum pump's catch hose to the bleed valve on the brake caliper (**Figure 8**).

> *NOTE*
> *When using a vacuum pump, watch the brake fluid level in the reservoir. It will drop quite rapidly, particularly the rear reservoir, which does not hold as much brake fluid as the front. Stop often and check the brake fluid level. Maintain the level at 10 mm (3/8 in.) from the top*

of the reservoir so air will not be drawn into the system.

8. Operate the vacuum pump to create vacuum in the hose.

9. Use a wrench to open the bleed valve. The vacuum pump should pull fluid from the system. Close the bleed valve before the brake fluid stops flowing from the system or before the master cylinder reservoir runs empty. Add fluid to the reservoir as necessary.

10. Operate the brake lever or brake pedal a few times, and release it.

11. Repeat Steps 7-10 until the fluid leaving the bleed valve is clear and free of air bubbles. If the system is difficult to bleed, tap the master cylinder and caliper housing with a soft mallet to release trapped air bubbles.

> *NOTE*
> *The setting on the front brake lever adjuster affects bleeding. Initially bleed the front brakes with the adjuster turned to the No. 5 setting. Once the brakes feel solid; check the feel with the adjuster in several settings. If the lever feels soft at any setting or if the lever hits the handlebar, air is still trapped in the system. Continue bleeding.*

12. Test the feel of the brake lever or brake pedal. It should feel firm and offer the same resistance each time it is operated. If the lever or pedal feels soft, air is still trapped in the system. Continue bleeding.

13. When bleeding is complete, disconnect the hose from the bleed valve, and tighten the valve to specification (**Table 1**).

14A. When bleeding the front brakes, repeat Steps 2-11 on the opposite front caliper. Also repeat Steps 2-12 at the bleed valve (**Figure 8**) on the front brake master cylinder.

14B. When bleeding the rear brakes, repeat Steps 2-11 at the bleed valve (**Figure 7**) on the caliper.

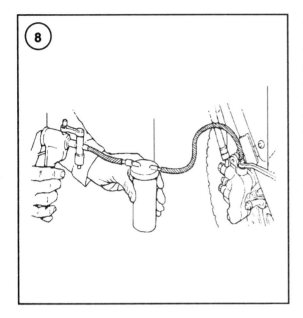

15. When bleeding is complete, disconnect the hose from the bleed valve, and tighten the valve to specification (**Table 1**).

16. Add fresh DOT 4 brake fluid to the master cylinder to correct the fluid level.

17. Install the diaphragm, diaphragm plate (front brake) and top cap. Be sure the cap is secured in place. Install the clamp onto the front brake master cylinder.

18. Test ride the motorcycle slowly at first to make sure the brakes are operating properly.

DRAINING BRAKE FLUID

Before disconnecting a brake hose, drain the brake fluid from the front or rear brakes as described below. Draining the fluid reduces the amount of fluid that can spill out when system components are removed.

Manual Draining

1. Remove the dust cap (**Figure 2**) from the bleed valve on the caliper assembly. Remove all dirt from the valve and its outlet port.

2. Connect a length of clear hose to the bleed valve on the caliper. Insert the other end into a container (**Figure 1**, typical).

3. Apply the front brake lever or the rear brake pedal until it stops. Hold the lever or pedal in this position.

4. Open the bleed valve with a wrench, and let the lever or pedal move to the limit of its travel. Close the bleed valve.

5. Release the lever or pedal, and repeat Step 3 and Step 4 until brake fluid stops flowing from the bleed valve.

6. When bleeding the front brakes, repeat Steps 2-5 on the opposite front caliper. Also repeat Steps 2-11 at the bleed valve (**Figure 8**) on the front brake master cylinder. When draining the rear brakes, repeat this on the second bleed valve.

7. Discard the brake fluid.

Vacuum Draining

1. Connect the pump's catch hose to the bleed valve on the brake caliper.

2. Operate the vacuum pump to create vacuum in the hose.

3. Use a wrench to open the bleed valve. The vacuum pump should pull fluid from the system.

4. When fluid has stopped flowing through the hose, close the bleed valve.

5. Repeat Steps 2-4 until brake fluid no longer flows from the bleed valve.

6. When bleeding the front brakes, repeat Steps 2-5 on the opposite front caliper. Also repeat Steps 2-4 at the bleed valve (**Figure 7**) on the front brake master cylinder. When draining the rear brakes, repeat this on the second bleed valve.

7. Discard the brake fluid.

BRAKE PAD INSPECTION

Brake pad wear depends greatly upon riding habits and conditions. Check the brake pads frequently.

To maintain even brake pressure on the disc, always replace all pads in a caliper at the same time. When replacing the front brake pads, replace all pads in both front calipers *at the same time*.

The brake hose does not need to be disconnected from the caliper during brake pad replacement. If the hose is removed, the brakes will have to be bled as described in this chapter. Disconnect the hose only when servicing the brake caliper.

Refer to Brake service *in this chapter.*

> *CAUTION*
> *Check the pads more frequently as the brake pads approach the bottom of the wear mark (**Figure 9**). On some pads, the wear limit marks are very close to the metal backing plate. If pad wear happens to be uneven, the backing plate may contact the disc and cause damage.*

14

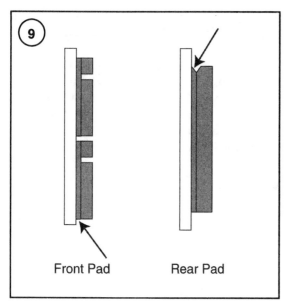

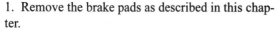

Front Pad   Rear Pad

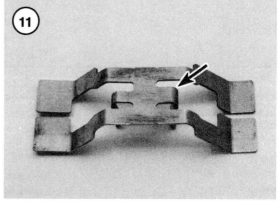

1. Remove the brake pads as described in this chapter.

2. Inspect the brake pads as following:

   a. Inspect the friction material (**Figure 10**, typical) for light surface dirt, grease and oil contamination. Remove light contamination with sandpaper. If contamination has penetrated the surface, replace the brake pads.

   b. Inspect the brake pads for excessive wear or damage. Replace the brake pads if either pad is worn to the bottom of the wear groove.

   c. Inspect the friction material for uneven wear, damage or contamination. All pads in a caliper should show approximately the same amount of wear. If the pads are wearing unevenly, the caliper may not be operating correctly.

   d. Inspect the metal plate on the back of each pad for corrosion and damage.

3. Use brake parts cleaner and a fine grade emery cloth to remove all road debris and brake pad residue from the brake disc surface.

4. Inspect the brake disc as described in this chapter.

5. Check the friction surface of the new pads for any foreign matter or manufacturing residue. If necessary, clean the pads with an aerosol brake cleaner.

6. Check the pad springs for wear or fatigue. Examine the spring in a front caliper, (**Figure 11**) or rear caliper (**Figure 12**). Replace the pad springs if any shows any sign of damage or excessive wear.

7. Thoroughly clean any corrosion or road dirt from the pad spring(s) and pad pin (where installed).

8. Inspect the pad pin (**Figure 13**). Replace a pin that is bent or worn.

9. Service the brake disc as follows:

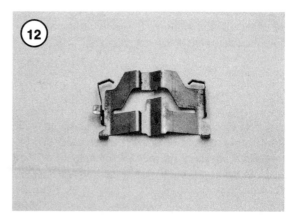

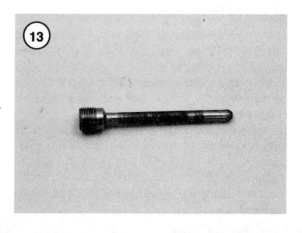

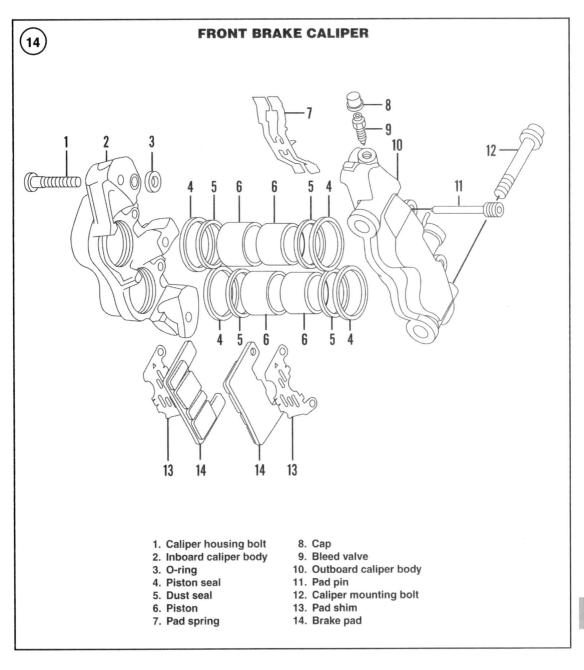

FRONT BRAKE CALIPER

1. Caliper housing bolt
2. Inboard caliper body
3. O-ring
4. Piston seal
5. Dust seal
6. Piston
7. Pad spring
8. Cap
9. Bleed valve
10. Outboard caliper body
11. Pad pin
12. Caliper mounting bolt
13. Pad shim
14. Brake pad

NOTE
A thorough cleaning of the brake disc is especially important when changing brake pad compounds. Many compounds are not compatible with each other. When purchasing new pads, make sure the compound of the new pads is compatible with the disc material.

a. Use brake cleaner and a fine grade emery cloth to remove all brake pad residue and any rust from the brake disc. Clean both sides of the disc.

b. Check the brake disc for wear as described in this chapter.

FRONT BRAKE CALIPER

Refer to **Figure 14** and read *Brake Service* in this chapter.

Brake Pad Removal/Installation

CAUTION
Check the pads more frequently as the pad thickness approaches the wear

*limit line (**Figure 15,** typical). The limit line is very close to the metal backing plate. If pad wear happens to be uneven for some reason, the backing plate could come in contact with the disc and cause damage.*

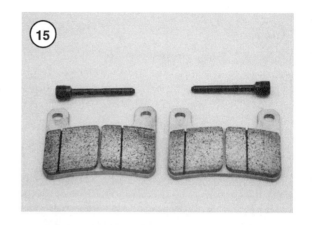

NOTE
The following photographs show brake pad replacement in a caliper that has been completely removed from the motorcycle. The pads can be replaced while the brake line is connected to the caliper.

1. Support the motorcycle on a level surface.
2. To prevent the front brake lever from being applied, secure a block of wood or another spacer between the brake lever and the throttle grip so the brake lever cannot be inadvertently squeezed.
3. Loosen each pad pin (A, **Figure 16**) from the caliper.
4. Remove the caliper mounting bolts (B, **Figure 16**), and lift the caliper (C) off the brake disc.

NOTE
Always replace both pads in both calipers as a set.

5. Remove the inboard and the outboard pads (**Figure 17**) from the caliper.
6. Remove the pad spring (**Figure 18**). Note that the side with the wider tang (**Figure 19**) faces toward the caliper bleed valve.
7. Inspect the brake pads as described in this chapter.
8. When new pads are installed in the calipers, the master cylinder brake fluid level rises as the caliper pistons are repositioned. If installing new brake pads, perform the following:

   a. Position the handlebars so the master cylinder reservoir is level.
   b. Remove the mounting screw (A, **Figure 3**) from the front master cylinder.
   c. Clean the top of the master cylinder of all dirt and foreign matter.
   d. Remove the top cover, diaphragm plate and diaphragm (B, **Figure 3**).
   e. Use a syringe to remove approximately half of the brake fluid from the reservoir.
   f. Temporarily install both old brake pads into the caliper and seat them against the pistons.
   g. Grasp the caliper and brake pad with a large pair of slip-joint pliers and squeeze the pistons back into the caliper. Pad the caliper with a shop cloth to prevent scuffing. Repeat for each side until the pistons are completely in the cali-

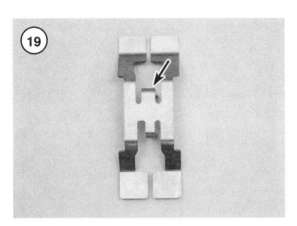

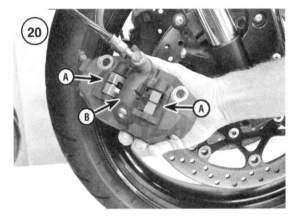

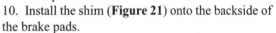

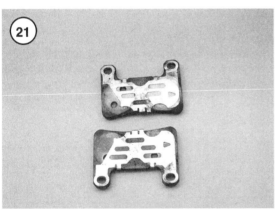

per. Constantly check the reservoir and make sure the fluid does not overflow. Draw out excess fluid as necessary.

   h. The pistons should move freely. If they do not, remove and service the caliper as described in this chapter.

   i. Remove the old brake pads.

   j. Install the diaphragm, top cover and screws.

9. Seat the pad spring in the caliper as follows:

   a. Position the spring so the side with the wider tang (**Figure 19**) faces the caliper bleed valve.

   b. Install the pad spring so the tangs (A, **Figure 20**) straddle the boss (B) in the bottom of the caliper.

10. Install the shim (**Figure 21**) onto the backside of the brake pads.

11. Align brake pad holes with the pad pin holes in the caliper, and install the brake pads (**Figure 22**).

12. Install each pad pin. Make each pin passes through the holes in both brake pads and into the inboard side of the caliper.

13. Carefully separate the brake pads (**Figure 23**) to allow room for the brake disc.

14. Lower the caliper assembly onto the disc. Exercise caution so the leading edges of the brake pads are not damaged.

15. Install the caliper mounting bolts (B, **Figure 16**) and tighten to specifications (**Table 2**).

16. Repeat Steps 9-15, and replace the front brake pads in the other front caliper.

17. Remove the spacer from the front brake lever.

18. Pump the front brake lever to reposition the brake pads against the brake disc. Roll the motorcycle back and forth and continue to pump the brake lever as many times as it takes to refill the cylinders in the calipers to correctly locate the brake pads against the disc.

19. Refill the master cylinder reservoir, if necessary, to maintain the correct fluid level as indicated on the side of the reservoir. Install the diaphragm, diaphragm plate, and the top cover (B, **Figure 3**).

20. Install the front master cylinder mounting screw (A, **Figure 3**) and tighten securely.

Caliper Removal/Installation

1. Support the motorcycle on a level surface.
2. If the caliper will be disassembled for service, perform the following:
   a. Remove the brake pads (this section).
   b. Drain the brake fluid from the front brakes as described in this chapter.
   c. Remove the banjo bolt (A, **Figure 24**) and sealing washers attaching the brake hose(s) to the caliper assembly. There are two sealing washers on the left caliper, and three on the right.
   d. Place the loose end of the brake hose(s) into a plastic bag so residual brake fluid to keep residual fluid leaking onto the motorcycle.

NOTE
The caliper hose as well as the cross-over hose attach to the right caliper. Consequently, the banjo bolt on the right caliper is longer than the banjo bolt on the left caliper.

   e. Loosen the caliper housing bolts (B, **Figure 24**).
3. Remove the caliper mounting bolts (B, **Figure 24**), and lift the brake caliper from the disc.
4. If necessary, disassemble and service the caliper assembly as described in this chapter.
5. Install the caliper by reversing these removal steps. Note the following:
   a. Lower the caliper assembly onto the disc. Exercise caution so the leading edges of the brake pads are not damaged.
   b. Install the caliper mounting bolts (B, **Figure 24**) and tighten to 35 N•m (25.5 ft.-lb.).
   c. Install the brake hose onto the caliper. On a right caliper, install the master cylinder hose and then install the crossover hose. Install a new *sealing washer on each side of the brake hose fitting(s) and install the banjo bolt (A,* **Figure 24**). Install two new sealing washers on a left caliper, three *new* sealing washers on a right caliper.
   d. Position the brake hose neck(s) so they rest against the caliper stop post (**Figure 25**). Tighten the banjo bolt to 23 N•m (17 ft.-lb.).
   e. Bleed the brakes as described in this chapter.

Disassembly

Refer to **Figure 26**.

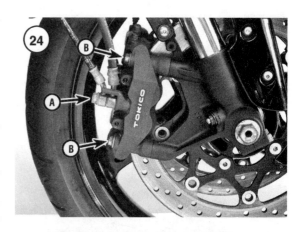

1. Remove the brake pads and caliper as described in this chapter.
2. Remove the caliper housing bolts (**Figure 27**).
3. Separate the caliper body halves. Remove and discard the O-ring(s) from the fluid port in the caliper half. A *new* O-ring must be installed during assembly.

NOTE
If the pistons were partially forced out of the caliper body during removal, steps 4-6 may not be necessary. If the pistons or caliper bores are corroded or very dirty, compressed air may be necessary to completely remove the pistons from the bores.

4. Tighten the bleed valve securely.

WARNING
In the next step, the piston may come out of the caliper body with considerable force. Protect yourself with shop gloves and safety goggles.

5. Place the caliper body face down on a rubber mat. The mat helps seal the fluid passages. Press the caliper firmly into the mat, and apply the air pressure in

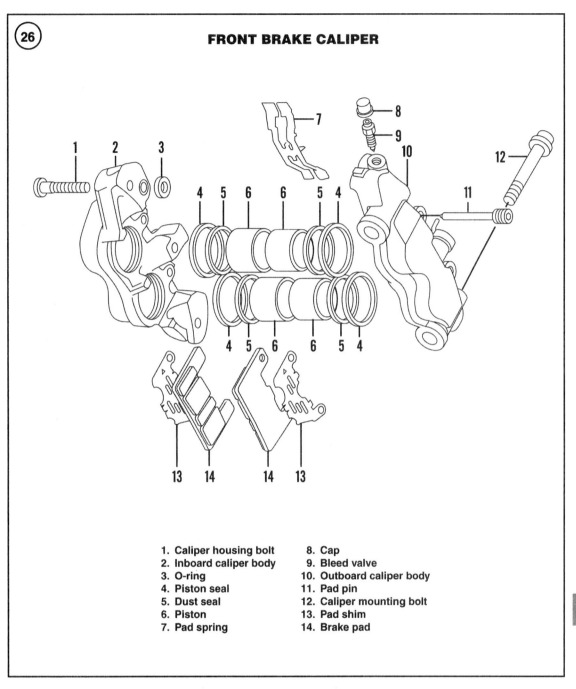

FRONT BRAKE CALIPER

1. Caliper housing bolt
2. Inboard caliper body
3. O-ring
4. Piston seal
5. Dust seal
6. Piston
7. Pad spring
8. Cap
9. Bleed valve
10. Outboard caliper body
11. Pad pin
12. Caliper mounting bolt
13. Pad shim
14. Brake pad

14

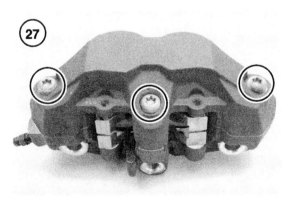

short spurts to hydraulic passageway on the caliper body (**Figure 28**). Repeat this process for the other caliper body half.

6. If only one piston comes out of the caliper body, perform the following:

    a. Push this piston back into the caliper body, and set the caliper body face down on the mat.

    b. Place a flat piece of plastic or a wooden shim under the piston that came out.

    c. Press the caliper firmly into the mat, and apply air to the banjo fitting as described in Step 5. The shim will prevent the easy piston from coming out too far so that both pistons can be driven from their respective bores.

   d. Remove each piston (**Figure 29**) from its bore by hand.

7. Repeat the Steps 4-6 for the other caliper half.

CAUTION
In the following step, do not use a sharp tool to remove the dust and piston seals from the caliper cylinders. Do not damage the cylinder surface.

8. Use a piece of wood or plastic scraper and carefully push the dust seal (A, **Figure 30**) and the piston seal (B) in toward the caliper cylinder and out of their grooves. Remove the dust and piston seals from each cylinder in each caliper half, and discard all seals.

9. If necessary, unscrew and remove the bleed valve.

10. Inspect the caliper assembly (this section).

Assembly

1. Soak the *new* dust and piston seals in fresh DOT 4 brake fluid.

2. Coat the cylinder bores and pistons with clean DOT 4 brake fluid.

3. Carefully install a piston seal (**Figure 31**) into the lower groove in each cylinder. Make sure each seal is properly seated in its respective groove.

4. Carefully install a *new* dust seal (**Figure 32**) into the upper groove in each cylinder. Make sure all seals are properly seated in their respective grooves.

5. Repeat Step 3 and Step 4 for the other caliper body half.

6. Position the pistons with the open ends facing out, and install the pistons into the caliper cylinders (**Figure 33**). Push the pistons in until they bottom.

7. Repeat Step 6 for the other caliper body half. Make sure all pistons are installed correctly.

8. Set the pad spring into place in the outboard caliper half so the pad spring fingers (A and B, **Figure 34**) straddle the center boss. Make sure the wider finger (A, **Figure 34**) faces the bleed valve (C) end of the caliper.

9. Coat the *new* O-ring(s) in DOT 4 brake fluid and seat the O-ring(s) (D, **Figure 34**) into the fluid port depression in the caliper half.

10. Lower the outboard caliper half over the inboard caliper half. Make sure the O-ring remains properly seated.

11. Install the caliper housing bolts (**Figure 27**). Evenly tighten the bolts to 22 N•m (16 ft.-lb.).

12. If removed, install the bleed valve assembly (C, **Figure 34**) and tighten to 7.5 N•m (66 in.-lb.).

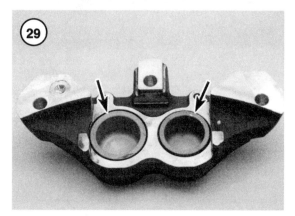

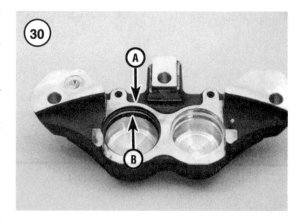

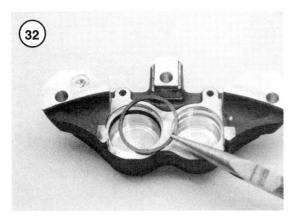

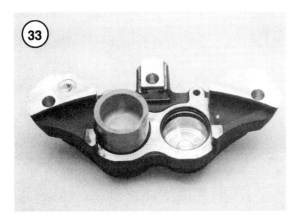

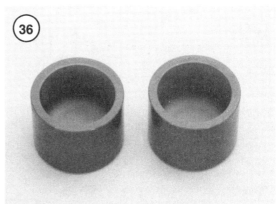

13. Install the caliper and brake pads as described in this section.
14. Bleed the brake as described in this chapter.

Inspection

1. Clean both caliper body halves (A, **Figure 35**) and all pistons (**Figure 36**) in fresh DOT 4 brake fluid or isopropyl alcohol. Thoroughly dry the parts with compressed air.
2. Make sure the fluid passageways in the base of the cylinder bores are clear. Apply compressed air to the openings to make sure they are clear. Clean out the passages, if necessary, with fresh brake fluid.
3. Make sure the fluid passageways in the caliper body halves are clean. Apply compressed air to the openings to make sure they are clear. Clean them with fresh brake fluid, if necessary.
4. Inspect the dust seal groove (B, **Figure 35**) and piston seal groove (C) in all cylinder for damage. If any groove is damaged or corroded, replace the caliper assembly.
5. Inspect the cylinder walls (D, **Figure 35**) and pistons (**Figure 36**) for scratches, scoring or other damage.
6. Measure the cylinder bores with a bore gauge or vernier caliper. Refer to the specifications listed in **Table 1**.
7. Measure the outside diameter of the pistons with a micrometer (**Figure 37**) or vernier caliper. Refer to the specifications listed in **Table 1**.
8. Inspect the banjo bolt threaded hole and the bleed valve threaded hole. If either is worn or damaged, clean it out with a metric thread tap or replace the caliper assembly.
9. Apply compressed air to each opening and make sure it is clear. Clean out if necessary with fresh brake fluid.
10. Inspect both caliper bodies for damage. Inspect the threads of the caliper housing bolt holes (E, **Figure 35**) and the caliper mounting bolt holes.

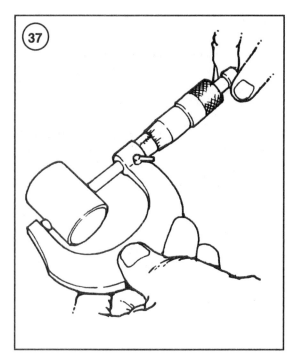

Clean any thread with an appropriate size metric tap or replace the caliper assembly.

FRONT BRAKE MASTER CYLINDER

Removal

> *NOTE*
> *The front fairing is shown removed in the following steps. It is not necessary, but it does allow additional working space.*

Refer to *Brake Service* in this chapter.

1. If the master cylinder will be serviced, perform the following:
   a. Drain the brake fluid from the front brakes as described in this chapter.
   b. Place a rag beneath the banjo bolt and remove the bolt (**Figure 38**) and separate the brake hose from the master cylinder. Account for the two sealing washers, one from each side of the brake hose fitting.
   c. Disconnect the reservoir hose from the fitting on the master cylinder (A, **Figure 39**). Be prepared to catch any residual brake fluid that dribbles from the hose.
   d. Place the loose end of the brake hose in a plastic bag to keep residual brake fluid from leaking on the motorcycle.
2. Disconnect the brake light switch electrical connectors from the front brake switch (**Figure 40**).

3. Unscrew the reservoir bolt (B, **Figure 39**) and separate the reservoir from its mounting bracket.
4. Remove the master cylinder clamp bolts (**Figure 41**), and remove the master cylinder from the handlebar.
5. If the master cylinder will be serviced, drain any residual brake fluid from the master cylinder and reservoir. Dispose of fluid properly.

Installation

1. Set the front master cylinder onto the right handlebar so its clamp mating surface aligns with the indexing dot (**Figure 42**).

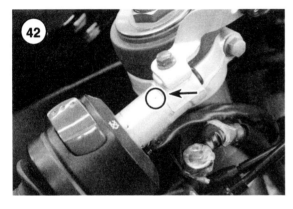

2. Mount the clamp with the UP mark facing up, and install the master cylinder clamp bolts (**Figure 41**). Tighten the upper clamp bolt first, then the lower bolt leaving a gap at the bottom. Tighten the master cylinder clamp bolts to 10 N•m (89 in.-lb.).

3. Connect the brake light switch electrical connector to the brake light switch (A, **Figure 41**).

4. Set the reservoir into place on its mounting bracket. Install the mounting bolt (B, **Figure 39**) securely.

5. Install the brake hose onto the master cylinder fitting (**Figure 38**). Install a *new* sealing washer onto each side of the hose fitting, and tighten the banjo bolt (**Figure 38**) to 23 N•m (17 ft.-lb.).

6. Refill the master cylinder reservoir, and bleed the brake system as described in this chapter.

Disassembly

Refer to **Figure 43**.

1. Remove the master cylinder (this section).

2. Release the hose clamp (A, **Figure 44**) and disconnect the reservoir hose from the master cylinder.

3. Remove the cap (B, **Figure 44**), diaphragm plate and diaphragm from the reservoir.

4. Slide the dust cover (**Figure 45**) away from the fluid port on the master cylinder.

5. Remove the snap ring (A, **Figure 46**), and lift the hose fitting (B) from the port.

6. Remove and discard the O-ring (A, **Figure 47**).

7. Loosen the mounting screw (A, **Figure 48**), and remove the front brake light switch.

8. Remove the nut (B, **Figure 48**) and washer from the brake lever pivot bolt.

9. Remove the brake lever pivot bolt (A, **Figure 49**), and slide the lever from the master cylinder bracket.

10. Roll the rubber boot (A, **Figure 50**) from the cylinder bore, and remove the boot/pushrod assembly (B).

11. Press the piston into the cylinder bore, and remove the snap ring (A, **Figure 51**).

12. Remove the piston (A, **Figure 52**) and the spring (A, **Figure 53**) from the cylinder bore. Watch for the spring guide (B, **Figure 53**).

Assembly

1. Soak the *new* cups and the *new* piston assembly in fresh DOT 4 brake fluid for at least 15 minutes to make them pliable. Coat the inside of the cylinder bore with fresh brake fluid prior to the assembly of parts.

2. Install the spring (A, **Figure 53**) into the piston so the spring guide (B, **Figure 53**) engages the dimple in the cylinder bore (A, **Figure 54**).

CAUTION
When installing the piston assembly, do not allow the cups to turn inside out. They will be damaged and allow brake fluid to leak within the cylinder bore.

3. Lubricate the piston (A, **Figure 52**) with fresh DOT 4 brake fluid, and install the piston over the spring (B) and into the cylinder bore.

4. Press the piston into the bore, and secure it in place with a *new* snap ring (A, **Figure 51**). Completely seat the snap ring init groove inside the cylinder bore.

5. Lubricate the boot with fresh DOT 4 brake fluid. Carefully roll the boot over the pushrod (A, **Figure 55**).

6. Apply grease (Suzuki Super Grease A or an equivalent) to the round end of the pushrod, and insert this end into the seat of the piston (B, **Figure 51**).

7. Carefully roll the dust boot (A, **Figure 50**) onto the master cylinder so its lips are properly seated in the bore.

8. Install the brake lever as follows:

   a. Lubricate the pivot bolt with grease (Suzuki Super Grease A or an equivalent).

   b. Install the brake lever/adjuster assembly into the lever bracket so the pushrod engages the

14

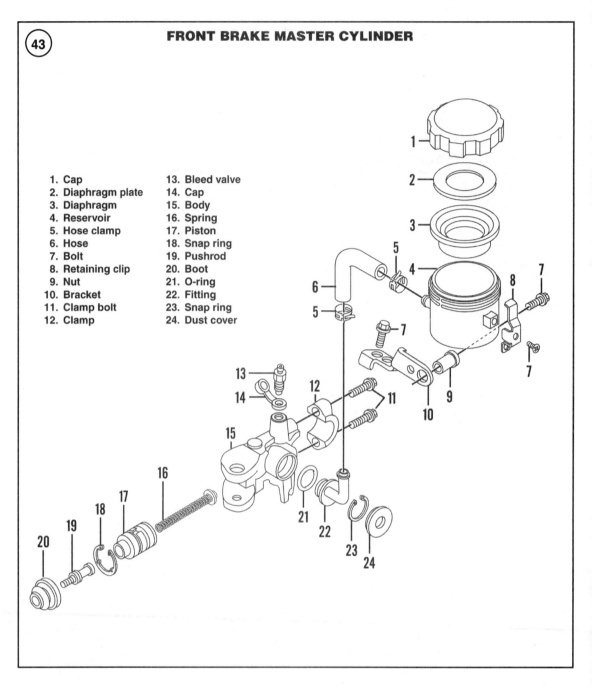

FRONT BRAKE MASTER CYLINDER

43

1. Cap
2. Diaphragm plate
3. Diaphragm
4. Reservoir
5. Hose clamp
6. Hose
7. Bolt
8. Retaining clip
9. Nut
10. Bracket
11. Clamp bolt
12. Clamp
13. Bleed valve
14. Cap
15. Body
16. Spring
17. Piston
18. Snap ring
19. Pushrod
20. Boot
21. O-ring
22. Fitting
23. Snap ring
24. Dust cover

lever hole (B, **Figure 49**), and install the pivot bolt (A).

  c. Install the nut (B, **Figure 48**) and washer onto the brake lever bolt, and tighten the nut securely. Check that the brake lever moves freely. If there is any binding or roughness, remove the piston bolt and brake lever and inspect the parts.

9. Install the front brake switch, and tighten the screw (A, **Figure 48**) securely.

10. Lubricate a *new* O-ring (A, **Figure 47**) with DOT 4 brake fluid, and install it into the fluid port (B) on the master cylinder.

11. Seat the fitting (B, **Figure 46**) into the port, and install the snap ring (A). Make sure the snap ring is completely seated in the grove.

12. Slide the dust cover down on the fitting, and seat it into the port (**Figure 45**).

13. Connect the reservoir hose to the fitting and install the clamp (A, **Figure 44**).

14. If removed, install the bleed valve assembly (C, **Figure 44**). Tighten the valve to 6.0 N•m (53 in.-lb.).

15. Install the cap (B, **Figure 44**) onto the reservoir.

16. Install the master cylinder (this section).

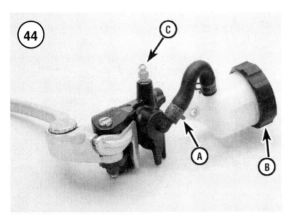

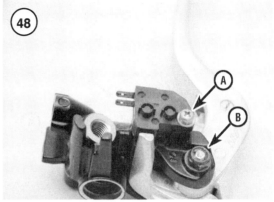

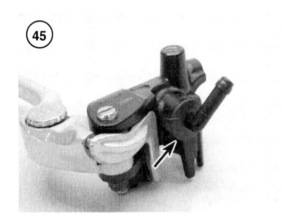

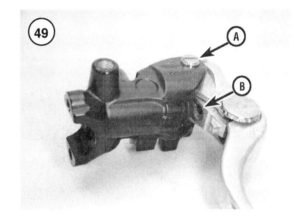

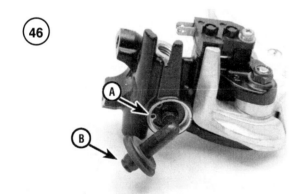

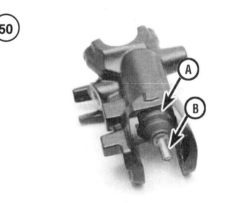

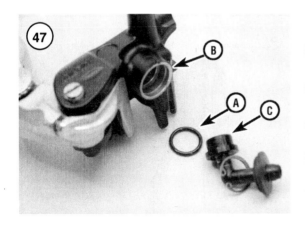

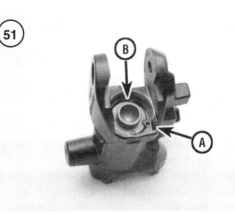

14

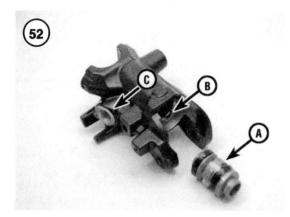

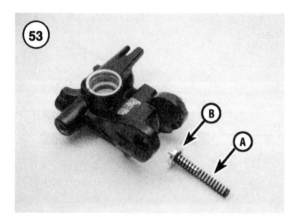

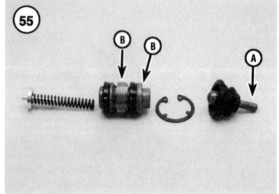

Inspection

Compare any measurements to the specifications in **Table 1** or **Table 2**. Replace any part that is worn, damaged or out of specification.

1. Clean all parts in fresh DOT 4 brake fluid or in isopropyl alcohol. Inspect the cylinder bore surface (B, **Figure 54**) and piston contact surfaces for signs of wear or damage. If less than perfect, replace the master cylinder assembly. The body cannot be replaced separately.

2. Inspect the fluid passageway in the master cylinder inlet port bore (A, **Figure 56**) and in the piston inlet fluid port (C, **Figure 54**). Blow clear as needed.

3. Measure the cylinder bore with a bore gauge or vernier caliper.

4. Inspect the primary cup (A, **Figure 57**) and secondary cup (B) for wear and damage. If necessary, replace the piston assembly. Individual cups cannot be replaced.

5. Inspect the contact surfaces of the piston (B, **Figure 55**) for signs of wear and damage. If necessary, replace the piston assembly.

6. Check the end of the piston for wear caused by the hand lever or push rod. If worn, replace the master piston assembly.

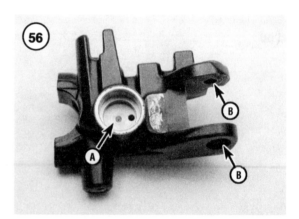

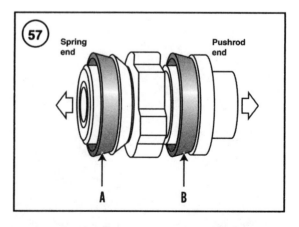

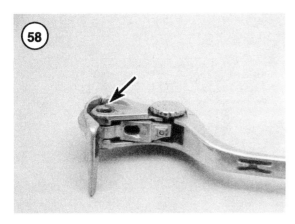

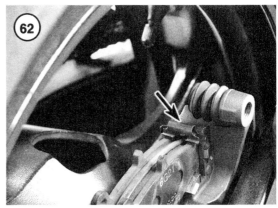

7. Measure the outside diameter of the piston with a micrometer (**Figure 37**).

8. Check the hand lever pivot lugs (B, **Figure 56**) on the master cylinder body for cracks or elongation.

9. Inspect the pivot hole (**Figure 58**) in the hand lever for cracks or elongation.

10. Inspect the banjo bolt threads in the brake hose port (C, **Figure 52**). Clean the threads with an appropriate size metric thread tap or replace the master cylinder assembly.

11. Inspect the reservoir hose fitting (C, **Figure 47**) for damage and deterioration.

12. Check the top cover, diaphragm and diaphragm plate for damage and deterioration; replace as necessary.

13. Inspect the adjuster on the hand lever. If worn or damaged replace the hand lever as an assembly.

14. Check the reservoir and hose (**Figure 59**) for damage and deterioration.

REAR BRAKE CALIPER

Refer to *Brake Service* in this chapter.

14

Brake Pad Removal/Installation

1. Securely support the motorcycle on a level surface.

2. Remove the pad pin (**Figure 60**).

3. Remove the caliper mounting bolt (A, **Figure 61**) and the sliding pin bolt (B).

4. Slide the caliper (C, **Figure 61**) up and off the brake disc.

5. Pivot both brake pads up at the rear and release them from the mounting bracket spring (**Figure 62**). Remove both brake pads.

6. Inspect the brake pads (this section).

7. When *new* pads are installed in the caliper, the fluid level rises in the rear master cylinder reservoir. Remove the hydraulic fluid from the reservoir and

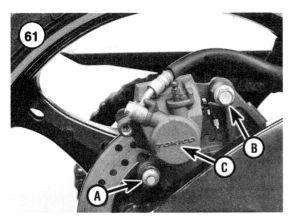

reposition the caliper pistons by performing the following:

   a. Remove the mounting bolt (**Figure 63**) and move the master cylinder away from the frame to access the top cover.

   b. Make sure the top of the reservoir is level.

   c. Remove the screws, top cover, and diaphragm (**Figure 64**).

   d. Use a syringe to remove approximately half of the fluid from the reservoir.

   e. Temporarily install one of the old brake pads into the caliper and seat it against the piston.

   f. Press the pad against the piston, and slowly push the caliper piston all the way into the caliper. Constantly check the reservoir to make sure brake fluid does not overflow. Remove fluid, if necessary, to prevent any overflow.

   g. The piston should move freely. If it does not, the caliper should be removed and serviced as described in this chapter.

   h. Install the diaphragm, top cover and screws.

8. Install the inboard brake pad (**Figure 65**) and the outboard brake pad (**Figure 66**).

9. Hook the brake pad ears (A, **Figure 67**) under the mounting bracket spring, and push the rear of the brake pads down into place on the brake disc and mounting bracket (B).

10. Check that both brake pad ears are located within the mounting bracket spring (**Figure 62**).

11. Install the caliper (C, **Figure 61**) onto the disc being careful to not damage the leading edges of the brake pads.

12. Install the caliper mounting bolt (A, **Figure 61**) and the sliding pin bolt (B). Do not tighten at this time.

13. Install the pad pin (**Figure 68**) into the caliper. Push down on the brake pads and push the pad pin through both brake pads and caliper (**Figure 60**). Tighten to 18 N•m (13 ft.-lb.).

14. Tighten the caliper mounting bolt (A, **Figure 61**) to to 18 N•m (13 ft.-lb.). Tighten the sliding pin bolt (B) to 33 N•m (24 ft.-lb.).

15. Pump the rear brake pedal to reposition the brake pads against the brake disc. Monitor the fluid level in the reservoir. Add fluid as necessary so air will not be drawn into the system.

16. Refill the master cylinder reservoir, if necessary, to maintain the correct fluid level as indicated on the side of the reservoir. Install the diaphragm and the top cover (**Figure 64**) and tighten screws securely.

17. Move the master cylinder back into position in the frame. Install the mounting bolt (**Figure 63**) and tighten securely.

Caliper Removal/Installation

1. If the caliper assembly is going to be disassembled for service, perform the following:

   a. Remove the brake pads (this section).

CAUTION
Do not let the piston contact the brake disc. If this happens the piston may scratch or gouge the disc during caliper removal.

NOTE
By performing Step b, compressed air may not be necessary for piston removal during caliper disassembly.

   b. Apply the brake pedal to push the piston part way out of caliper assembly for ease of removal during caliper service.

   c. Remove the banjo bolt and sealing washers and disconnect the brake hose (A, **Figure 69**) from the rear brake caliper. Place the loose end of the brake hose into a plastic bag to keep residual brake fluid from leaking onto the motorcycle.

2. Remove the caliper mounting bolt (B, **Figure 69**), and sliding pin bolt (C).

3. Slide the caliper (D, **Figure 69**) up and off the brake disc.

4. If necessary, disassemble and service the caliper assembly as described in this section.

5. Install the caliper onto the disc. If the caliper was not serviced, be careful not to damage the leading edges of the brake pads.

6. Install the caliper mounting bolt (A, **Figure 69**) and the sliding pin bolt (B). Tighten the caliper mounting bolt (A, **Figure 69**) to to18 N•m (13 ft.-lb.). Tighten the sliding pin bolt (B, **Figure 69**) to 33 N•m (24 ft.-lb.).

7. Install the brake hose to the caliper with the banjo bolt (A, **Figure 69**). Install a *new* sealing washer onto each side of the brake hose fitting, and tighten the banjo bolt to 23 N•m (17 ft.-lb.). Position the brake hose so its neck fits into notch (**Figure 70**) on top of the caliper body.

8. Refill the reservoir and bleed the brake as described in this chapter.

Disassembly

   Refer to **Figure 71**.

1. Remove the brake pads and rear caliper as described in this chapter.

14

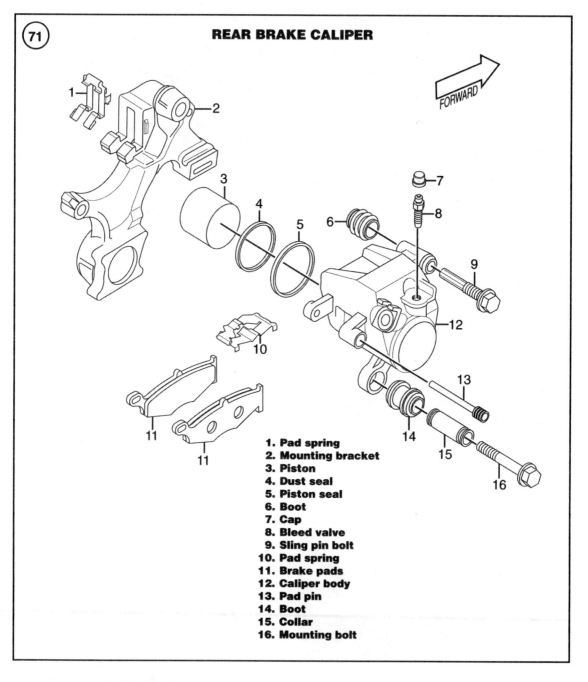

REAR BRAKE CALIPER

FORWARD

1. Pad spring
2. Mounting bracket
3. Piston
4. Dust seal
5. Piston seal
6. Boot
7. Cap
8. Bleed valve
9. Sling pin bolt
10. Pad spring
11. Brake pads
12. Caliper body
13. Pad pin
14. Boot
15. Collar
16. Mounting bolt

NOTE

If the pistons were partially forced out of the caliper body during removal, Step 1, Step 2 and 3 may not be necessary. If the piston or caliper bore is corroded or very dirty; a small amount of compressed air may be necessary to completely remove the pistons from the body bores.

2. Place a piece of soft wood or folded shop cloth over the end of the piston and the caliper body. Turn

this assembly over with the piston facing down onto the workbench top.

WARNING

In the next step, the piston may come out of the caliper body with considerable force.

Protect yourself with shop gloves and safety goggles.

3. Apply the air pressure in short spurts to the hydraulic fluid passageway and force the piston out of the caliper bore.

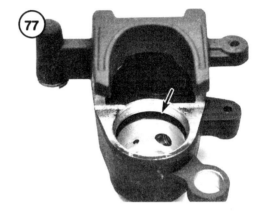

4. If necessary, remove the bleed valve (**Figure 72**).
5. Remove the collar (A, **Figure 73**) from the mounting bolt boot. Remove the boot (B, **Figure 73**) from the caliper.
6. Remove the pad spring (**Figure 74**).
7. Remove the piston (**Figure 75**) from the bore.

CAUTION
Do not use a sharp tool to remove the dust and piston seals from the caliper cylinders. These tools could damage the cylinder surface.

8. Use a piece of wood or plastic scraper and carefully push the dust seal (**Figure 76**) and the piston seal (**Figure 77**) in toward the caliper cylinder and out of their grooves. Remove the dust and piston seals from the other caliper half and discard all seals.
9. Inspect the caliper assembly (this section).

Assembly

1. Soak the *new* dust and piston seals in fresh DOT 4 brake fluid.
2. Coat the piston bores and pistons with clean DOT 4 brake fluid.
3. Carefully install the *new* piston seal (**Figure 77**) into the inner groove in the cylinder bore.

14

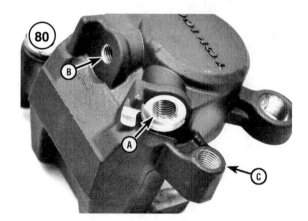

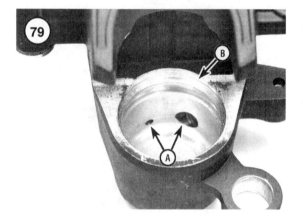

4. Install the *new* dust seal (**Figure 76**) into the outer groove. Make sure both seals are properly seated in their respective grooves.

5. Position the piston with the open end facing out (**Figure 75**). Manually turn the piston into the caliper cylinder so the seals will not be damaged. Press the piston into the cylinder until it bottoms (**Figure 78**).

6. Install the pad spring (**Figure 74**) and press it down until it locks into place.

7. Install the boot (B, **Figure 73**) into the caliper boss.

8. Install the collar (A, **Figure 73**) into the mounting bolt boot, and make sure it is seated correctly within the boot.

9. If removed, install the bleed valve (**Figure 72**) and tighten to 7.5 N•m (66 it.-lb.).

10. Install the caliper and brake pads as described in this chapter.

11. Bleed the brake as described in this chapter.

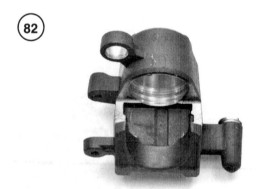

Inspection

Compare any measurements to the specifications in **Table 1** or **Table 2** when inspecting brake components. Replace any part that is worn, damaged or out of specification.

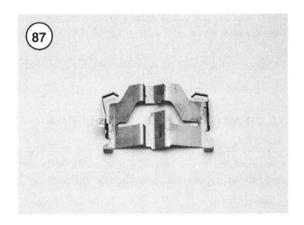

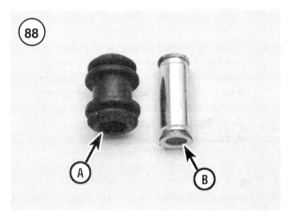

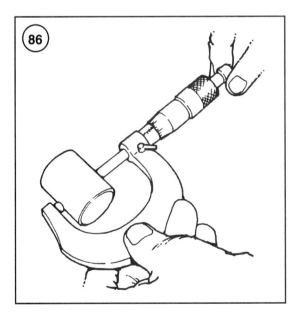

1. Clean both caliper body halves and pistons in fresh DOT 4 brake fluid or isopropyl alcohol. Dry the parts with compressed air.

2. Inspect the fluid passageways (A, **Figure 79**) in the base of the cylinder bore. Apply compressed air to the openings to make sure they are clear. Clean them with fresh brake fluid if necessary.

3. Inspect the piston seal and dust seal grooves (B, **Figure 79**) in the caliper body for damage or corrosion.

4. Inspect the threads in the banjo bolt hole (A, **Figure 80**), the bleed valve holes (B) and pad pin hole (C). If worn or damaged, dress the threads with a metric tap or replace the caliper assembly.

5. Inspect the bleed valve (A, **Figure 81**) and banjo bolt (B). Apply compressed air to the openings and make sure each is clear. Clean either part with fresh brake fluid if necessary.

6. Inspect the caliper (**Figure 82**) for damage.

7. Check the mounting bosses (**Figure 83**) for cracks or damage.

8. Inspect the cylinder wall (**Figure 84**) and piston (**Figure 85**) for scratches, scoring or other damage.

9. Measure the inside diameter of the cylinder bore with a bore gauge or vernier caliper.

10. Measure the outside diameter of the piston with a micrometer (**Figure 86**) or vernier caliper.

11. Inspect the pad spring (**Figure 87**) for cracks or fatigue for wear and damage.

12. Check the mounting bolt boot (A, **Figure 88**) for tears or deterioration. Inspect the inner surface of the collar (B, **Figure 88**) for corrosion or burrs. Clean out if necessary with a small spiral wire brush, and apply DOT 4 brake fluid.

14

13. Check the pad pin (**Figure 89**) for wear or corrosion. Clean with emery cloth and apply DOT 4 brake fluid.

14. Inspect the brake pads as described in this chapter.

REAR BRAKE MASTER CYLINDER

Before beginning work, note how the rear brake hose is routed to the from the rear master cylinder, along the swing arm and onto the rear caliper.

Removal

> *CAUTION*
> *Cover the swing arm and rear wheel with a heavy cloth or plastic tarp to protect them from accidental brake fluid spills. Brake fluid erodes the finish on any plastic, painted or plated surface. Wash any spilled brake fluid off these surfaces immediately. Use soapy water, and rinse the area completely.*

1. Support the motorcycle on a level surface.

2. Remove the master cylinder reservoir mounting bolt (**Figure 90**) and move the master cylinder away from the frame (**Figure 91**).

3. Drain the brake fluid from the rear brake as described in this chapter.

4. Remove the brake hose banjo bolt (**Figure 92**), separate the brake hose from the port on the top of the master cylinder. Be prepared to catch residual brake fluid that leaks from the brake hose. Discard the sealing washer from each side of the brake hose fitting.

5. Insert the brake hose end into a plastic bag to keep moisture and foreign matter out of the system. Seal the bag around the hose.

6. Remove the foot guard mounting bolts (A, **Figure 93**) and remove the foot guard (B).

7. Remove the cotter pin from the inboard end of the clevis pin. Withdraw the clevis pin (**Figure 94**) from the clevis pin. Watch for the washer behind the pushrod clevis.

8. Release the lower clamp (A, **Figure 95**) on the reservoir hose, disconnect the hose (B) from the fitting on the master cylinder. Remove the reservoir and hose from the motorcycle. Be prepared to catch residual brake fluid that dribbles from the reservoir hose.

9. Remove the master cylinder mounting bolts (C, **Figure 95**) and remove the master cylinder from the footpeg mounting bracket.

10. Wash any spilled brake fluid immediately.

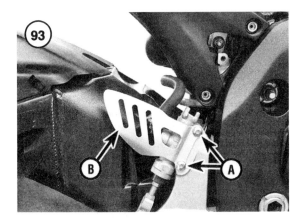

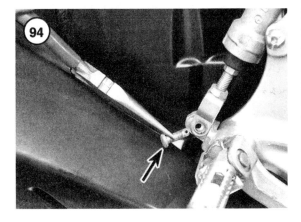

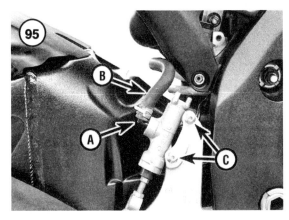

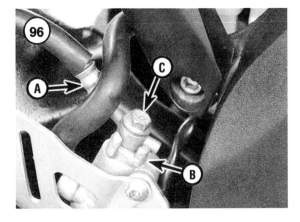

Installation

1. Correctly position the master cylinder against its mount on the footpeg bracket. Install the mounting bolts (C, **Figure 95**), and tighten securely.

2. Install the reservoir and hose onto position in the frame. Install mounting bolt (**Figure 90**) and tighten securely.

3. Connect the reservoir hose (B, **Figure 95**) onto the master cylinder fitting and secure it with the clamp (A).

4. Align the pushrod clevis with the brake pedal, and install the clevis pin (**Figure 94**) through both parts. Slide the washer over the end of the clevis pin, and install a *new* cotter pin. Bend over the pin ends completely.

5. Install the foot guard (B, **Figure 93**) and mounting bolts (A). Tighten the bolts securely.

6. Correctly position the brake hose under the reservoir hose (A, **Figure 96**).

7. Install a *new* sealing washer onto each side of the brake hose fitting, and index the fitting against the locating tab (B, **Figure 96**) on the master cylinder. Install the banjo bolt (C, **Figure 96**) and tighten to 23 N•m (17 ft.-lb.).

8. Add brake fluid to the reservoir, and bleed the rear brake as described in this chapter.

Disassembly

Refer to **Figure 97**.

1. Remove the rear master cylinder as described in this chapter.

2. If still attached, remove the snap ring (A, **Figure 98**) and separate the reservoir hose fitting and hose (B) from the master cylinder body. Remove and discard the O-ring from the port.

3. Roll the rubber boot (**Figure 99**) down the pushrod.

4. Remove the pushrod snap ring (A, **Figure 100**) from the master cylinder body with snap ring pliers.

5. Withdraw the pushrod (B, **Figure 100**), piston and spring assembly from the master cylinder.

6. Remove the top cover (A, **Figure 101**), diaphragm plate (B), and diaphragm (C) from the fluid reservoir (D). Pour out any residual brake fluid and discard it appropriately.

7. If necessary, loosen the clevis locknut (A, **Figure 102**), and unscrew the clevis (B) and nut (C) from the pushrod (D).

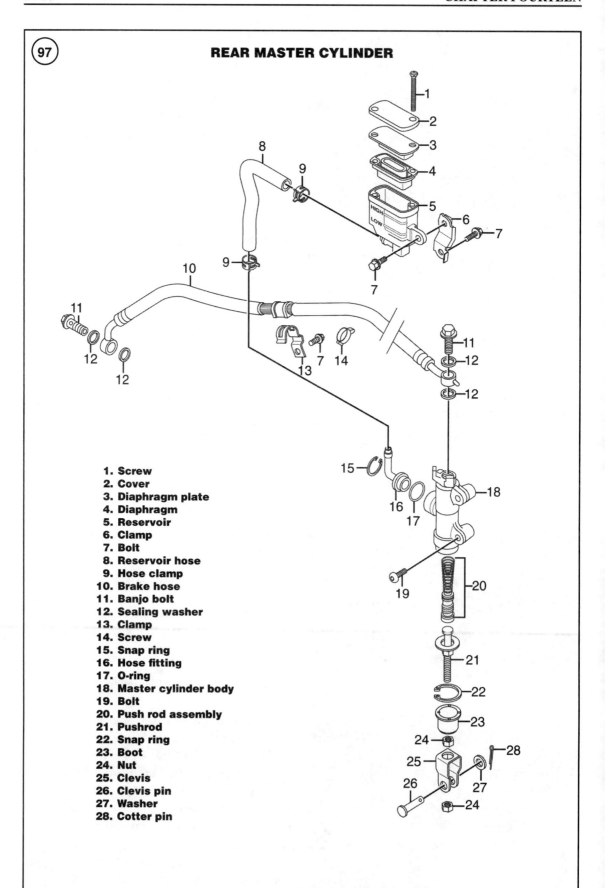

REAL MASTER CYLINDER

97

1. Screw
2. Cover
3. Diaphragm plate
4. Diaphragm
5. Reservoir
6. Clamp
7. Bolt
8. Reservoir hose
9. Hose clamp
10. Brake hose
11. Banjo bolt
12. Sealing washer
13. Clamp
14. Screw
15. Snap ring
16. Hose fitting
17. O-ring
18. Master cylinder body
19. Bolt
20. Push rod assembly
21. Pushrod
22. Snap ring
23. Boot
24. Nut
25. Clevis
26. Clevis pin
27. Washer
28. Cotter pin

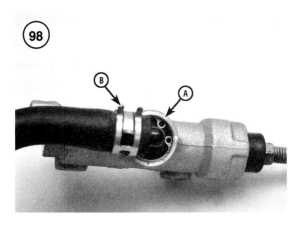

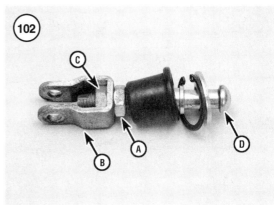

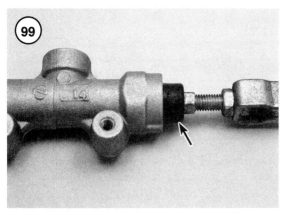

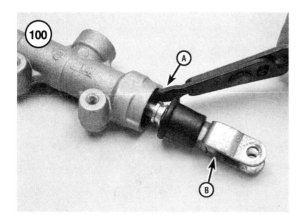

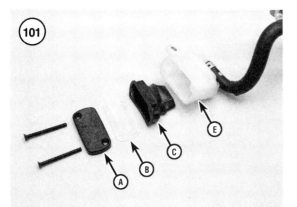

Assembly

1. If removed, install the clevis (B, **Figure 102**), and nut (C) onto the pushrod (D). Tighten the locknut securely (A, **Figure 102**).

2. Soak the piston assembly (**Figure 103**) in fresh DOT 4 brake fluid to make the cups pliable.

3. Coat the inside of the cylinder bore with fresh DOT 4 brake fluid prior to the assembly of parts.

> *CAUTION*
> *When installing the master piston assembly, do not allow the cups to turn inside out. They will be damaged and allow brake fluid leakage within the cylinder bore.*

4. Insert the spring (A, **Figure 104**) and piston assembly (B) into the cylinder bore. Press the assembly into the cylinder until it bottoms.

5. Install the pushrod assembly (**Figure 105**) so the push rod engages the end of the piston, and press the pushrod assembly all the way into the cylinder.

6. Press down on the pushrod assembly (B, **Figure 100**) in this position, and install the snap ring (A). Make sure the snap ring is correctly seated in its groove.

14

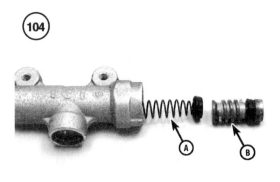

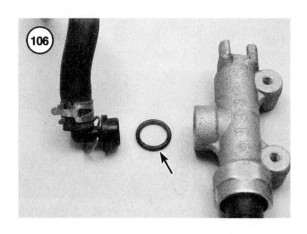

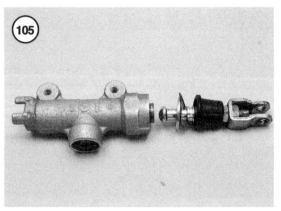

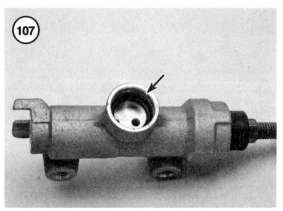

7. Install the rubber boot (**Figure 99**) into the body so it is completely seated in the cylinder.

8. Install a *new* O-ring (**Figure 106**) into the hose port in the master cylinder body. Apply a light coat of fresh brake fluid to the O-ring (**Figure 107**).

9. Install the reservoir hose fitting and hose (B, **Figure 98**) onto the master cylinder body. Install the snap ring (A, **Figure 98**) and make sure the snap ring is correctly seated in its groove

10. Install the master cylinder as described in this chapter.

11. Adjust the brake pedal height (Chapter Three).

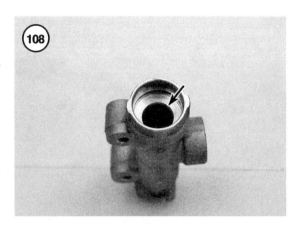

Inspection

During inspection, compare any measurements to the specifications in **Table 1** and **Table 2**. Replace any part that is out of specification, worn or damaged.

1. Clean all parts in fresh DOT 4 brake fluid or isopropyl alcohol.

2. Inspect the cylinder bore surface (**Figure 108**). If it is less than perfect, replace the master cylinder assembly. The body cannot be replaced separately.

3. Make sure all fluid passages (**Figure 109**) in the master cylinder body are clear. Clean it if necessary.

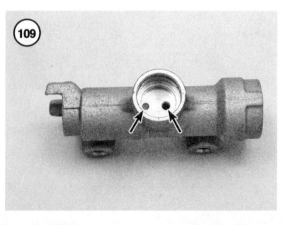

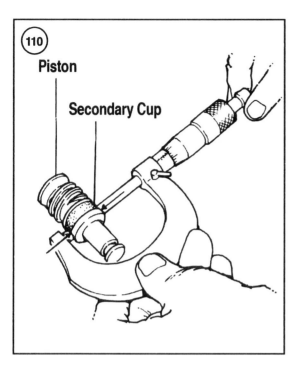

6. Check the entire master cylinder body for wear or damage. If damaged in any way, replace the master cylinder assembly.

7. Inspect the piston cups (**Figure 103**) for signs of wear and damage. If less than perfect, replace the piston assembly. The cups cannot be replaced separately.

8. Check the end of the piston (**Figure 111**) for wear caused by the pushrod.

9. Inspect the piston push rod assembly for wear or damage. Replace the piston assembly if necessary.

10. Inspect the push rod end (A, **Figure 112**) for wear or damage. Make sure the boot (B, **Figure 112**) is in good condition.

11. Inspect the banjo bolt threads (**Figure 113**) and mounting bolt threads (**Figure 114**) in the master cylinder. If damaged, clean the threads with a metric thread die or replace the bolt.

12. Check the reservoir hose fitting (A, **Figure 115**) for damage.

13. Inspect the reservoir, top cover, diaphragm plate and diaphragm (**Figure 116**) for wear or damage.

14. Inspect the brake hose and reservoir hose (B, **Figure 115**) for wear or deterioration.

14

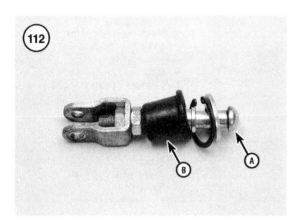

4. Measure the cylinder bore with a bore gauge or vernier caliper.

5. Measure the outside diameter of the piston with a micrometer (**Figure 110**).

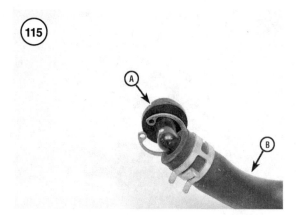

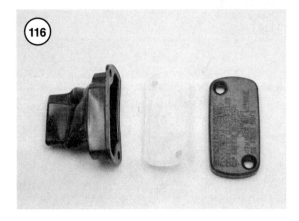

BRAKE PEDAL/FOOTPEG ASSEMBLY

Removal/Lubrication/Installation

Refer to **Figure 117**.

1. Support the motorcycle on a level surface.

2. Remove the rear brake master cylinder as described in this chapter.

3. Use a wire or bungee cord to suspend the master cylinder from the frame so the brake hoses with not be strained.

4. Remove the footpeg mounting bracket No. 1 bolts (A, **Figure 118**), and remove the brake pedal/footpeg assembly (B) from the motorcycle.

5. Inspect the brake pedal/footpeg assembly (**Figure 119**) for cranks or damage and replace it if necessary.

6. Unhook the rear brake light switch spring (A, **Figure 120**) and brake pedal return spring (B) from the brake pedal.

7. Remove the E-clip (A, **Figure 121**) from the footpeg pivot pin. Remove the pivot pin and the footpeg (B, **Figure 121**) from the footpeg holder.

8. Remove the footpeg holder Allen bolt (C, **Figure 120**) from the inboard side of the footpeg bracket.

9. Remove the footpeg holder (C, **Figure 121**) and rear brake pedal assembly (D) from the footpeg mounting bracket No. 2.

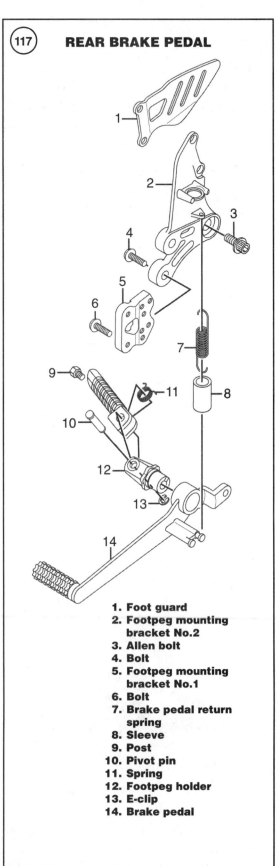

REAR BRAKE PEDAL

1. Foot guard
2. Footpeg mounting bracket No.2
3. Allen bolt
4. Bolt
5. Footpeg mounting bracket No.1
6. Bolt
7. Brake pedal return spring
8. Sleeve
9. Post
10. Pivot pin
11. Spring
12. Footpeg holder
13. E-clip
14. Brake pedal

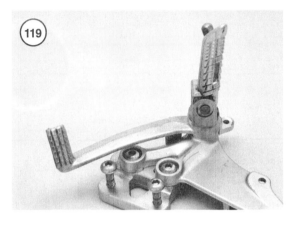

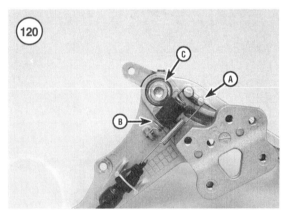

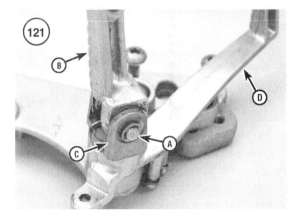

10. Clean the footpeg bolt with solvent, and inspect it for wear or damage. Replace if necessary.

11. Install the pedal by reversing these removal steps. Note the following:

    a. Lubricate the brake pedal pivot and spring with grease (Suzuki Super Grease A or equivalent).

    b. Tighten the footpeg holder bolt (C, **Figure 120**) securely.

    c. Install each footpeg bracket No. 1 bolt (A, **Figure 118**), and tighten the bolts to 23 N•m (17 ft.-lb.).

    d. Use a *new* E-clip (A, **Figure 121**) on the footpeg pivot pin.

    e. Adjust the rear brake pedal height (Chapter Three).

BRAKE DISC

The brake discs are separate from the wheel hubs and can be removed once the wheel is removed from the motorcycle.

Inspection

Small nicks and marks on the disc are not important, but radial scratches deep enough to snag a fingernail reduce braking effectiveness and increase brake pad wear. If these grooves are evident and the brake pads are wearing rapidly, replace the disc.

Specifications for the standard and wear limits are listed in **Table 1** and **Table 2**. On some models, the minimum (MIN) thickness is stamped on the disc face). If the specification stamped on the disc differs from the wear limit listed in the tables, use to the specification on the disc for inspection purposes.

Do not machine a disc to compensate for any warp. If a disc is warped, the brake pads may be dragging on the disc due to a faulty caliper and causing the disc to overheat. Overheating can also be caused when there is unequal pad pressure on the sides of the disc. If a disc is overheating, troubleshoot the brakes as described in Chapter Two.

NOTE
The brake disc can be measured with the wheel mounted on the motorcycle.

1. Make sure the disc mounting bolts (A, **Figure 122**) are tight before performing this inspection. Refer to the specifications in **Table 3**.

2. Measure the thickness of the disc at several locations around the disc (**Figure 123**).

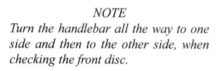

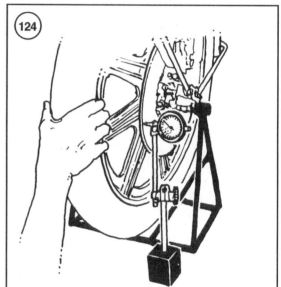

NOTE
Turn the handlebar all the way to one side and then to the other side, when checking the front disc.

3. Slowly rotate the wheel and measure the disc runout with a dial indicator (**Figure 124**). If runout is excessive, check for loose brake disc bolts, inspect the wheel bearings, and examine the surface of the brake disc. If these are in good condition, replace the brake disc.

4. Clean any rust or corrosion from the disc, and wipe it clean with lacquer thinner. Never use an oil-based solvent that may leave an oil residue on the disc.

5. On the front wheel, inspect the floating disc fasteners (B, **Figure 122**) between the outer and the inner rings of the discs. If damaged, replace the disc.

Removal/Installation

CAUTION
*Do not set the wheel down on the disc surface, as it may get scratched or warped. Set the wheel on 2 wooden blocks (**Figure 125**).*

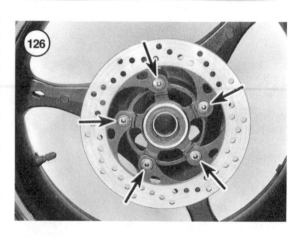

1. Remove the front or rear wheel (Chapter Eleven).

2. Insert a spacer between the brake pads. This way, if the brake lever or pedal is inadvertently applied, the pistons will not be forced out of the cylinders.

3. Remove the brake disc bolts (**Figure 126**), and remove the disc from the hub.

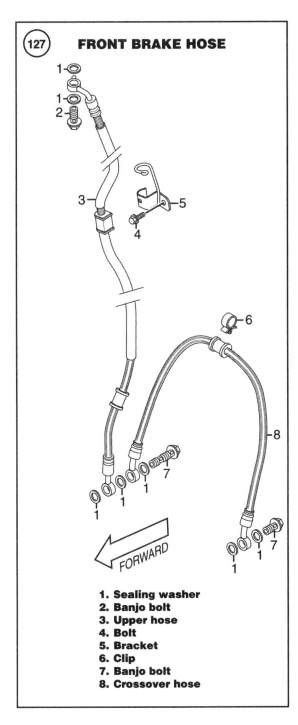

127 **FRONT BRAKE HOSE**

FORWARD

1. Sealing washer
2. Banjo bolt
3. Upper hose
4. Bolt
5. Bracket
6. Clip
7. Banjo bolt
8. Crossover hose

4. Install by reversing these removal steps. Note the following:

   a. Position the disc so its direction arrow points in the direction of tire rotation.

   b. Apply threadlock (Suzuki Thread Lock Super 1360 or equivalent) to the threads of the disc bolts.

   c. Tighten brake disc bolts to the specification in **Table 3**.

BRAKE HOSE

Removal/Installation

Front brake hoses

Refer to **Figure 127**.

1. Remove the front fairing (Chapter Fifteen).

2. Drain the fluid from the front brakes as described in this chapter.

3. Remove the brake hose holder bolt (**Figure 128**), and release the brake hose from the lower fork bridge.

4. Release the master cylinder brake hose (**Figure 129**) from the holder on the right side of the fender.

5. On the right side, perform the following:

   a. Remove the banjo bolt (A, **Figure 130**) and sealing washers, and disconnect the crossover hose (B) and master cylinder hose (C) from the right caliper. Catch any brake fluid that leaks from the hose fittings.

   b. Place the end of the each brake hose into a plastic bag so brake fluid will not leak onto the motorcycle. Discard the sealing washers.

6. On the left side, perform the following:

   a. Release the crossover brake hose (A, **Figure 131**) from the holder on the backside of the fender.

14

b. Remove the banjo bolt (B, **Figure 131**) and sealing washers, and disconnect the crossover hose (C) from the left caliper.

c. Place the end of the brake hose into a plastic bag so brake fluid will not leak onto the motorcycle. Discard the sealing washers.

7. At the master cylinder, perform the following:

a. Remove the banjo bolt (**Figure 132**) and sealing washers, and disconnect the hose from the master cylinder.

b. Place the end of the brake hose into a plastic bag so brake fluid will not leak onto the motorcycle. Discard the sealing washers.

8. Remove master cylinder hose down and out from behind the throttle cables on the right side.

9. Install *new* hoses in the reverse order of removal while noting the following:

a. Route each hose along the path noted during removal.

b. Position the brake hoses so their necks sit against the stop post on each caliper.

c. Install *new* sealing washers onto each side of the hose fittings. Use three sealing washers when securing the master cylinder hose (C, **Figure 130**) and crossover hose (B) to the right brake caliper.

d. Tighten the banjo bolts to the 23 N•m (17 ft.-lb.).

e. Refill the master cylinder reservoir and bleed the front brakes as described in this chapter.

Rear Brake Hose

1. Note how the brake hose is routed along the top of the swing arm. The brake hose must be rerouted along the same path during master cylinder installation.

2. Drain the brake fluid as described in this chapter.

3. Release the brake hose from the hose holder (**Figure 133**) on the swing arm.

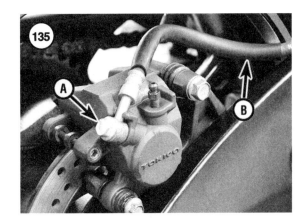

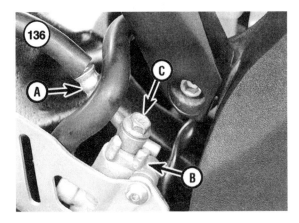

into a plastic bag so brake fluid will not leak onto the motorcycle. Discard the sealing washers installed on each side of the hose fitting.

5. Remove the banjo bolt (A, **Figure 135**) and disconnect the brake hose from the rear caliper. Take the precautions mentioned in Step 3 so brake fluid does not dribble onto the motorcycle.

6. Remove the brake hose assembly (B, **Figure 135**) from the swing arm.

7. Install a *new* hose, *new* sealing washers and banjo bolts in the reverse order of removal while noting the following:

   a. Correctly position the brake hose under the master cylinder reservoir hose (A, **Figure 136**).

   b. Install a *new* sealing washer onto each side of the brake hose fitting, and index the fitting against the locating tab (B, **Figure 136**) on the master cylinder. Install the banjo bolt (C, **Figure 136**) and tighten to 23 N•m (17 ft.-lb.).

   c. Refill the master cylinder reservoir and bleed the rear brake system as described in this chapter.

4. Remove the banjo bolt (**Figure 134**) and disconnect the brake hose from the rear master cylinder. Be prepared to catch residual brake fluid that leaks from the brake hose. Place the end of the brake hose

Table 1 BRAKE SPECIFICATIONS (2006-2007 MODELS)

Item	Standard mm (in.)	Service limit mm (in.)
Brake fluid	DOT 4	-
Brake disc runout (front and rear)	–	0.30 (0.16)
Brake disc thickness		
Front	5.3-5.7 (0.209-0.224)	5.0 (0.20)
Rear	4.8-5.2 (0.189-0.205)	4.5 (0.18)
Front master cylinder		
Cylinder bore	19.050-19.093 (0.7500-0.7517)	–
Piston diameter	19.018-19.034 (0.7487-0.7494)	–
Front brake caliper		
Cylinder bore		
Leading	30.280-30.356 (1.1921-1.1951)	–
Trailing	34.010-34.086 (1.3390-1.3420)	–
Piston diameter		
Leading	30.150-30.200 (1.1870-1.1890)	–
Trailing	33.884-33.934 (1.3340-1.3360)	–
Rear master cylinder		
Cylinder bore	14.000-14.043 (0.5512-0.5529)	–
Piston diameter	13.957-13.984 (0.5495-0.5506)	–
(continued)		

14

Table 1 BRAKE SPECIFICATIONS (2006-2007 MODELS) (continued)

Item	Standard mm (in.)	Service limit mm (in.)
Rear brake caliper		
Cylinder bore	38.180-38.256 (1.5031-1.5062	–
Piston diameter	38.098-38.148 (1.4999-1.5019)	–
Brake pedal height	60-70 (2.4-2.8)	–

Table 2 BRAKE SPECIFICATIONS (2008-2009 MODELS)

Item	Standard mm (in.)	Service limit mm (in.)
Brake fluid	DOT 4	–
Brake disc runout (front and rear)		– 0.30 (0.16)
Brake disc thickness	4.8-5.2 (0.189-0.205)	4.5 (0.18)
Front master cylinder		
Cylinder bore	17.460-17.503 (0.6874-0.6891)	–
Piston diameter	17.417-17.444 (0.6857-0.6868)	–
Front brake caliper		
Cylinder bore		
Leading	30.280-30.330 (1.1921-1.1941)	–
Trailing	32.080-32.130 (1.2630-1.2650)	–
Piston diameter		
Leading	30.167-30.200 (1.1877-1.1890)	–
Trailing	31.967-32.004 (1.2585-1.2598)	–
Rear master cylinder		
Cylinder bore	14.000-14.043 (0.5512-0.5529)	–
Piston diameter	13.957-13.984 (0.5495-0.5506)	–
Rear brake caliper		
Cylinder bore	38.180-38.256 (1.5031-1.5062	–
Piston diameter	38.098-38.148 (1.4999-1.5019)	–
Brake pedal height	60-70 (2.4-2.8)	–

Table 3 BRAKE TORQUE SPECIFICATIONS

Item	N•m	in.-lb.	ft.-lb.
Brake bleed valve			
Front master cylinder	6.0	53	–
Front caliper	7.5	66	–
Rear caliper	7.5	66	–
Brake disc bolt*			
Front	23	–	17
Rear	35	–	26
Brake hose banjo bolt	23	–	17
Footpeg bracket bolt, front and rear	23	–	17
Front caliper			
Brake pad pin	16	–	11.6
Housing bolt	22	–	16
Mounting bolt	35	–	26
Front master cylinder clamp bolt	10	89	•
Rear brake pad pin	16	–	11.6
Rear caliper			
Brake pad pin	18	–	13
Mounting bolt	18	–	13
Sliding pin bolt	33	–	24
Rear master-cylinder-rod locknut	18	–	13

* Apply threadlock (Suzuki Thread Lock Super 1360, or equivalent).

CHAPTER FIFTEEN

BODY AND FRAME

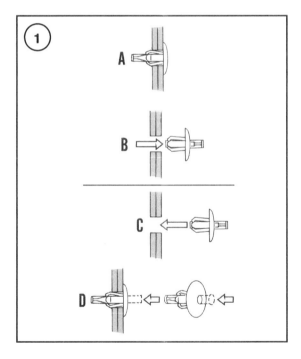

This chapter covers the seats, mirrors, fairing panels, fenders and sidestand.

As soon as a panel is removed from the motorcycle, reinstall all mounting hardware onto the removed panel. This assures the fasteners will be reinstalled in their correct locations.

After a panel is removed from the frame, wrap it in a towel or blanket, and store it in a safe place where it will not be damaged.

Table 1 is at the end of this chapter.

BODY PANEL FASTENERS

Several types of fasteners are used to attach the various body panels to each other and to the frame. Note the type of fastener used before removing a panel. An improperly released fastener can damage a body panel.

Trim Clip

Quick release trim clips are used at various locations. The plastic trim clips degenerates with heat, age and use. Installing a worn trim clip through the mounting hole(s) can be very difficult. The ends may break off or become distorted so the clip cannot be inserted into the body panel holes.

Replace trim clips as necessary. To remove a trim clip, push the center pin into the head with a Phillips screwdriver (A, **Figure 1**). This releases the inner lock so the trim clip can be withdrawn from the panel (B, **Figure 1**).

To install a trim clip, push the center pin outward so it protrudes from the head (C, **Figure 1**), and insert the clip through the opening in the plastic panel. To lock the trim clip into place, push the pin into the clip (D, **Figure 1**) so the pin sits flush with the top of the head.

15

Quick Fastener Screw

The quarter-turn quick fastener screws (DZUS fasteners) are used mainly to secure one body panel to one another. Use a Phillips screwdriver and turn the fastener ¼-turn counterclockwise to release it from an adjacent body panel. The screw will usually stay with the outer body panel as it is held in place with a plastic washer. This screw can be reused many times.

Flat Head Clip

To remove a flat head clip, insert a screwdriver under the head, and pry the head out of the clip. This releases the pawls in the clip (A, **Figure 2**). Remove the flat head clip from the panel.

To install a flat head clip, with the head protruding from the clip, insert the clip into the panel. Press the head into the clip to open the pawls and lock the clip in place.

A worn out flat head clip (B, **Figure 2**) can be difficult to install. These are relatively inexpensive and should be replaced as necessary.

Special Nut

A special nut (Tinnerman clip) is a U-shaped metal clip (**Figure 3**) that is pushed onto the edge of a body panel. It usually remains secured to the body panel during removal. If a special nut falls off, lightly crimp it together and push it back into place on the panel.

RIDER'S SEAT

Removal/Installation

Refer to **Figure 4**.
1. Support the motorcycle on a level surface.
2. Remove the bolt (A, **Figure 5**) from each side.
3. Lift the front of the seat (B, **Figure 5**) and pull it forward until the seat hooks disengage from the frame.
4. Inspect the plastic base on the underside of each seat for cracks or damage. Make sure seat hooks (A, **Figure 6**) and bolt bosses (B) are not damaged.
5. To install the front seat, perform the following:
   a. Insert the rear of the seat into the frame cover opening.
   b. Slide the seat rearward until the seat hooks engage the seat retainer on the frame.
   c. Install the bolts (A, **Figure 5**), and tighten securely. Check that the seat is firmly bolted into place.

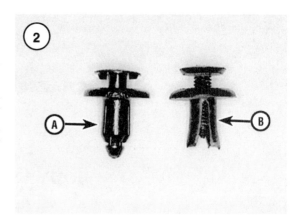

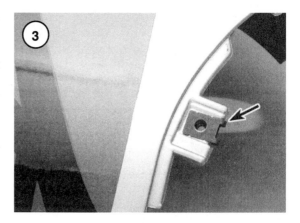

PASSENGER SEAT/TAIL COVER

Removal/Installation

Refer to **Figure 4** and **Figure 7**.

Either a passenger seat or a tail cover fits onto the rear of the tail piece. The following procedure describes the removal and installation of a tail cover. The procedure is identical for a passenger seat.
1. On the left side of the frame cover, insert the ignition key into the lock (**Figure 8**) on the left side of the frame cover.
2. Turn the key clockwise and lift the front of the seat (**Figure 9**), or cover until its posts clear the lock.
3. Pull the seat or, tail cover forward, and remove it.

> *WARNING*
> *Do (bold ital)not try to repair any damaged seat hook. These hooks are molded into the seat base and must be solid with no fractures or cracks in order to secure the seat/tail cover. A repaired hook may create a false sense of security that may lead to a seat working loose during a ride.*

4. Inspect the seat hook (A, **Figure 10**) and locking posts (B) on the underside of the seat or tail cover.

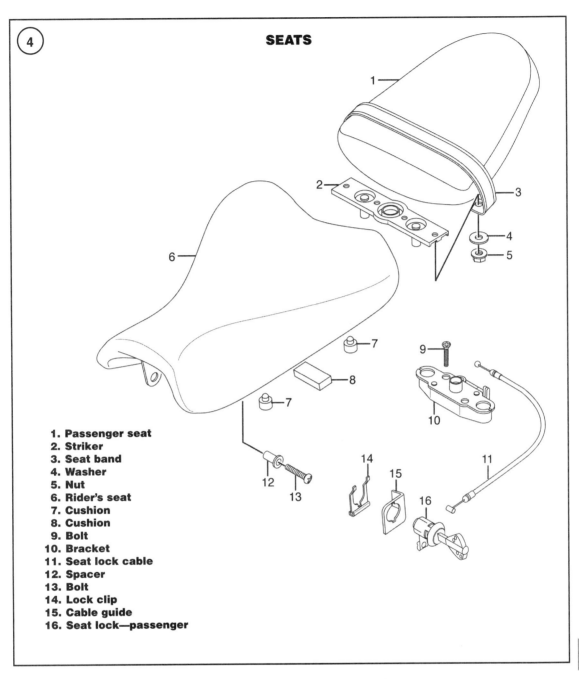

SEATS

4

1. Passenger seat
2. Striker
3. Seat band
4. Washer
5. Nut
6. Rider's seat
7. Cushion
8. Cushion
9. Bolt
10. Bracket
11. Seat lock cable
12. Spacer
13. Bolt
14. Lock clip
15. Cable guide
16. Seat lock—passenger

15

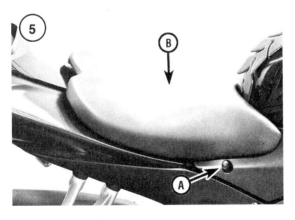

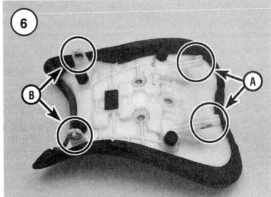

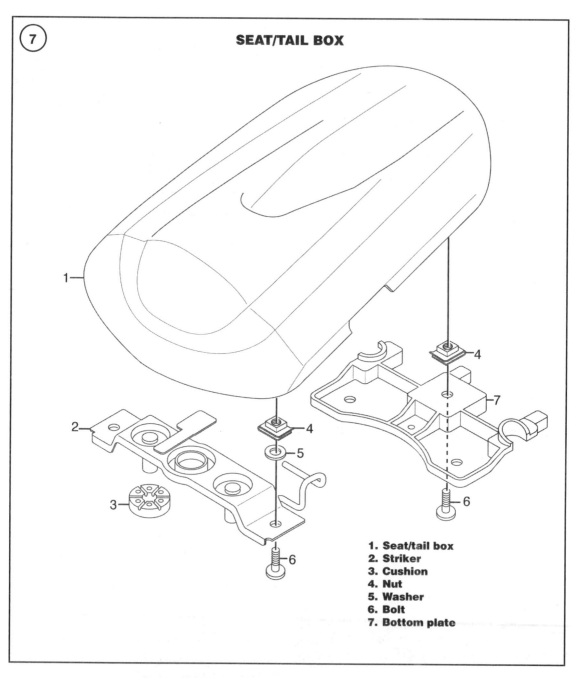

SEAT/TAIL BOX

1. Seat/tail box
2. Striker
3. Cushion
4. Nut
5. Washer
6. Bolt
7. Bottom plate

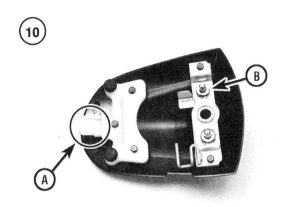

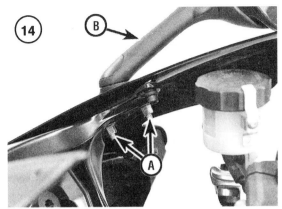

Replace the seat or tail cover if the hook or lock posts are damaged.

5. To install the rear seat, perform the following:

   a. Slide the tail cover rearward until the seat hook engages the seat retainer (**Figure 11**) on the frame.

   b. Push the front of seat, or tail cover down until it locks in place.

   c. Check that the seat, or tail cover, is firmly secured in place.

MIRROR

Removal/Installation

1. Remove the windshield (**Figure 12**) to gain access to the mirror mounting nuts as described in this chapter.

2. Disconnect the front turn signal electrical connector (**Figure 13**).

3. Remove the mirror mounting nuts (A, **Figure 14**), and remove the mirror (B) from the front fairing and mounting bracket.

4. Align the holes in the front faring with the mounting bracket, and install the mirror mounting studs through both parts.

NOTE
Do not substitute a different type of mounting nuts as they will not properly locate the mirror mounting studs within the mounting bracket recess.

5. Install the shoulder nuts (A, **Figure 14**) and tighten to 10 N•m (89 in.-lb.).

6. Connect the front turn signal electrical connector (**Figure 13**).

7. Install the windshield (**Figure 12**) as described in this chapter.

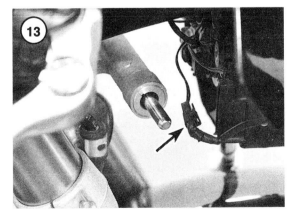

15

WINDSHIELD

Removal/Installation

1. Support the motorcycle on a level surface.
2. Remove the perimeter mounting screws (A, **Figure 15**) on each side.
3. Remove the windshield (B, **Figure 15**) from the front fairing.
4. Installation is the reverse of removal. Tighten the screws securely, but do not overtighten as the plastic may fracture.

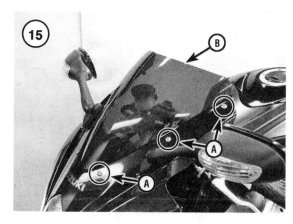

CENTER COVERS

Removal/Installation

Refer to **Figure 16** and **Figure 17**.
1. Support the motorcycle on a level surface.
2. Remove the clips securing the left side center cover (A, **Figure 18**) to the side fairing.
3. Disengage the rear clips securing the side cover to the side fairing and remove the center side cover.
4. Repeat Step 2 and Step 3 for the right side cover.
5. Remove the screws securing the center cover (B, **Figure 18**), and lower it from the front fairing.
6. Installation is the reverse of removal.

FAIRING SIDE PANEL

Removal/Installation

Refer to **Figure 19** and **Figure 20**.

NOTE
The fairing side panels are to be re-moved as an assembly. If necessary, they can be separated after removal from the frame.

1. Support the motorcycle on a level surface.
2A. On 2006-2007 models, remove the four fasteners (**Figure 21**) securing the side panel to the frame.
2B. On 2008-2009 models, remove the two upper fasteners (**Figure 22** and **Figure 23**), and lower fastener securing the side panel to the frame.
3. Pull straight out and release the four locating pins from the frame grommets. Remove the fairing side panel from the frame.
4. If necessary, remove the mounting screws and separate the front and rear side fairing panels. Account for the grommet adjacent to the mounting bosses.

FRONT FAIRING

Removal/Installation

Refer to **Figures 24-26**.
1. Remove each fairing side panel as described in this chapter.
2. Remove the center covers as described in this chapter.
3. Remove the combination meter (chapter Nine).
4. Remove both mirrors as described in this chapter.
5. Disconnect the turn signal harness connectors (**Figure 27**) from its harness mate.
6. On 2007-2008 models, disconnect the steering damper harness connector (**Figure 28**) from its harness mate.
7. Pull back the sleeve (A, **Figure 29**) and disconnect the harness connectors (B) from its harness mate. Remove the wire clamp (C, **Figure 29**) from the underside of the front fairing.
8. Remove the mounting screw (**Figure 30**) on each side securing the front fairing to the mounting bracket.

NOTE
The air intake pipe assemblies will re-main attached to the front fairing.

9. Spread the fairing ears so they clear the mounting bracket on both sides.
10. Pull the front fairing and air intake pipe assembly straight forward and remove the assembly.
11. Inspect the front fairing for damage.
12. Installation is the reverse of removal. Note the following:
   a. Ensure the air intake pipe dust boot (A, **Figure 31**) is in place on each side of the front fairing.
   b. Slide the front fairing rearward until each dust boot seals on the intake receptacle of the frame.

⑯ INNER FAIRING (2006-2007 MODELS)

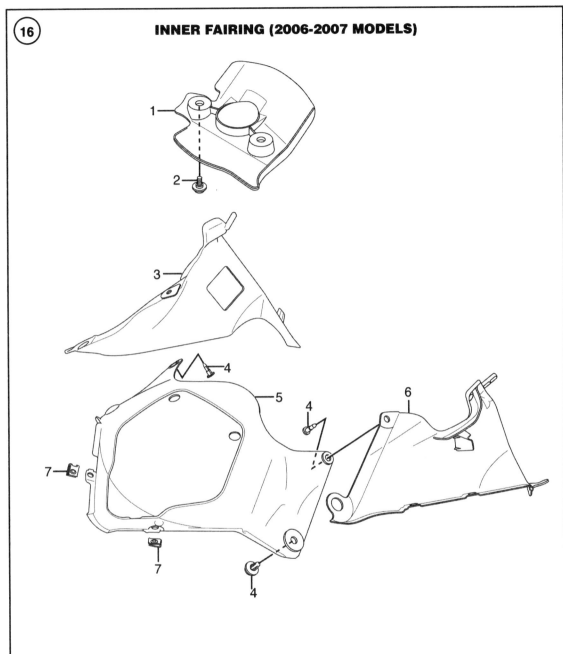

1. Bracket
2. Screw
3. Clip
4. Cover—right side
5. Center cover
6. Cover—left side
7. Tinnerman clip

15

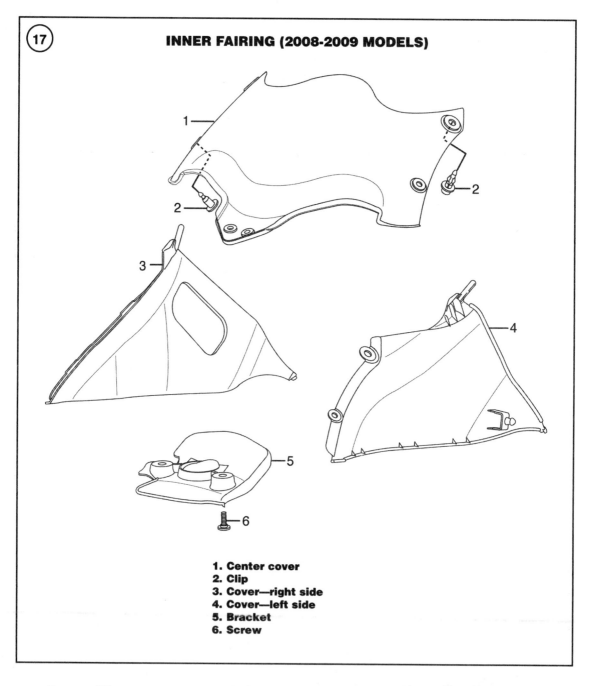

INNER FAIRING (2008-2009 MODELS)

1. Center cover
2. Clip
3. Cover—right side
4. Cover—left side
5. Bracket
6. Screw

c. Connect all harness connectors onto its harness mate.

AIR INTAKE PIPE AND COVER

Removal/Installation

Refer to **Figure 25** or **Figure 26**.

1. Remove the front fairing as described in this chapter.

2. Remove the rear mounting screw (B, **Figure 31**), and front mounting screw (**Figure 32**), and slide the

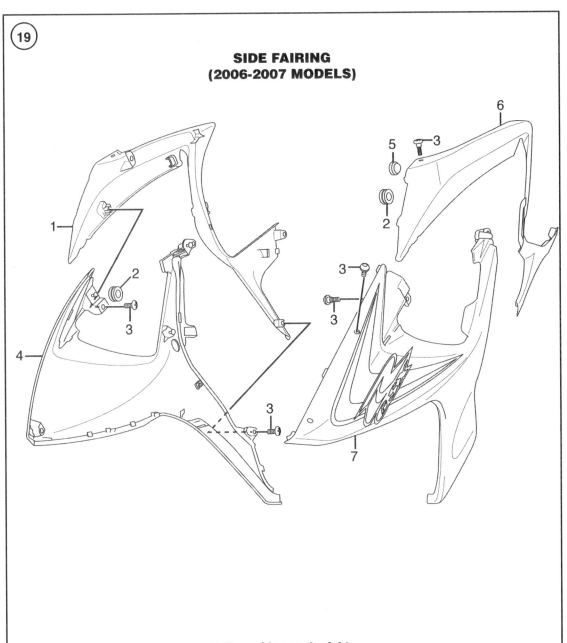

(19)

**SIDE FAIRING
(2006-2007 MODELS)**

1. **Rear side panel—right**

15

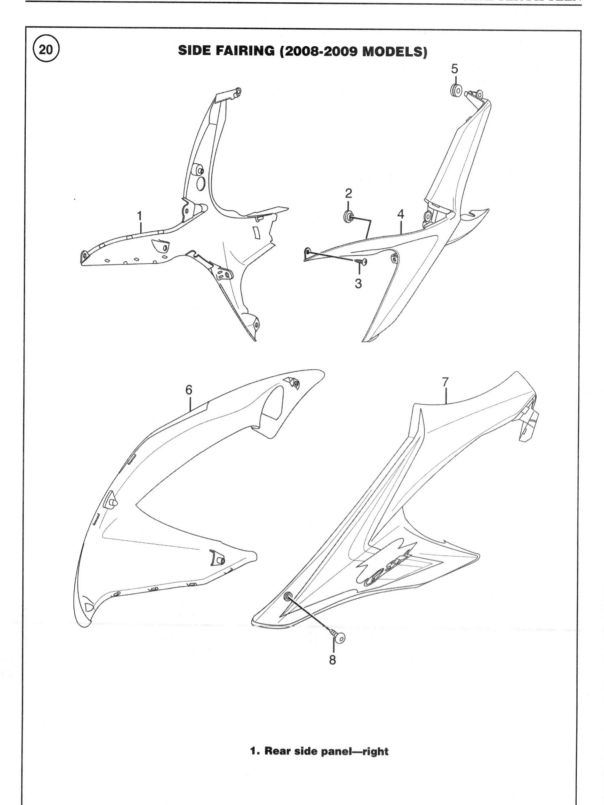

(20)

SIDE FAIRING (2008-2009 MODELS)

1. Rear side panel—right

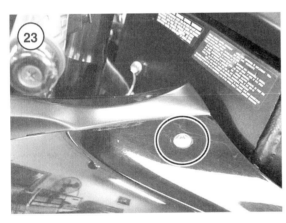

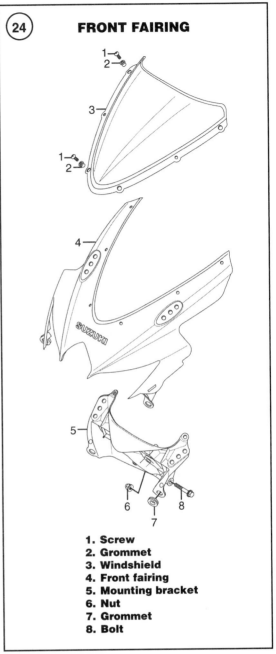

FRONT FAIRING

1. Screw
2. Grommet
3. Windshield
4. Front fairing
5. Mounting bracket
6. Nut
7. Grommet
8. Bolt

15

intake pipe from the front fairing port and remove it.

3. Inspect the air intake pipes (A, **Figure 33**) for damage. Clean out any debris in the intake screen (**Figure 34**).

4. Inspect the air intake pipe covers (B, **Figure 33**) for damage. If necessary, remove the screw and clip and separate the two parts.

5. Installation is the reverse of removal.

FRONT FAIRING BRACKET

Refer to **Figure 24**.

Removal/Installation

1. Remove the front fairing and side fairing panels as described in this chapter.
2. Remove the combination meter (**Figure 35**) (Chapter Nine).
3. Remove the fairing bracket nuts and bolts (**Figure 36**) on each side, and remove the bracket from the steering head.

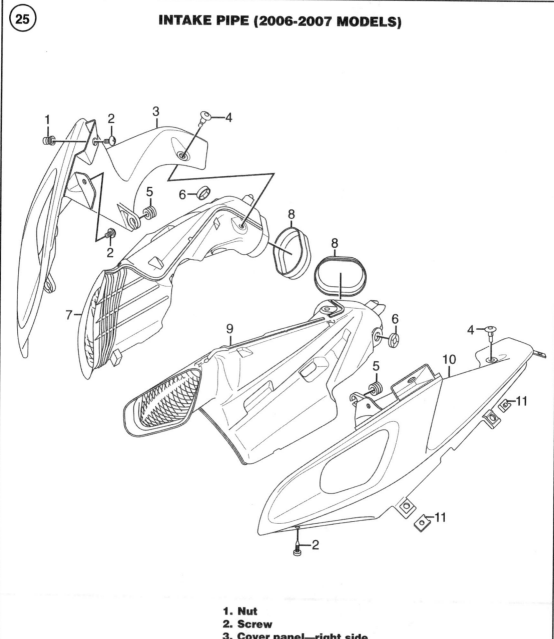

INTAKE PIPE (2006-2007 MODELS)

1. Nut
2. Screw
3. Cover panel—right side
4. Screw
5. Grommet
6. Plug
7. Air intake pipe—right side
8. Dust boot
9. Air intake pipe—left side
10. Cover panel—left side
11. Tinnerman clip

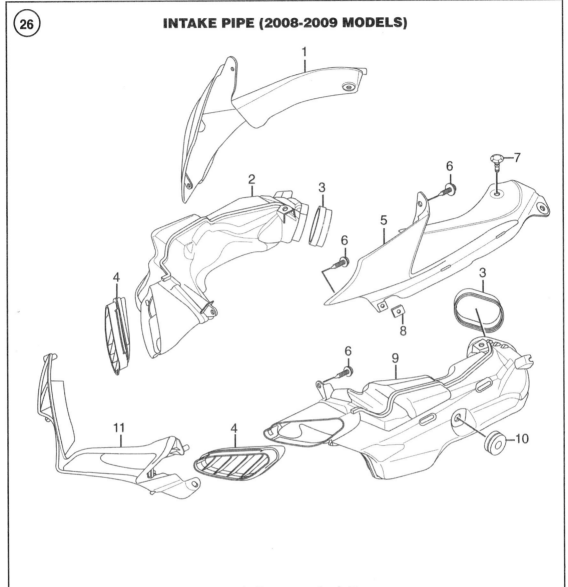

26 **INTAKE PIPE (2008-2009 MODELS)**

1. Cover panel—right

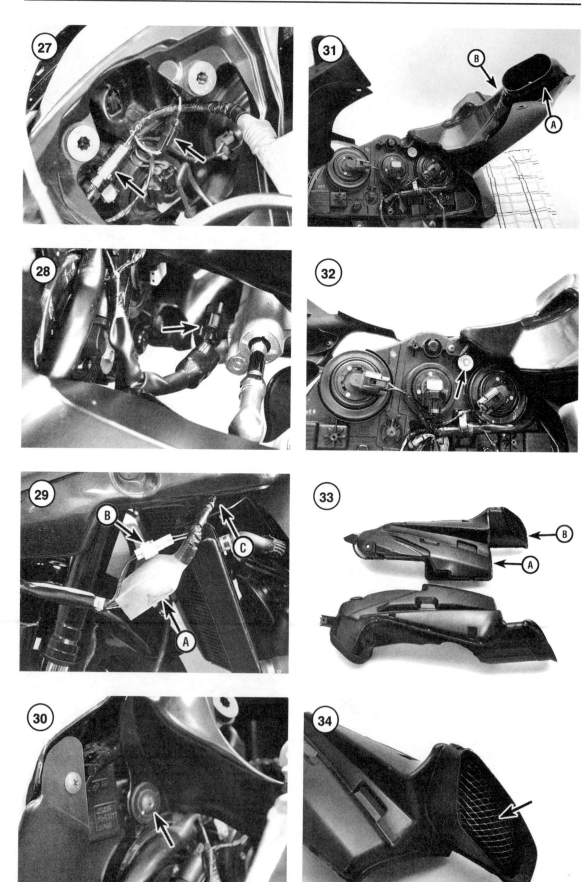

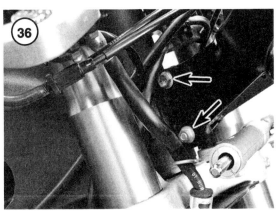

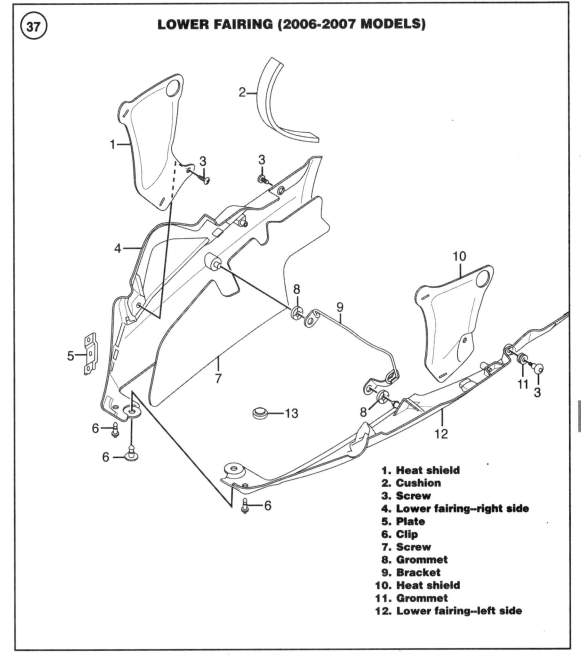

LOWER FAIRING (2006-2007 MODELS)

1. Heat shield
2. Cushion
3. Screw
4. Lower fairing--right side
5. Plate
6. Clip
7. Screw
8. Grommet
9. Bracket
10. Heat shield
11. Grommet
12. Lower fairing--left side

15

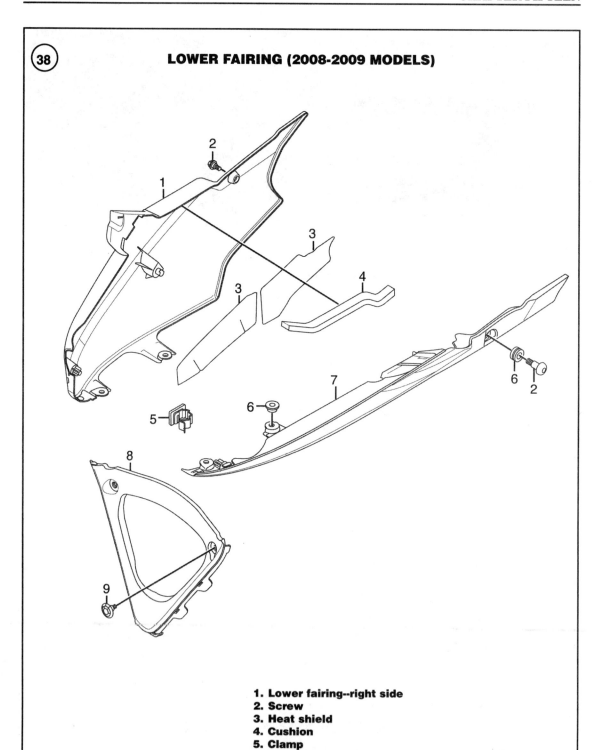

LOWER FAIRING (2008-2009 MODELS)

1. Lower fairing--right side
2. Screw
3. Heat shield
4. Cushion
5. Clamp
6. Grommet
7. Lower fairing--left side
8. Center panel
9. Clip

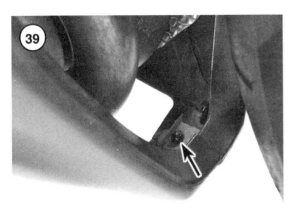

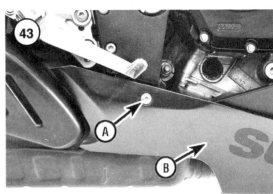

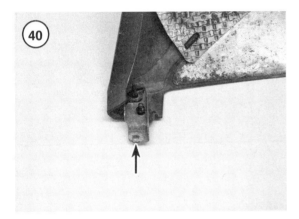

4. Installation is the reverse of removal. Tighten the fairing bracket bolt/nut to 23 N•m (17 ft.-lb.).

LOWER FAIRING

Removal/Installation

Refer to **Figure 37** or **Figure 38**.

NOTE
On 2006-2007 models, each individual lower fairing panel can be removed separately or as an assembly

1. Support the motorcycle on a level surface.
2. Remove the side fairing panels as described in this chapter.
3A. On 2006-2007 models, to remove the lower fairing panels separately, perform the following:
   a. Remove one of the screws (**Figure 39**) securing the two lower fairing panels together at the front. The bracket (**Figure 40**) will stay with the remaining panel.
   b. Reach under the lower fairing and disconnect the panel from the bracket grommet (**Figure 41**).
3B. On 2008-2008 models, remove the screws (A, Figure 42) securing the lower faring to the center panel (B).
4. Remove the rear mounting screw (A, **Figure 43**) and remove the lower fairing panel(s).
5. Installation is the reverse of removal.

FRAME COVER

Removal/Installation

Refer to **Figure 44** or **Figure 45**.
1. Support the motorcycle on a level surface.
2. Remove the rider's seat and the passenger seat/tail cover as described in this chapter.

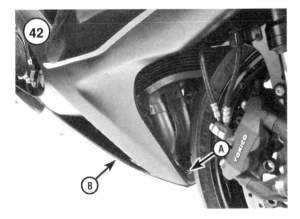

15

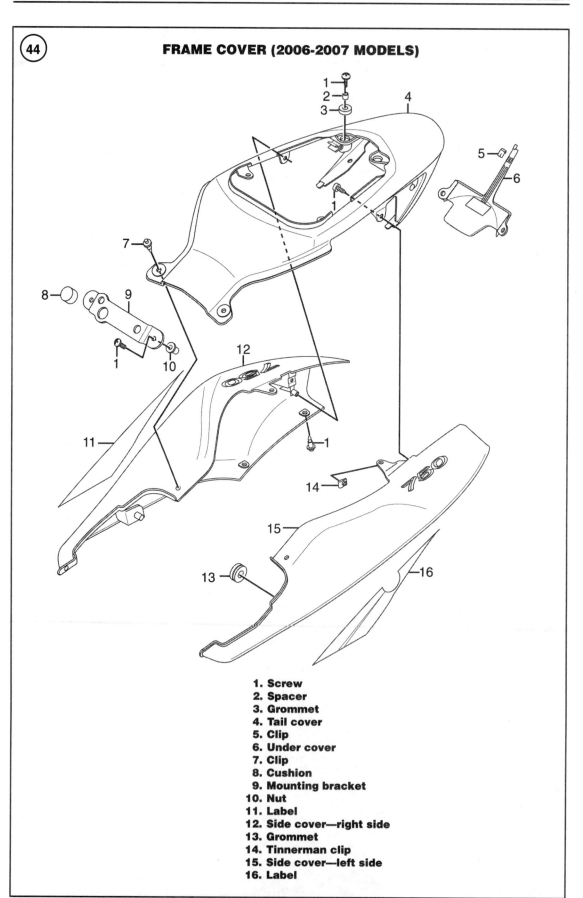

44 **FRAME COVER (2006-2007 MODELS)**

1. Screw
2. Spacer
3. Grommet
4. Tail cover
5. Clip
6. Under cover
7. Clip
8. Cushion
9. Mounting bracket
10. Nut
11. Label
12. Side cover—right side
13. Grommet
14. Tinnerman clip
15. Side cover—left side
16. Label

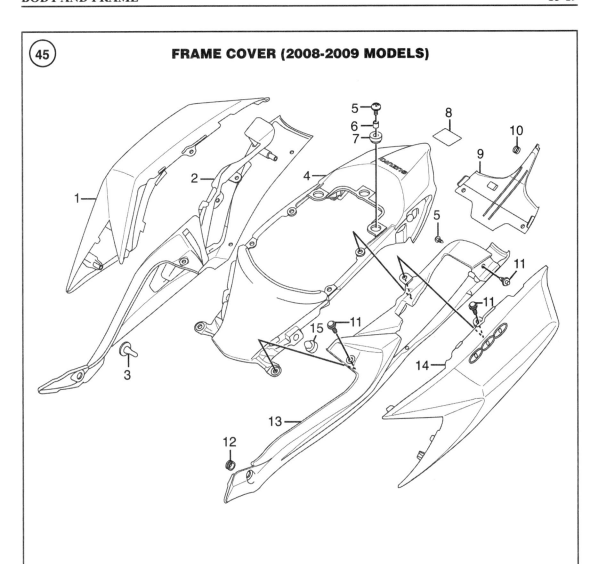

FRAME COVER (2008-2009 MODELS)

45

1. Side cover—right side
2. Frame cover—right side
3. Cushion
4. Tail cover
5. Screw
6. Spacer
7. Grommet
8. Foam tape
9. Under cover
10. Clip
11. Clip
12. Cushion
13. Frame cover—left side
14. Side cover—left side
15. Cushion

15

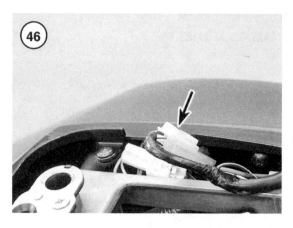

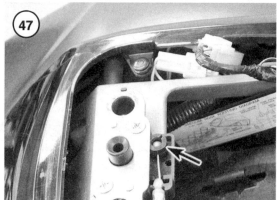

3. Disconnect the 3-pin rear combination light connector (**Figure 46**) from its harness mate.

4. Disconnect the passenger seat cable end (**Figure 47**) from the release mechanism.

5. On 2006-2007 models, remove the rear lower screw.

6. Remove the upper and lower retaining clips (**Figure 48**).

7A. On 2006-2007 models, perform the following:

   a. Pull straight out and release the front interior post from the frame grommet.

   b. Remove the side cover (**Figure 49**) from the tail cover. Repeat for the other side, if necessary.

7B. On 2008-2009 models, perform the following:

   a. Remove the top clip (**Figure 50**) securing the side cover to the frame cover.

   b. Pull the side cover toward the rear and disengage the rear clip (**Figure 51**) from the locating notch in the frame cover. Remove the side cover.

   c. To remove the frame cover, disconnect and remove all of the electrical connectors and components (A, **Figure 52**) secured to the left side. Remove all fasteners and remove the frame cover(s) (B, **Figure 52**).

8. Remove the screws (**Figure 53**, typical) securing the rear of the tail cover. Remove the cover, and account for the spacer located within the grommets.

9. Installation is the reverse of removal. Install a collar and damper where noted during removal.

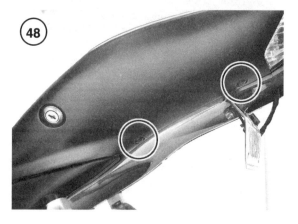

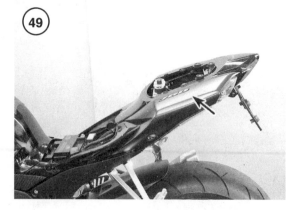

FRONT FENDER

Removal/Installation

1. Support the motorcycle on a level surface.

2. Release the brake hose (A, **Figure 54**) from the holder on the right side, and the top of the fender (B).

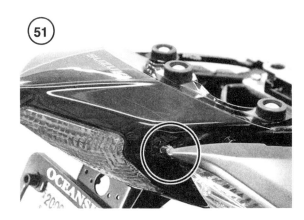

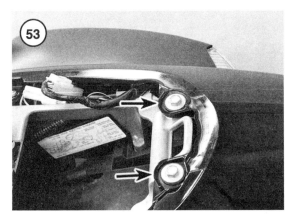

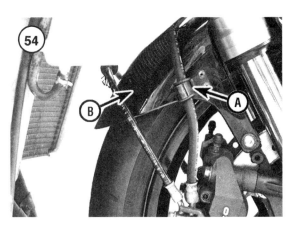

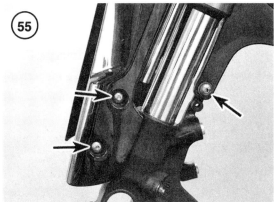

3. Remove the front wheel (Chapter Eleven).

4. Remove the front fender mounting screws (**Figure 55**) from each side.

5. Lift the fender down and out from between the fork legs, and remove the fender.

6. Installation is the reverse of removal. Tighten the fender screws securely, but do not overtighten them. The plastic fender may fracture.

REAR FENDER/UPPER (2008-2009 MODELS)

Removal/Installation

Refer to **Figure 56**.

1. Support the motorcycle on a level surface.

2. Disconnect the 3-pin rear combination light connector (**Figure 46**) from its harness mate.

3. Remove the mounting bolts and plate, lower the rear fender down and remove the fender.

4. If necessary, remove the mounting bolts and remove the front rear fender.

5. Installation is the reverse of removal.

REAR FENDER

Removal/Installation

Refer to **Figure 57** or **Figure 58**.

1. Support the motorcycle on a level surface.

2. Remove the rider's seat and the passenger seat/tail cover as described in this chapter.

3. Remove the rear fender/upper (2008-2009 models), and frame cover as described in this chapter.

4. Remove the fasteners securing the rear fender/lower, lower and remove it from the rear fender/upper.

5. Remove all electrical components and the battery (**Figure 59**) located with the top surface of the rear fender/upper (Chapter Nine).

15

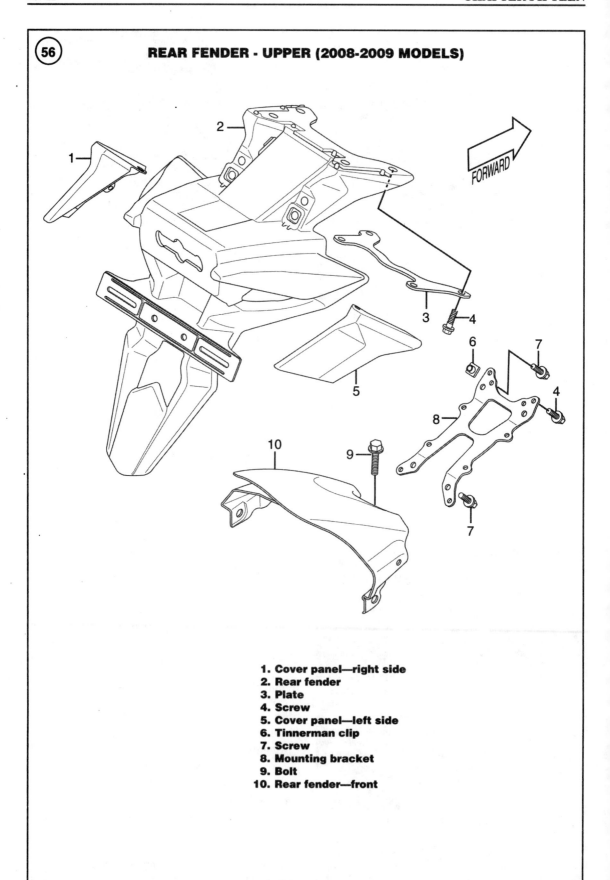

56 **REAR FENDER - UPPER (2008-2009 MODELS)**

FORWARD

1. Cover panel—right side
2. Rear fender
3. Plate
4. Screw
5. Cover panel—left side
6. Tinnerman clip
7. Screw
8. Mounting bracket
9. Bolt
10. Rear fender—front

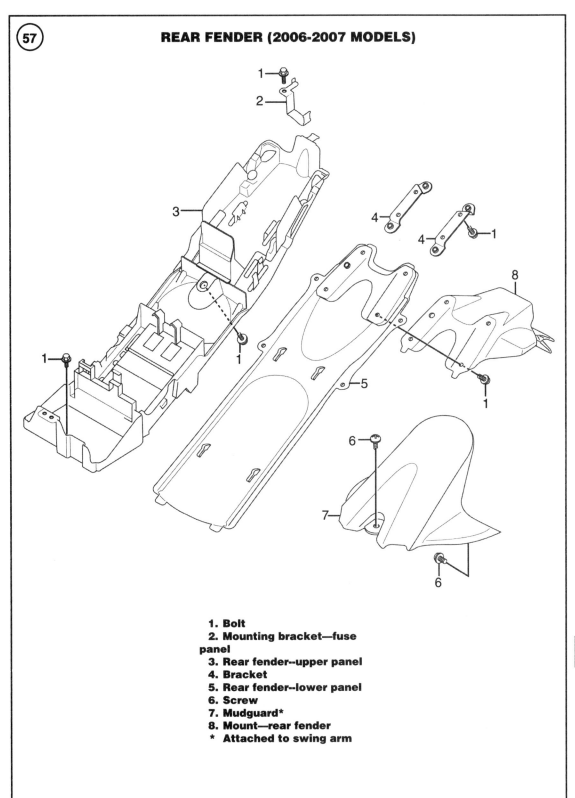

57

REAR FENDER (2006-2007 MODELS)

1. Bolt
2. Mounting bracket—fuse panel
3. Rear fender--upper panel
4. Bracket
5. Rear fender--lower panel
6. Screw
7. Mudguard*
8. Mount—rear fender
* Attached to swing arm

15

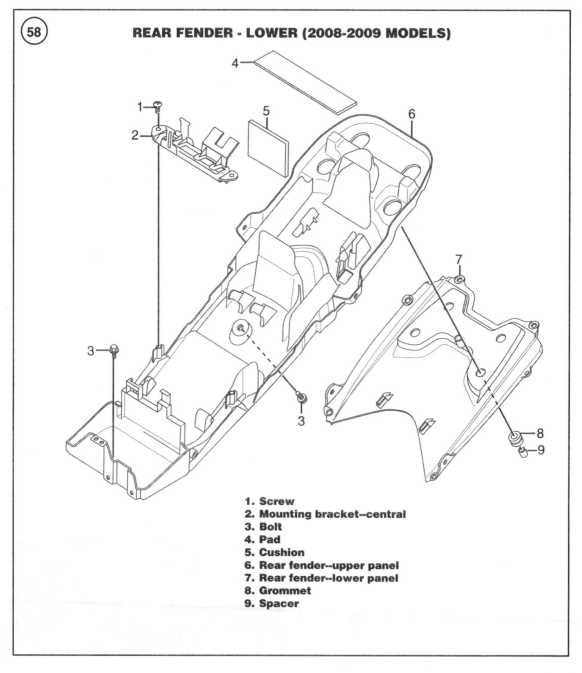

REAR FENDER - LOWER (2008-2009 MODELS)

1. Screw
2. Mounting bracket--central
3. Bolt
4. Pad
5. Cushion
6. Rear fender--upper panel
7. Rear fender--lower panel
8. Grommet
9. Spacer

6. Remove the fasteners securing the rear fender to the rear frame.

7. Ensure that all fasteners and electrical have been disconnected or removed. Lower and remove the rear fender.

8. Installation is the reverse of removal.

FOOT RESTS

Removl/Installation (Front)

Refer to **Figure 60** and **Figure 61**.

1. Support the motorcycle on a level surface.

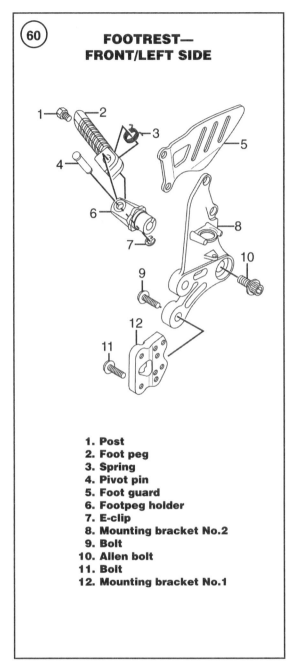

**FOOTREST—
FRONT/LEFT SIDE**

1. Post
2. Foot peg
3. Spring
4. Pivot pin
5. Foot guard
6. Footpeg holder
7. E-clip
8. Mounting bracket No.2
9. Bolt
10. Allen bolt
11. Bolt
12. Mounting bracket No.1

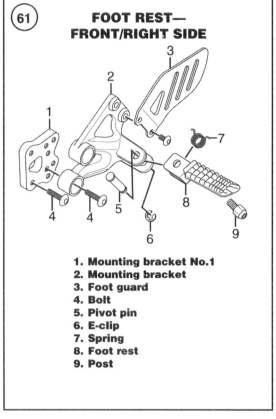

**FOOT REST—
FRONT/RIGHT SIDE**

1. Mounting bracket No.1
2. Mounting bracket
3. Foot guard
4. Bolt
5. Pivot pin
6. E-clip
7. Spring
8. Foot rest
9. Post

2. On the left side, remove the mounting bolts (A, **Figure 62**) and remove the foot rest (B) from the frame.

3. On the right side, perform the following:
   a. Remove the rear brake lever (Chapter Fourteen).
   b. Remove the footpeg mounting bracket No. 1 bolts (A, **Figure 63**), and remove the brake pedal/footrest assembly (B) from the motorcycle.

4. Inspect the brake pedal/footrest assembly (**Figure 64**) for cranks or damage and replace it if necessary.

5. Installation is the reverse of removal. Tighten the mounting bolts to 23 N•m (17 ft.-lb.).

Removal/Installation (Rear)

Refer to **Figure 65**.

1. Support the motorcycle on a level surface.

2. Remove the mounting bolts (A, **Figure 66**) and remove the foot rest (B) from the rear frame.

3. Installation is the reverse of removal. Tighten the mounting bolts to 23 N•m (17 ft.-lb.).

15

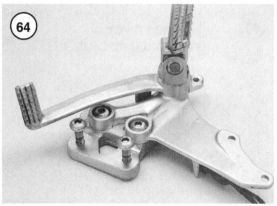

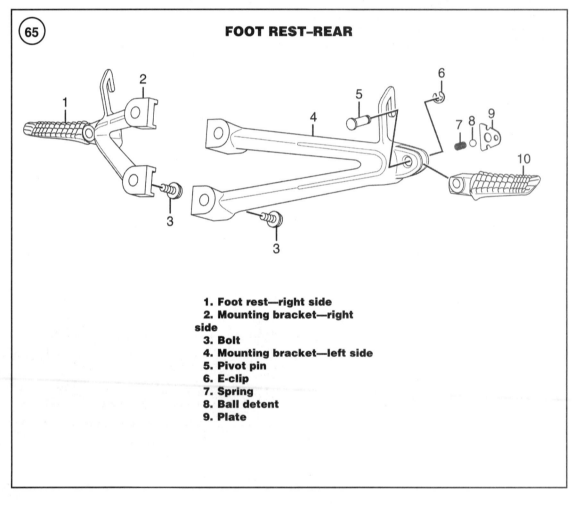

FOOT REST–REAR

1. Foot rest—right side
2. Mounting bracket—right side
3. Bolt
4. Mounting bracket—left side
5. Pivot pin
6. E-clip
7. Spring
8. Ball detent
9. Plate

Disassembly/Assembly

1. On front footrest, remove the E-clip (A, **Figure 67**), withdraw the clevis pin (B) and remove the footrest (C) from the mounting bracket. Account for the spring located within the footrest pivot area

2. On the rear footrest, remove the E-clip withdraw the clevis pin and remove the footrest from the mounting bracket. Account for the spring, ball detent and plate located within the footrest pivot area.

3. Installation is the reverse of removal.

SIDESTAND

Removal/Installation

1. Support the motorcycle on a level surface.

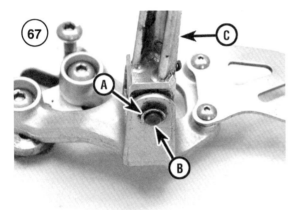

2. Remove the lower fairing as described in this chapter.

3. To replace only the spring, perform the following:
   a. Place the sidestand in the raised position.
   b. Use locking pliers to disconnect the springs from the post on the side stand and the post on the inboard side of the sidestand bracket.
   c. Install the *new* springs onto the posts.

4. Remove the air filter assembly (Chapter Eight).

5. Follow the sidestand switch wiring up the left side of the frame and locate the 2-pin electrical connector adjacent to the fuel rail.

6. Disconnect the 2-pin sidestand switch connector from its harness mate.

7. Lower the sidestand.

8. Remove the two mounting bolts (A, **Figure 68**), and lower the sidestand (B) from the frame member.

9. Check the sidestand for damage and make sure the nut is tight on the pivot bolt.

10. Inspect the spring mounting posts (**Figure 69**) for cracks or damage.

11. If necessary, remove the sidestand switch mounting bolts (A, **Figure 70**) and remove the switch (B).

12. Apply grease (Suzuki Super Grease A or equivalent) to the spring mounting posts and to the pivot on the sidestand.

13. Correctly position the sidestand against the frame and install the bolts (A, **Figure 68**).

14. Apply threadlock (Suzuki Thread Lock 1342 or equivalent) to the threads of the mounting bolts.

15. Tighten the sidestand mounting bolts (A, **Figure 68**) to 50 N•m (36 ft.-lb.).

16. Move the sidestand up and down to check for freedom of movement.

15

SEAT RAIL

Removal/Installation

Refer to **Figure 71** and **Figure 72**.
1. Support the motorcycle on a level surface.

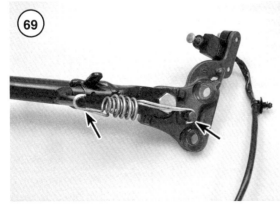

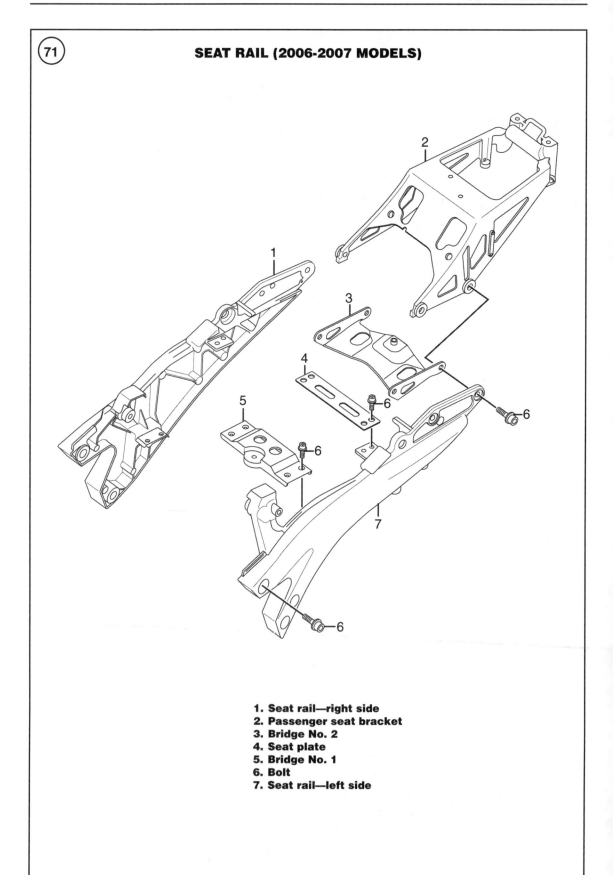

SEAT RAIL (2006-2007 MODELS)

(71)

1. Seat rail—right side
2. Passenger seat bracket
3. Bridge No. 2
4. Seat plate
5. Bridge No. 1
6. Bolt
7. Seat rail—left side

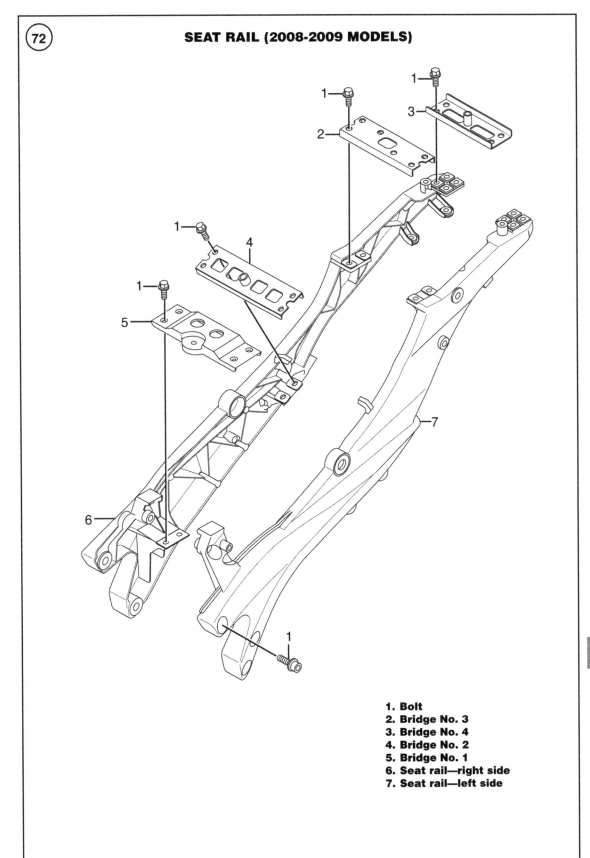

SEAT RAIL (2008-2009 MODELS)

1. Bolt
2. Bridge No. 3
3. Bridge No. 4
4. Bridge No. 2
5. Bridge No. 1
6. Seat rail—right side
7. Seat rail—left side

2. Remove the rider's seat and the passenger seat/tail cover as described in this chapter.

3. Remove all body components attached to the seat rail as described in this chapter.

4A. To remove the seat rail as an assembly, perform the following:

    a. Have an assistant secure the end of the seat rail.

    b. Remove the bolts (A, **Figure 73**), on each side securing the seat rail to the main frame.

    c. Pull the seat rail assembly (B, **Figure 73**), forward the rear and remove it.

4B. To remove the seat rail components, perform the following:

    a. On 2006-2007 models, remove the bolts securing the passenger seat bracket and remove the bracket.

    b. Remove the bolts securing the bridge plates as necessary.

    c. Remove the bolts (A, **Figure 73**), securing the seat rail to the main frame.

    d. Remove the seat rail (B, **Figure 73**), from the main frame and remove it.

5. Installation is the reverse of removal. Tighten the seat rail mounting bolts (A, **Figure 73**) to 50 N•m (36 ft.-lb.).

Table 1 BODY AND FRAME TORQUE SPECIFICATIONS

Item	N•m	in.-lb.	ft.-lb.
Fairing bracket bolt/nut	23	–	17
Foot rest mounting bolt	23	–	17
Mirror mounting nut	10	89	–
Seat rail bolt	50	–	36
Sidestand			
Mounting bolt	50	–	36
Pivot bolt	50	–	36

INDEX

16

16

16

2006-2007 GSX-R600/750 U.S., CALIFORNIA AND CANADA MODELS

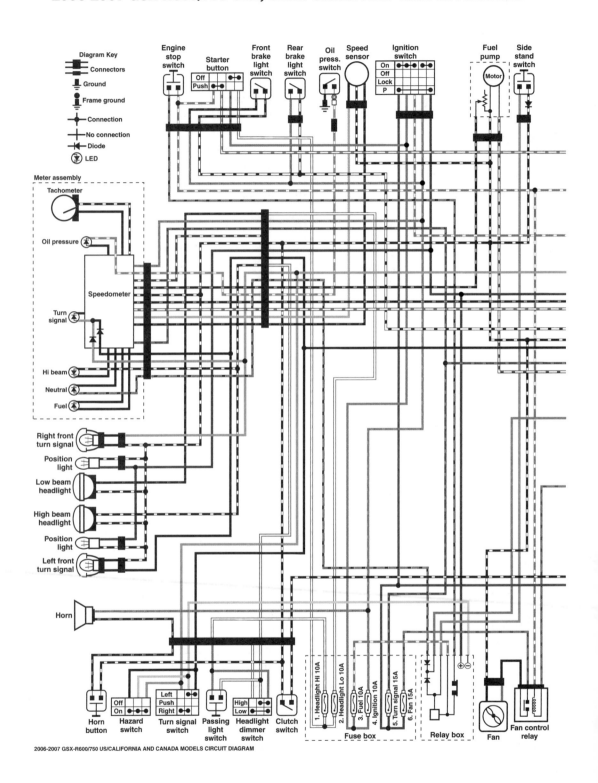

2006-2007 GSX-R600/750 US/CALIFORNIA AND CANADA MODELS CIRCUIT DIAGRAM

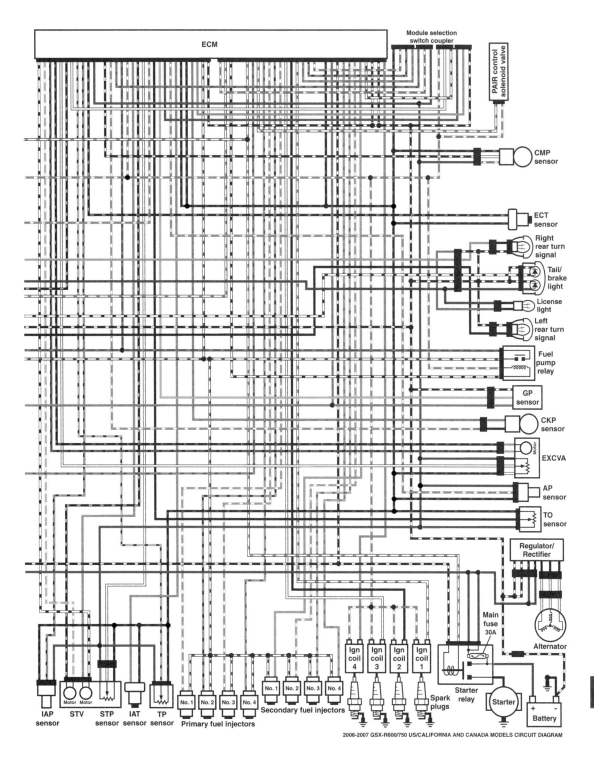

2006-2007 GSX-R600/750 US/CALIFORNIA AND CANADA MODELS CIRCUIT DIAGRAM

17

2006-2007 GSX-R600/750 U.K., EUROPE AND AUSTRALIA MODELS

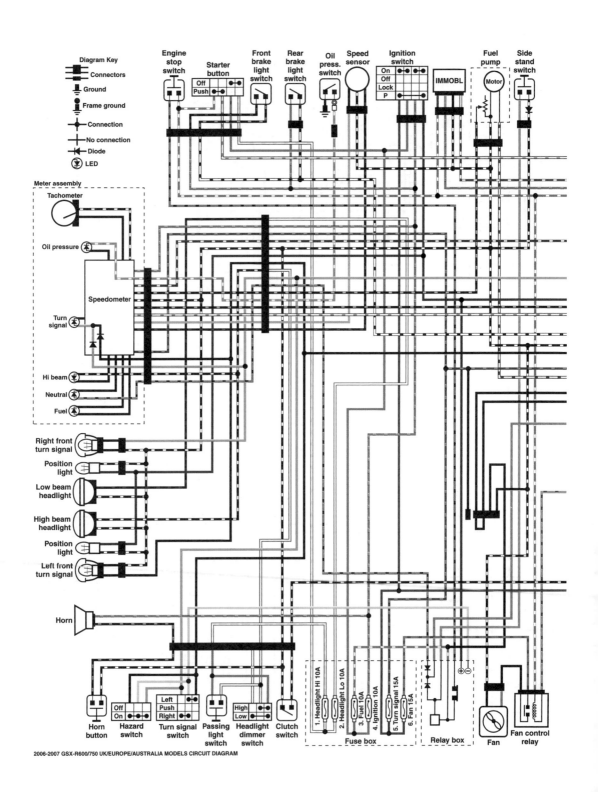

2006-2007 GSX-R600/750 UK/EUROPE/AUSTRALIA MODELS CIRCUIT DIAGRAM

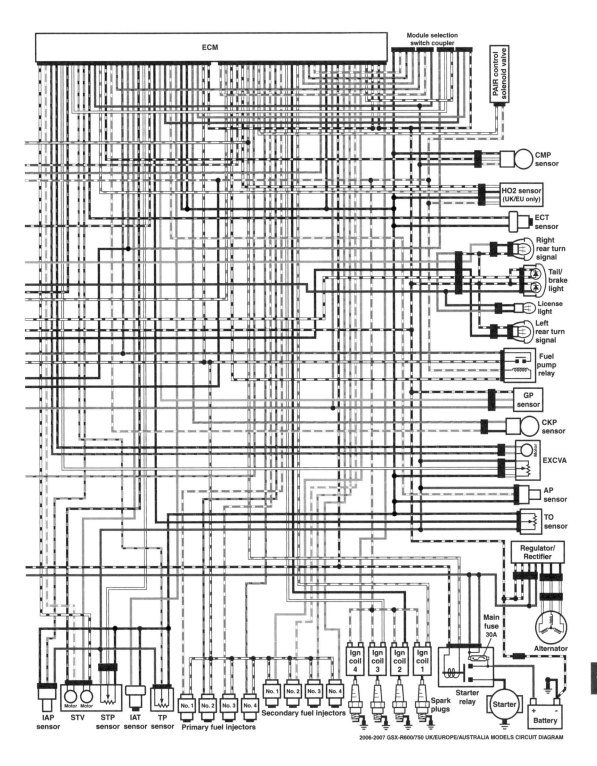

2006-2007 GSX-R600/750 UK/EUROPE/AUSTRALIA MODELS CIRCUIT DIAGRAM

2008-2009 GSX-R600/750 MODELS

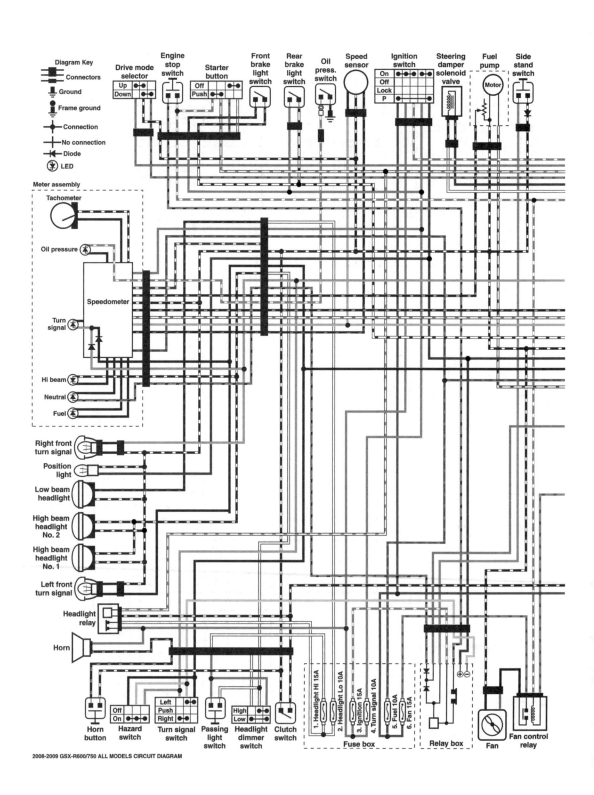

2008-2009 GSX-R600/750 ALL MODELS CIRCUIT DIAGRAM

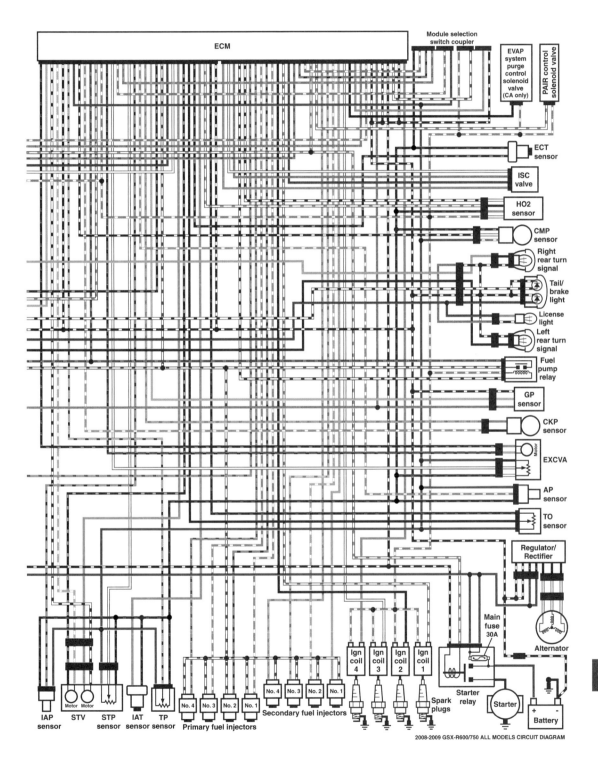

2008-2009 GSX-R600/750 ALL MODELS CIRCUIT DIAGRAM

Notes